# Handbook for Screening Adolescents at Psychosocial Risk

# Handbook for Screening Adolescents at Psychosocial Risk

*Edited by*

Mark I. Singer
Lynn T. Singer
Trina M. Anglin

LEXINGTON BOOKS
*An Imprint of Macmillan, Inc.*
NEW YORK

Maxwell Macmillan Canada
TORONTO

Maxwell Macmillan International
NEW YORK   OXFORD   SINGAPORE   SYDNEY

Library of Congress Cataloging-in-Publication Data

Handbook for screening adolescents at psychosocial risk / edited by
   Mark I. Singer, Lynn T. Singer, Trina M. Anglin.
      p.      cm.
   Includes bibliographical references and index.
   ISBN 0-669-24827-4
   1. Teenagers—Mental health.   2. Behavioral assessment of
teenagers.   3. Teenagers—Health risk assessment.   I. Singer, Mark
I.   II. Singer, Lynn T.   III. Anglin, Trina M.
RJ503.H26   1993
616.89′022—dc20                                                              92-38230
                                                                                   CIP

Lexington Books
An Imprint of Macmillan, Inc.
866 Third Avenue, New York, N.Y. 10022

Maxwell Macmillan Canada, Inc.
1200 Eglinton Avenue East
Suite 200
Don Mills, Ontario M3C 3N1

Macmillan, Inc. is part of the Maxwell Communication
Group of Companies.

Printed in the United States of America

printing number
1   2   3   4   5   6   7   8   9   10

# Contents

# Preface

Adolescence—the bridge between childhood and adulthood—represents a significant developmental period, characterized by marked changes in physiology, cognition, and behavior. For those in the field of human services, working with adolescents represents a particular challenge, as the transition from childhood is often fraught with difficulties. Accidents, homicide, and suicide—the three leading causes of death among adolescents—are all largely preventable and are directly related to psychosocial and developmental issues. Additionally, adolescents are at high risk for sexually transmitted diseases, HIV/AIDS, substance abuse, mental and emotional disorders, gang involvement, and physical and sexual abuse.

Early recognition of problems during adolescence is critical to the provision of timely intervention. Individuals working with adolescents, however, often do not enjoy the benefit of a long history of past behaviors and problems from which to make clinical judgments; yet, in the context of minimal historical information, and in the face of possible serious sequelae, such judgments must be made.

The challenges of identifying and addressing adolescents' developmental needs, health, mental health, and social problems span many disciplines. For example, school counselors need to understand reproductive health issues and how to recognize depression, for they may be the first called on to provide preliminary evaluation of a psychotic teenager who has disrupted a classroom. Nurses and social workers who work in urban hospital emergency departments frequently encounter youths who are involved in gang violence and substance abuse, who are depressed, who have attempted suicide, and who have been sexually assaulted. Youth workers and probation officers in the juvenile justice system and social workers for departments of human services all need to recognize the multiple problems in which their charges are involved, such as sexual risk-taking, substance abuse, delinquency, and violence. The majority of these youngsters have problematic family backgrounds, and many of them have experienced physical or sexual abuse.

It is the purpose of this book to acquaint professionals with the information necessary to recognize many of the major psychosocial problems of adolescence. It is designed to serve as a single-volume resource for professionals working with youngsters who may have multiple problems. Each chapter is written by an experienced clinician or research scientist who is a recognized expert in his or her designated problem area. The chapters are designed to present youth-serving professionals with the information necessary to understand and identify a wide range of psychosocial problems of adolescence. Problem areas addressed in this book include family problems, substance abuse, attention deficit hyperactivity disorder, traumatic brain injury, eating disorders, sexual and physical abuse, gang involvement, antisocial behavior, reproductive health, psychosis, depression, and suicide.

Each chapter presents the criteria necessary for the recognition of a specific psychosocial problem as well as pertinent knowledge about its etiology and the subgroups at high risk. A unique feature of this volume is the inclusion of specific screening techniques regularly used by the researchers or practitioners themselves, giving "hands-on" information about how the instruments are usually employed and what results can be expected. Because so many professionals working with adolescents today are often called on to help families find the most appropriate referral sources, most chapters contain treatment options for the identified problem area. In concert with the "hands-on" approach, case vignettes have also been included whenever possible.

Many professionals who routinely encounter adolescents as part of their job assignment have not received formal training in the numerous issues pertinent to this age group and may not feel sufficiently prepared to recognize adolescents' needs. We hope that this *Handbook* will enhance these professionals' feelings of self-efficacy, and will help them become more comfortable in screening adolescent students, clients, and patients for problem behaviors and for mental health problems. Above all, we hope that the information and suggested screening techniques contained in the *Handbook* impart the challenge, excitement, and personal satisfaction the editors and authors have experienced through their work with adolescents.

We would like to thank the Center for Practice Innovations at the Mandel School of Applied Social Sciences for supporting this work. The efforts of Pat Kilrain and Sharon Hoskins are much appreciated. The patience and motivation provided by Margaret Zusky at Lexington Books were a great help to us. A special debt of gratitude is owed to Rose Marie Ashley, who worked tirelessly on behalf of this book.

*Mark I. Singer*
*Lynn T. Singer*
*Trina M. Anglin*

# 1
# Assessing the Family

*Kathleen Cole-Kelly*
*David Kaye*

A s in the joke about how many people are dead in that cemetery (answer: all of them), all adolescents have some form of ongoing, and typically continuous, relationships with their families. Adolescents grapple with issues of identity, separation individuation, and sexuality within the crucible of the family. While adolescents frequently look like adults, walk like adults, and talk like adults, they remain dependent on their families in countless ways. Because of these facts, many mental health professionals attempt to work solely with the family-with-adolescent (i.e., family therapy) when confronted with the situation in which an adolescent is presenting difficulties. Other professionals argue that because adolescents are struggling for separation from their families of origin, one should respect this by meeting with the adolescent individually (typically in "individual therapy"). Prevailing models increasingly recognize both perspectives and combine treatment modalities. Regardless of emphasis, all approaches require an assessment of the current family functioning. In fact, no one would pretend to understand an adolescent without an understanding of his or her family context. We would further argue that to truly understand a given adolescent, one must also understand the larger social/cultural/world/historical context, but in the interest of keeping this chapter at a reasonable length, we will not address those crucial issues here. In this chapter we will focus on an approach to assessing the families of adolescents that will assist front-line professionals in being useful to the adolescent and family.

We have already glossed over a number of thorny issues that we would like briefly to clarify. First, what do we mean by "family" in this country, at this time? As with Heinz, there are at least fifty-seven varieties, and we by no means assume that this chapter will apply to all of them to the same degree. We have tried to be sensitive to these issues without making so many exceptions that the entire chapter becomes meaningless. What we are writing applies most to your garden-variety, middle-class North American family living in the latter days of the twentieth century. Further, it is recognized that what we believe to be healthier qualities in families are inextricably intertwined with the kinds of qualities healthier adults require in our culture. As so elegantly described by Erikson, approaches to child rearing differ widely depending on the kind of adults the society values and needs (Erikson, 1950). A second point to be made is that it must be recognized that the family assessment we will be describing here is a cross-sectional one. In other words, it is an assessment of the family in the here and now, with relatively little attention paid to the changes in family functioning that occur over time. While we assume that substantial changes may well have occurred, as family therapists we also assume that there is a stability to the most salient patterns of family interaction and that therefore even a single interview with a family will reveal important and durable patterns.

With these various caveats said, let us now move on to some thoughts on the theory of assessment. First, one cannot observe everything; one cannot assess every aspect of a given situation. We must narrow our focus so that we collect the information necessary to do something useful. Therefore, we must ask, What are we trying to do? What questions are we trying to answer? We assume that the reader of this chapter primarily needs to make triage decisions regarding large numbers of adolescents and their families. In other words, one needs to screen the families and make preliminary judgments as to which broad resources are most likely to benefit a given adolescent and family. Like the triage nurse in an emergency room, one needs to know which patients are hemorrhaging and require immediate intensive treatment; which ones have less acute problems that can wait; and which ones have specialized or unusual problems that require services available at another facility. Second, as all assessments are based on a model of health, our assessments are based on our own model of healthier family functioning. We would see the healthier family as exhibiting the following qualities and characteristics:

1. *A sense of the whole or team spirit.* This is typically the most important indicator of healthier family functioning. Healthier families develop a kind of family nationalism or team spirit and have a sense of their wholeness. Many of the qualities that follow overlap with or contribute to this sense of wholeness. Especially powerful determinants of this sense of the whole are their responsiveness to the individual, their ability to play, the respect for individual private style, the encouragement of affected expression, and successful conflict resolution. (See below for further descriptions of these qualities.)

2. *The whole is responsive to the individual.* In the healthier family, the group as a whole is sensitive to and responds to both the difficulties and the successes of the individual members. This includes an appreciation for the natural process of regression in the face of difficulty. The healthy family is able to pass around the family cuddle blanket at these times.

3. *Respect for the individual.* Although in all families there is always

some tension between belongingness and individuation, the healthier family is marked by the mutual respect for individual styles, pursuits, and privacy. This cuts both ways; that is, the parents respect the children and the children respect the parents.

4. *Family rituals.* Although these may be religious, the healthier family develops unique idiosyncratic rituals that contribute to their sense of history and team spirit. Rituals in these families retain flexibility and evolve over time. In other words, the family retains a responsiveness to circumstances so that rituals do not degenerate into meaningless exercises in obedience.

5. *The ability to play.* This is a hallmark of the healthier family. The deadly serious family in which one feels constrained to smile or tell a joke is in deep trouble. Playfulness, the ability to play, and the related sense of humor are perhaps the most important counterbalances to the inevitable sufferings of life. Without these qualities, families drown in sorrow, anger, bitterness, and pain. As Keith has offered, it allows families to see over the tops of their pain (Keith, personal communication, Sept. 14, 1989).

6. *Encouragement of affective expression.* Healthier families encourage a range in the expression of affect. This includes not only anger but also sadness, fear, yearning, joy, and so forth. The healthier family has the ability to accept, contain, and productively channel these emotions. While families differ widely in their temperament (e.g., the stereotypical "expressive" Italian family versus the "reserved" Scandinavian family), it is most important that there be some flexibility in the range of expressiveness. As an aside, this does not refer to those families who hide their destructive expressions of anger under the cloak of "open and honest" communication.

7. *Productive conflict resolution.* Because families are composed of individuals with their own desires, needs, abilities, shortcomings, and so forth, conflict is inevitable. Healthier families recognize (and at times value) these differences and—unlike many families that claim to be "close"—do not attempt to hide them. Healthier families are able to resolve differences fairly without resorting to physical abuse, intimidation, or psychological coercion.

8. *Generation gap.* Contrary to our culture's consternation in the 1960s at the recognition of this phenomenon, we believe that healthier families show a clear generation gap. The healthier family is not a democracy; there are boundaries, and different ranks exist. The parents are the parents (and the grandparents, parents, and children recognize this), and the children are the children (and the grandparents, parents, and children recognize this as well).

9. *Flexible roles.* Hand in hand with the separation of the generations is the presence of flexibility of roles. Healthier families demonstrate a freedom of choice in periodic role selection, and each role is available to any member. As Whitaker and Keith have stated, "Father can be a 5 year old, mother can be a 3 year old, the 3 year old can be a father, the father can be a mother, depending on the situation, with each family member protected by an im-

plicit 'as if' clause" (Whitaker & Keith, 1980). In these situations, Junior *becomes* Daddy, Susie *becomes* Mom, and Mom *becomes* sister.

10. *Sibling subgroup.* In healthier families, the siblings form their own subgrouping, separate from the adults. This provides the forum for interactional exploration of issues involving persons of equal rank (e.g., competition, cooperation, support). Example: The children of a colleague developed a secret code to talk among themselves, excluding the parents. To do this, they used the words *rents* extensively: "Don't do it now; the rents are coming," or "You go out to the store, and I'll watch for the rents." It wasn't until many months later that our colleagues broke the code and discovered that *rents* was short for *parents.*

11. *Rotating scapegoat.* In the healthier family there is an awareness that each person has strengths and weaknesses, good points and bad points, abilities and disabilities. They are allergic to the idea that one member may be the repository of everything bad in the family (or the flip side of the same coin: that one member represents everything good and is idealized). Thus, they are free to blame whomever as the situation arises and as circumstances dictate.

12. *Growth.* Although this is subsumed by many of the preceding qualities, it is distinct enough to warrant separate mention. In short, healthier families show an evolution over time. Over the course of time, they learn to increase the flexibility of their roles, solidify the generation gap, augment their ability to play, increase their responsiveness to individuals, improve conflict resolution, encourage affective expression, solidify family rituals, and so on. This sense of movement leaves family members with hope, which is a significant contributor to the overall sense of team spirit.

In addition to these qualities and characteristics, there are other important family systems considerations for anyone working with adolescents. In this portion of the chapter we are going to discuss two such considerations: the family life cycle and the family genogram.

Family therapists and sociologists have described the importance of the family life cycle concept in working with families, in family research, and in family systems curriculum development. The traditional stages of the family life cycle include the unattached adult, the newly formed family, the family with young children, the family with adolescents, the launching children family, and the family in later life (Carter & McGoldrick, 1988).

Identifying a family's current life cycle stage is a valuable component of any family assessment process. Equipped with an understanding of the concomitant emotional adjustments a family goes through as it makes transitions from one stage of the life cycle to the next, the professional can help families both anticipate and understand many of the issues they currently or will encounter. Although every family follows a unique course through the stages of the life cycle, there are useful generalizations about each stage. Most families with adolescent children will have many similar family issues to resolve, both as they enter this stage and before they are able to move on as a family to the next stage of the life cycle. In contrast to the more peaceful phase of the family with young children, the family with adolescents often will experience turmoil, excitement, growth, and tension. This portion of the chapter will look at family life cycle issues valuable to consider when assessing the family with adolescents.

The fact that couples have the fastest growth in divorce rates at the adolescent family phase of the life cycle reflects the significant stress often accompanying this phase (Carter & McGoldrick, 1988). It is at this stage of the life cycle that families are often required to make major adjustments in a variety of domains. Not since the couple gave birth to the first child has the parent or parents had to juggle so many transitions at once. The transitions the family must endure include the adolescent moving from being dependent to being less so, the potentially new and threatening emphasis on the marital relationship as the children's dependency needs diminish, the increasing needs and problems of the parents' aging parents, the increase in influence of the children's peer culture, and midlife evaluation of each parent about his or her own life (career). It is incumbent on anyone working with the adolescent family to consider the enormous challenges this stage of the life cycle presents for many families.

Up until this point in a family's life cycle, most parents may have felt they were somewhat "in control" of the family dance. As the family tumbles into this roller-coaster adolescent phase, it finds that many of the rules it had for proceeding no longer work. Carter and McGoldrick speak of the value of parents remembering the AA adage at this stage of the life cycle: "May I have the ability to accept the things I cannot change, the strength to change the things I can, and the wisdom to know the difference" (Carter & McGoldrick, 1988). The parents at this stage have a delicate balancing act to execute: to maintain some control and influence over the adolescent while encouraging and providing opportunities for developmentally expected demonstrations of independence and autonomy.

Openness to new or different values, altered family boundaries, and increased rule negotiation are just a few of the demands implicitly or explicitly made by the teens. Parents have not had much preparation for these new phase demands and are often ill-prepared for the developmental punches they find themselves receiving. To accommodate to this phase, parents usually draw on their own experience of being a teen to adjust to their children's challenges. Thus, the professional working with the family at this phase of the life cycle is well advised to inquire about the parents' own experiences when they were adolescents in their family of origin. Gathering a family tree or genogram (see Figure 1) can be a vehicle for guiding both family members and helping professionals in understanding how the parents' own parents dealt with this phase of the life cycle. This process not only encourages each

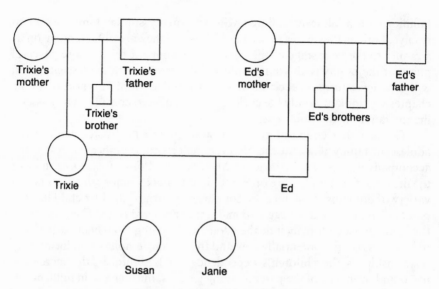

Figure 1. The Norton Family

parent's better understanding of the family of origin rules he or she may be using to respond to current difficult issues but also can help teens gain a historical context for the parents' responses.

Mr. and Mrs. Norton met with the school counselor, Mr. Page, who had met individually with Janie Norton, a sophomore in the high school. Janie had come to the counselor to complain about the extreme restrictions that had been imposed on her since midsemester. The counselor encouraged Mr. and Mrs. Norton to come in for a meeting about Janie's concerns. In the beginning of the meeting, Mr. Page requested that the parents help him gather a three-generational family genogram (see Figure 1). Mr. Page explained that the genogram would help him better understand Janie and her problem in the context of her family. Mr. Page paid special attention to both parents' experiences in their families of origin. He asked each of them questions, while looking at the family tree, about their own parents' approach to dealing with them as teenagers. In talking about her own experience as a teen, Mrs. Norton stated that her parents made her come home directly from school each day, forbidding her from talking with friends, watching TV, or playing after-school sports. Mrs. Norton had done well in school, but with gentle prodding she acknowledged that she was quite unhappy during her adolescence. Mr. Norton's experience was the antithetis. His parents were extremely laissez-faire in their approach to him and his brothers. He barely made it through high school and was in fact the only sibling to go on to college. Relying on these two contradictory models for dealing with teenagers, the Nortons decided that a severe approach was the best to take. Janie had no idea about the parents' own experience of being teens in their families of origin. She was curious to hear more details of her parents' lives as teens. The counselor spent two sessions helping the family members negotiate a more moderate approach to limit setting of Janie's after-school activities. The family took the copy of the family genogram home to share with their other child.

The genogram reveals multigenerational patterns that can be predictive of how a family will respond to the adolescent phase of the life cycle. Another consideration when gathering the genogram is to look at the ethnic background of the parents. Family beliefs about dealing with adolescents and coping with the developmental thrust toward independence and autonomy often have a cultural, ethnic heritage that goes beyond the three generations. Exploration of these beliefs is critical in gaining better understanding of the struggles confronting any family with adolescents. The adolescent's yearning for greater independence is often counter not just to the parents' and grandparents' beliefs or experience but to the culture from which they come. In *Ethnicity and Family Therapy,* McGoldrick, Pearce, and Giordano (1982) discuss in detail the influence of ethnic background on family process, family response to therapy, and family response to illness issues and problem solving. Conflicts around independence, openness, and differing values are often deeply rooted in historical/cultural contexts. The helping professional is encouraged to explore the particular ethnic backgrounds represented by the family of the adolescent to better understand the impact of the ethnic beliefs on the family. A careful assessment of the impact of the family's culture(s) of origin is critical to a thorough understanding of the adolescent family.

Mr. and Mrs. Lugano came to the West Side Mental Health Center to see a counselor about their fifteen-year-old daughter Clara. When requested to tell the counselor what they felt was the problem in the family, Mr. Lugano quickly asserted that his oldest daughter was getting a little too independent for her own good. Clara rolled her eyes as her father talked, looked pleadingly at her mother, and moved her chair as far from her father as possible without crushing the chair against the wall. When the counselor asked Clara for her view on the problem, she said, "Frankly, I think he still would like me to be the little girl that he can take with him every Friday night to Grandma's for dinner." Clara gave other examples of activities which previously had been family ventures but in which she no longer wanted to participate. Mrs. Lugano was noticeably silent throughout this discussion, although she did maintain frequent eye contact with Clara. After gathering a genogram of the family and learning that the parents had quite different experiences in their own families of origin, the counselor asked each parent about his or her ethnic background. Mr. Lugano piped up enthusiastically that he was 200 percent Italian and was proud of both being referred to as "Mr. Machismo" and being a provider for his fine family. He spoke of how he, like his father and grandfather, loved his wife and children more than pasta. He explained he had always provided everything for them as best he could and had never before had much trouble with any of his children.

Mrs. Lugano was British. She spoke of how her brother had gone off to boarding school at a young age, as was common in Britain; she had not gone, due to a prolonged bout of pneumonia during her adolescence. She indicated, however, that in her family children were encouraged to move on, literally and figuratively. This was in stark contrast with Mr. Lugano's cultural tradition, wherein females particularly were not encouraged to be independent or free of restrictions. Mr. Lugano said he remembered his mother telling him stories of her adolescence in a small Italian village where all the girls would stroll in the village square each night while the parents were also strolling. Mr. Lugano found Clara's requests to spend weekend evenings "out, somewhere . . . I don't know . . . just with my friends" as totally inappropriate. Mr. Lugano also was firm in his belief that children, whatever their age, should not talk back or challenge the parental authority.

Only by a thorough appreciation of the impact of Mr. and Mrs. Lugano's cultural beliefs and influences will the counselor be successful in addressing the common adolescent-family struggle around independence, challenging of authority, and desire for increased privacy. A culturally sensitive approach will enable the counselor to see Mr. Lugano's response to his daughter's pleas as a culturally consistent and predictable response, rather than merely a rigid, controlling response to this daughter. Further exploration of the struggles between Mr. and Mrs. Lugano around their very different cultural heritages will additionally highlight the challenges this family will face during this life cycle phase.

Routine incorporation of the family life cycle and the genogram into any preliminary assessment of a family with adolescents will ensure that the presenting problem is considered in a broader context. Before we go on to present the specific dimensions of general family functioning in the screening guide, three special but common family situations deserve detailed discussion. These situations require incorporation of the above considerations, as well as some specific areas of assessment. The special family situations are the blended or remarried family, the single-parent family, and the family with chronic illness.

## Special Considerations for Family Subtypes

### The Blended or Remarried Family

According to a study by Visher and Visher (1979), teenage children, more than children of other ages, have the most difficulty adjusting to remarriage. Coupling the findings of this research with the prediction that in the 1990's, over 35 percent of children in the United States can expect to live with a stepparent for some time before age eighteen (Carter & McGoldrick, 1988), helping professionals must understand the issues confronting the stepfamily with adolescent children.

Consider the following example:

Mr. Fish and Ms. Logan met at a national convention. They each were divorced and were prime candidates for romantic involvement. Mr. Fisk had been divorced for less than a year and was in the midst of resolving his joint custody request. He was the father of Brian, fourteen, and Susan, sixteen. Ms. Logan, twelve years younger than Mr. Fisk had a seven-year-old son, John, for whom she had sole custody.

After a year of primarily out-of-town weekend get-togethers or weekly conference meetings, Ms. Logan and Mr. Fisk became engaged and were married a week before Susan's seventeenth birthday. Susan had threatened her father (with whom she had a good relationship prior to his commitment to Ms. Logan) that she would not participate in his wedding. Susan started staying out late, ignoring her curfew, being abrupt and harsh with Ms. Logan, belittling her father's attention to Ms. Logan, and chiding John at every occasion.

Brian was much less outward about his discomfort with the new arrangement. He, however, started requesting fewer outings with his father, spending more time in his room, listening to music, and talking at length with his girlfriend on the phone. John, who had never had much attention from his natural father, was delighted with the new arrangement. He was very demanding of Mr. Fisk's attention, continuously asking him to play a sport with him at every occasion. He asked to call Mr. Fisk "Dad" and wanted to hold his hand whenever he went with him anywhere.

On Susan's seventeenth birthday she told her dad she was going out with her boyfriend and other friends to a movie and a party. She didn't come home that night, and her father spent hours tracking her down. When Mr. Fisk finally found Susan at a friend's, she stated that she wanted to live with her mother full-time. Mr. Fisk was devastated, because he didn't want to lose the relationship with Susan. He asked her if she would be willing to see a family counselor to discuss what could be done.

The family therapist or other helping professional has his or her work already cut out in meeting with a remarried family. This example highlights many of the most common issues that need to be assessed when meeting with any of the members of a remarried system. Issues of boundary ambiguity, role changes, loyalty conflicts, and integration of different life cycle phases are particularly important to assess in the remarried family system.

**Boundaries.** Boundaries are the invisible lines that give definition to family relationships. Each family has its own implicit boundary rules that define who belongs in each family system and subsystem. Boundaries separate nuclear family from extended family and others in the larger community. At the phase of the life cycle of adolescents, boundary rules are challenged as the adolescent both brings peers into the family and begins to spend more time outside the boundary of the family system. Boundary controversy is magnified with the reorganization of a remarried system. In the above example, Ms. Logan and John intruded in the boundary of the system created between Mr. Fisk, Susan, and Brian. For this remarried system to coalesce, Ms. Logan and John would have to be included in the well-established system of the Fisks. This is not done without struggle and negotiation, often fraught with conflict. Concrete boundary issues are exposed as John tries to create a new subsystem with his stepfather. Brian perhaps experiences this as John's attempt to push Brian out of bounds from his dad. Brian retreats to the bounds of his own bedroom to take refuge and avoid observing his assumed replacement. Susan is taking the boundary limits to the extreme. She is threatening to leave the former established boundary of the family group and retreat to her mother's home.

**Role Changes.** In the remarried family, countless role changes occur as the new members share one household. Not only parental but also children's roles are altered. For the Fisk-Logan system, Ms. Logan is suddenly propelled into a role for which she has had no desensitization training—dealing with an adolescent. Most parents have little preparation for confronting adolescent children, but a relationship with a lifelong history can encourage a parent to press through the challenges: "I've invested a lot in this relationship; I'm not going to give up now." With a stepparent relationship, such as exists between Susan and Ms. Logan, there is little foundation to absorb the adolescent challenges. Ms. Logan is ill-equipped to handle this new role. She and Susan might see each other as competitors for key roles in the household. Perhaps Susan had assumed most of the cooking and shopping responsibilities when she was at her father's home. Seeing herself as a young woman in the family, Susan may feel quite special in this role with her father. Ms. Logan innocently assumes when she enters this system that she will do the cooking, shopping, and so forth. Role conflicts in this situation are inevitable. What is Ms. Logan's role in disciplining Mr. Fisk's adolescent children, and what is Mr. Fisk's responsibility with John? In addition to the parents feeling quite lost in their newfound roles, the children obviously are also suffering. Brian had treasured his position as his dad's youngest child and his only son; he had a special role as his dad's companion, watching or playing sports. John, eager to attach to Mr. Fisk, challenges John's special role in the remarried family. The multiplicity of role changes extends to the grandparents and other family members. Who comes to the school plays? Who flies down for Grandpa's eighty-fifth birthday? Adaptability in role changes can frequently be a challenge to the remarried family system.

**Loyalty Conflicts.** Bray (1986) found that girls in stepfamilies reported more negative stress than boys in stepfamilies or girls in nuclear families. It is hypothesized that this stress reflects the intense emotional involvement that girls most often feel in family relationships. Due to these feelings, the girls often experience a loyalty pull between the parents. Additionally, the girls feel particularly protective of their biological mother when relating to a stepmother. The pull of loyalty conflicts isn't restricted to the domain of the female. In the above vignette, Mr. Fisk would feel tremendous loyalty struggles in wanting to attend to his daughter's unhappiness while trying to keep his new wife from feeling she had caused all the problems. Mr. Fisk would also feel a loyalty pull when John enthusiastically demanded his attention but Mr. Fisk saw Brian needing his attention. Loyalty struggles often result from poorly articulated expectations of new relationships. All the members of the Fisk-Logan system have countless loyalty issues to address. Ahrons's research shows that children function best after divorce if they are able to maintain satisfactory contact with both parents (1981). This research suggests that by keeping in good contact with both parents, the loyalty struggles may be somewhat minimized. If a child is able to maintain contact with only one parent, he or she may feel disloyal to the absent parent. Keeping in mind, professionals working with adolescents and their families must inquire how the loyalty dilemmas are being handled in family systems.

**Different Life Cycle Phases.** McGoldrick and Carter (1988) claim that the wider the discrepancy in family life cycle between the two uniting systems, the greater the difficulty in transition to a remarried family group. Mr. Fisk and Ms. Logan have been living at distinctly different stages of the life cycle—that is, Mr. Fisk, with teens, is seeing his active parenting days soon to come to a close, whereas Ms. Logan, with seven-year-old John, is involved with meeting her son's natural requirements for more active parental involvement. These two stages are discrepant. Examples abound of blended families in which the discrepancy is even more extreme. Situations in which one parent who has finished raising and launching his or her children and now becomes involved with a family of new teens require that the adult partners address the challenges in merging these two life cycle phases. This will call for the stepparents to discuss their different expectations for discipline, rules, roles, and so on. The helping professional's inquiry to the problems of the remarried adolescent life cycle family must include discussion of the discrepant phases.

For children living in remarried families, school problems, pronounced family conflicts, acting out, or severe peer problems might be reflective of reorganizational crises. Any engagement of a remarried family for assessment must include each of these areas of exploration.

## The Single-Parent Family

This discussion will focus on female single-parent households, since they compose the majority of single-parent systems. For a discussion of male single-parent households, see Hetherington, Cox, and Cox (1976). The National Center for Health Statistics has estimated that approximately half of all American school-aged children live in households with either one parent or a stepparent (*Family Therapy News,* 1984). It is inevitable that helping professionals providing family assessments will encounter many single-parent families with adolescents. The issues relevant to consider for such families include financial strains, emotional and physical exhaustion and anxiety about the teen's separation.

**Financial Strains.** A teenager who doesn't request (if not demand) money from his or her parents is a rare breed. Name-brand shoes and clothes, movies, transportation, books, and food are among the items for which the adolescent indignantly bellows, "I need them *now*; come on, everyone *else* has them." The single parent of the adolescent is commonly in a difficult financial situation that makes it hard to respond to these needs. What often ensues is a torrent of debate between teen and parent about what can and cannot be afforded. The result of debate is often resentment or disappointment from the teen and guilt, rage, or depression from the parent. Conflicts over financial strains can produce frequent tension between the family members. Considering that the average income for single-parent (female-headed) households is $9,000 (*Family Therapy News,* 1984) for those who receive support and $6,000 for those who do not, financial problems are likely to be a major source of anxiety and conflict.

**Emotional and Physical Exhaustion.** The financial worries confronting the mother heading the single-parent household often motivate the parent to work full-time to make ends meet. Working all day and then returning home as the sole parent, the mother often feels drained and unable to provide necessary emotional or instrumental support. The demands of teenagers to engage in prolonged debates about going out on a weeknight, needing a ride to a football game, or wanting to go shopping at the last minute for a prom dress can all be experienced as overwhelming demands for the exhausted single parent, who dreams of turning to a supportive other, saying, "Can you do that tonight? I'm wiped." Often the outcome of the emotional and physical exhaustion is a conflict, since teens have little tolerance either for waiting or for ambiguous statements, as in the mother saying, "I would like to take you to look for the shoes, but I am not sure if we have enough money right now and I'm less sure if I have the energy to do that tonight." Such legitimate claims by the parent can fuel an outburst of intolerance from the adolescent.

**Difficulty in Separation.** A critical task for the adolescent in any family system is to become increasingly independent. Often the adolescent executes this transition with small explosions rather than gentle moves. The single-parent household experiences these shocks with various responses, depending on the parental situation. The history of the parent-child relationship is important to assess. If the teen has previously been a source of emotional and instrumental support to the single-parent mom, the declarations of independence can be difficult to absorb. The growing thrust toward separation may, for the single parent, feel like another abandonment. The adolescent's dating, private conversations, and reluctance to share information can all trigger separation anxiety in the single parent if other support persons are not available. Conversely, the single parent can stir separation anxiety in the adolescent. In situations where the single parent, formerly quite dependent on the teen, now becomes less available, separation can be distressing to the adolescent.

> Mrs. June Belsky lived with Sarah, sixteen, and Sean, nine. The first few years after her divorce from her husband, June had trouble coping with her single-parent status. During these years, she leaned heavily on Sarah for support and energy to deal with her own issues as well as the demands of active Sean. Sarah had always been the "good" daughter June had hoped she could be. In the past year, June had got involved with a support group for single parents, as well as having become an active member of Parents without Partners. At Parents without Partners June met a man about whom she was very excited. Recently she had a distracted demeanor when she was talking with Sarah and was home much less often than usual. This involvement coincided with Sarah's natural inclination to explore a

less "good" world—dating, experimenting with alcohol, and being less motivated to study. The lack of predictability about Sarah's mother left her, however, feeling quite unstable. If she was to wander from her anchor, she wanted to be reassured that the anchor was definitely there. Sarah had decided to be more extreme in her experimentation, in the hope that it would bring her mother back into her own orbit.

Separation issues are difficult to resolve, even in resource-rich environments. For the single-parent household, these issues can exert problematic pressures that need to be understood and addressed.

## The Family with Chronic Illness.

Two aspects of chronic illness affecting the family with adolescents will be briefly explored: the family with a chronically ill adolescent and the family with adolescents and a chronically ill parent.

Elizabeth had been diagnosed with juvenile diabetes at the age of eight. She had adjusted fairly well to the required insulin-dependent regimen she was forced to accept. She was compliant when her mother needed to test her blood sugars at the younger ages. She had agreed at age ten to go off to a diabetic summer camp, where she developed some greater self-care skills—learning to do her own testing and monitoring. Her mother had a little trouble allowing her such autonomy but was able to adjust when Elizabeth and she struck a compromise: Elizabeth would do the testing on her own every day, and twice a week Mom would watch and confirm her results. Elizabeth's mom had taken full responsibility for the cooking of foods and the purchasing of groceries, thus ensuring a pretty tight control on the incoming food items stocking the pantry shelves and refrigerator racks. The system was working quite well until Elizabeth entered high school. It was at this time that Elizabeth's mom called the school counselor for help. "I'm worried that she is going to really harm herself if she doesn't resume the same strict control we had her under before she came to the high school," Mrs. Leader, in an exasperated tone, said to the counselor.

Issues related to an adolescent's coping with chronic illness often reverberate throughout the entire family system. Elizabeth is demonstrating a prevalent response to chronic illness. It would be quite natural for Mrs. Leader to tell the counselor that Elizabeth is sometimes missing her testing and being less rigid in her insulin injection times—sometimes sleeping too late and giving herself the insulin at the outer edge of safe time. Of gravest concern, Mrs. Leader might be worried that Elizabeth is abandoning her former control around her sugar-free diet. Her worst fear would be that Elizabeth will start drinking or smoking.

When a child has been coping with a chronic illness over an extended period, several conflicts inevitably emerge as he or she enters adolescence. Conflicts over autonomy—self-control—are common. The teenager has the desire to reject the control and the consistent care needed in many illness regimens. As is well established throughout this book, the teenager's ambivalent quest for autonomy inevitably includes a rejection of former compliant behaviors. Elizabeth no longer wants to be her mother's good daughter who takes such good care of her diabetes. She certainly would no longer want her mother intruding into her care of the diabetes. Elizabeth desires privacy for her phone calls and her friends' visits, and so of course she would want similar privacy for her personal care, which includes her diabetes. Additionally, Elizabeth desires more autonomy from parental expectations on weekends—"I'm going with my friends to Wendy's and then to a movie and afterward to get something to eat." Each of these activities includes possibilities of great intake of sugar. Elizabeth's mother's response to her projected plans could greatly affect her behavior. If her mother is respectful and encouraging of her good judgment, Elizabeth will have less reason to rebel against her perception of her mother being too controlling with her diet. If, however, her mother starts lecturing to her about the dangers of her being careless and so on, she might well be tempted to say to herself (or to her mother directly), "Well, screw you. I am in charge of my body, not you or Dr. Post; I'll eat what I damn please."

The interaction between an adolescent with a chronic illness and a family system requires exquisitely sensitive communication between the parents and the adolescent so that the illness does not become the object of conflict around control. Hopefully, other control issues—dress, a clean room, homework, the use of the car—will provide enough opportunities for teen-parent conflicts that the teens can deal with their disease more and more on their own. If teens feel unable to assert themselves in any other area, the disease can become the battleground for a "war" of independence. The counselor meeting with the family and teen coping with the chronic illness must explore how control/autonomy issues are being addressed at this fragile stage. The impact of the disease on the teen's ability to function as other peers do is also worthy of exploration. For the most comprehensive discussion of the impact of the chronic illness on the family system, the reader is encouraged to read John Rolland's *Helping Families with Chronic and Life Threatening Disorders* (1992).

The Homans family consisted of Linda, forty; Don, thirty-nine; Sandy, seventeen; and Daniel, ten. Two years ago Don had been diagnosed with multiple sclerosis after a prolonged period of extreme fatigue, occasional difficulty walking, and general malaise. Unlike that for many other victims, Don's course seemed to be progressing rapidly. He often felt too exhausted to work and was having trouble walking. Don had worked as a letter carrier for the past fifteen years and loved both the job and the security it provided to him and his family. Linda worked part-time as an occupational therapist at a local hospital. She worked part-time in order to giver herself additional time to attend to both of her parents: her mother in a nursing home and her father living in his home. With the onset of Don's disease process and its steadily worsening course, Linda needed to rely more and more on Sandy to do many of the house-tending activities that Don had done when he was healthy. His mail delivery job had allowed him to be home early in the afternoon so that he could pick up the slack while Linda attended to her parents. Now that her dad was sick, Sandy was busy making meals, doing the grocery shopping and the laundry, and driving Daniel to his various activities. Before Don's course worsened, Sandy had hoped to go to college on the East Coast but was now procrastinating about filling out any of her forms. Although her parents both encouraged her to get the applications off, Sandy merely gave myriad excuses why she couldn't do them. One afternoon Mrs. Homans received word from the school counselor, who had been contacted by several of Sandy's teachers noting a gradual decline in her work. The counselor called to see if Sandy's parents would be open to meeting at the school.

A chronic illness is never a timely occurrence for any family system. The family with adolescents has its own important issues to resolve when a parent of adolescent children is dealing with chronic disease. In the Homans family, many classic family issues are evident. For Sandy to feel that she can comfortably be launched from her family system, she needs to feel that her parents can spare her. In this situation, it is unclear who will fulfill the roles that she has assumed since her father became so ill. Assuming that Sandy typically would like to be out with her friends and sometimes be a little less adultlike and responsible, she now has little opportunity to assert her independent spirit. Her sabotaging the college application process has several outcomes for this family. If Sandy were to move off her position in the family mobile, major shifts would have to occur for others in the family: Daniel taking new responsibilities, Linda finding alternative ways of being attentive to her parents, and Don seeing new methods of involvement in the family. This family would have to address these significant role changes before Sandy could feel free to "abandon" this fragile ship she is so instrumental in keeping afloat. By Sandy not getting her college applications done, she is rebelling in a way that causes no change for anyone else in the family. Sandy's reluctance to finish her applications can become a major focus of family controversy. As long as the family can organize around this problem, the family does not have to address any of the more powerful situations confronting the system—nursing home decisions, Mother's job stress, and, most importantly, Dad's disease. Perhaps Sandy's concern about the financial strain her college venture would put other family members under contributes to her procrastination. Only through an open discussion of the impact of the chronic illness on this family system can the adolescent and parents resolve the complex decisions facing them.

Thus far, we have presented many consideration is for the professional engaged in assessment of the adolescent and family system. We have presented general qualities and characteristics, as well as the family life cycle, the genogram, and special elements of family systems to consider when assessing a single-parent family, a remarried family, or a family with chronic illness. Being mindful of these family considerations will ensure a rich and thorough assessment of a family system. We next want to present a concrete guide to help professionals carry out a systematic assessment of the family with adolescents.

## "The Guide to Family Observation and Assessment"

In an effort to provide a systematic and organized conceptual framework for assessing families, we developed "The Guide to Family Observation and Assessment," or GFOA (see the Appendix). This guide provides school counselors, mental health professionals, probation workers, and crisis intervention counselors with a systematic and thorough approach to a family with adolescents. We recommend that these helping professionals routinely use the guide when needing to make a family assessment, until the family concepts covered in the guide are naturally integrated. Each of the twenty-one dimensions in the guide are described in straightforward terms that avoid jargon. The simplicity of the language and concepts should make the guide user-friendly. Each dimension has anchor points that guide professionals in assessing the family on a certain aspect of family functioning. These anchor points present a range of descriptors. The intention of the guide is to expand, not reduce, the way counselors, therapists, and others see a family system. We chose the twenty-one dimensions we felt were most important to consider when assessing families. The guide evolved as a method to teach residents in primary care and psychiatry an organized way to think about and approach a family assessment interview. We encourage readers of this chapter to see if this provides them with a useful outline and valuable content areas when interviewing a family. We hope it serves both as a guide to families for those working currently with family systems and as a teaching instrument from which individuals new to the field of family systems can feel better oriented. The time to complete the guide will vary, depending on one's familiarity with the terms and the depth of detail one uses in the "Describe" section. In this part of the chapter we will review the categories of the GFOA and provide some ideas about what to ask and observe during the interview to assess families.

1. *Family nationalism.* An assessment of the sense of the whole is gained primarily from observations of the family. Direct questions are generally of less value here. We would observe the overall level of energy in the family, the sense of trust they demonstrate in one another, and the family affect when all together. We wonder, Do they seem to like one another? Do they seem to have respect for one another? Is there an openness to one another's thoughts and feelings? We also take keen notice of our own feelings in being in the presence of the family. Dysphoric affect (i.e., depression, anger, irritability, tension, fear, etc., but not mere sadness) in the observer/evaluator is generally a sign of deficits in family nationalism. One last note to keep in mind is that while parents typically set the tone for all family relationships, children, especially adolescents, in turn exert a major influence on the parents. Certain adolescents, particularly those with serious psychiatric or developmental disturbances, may wreak havoc on the overall sense of family nationalism. Thus, this category may be rated problematic while many or even most other categories remain quite adequate.

2. *Family involvement.* Under this section we attempt to answer three questions: (a) Are family members companions for one another? That is, how much time do they actually spend with one another? (b) Are family members emotionally supportive of and able to listen to one another? (c) Do family members offer themselves for material support? For example, do they support one another financially, if necessary? Would they help another member move into a new apartment?

Observations that we find helpful in this would be:

(a) Do family members touch one another? in the waiting room? after they leave the office?
(b) Is the contact gentle and loving, or is it harsh and/or abrupt?
(c) Do family members sit near to one another? Do they make eye contact with one another?
(d) When there is expression of sadness or pain, do others offer comfort?

Direct questions we have found useful to assess this area including the following:

(a) What do you do for fun with one another? with Father? with Mother? with siblings? with your grandparents?
(b) If Johnny were troubled about something that happened, what would he do? Would he talk to someone? if so, who?

(c) If Johnny needed help with homework what would he do? Would he ask Mother? Father? What would they do?

3. *Family's respect for the individual.* In this area we are trying to assess whether the family has respect for each individual's privacy and autonomy, as well as the universal desire to feel in charge of one's self/life. It is recognized that at times it is appropriate for parents to intrude in their children's lives. What would trouble us would be a general pattern of interaction that disregarded the developmental status of the child, situational factors, or the child's appropriate sense of autonomy.

We make the following observations to assess this area:

(a) Do family members speak for one another without invitation?
(b) Do family members touch one another in unwanted ways?
(c) Do family members interrupt one another during conversation?

Useful questions to ask include:

(a) Is there a history of sexual abuse?
(b) How do the parents feel about closed doors?
(c) Do parents listen in on children's phone conversations?
(d) Do family members offer opinions when not asked?

4. *Parental appreciation of developmental needs.* This area assesses whether the parents have a reasonably accurate appreciation for what it's like to be an adolescent in this culture at this time. We especially look for parents' appreciation of adolescents' struggle for separation from their families, their need to feel competent, a sense that they are in charge of their own lives, the need to gradually and healthily learn about sexuality, and the need to establish an independent identity. An independent identity involves a personal grappling with such issues as What are my values? my worldview? my priorities? What is a friend? Who are my friends? What is love? What is a lover? What are my career/vocational goals? my educational goals? Healthier parents recognize that these issues cannot be decided for an adolescent, though at the same time they recognize that their experience and opinion may be invaluable in helping the adolescent come to his or her own resolutions. Although we would also see the learning of accountability as being a developmental need of the adolescent, this area is addressed in items 6, 7, and 10. In less healthy families, parents attempt to rigidly control the adolescent's life, with little or no sense of the need for a gradual increase in responsibility. Independent opinions are experienced as threatening and hence are discouraged. Another less healthy version would be the parents who ignore the adolescent and provide no structure, under the guise of encouraging the child's independence (see also item 9).

Observations of the family that are helpful include the following:

(a) Do parents convey respect for the adolescent's opinions and feelings?
(b) Do parents encourage the adolescent to speak for him- or herself?
(c) Do parents' expectations leave the child in a position of feeling competent about him- or herself?

Questions that may be useful include the following:

(a) At what age can an adolescent date?
(b) In ten years, what will this adolescent be doing? be married? have children? work?
(c) What is the adolescent's curfew?
(d) Does the adolescent receive an allowance?
(e) What activities do the parents and adolescent do together? In recognition of the fact that two parents may have different levels of appreciation of an adolescent's needs, we have created separate evaluations for each. This approach also applies to 5 and 6.

5. *Parental appreciation of adolescent's abilities.* Adolescents, like all human beings, have differing abilities/disabilities, vulnerabilities/strengths, and talents/deficits. Further, adolescents develop physically, emotionally, socially, and cognitively at different rates and in their own pattern. The parents' ability to see their adolescent accurately and respond accordingly in this regard is a hallmark of healthier functioning. Some adolescents are ready for a driver's license at sixteen, while others are not; some are able to hold a job and go to school, while others need a single focus; some are ready to date at fourteen, while others aren't until nineteen. These are but a few of the myriad considerations that arise. What we look for is whether the parents display an accurate reading of their children—in other words, a recognition of "who they are." Healthier parents regularly and accurately recognize their child's abilities, with a minimum of distortion due to their own needs to see a child in a particular light. Less healthy families show greater rigidity in their responses to an adolescent, basing them on outdated expectations from their own upbringing or on childhood (or adulthood) disappointments that the parent hoped would be made up for by the adolescent (and inevitably are not). The most troubled families have virtually no ability to see the adolescent outside of the expectations and needs of the disappointed parent, leading to grave shame-inducing interactions. The following serves as an illustration of this point:

Suzy was the older of two children living with her parents. Although at fifteen she was interested in boys, she showed no interest in dating per se or in having a boyfriend. Separately, she had told the therapist that she had no interest in kissing boys and that a sexual relationship frightened her. Despite this, her father repeatedly made efforts to rigidly control her whereabouts, associates, curfew, and so forth. Although he initially would not acknowledge why, it became clear that he was certain she was having sex indiscriminately. It later came out that father had impregnated a girl when he was sixteen, yet he had no sense that this was the source of his concern regarding his daughter; rather, he insisted that "You know, that's the way girls are these days!"

In assessing this area, observations are more helpful than direct questions, although it can be instructive to ask what the parent thinks the adolescent is "good at" and "not good at." In the course of the interview, we mainly look for a congruence (or lack thereof) between our own perceptions of the adolescent and the parents' descriptions of and responses to the child. When these are consistent with each other, it is a sign of higher functioning; the more inconsistently these perceptions approach each other, the more dysfunctional the family.

6. *Parental acknowledgment of positive behavior.* Under this category we assess the extent to which the parents recognize desired behavior, healthy behavior, good intentions, and accomplishments. Healthier parents do this regularly and directly (i.e., openly and with words). Less healthy parents rarely acknowledge these behaviors. Instead, the behaviors are entirely overlooked or ignored, as the parents appear to be consumed with their own concerns. Often in these situations praise or other positive recognition is given for oppositional or noncompliant behavior with others (outside the family) and is further reinforced by the protracted negative attention this behavior receives when directed at the parents observations that are helpful include:

(a) Do the parents make any positive comments about the adolescent?
(b) Do the parents make positive comments about any adolescent achievement referred to during the interview?
(c) Do the parents recognize the adolescent's good intentions or desired behavior occurring during the interview?

Direct questions that may be helpful include the following:

(a) What do the parents do when the adolescent does well in school? Does the adolescent feel recognized for any of his or her achievements(e.g., sports, art, music, peers, clubs, church?
(b) Does the adolescent feel appreciated for his or her genuine efforts?

7. *Parental alliance.* This category addresses whether parents are in major agreement with each other about their values and approaches in child rearing. We are also attempting to assess whether they are able to support each other in accomplishing their goals as parents. Healthier parents share common values, priorities, and worldviews, while generally acting in ways that support each other. Less healthy parents have major differences in the preceding areas and are unable to resolve these differences, leading to repeated or continuous undermining of each other. The most common version of this is the situation in which Mother feels that Father is too harsh and therefore acts in overly "soft" ways; in the meantime, Father feels he must respond to Mother's softness by becoming increasingly punitive. During the interview, observations can be made when the parents discuss any issue regarding parenting (e.g., curfew, use of the car, house rules). This allows the interviewer to gain firsthand knowledge of how the parents approach this kind of problem, the types of differences that come up, and their methods of resolving them.

Direct questions that may be helpful include the following:

(a) Do the parents generally agree about a broad approach in raising children?
(b) What happens when the parents disagree with each other? How do they resolve differences?
(c) How often do the parents disagree?
(d) What typically happens if the parents can't agree?

8. *Parental perception of children as a subgroup.* Parents' perceptions of their children are always a reflection of the child's traits as seen through the *parents'* eyes. While all children are different (and hence are responded to differently), healthier parents exhibit a basic sense of balance and fairness in their interactions with their children. There is a recognition that no child is the repository of all bad in the family, just as no child is the repository of all good. Whether recognizing accomplishments, settling differences, or buying presents, healthier parents display an evenhandedness in the process. Less healthy parents reveal an inconsistency in this area that typically leads to frequent sibling bickering, conflict, and charges of unfairness. In the most disturbed situations, one child is seen by at least one parent as all bad, hateful, evil, or, in the worst situations, subhuman (e.g., the child may be referred to as "It"). Direct questions regarding this category are generally unnecessary, as the relevant observations are usually readily made in the course of any family discussion in which all members are present.

9. *Sibling alliance.* Under this category we assess whether siblings are available to one another for support, discussion, companionship, or material aid. In healthier families, siblings are able to form at least one supportive, confirming relationship. In the least healthy situations, children are in chronic

conflict, treat one another sadistically, dislike one another, and have little or no empathy for one another.

Observations that are helpful in this area include:

(a) What is the tone of the relationships between the siblings?
(b) Is there a sense of respect for one another?
(c) Is there a demonstrated interest in one another's feelings and opinions?

Direct questions that are helpful include:

(a) What do you do for fun with your brother/sister?
(b) If you had a problem, would you discuss it with a brother or sister? Would they be responsive?
(c) If you needed something—for example, money, help with homework, or a ride—would you ask a brother or sister? Would they respond?

10. *Generation distinctions.* This item refers to the clarity in the family between generations. In other words, do the parents know they are the parents and the children know they are the children? What appears to be important for healthy family functioning is a general family orientation in which parents are a distinct subsystem, with their own set of rules, sense of teamship, and shared roles, while children are children, with a similar subsystem identity. If the children are in charge within the family and there is no discernible distinction between the generations, one must be concerned about the role of parental guidance, nurturance, and limit setting. The setting of appropriate limits is one key indicator of there being a gap in generations in the family system. If children have no sense of rules, if there is no one making or enforcing the rules, the problem may well reflect a lack of clear generations in the family. If a grandparent is dictating consequences for a teen's behavior and circumventing the parental authority, a problem in generational clarity exists. Flexibility in the degree of clarity of the boundaries between the generations is expected in situations of single parenting or chronic illness, as discussed above. In these situations, children might sometimes need to act in a role more similar to that of the parental generation. Even in these situations, however, it is also important that the children (adolescents and younger offspring) know that they are the children and that the parent or parents are the parents. Families, depending on their ethnic and cultural heritage, will vary in the degree of hierarchical authority and democratic process between children and parents. This is again where the concept of generation distinction needs to be flexible enough to allow such variation yet still keep parents separate from the children in their role function. We are not proposing that a family look like a military boot camp, and we will concede that

many "healthy" families don't have rigid generational distinctions; however, we are also aware that in many families there are casualties (primarily sexual abuse) when inadequate distinctions exist between generations.

Observations that are helpful in this area include:

(a) In a discussion of a rule infraction, do the parents tell the adolescent clearly and unequivocally to stop?
(b) Do the parents provide consequences for broken rules?
(c) Do the parents follow through with the consequences?

Direct questions that may be helpful are:

(a) What do you [the parents] expect your adolescent to do at home in the way of chores?
(b) Are there any other rules you expect your adolescent to follow?
(c) Who decides what the rules will be for your adolescent?
(d) How do you decide?
(e) What do you do if a chore is not done or a house rule is not followed?

11. *Adult/spousal alliance available.* It is important to assess whether the adults in the family sense that there is an adult alliance for them. In this dimension we are interested both in the availability of someone to do something with or get support from and in the availability of someone to talk with. If there are two parents in the home, one would look to that relationship offering a strong alliance for each adult. Unlike item 7 (parental alliance), this dimension is not solely focused on parenting; rather, it concerns the adult feeling that the parent has another adult to turn to for a variety of areas of support. For a single parent, this alliance might come through several people—for instance, a girlfriend for emotional support around dating, parenting, and the like, and a parent for financial, emotional, or child-care support. The presence of a support adult can reduce the stress experienced by the parent at this stage of the life cycle. The presence of an alliance can also reduce the inclination for a parent to form a significantly dependent relationship with one of the children.

Observations that are helpful in this area include:

(a) Does the parent(s) in the system mention another adult in or outside the family system to whom he or she can turn for support—emotional, recreational, physical, if needed?
(b) Do the adults in the system seem to agree with each other and acknowledge each other, or are they working as isolated units?
(c) Does the parent(s) talk of other adults as sources of support or as sources of stress?

Direct questions that are useful to ask each adult include:

(a) To whom do you turn for support?
(b) Do you feel you have a sense of teamship with any other adults?
(c) To whom do you turn when you are feeling very stressed?
(d) If you are struggling with your teen around a curfew or a room-cleanup issue, with whom would you talk about it?
(e) If you wanted to go out for a little while with someone else, to whom would you turn for company?

12. *Family communication.* Members of the family system feel that there is someone else in the family to talk with if they desire that communication. It is helpful to look for the following:

(a) Each family member acknowledges that he or she has someone to talk with if needed. Each is satisfied with the communication in the family.
(b) Family members acknowledge that some members in the family feel satisfied with intrafamily communication and some do not.
(c) No one feels satisfied with the communication in the family.

Talking and feeling listened to are two important aspects of communication that should be accessible to all family members. Certainly, at different stages of the life cycle children are going to be less inclined to be extremely communicative to parents and siblings. The critical element in this dimension, however, is that all family members perceive that there is a general disposition in the family to being able to talk to someone if one needs to and to be listened to. There are great variations in family and ethnic styles as to the range of feelings expressed and the degree of openness endorsed in communicating with family members. It is our contention, however, that for a family to function in an adequate way, having someone to talk to and having someone who will listen are critical. Satisfaction indicates feeling understood or responded to.

Observations that we find helpful in this area would be:

(a) When individual family members start talking, other family members listen.
(b) Family members seem comfortable talking to one another, versus stopping midsentence or mididea with the assumption that people don't want to listen.
(c) Family members listen without frequent interruptions that make the completion of an idea impossible.

Direct questions that we have found useful to assess this area include the following:

(a) Do you each feel that there is someone in the family to whom you can talk and who will listen to you?
(b) When you try to express a thought, feeling, or idea to another family member, do you feel satisfied that the person is interested and understands?
(c) Do you feel that there is no one to talk to or to listen to you in your family?

13. *Involvement with grandparents' well-being.* Increasing numbers of parents are finding themselves in what the media has referred to as the "sandwich generation." With men and women living longer and couples often making the decision to have children later, many parents of teenagers find the demands of adolescents coinciding with the demands of their own aging parents. Caring for aging grandparents can be complex and time-consuming. It is important to explore the emotional or physical demands of caring for grandparents and the degree to which these demands limit the parents' ability to attend to the needs of their children.

Observations that may prove helpful are:

(a) When either parent talks about the grandparents, do the children look sad, seem angry, or avoid eye contact?
(b) Do the parents seem overwhelmed by the combined demands of caring for children and grandparents?

Direct questions include:

(a) To the parents: Can you tell us a little about your parents? Are they in good health? Do you have many responsibilities for them at this stage of your life? Do these responsibilities make it difficult for you at home?
(b) To the adolescent: Does it seem like your parents are spending lots of time attending to your grandparents?

14. *Family problem-solving skills: Being competent to meet everyday needs—demonstrating flexibility.* Often what is stated as the family's current problem reflects a paucity of problem-solving skills in the family system. A family with a limited repertoire for solving difficult situations frequently gets into a vicious circle that only promotes rather than resolves the problem. Many times a family will use the same solution to a particular problem instead of trying out alternative solutions. One of us recollects Rita Mae Brown having said that the definition of craziness is doing the same thing over and

over again and expecting a different result. With teenagers, there are count-less opportunities for a parent's repertoire of problem-solving skills to be tested. A family system that generates alternative solutions to old problems demonstrates a flexibility and innovativeness that will allow it to resolve the encountered challenges.

The ability of family members to adapt to new roles is one of the most important aspects of problem solving to assess within the family. For in-stance, in a situation where a mother's role has always been that of caretaker, if she becomes ill, can another member of the family incorporate some of the elements of that role? For the teenager, this is particularly important. As the child becomes a teen, new role expectations are often part of the growing-up agreement in the family. Is the family able to encourage and/or allow new roles for the emergent teen? If a parent can no longer function in a respon-sible parental role due to an accident or illness, is the teen able to modify his or her desire to be independent and free and assume more parental respon-sibilities? How the family manages problems that require role adaptability reveals the presence of family problem-solving skills.

Observations that are helpful in this area include:

(a) As family members discuss a problem, do they refer to a variety of approaches they have used in trying to resolve it?
(b) Do most members participate with ideas about resolving cur-rent problems?
(c) Are family members adapting to necessary role shifts that can help the family function (as in the case of a chronically ill par-ent)?

Direct questions that are helpful include:

(a) Can you identify a situation that has been problematic for you in the recent past?
(b) Can you tell me the approach or approaches you used to resolve the problem? Who was involved; who wasn't? Were there var-ious approaches you took? What were they?

Specific questions about role adaptability include:

(c) Has anyone in the family recently needed to change roles?
(d) Are there any roles currently not filled in the family system?
(e) Who used to fill that role, and what prevents someone else from filling it now?

15. *Conflict resolution skills.* Resolving conflicts is one of the most sig-nificant challenges to family systems. With the advent of teenagers, who are

often quite determined to assert their own will and self-appointed authority, the opportunity to exercise conflict resolution skills is often limitless. All families have their idiosyncratic methods of resolving conflicts, and many approaches can work. Ethnic and cultural influences often dictate some of the rules for resolving conflicts. It is not realistic to expect that every teenager is going to feel that in each conflict resolved, he or she received fair and just treatment; however, a sense that, over time, individuals in the family are treated justly is very important. The use physical force, such as hitting, slapping, kicking, or throwing, as a source of intimidation to resolve conflicts is not regarded as a positive approach to conflict resolution. Further, the use of psychological coercion through the expression of verbal threats, such as statements of abandonment ("If you don't stop arguing with me, I'll send you to a foster home tomorrow, and I mean it"), name-calling ("You are such a baby, just like your father was"), verbal put-downs ("You're too dumb to even stay in high school; how could you think of college?"), or shaming statements ("You're no good; in fact, you're just a pathetic example of the human race") are important to be attentive to in looking at this dimension of family functioning.

Observations that are helpful in this area include:

(a) Does anyone start to raise a hand or stand up against someone else in the family when a controversial discussion occurs?
(b) Do you hear any family members saying harsh put-downs or name-calling statements to other family members?
(c) Do you see any family member repeatedly trying to shame another family member?

Direct questions that are helpful include:

(a) After you have had a conflict between two or more members of the family, do you feel that individuals have been treated fairly? Is that how you would describe it most of the time? or rarely?
(b) Can you give an example of a conflict situation in which two or more members of the family were engaged? Who became involved? What happened? How did people talk to one another? How did family members treat one another?
(c) When conflicts erupt, is anyone in the family afraid of being physically hurt?
(d) When there are conflicts in the family, does one or more family members use a lot of words that make you feel respected? or scared? Can you give examples?

16. *Family rituals.* Family rituals help families negotiate difficult life cycle transitions, as well as encouraging family members to celebrate jointly important traditions and celebrations. Imber Black distinguishes between

three categories of rituals that family systems participate in: (a) everyday rituals, such as the good-night kiss; (b) traditions, such as Seder or Easter dinner; and (c) family celebrations, such as anniversaries, birthdays, and weddings (Roberts, 1988). Every family has opportunities to incorporate some aspect of each of these ritual categories in their family life. Imber Black and others (Wolin, Bennett, & Jacobs, 1988) have noted that rituals play a key role in family systems. The observation or celebration of a ritual helps give family members a sense of family identity and can often assist family members in healing during difficult transitions. It is important to assess the family's ritual life. Is this a family that is "underritualized" or is it one that is rigidly hanging onto rituals that no longer have any meaning to the family? In a remarried family system, sensitive negotiation must occur to decide what aspects of each family's holiday tradition will be included in the remarried family's tradition. In a time of a family coping with an acute phase of an illness, does the family remember to continue significant family rituals—say, lighting the candles for Shabbat, having a birthday party for the four-year-old, or reading a bedtime story? Such rituals all provide a sense of predictability and security for family members.

A harsh blow to a family system can occur when the teenager pronounces to the other family members, "I won't be home this Friday for family night. I'll be going to the basketball game with my friends." The family of the adolescent needs to do a careful assessment of what is realistic for this family at this stage of the life cycle. A common struggle for a family that has recently immigrated to this country occurs between the teenage children and the Old World parents. The parents often yearn to hold onto the age-old traditions and rituals that help them feel connected to their family and country of origin, whereas the teenagers, eager to fit in with their peer group, reject certain of the rituals, perceiving them as promoting isolation rather than the integration they seek with friends. This sensitive issue needs to be addressed with families of diverse ethnic backgrounds.

Research reveals that families enduring difficult family crises, such as alcoholism, are less severely affected by the crisis if the family maintains its family rituals (Vaillant, 1983). Careful assessment of both the inclusion of family rituals (daily traditions and celebrations) in the family system and the appropriateness of the continuation of the ritual at the adolescent phase of the life cycle is an important part of any family evaluation.

Direct questions that are helpful include:

(a) Do you have dinner together? Is there a special routine for going to bed? Are there special things you like to do with your parents?

(b) What are the daily or weekly rituals of your family at this time? Have there been many changes in your rituals as you enter the adolescent phase of the life cycle?

(c) What are the important family traditions that you celebrate as a group? Has anything changed in the manner or occurrence of the celebrations?

(d) Are there any important events that were celebrated in the past but are no longer celebrated?

(e) Have family members experienced any significant transition that needed a ritual to help facilitate the transition but didn't have one?

17. *Sense of humor and play.* A sense of humor and a sense of play can help families negotiate difficult life transitions. The presence of laughter, joking, and playful interaction in families reveals a family that has humor and play as resources to counter the natural difficulties that every family meets. The sense of play provides children with access to parents and vice versa in a way that can temporarily diminish distance between family members. In some families, however, joking is perceived as a lack of respect; in these families a rigidity of interaction makes it impossible for children and parents to enjoy each other's company and to engage in a playful manner with members of different generations.

Observations that are helpful in this area include:

(a) Is a tone of play or humor ever evident in this family?

(b) Can people joke with one another or be playful without it being mean or teasing?

(c) Do parents tolerate or encourage children joking with them, or do they interpret this as a sign of lack of respect?

Direct questions that are helpful include:

(a) How does your family play, have fun?

(b) Is playful behavior tolerated or encouraged by family members?

(c) Does humor help the family get through difficult situations?

18. *Substance abuse.* The topic of adolescent substance abuse is addressed in a separate chapter of this book. An assessment of the family system must include an inquiry about substance abuse of all members of the family system. A substance-abusing parent presents a difficult situation for children at any age. At the adolescent phase, the presence of such a parent has an impact in several ways: through the role-modeling, by the lack of stability at home at a time when most teens feel generally less stable, and the risk of the nonabusing parent's dependency on the teen. A substance-abusing family member has an extreme effect on the functioning of the whole family system and cannot be ignored.

The last area of assessment concerning substance abuse in the family pertains to the siblings of the identified patient. If the parents meet with a school counselor about a student's drop in grades, the counselor should inquire about any substance abuse in other family members, including the other children. The presence of alcohol or chemical abuse might be causing great disruption in the family system, with the parents overly focused on the substance-abusing child. The adolescent who has come to the attention of the counselor for possible depression might be reflecting the lack of attention available in a system consumed with one child's abuse problem.

Observations that are helpful in this area include:

(a) Do family members allude to anyone having currently or having had a drug or alcohol problem?

(b) Do people in the family seem extremely protective of one member of the family when questions of chemical abuse are raised?

Direct questions that are helpful include:

(a) Is there currently anyone in the family with a substance abuse problem?

(b) Has there been a history of substance abuse in this family system?

(c) Does anyone feel concerned that another family member might have a drug or alcohol problem?

(d) Has anyone ever been arrested because of being intoxicated?

(e) Has anyone lost a job or relationship because of drugs or alcohol?

(f) Has anyone had health problems related to drug or alcohol abuse?

19. *Current violence.* The presence of violent behaviors—either sexual or physical—is extremely important to assess. (Chapter 4 of this book present a comprehensive discussion of this as it relates to the adolescent. As with substance abuse, it is equally important to assess the presence of sexual or physical abuse by a parent or sibling.

Observations that are helpful in this area include:

(a) Do family members appear extremely cautious with one another?

(b) Is there sexual touching between adults and children?

(c) Is there talk of harsh physical threats by parents to children or by children to parents or other children?

Direct questions that are helpful include:

(a) Are any adults or children feeling fearful for their personal safety?

    (b)  Has there been a history of either sexual or physical abuse in this family system?

    (c)  Is anyone in the family worried about someone acting violently?

    (d)  Is anyone hitting, kicking, or throwing things at any other family member?

    (e)  Is anyone being touched by anyone else without permission?

20. *Additional sources of family stress.* There is a growing body of research on family systems and family adjustment talk is of the impact of stress on family functioning generally and on health outcomes specifically. It is important that any assessment of a family include assessment of past and current sources of stress. Chronic care of an ill family member, remarried family issues, death, the presence of a psychiatric illness like schizophrenia or manic depression, persistent poverty, and unemployment are just a few sources to be inquired about when meeting with a family system.

Direct questions that may be helpful include the following:

    (a)  What are current sources of stress in your family?

    (b)  Does it seem like your family is having harder times now than six months ago? a year ago? What seems different?

    (c)  If you could wave a magic wand and remove a current stress in the family, what would that be?

    (d)  What have been some of the major problems this family has encountered?

21. *Family involvement with community resources.* For many families, reliance on community resources is critical to healthy family functioning. An example of this would be a family with a chronically ill parent or child learning to take advantage of respite care services available or a single mother wanting to enroll in a GED tutoring program in order to get off welfare and start working. Attendance at AA meetings and participation in church bingo games for social contact are additional examples of important community resources to be taken advantage of by a family. It is important to learn if the family is aware of the community resources available and if the family has the means to mobilize or utilize the necessary resources.

Direct questions that may be helpful include the following:

    (a)  Are there any people in the community or in agencies that you have contact with? Who are they?

    (b)  Do you think that your family could benefit by being linked to some resource in the community? What would that be?

    (c)  Do you know where to go for help with any of your family's current needs—for example, VNA, AA, GED tutoring, Head Start?

## Treatment Options and Recommendations

We will conclude this chapter with a few notes on treatment recommenda-tions. They can be thought of as Cliff Notes (abbreviated ones at that) to treatment planning. The front-line professional involved with adolescents generally needs to be able to make triage decisions regarding treatment for adolescents and their families. With this in mind, we have developed a flow chart (see Figure 2) to aid in this process. As with any flow chart, we would caution readers not to take it so seriously that they lose sight of the fact that people are involved. Whenever people are involved, one is well advised not to become too rigid about fitting them into any cookie-cutter theory of assess-ment or treatment. Nevertheless, we find this approach useful and hope that, as readers become more familiar with it, they will be able to use it flexibly to help adolescents.

As one can see at the top, our first priority is to assess the degree of physical danger present in the situation. This assessment of danger is more

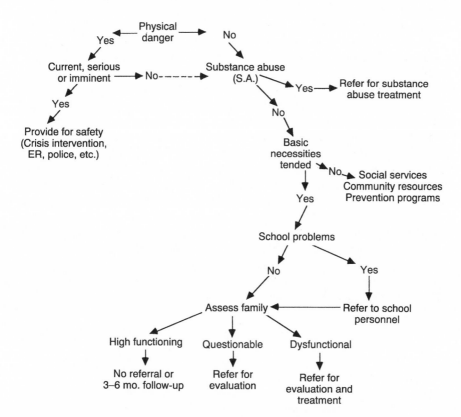

Figure 2. Flow Chart for Triage Treatment Decisions

fully addressed in a separate chapter of this volume; the reader is referred there for further information. If violence to or by the adolescent is felt to be imminent, then one must act to ensure the safety of those involved. In the immediate situation, this means calling in emergency help (i.e., other staff close at hand), or, if the situation can be stabilized for a few minutes or hours, other resources can be called on (e.g., crisis services, emergency rooms, police, shelters). If it has been determined that the adolescent is not in imminent danger, the next step is to attain some sense as to whether substance abuse is currently a problem (i.e., within the past year) for the adolescent or for other family members. If so, it is virtually mandatory that the family be referred for substance abuse assessment and probably treatment. It is our belief that without treatment and complete cessation of substance usage, *any* other treatment effort will be unsuccessful and wasted. If substance abuse is not a current concern, the next area to be addressed is whether the basic necessities of life (safety, food, clothing, shelter, education, medical care, etc.) are being provided adequately. Communities often have programs to meet these needs; such needs should be trended to *before* recommendations for any mental health treatment are made. Departments of social services, hospitals, public or private agencies serving children, and churches, among others, often provide these types of services and are good referral resources. Once these areas are addressed (or if they were not initially of concern), the next area to assess is whether the adolescent is experiencing substantial school problems. Adolescents' lives are so intimately related to school (remember, they typically spend 60 to 75 percent of their waking hours there) that this area must not be overlooked. Because education is crucial to the entire future functioning of most adolescents, even in situations where an adolescent is no longer in school (the most obvious indicator of the presence of "school problems"), professionals need to take care to ensure every opportunity for an adolescent to have a successful school experience. Most school districts have many specialized programs to meet the needs of students "off the beaten track." Principals, school psychologists, and social workers in the child's home school are good resources to contact when the child exhibits problems. Once school programming issues have been addressed (or if they were never an issue), one can look more specifically at family functioning. Using the GFOA, one can make a rough estimate of overall family functioning. Generally, families with adequate "family nationalism" ("a" or "b" on item 1), no history of violence or substance abuse, and the ability to meet most material needs (item 18) are most likely to be categorized as higher-functioning. A follow-up visit in three to six months may be all that is necessary. These families may alternatively benefit from periodic guidance and/or support in adjusting to a dysfunctional adolescent. Only under rare circumstances (e.g., a solidly high-functioning family that has a good understanding of their adolescent's needs and abilities, a high level of ability to resolve conflict, good limit-setting skills, and, strong spousal alliance and that already has had substantial family therapy and desires no more) would we recommend no follow-up with the family of an adolescent who has been identified as troubled. Families that have the ability to meet most material needs, have no history of violence or substance abuse, but have a family team spirit rated as "c" or lower would generally be considered midrange cases. These should be referred to a mental health professional for more detailed evaluation. Families with any history of violence or substance abuse, substantial difficulties meeting their material needs, or any "c" responses on other items are generally seen as dysfunctional and are virtually always in need of further family evaluation and treatment by a mental health professional.

In this chapter we have described a thorough approach for evaluating families with adolescent children. What determines a healthy family is a difficult issue for mental health professionals. Four family therapists from different settings might have varying concepts of what constitutes the healthy family. In this chapter we have presented what we believe are useful concepts to consider in trying to gain a more thorough understanding of how a family with adolescents is functioning. We are aware of the dangers of thinking too rigidly about what constitutes either a "healthy" or an "at risk" family and believe that the model set forth in this chapter will guide and encourage flexible consideration of any family being evaluated.

## Appendix
## Guide to Family Observation and Assessment
(Family with Adolescents)
    Kathleen Cole-Kelly, MS, MSW and David Kaye, MD

1. **Family Team Spirit:** "We are the Smiths—ta da!!!!"
   Family members share a sense of pride in being connected as a group.
   a. Strong sense of family pride
   b. Ambivalent connectedness
   c. Covert tension
   d. Overt tension and antagonism
   e. Disconnected or chaotic
   Describe:

2. **Family Involvement:** Family members offer emotional availability, companionship or information to other family members.
   a. Family members involved with one another
   b. Excessive family involvement
   c. Limited family involvement
   d. No family involvement
   Describe:

3. **Family's Respect for the Individual:** Individual's rights, privacy, growth and development are respected and encouraged by other family members.
   a. Respect for individual boundaries
   b. Intermittent respect for individual boundaries
   c. Virtually lacking respect for individual boundaries
   Describe:

4. **Parental Appreciation of Developmental Needs:** Parents are sensitive to the needs of the adolescent(s)
   Father:
   a. Good enough or accurate appreciation
   b. Inconsistent appreciation
   c. Minimal/no appreciation
   Mother
   a. Good enough and accurate appreciation
   b. Inconsistent appreciation
   c. Minimal/no appreciation

   Describe for mother and for father:

5. **Parental Appreciation for Adolescent's Abilities:** Parents have accurate perception of adolescent's skills, abilities and limitations.
   Father
   a. Good enough and accurate appreciation
   b. Inconsistent appreciation
   c. Minimal/no appreciation
   Mother
   a. Good enough and accurate appreciation
   b. Inconsistent appreciation
   c. Minimal/no appreciation

   Describe for mother and for father:

6. **Parental Acknowledgement of Positive Behavior:** Parents compliment and note good or appropriate behavior of the children.
   Father
   a. Consistent acknowledgement
   b. Inconsistent acknowledgment
   c. Minimal/no acknowledgment
   Mother
   a. Consistent acknowledgement
   b. Inconsistent acknowledgement
   c. Minimal/no acknowledgement

   Describe for mother and for father:

7. **Parental Alliance:** Parents are mutually supportive (can work cooperative in parenting) even if living separately.
   a. Strong alliance
   b. Moderate or inconsistent alliance
   c. Weak alliance (frequent subtle sabotage or overt conflict around parenting)
   Describe:

8. **Parental Perception of Children as Subgroup:** Fairness in perception of children in the family.
   Father
   a. Consistent fairness to all children
   b. Inconsistent fairness to all children
   c. Unfair or biased perception
   Mother
   a. Consistent fairness to all children
   b. Inconsistent fairness to all children
   c. Unfair or biased perception
   Describe:

9. **Sibling Alliance:** Siblings in family have a sense of each other being generally supportive and caring.
   a. Strong alliance—each sibling can name at least one other sibling in the family who is a source of support.
   b. Weak alliance or chronic conflict with no apparent appreciation of each other
   Describe:

10. **Generation Gap:** Clarity in family system between generations
    a. Good clarity—children know the parents are the parents
    b. Inconsistent clarity—some situations clearly evident, some less so
    c. Poor clarity or consistently reversed generations—children and parents act as if children are the parents.
    d. Excessive differentiation to the point of oppressing the younger generation
    Describe:

11. **Adult/Spousal Alliance Available:** Each adult in system has another supportive adult accessible—this could include a spouse, an extended family member, reliable friend, boyfriend/girlfriend.
    a. Strong alliance
    b. Moderate or inconsistent alliance
    c. Weak or nonexistent alliance
    Describe:

12. **Family Communication:** Members of the family system feel there is someone else in the family to talk with if they desire that communication.
    a. Each family member acknowledges that they have someone to talk with if needed. Family members are satisfied with the communication in the family.
    b. Family members acknowledge that some members in the family feel satisfied with the communication and some do not.
    c. No one feels satisfied with the communication in the family.
    Describe:

13. **Parent/s' involvement with grandparents' well-being:** Degree to which family members are emotionally and physically involved with care of grandparents.
    a. Involvement with grandparent/s does not interfere with tending to primary parental functions with children.

    b. Involvement with grandparent/s minimally interferes with tending to primary parental functions with children.

    c. Involvement with grandparent/s is sporadically demanding so that one or both parents is less available to other family members.

    d. One or both parents are consumed by grandparent/s needs to the exclusion of child's needs on a continual basis.

Describe:

14. **Family Problem Solving Skills:** Family's ability both to generate solutions to problems and to try alternative solutions if necessary.
    a. Able to generate and try
    b. Inconsistent ability
    c. Limited ability to generate or try

Describe:

15. **Conflict Resolution Skills:** The family has skills to regularly resolve differences without resorting to physical or psychological coercion. Over time, there is a general sense of fairness about the way conflicts are resolved
    a. Conflicts resolved with infrequent use of shame, with no threats of bodily harm or abandonment and a general sense, over time, that rights are balanced in the family.
    b. Conflicts resolved without threats of physical intimidation or abandonment but shaming used more frequently and family members feeling dissatisfied with the process.
    c. Occasional threats of abandonment, extreme shaming or bodily harm made and a general dissatisfaction with conflict resolution.
    d. Threats of abandonment, extreme shaming or bodily harm are the dominant modality of conflict resolution.

Describe:

16. **Family Rituals:** Family maintains meaningful rituals and traditions.
    a. Consistently maintaining meaningful rituals
    b. Inconsistently maintaining meaningful rituals
    c. Minimal or no rituals

Describe:

17. **Sense of Humor and Play:** Family can playfully joke and have fun together.
    a. Playful and clearly demonstrated sense of humor
    b. Limited display, but clearly part of family's repertoire display
    c. Minimal or none (Life is a bitch and then you die!)

Describe:

18. **Substance Abuse:** Involvement with drugs and/or alcohol
    a. No family history of substance abuse (in members of immediate family)
    b. Does not currently exist, but has in the past
    c. Currently exists in one or more family members

Describe: (Include who—mother, father, child, grandparent)

19. **Domestic Violence:** Physical and/or Sexual Threat or Action
    a. No history of domestic violence
    b. Does not currently exist, but has in the past
    c. Exists currently
    Describe: (Include who—mother, father, child, grandparent)


20. **Additional Sources of Family Stress:** Chronic Illness, Poverty, Trauma/ Loss, Unemployment, History of Psychiatric illness, Remarried Family, Multiple Moves, Inadequate Housing.
    a. Minimal or no sources of family stress
    b. Moderate sources of stress
    c. Significant family stressors
    Describe:


21. **Family Involvement with Community Resources:**
    a. Family has identified and availed itself of resources to meet most needs.
    b. Family has identified needs but cannot find resources.
    c. Family has neither identified needs nor can find adequate resources.
    Describe:

---

## References

Ahrons, C. (1981). The continuing coparental relationship between divorced spouses. *American Journal of Orthopsychiatry, 51,* 315–328.

Bray, J. (1986 Dec. 9) Reported in *Marriage and Divorce Today.*

Carter, B., & McGoldrick, M. (1988). *The changing family life cycle.* New York: Gardner.

Erikson, Erik (1950). *Childhood and society.* New York: Norton

*Family Therapy News* (1984). Changing USA Families, 15(2), 16.

Hetherington, E. M., Cox M., & Cox, R. (1976). Divorced fathers. *The Family Co-ordinator, 25,* 417–428.

McGoldrick, M., & Carter, B. (1988). Forming a remarried family. In B. Carter & M. Goldrick (Eds.), *The changing family life cycle.* New York: Gardner.

McGoldrick, M., Pearce, J. K., & Giordana, J. (Eds.). (1982). *Ethnicity and family therapy.* New York: Guilford.

Roberts, J. (1988). Setting the frame: Definition, functions, and typology of rituals. In E. Imber-Black, J. Roberts, & R. Whiting (Eds.), *Rituals in families and family therapy.* New York: Norton.

Rolland, J. (1992). *Helping families with chronic and life threatening disorders.* New York: Basic.

Rolland, J. (1987) Chronic illness and the life cycle: A conceptual framework. *Family Process, 26,* 203–221.

Vaillant, G. E. *The natural history of alcoholism.* Cambridge, MA: Harvard University Press

Visher, E. B., & Visher, J. (1979). *Stepfamilies: A guide to working with step-parents and step-children.* New York: Brunner/Mazel.

Whitaker, C., & Keith, D. (1980). Symbolic-experiential family therapy. In A. Gurman & D. Kniskern, (Eds.), *The handbook of family therapy.* New York: Brunner/Mazel.

Wolin, S., Bennett, L., & Jacobs, J. (1988). Assessing family rituals. In E. Imber-Black, J. Roberts, & R. Whiting (Eds.), *Rituals in families and family therapy.* New York: Norton.

# 2
# Psychoactive Substance Use and Abuse

*Trina M. Anglin*

## Introduction

Professionals* who encounter adolescents must learn how to assess young people's use of alcohol and drugs. We know that the large majority of teenagers in the United States have used mood-altering substances by the time they reach twelfth grade (NIDA, 1992).

Most adolescents who have used alcohol and drugs do not develop dependence (Newcomb & Bentler, 1989). In fact, experimental use of alcohol and even marijuana may be considered normative experiences for teenagers living in the United States, because such large proportions of youth have tried these substances at least once. Developmentally, youngsters who experiment with substances but do not use them on a regular basis have been found to demonstrate better psychological adjustment than adolescents who by age eighteen have never experimented with drugs. Predictably, however, this study found that teenagers who frequently used drugs were not well adjusted and demonstrated emotional distress, a sense of alienation from others, and poor impulse control (Shedler & Block, 1990). National survey data, however, indicate that 4 percent of high school seniors graduating in 1991 drank alcohol daily and that 2 percent used marijuana on a daily basis (NIDA, 1992). Further information about the scope of adolescent substance use is provided in the next section.

The professional also needs to recognize that several other serious adolescent problems are linked to the use of alcohol and drugs. Several examples follow. Nonintentional trauma, including motor vehicle accidents, drown-

---

This chapter was adapted from the article "Interviewing Guidelines for the Clinical Evaluation of Adolescent Substance Abuse," Pediatric Clinics of North America 34(2) :381-398, 1987. Permission to adapt and to update this article for publication as a chapter in this book has been granted by W. B. Saunders Company, Philadelphia.
* The general term *professional* will be used throughout this chapter. It recognizes that helping professionals who work with adolescents represent a variety of disciplines, including counseling, education, law enforcement, medicine, nursing, psychology, and social work.

ings, and falls, is clearly associated with the use of alcohol and drugs (e.g., Centers for Disease Control, 1982, 1983a, 1983b; Halperin, Bass, Mehta & Betts., 1983; Owens, McBay, & Cook, 1983; Roizen, 1982; Williams, Peat, Crouch, Wells & Finkle, 1985). Both depression and suicidal behavior, each a common problem among adolescents living in the United States, are strongly linked with substance abuse (Joshi & Scott, 1988; Crumley, 1990; Zarek, Hawkins, & Rogers, 1987; Newcomb & Bentler, 1989; Alcohol, Drug Abuse and Mental Health Administration, 1989). Interpersonal violence, including fights between peers and among family members, and homicide are also strongly linked to the use of drugs and alcohol (Centers for Disease Control, 1992). It has also been established that teenagers who have been victimized by physical abuse and/or sexual abuse during childhood are at heightened risk for substance abuse (Dembo, et al., 1990; Zarek, Hawkins, & Rogers, 1987). There is a definite association between delinquency and substance use (Elliott, Huizinga, & Ageton, 1985; Elliott, Huizinga, & Menard, 1989; Newcomb & Bentler, 1989). Finally, homeless street youth are at high risk for substance use, as well as for multiple other serious problems (Cohen, MacKenzie, & Yates, 1991).

Given the broad implications of these problems, professionals have a moral imperative to learn to identify adolescents who use mood-altering substances. At the very minimum, this knowledge will help professionals to provide focused educational counseling for teenagers and their families. Professionals must also learn to recognize when adolescents' use of chemicals is causing functional impairment. Is use interfering with normal adolescent development? In general, if a professional uncovers problems relating to inappropriate use of substances or believes that an individual youngster is at high risk for abusing chemicals, he or she should share this assessment with the adolescent and his or her family in order to guide them to appropriate resources for further evaluation and/or for treatment. The majority of helping professionals do not have the personal expertise or resources necessary to provide ongoing counseling or treatment to adolescents harmfully engaged in chemical use. As trusted advisers, however, they can help ensure that youngsters and their families do receive appropriate treatment for the substance abuse, as well as for any underlying or coexisting problems.

Bright, Hawley, and Siegel (1985) have summarized why assessment of adolescent substance abuse can be difficult. Compared with adults, adolescents have a relatively short history of chemical use and therefore have not always experienced numerous negative consequences from it. There is normative acceptance of excessive levels of alcohol and drug use among groups of substance-abusing youth, so that a single adolescent who consumes similar quantities will not consider his or her use abnormal or deviant. The psychological, familial, and social dysfunction that is frequently found as part of a substance abuse problem may have existed prior to the chemical use or may have been caused by the abuse. Finally, most adolescents' cognitive skills are not yet fully developed. Self-definition and effective problem-solving skills may be limited by the adolescent's cognitive immaturity.

The primary goal of this chapter is to help professionals develop their interviewing skills relevant to assessing adolescents for harmful involvement with drugs and alcohol. Professionals who are sensitive to the issues of substance abuse and who have well-developed interviewing skills should be able to detect youngsters at risk for harmful involvement with chemicals prior to the development of major problems (Macdonald, 1986). The chapter will address the major substantive areas that require evaluation and will provide suggestions for organizing the interview process and for phrasing specific questions. The chapter will also present national survey data outlining the extent of and chronological trends in adolescent substance abuse, discuss the use of written screening questionnaires and the utility of physiological and pharmacological screening measures, and provide a brief overview of treatment options.

## Scope of and Chronological Trends in Adolescent Substance Use

The most useful and widely cited information regarding adolescent substance use in the United States comes from a national survey of high school seniors conducted annually by the University of Michigan's Institute for Social Research. It is part of an ongoing research and reporting program called "Monitoring the Future: A Continuing Survey of the Lifestyles and Values of Youth." The study itself is named the High School Senior Survey. It consists of a representative cluster sample of public and private schools in various geographic sections of the country that are located in communities of different population densities and sizes (e.g., urban, suburban, rural). Data from approximately 16,000 students are collected in classroom settings during the spring of the senior year (NIDA, 1992). It is considered a self-report survey and consists of a questionnaire; students answer questions using a pencil-and-paper format. The survey has been conducted annually since 1975. It is important to remember that a new class of high school seniors is studied each year.

Although there has been a recent gratifying decrease in the proportions of high school seniors who report having used drugs on both experimental and regular bases and alcohol on a regular basis (experimental use of alcohol remained at a relatively constant level between 1975 and 1991), the numbers of teenagers who are harmfully involved in substance use remains unacceptably high. Table 1 summarizes this information. It has three components, which correspond to the concepts of experimental use, probable misuse, and actual abuse of drugs and alcohol. The first, labeled "Lifetime Prevalence," includes youngsters who reported at least one experience with a designated category of substance. Inspection of the remaining components of the table, "Thirty-Day Prevalence" and "Daily Prevalence," demonstrates that far smaller proportions of students self-reported these high-frequency use rates. Although high-frequency users are included in those reporting any lifetime experiences, it is clear that the majority of students included in this component demonstrate experimental use.

An independent, cross-sectional, national survey of adolescent students that used a geographically representative cluster sampling frame was conducted during late 1987 and early 1988. Called the National Adolescent Student Health Survey, it was cosponsored by private organizations that received federal funding (American School Health Association, Association for the Advancement of Health Education, & Society for Public Health Education, Inc., 1989). This study focused on eighth- and tenth-grade students and addressed a variety of adolescent health concerns, including substance abuse. Other issues included injury prevention, suicide, AIDS, sexually transmitted disease, violence, nutrition, and consumer skills. Slightly more than 12,000 students participated in this study. The large majority ranged in age from thirteen to sixteen years. Therefore, compared with the High School Senior Survey, this study was able to report on substance use patterns of younger teenagers. Its findings, however, were quite similar to those of the High School Senior Survey. Overall, this study found that 83 percent of students reported at least one lifetime experience with alcohol, 25 percent reported at least one lifetime experience with marijuana, and 6 percent had used cocaine at least once. When usage during the previous month (which may indicate a problem with substance abuse) was examined, 42 percent of this younger age-group reported recent use of alcohol, 10 percent recent use of marijuana, and 3 percent recent use of cocaine. In addition, almost one-third (32 percent) of students reported binging on alcohol (consuming at least five drinks on one occasion) during the preceding two weeks.

In summary, helping professionals can use the presented national data to help estimate the prevalences of substance use and substance abuse by the groups of teenagers they encounter. It should be remembered, however, that local communities may have patterns of substance use that differ from national averages and that separate groups of teenagers may also display differing patterns of use.

## Psychosocial Assessment

All teenagers should be screened for their risk for harmful involvement with chemicals as part of health maintenance care (American Academy of Pediatrics, 1982), on entering into mental health counseling, as part of the evaluation process for poor or deteriorating scholastic performance, and as part of the intake process into the juvenile justice system. A complete assessment

## Table 1.
## Trends in Prevalence of Substance Use by High School Seniors Living in the United States[1]

| Substance[2] | Lifetime Prevalence (% ever used) | | | | |
|---|---|---|---|---|---|
| | 1975[3] | 1979 | 1983 | 1987 | 1991 |
| Alcohol | 90 | 93 | 93 | 92 | 88 |
| Marijuana | 47 | 60 | 57 | 50 | 37 |
| Total cocaine[4] | 9 | 15 | 16 | 15 | 8 |
| Inhalants | NA[5] | 18 | 18 | 19 | 18 |
| Stimulants | 22 | 24 | 27 | 22 | 15 |
| Sedatives | 18 | 15 | 14 | 9 | 7 |
| Hallucinogens | 16 | 18 | 14 | 11 | 10 |

| Substance[2] | Thirty-Day Prevalence (% used within last 30 days) | | | | |
|---|---|---|---|---|---|
| | 1975[3] | 1979 | 1983 | 1987 | 1991 |
| Alcohol | 68 | 72 | 69 | 66 | 54 |
| Marijuana | 27 | 36 | 27 | 21 | 14 |
| Total cocaine[4] | 2 | 6 | 7 | 4 | 1 |
| Inhalants | NA[5] | 3 | 2 | 4 | 3 |
| Stimulants | 8 | 10 | 9 | 5 | 3 |
| Sedatives | 5 | 4 | 3 | 2 | 2 |
| Hallucinogens | 5 | 5 | 4 | 3 | 2 |

| Substance[2] | Daily Prevalence (% used for at least 20 days in the last month) | | | | |
|---|---|---|---|---|---|
| | 1975[3] | 1979 | 1983 | 1987 | 1991 |
| Alcohol | 6 | 7 | 6 | 5 | 4 |
| Marijuana | 6 | 10 | 6 | 3 | 2 |
| Total cocaine[4] | 0.1 | 0.2 | 0.2 | 0.3 | 0.1 |
| Inhalants | NA[5] | 0.2 | 0.2 | 0.4 | 0.5 |
| Stimulants | 0.5 | 0.6 | 0.8 | 0.3 | 0.2 |
| Sedatives | 0.3 | 0.1 | 0.2 | 0.1 | 0.1 |
| Hallucinogens | 0.1 | 0.2 | 0.2 | 0.2 | 0.1 |

[1] Information summarized from National High School Senior Drug Survey 1975–1991, "Monitoring the Future Survey. NIDA Capsules, ADAHMA, USDHHS, 1992.

[2] Selected categories of substances are presented. The actual survey addressed 16 classes and subclasses of substances, including cigarettes, heroin and other opiates, and anabolic steroids.

[3] Although this survey has been conducted annually since 1975, the information presented in this table represents data from every fourth year.

[4] Total cocaine includes crack, although specific questions addressing the use of crack were not included until 1986.

[6] The survey did not include questions about inhalants until 1976.

of an adolescent for substance abuse requires commitment on the part of the professional and family. For example, Jones (1985) recommended a minimum of three separate visits with a health care professional for the evaluation, including gathering of historical information from the adolescent and his or her family, physical examination and laboratory testing, and interpretation of the assessment to the adolescent and family. In general, however, basic screening by interview can frequently be completed within one or two sessions. Some important techniques of interviewing adolescents are summarized in Table 2.

A general psychosocial assessment of an adolescent provides the infrastructure for addressing actual chemical use. It helps to answer the questions, What roles do psychoactive substances play in the adolescent's life? Are they present at all? How do they fit into, influence, or direct the adolescent's life? This assessment provides the specific information that will help the professional determine whether an adolescent is at risk for abusing chemicals, whether the adolescent is making satisfactory developmental progress, whether the adolescent's adaptive functioning skills are impaired, and whether the adolescent has experienced any negative consequences from chemical use. Table 3 outlines the key substantive areas of exploration.

## Substance Use History

### Initial Exploration

People who abuse chemicals tend to minimize their involvement with them. On the other hand, skillful interviewers believe that if the substance abuser perceives the professional as a helping person, then the history given will be

## Table 2.
## Suggested Interviewing Techniques

Interview the adolescent privately.

Discuss the parameters of confidentiality.

Avoid parental subterfuge.

Ask open-ended questions.

Do not barrage the adolescent with questions.

Do not lecture or moralize.

Be sensitive to the adolescent's responsiveness to your style and to specific questions.

Determine what types of information the adolescent would like to learn or verify, and then provide it.

If the adolescent has no questions, offer information that is developmentally appropriate, using the technique of generalization.

## Table 3.
## Substantive Areas of Psychosocial Assessment

Home and family relationships (constellation, shared activities, respect for parents, organization of family's daily life, isolation, conflict, breaking of family rules, running away)

Family history (use by parents, siblings, and relatives)

School (performance and classroom placement, attendance, behavior, ability to concentrate and remember, involvement in sports and extracurricular activities)

Peers (developmental appropriateness, shared activities, fighting, substance use, involvement in gang activities and gang membership, legal involvement, motor vehicle accidents and traffic citations)

Sexual behavior (romantic involvement, use by boyfriend/girlfriend, risk for pregnancy/fatherhood and sexually transmitted infections, number of partners, prostitution, trading sex for drugs)

Leisure activities (fun, relaxation, preferred music and video genres, community organizations and service)

Employment (where works, position, work schedule, disposition of earnings)

Role of religion (religiosity of parents and adolescent, any unique beliefs associated with their religion's tenets, involvement with youth-group activities)

Physical health (general health and somatic concerns, symptoms of withdrawal, toxic reactions to specific drugs and to alcohol, overdoses, blackouts, history of trauma and injuries, bulimic binging and purging)

History of victimization by abuse (physical, sexual)

Motor vehicle history (driving record, accidents and near misses, traffic citations)

Access to weapons (family, peers, firearm ownership)

Police and court involvement (probation status, history of illegal activities, incarceration, pattern of charges and offenses)

Mental health (depression and moods, alienation, anxiety, hallucinations, suicidal ideation/attempts, anger, impulsivity, history of intervention and hospitalization)

Aspirations and goals for the future (hopes and plans for beyond high school)

Self-perception (self-liking and satisfaction with current life)

valid (Senay, 1983). In particular, most teenagers whose life-styles do not revolve around their use of substances will provide sufficient information about their use of alcohol and drugs to allow the professional to complete an accurate evaluation (Schonberg, 1985). It is critical, however, for the professional to establish an appropriate atmosphere for the interview and to convey trustworthiness and sincerity. The purpose of initial, exploratory inquiries is to help establish the tone of this section of the interview. During this process, the interviewing professional may be tested by the adolescent patient. If the interviewer appears to register disapproval, dismay, or condescension in reaction to initial disclosure statements, it is doubtful that the adolescent will provide accurate information regarding his or her own use (American Academy of Pediatrics, 1982). The professional will have failed the teenager's test and will not be deemed trustworthy or credible. During this exploratory phase, the interviewer can additionally measure the adolescent's willingness to provide open information.

Exploratory issues are phenomenological; they address the adolescent's perceptions of how widely drugs and alcohol are used by other teenagers. Specifically, the interviewer can inquire whether many students at the teenager's school are drinking or doing drugs. If someone wanted to buy marijuana, crack, or uppers, how easy would it be? What happens at parties the teenager has heard about? at parties the teenager has personally attended? This approach is less threatening to adolescents, because it does not ask them to disclose information about their personal involvement with substances. If, however, a teenager disavows general knowledge about the prevalence of substance use among adolescents in his or her community, or denies that drinking and drug use exist, the professional will recognize that a trusting relationship has not been established.

### Elements of a Formal Substance Use History

The goal of this set of questions is to determine the quality and depth of relationship the adolescent has with substances. Minimal time is needed to discuss these issues with a teenager who is functioning well and who admits to little or no use of alcohol and drugs. These questions are useful, however, when the professional needs to explore an adolescent's use of substances more intensively. Table 4 summarizes the elements of a substance use history.

When asking an adolescent to discuss his or her personal use of alcohol and drugs, it is less threatening to use a historical perspective. Before addressing current use patterns, find out about the teenager's first experiences with alcohol and with marijuana: "Tell me about the first time you ever had anything to drink. What was the experience like?" "When was the first time you

**Table 4.**
**Elements of a Substance Use History**

First use: age, circumstances, feeling effects

Past substance use patterns

Current motivation to use (perceived benefits of use)

Current feeling effects of use (included both pleasant and negative experiences)

Current patterns of use (substances used, frequency, binging behavior, circumstances of use)

Current frequency of intoxication/becoming "high"

Tolerance (how much alcohol does it take to get high now? What about six months ago? a year ago?)

Substances of choice

Personal limits to categories of substances willing to try

How substances obtained

Financial resources

Dealing activities

Perceptions of significant others about use (family members, peers, boyfriend/girlfriend)

ever got really high?" The interviewer is trying to accomplish three goals with these questions: (a) to help the adolescent disclose accurate information, to gather facts, and (c) to determine whether the adolescent is preoccupied with the experience of getting high. Although one cannot ask any specific questions that directly address the third goal, one can frequently document such preoccupation through the adolescent's enthusiastic descriptions of what it feels like to be high.

The interviewer should gradually move the questions to the present time. It is useful to have the teenager compare usage patterns: "About how much are you drinking now, compared with last fall when school started?" In identifying patterns of use, the professional will need to learn how frequently the adolescent uses particular substances and how much is consumed at a time: "How many times did you get high in the last month?" Forced multiple-choice answers are a useful strategy for adolescents who find it difficult to answer spontaneously. For example, one could provide the choices "about every month, Saturday nights only, or three times a week?" When was the last time the teenager got high? Is the adolescent using substances on school nights, or is he or she limiting intake to weekends?

It may be less threatening to determine approximate quantities of substances consumed by using the concept of tolerance, rather than asking for this information directly. Increasing tolerance for specific agents is closely associated with more intense use. Tolerance can be addressed historically by determining the relative quantity it takes to get a little high and how much it takes to get really high. Have the teenager compare these amounts with what was necessary to get high six months ago and a year ago.

The interviewer should learn about the circumstances of use. Does the teenager use substances only during parties, or by him or herself? Has the teenager ever used substances at school? What does the adolescent gain from the experience of becoming high? Examples of possible questions that can explore this experience are as follows: "What is it like to be high?" "Has anything really good ever happened while you've been high?" "What does getting high do for you?" The professional should remember that the appetitive effects of substances serve as important motivators for individuals to continue their use once they experience initial pleasurable sensations. They develop a strong desire, or "appetite," for continued use of the substance in order to prolong or re-create the positive feelings. The appetitive model, however, even though it has clearly been invoked as an explanation for adult substance abuse, has not been well studied in or frequently used as an explanation for adolescent substance abuse (U.S. Congress, Office of Technology Assessment, 1991).

Another important area to explore concerns the benefits substance use may offer the teenager. Does intoxication relieve negative pressures and bring the ability to relax? Teenagers who have learned to turn to substances to help relieve anxiety are at special risk for developing more serious problems (Labouvie, 1986). These youngsters risk developing a dependent relationship with drugs and alcohol. In addition, they have not been able to learn healthy mechanisms for coping with stress or for addressing problematic issues (Obermeier & Henry, 1985). A possible exploratory question is, "How do you make yourself feel better when you're really upset or nervous about something?"

The concept outlined above—that adolescents who use substances perceive benefits from their use—was elaborated into a brief formal screening instrument by Petchers, Singer, Angelotta, and Chow (1988). It is discussed in more detail in the section "Clinical Screening Instruments"; however, the professional could incorporate the five items composing the empirically validated scale into the clinical interview by asking the teenager to what extent drugs and alcohol help him or her relax, be friendly, be with friends who drink, forget problems, and feel good about him- or herself. When used in this manner, these questions are meant to enrich clinical information and help youngsters gain preliminary insight into their relationships with substances but are not meant to serve as a formal screening instrument.

Learning how a teenager obtains his or her drugs and/or alcohol may not be possible unless a trusting relationship has developed between professional and adolescent. To obtain supplies, youngsters who have become chemically dependent frequently resort to deviant and illegal behaviors, such as stealing, dealing, and prostituting. It should be obvious that if an adolescent engages in these types of activities, he or she has a serious problem. (Note, however, that youthful, contemporary, successful dealers may not use substances, in order to retain their sharp business acumen.) There is an excellent chance that such an adolescent will exhibit dysfunctional behavior in other areas.

It is frequently enlightening to learn who is concerned about an adolescent's use of alcohol and drugs. Family members, friends, and boyfriends or girlfriends who worry that an adolescent is using alcohol or drugs excessively are usually accurate in their perceptions. The professional should be aware, however, that heightened media publicity about drug use may overly sensitize cautious parents about an adolescent's experimentation. A teenager who abuses substances may be able to admit that a parent is anxious about the use, even though he or she may minimize or belittle the concern. It is quite unusual, however, for an adolescent who is harmfully involved with chemicals to admit spontaneously that his or her involvement is dysfunctional, even when use has caused significant problems.

## Dysfunctional Consequences

Even though adolescents who are abusing alcohol and drugs may not recognize dysfunctional consequences associated with the abuse, helping professionals can play an important role by pointing out to both the family and the adolescent that use has caused problems. The impact of associating a negative consequence with use of substances is more powerful if it occurs close to the time the consequence occurred. For example, as a youngster is recovering from the ill effects of an overdose or acute intoxication, he or she and the family may be receptive to associating the negative event with use, and ultimately be receptive to intervention. The need for an emergency room visit or hospitalization for chemically associated trauma, behavioral aberration, or decreased consciousness is a medical consequence a profession should target (Stephenson, Moberg, Daniels & Robertson, 1984). Such a consequence can be particularly helpful to convince a family that a substance abuse problem exists. An intensive medical experience can be frightening. When people are frightened, they are frequently vulnerable and consequently more open to receiving help. For example, professionals should be aware that adolescents admitted to inpatient substance abuse treatment programs are frequently in crisis. One study, conducted on the chemical dependency unit of a psychiatric hospital, found that approximately 90 percent of admissions had been precipitated by a crisis. The majority of patients (about 60 percent) had exhibited acute conduct and behavioral disturbances and had been admitted because of these problems; substance abuse had not been recognized as a primary reason for admission. Only about 30 percent of patients had admission precipitants that had clearly been identified at the time of admission as being related to drug or alcohol use (Williams, Feibelman, & Moulder, 1989). In addition, this study reported that parents had been aware of their adolescent children's substance abuse for a mean duration of 1.8 years prior to the crisis that had precipitated admission. This study emphasizes the point that substance-using teenagers and their families may be more receptive to help during times of acute crisis than they are at other times and that, unfortunately, they may not seek help until a crisis erupts.

The interviewer should look for other common consequences associated with the use of substances by focused interview questions. Table 5 outlines areas that should be explored.

## Synthesizing Interview Information

The professional, through use of indirect measures, must judge the accuracy of information provided by an adolescent. The interviewer can compare the adolescent's individual historical use of substances with empirical information that supports the "stepping-stone theory." It has been hypothesized and empirically demonstrated that most adolescents follow a specific sequence of substance use. They practically never begin with an illicit drug. The usual sequence is beer or wine, tobacco, hard liquor, and then marijuana. The use of these substances precedes involvement with other drugs, such as cocaine (Donovan & Jessor, 1983; Kandel, 1982; Yamaguchi & Kandel, 1983; Yamaguchi & Kandel, 1984; Voss & Clayton, 1987). For example, if there is

**Table 5.**
**Exploration for Consequences of Substance Use**[1]

Medical and physical
  Somatic symptoms
  Blackouts
  Trauma and unintentional injury
  Visits to emergency facility for intoxication or overdose
Social
  Motor vehicle accidents and near misses
  Conflict with family
  Loss of friends
  Loss of a romantic relationship
  Fighting
  Impulsive sexual behavior
  Destruction of property
  Theft
  School failure
  Disciplinary action (DWI, other legal involvement, school suspension, dropped from sports team)

[1] Note that these common examples of consequences of substance use are embedded in the psychosocial history.

evidence that a youngster has used amphetamines and he or she admits only to using that particular drug, this information is not consistent with empirically described patterns. In addition, even though a youngster may have a substance of choice, he or she does not usually discontinue other drugs previously used on a regular basis. There is more likely to be an addition of a chemical than a substitution of one. Adolescents may, however, clearly avoid categories of substances that caused unpleasant or frightening effects for them.

The professional must synthesize information learned during the substance use history with the general psychosocial assessment. The purpose of the psychosocial assessment is to determine whether the adolescent appears at risk for harmful involvement with drugs and alcohol and whether the adolescent's behavior is dysfunctional. Can the dysfunctional behavior be linked to the use of substances? The substance use history can provide the key to explaining a set of disturbing behaviors. The following example demonstrates this point:

A sixteen-year-old was evaluated by her pediatrician because she frequently appeared pale, listless, and withdrawn to her concerned grandmother. The family had experienced a tumultuous year. An older sibling had been killed accidentally several months earlier, and the parents were currently seeking a divorce. Her visiting grand-mother appreciated that the girl was depressed but thought a medical problem might be present, because a previous mental health evaluation had not been helpful. A careful history revealed that this youngster was going out at least three times a week with her friends, most of whom were eighteen to twenty-one years old. The group would drink until late at night. It was not unusual for the girl to consume eight to ten bottles of beer at a sitting; it required at least this quantity to feel even slightly high. Her school performance had not changed over the past year; she maintained her low-C average. She admitted that she frequently attended school with a hangover and suffered from hangovers on most weekends (when her grand-mother visited). About once a week she shared marijuana joints with her friends but didn't really like the effects. She and her parents saw nothing dysfunctional about her use of alcohol. A short trial of abstinence, however, improved her activity level and facial color. The girl and her grandmother acknowledged the improvement. She was able to associate her appearance and concerning behavior to staying out late, drinking, and suffering hangovers.

Shortly after this assessment the teenager moved in with her grandmother. Within several months her school grades had improved to a B average, and her drinking behavior ended. She started to explore the possibility of attending college.

## Confidentiality

Confidentiality of patient care is a maxim of adolescent medicine. Other professional groups (e.g., law enforcement and justice system staff) may not, however, use a similar guiding principle. In general, clinical practitioners honor the confidentiality of adolescent patients unless there is concern that the adolescent is engaging in life-jeopardizing or serious health-compromising behavior. Substance abuse is clearly a health-compromising behavior. Most professionals would agree that parents need to be included if an adolescent is experiencing serious behavioral dysfunction from substance use or if referral to a treatment program is necessary. It should be recognized, however, that state laws vary regarding the need for parental consent for treatment (Weger & Diehl, 1984). In general, parental consent is legally necessary if treatment requires overnight stay or if medication is administered. In practice, financial responsibility usually necessitates parental involvement. Certain situations may make parental consent meaningless, however. For example, an older adolescent who is still a minor may agree to enter a day treatment program on the condition that his or her parents not be notified. The program receives extramural funding that allows indigent clients to receive services. The professional recognizes that the family itself is severely dysfunctional. The statutes and agency regulations of the adolescent's state of residence do not address the issue of minority. In this set of circumstances, the professional would probably decide to refer the youngster to the treatment agency without involving the family.

More commonly, a professional may be faced with the realization that an adolescent drives while intoxicated or accepts automobile rides from an intoxicated driver. The parents do not seem aware of these practices. Except for this risky behavior, the teenager appears to be functioning well. How can a professional intervene effectively? Should parents be warned? In this situation, the professional may well decide that directly informing the parents would be counterproductive. An alternative approach is to involve the parents and adolescent in a discussion of prevention of unsafe driving practices and passengership. Have the family unit decide how it would handle a future request from an intoxicated adolescent/child for help getting home (Schonberg, 1985). As part of health counseling or anticipatory guidance, the professional can help parents and teenagers to prepare for risky situations and to appreciate that this preparation is helpful for adolescents' maturation into adulthood.

## Clinical Screening Instruments

Professionals who feel uncomfortable with conducting or lack the time to conduct more comprehensive interviews of adolescents may benefit from using previously developed formal clinical screening instruments. Although multiple instruments have been developed to screen adults for alcohol and/or drug use, this section will focus on four that were specifically developed for use with teenagers and that have been published. (Note that the majority of well-known instruments, such as the CAGE [Ewing, 1984] and MAST [Michigan Alcoholism Screening Test] [Selzer, 1971], were standardized on adults and may not have empirical validity for teenagers.) The first screening instrument outlined below is an older scale that focuses on alcohol use; two of the screening instruments were developed to help clinicians quickly assess whether a possible problem exists with alcohol and/or drugs; and the final screening device is actually a screening system.

Prior to summarizing and discussing each instrument, it is useful to consider the concepts underlying screening for substance use and abuse. Use of formal instruments provides a highly structured and efficient approach to screening. In contrast, the detailed clinical interview, as outlined in earlier sections, is descriptive, open-ended, and interactive. If conducted skillfully, it can also offer a contextual richness that is missing from more structured approaches. Although the clinical interview has not been empirically validated, it is generally accepted as a valid and time-honored procedure. In contrast, some of the formal screening instruments have been empirically validated against self-report written questionnaires and may be less time-consuming. Both approaches to the process of assessment will, however, help the professional achieve the following goals: (a) to describe the teenager's presenting problems sufficiently clearly to provide a clinical understanding; (b) to identify the pattern of behavioral, psychological, and physiological conditions associated with the substance use; and (c) to refer the adolescent to an appropriate facility for further evaluation and intervention (Donovan, 1988).

Different levels of screening measurement exist and have been described as forming a "behavioral assessment funnel" (Donovan, 1988). The top of the funnel represents the first level of assessment, a broad, relatively brief screening that identifies general problem areas. Such screening should be relatively low-cost; however, it may sacrifice depth and accuracy of measurement. Three of the screening instruments discussed below represent this first level of assessment. The results of a preliminary screen will help determine which adolescents require the second level of "basic assessment." Professionals involved at this level define the nature and extent of the problems associated with substance abuse and make tentative decisions regarding treatment intervention. They may also formulate ideas about which conditions and issues help an adolescent maintain the substance use, as well as which ones may be helpful in addressing the problems. As described in preceding sections, the clinical interview represents the second level of assessment. The final level of evaluation, called "specialized assessment," involves gathering detailed information in order to target specific aspects of the substance use behavior across their behavioral, social, psychological, and physiological dimensions. This specialized assessment is usually conducted by personnel staffing substance abuse intervention programs, and it frequently includes the administration of standardized psychological tests. It may take days to weeks to gather this information. The specialized assessment is comprehensive, time-consuming, and relatively expensive. It serves as a prelude to and forms the basis for specific interventions (Donovan, 1988).

Sobell, Sobell, and Nirenberg (1988) have recommended that a clinician consider two issues before selecting an instrument to help evaluate substance use. First, the instrument should possess satisfactory psychometric characteristics in order to provide valid and reliable information. Second, in order for the instrument to be clinically useful, it needs to offer what the clinician wants to know about the teenager. For example, if the professional already knows that a serious substance abuse problem exists, simple preliminary screening tests will not add extra information.

## Adolescent Alcohol Involvement Scale

The Adolescent Alcohol Involvement Scale (AAIS) was developed in 1979 as a fourteen-question, self-reporting written questionnaire that measures teenagers' use and misuse of alcohol. Its intent is to identify adolescents who are

## Table 6.
## Questions Contained in the Adolescent Alcohol Involvement Scale and Examples of Its Multiple-Choice, Ranked Responses

1. How often do you drink?
   Score range 0–5
   Examples of ranked responses: never, once or twice a year, once or twice a month, every weekend, every day.

2. When did you have your last drink?
   Score range 0–6
   Examples of ranked responses: never drank, not for over a year, several weeks ago, last week, yesterday, today.

3. I usually start to drink:
   Score range 0–5
   Examples of ranked responses: because I like the taste; to feel like an adult; because I feel sad, lonely, sorry for myself.

4. What do you drink?
   Score range 0–5
   Examples of ranked responses: wine, beer, mixed drinks, hard liquor, a substitute for alcohol (paint thinner, cough medicine, etc.).

5. How do you get your drinks?
   Score range 0–5
   Examples of ranked responses: supervised by parents, from brothers or sisters, from home without parents' knowledge, from friends, buying it with false identification.

6. When did you take your first drink?
   Score range 0–5
   Examples of ranked responses: never, recently, after age 15, between ages 10 and 13, before age 10.

7. What time of the day do you usually drink?
   Score range 0–5
   Examples or ranked responses: with meals, at night, afternoons, mostly in the morning, I often get up during my sleep and drink.

8. Why did you take your first drink?
   Score range 0–5
   Examples of ranked responses: curiosity, parents or relatives offered, encouragement from friends, to feel more like an adult, to get drunk or high.

9. How much do you drink, when you do drink?
   Score range 0–5
   Examples of ranked responses: 1 drink, 2 drinks, 3–6 drinks, 6 or more drinks, until high or drunk.

10. Whom do you drink with?
    Score range 0–5
    Examples of ranked responses: parents/relatives only, brothers/sisters only, friends own age, older friends, alone.

11. What is the greatest effect you have had from alcohol?
    Score range 0–5
    Examples of ranked responses: loose, easy feeling; moderate "high"; drunk; passed out; was drinking heavily and the next day didn't remember what happened.

12. What is the greatest effect drinking has had on your life?
    Score range 0–8
    Examples of ranked responses: no effect, prevented me from having a good time, has interfered with my school work, have lost friends because of drinking, was in a fight or destroyed property, has resulted in an accident, an injury, arrest, or being punished at school for drinking.

Table 6. (*continued*)

13. How do you feel about your drinking?
    Score range 0–6
    Examples of ranked responses: no problem at all, I can control it and set limits on myself, I often feel bad about my drinking, I need help to control myself, I have had professional help to control my drinking.

14. How do others see you?
    Score range 0–5
    Examples of ranked responses: can't say, a normal drinker for my age, my family and friends advise me to control or cut down on my drinking, my family or friends tell me to get help for my drinking, my family or friends have already gone for help for my drinking.

Source: The complete Adolescent Alcohol Involvement Scale is contained in J. E. Mayer and W. J. Filstead, *Adolescents and Alcohol.* Cambridge, MA: Ballinger Publishing Company, 1980

misusing alcohol, but it cannot diagnose alcoholism. It was designed to measure disruption in three domains of an adolescent's life: psychological functioning, social relations, and family living (Mayer & Filstead, 1980). Completion of the written questionnaire yields a total score with a potential range from 0 to 76. Alcohol misuse should be considered for scores higher than 41 points. This instrument has been well validated on adolescents being treated for alcoholism and on general populations of high school students.

The AAIS is short and uncomplicated. All answers are grounded in descriptive phrases. It does not, however, address drug use; hence, in its published form it cannot be used as a global screen for substance abuse. As reported by Winters (1990), however, Moberg recast the AAIS items to reflect general drug use rather than focusing only on involvement with alcohol. Moberg titled the modified instrument the Adolescent Drug Involvement Scale and conducted preliminary tests of its psychometric properties but has not yet published his work (Winters, 1990). The questions composing the AAIS are outlined in Table 6.

## Perceived Benefits Scales

The Perceived Benefit of Drinking Scale and the Perceived Benefit of Drug Use Scale were developed to be quickly and easily administered screening instruments that could serve as proxy measures of adolescents' substance abuse (Petchers, Singer, Angelotta, & Chow, 1988). The authors reasoned that a phenomenological approach could yield valuable information regarding substance use without needing to elicit information about the teenager's specific patterns of substance use or negative consequences resulting from alcohol and drug use. Such information can be difficult to obtain accurately during an initial interview, because the adolescent may not trust the interviewer or may deny heavy use patterns or the occurrence of negative consequences. The questions from these scales were briefly presented as a strategy to supplement and help enrich other clinical information in the section "Elements of a Formal Substance Use History." This section will review the empirical validity of the Perceived Benefits Scales and discuss their clinical utility when used as a formal instrument to screen for adolescent substance abuse. The alcohol and the drug scales each contain five parallel questions:

1. Drinking (drugs) helps me to relax
2. Drinking (drugs) helps me to be friendly
3. Drinking (drugs) helps me to be with friends who drink
4. Drinking (drugs) helps me to forget my problems
5. Drinking (drugs) helps me to feel good about myself

Adolescents' answers are dichotomized; that is, replies are given in a yes-or-no format. Each separate item receives a score of 1 if an adolescent endorses it. The two instruments were designed as paper-and-pencil questionnaires. Their validities were assessed by administering them to approximately 1,400 secondary school students in classroom settings as part of a larger questionnaire that asked students to (a) self-report their alcohol and drug use and any adverse consequences and (b) provide sociodemographic information. Responses for the two Perceived Benefits Scales were analyzed only for students who reported some experience with drinking or drug use. Each scale met empirical criteria for unidimensionality and demonstrated adequate reliability. Importantly, each scale was able to differentiate adolescents by the frequency of being high or drunk, by whether they had experienced trouble in school due to drinking or drugs, by whether they reported trouble with the police or courts, and by whether they perceived that drinking or using drugs was causing problems for them. The authors recommended that a cutoff score of 3 be used for each scale, so that scores of 3 or higher would suggest an abuse problem (Petchers et al., 1988). Using this cutoff score yielded a mean accuracy rate of 77 percent for the Perceived Benefit of Drinking Scale and 80 percent for the Perceived Benefit of Drug Use Scale.

The Perceived Benefit Scales have been carefully validated and may represent the only recently developed, brief, empirically validated instrument for screening adolescents for substance abuse (Winters, 1990). As discussed above, the individual questions composing these scales can help to strengthen a clinical interview. The professional must consider several issues, however, prior to using the perceived benefit scales as clinical screening instruments. The authors have not provided guidance on these points. First, the scales were validated in a classroom setting, rather than in an individual clinical setting; it is not clear how well the scales would perform for individual youngsters. Second, the scales were validated only for teenagers who self-reported some life experience with alcohol or drugs; they are not appropriate for youngsters who have not used substances. In addition, the scales could not be used to differentiate youngsters with no life experience with substances, because each individual question presumes use. Youngsters who don't use alcohol and/or drugs but who are requested to answer these questions may feel alienated because a false assumption was made about them. Each scale was validated independently. Clinically, however, youngsters may become impatient in answering two sets of parallel questions. The scales were validated based on a pencil-and-paper format. Some clinicians may choose to administer the questions composing the scales verbally (i.e., by interview), but there is no information regarding the validity of these scales with an altered mode of administration. Finally, neither scale predicts perfectly; each scale has a mean error rate of approximately 20 percent. In summary, the Perceived Benefit Scales can serve as a useful adjunct to interviewing youngsters who are already known to have some life experience with substance use. They probably function best for adolescents who are known to use drugs and/or alcohol currently.

### RAFFT Screen for Substance Use

The RAFFT screen was developed by Project Adept at Brown University as a five-question clinical instrument to help determine whether an adolescent is harmfully involved with alcohol and drugs (Riggs & Alario, 1989). This instrument covers a much broader range of issues than the Perceived Benefit Scales do. It quickly addresses perceived benefits, one pattern of drinking behavior, peer use, genetic issues, and psychosocial consequences. RAFFT is an acronym: the R stands for Relax, the A for Alone, the first F for Friends, the second F for Family, and the T for Trouble. The actual suggested screening questions are outlined below (Riggs and Alario, 1989):

1. Do you drink or use drugs to RELAX, feel better about yourself, or to fit in? [Note that this question set is asking about the perceived benefits of using substances.]
2. Do you ever drink alcohol or use drugs while you are by yourself, ALONE?
3. Do you or any of your closest FRIENDS drink or use drugs?
4. Does a close FAMILY member have a problem with alcohol or drug use?
5. Have you ever gotten into TROUBLE from drinking or drug use (i.e., skipping school, bad grades, trouble with the law or parents)?

In summary, the RAFFT appears to have been developed for the professional who has extremely limited time but who wants to screen adolescents for possible substance use problems as part of an interview. It briefly covers several substantive areas that this chapter has described as being important to a detailed substance abuse assessment by interview. Although it appears to be a clinically useful tool and has been anecdotally successful, it does have several limitations. First, it does not appear to have been validated empirically, so that the professional cannot know whether this set of questions can be depended on to yield accurate and reliable information. Is it a sufficiently sensitive screen, so that it is capable of identifying virtually all adolescents who may need a more detailed evaluation of their substance use? Second, no scoring system has been developed, so that the professional must rely on his or her clinical judgment regarding seriousness of risk for a substance abuse problem. For example, does a positive answer to any single question serve as a "red flag"? How many positive answers are required to make the judgment that an adolescent may indeed have a substance abuse problem and deserves further assessment? Third, the questions are framed dichotomously, so that the adolescent would be expected to answer yes or no. Skilled interviewers always attempt to phrase questions so that an adolescent's response is descriptive and requires at least a phrase or a sentence to complete. In addition, the first and third questions actually have more than one component, so that an adolescent may become confused about how to answer, because his or her answers may be internally contradictory to other components of the question. Finally, the first two questions assume that the adolescent actually drinks or uses drugs, so that the professional may discover that he or she has created an awkward interview situation and may need to work hard to reestablish rapport with an adolescent who actually does not use substances and feels offended by the presumption that he or she does use them.

## AARS (Adolescent Assessment/Referral System Manual)

The National Institute on Drug Abuse (NIDA) recently published "The Adolescent Assessment/Referral System Manual" (AARS) (Rahdert, 1991), which uses the concept of a "behavioral assessment funnel." NIDA's goal was to identify, collect, and organize all appropriate materials associated with the assessment and treatment referral of troubled youths ages twelve through nineteen (Rahdert, 1991). The AARS targets multiple functional areas for evaluation in order to help professionals match appropriate treatment resources to the needs of individual adolescents. It was designed to screen and evaluate individual youngsters suspected of using illicit drugs. Such youth could be identified by school personnel, family members, health care professionals, or justice system personnel. A major purpose was to provide a standardized approach to assessment, so that individuals who are not experts in the field of substance abuse could determine which youngsters need more extensive evaluation.

Initial screening, or the top of the assessment funnel, is accomplished by the completion of two written questionnaires by individual adolescents. The first is the Problem Oriented Screening Instrument for Teenagers (POSIT). It was designed by a consensus panel of "expert clinician researchers" and consists of 129 questions with dichotomized responses (yes or no). POSIT screens ten functional areas for problems: substance use/abuse, physical health status, mental health status, family relationships, peer relations, educational status, vocational status, social skills, leisure and recreation, and aggressive behavior/delinquency. It is scored using a template; each functional area has been assigned a cutoff score that indicates an individual adolescent may be experiencing a problem in that area and probably needs further assessment. Certain items are "red flags" that by themselves indicate an adolescent is at high risk for a problem and deserves further assessment in that functional area.

Although POSIT has not yet been field-tested or validated empirically, a preliminary study comparing responses of 216 adolescents in substance abuse treatment with 633 junior and senior high school students demonstrated that its clinically derived scoring system could discriminate between youngsters diagnosed with substance abuse and adolescents from a general school population. That is, each of the mean scores for the ten functional areas were significantly higher for the group of adolescents diagnosed as having substance abuse than for the school group. Large proportions of the school group of adolescents, however, also demonstrated possible problems in each functional area (e.g., substance use/abuse, approximately 50 percent; mental health, approximately 80 percent; social skills, approximately 60 percent; aggressive behavior, approximately 70 percent).

In summary, POSIT cutoff scores were designed to be very sensitive, to allow complete detection of problems; however, such sensitivity may falsely identify adolescents who actually have no problems. Other possible issues that POSIT presents include its dichotomization, which may make it more difficult for youngsters to endorse both high- and low-risk answers, and the reading level needed to understand certain questions. Finally, POSIT cannot be scored without use of its template. POSIT is available in both English and Spanish.

The second component of the initial screening of youngsters suspected of having possible substance use or abuse problems is the Client Personal History Questionnaire, which elicits demographic information, as well as information about religion, living status, school performance, employment status, membership in a street gang, health status and behavior, familial socioeconomic status, adolescent and familial involvement with the justice system, substance use by family members, treatment by a mental health professional, and special education needs. The Client Personal History Questionnaire also helps to determine the adolescent's exposure to forty stressful life events, in order to profile the current level of stress in the adolescent's life and environment. This questionnaire asks the teenager to share very sensitive information in a written format; if it is used as part of an intake process in the absence of skilled interviewing, it is possible that the adolescent would be too threatened to disclose some information accurately.

If the POSIT has indicated that a possible problem exists in any of its ten functional domains, the AARS recommends two specific tools to further define the problem. Together, these nineteen instruments (in general, two are recommended for each domain) compose the Comprehensive Assessment Battery (CAB). These instruments represent the second level of basic behavioral assessment. The tools composing the CAB were recommended by national experts; the majority have been psychometrically validated on adolescents and successfully used in clinical settings. The experts attempted to recommend instruments that are readily available and can be administered and scored with a minimum of training (Rahdert, 1991). But because many of these tests are time-consuming and carry monetary costs, the professional is cautioned to exercise judgment in their application. They are listed in Table 7. Purchase information is contained in the AARS (Rahdert, 1991). Many of these instruments may be familiar to the reader; however, the Personal Experience Inventory (PEI) and the Adolescent Diagnostic Interview (ADI) have recently been developed, the former published in 1989 (Winters & Henly, 1989), and the latter in 1991 (Winters & Henly, 1991).

**Table 7.**
**Comprehensive Assessment Battery Tools**

| Functional Area | Assessment Tools |
|---|---|
| Substance use/abuse | Personal Experience Inventory (PEI)<br>Adolescent Diagnostic Interview (ADI) |
| Physical health status | Physical examination and laboratory studies |
| Mental health status | Diagnostic Interview Schedule for Children (DISC)-2.1C)<br>Brief Symptom Inventory (BSI-53) |
| Family relationships | Family Assessment Measure (FAM)<br>Parent Adolescent Relationship Questionnaire (PARQ) |
| Peer relations | Piers-Harris Self-Concept Scale<br>Behavior Problem Checklist |
| Educational status | WAIS-R, WISC-R,<br>Woodstock-Johnson Psychoeducational Test Battery |
| Vocational status | Career Maturity Inventory (CMI)<br>Generalizable Skills Curriculum |
| Social skills | Social Skills Rating System (SSRS)<br>Matson Evaluation of Social Skills with Youngsters (MESSY) |
| Leisure and recreation | Leisure Diagnostic Battery,<br>Physical Activity Assessment,<br>Social Adjustment Inventory for Children and Adolescents (SAICA) |
| Aggressive behavior/delinquency | Youth Self-Report of the Child Behavior Checklist (YSR)<br>National Youth Survey Delinquency Scale |

Source: Adapted from Table 2 in the Adolescent Assessment/Referral System Manual. Editor: E. R. Rahdert, NIDA, U.S. Department of Health and Human Services, ADAMHA, 1991.

The Personal Experience Inventory is a self-reporting written, structured questionnaire geared for a sixth-grade reading level. It has been extensively validated for both construct validity and reliability. It is divided into two sections: chemical use problem severity and psychosocial risk factors. It contains a total of eighteen indices, reviews drug use history, and screens for six clinical problems, such as physical and sexual abuse. It also contains questions that allow the scorer to determine whether the teenager is answering question sets accurately or whether the answers represent a response set. The Adolescent Diagnostic Interview follows a structured format and addresses the symptoms of psychoactive substance use disorders covered by the American Psychiatric Association's *Diagnostic and Statistical Manual of Mental Disorders*, Third Edition, revised (1987). It also measures psychosocial stressors and level of functioning. It was designed to be able either to supplement the PEI or to be used as an independent assessment for substance abuse (Rahdert, 1991).

In summary, the AARS provides an integrated approach to help clinicians evaluate adolescents for possible substance abuse. Although its goals are laudable, too little evaluative research has been conducted to determine its validity and clinical utility. For example, it is possible that busy clinicians will refer a youngster for further evaluation if they are concerned about the results of POSIT, rather than attempting the second level of basic assessment themselves. Professionals should also remember that in clinical circumstances, structured questionnaires cannot be administered in the absence of individual interaction with the clinician.

## Physical and Physiological Screening

Unless an adolescent is experiencing the effects of an overdose and seeks help from a free clinic or a hospital emergency department, it is unusual to be able to diagnose substance abuse by physical examination findings. Clearly, individuals suffering from acute effects, overdoses, and withdrawal from alcohol and specific classes of drugs have known constellations of physical and mental status findings. It is beyond the scope of this chapter to discuss the acute medical presentations of substance abuse. Yet adolescents can experience many physical symptoms, largely related to specific classes of substances. (A symptom is experienced by an individual as a health problem or a sensation that is a departure from normal.) An astute health care clinician may suspect that an adolescent has a substance abuse problem based on several simultaneous health concerns that cannot otherwise be explained. Although certain symptoms are clearly linked to specific classes of substances, others are more general and may be caused by more than one type of substance. Table 8 lists chronic or recurrent physical symptoms that may propel an adolescent substance user to seek medical care.

Some symptoms represent the acute effects of use (e.g., cocaine causes a

## Table 8.
## Recurrent Physical Symptoms That May Be Related to Substance Use

*General*

Fatigue

Poor appetite

Weight loss

Malnutrition

Insomnia

Increased sleeping

*Respiratory*

Cough

Laryngitis

Bronchitis

Wheezing

Coughing of blood

*Mucous membranes and nose*

Conjunctival irritation

Nasal congestion

Nosebleeds

Sinusitis

*Cardiac*

Rapid heart rate

Palpitations

Chest pain

*Gastrointestinal*

Abdominal pain

Vomiting

Constipation

*Neurologic*

Headaches

Blackouts (amnesia)

Dizziness

Fainting

Seizures

*Hormonal and reproductive*

Abnormal menstrual cycles

Male sexual dysfunction

Enlarged breasts in males

*Skin*

Skin infections

rapid heartbeat), and some represent complications of use (e.g., cocaine can cause cardiac arrhythmias, which can be experienced as palpitations, as well as narrowing of the blood vessels supplying the heart, which can cause chest pain). Other symptoms, such as fatigue and disordered sleep, do not have such straightforward explanations.

A medical evaluation, including physical examination, is recommended as part of the assessment process for adolescent substance abusers. It has several goals: First, many teenagers who have used substances do not receive regular health care and deserve age-appropriate screening and immunizations. Second, although organ system damage is unusual among adolescent substance abusers, it can occur. Youngsters with specific symptoms (e.g., upper abdominal pain) should be evaluated carefully to ensure that complications of alcohol use (such as gastritis or pancreatitis) are not causing it. Finally, youngsters who abuse substances are at risk for multiple problems, largely because of their life-styles. For example, they are at risk for sexually transmitted infections, pregnancy, and sexual assault. They also experience disproportionately high rates of unintentional trauma. Chronic users of certain classes of drugs may be at risk for malnutrition (Rahdert, 1991).

It is generally agreed that laboratory testing of adolescents' body fluids (e.g., blood) does not provide a valid technique to diagnose chronic alcohol and marijuana use (Farrow, Rees, & Worthington-Roberts, 1987). In contrast, adults with chronic alcoholism may demonstrate elevation of certain hepatic enzymes, increased mean volume of their red blood cells, and changes in their high-density lipoproteins. None of these physiologic changes, however, is sufficiently sensitive or specific to serve as a marker for alcoholism (Leigh & Skinner, 1988). No similar physiological parameters have been identified in individuals of any age who have used other categories of substances.

Therefore, routine laboratory testing to search for standing physiological changes is not recommended. In contrast, however, adolescent substance abusers may be nutritionally deficient and should be screened for anemia. In addition, they deserve careful and appropriate laboratory and imaging assessment of medical symptoms and any abnormal physical findings. Some adolescents (e.g., those who inject drugs by needle) need a comprehensive evaluation for systemic infections (e.g., hepatitis and HIV infection) and organ system damage. Finally, substance-abusing adolescents should be screened for such problems as sexually transmitted infections, for which their behavior enhances their risk.

## Pharmacological Screening

Pharmacological or drug screening of body fluids for substances of abuse is a technologically sophisticated but controversial procedure. Public and institutional policies that mandate involuntary, obligatory, and random urine testing for substances of abuse continue to be debated. The focus of this section is clinical screening. That is, it discusses the pharmacological screening of individual teenagers for clinical purposes. It should be remembered that drug testing can differentiate only between individuals who have used a drug and those who have not had such exposure. Drug tests cannot provide information about the abuse of or dependence on drugs or about any physical or mental impairment that may result from drug use (American Medical Association, 1987). (In contrast, blood alcohol concentration levels are correlated with degrees of neurological impairment.) In addition, because the majority of substances and their metabolic products have relatively short half-lives, the window of time during which they can be detected is quite limited. Therefore, a negative test cannot prove or guarantee that the adolescent does not use substances. Retention times vary by class of substance and range from approximately ten hours (alcohol), to two to four days (cocaine), to three to ten days (occasional use of marijuana), to one to two months (daily use of marijuana) (MacKenzie & Kipke, 1992).

Several clinical circumstances necessitate drug screening in adolescents. They include psychiatric symptoms, mental status and performance changes, acute onset behavior states, recurrent and unexplained nonintentional trauma (e.g., motor vehicle accidents and falls), recurrent respiratory symptoms, and unexplained somatic symptoms. In addition, many professionals would obtain drug screens on adolescents in legal-social crisis, such as running away and engaging in delinquent behaviors. Teenagers with these problems are considered to be at high risk for substance abuse (MacKenzie & Kipke, 1992). Finally, any adolescent who sustains trauma serious enough to warrant care by a hospital emergency department deserves to have pharmacological screening for alcohol and drugs conducted at the time of his or her visit. To emphasize this point, the major findings of several studies examining this issue are presented. A recent prospective study found that at least one-third of acute trauma patients, including victims of both vehicular and non-vehicular trauma, had used alcohol, marijuana, or both prior to the injury. In addition, the severity of the injury was not correlated with the presence or absence of substances (Soderstrom, Trifillis, Shankar, Clark, & Cowley, 1988). Similarly, 42 percent of a consecutive series of patients with mild head injuries had positive blood alcohol tests, but this study did not screen for other substances (Rutherford, 1977). When laboratories have studied the results of specimens submitted to them by emergency department staffs on patients clinically suspected of being intoxicated, the prevalence of positive results has been even greater. At least 80 percent of such screens have been found to be positive for at least one substance (Taylor, Cohan, & White, 1985; Sloan, Zalenski, Smith et al., 1989). Taylor and colleagues (1985) also documented multiple drug use in 28 percent of patients with positive results. Not surprisingly, recent studies examining the prevalence of cocaine in urban trauma victims have determined relatively high rates of use: 54 percent positivity in patients admitted to the trauma service in a Philadelphia hospital (Lindenbaum, Carroll, Daskal, & Kapusnick, 1989) and 18 percent positivity among motor vehicle fatalities in New York City (Marzuk, Tardiff, Leon, Stajik, Morgan, & Mann, 1990).

In contrast, it is not recommended that all adolescents be screened or that pharmacological screening for drugs be conducted as part of routine adolescent health care (MacKenzie, Cheng, & Haftel, 1987). In these circumstances, screening by interview has actually been found to be more sensitive than testing body fluids, because it also considers use at more remote points in time; however, a study of adolescents seeking health care who admitted only to using marijuana more than a month earlier found that one-third of this group tested positive (Silber, Getson, Ridley, Iosefsohn, & Hicks, 1987). Despite the recognition that a certain proportion of substance-using adolescents will not accurately describe their usage patterns during a single interview encounter, most professionals would argue that obtaining drug screens on youngsters who are basically free of acute behavioral problems and physical symptoms is counterproductive. As pointed out by MacKenzie and Kipke (1992), merely confronting substance abusers with objective evidence of their use (e.g., positive drug screens) has little impact on their behavior and little chance of motivating them to stop using. Pharmacological screening should be incorporated into a comprehensive plan of assessment, rather than be conducted independently.

## Counseling Strategies for Referral of Adolescents with Substance Abuse Problems

Most helping professionals will not and probably should not assume the responsibility for actual treatment of substance-abusing adolescents and their families. They can, however, employ counseling strategies to ensure effective communication and referral of appropriate adolescents for more detailed evaluation and treatment. The helping professional should remember that many substance-abusing adolescents and their families have not previously considered the use to be problematic, even though it is objectively associated with dysfunctional consequences. These teenagers and their families may be less able to accept the recommendation that treatment intervention would be helpful. Using the "stages of change" model, these individuals may be placed into the "precontemplative" stage, which describes the substance use pattern that exists prior to any active consideration of change (Marlatt, 1988). The professional may need to modify the counseling goal for these youngsters and their families. He or she may need to accept success in calling the teenager's and family's attention to the substance abuse as a problem behavior, which may allow them to proceed to the "contemplation," or "motivation and commitment," stage. Although individuals in this stage are clearly considering addressing the substance abuse problem, they may also experience motivational conflict and ambivalence. The professional's goal for teenagers and their families who are at this second stage is to move them forward to the "action" stage, in which they make active attempts to change (Marlatt, 1988). A successful counseling outcome for these adolescents and their families would be acceptance of the screening evaluation and follow-through with the recommendation for full assessment and therapeutic intervention.

The helping professional should be aware of clinical guidelines that have been developed to help enhance the probability of a successful treatment outcome. In attempting to link individual adolescents with appropriate treatment programs, it is helpful to involve them in their own treatment planning. As outlined by Sobell, Sobell, and Nirenberg (1988), such involvement is important for several reasons. First, the teenager can provide important information regarding the feasibility and ease with which various treatment options can be implemented. Second, involvement of the teenager in the process of goal setting and planning promotes continued involvement, or adherence to the treatment plan. In part, enhanced compliance is due to the mutual determination of treatment goals. Finally, involvement allows teenagers to have a sense of mastery over their problems.

There are several substantive issues professionals should consider in linking teenagers with different treatment options. This discussion has been adapted from recommendations made for the planning of behavioral treatment by Sobell, Sobell, and Nirenberg (1988). First, the teenager should be placed in the "least restrictive environment," if alternative strategies are considered to be equally effective. This recommendation is in accord with the mental health regulations of most states (Chatlos & Tufaro, 1911). In practice, however, this determination is usually made on space and financial availability. Second, the teenager's life-style and cultural background should be considered. Third, the teenager's personal strengths and resources should be identified in order to build success into early treatment experiences and to prepare the youngster to address more difficult problems. A fourth area of importance for linking treatment service options with individual adolescents' needs is motivation. Substance abuse treatment agencies can enhance compliance by setting goals mutually with the individual teenager and by assuring that the goals are specific and attainable. Unrealistic goals may heighten the chance for failure, which can then be seen as lack of commitment by the adolescent to the treatment process (Sobell, Sobell, & Nirenberg, 1988).

This section outlines a practical approach professionals can adopt in helping teenagers and their families make the transition to a drug abuse treatment agency. These strategies are summarized in Table 9 and are partly adapted from work by Riggs and Alario (1989).

First, the professional should permit the adolescent to describe his or her understanding of the substance use and what types of problems it may be causing for him or her. Regardless of the adolescent's perspective, the pro-

## Table 9.
### Helpful Counseling Strategies

Allow the adolescent to describe his or her understanding of the substance use.

Summarize information disclosed as part of the interview and from any collateral sources, using a nonconfrontational style.

Clarify the problem behavior(s) regarding the substance use.

Provide clear information about dysfunctional consequences, including medical and psychosocial problems, that have resulted from substance use, but do not moralize.

Communicate concern for the adolescent's well-being.

Allow the adolescent and family to express their responses to your summary and synthesis of the problems.

Clarify your role in the evaluation/intervention process.

Provide concrete assistance to the adolescent and family to enhance the likelihood that successful completion of a referral to a treatment agency will occur.

If necessary, assume responsibility for acting as an intermediary between the adolescent and parents.

Assume responsibility for initiating the referral to a treatment agency.

fessional should then proceed to summarize the information that was disclosed during the assessment. This approach demonstrates respect for the adolescent and allows the professional to adapt his or her style in order to respond most effectively to the adolescent's concerns. In addition to preparing the adolescent and family for future steps, summarization ensures that the professional understands the historical information and is able to communicate the problem accurately. A descriptive summary allows the interviewer to provide a clear statement of the problem behaviors to the adolescent and family. It is particularly helpful to outline dysfunctional behavior in the context of substance use. An example of this approach is as follows: "I know that many teenagers occasionally smoke marijuana. Nevertheless, since this school year started, when you have been using it more frequently than you did last year, a lot of concerning things have happened. First, you haven't been feeling well—you are tired all the time and have been coughing a lot every day. Second, school isn't going well for you—you've already been suspended twice for fighting, you dropped out of the debating club and quit soccer, and your grades are down. Third, you were really shaken up last week by that traffic accident. Fourth, you have been feeling very sad, and other people see you as being angry all the time." Communicate concern for the adolescent's well-being: "I am very worried about you."

The next step is to provide clear information without moralizing or lecturing: "When a person becomes really involved with drinking or doing drugs, without realizing it or even wanting it to happen, the alcohol and drugs can take over a person's life. This is what I believe is happening to you." At this point, the teenager may again need a chance to express his or her perceptions as part of the discussion. As outlined above, however, do not expect your assessment to be automatically accepted by either the teenager or the family, even if the adolescent is experiencing serious dysfunction.

Clarify your role, as you facilitate the referral process. Try not to allow the teenager and family to perceive the referral as rejection by you. Two techniques you can use to avoid this issue are (a) commitment to continued appropriate involvement with the adolescent and (b) personalization of the referral process: "I believe that it would really help you to feel better if you and your family learned more about chemical dependency, and enrolled in a treatment program for teenagers who have problems with drugs and alcohol. I would like you to meet a friend of mine who knows a lot about teenagers, families, and the problems that drugs and alcohol can cause. I don't have the background to give you really expert help for this problem. I will continue to be here for you, but you also need counseling help."

It may be necessary to provide concrete assistance to an adolescent's family or to the teenager in facilitating referral to a treatment agency. The professional needs to become familiar with resources in his or her community. He or she should learn about programs' philosophies of treatment, the actual services they provide, and their fee schedules. Establish personal contact with appropriate members of treatment programs' staffs. This firsthand knowledge will help you to project confidence. Teenagers and families commonly feel overwhelmed and powerless when they are confronted with serious problems. Your potency will help provide the stimulus they need to complete the referral successfully. You may want the patient or family to telephone the counseling professional or treatment agency from your office. Ask the family to call you after their first appointment. Let them know you will have the agency or counselor contact you if the adolescent misses his or her first appointment.

## Treatment Services

Teenagers require professional services to treat their substance use if they develop physical, social, or emotional problems. Broad treatment goals include the elimination of substance abuse and any accompanying undesirable behaviors and the restoration of the teenager to a functional and healthy status (U.S. Congress, Office of Technology Assessment, 1991). Helping professionals should become familiar with the substance abuse treatment resources in their communities, so that they can make knowledgeable referrals of substance-abusing adolescents.

There are four categories of substance abuse treatment programs. Some of them overlap, or a single agency may offer more than one type of program, or an individual youngster may participate in more than one type of service during the course of treatment. Virtually all programs, however, share the belief that treatment begins with cessation of use and requires stable maintenance of sobriety, and have the goal of a substance-free life-style (Wheeler & Malmquist, 1987). Each category of service is described below.

## Self-Help Groups

These programs are community-based and are frequently used as adjuncts to professional substance abuse treatment programs. Participating substance abusers count on peer support and are often paired with individual sponsors who are more experienced group members and are available for emotional support in crisis intervention. Alcoholics Anonymous (AA) and Narcotics Anonymous (NA) represent the largest and best-known self-help groups. AA has widely promoted its twelve-step model of recovery, which regards substance dependence as a chronic disease process from which recovery (never cure) is a continuous, lifetime exercise maintained by total abstinence. Individuals must acknowledge their personal powerlessness and accept a spiritual (nonsectarian) power as a key to the recovery process. Filstead and Anderson (1983) have explained why the AA philosophy is helpful to adolescents. They pointed out that teenagers have expressed the belief that AA provides both a structure that can enhance the recovery process and an explanation for "how things got the way they are." That is, AA offers a framework of understanding for teenagers. Even though these groups are virtually always included as part of adolescents' treatment programs, no outcome research data are available on adolescents. There is, however, a high attrition rate from these self-help programs (U.S. Congress, Office of Technology Assessment, 1991). In addition, a recent randomized study of alcoholic adults found that a large percentage of those originally assigned only to compulsory attendance at AA meetings required additional inpatient treatment because of relapse. This outcome was especially true for adults who had also abused cocaine (Walsh, Hingson, Merrigan et al., 1991).

## Outpatient Substance Abuse Treatment Programs

Outpatient treatment programs for adolescents use counseling as their major therapeutic intervention. Their goal is to limit the progression of substance abuse (Wheeler & Malmquist, 1987). Their counseling strategies frequently include both individual and group sessions and help youngsters develop social skills. Outpatient programs are thought to be most effective for highly motivated adolescents during early stages of substance dependency. These programs are often incorporated into comprehensive youth service centers and community mental health centers and are therefore usually available to teenagers from low-income families.

Some outpatient treatment programs serve as aftercare programming for adolescents who have previously received inpatient treatment. In this context, outpatient aftercare programs are considered part of a total treatment package and can be quite costly (U.S. congress, Office of Technology Assessment, 1991). The goal of aftercare programs is to prevent relapse of substance abuse by providing ongoing support to the adolescent. Aftercare efforts help teenagers maintain a substance-free life-style in their home communities. For example, aftercare programs include family members to help maintain family support of the teenager, promote skills to help adolescents cope with interpersonal situations in which they are pressured to use substances, and facilitate teenagers' involvement in recreational and leisure activities that do not involve the use of substances (Hawkins & Catalano, 1985).

Day treatment programs represent the most intensive form of outpatient treatment. They function similarly to inpatient programs, utilize structured and therapeutic activities, and provide education on-site. Teenagers return home in the evening to sleep. Day treatment programs supported by public funding may provide an alternative to residential treatment or inpatient treatment for adolescents from low-income families.

### Residential Substance Abuse Treatment Programs

Residential programs provide continuous supervision to substance-dependent adolescents by adults and recovering peers. There are several models, but in general they include daily structured activities, on-site education, and therapeutic groups. They provide a high level of structure, especially in the initial stages of participation, but usually permit teenage clients to earn privileges and to progress to greater independence through continuous demonstration of responsible behavior. One goal of residential programs is to remove teenagers from environments, either community or familial, that encourage or enable substance use. The staff of residential programs provide immediate confrontation for any substance use or other self-defeating behavior. These programs frequently use a relatively high proportion of paraprofessional staff who are recovering themselves.

Three models of residential treatment are briefly described. The halfway house model provides adult supervision and structured therapeutic activities but usually allows adolescents to participate in community activities and attend a public school. Adolescents frequently remain at a halfway house for six to nine months (Wheeler & Malmquist, 1987). Such facilities help teenagers prepare for return to their home communities. The second model of residential treatment is the therapeutic community. It emphasizes global changes in conduct, values, and attitudes. As adolescents successfully progress through the program, they receive increasing levels of privileges and responsibilities, including authority over newer program participants. This type of program can be highly confrontational in its approach. The mean length of enrollment in one adolescent-oriented therapeutic community is thirteen months (Macdonald, 1989). A third model of residential treatment is the wilderness challenge program. This type of program has been developed for disadvantaged adolescents living in high-risk, urban environments. Teenagers and adult counselors live in a primitive camp setting. Participants are helped to master unfamiliar environmental conditions, learn wilderness survival skills, and learn to trust their peers (U.S. Congress, Office of Technology Assessment, 1991).

### Inpatient Substance Abuse Treatment Programs

Inpatient programs can be based in general hospitals, in psychiatric hospitals, and in freestanding facilities specializing in addiction. Many hospital-based inpatient programs have locked units. These programs are usually comprehensive and provide intensive, short-term treatment. Adolescents usually remain hospitalized for a maximum of four to six weeks. In addition to providing therapeutic groups, individual counseling, structured recreation, on-site education, and family treatment, hospital-based programs typically include medical services, such as detoxification, as part of the treatment package. Teenagers who are thought to benefit best from hospitalization include those who are substance-dependent and exhibit daily preoccupation with alcohol and/or drugs, have failed less intensive treatment modalities, have poor support systems, are medically at risk, or have been dually diagnosed (U.S. Congress, Office of Technology Assessment, 1991). Staffing is multidisciplinary and consists of chemical dependency counselors, consulting psychologists and psychiatrists, medical physicians and nurses, teachers, and occupational/recreational therapists. In general, hospital-based programs are expensive and require private, third-party insurance coverage. Youngsters from low-income families are frequently restricted to less intensive treatment programs, conducted in outpatient settings that receive public funding, regardless of the severity of their problems. Some low-income adolescents may be admitted by "scholarship" to a hospital's "charity bed." In addition, some states have developed "wraparound" services for adolescents from indigent families as cooperative projects between their Medicaid programs and bureaus of mental health or substance abuse.

Dual diagnosis programs deserve special note. Many teenagers who abuse substances have independent or coexisting psychiatric or behavioral problems. Examples include depression, posttraumatic stress disorder, eating disorders, bipolar disorders, schizophrenia, conduct disorders, and attention deficit hyperactivity disorders. In addition, some adolescents with a substance abuse problem may be diagnosed as having a borderline personality disorder (Chatlos & Tufaro, 1991; Marrison & Smith, 1987; Hoffmann, Sonis, & Halikas, 1987). Recognition of the interface between substance abuse and primary mental health disorders is relatively recent. The traditional perspective of the substance abuse treatment community identified the individual's loss of control over substance use as the primary problem ("disease") and, until recently, insisted that other problems could not be addressed until the individual's substance abuse had been checked. Historically, the substance abuse community has been dissatisfied with the mental health professional community and has cited it for failure to recognize the severity of substance abuse problems in their own right and to provide effective treatment (Hoffman et al., 1987). Over the past two decades, however, there has been a movement toward a convergence of philosophies, so that the substance abuse community has been willing to broaden its perspective as the mental health community has accepted substance abuse as an independent diagnostic entity and as a field requiring specialized expertise (Bailey, 1989). Dual diagnosis programs are an outgrowth of this mutuality. They are able to identify and address individual adolescents' problems and to design specific treatment programs for each youngster that reflect both the psychiatric issues and the substance abuse.

## Issues Regarding Treatment

The helping professional should be aware of several issues regarding treatment services for adolescents with substance abuse problems.

1. Treatment program philosophy is monolithic, and there is a limited ability to individualize treatment for adolescents. There is one prevailing philosophy of substance abuse and its treatment in the United States. It is based on the concept of substance abuse as a unidimensional "disease" that follows a specific downward course (Marlatt, 1988). The majority of treatment programs have been adapted from the Minnesota model, which is founded on the philosophy of AA and believes in the need to intervene in a substance abuser's system of denial and to use peer groups as a strategy to confront these defenses (Wheeler & Malmquist, 1987). Until recently, there was little thought given to individual teenagers' needs. All adolescents received the same treatment package, without considering the function of the presenting problem or the characteristics of the adolescent, the family, or the surrounding environment (U.S. Congress, Office of Technology Assessment, 1991; Marlatt, 1988). The concept of "client-treatment matching" is relatively new. It is based on the notion that treatment for addiction problems should be graded in intensity and relevant to the set of presenting problems (Marlatt, 1988). Little empirical information, however, is available on matching treatment services for adolescents. Rahdert (1991) was unable to provide specific recommendations for matching youngsters who have differing diagnostic profiles with different therapeutic programs, as such a prescription would be based on inadequate scientific evidence. Given the single basic treatment model, the Office of Technology Assessment (U.S. Congress, 1991) wondered how treatment services can even be matched with the needs of individual clients. Some national organizations, however, have developed

standards and guidelines for placement and treatment in the context of levels of care (U.S. Congress, Office of Technology Assessment, 1991).

2. Access to more intensive services (inpatient or residential) may be limited to adolescents from low-income families. In addition, if publicly funded mental health and substance abuse programs receive monetary support from different funding sources (e.g., separate state bureaus or departments), it is possible that teenagers with dual diagnoses may be denied needed treatment for one condition while enrolled in a program for the other problem (U.S. Congress, Office of Technology Assessment, 1991).

3. Many communities do not offer substance abuse treatment services specifically for adolescents. Teenagers are frequently treated in programs designed originally for adults. In addition, even programs developed for adolescents do not appear to differentiate among adolescents at different stages of maturation, so that early, middle, and late adolescents may be treated similarly (U.S.Congress, Office of Technology Assessment, 1991). The helping professional needs to learn which programs' staffs are knowledgeable about adolescents and adolescent development and enjoy working with teenagers.

4. Little empirical information is available concerning treatment for substance-abusing adolescents who come from racial and ethnic minority groups. It is not clear whether teenagers coming from different groups have special or unique treatment needs. We need to learn what cultural meanings different ethnic groups attach to adolescent substance use and how these perceptions influence the treatment needs of youngsters coming from these groups (Hanson, 1985). In addition, treatment programs must help youth coming from racial and ethnic minority backgrounds to become biculturally competent, in order to achieve comfort in the two worlds in which they reside (Moncher, Holden, & Trimble, 1990). It has been suggested that minority youth experience stress as they try to develop adaptive skills that will allow them to interact successfully and appropriately within both the minority and majority cultures. Substance use can be a coping response for stress (LaFromboise, 1988). These questions are clinically important and are necessary for the helping professional to attempt to address, even though research findings cannot provide guidance in this area.

5. Helping professionals should be aware of the staffing patterns and staff members' credentials in substance abuse treatment agencies (Macdonald, 1989). Many states now require certification for substance abuse professionals (e.g., certified alcohol counselor, certified drug counselor, certified addictions counselor). Physicians with significant experience in the field of alcoholism and drug dependence may also be eligible to sit for a certification examination. Many programs have a blended counseling staff and employ both those with educational degrees in addictions counseling and those who are themselves recovering but may not have received formal education in this arena. Some agencies, especially those receiving public support, may suffer

from funding limitations and small staff-to-client ratios. Clearly, a restricted staff size affects the quality of programming and individual attention that adolescents receive (U.S. Congress, Office of Technology Assessment, 1991).

## Summary

Helping professionals can learn to assess adolescent patients' use of drugs and alcohol. Their most important task is to determine whether use of substances is causing behavioral impairment. A general psychosocial assessment of an adolescent's functioning is the most important component of an evaluation for substance abuse. It provides the foundation for determining whether behavioral dysfunction exists. The professional should address several topical areas: family relationships, school performance and attendance, peer relationships, involvement in gang activities, legal difficulties, leisure activities and employment, mental health status, and self-perception. In addition, it is now recognized that youngsters who have been physically or sexually abused, as well as youngsters with bulimia, may be at risk for involvement with drugs and alcohol. Finally, youngsters who have abused substances may also have serious primary mental health problems, such as depression, that require coordinated evaluation and treatment.

The substance use history helps the professional in two ways. In general, it helps to focus educational counseling about the risks of substance use. It also helps the professional to determine whether substance abuse is the cause of or related to any behavioral dysfunction that may have been discovered during the general psychosocial assessment. Strategies to enhance more accurate disclosure of substance use by adolescents include postponing this section of the interview until rapport has been developed with the teenager, ordering questions so that illicit substances are addressed later, exploring peer involvement with substances as an antecedent to discussing the adolescent's personal use, and using a historical perspective, so that the teenager is asked to describe his or her initial experience with each substance class prior to addressing current use patterns. Because they represent crises, dysfunctional consequences of substance use, such as trauma and disciplinary action, may present opportunities for adolescents and their families to accept intervention.

Formal screening instruments, conducted by interview or as a pencil-and-paper exercise, can be helpful for a professional who has limited time to interview adolescents around substance abuse issues. Physiological and pharmacological measures, however, are not recommended as general screening strategies for teenagers thought to be harmfully involved with alcohol or drugs. In contrast, though, drug screens are clinically useful in certain circumstances, such as the onset of psychiatric symptoms; mental status changes; trauma; recurrent, unexplained somatic symptoms; and medical-legal crises.

If the professional believes that an adolescent would benefit from a more comprehensive evaluation and a treatment program, the following steps will help ensure successful completion of the referral. The professional should summarize information learned during the evaluation that is relevant to the problem behaviors but also needs to hear the adolescent's perspective. Try to outline the dysfunctional behavior in the context of substance use. Communicate concern for the teenager's well-being. Provide information without moralizing or lecturing. Clarify your own role and involvement. Try to personalize the referral process, to prevent feelings of rejection by the adolescent and family. If necessary, provide concrete assistance to the family to facilitate the referral process.

There are several categories of treatment services for adolescents who abuse substances, but they are all based on the "disease" model of chemical dependency. Participation in self-help groups, such as AA, is usually included in other treatment programs, but its efficacy as a single treatment strategy has not been proved. Outpatient counseling programs are most appropriate for motivated teenagers during the early stages of substance abuse. They are frequently supported by public funding and are usually financially accessible to youth from families with low incomes. Residential programs include several subtypes but represent a more intensive treatment format. Adolescents frequently remain in residential programs for several months, during which time they progress through structured stages as they prepare for a return to their own homes and communities. Inpatient substance abuse treatment programs represent the most intensive format. They provide short-term services that include medical care and detoxification, as well as counseling and engagement in structured activities. Teenagers who require hospitalization exhibit evidence of severe chemical dependency and may have failed less intensive treatment formats. Dual diagnosis inpatient units for teenagers are a relatively recent phenomenon. They are able to address the needs of teenagers who have both psychiatric or behavioral problems and substance abuse problems. Because many inpatient programs accept only private insurance, teenagers from low-income families may have limited financial access to them. Client-treatment matching is a relatively new concept, recognizing that treatment options should be graded in level of intensity and should be relevant to individual teenagers' problems and needs. Because, however, the majority of substance abuse treatment programs offer a uniform treatment "package," there is little practical experience or empirical information currently available to guide the clinical application of client treatment matching.

## References

Alcohol, Drug Abuse and Mental Health Administration (1989). *Report of the Secretary's Task Force on Youth Suicide. Volume 2: Risk Factors for Youth Suicide.* DHHS Pub. No. (ADM) 89–1622. Washington, D.C.: Superintendent of Documents, U.S. Government Printing Office.

American Academy of Pediatrics. Committee on Adolescence (1982). The role of the pediatrician in substance abuse counseling. *Pediatrics, 72,* 251–252.

American Academy of Pediatrics. Committee on Adolescence, Committee on Bioethics, and Provisional Committee on Substance Abuse (1989). Screening for drug abuse in children and adolescents. *Pediatrics, 84,* 396–398.

American Medical Association, Council on Scientific Affairs (1987). Scientific issues in drug testing. *Journal of the American Medical Association, 257,* 3110–3114.

American Psychiatric Association (1987). *Diagnostic and Statistical Manual of Mental Disorders,* 3rd ed., revised. Washington, D.C.

American School Health Association, Association for the Advancement of Health Education, Society for Public Health Education, Inc. (1989). *The National Adolescent Student Health Survey: A Report on the Health of America's Youth;.* Oakland, CA: Third Party Publishing Company.

Bachman, J. G., Johnston, L. D., & O'Malley, P. M. (1981). Smoking, drinking, and drug use among American high school students: Correlates and trends, 1975–1979. *American Journal of Public Health, 71,* 59–69.

Bailey, G. W. (1989). Current perspectives on substance abuse in youth. *Journal of the American Academy of Child and Adolescent Psychiatry, 28,* 151–162.

Bright, G. M., Hawley, D. L., & Siegel, P. P. (1985). Ambulatory management of Adolescent alcohol and drug abuse. *Seminars in Adolescent Medicine, 1,* 279–292.

Centers for Disease Control (1982). Alcohol-related highway fatalities among young drivers—United States. *Morbidity and Mortality Weekly Reports, 31,* 641–644.

Centers for Disease Control (1983a). Patterns of alcohol use among teenage drivers in fatal motor vehicle accidents. *Morbidity and Mortality Weekly Reports, 32,* 344–347.

Centers for Disease Control (1983b). Blood alcohol concentrations among young drivers—United States, 1982. *Morbidity and Mortality Weekly Reports, 32,* 646–648.

Centers for Disease Control (1992). Homicide surveillance, 1979–1988. In CDC Surveillance Summaries. *Morbidity and Mortality Weekly Reports, 41* (No. SS-3), 1–33.

Chatlos, J. C., & Tufaro, J. B. (1991). Treatment of the dually diagnosed adolescent. In M. S. Gold & A. E. Slaby (Eds.), *Dual Diagnosis in Substance Abuse* (pp. 253–288). New York: Marcel Dekker, Inc.

Chychula, N. M. (1984). Screening for substance abuse in the primary care setting. *Nurse Practitioner, 9,* 15–24.

Cohen, E., MacKenzie, R. G., & Yates, G. L. (1991). HEADDS, a psychosocial risk assessment instrument: Implications for designing effective intervention programs for runaway youth. *Journal of Adolescent Health, 12,* 539–544.

Comerci, G. (1990). Substance abuse. In J. A. Stockman (Ed.), *Difficult Diagnosis in Pediatrics* (pp 149–161). Philadelphia: W. B. Saunders Company.

Crumley, F. E. (1990). Substance abuse and adolescent suicidal behavior. *Journal of the American Medical Association, 263,* 3051–3056.

Dembo, R., Williams, L., La Voie L., Schmeidler, J., Kera, J., Getreu A., Berry, E., Genhng, L., & Wish, E. D. (1990). Longitudinal study of the relationships among alcohol use, marijuana/hashish use, cocaine use, and emotional/psychological functioning in a cohort of high-risk youths. *The International Journal of the Addictions, 25,* 1341–1382.

Donovan, D. M. (1988). Assessment of addictive behaviors. Implications of an emerging biopsychosocial model. In D. M. Donovan & G. A. Marlatt (Eds.), *Assessment of Addictive Behavior* (pp. 3–48). New York: The Guilford Press.

Donovan, J. E., & Jessor, R. (1983). Problem drinking and the dimension of involvement with drugs: A Guttman scalogram analysis of adolescent drug use. *American Journal of Public Health, 73,* 543–552.

Elliott, D. S., Huizinga, D., & Ageton, S. S. (1985). *Explaining Delinquency and Drug Use.* Beverly Hills: Sage Publications.

Elliott, D. S., Huizinga, D., & Menard, S. (1989). *Multiple Problem Youth: Delinquency, Substance Abuse, and Mental Health Problems.* New York: Springer-Verlag.

Ewing, J. A. (1984). Detecting alcoholism. The CAGE questionnaire. *Journal of the American Medical Association, 252,* 1905–1907.

Farrow, J. A., Rees, J. M., & Worthington-Roberts, B. S. Health, developmental and nutritional status of adolescent alcohol and marijuana abusers. *Pediatrics, 79,* 218–223.

Felice, M. E., & Friedman, S. B. (1982). Behavioral considerations in the health care of adolescents. *Pediatric Clinics of North America, 29,* 399–413.

Filstead, W. J., & Anderson, C. L. (1983). Conceptual and clinical issues in the treatment of adolescent alcohol and substance misusers. In R. Isralowitz & M. Singer (Eds.), *Adolescent Substance Abuse: A Guide to Prevention and Treatment* (pp. 103–116). New York: The Haworth Press.

Friedman, L. S., Johnson, B. A., & Brett, A. S. (1990). Evaluation of substance-abusing adolescents by primary care physicians. *Journal of Adolescent Health Care, 11,* 227–230.

Greenberger, E. E., & Steinberg, L. (1986). *When Teenagers Work: The Psychological and Social Costs of Adolescent Employment.* New York, Basic Books.

Halperin, S. F., Bass, J. L., Mehta, K. A., Betts, K. D. (1983). Unintentional injuries among adolescents and young adults: A review and analysis. *Journal of Adolescent Health Care, 4,* 275–281.

Hanson, B. (1985). Drug treatment effectiveness: The case of racial and ethnic minorities in America—Some research questions and proposals. *The International Journal of the Addictions, 20,* 99–137.

Hawkins, J. D., & Catalano, R. F. (1985). Aftercare in drug abuse treatment. *The International Journal of the Addictions, 20,* 917–945.

Hoffman, N. G., Sonis, W. A., & Halikas, J. A. (1987). Issues in the evaluation of chemical dependency treatment programs for adolescents. *Pediatric Clinics of North America, 34,* 449–459.

Jessor, R., Chase, J. A., & Donovan, J. E. (1980). Psychosocial correlates of marijuana use and problem drinking in a national sample of adolescents. *American Journal of Public Health, 70,* 604–613.

Jones, R. (1985). Identification and management of the toxic adolescent. *Seminars in Adolescent Medicine, 1,* 239–245.

Joshi, N. P., & Scott, M. (1988). Drug use, depression and adolescents. *Pediatric Clinics of North America, 35,* 1349–1364.

Kandel, D. B. (1982). Epidemiological and psychosocial perspectives on adolescent drug use. *Journal of the American Academy of Child and Adolescent Psychiatry,* 21, 328–347.

Labouvie, E. W. (1986). Alcohol and marijuana use in relation to adolescent stress. *The International Journal of the Addictions,* 21, 333–345.

LaFromboise, T. D. (1988). American Indian mental health policy. *American Psychologist,* 43, 388–397.

Leigh, G., & Skinner, H. A. (1988). Physiologic assessment. In D. M. Donovan & G. A. Marlatt (Eds.), *Assessment of Addictive Behavior* (pp 112–136). New York: The Guilford Press.

Lindenbaum, G. A., Carroll, S. F., Daskal, I., & Kapusnick, R. (1989). Patterns of alcohol and drug abuse in an urban trauma center: The increasing role of cocaine abuse. *The Journal of Trauma,* 29, 1654–1658.

Macdonald, D. I. (1984). Drugs, drinking, and adolescence. *American Journal of Diseases of Children,* 138, 117–125.

Macdonald, D. I. (1986). Prevention of adolescent smoking and drug abuse. *Pediatric Clinics of North America,* 33, 995–1005.

Macdonald, D. I. (1989). Diagnosis and treatment of adolescent substance abuse. *Current Problems in Pediatrics,* 19, 395–444.

MacKenzie, R. G., Cheng, M., & Haftel, A. J. (1987). The clinical utility and evaluation of drug screening techniques. *Pediatric Clinics of North America,* 34, 423–436.

MacKenzie, R. G., & Kipke, M. D. (1992). Substance use and abuse. In S. B. Friedman, M. Fisher, & S. K. Schonberg (Eds.), *Comprehensive Adolescent Health Care* (pp. 765–786). St. Louis: Quality Medical Publishing, Inc.

Manno, J. E. (1986). Specimen collection and handling. In R. L. Hawks & C. N. Chiang (Eds.), *Urine Testing for Drugs of Abuse, NIDA Research Monograph 73* (pp. 24–29). Rockville, MD: Department of Health and Human Services, National Institute on Drug Abuse, DHHS Publication No. (ADM) 87–1481.

Marlatt, G. A. (1988). Matching clients to treatment. Treatment modules and stages of change. In D. M. Donovan & G. A. Marlatt (Eds.), *Assessment of Addictive Behavior* (pp. 474–483). New York: The Guilford Press.

Marzuk, P. M., Tardiff, K., Leon, A., Stajic, M., Morgan, E. B., & Mann, J. J. (1990 Prevalence of recent cocaine use among motor vehicle fatalities in New York City. *Journal of the American Medical Association,* 263, 250–256.

Mayer, J. E., & Filstead, W. J. (1980). Empirical procedures for defining adolescent alcohol misuse. In J. E. Meyer & W. J. Filstead (Eds.), *Adolescence and Alcohol* (pp. 51–68). Cambridge, MA: Ballinger Publishing Company.

Mensch, B. S., & Kandel, D. B. (1988). Dropping out of high school and drug involvement. *Sociology of Education,* 61, 95–113.

Miller, W. R. (1985). Motivation for treatment: A review with special emphasis on alcoholism. *Psychological Bulletin,* 98, 84–107.

Moncher, M. S., Holden, G. W., & Trimble, J. E. (1990). Substance abuse among Native-American Youth. *Journal of Consulting and Clinical Psychology,* 58, 408–415.

Morrison, M. A., & Smith, Q. T. (1987). Psychiatric issues of adolescent chemical dependence. *Pediatric Clinics of North America,* 34, 461–480.

National Institute on Drug Abuse. (1992). National high school senior drug abuse survey 1975–1991. Monitoring the future survey. *NIDA Capsules.* U.S. Department of Health and Human Services, Alcohol, Drug Abuse and Mental Health Administration.

Newcomb, M. D., & Bentler, P. M. (1988). *Consequences of Adolescent Drug Use.* Newbury Park, CA: Sage Publications.

Newcomb, M. D., & Bentler, P. M. (1989). Substance use and abuse among children and teenagers. *American Psychologist, 44,* 242–248.

Obermeier, G., & Henry, P. (1985). Inpatient treatment of adolescent alcohol and polydrug abusers. *Seminars in Adolescent Medicine, 1,* 293–301.

Oetting, E. R., & Beauvais, F. (1990). Adolescent drug use: Findings of national and local surveys. *Journal of Consulting and Clinical Psychology, 58,* 385–394.

Owens, S. M., McBay, A. J., & Cook, C. E. (1983). The use of marijuana, ethanol, and other drugs among drivers killed in single-vehicle crashes. *Journal of Forensic Science, 28,* 372–379.

Petchers, M. K., Singer, M. I., Angelotta, J. W., & Chow, J. (1988). Revalidation and expansion of an adolescent substance abuse screening measure. *Journal of Developmental and Behavioral Pediatrics, 9,* 25–29.

Rahdert, E. R. (ed.). (1991). *The Adolescent Assessment/Referral System Manual.* Washington, D.C.: U.S. Department of Health and Human Services, Alcohol, Drug Abuse and Mental Health Administration, National Institute on Drug Abuse, DHHS Publication No. (ADM) 91–1735.

Riggs, S. G., & Alario, A. J. (1989). Adolescent Substance Use. Instructor's Guide. In C. E. Dube, M. G. Goldstein, D. C. Lewis, E. R. Myers, & W. R. Zwick (Eds.), *The Project ADEPT Curriculum for Primary Care Physician Training.* Providence: Project ADEPT, Brown University.

Roizen, J. (1982). Estimating alcohol involvement in serious events. In *Alcohol Consumption and Related Problems, Alcohol and Health Monograph I.* Washington, D.C.: National Institute on Alcohol Abuse and Alcoholism. D.H.H.S. Publ. No. (ADM) 82–1190, U.S. Government Printing Office.

Rutherford, W. H. (May 14, 1977). Diagnosis of alcohol ingestion in mild head injuries. *The Lancet, 1(8020),* 1021–1023.

Schonberg, S. K. (1985). Perspective on the role of the pediatrician in the management of adolescent drug use. *Pediatrics in Review, 7,* 131–132.

Schwartz, R. H., Cohen, P. R., & Bair, G. O. (1985). Identifying and coping with a drug-using adolescent: Some guidelines for pediatricians and parents. *Pediatrics in Review, 7,* 133–139.

Swhwartz, R. H. Hayden, G. F., Getson, P. R., & DiPaola, A. (1986). Drinking patterns and social consequences: A study of middle-class adolescents in two private pediatric practices. *Pediatrics, 77,* 139–143.

Selzer, M. L. (1971). The Michigan Alcoholism Screening Test: The quest for a new diagnostic instrument. *American Journal of Psychiatry, 127,* 1653–1658.

Senay, E. C. (1983). *Substance Abuse Disorders in Clinical Practice.* Boston, John Wright—PSG, Inc.

Shedler, J., & Block, J. (1990). Adolescent drug use and psychological health. A longitudinal inquiry. *American Psychologist, 45,* 612–630.

Silber, T. J. Getson, P., Ridley, S., Iosefsohn, M., & Hicks, J. M. (1987). Adolescent marijuana use: Concordance between questionnaire and immunoassay for cannabinoid metabolites. *Journal of Pediatrics, 111,* 299–302.

Sloan, E. P., Zalenski, R. J., Smith, R. F., Sheaff, C. M. Chen, E. H., Keys, N. I.,

Crescenzo, M., Barrett, J. A., & Beman, E. (1989). Toxicology screening in urban trauma patients: Drug prevalence and its relationship to trauma severity and management. *The Journal of Trauma, 29,* 1647–1653.

Sobell, L. C., Sobell, M. B., & Nirenberg, T. D. (1988). Behavioral assessment and treatment planning with alcohol and drug abusers: A review with an emphasis on clinical application. *Clinical Psychology Review, 8,* 19–54.

Soderstrom, C. A., Trifillis, A. L., Shankar, B. S. Clark, W. E., & Cowley, R. A. (1988). Marijuana and alcohol use among 1023 trauma patients. *Archives of Surgery, 123,* 733–737.

Stephenson, J., Moberg, D., Daniels, B., & Robertson, J. F. (1984). Treating the intoxicated adolescent. *Journal of the American Medical Association, 252,* 1884–1888.

The Task Force on Pediatric Education. (1978). *The Future of Pediatric Education.* Denver: Hirschfeld Press.

U.S. Congress, Office of Technology Assessment. (1991). Alcohol, tobacco and drug abuse: Prevention and services. *Adolescent Health—Volume II: Background and the Effectiveness of Selected Prevention and Treatment Services.* OTA-H-468 (pp. 499–578). Washington, D.C.: U.S. Government Printing Office.

Taylor, R. L., Cohan, S. L., & White, J. D. (1985). Comprehensive toxicology screening in the emergency department: An aid to clinical diagnosis. *American Journal of Emergency Medicine, 3,* 507–511.

Voss, H. L., & Clayton, R. R. (1987). Stages in involvement with drugs. *Pediatrician, 14,* 25–31.

Walsh, D. C., Hingson, R. W., Merrigan, D. M., Levenson, S. M., Cupples, A., Heeren, T., Coffman, G. A., Becker, C. A., Barker, T. A., Hamilton, S. K., McGuire, T. G., & Kelly, C. A. (1991). A randomized trial of treatment options for alcohol-abusing workers. *New England Journal of Medicine, 325,* 777–782.

Wechsler, H., & Isaac, N. (1992). "Binge" drinkers at Massachusetts colleges: Prevalence, drinking style, time trends, and associated problems. *Journal of the American Medical Association, 267,* 2929–2931.

Weger, C. D., & Diehl, R. J. (1984). *The Counselor's Guide to Confidentiality.* Honolulu: Program Information Associates.

Wheeler, K., & Malmquist, J. (1987). Treatment approaches in adolescent chemical dependency. *Pediatric Clinics of North America, 34,* 437–447.

Williams, A. F., Peat, M. A., Crouch, D. J., Wells, J. K., & Finkle, B. S. (1985). Drugs in fatally injured young drivers. *Public Health Reports, 100,* 19–25.

Williams, R. A., Feibelman, N. D., & Moulder, C. (1989). Events precipitating hospital treatment of adolescent drug abusers. *Journal of the American Academy of Child and Adolescent Psychiatry, 28,* 70–73.

Winters, K. (1990 The need for improved assessment of adolescent substance involvement. *Journal of Drug Issues, 20,* 437–502.

Winters, K. D., & Henly, G. A. ()1989). *Personal Experience Inventory test and manual.* Los Angeles: Western Psychological Services.

Winters, K. C., & Henly, G. A. (1991). *Adolescent Diagnostic Interview schedule and manual.* Los Angeles: Western Psychological Services.

Yamaguchi, K., & Kandel, D. B. (1984). Patterns of drug use from adolescence to young adulthood: II. Sequences of progression. *American Journal of Public Health, 74,* 668–672.

Yamaguchi, K., & Kandel, D. B. (1984). Patterns of drug use from adolescence to young adulthood: III. Predictors of progression. *American Journal of Public Health, 74,* 673–681.

Zarek, D. J., Hawkins, D., & Rogers, P. D. Risk factors for adolescent substance abuse: Implications for pediatric practice. *Pediatric Clinics of North America, 34,* 481–493.

# 3
# Eating Disorders: Anorexia Nervosa and Bulimia Nervosa

*Sonia Minnes*
*Pamela Senders*
*Lynn T. Singer*

ating disorders have increasingly come to public attention over the past decade through numerous magazine articles and television movies. Karen Carpenter, Jane Fonda, and even Princess Diana are only a few of numerous media stars whose struggles, not all successful, with anorexia nervosa and bulimia nervosa have been publicized. Media attention has led to heightened awareness and increased research efforts into prevention and treatment. As eating disorders are most likely to have their onset in adolescence (Fairburn & Cooper, 1982; Halmi, Casper, Eckert, Goldberg, & Davis, 1979), recent medical emphasis on adolescent health has led to greater attention to these problems.

Identifying adolescents at risk and accurately assessing the behaviors and beliefs associated with eating disorders are essential for prevention and successful treatment. This chapter will provide an overview of the disorders of anorexia nervosa and bulimia nervosa, including a discussion of causal theories, risk groups, treatment alternatives, and a method for assessing symptoms of eating disorders using the Eating Disorders Inventory 2 (EDI 2).

## Overview of Anorexia and Bulimia Nervosa

Formerly thought to occur only rarely, eating disorders are now believed by many researchers to be on the rise (Jones, Fox, Babigan, & Hutton, 1980; Willi & Grossman, 1983). Whether there is a real rise in incidence, versus artifactual changes in definition or reporting, has, however, been debated (Johnson, Tobin, & Lipkin, 1989; Schwartz, Thompson, & Johnson, 1981). While clinical case reports of eating disorders have been noted for centuries, treatment focus on them as distinct clinical entities has been relatively recent. Bulimia nervosa, for example, was initially conceptualized by Russell (1979), with concerted efforts at treatment developed in the 1980s. Current estimates suggest that up to 1 percent of young women have anorexia nervosa (American Psychiatric Association, 1987). From 4 to 19 percent, depending on the criteria and population used, have significant symptoms of bulimia (Pyle et al., 1983; Halmi, Falk, & Schwartz, 1981), with females composing over 90 percent of all cases (Halmi, 1974; Halmi et al., 1981). Both anorexia nervosa and bulimia nervosa are considered "classic" disorders of adolescence, since most patients are likely to develop these disorders in the teenage years. Anorexia nervosa has been shown to be more likely to have an onset at ages fourteen and eighteen (Halmi, Casper, Eckert, Goldberg, & Davis, 1979) and is usually considered a disorder of early adolescence. Bulimia nervosa tends to occur in older adolescents (Mitchell, Hatsukami, Eckert, & Pyle, 1985), although recent studies suggest that it may occur earlier. For example, Singer, Yamashita, Benson-Szekely, and Jaffe (1990) found their sample of adolescent pediatric patients with bulimia nervosa to have onset at a mean age of 15.2 years.

While the majority of reported cases of eating disorders have been among white, higher-social-class populations, recent evidence suggests that the disorders may be becoming more prevalent in middle and lower social classes and among minority populations (Gowers & McMahon, 1989). Eating disorders are also disproportionately found among groups engaged in certain recreational and professional pursuits, such as college athletics (Rosen, McKeag, Hough, & Curley, 1986). Although eating disorders can and do occur in male adolescents, because the overwhelming majority of patients are female, throughout this chapter we will use the pronoun *she* when referring to an individual patient.

The phrase "eating disorder" refers to abnormal beliefs and behaviors related to intake of food and weight regulation. Often eating disorders interfere with an adolescent's ability to function socially and academically and cause psychological distress and/or medical complications. Because of their significant effects on both medical and psychological components of an individual's health, eating disorders can be considered a prototype of psychosomatic or psychophysiological disorders, as they require adequate professional attention to both aspects of functioning.

**Table 1.**
**Anorexia Nervosa**

1. Body weight at least 15% below what would be expected for age and height. Weight loss is a result of willful restriction of food intake.

2. Irrational fear about becoming fat or gaining weight even when obviously below normal body weight.

3. Inaccurate perception of body image.

4. Amenorrhea for at least three menstrual cycles in a row.

## Table 2.
## Bulimia Nervosa

1. Ingestion of large amounts of food (bingeing) in a short period of time. Usually several thousand calories of foods typically avoided are consumed during a binge. This occurs at least twice a week for three months.
2. Eating behavior during binges is being experienced as out of control.
3. Binges are usually followed by self-induced vomiting, use of laxatives or diuretics, strict dieting or fasting, or vigorous exercise, in order to prevent weight gain.
4. Ongoing concern about body weight and shape.

Different diagnostic criteria for eating disorders have been used in clinical settings and for research. The most recent and widely accepted diagnostic criteria were published in the American Psychiatric Association's *Diagnostic and Statistical Manual of Mental Disorders* III-R (1987), although work toward clarifying these criteria is currently in progress (Walsh, 1992). The three major diagnostic categories for the eating disorders commonly seen in adolescents are anorexia nervosa, bulimia nervosa, and eating disorders not otherwise specified (NOS). Their symptoms are described in Tables 1–3.

*Anorexia* literally means "loss of appetite." As it is used in "anorexia nervosa," the term refers to a somewhat different phenomenon, as actual loss of appetite in the disorder is rare. Rather, willful and conscious refusal to ingest adequate calories, or maintain a healthy body weight, and failure to achieve expected weight gains during periods of maturation are the central features of anorexia nervosa. An individual with anorexia nervosa has an overwhelming fear of becoming fat and continues to restrict caloric intake even when she is underweight. Distortions exist in the way actual body weight is perceived. For example, an adolescent may believe that her hips are much too fat, even though she is severely emaciated and no excess fat exists. Another diagnostic criterion for anorexia nervosa is the absence of three or more consecutive menstrual cycles. Menstrual irregularities are common, due to the hormonal changes secondary to starvation.

Bulimia nervosa is an eating disorder in which rapid consumption of

## Table 3.
## Eating Disorder, Not Otherwise Specified

Disturbances of eating that do not meet the criteria for anorexia nervosa or bulimia nervosa, yet have psychological and medical consequences. For example:

1. A person who has lost at least 15% of average body weight and has other characteristics of anorexia nervosa but still has regular menstrual cycles.
2. A person who has episodic binge eating and purging, but only once weekly and therefore less frequently than in bulimia nervosa.

large quantities of food occur episodically. During the binges, thousands of calories can be consumed in a very short time. The individual feels as if she has no control over the amount of food consumed during the binge. Yet she feels terribly distressed over the ingestion of so many calories, because body weight and shape are of major concern. Binges are followed by periods of purging, either through self-induced vomiting, use of laxatives or diuretics, or vigorous exercise or fasting to prevent weight gain. For the individual to be diagnosed with bulimia nervosa, all of these symptoms must be present and at least two binge episodes must occur per week.

The distinction between anorexia and bulimia nervosa is sometimes confusing, as the two disorders may overlap, or occur in the same adolescent at different times. For example, an adolescent with anorexia nervosa may use self-induced vomiting or other purgatives to lose weight faster, or she may rely solely on reduced food intake. For this reason, anorexia nervosa is often categorized as "restrictor" type or "bulimic" type, based on the differing symptoms. Proposed diagnostic criteria for DSM IV include a distinction of these two subtypes of anorexia nervosa (Walsh, 1992). An adolescent with bulimia nervosa may also use self-induced vomiting to rid herself of calories, but this occurs usually after consuming large quantities of food and experiencing overwhelming feelings of being out of control. Additionally, in bulimia nervosa the adolescent may maintain above-average weight, be of average weight, or even be slightly underweight. Proposed DSM IV diagnostic criteria for bulimia nervosa include an option to classify the disorder into purging (self-induced vomiting, laxative or diuretic use) or nonpurging (strict dieting, fasting, or vigorous exercise but not purging) types (Walsh, 1992). Severe weight loss (15 percent below norms for height and sex) is necessary to diagnose anorexia nervosa. Preoccupation with body shape and weight are characteristic of both disorders. Some restrictor anorexics develop normal-weight bulimia over time (Crisp, Hsu, Harding, & Hartshorn, 1980), and up to 50 percent of normal-weight bulimics may have a history of anorexia nervosa (Hsu & Holder, 1986).

What may further complicate diagnosis is that some obese individuals may engage in compulsive overeating similar to bulimia nervosa but not experience the same preoccupation with thinness or overwhelming need to purge themselves of the food. Apparently, this condition is common among those in hospital-affiliated weight control programs. As a result a new diagnosis, Binge Eating Disorder, has been proposed and is currently under evaluation as a distinct disorder to be included in DSM IV (Spitzer et al., 1992). A clear understanding of diagnostic criteria and an accurate assessment of symptoms are essential for treating eating disorders.

The following are sample case studies of female adolescents who developed an eating disorder, one with anorexia nervosa and the other with bulimia nervosa. The examples will illustrate some differences between the two disorders.

*Adolescent with Anorexia Nervosa*

Rebecca was the youngest of three children. Her older sister and brother were successful academically and launched in their new careers. At age fifteen, Rebecca noticed that she wore a larger size in clothes than her older sister, and had much larger hips and breasts. At five feet, six inches and weighting 130 pounds, Rebecca was of average weight for her height and age. Eventually she began to equate her sister's success with her petite stature and decided to lose enough weight to wear the same clothing size as her sister. When Rebecca limited her caloric intake to 800 calories a day, she quickly began to lose weight. Pleased with her success, she began to take an almost compulsive interest in academics, studying constantly. Eventually she stopped menstruating, felt constantly cold, and used her studies as an excuse to be more and more reclusive. Rebecca enjoyed the compliments others made when she resisted high-calorie foods and proudly announced her small size. When her weight dropped to 105 pounds, more than 15 percent below her original body weight, her parents and teachers commented that she was much too thin. Rebecca insisted that she needed to lose just a little more, to be just right.

*Adolescent with Bulimia Nervosa*

Jennifer was always just a little heavy as a child. She recalled other children's mothers referring to her as "chunky" and having to shop with her mother for "plus" sizes in pants. Until junior high school, it was always OK to eat just what she wanted. With a healthy appetite, she regularly helped herself to seconds and desserts. Shortly after her thirteenth birthday, at five feet, two inches tall and weighing 123 pounds, she began her first diet, on the suggestion of her father to cut down on sweets. He said, "Then you won't have to worry about your weight." At parties and sleepovers, Jennifer politely refused cake, chips, and pizza, which she considered part of the forbidden group of foods. This diet plan quickly produced results. Jennifer lost 13 pounds, she was no longer called "chunky," and her clothes size dropped to a 5. With these results, Jennifer eventually began to place further eating restrictions on herself. A set of beliefs about what could be eaten and about her ideal weight also developed as she formulated the rules for staying slender. One problem, however, was that she was chronically hungry.

At a family gathering, she could no longer maintain her fast. The relief from hunger she felt from the first taste started a frenzy of eating. Jennifer was embarrassed and tried not to look conspicuous as she loaded her plate. She offered to clean up, which gave her access to all her "forbidden" foods in private. As she estimated the damage, she computed that she had consumed 7,000 calories. Panic-stricken, Jennifer searched for solutions to rid herself of the extra calories and cried secretly all the way home in shame and disgust. As soon as she returned home, she took laxatives from her parents' medicine cabinet to help the food quickly pass through her digestive system. What followed were many days when the compulsion to eat the forbidden, fattening foods could no longer be resisted, but her obsession with slenderness was maintained. Her weight usually stayed around 112 pounds. Binges occurred three to four times a week, usually at home before her parents arrived home from work. Eventually Jennifer experimented with self-induced vomiting, a method she found less aversive and more effective than laxative use. Each binge brought feelings of anxiety, self-hatred, and depression. This cycle continued secretly until six years later, when Jennifer was in college and the resulting depression became so severe that she found it difficult to function academically or socially.

## History

A close look at anorexia nervosa demands some recognition of its precursors. Brumberg's work *Fasting Girls* (1988) provides a detailed review of the development of anorexia nervosa as a modern disease. In medieval times, female saints often abstained from food and drink and reportedly subsisted on minimal intake. The most famous of these, Catherine of Siena, existed on spoonfuls of herbs. These early, religiously motivated abstainers were said to exhibit "anorexia mirabilis" (miraculously inspired loss of appetite). In the seventeenth and eighteenth centuries, fasting declined and was considered the work of the devil. Clerics and physicians began to scrutinize the "fasting maids" for signs of surreptitious food intake. By the nineteenth century, abstinence was viewed as a medical problem. Famous cases such as Ann Moore, the "Fasting Woman of Tutbury," and Sara Jacob, the "Welsh Fasting Girl," were unraveled by around-the-clock surveillance that proved the girls had eaten some food after all. The phrase "fasting girl" came to be used in the late 1800s to signify a case of abstinence in which the etiology of the fasting and the intent of the faster were unclear. Sometimes there were religious undertones, claims of mystic powers and clairvoyance, or desires for monetary gain.

The term *hysteria* came to be applied more and more often to young women who refused food. On occasion it was recommended that they be removed from their home environment to hospital settings where their intake could be monitored, and force-feedings were introduced when the situations became life-threatening. The implication was that the families colluded with the abstainers on religious or other grounds to the detriment of their own child's well-being. Gradually over the nineteenth century, food refusal was transformed from an act of religious piety to the realm of disease and what came to be known as "anorexia nervosa."

In October 1873 William Gull lectured on girlhood emaciation, which he considered a perversion of the will, accompanied by marked restlessness. He referred to the disease as anorexia nervosa and recommended rest, re-feeding, special nursing, and, in some cases, separation from the family. While Gull's views were primarily focused on medical aspects of differential diagnosis, a French physician, Charles Lasegue, addressed the issues of anorexia from a more family-oriented perspective. He too suspected emotional causes in the family environment, pressures regarding marriage and suitors, and the prolonged dependence of the new bourgeois life-style to be contributing factors. He believed the young women could express their concerns and displeasures by rejecting food and disrupting family life.

The early 1900s saw a move toward new medical treatment for anorexics, an increased focus on body beauty, dieting, and healthy eating. These trends waxed and waned with the arrivals of the world wars and the depression. After World War II, the ideals for feminine beauty and the sociocultural push toward dieting increased. The 1960s and 1970s brought an explosion in dieting techniques and information, along with extremely slim models, such as Twiggy, and thinner ideals of beauty manifest in the decreasing size of Miss America contestants. Today social changes and expectations for food intake and sexuality continue to apply subtle and not-so-subtle pressures to young women to perfect their bodies through dieting and athletics. Changes in classic analytic thinking based on contributions by Hilde Bruch (1973) linked overeating and undereating as indicators of family patterns, personality development, and pathological ways to respond to needs for autonomy and individual development. It became clear that anorexia nervosa was not a lose of appetite but rather a denial of appetite for complex intrapsychic and social reasons.

If anorexia is denial and suppression of appetite, then bulimia nervosa can be characterized as a repeated indulgence of appetite with subsequent "denial" through purging. Early reports of bulimic behavior date back to the late 1800s; however, the phrase "bulimia nervosa" did not appear until 1979, when coined by Gerald Russell. As the upcoming version of DSM IV will include a new and separate disorder called Binge Eating, the "history" of eating disorders is still in the making.

## Etiologic Theories

Several causal factors accounting for anorexia and bulimia nervosa have been proposed, although currently no specific etiologic theory can solely account for the disorders. As a movement toward a coherent theory of etiology, some researchers have come to believe that anorexia and bulimia nervosa are complex, multidetermined disorders in which patterns of symptoms result from distinctly different developmental factors. These factors include biological and genetic makeup, sociocultural and psychodynamic influence, and cognitive, behavioral, family, and learning variables (Garner, 1991). Hsu (1990) further suggests that the initiation of conscious weight reduction by an adolescent, regardless of the reason, serves as an entry or a final common pathway, into an eating disorder. Once dieting and weight loss are initiated, other factors intensify preoccupation with weight and food intake, increasing the risk of developing an eating disorder.

## Biological and Genetic Factors

Biological investigations of eating disorders have evaluated predisposing physical factors, psychophysiological effects of the disorder, and the physiological effects of starvation. Biological differences in individuals with an eating disorder can precede, accompany, or result from behavioral changes in eating. Therefore, interpretation of the biological differences found among individuals with eating disorders has been quite difficult.

There is evidence for endocrine disturbances in both anorexia nervosa and bulimia nervosa (Kaplan, 1990). Sometimes these disturbances are expressed as medical complications, such as lack of or irregular menstrual cycles. Usually endocrine disturbances are considered to be a consequence of malnutrition and weight loss, rather than a primary cause of eating disorders. Endocrine and neurotransmitter dysfunctions observed in bulimia nervosa are thought to result from restrained eating. Eventually these disturbances lead to binge eating and the compulsion to purge the unwanted calories.

Some biological investigations of anorexia and bulimia nervosa have focused on central nervous system neurotransmitters—such as serotonin, dopamine, norepinephrine, opioids, and gastrointestinal hormones—that are known to be involved in the regulation of eating behaviors (Fava, Copeland, Schweiger, & Herzog, 1989). Interestingly, these neurotransmitters have also been implicated in the symptoms of depression and anxiety that often accompany eating disorders. To date no primary deficit in a central nervous system neurotransmitter has been identified in either anorexia or bulimia nervosa. While changes in neurotransmitter systems have been found in both disorders, they are thought to occur sometime after the onset of weight loss. Anorexia is associated with changes in the noradrenergic, serotonergic, and opioid systems. Alterations in serotonin and norepinephrine activity are associated with bulimia nervosa (Fava et al., 1989).

The noradrenergic neurotransmitter system is believed to be involved in the regulation of feeding behaviors and is thought to provide important neural substrates for the psychological symptoms of depression and anxiety frequently observed in eating disorders. Serotonin acts on what is considered the satiety system. The serotonergic system is also related to anxiety, depression, and obsessive-compulsive symptoms, which are often features of both anorexia and bulimia nervosa. The opioid system is closely linked to the dopamine system in the neuroregulation of feeding.

The search for a genetic component of eating disorders has been investigated through twin and family risk studies. Family studies indicate that female relatives of an individual with anorexia or bulimia nervosa have up to a five times greater risk of developing an eating disorder than those with nonaffected relatives (Strober, Morrell, Burroughs, Salkin, & Jacobs, 1985). Other psychological disorders, especially depression, have been found to occur at up to three times the rate in relatives of patients with eating disorders (Strober, 1991). There is also evidence of greater incidence of substance abuse among relatives of patients with eating disorders (Biederman et al., 1985; Hudson, Pope, Jonas, & Yurgelun-Todd, 1983), although these findings are inconclusive.

Researchers sometimes investigate genetic influences of a disorder by determining the percentage of monozygotic (identical) and dizygotic (not identical) twins who both have the disorder. A higher concordance rate among identical twins implies a strong genetic factor accounting for the occurrence of the disorder. A review of studies of identical twins by Hsu (1990) found that there was a consistently higher rate of concordance for identical twins than for nonidentical twins in anorexia nervosa. The support for a genetic link in bulimia nervosa is not as strong. The few existing data show low rates of concordance for identical twins and none for nonidentical twins. In all twin studies, the mechanism of genetic predisposition is confused by the fact that family members not only carry genetic information but significantly influence the environment in which a child is raised. Teasing apart this intricate interaction has not been possible.

## Sociocultural Influences

The prevalence of people on weight reduction diets in a population is directly proportional to the occurrence of eating disorders in that population (Hsu, 1990). Western industrial societies such as the United States have increasingly come to value thinness and to emphasize the need to reduce caloric intake and exercise more. This drive to be thin is easily observed by reviewing the number of diet-food products, the popular literature and media coverage of dieting, and visible slender role models such as actresses and athletes.

The value to women of being thin and women's general body dissatisfaction were cleverly demonstrated by researchers (Fallon & Rosen, 1985) in a sample of some 500 male and female undergraduate students. The researchers used a set of nine figure drawings, ranging from emaciated-looking to very heavy. All the students were asked to choose a figure that matched their current figure, their ideal figure, and the figure they believed would be most attractive to the opposite sex. Men rated their current, ideal, and most attractive figures as about the same. In contrast, for women the current figure was heavier than the most attractive one and was even heavier than their ideal.

There is some concern among eating disorder researchers that the emphasis on thinness may be intensifying for adolescents and generalizing to children at a younger age. For example, Garner, Garfinkel, Schwartz, and Thompson (1980) found several indications of an increased societal emphasis on slimness during a twenty-year period, including a sixfold increase in the number of diet articles in popular women's magazines and a progressive decrease in body size of beauty pageant contestants and centerfold models between 1959 and 1978.

Other researchers (Cavior & Dokecki, 1973; Cavior & Lombardi, 1973) investigated attitudes of children of seven or eight years of age and found their judgments of physical attractiveness to be similar to those of older adolescents. In a survey of 318 girls and boys in grades three to six, Maloney, McGuire, Daniels, and Specker (1989) found that 45 percent wanted to be thinner and that 37 percent had already tried to lose weight. The attitudes are similar to those of young adolescents, ages twelve to thirteen, who express significant concerns about being too fat (Wardle & Beales, 1986). These findings suggest that even very young children are aware of cultural values placed on slimness. Although sociocultural influences do not explain eating disorders in our culture, they can impact on the number of adolescents who initiate weight loss programs, placing themselves at greater risk for developing an eating disorder.

*Feminist Psychoanalytic Theory*

The feminist psychoanalytic theory of etiology is based on the fact that eating disorders have affected primarily women in increasing numbers over the past decade. A female's passage from girlhood to maturity in modern society creates a psychology unique to women. This passage is conceptualized as an important determinant in the development of an eating disorder. The mother-daughter relationship is seen as crucially important to developing a sense of self. Feminist therapists postulate that feminine maturity includes three basic demands: feminine deference to others, the anticipation and meeting of the needs of others, and self definition through connection with another (Orbach, 1985). Implicit in these demands is self-denial. As a female adolescent strives to meet the basic demands of feminine maturity, a conflict arises in being able to develop a true sense of her own needs. One result may be that she develops insecurity, especially about her changing body during adolescence. Striving for the "correct" body can become a central goal. The symptoms of anorexia nervosa are considered part of an elaborate defense structure that develops to protect a severely underdeveloped sense of self.

*Family Factors*

In addition to the genetic contribution of parents, a family's interactional style and attitudes have been implicated in the onset of eating disorders in those adolescents who are at risk. To date most research on familial environments and interactions has investigated families after the onset of an eating disorder. This type of research is problematic, since differences—such as abnormal attitudes toward weight—found in families in which a member has an eating disorder cannot be considered causal, only related. The direction of current research is toward prospective studies that investigate base rates of eating problems in childhood and test specific hypotheses regarding family characteristics and the development of eating disorders in adolescence (Crawford & Watts, 1992).

Clinical observations of families of adolescents with anorexia nervosa typically describe white, upper-middle-class families concerned with outward appearances, such as displays of harmony and physical fitness (Yager, 1982). Adolescents who develop anorexia nervosa commonly have been models of compliance in childhood (Bruch, 1973). Bruch (1973) asserts that anorexia nervosa results from early core developmental deficits that prevent the child from understanding her own needs and wishes. At puberty, the tasks of individuation, including achievement of separation and autonomy from the family, stress the adolescent's faulty defense system. Rigid family rules are upheld at the expense of communication, and family members assume that they know each other's feelings. It is believed that an adolescent brought up in this type of environment will have a difficult time with such important developmental tasks as autonomy, independence, achievement of personal identity, and negotiation of physical and emotional changes related to the onset of puberty (Garner, 1991; Hsu, 1990).

Family disturbances in bulimia nervosa have also been described. Some investigators characterize the family environment of bulimia patients as constricting the adolescent psychologically (Lambley & Scott, 1988). For example, wishes by an adolescent to explore career alternatives in music might be met with undervaluation of the idea, such as "You could never count on making a living that way." This type of response does not allow independent exploration by the adolescent to continue. (Johnson & Flach, 1985). Family characteristic based on perceptions of 105 patients with bulimia, were reported to include a lack of emphasis on assertive, independent behavior and open expression of feelings. Isolation and preoccupation with outward appearance were also described as characteristic of their families. In both anorexia and bulimia nervosa, abnormal parental attitudes toward diet and shape have been suspected (Kalucy, Crisp, & Harding, 1977; Schwartz, Thompson, & Johnson, 1981).

Some family therapists believe that certain transactional patterns are characteristic of families that have a member with anorexia nervosa, terming them "psychosomatogenic families" (Minuchin, 1974). In this model, the development of anorexia nervosa, or any somatic illness in an identified member, is the expression of a dysfunctional family, characterized by enmeshment, overprotectiveness, rigidity, and lack of conflict resolution. Involvement of the child in conflict between parents is also considered a characteristic in this model of a dysfunctional family. Such characteristics and models, however, have not been subjected to adequate empirical research to support or refute them and thus remain speculative.

## Cognitive/Behavioral Theories

Without clear evidence for a biological, sociocultural, or psychodynamic etiology, behavior therapists contend that a cognitively focused model of bulimia nervosa best fits the data (O'Leary & Wilson, 1987). Central to this theory is that an individual who suffers from psychological distress usually has abnormal beliefs or thoughts. An adolescent with bulimia nervosa expresses abnormal attitudes and beliefs about weight regulation. For example, she may believe she should only have one meal a day to achieve or maintain her ideal weight. She becomes preoccupied with this diet and evaluates her self-worth based on her weight and dieting standard. Eventually, through biological changes due to starvation or as a response to stressful circumstances, a binge is triggered. Strict belief in her dieting standard and fear of gaining weight may cause her to purge the unwanted calories through vomiting, laxative abuse, or physical exertion.

A person with anorexia nervosa is similarly thought to have abnormal attitudes and beliefs about ideal weight and dieting. One conceptualization of anorexia nervosa is that of a weight phobia, or intense fear and avoidance of a mature weight and shape (O'Leary & Wilson, 1987). Dieting continues in order to avoid the feared stimulus of fatness and associated meanings attached to fatness, such as sexual activity, pregnancy, and maturity. Strict dieting behavior continues because the woman is reinforced positively with thinness and gains a sense of gratification and self-control. Distortions in the eating-disordered person's thinking, such as overgeneralization ("All successful people are thin") and catastrophizing ("Eating this cake will make me fat"), help maintain abnormal dieting behaviors.

Cognitive behavioral theories provide some insight into the beliefs and thoughts of individuals with anorexia and bulimia nervosa but do not incorporate important biological, sociocultural, or psychological variables that affect the development or maintenance of eating disorders. Nevertheless, some useful treatment approaches have been developed based on cognitive behavioral principles. Certain of these interventions will be addressed later in the chapter.

## Risk Groups

Not all adolescents who try to lose weight develop an eating disorder; nor are all adolescents equally concerned with achieving a slim, narrow-hipped figure. Epidemiological studies of the incidence, prevalence, and correlates of eating disorders in different populations have identified groups at higher risk for developing eating disorders.

### Cross-Cultural and Socioeconomic Differences

Societal emphasis on thinness appears to be a sociocultural and socioeconomic phenomenon. Where money and food supplies are sparse, as in Eastern, nonindustrialized countries, the emphasis on a slim ideal does not appear to be so prevalent. While eating disorders do occur in non-Western cultures, they occur primarily among individuals of higher-social-class background (Hsu, 1990).

Typically, abundance of food is associated with an increased standard of living and a consequent increase in average weight in the population. In the West, higher social status and education are, however, associated with the desire to be slim, a reversed situation (Hsu, 1990). A study by Dornbusch and colleagues (1984) surveyed over 7,000 youths ages twelve to seventeen in a national sample. Girls whose parents were of higher education and social status wanted to be thin more often than those in lower-social-status groups. In contrast, no relationship between social class and the desire to be thin was found for males. Although eating disorders have traditionally been associated with white, higher-socioeconomic-status adolescents, they may be on the rise in other socioeconomic and minority groups. For example, a recent report (Rosen et al., 1988) found a significant proportion of Native American women trying to lose weight (74 percent), with 12 percent using harmful purging techniques such as self-induced vomiting. The previously reported low incidence of eating disorders in minority women may be a result of sampling and research biases, and no accurate assessment of the number of cases can be made at this time (Dolan, 1991).

### "Body-Focused" Subgroups

Inherent in some professions and hobbies is a focus on the body, particularly weight and percentage of lean body mass. Among such subgroups are athletes, dancers, models, actresses, and jockeys. Since adolescents are typically encouraged to pursue extracurricular activities such as sports or drama, they are often compelled to become part of a body-focused subgroup.

Strenuous physical activity and low body fat are goals for many athletes. In some sports in which low body weight is particularly desirable for aesthetic or performance reasons, female athletes engage in moderate to severe diet restriction (Hamilton, Brooks-Gunn, & Warren, 1985). Studies of dancers have reported an increased incidence of eating disorders. Garner and colleagues (1987) assessed fifty-five female students, eleven to fourteen years of age, enrolled in a competitive professional ballet school in North America. The girls were assessed using the Eating Disorders Inventory (EDI), and thirty-five were followed up two years later through a personal interview. Fourteen were found to have some form of an eating disorder: nine with anorexia nervosa, one with bulimia nervosa, and four with partial symptoms of both disorders. These findings are consistent with an earlier study identifying dancers to be at particularly high risk for developing an eating disorder (Garner & Garfinkel, 1980).

Other subgroups of athletes have been evaluated to assess the prevalence of eating disorders. In a survey of 182 female college athletes competing in several different sports, including gymnastics, swimming, field hockey, and track, an average of 32 percent employed at least one pathological eating behavior, such as self-induced vomiting or laxative use (Rosen et al., 1986). Male athletes are also at increased risk for pathological weight control behaviors. Male wrestlers (Enns, Drewnowski, & Grinker, 1987) scored higher on scales of dieting restraint and had more aberrant eating attitudes than swimmers and skiers. While the vast majority of adolescents with eating disorders are female, these data suggest that wrestlers may represent a male, athletic population at risk. An interview of sixty male marathon runners (Yates, Leehey, & Shisslak, 1983), classified as obligatory runners, found them to have family backgrounds and psychological themes similar to those of female anorexics.

### "Medical" Subgroups

The co-occurrence of eating disorders among individuals with chronic illnesses such as diabetes and cystic fibrosis is not unheard of. In fact, chronic illnesses with an onset in early childhood may precipitate psychological distress (Nielsen, Borner, & Kabel, 1987). The potentially deadly combination of insulin-dependent diabetes mellitus (IDDM) and either anorexia or bulimia nervosa has been brought to medical attention through several case reports in the literature. In a review of the cases, Hillard and Hillard (1984) note that the concurrence of these disorders may be more common than previously thought, since patients with diabetes can manipulate doses of insulin to encourage weight loss.

Individuals with cystic fibrosis, the most common lethal genetic illness of Caucasian children, have also been identified as potentially at risk for the development of an eating disorder. Increased depression, anxiety, and social isolation have been noted in adolescents with cystic fibrosis (Gayton & Friedman, 1981). Pumariega and colleagues (1986) identified thirteen female patients with cystic fibrosis who were referred for psychiatric consultation because of anorectic-like symptoms. None of the patients met the strict diagnostic criteria for an eating disorder, but did meet diagnostic criteria for major depression or dysthymia.

### Family History Factors

Several risk factors associated with family history have also emerged, including greater incidence of depressive disorders and substance abuse among relatives of individuals with an eating disorder (Rivinus, et al., 1984, Strober et al., 1985). Adolescents who begin to lose weight and who also have a positive family history for depression or eating disorders may be at increased risk for developing an eating disorder. Genetic vulnerability to obesity may also increase a teenager's perceived need for dieting. For example, one fifteen-year-old's intense and early focus on dieting stemmed from her knowledge that her grandfather had died of morbid obesity.

Other risk factors associated with family history may be more obscure. For example, poor interpersonal communication, negativity, rigidity, and other factors characteristically used to describe families of patients with eating disorders are potentially learned and passed from one generation to the next. When the confluence of adolescent dieting and these family factors come into play, the adolescent may be at greater risk for developing an eating disorder. Or if an adolescent is raised in a family with particular interpersonal characteristics, she may be more likely to use dieting to gain some control over her life.

## Consequences of Eating Disorders

Patients with eating disorders tend to minimize or deny their negative physical and psychological symptoms. Even professionals and parents of adolescents may be tempted to glamorize the disorder, minimize its severity, and hope that it is just a "phase" the adolescent is going through or something or she will "grow out of." Although these attitudes sound hopeful, they may prove dangerous for the teen suffering from an eating disorder. Numerous medical and psychological complications of eating disorders range from abdominal discomfort, swollen cheeks, and feeling sad to severe depression, suicide, or serious medical complications, such as cardiac irregularities. Clearly, any adolescent who is suspected of having an eating disorder and who displays any of the symptoms described below should be taken seriously, interviewed in detail about foods and weight-related habits, assessed for related psychological disorders, and referred for a full physical examination with laboratory testing.

## Medical Consequences of Anorexia Nervosa

Emaciation, the hallmark of anorexia nervosa, can be spotted readily. Other signs, however, may exist prior to extreme weight loss. An adolescent with anorexia nervosa may have dry skin, a yellowish discoloration to the skin (hypercarotenemia), or a covering of fine hair over the face, trunk, and extremities (lanugo) (Hsu, 1990). She may experience cold and have lower-than-normal body temperatures, (< 35.5°C) edema, slowed heartbeat (bradycardia), or low blood pressure (hypotension) (Palla & Litt, 1988), the last of which conditions may result in dizziness or fainting. Bone loss (osteopenia) can result in pathological fractures (Rigotti, Nussbaum, Herzog, & Neer, 1984) and, in those with early onset of the disorder, stunted growth (Pfeiffer, Lucas, & Ilstrup, 1986). Exercising to the point of exhaustion and problems with constipation and hair loss (Giannini, Newman, & Gold, 1990) are other complications.

Further medical complications may involve one or several organ systems. Endocrine disturbances resulting from starvation can prompt a decrease in hypothalamic-pituitary-ovarian axis functioning that can cause amenorrhea (absence of menstruation). Elevated activity in the hypothalamic-pituitary-adrenal axis can cause an increase in plasma cortisol levels, and dexamethasone nonsuppression has been reported (Hsu, 1990). Disruptions of the hypothalamic-pituitary-thyroid axis results in below-normal thyroxine (T4) and triiodothyronine (T3) levels, which may cause the patient to exhibit signs of hypothyroidism, such as cold intolerance, bradycardia, and constipation. In addition, growth hormone levels are elevated, and prolactin levels may be lower than normal at night (Hsu, 1990).

A person with anorexia nervosa may experience constipation or delayed gastric emptying of solids, and possibly liquids, as a result of disturbances in gastrointestinal hormone levels. This accounts for feelings of abdominal fullness and distension. Some recent research points to disturbances in central nervous system transmitters, such as deficits in serotonin function (see Fava, Copeland, Schweiger, & Herzog, 1989, for a detailed discussion of neurochemical effects).

Most of these complications in anorexia nervosa can be reversed at varying rates of recovery once the patient initiates a program of weight gain. Amenorrhea may persist due to the time lag in reestablishing the positive pituitary feedback response to estrogen, but normal menstrual function eventually returns.

Unusual lab findings for patients with anorexia nervosa are the result of starvation. These may include anemia, leukopenia (low white cell count), pyuria (white blood cells in urine), proteinuria (protein in urine), hematuria (blood in urine), and compromised renal status (Palla & Litt, 1988). Changes in electrocardiograph results occur as well (Hsu, 1990; Palla & Litt, 1988). Cardiovascular deaths have been known to occur both during the initial phases of illness and during refeeding, if caloric intake is not supervised (Palla & Litt, 1988). Impaired breathing and low blood sugar from prolonged fasting have also been reported.

Electrolyte imbalances can be present if the person with anorexia nervosa also engages in purging activities. Electrolyte imbalances can cause serious damage to renal function and other systems. Additionally, abnormalities have been identified in brain CT and PET scans in patients with anorexia nervosa (Pomeroy & Mitchell, 1989), although further research is needed to establish the importance of these findings.

While the medical complications listed above do not constitute a complete list of findings for anorexics, they do highlight the potential seriousness of medical complications in anorexia nervosa and the need for close medical and laboratory monitoring, along with psychotherapeutic intervention. (For further details and references, see Hsu, 1990.)

## Medical Consequences of Bulimia Nervosa

The physical signs of bulimia nervosa differ from those of anorexia nervosa, since they stem primarily from the bingeing and purging aspects of the disorder, rather than from starvation. As with anorexia nervosa, most complications of bulimia resolve with treatment.

Repeated vomiting may cause patients with bulimia to have swollen salivary glands, which may be evident in puffy, "chipmunk" cheeks. Some adolescents who use vomiting as a means of purging themselves show signs of dental enamel erosion from repeated exposure to the acid in vomitus (Mitchell, Pomeroy, & Colon, 1990). Calluses on the back of the hand or fingers from repeated stimulation of a gag reflex may be present. Flushed cheeks and hemorrhages of the eyes or face can also occur shortly after self-induced vomiting.

Fatigue, headaches, nausea, swelling, lethargy, general weakness, dizziness, and bloating are also common symptoms with bingeing and purging behaviors. Resulting endocrine disturbances can interfere with regular menstrual cycles. Although cortisol levels are generally normal, some with bulimia exhibit dexamethasone nonsuppression (Walsh, Roose, Lindy, Gladis, & Glassman, 1987). Triiodothyronine (T3) levels may be lower in average-weight patients with bulimia compared with those in controls, indicating a state of biological starvation even though a normal weight exists (Hsu, 1990). Elevation in insulin and glucose levels are also sometimes detected. In addition to swollen salivary glands, the gastrointestinal system of a bulimic may show abnormalities that can interfere with the satiety response.

Electrolyte imbalances result from vomiting and from diuretic or laxative abuse. These imbalances may include hypokalemia (low potassium), with possible renal damage, hyponatremia (low sodium); proteinuria (protein in the urine); metabolic alkalosis (increased pH of body fluid); and hypochloremia (deficient chloride in the blood). Iron deficient anemia can result from rectal bleeding secondary to laxative abuse. Wasting of the heart muscle (cardiac myopathy) may result from abuse of syrup of ipecac, which contains a cardiotoxic ingredient. The cardiovascular system may also suffer from dehydration or hypotension.

Another possible medical complication is an accumulation of air in the tissues and organs between the sternum and the spinal column, (pneumomediastinum) or under the skin. Aspiration pneumonia has been known to occur when self-induced vomiting takes place in a semiconscious condition, perhaps induced by drug or alcohol use (Lipscomb, 1987). (For further details and references, see Hsu, 1990.)

## Psychological Consequences of Anorexia Nervosa

A significant psychological correlate of anorexia nervosa is severe depression. Patients may feel sad, have poor self-esteem, and withdraw socially and emotionally. Hsu (1990) reports that as many as 60 percent of patients with eating disorders also meet the criteria for depression, although the rate may be higher in patients with bulimia nervosa. Studies of anorexia nervosa patients indicate that suicide is the most common cause of death (Patton, 1988).

Obsessive thoughts, especially the preoccupation with food content and mealtimes, and compulsive or ritualistic behaviors are characteristic of anorexia nervosa and are probably the effect of starvation. Sometimes non-food-related obsessive-compulsive behaviors, such as hand washing or checking, may occur in an individual with anorexia. Significant social anxiety, usually concerning body weight or eating rituals, may occur, resulting in increasing reclusivness. Severe anxiety may also occur with disruptions of feeding rituals or attempts to force the person with anorexia to eat. Feelings of low self esteem, inadequacy, social insecurity, interpersonal distrust, wishes to retreat to childhood, maturity fears, and perfectionism are also recurrent psychological themes for adolescents with anorexia nervosa (Garner, 1991).

## Psychological Consequences of Bulimia Nervosa

A person with bulimia nervosa enters a cycle of fasting, bingeing, and purging. A period of dieting usually initiates the cycle and may continue for months or even years before the adolescent gives into an increased urge to eat. Usually accompanying this cycle are feelings of guilt, remorse, and anxiety after the binge. Continued feelings of failure, depression, and low self-esteem perpetuate the cycle (Heatherton & Polivy, 1992). Accompanying concurrent biological changes may increase the severity of coexisting depression among patients with bulimia nervosa.

Conduct problems, such as sexual promiscuity, stealing, and alcohol and drug abuse occur in about one-third of patients with bulimia nervosa (Hsu, 1990). Moreover, such personality characteristics as quickly changing moods, impulsivity, and manipulative and difficult interpersonal relationships are observed in some patients with bulimia nervosa. Psychological themes similar to those found in anorexia nervosa—such as social insecurity, low self-esteem, maturity fears, perfectionism, and feelings of ineffectiveness—are reported to be prevalent in bulimia (Garner, 1991).

## Associated Psychiatric Problems

Eating disorders have been associated with high rates of coexisting psychiatric disorders, particularly mood disorders, such as depression, drug dependence, and anxiety, and personality disorders (Mitchell, Specker, & Zwaan, 1991). Often it is quite difficult to determine which disorder occurred first; however, the greater incidence of mood disorders in relatives and the observed similarity of neurotransmitter disturbances in some psychiatric conditions and eating disorders have led researchers to investigate this area further.

### Mood Disorders

Mood disorders refer to a prolonged emotion that colors one's whole psychic life, such as depression (American Psychiatric Association, 1987). Since depression is commonly observed in patients with anorexia and bulimia nervosa, the relationship between the two disorders has been of much interest (see Chapters 5 and 6 of this volume). Basic questions remain as to whether such symptoms develop because of the social changes in eating habits or a relative state of starvation cause the depressive symptoms to occur. Laessle, Kittl, Fichter, Wittchen, and Pirke (1987) suggest that depression develops because of both biological and psychological risk factors associated with eating disorders. These risk factors include changes in neurotransmitter systems due to weight loss and psychological factors such as reduction in social activities. Others have hypothesized that eating disorders are variants of affective or mood disorders, although this idea has generally lost favor (Mitchell et al., 1991).

Some studies have looked at which disorder preceded the other when affective disorders and eating disorders coexist. Walsh, Roose, Glassman, Gladis, and Sadik (1985) found that 74 percent of patients with bulimia had their first episode of major depression simultaneously with or after the onset of bulimia. Whether depression precedes, occurs simultaneously with, or follows an eating disorder, its overall prevalence in this population suggests that it is an important factor.

## Substance Use and Dependence

Coexisting substance abuse is a significant problem in patients with bulimia nervosa. About one-third of a sample of 275 women with bulimia nervosa had a history of alcohol or drug problems, and nearly 18 percent had prior chemical dependency treatment (Mitchell, Hatsukami, Eckert, & Pyle, 1985). Compared with individuals with anorexia nervosa (Laessle, Wittchen, Fichter, & Pirke, 1989), those with all subtypes of bulimia nervosa had a higher lifetime prevalence of substance abuse. Thus, it is not surprising that a high prevalence of eating disorders in substance-abusing populations has also been documented (Beary, Lacey, & Merry, 1986; Jonas, Gold, Sweeney, & Pottash, 1987; Peveler & Fairburn, 1990).

## Personality Disorders

Such personality characteristics as mood lability, impulsiveness, being histrionic, and obsessiveness or compulsiveness can sometimes interfere with interpersonal relationships and daily functioning to such an extent that they are considered a personality disorder. Individuals with eating disorders, especially bulimia nervosa, are reported to have personality disturbances and often qualify for an additional diagnosis of a personality disorder (Mitchell et al., 1991).

Piran and colleagues (1988) report that, while personality disorders are prevalent in both anorexia and bulimia nervosa, the cluster types of personality disorders are characteristically different for the two eating disorders (see DSM III-R for a description of personality disorders). Their clinical assessments resulted in anorexic subjects most commonly demonstrating avoidant, passive-aggressive, dependent, and compulsive personality disorders. In patients with bulimia nervosa, borderline, histrionic, avoidant, and antisocial-dependent personality disorders were most common. Different theories of why eating disorders and personality disorders coexist have arisen. It may be that personality disorders predispose an individual to develop an eating disorder. Another possibility is that personality disorders are a consequence of eating disorders. Alternatively, both disorders may coexist, altering and exacerbating each other.

## Anxiety Disorders

Anxiety disorders range from simple phobias to panic attacks and obsessive-compulsive disorders. The comorbidity of anxiety disorders and eating disorders is common and has recently been investigated. Laessle and colleagues (1989) found 65 to 70 percent of their sample of patients with bulimia nervosa to have an anxiety disorder. This rate is greater than that in the general population, which has a prevalence rate estimated at 18 percent. Another longitudinal follow-up study found anxiety disorders in over 50 percent of patients with eating disorders (Toner, Garfinkel, & Garner, 1986). Among the restricting type of anorexia nervosa patients, obsessive-compulsive disorders and social phobias were most common. In the bulimic type of anorexia, agoraphobia, social phobia, and panic disorders were most common. Anxiety disorders also appear to be prevalent among those with eating disorders and may need to be assessed and treated parallel to the eating disorder.

### Family Dysfunction

As noted previously, family characteristics have been implicated in the etiology of both anorexia and bulimia nervosa. Awareness of an eating disorder in an adolescent sometimes intensifies family disharmony and maintains the illness. For the adolescent with anorexia nervosa, the efforts of parents to force or demand her to eat, gain weight, or stop "acting crazy" may intensify the adolescent's desire to reduce her weight and may create feelings of being misunderstood. The adolescent with bulimia nervosa fears being found out and considered weak, disgusting, or out of control by family members. Her shame often prevents her from discussing her behaviors with family or friends and may make therapy difficult when she relapses.

### Risk of Suicide

The risk of suicide in adolescents with eating disorders is considerable, especially since depression in both anorexia and bulimia nervosa and impulsivity, severe distress, and drug dependence in bulimia are prevalent, and these psychological factors may increase the risk. A fifteen-year outcome study (Patton, 1988) of patients with anorexia and bulimia nervosa compared mortality ratios with those of a normal adolescent population. A 600 percent increase was found in the mortality ratios for adolescents with anorexia nervosa. Six of the eleven deaths were a result of suicide. Significant predictors of death in the anorexia group were (a) more than one inpatient admission and (b) very low weight at admission. Three deaths occurred in the bulimia group, representing a 940 percent increase compared with ratios for the general population, yet these deaths were not from suicide; two deaths occurred in traffic accidents and the other as a result of very low weight. Another follow-up study (Swift, Ritholz, Kalin, & Kaslow, 1987) found that 90 percent of bulimic patients scored in the normal range for depression; however, 13 percent had made a suicide attempt, and 10 percent reported self-injurious behavior. In a review of outcome studies, the major causes of death in eighty-eight individuals with anorexia nervosa was found to be the disorder itself (approximately half) and 24 percent by suicide (Herzog, Keller, Lavori,

1988). Reports of suicidal feelings or wishes to be dead should always be taken seriously and evaluated further.

### Differential Diagnosis

In addition to assessing the adolescent for coexistent psychiatric disorders, eating disorders must be distinguished from other psychological disorders that cause weight loss. These disorders included conversion disorder, schizophrenia, depression, and obsessional disorder. These disorders primarily differ from eating disorders in that an intense drive for thinness is absent and body image is usually not disturbed (Garfinkel, Garner, Kaplan, Rodin, & Kennedy, 1983). (See also Chapter 5, of this volume.)

## Treatment Models

A wide array of treatment models have been proposed for eating disorders, generally corresponding to central etiologic theories. As no one etiologic theory explains the eating disorders, no one treatment model can provide the cure. Most often a combination of treatment methods are used, either simultaneously or separately in the course of successful treatment. Treatment requires combined attention to both physical and psychological aspects. The main treatment goals are the restoration of normal body weight and the establishment of healthy eating patterns. Other important goals include alteration of moods and thoughts that perpetuate the disorder, treatment of coexisting medical and psychiatric complications, and prevention of relapse. Relapse is of great concern, since about 50 percent of patients experience relapse within a year of inpatient treatment (Hsu, 1990), and such chronic conditions appear to become more resistant to treatment over time. It has been our experience that it is important to emphasize to the adolescent patient and her family the need for sustained commitment to a treatment program. Too frequently, parents and the adolescent think a "short" hospitalization will "cure" the problem quickly. In other cases, perhaps because of media attention, parents underestimate the severity of the disorder, minimizing the behaviors as a teenage "phase." Helping parents and the adolescent understand the medical and psychological risks of eating disorders and giving them realistic expectations about the typical duration and extent of therapies are important to successful treatment.

### Anorexia Nervosa

Increased caloric intake and normalization of eating patterns are life-preserving for an individual with anorexia nervosa and also seem to improve psychological factors that may maintain the disorder. In anorexia nervosa, the target weight should be a return to an individually determined healthy body weight at which regular menstrual cycles resume. Hsu (1990) maintains that weight restoration is generally successful in 85 percent of anorexic patients, provided that these treatment principles are fulfilled:

- Weight restoration occurs in conjunction with psychotherapy.
- Patient trusts that she will not be permitted to become overweight.
- Patient fear of loss of control over food is contained.
- Staff is available during meals to discuss fears and anxiety over food intake.
- Weight gain is gradual.
- Positive and negative reinforcement is used.
- Self-destructive behavior, such as vomiting, is confronted and controlled.
- Therapist works with family during mealtime sessions.

Behavioral techniques are effective and therefore often used to help a patient return to an average weight and resume normal eating patterns (Halmi, 1985). In this type of weight restoration treatment, positive reinforcement, such as increasing levels of activity and visiting privileges, are contingent on weight gain. Negative reinforcement is sometimes employed to eliminate vomiting in a patient with anorexia nervosa. The selection of positive or negative reinforcement must be based on what is pleasurable or disagreeable to a particular individual. Once a weight goal is reached, a behavioral program may change focus to reinforce maintenance of weight and healthy eating patterns. Halmi (1985) points out that almost all treatment programs contain an implicit if not overt behavioral component whose focus is on refeeding, weight restoration, and weight maintenance. For example, in hospitalization, discharge is usually implicitly contingent on patient weight gain. For outpatient adolescents, weight gain or maintenance goals are an integral part of treatment for anorexia nervosa, with participation in sports or exercise programs often contingent on goal achievement.

While not part of routine treatment, psychotropic medications have been used to induce weight gain and to correct central neurotransmitter dysfunction in anorexia nervosa. A summary of appropriately conducted studies indicates that some psychotropic medications, such as the antidepressant clomipramine, may have a minimal effect on the rate of weight gain in a patient with anorexia nervosa when used in conjunction with other forms of intervention (Hsu, 1990). It is important to keep in mind that rapid weight gain does not define meaningful improvement, as it may be uncomfortable, interfere with a therapeutic relationship, and have no bearing on long-term outcome. Usually symptoms such as depression and anxiety are considered a part of the eating disorder and are treated through psychotherapy rather than medication. Relaxation training, hypnosis, and imagery techniques are also often used to help patients cope with anxiety about eating and fears of fatness of both anorexia and bulimia nervosa patients.

## Bulimia Nervosa

Strict dieting or long periods without food, even in normal-weight individuals, can lead to binge-like eating and concern about accumulation of fat. For this reason, a restoration of normal eating patterns is critical in interrupting the bulimic cycle and in correcting endocrine disturbances that result from the cycle. Individuals with bulimia nervosa are usually instructed to eat three to four well-balanced meals daily to maintain average weight (Hsu & Holder, 1986) or 90 percent of the highest weight preceding their eating disorder.

One rationale for the use of antidepressant medication to treat bulimia nervosa stems from (a) the association between bulimia nervosa and the comorbidity of mood disorders such as depression and (b) the increased incidence of mood disorders among relatives (Kennedy & Goldbloom, 1991). Another rationale for the use of antidepressant medication is the possibility of chemical regulation of appetite behaviors. Reviews of studies that used antidepressants, such as imipramine or desipramine, to treat bulimia nervosa indicate that there is reduced frequency of binge behavior (Hsu, 1990; Kennedy & Goldbloom, 1991) and that prescribing them early in treatment may help reestablish a normal eating pattern.

## Cognitive Behavioral Interventions

Cognitive behavioral therapy is aimed at the dysfunctional behaviors that are maintained by disturbed beliefs and thoughts. A comprehensive intervention using cognitive behavioral therapy has been developed for individuals with bulimia nervosa (Fairburn, 1985). The aims of this treatment are to change the thought processes preceding a binge, to reduce bulimic behavior, and to improve negative self-concept. An assumption is that these factors perpetuate the binge-purge cycle. Cognitive behavioral therapy has been shown to be more effective than interpersonal psychotherapy or behavioral therapy in modifying outpatients' disturbed attitudes toward shape and weight and the use of dieting and vomiting to control shape and weight (Fairburn et al., 1991). One note of caution is that cognitive behavioral treatment has been used largely with adult populations; as yet there are few data documenting its effectiveness with adolescents. Highlights of this treatment approach are outlined below; More detailed information can be obtained by referring to Fairburn (1985).

Treatment goals are conceptually divided into three stages. During stage 1, the goals are to introduce a pattern of regular eating in order to interrupt the binge-purge cycle. An educational component also provides information about the relationship between starvation and binge eating and about the potentially dangerous consequences of purging. Patients are taught to closely monitor their food intake and to identify their eating as part of a meal or a binge. This eating record issued to further explore what happens before a binge. Table 4 illustrates the eating record of a fifteen-year-old girl with bulimia nervosa. As the record shows, antecedent events can be physiological, emotional, related to specific thoughts or beliefs, or situational.

Progression to stage 2 of treatment usually takes place when the patient has decreased the frequency of binges by about 75 percent. The aims at this stage are to maintain regularity of eating patterns, reduce dietary restraints, learn methods for coping with antecedents to bulimic behavior, and address beliefs about fatness. During this period of treatment, continued monitoring of all foods eaten continues. Two cognitive techniques are often used to deal with antecedents to a binge. One involves a model for problem solving, including defining the problem, identifying an alternative solution, identifying the implication of solutions, and implementing and evaluating the solution. Such problems often include how to prepare for an event during which quantities of "forbidden binge food" may be present. The other cognitive technique used is restructuring dysfunctional cognitions. Techniques for cognitive restructuring include decatastrophizing ("I will not be fat if I eat this dessert"), decentering ("Other people do not notice if I am three pounds heavier"), challenging "shoulds" ("Should I always do as others expect?"), and reattribution ("I feel fat because I have an eating disorder") (Hsu, 1990). Characteristic fear of fatness is also addressed through helping a patient to restructure irrational beliefs about slimness and sociocultural pressures on women to be thin.

Relapse prevention and preparation for termination of therapy are the aims of stage 3. The patient rehearses in self-instruction learned in the previous stage for solving problems and interrupting automatic thoughts that precede binges. While food monitoring is phased out in this stage, the patient is instructed to reinstate this practice if relapse occurs and eating is perceived to be out of control. At this stage, some patients may still have unresolved personal issues, even though the eating disorder is under control. Appropriate referrals or continued work with the therapist on these issues occurs at this stage.

An additional behavioral therapy for the treatment of binge-purge behaviors in bulimia nervosa is Exposure with Response Prevention, or ERP (Rosen & Leitenberg, 1985). Two basic components of this treatment are exposure to a feared stimulus (forbidden foods or amounts of foods) in the presence of a therapist and prevention of the habitual escape response (i.e., self-induced vomiting). ERP is based on the idea that binge eating and purging, usually self-induced vomiting, in bulimia nervosa are linked in a vicious circle by anxiety. Purging is an escape response reinforced by a reduction of anxiety after it occurs. Treatment begins with an assessment of foods that are

**Table 4.**
**Eating Record of 15-Year-Old Female with Bulimia Nervosa**

| Date | Time | Food and Liquid Consumed | Place | Thoughts, Situations, Emotions | Meal or Binge Outcome |
|------|------|--------------------------|-------|-------------------------------|-----------------------|
| 9/23 | 7:45 A.M. | Apple | Kitchen | Didn't finish homework | Meal |
| | 2:00 P.M. | Soft pretzel Diet Coke | Study hall | I'm hungry Hope I make it through swimming practice | Meal |
| | 6:03 P.M. | Broiled chicken Baked potato Broccoli (no butter) Water | At home with family | Need to study for chemistry test; anxious about test/ don't really understand it | Meal |
| | 8:00 P.M. | Apple Glass of water | In bedroom | Can't concentrate/ don't want to eat too much; feeling fat and ugly | Snack |
| | 8:10 P.M. | Bagel Cream cheese Jelly | In bedroom | Feel like eating a lot | Snack |
| | 8:15 P.M. | Bread with peanut butter Bowl of ice cream 8 cookies 2 doughnuts 3 glasses water | In bedroom | feel fat/ hate myself; need to study; wasting time | Binge/ vomited immediately after |
| 9/24 | 9:00 A.M. | Skim milk | Kitchen | Weigh 113 this A.M.; need to lose 3 pounds | Meal |
| | 11:00 A.M. | Diet drink Chewing gum | Mall | With friends; talking about boys at school; size 5 too tight | Meal |
| | 2:30 P.M. | 3 large chocolate chip cookies | Mall | Wish friends didn't buy cookies; feel fat; hungry; if I eat one, I'll blow it | Binge |
| | 4:15 P.M. | Box of vanilla wafers Leftover lasagna Chocolate pudding Ice cream | Home | Feel fat; shouldn't have eaten those cookies before; probably failed my test | Binge; vomited before Mom got home |
| | 6:30 P.M. | Mom offered dinner | Home | Can't eat anything else today; lied and told her that I ate dinner | |

avoided when purging is not possible, the type and amounts of food that usually result in vomiting, and irrational beliefs related to weight gain. Gradual exposure to the feared foods and amounts, takes place in the presence of a therapist. Vomiting is prevented by having the patient stay in the presence of the therapist until the anxiety subsides. Anxiety during and after intake of forbidden foods is monitored, and anxiety-provoking thoughts, such as "I am getting fatter as I eat this cake," are addressed. As treatment sessions progress and repeated exposure to feared foods occurs without vomiting, anxiety is decreased and a greater range of foods and more normal amounts can be eaten.

Cognitive behavioral treatment has been extensively evaluated because it was the first specific approach described in detail, supported by clinical data, and acceptable to patients and clinicians (Fairburn, 1988). Yet many questions remain about its efficacy compared with that of other forms of treatment. Fairburn et al. (1991) evaluated cognitive therapy, behavior therapy, and interpersonal psychotherapy in the treatment of bulimia nervosa. All three interventions were found to reduce some symptoms. One difference, however, was that cognitive behavior therapy was more effective in modifying disturbed attitudes about shape and weight and reducing extreme attempts to diet. It is unclear whether ERP adds significant benefits when used in conjunction with cognitive behavioral therapy (Fairburn, 1988). At this time, cognitive behavioral treatment is a suggested treatment for bulimia nervosa, although its effectiveness in relation to group therapy, drug treatment, or subgroups of patients such as adolescents is not clear.

Patients with bulimia nervosa share characteristics in common with those who have anorexia nervosa, especially if the individual with anorexia nervosa binges and purges, rather than solely restricting food intake. Cognitive behavioral approaches to be used in the treatment of anorexia nervosa must be lengthened and modified because of two main treatment barriers (Fairburn, 1985). The first barrier is poor motivation, since weight loss in a person with anorexia nervosa is consistent with her beliefs and values, rather than a source of distress. The primary need for weight gain, as opposed to stabilization of eating patterns, is another barrier to using cognitive behavioral intervention for patients with anorexia nervosa. While cognitive psychotherapy following initial weight restoration has been proposed for the patient with anorexia (Garner & Bemis, 1985), Fairburn (1985) suggests that until effective methods of increasing the motivation in the restricting anorexic have been developed, cognitive behavioral therapy in this group may be largely ineffective.

## Family Therapy

The goal of family therapy is to alter patterns of family interaction that are believed to maintain the eating-disordered behavior in the adolescent. Interesting models of family intervention have been developed (Minuchin, 1974; Palazzoli, Boscolo, Cecchin, & Prata, 1977) and used to treat eating disorders. Family therapy is typically recommended as one component of a comprehensive treatment intervention, especially for adolescents. An investigation of the efficacy of family therapy over individual supportive therapy indicates that family therapy may be superior (Russel, Szmukler, Dare, & Eisler, 1987) for patients whose onset of illness occurs before age nineteen and whose disorder is not chronic. Older, more severely ill patients seem to benefit more from supportive therapy. Until models of family therapy are verified through long-term follow-up and carefully conducted studies, family therapy should be used not as the sole treatment but as an important adjunct to it, especially for adolescents still living at home (Gilchrist, McFarlane, McFarlane, & Kalucy, 1986). A significant goal is to help other family members learn about and cope with the behavior of the adolescent so that therapeutic goals can be supported by the family milieu.

### Feminist Psychoanalytic Treatment

A feminist psychoanalytic approach to treatment of anorexia nervosa usually takes place in individual open-ended psychotherapy lasting two and a half to four years. Object constancy, providing a consistent and reliable environment, is a fundamental aspect of this treatment approach (Orbach, 1985). The process is one in which a developing adolescent creates a sense of self through therapy. Initial consultation is focused on developing openness about the particulars of food intake and on understanding feelings about food. In the initial phase of therapy, the therapist creates an atmosphere that allows the individual to disclose information without the fear of rejection. The goal at this stage of treatment is to enable the adolescent to live unafraid of food. The middle stage of therapy, after a treatment alliance has been achieved, enables the adolescent to regress and to evaluate herself from a new perspective. Also at this stage of therapy she learns that she has unmet emotional and physical needs, including her appetite. Learning to express herself in ways other than dramatic transformation of her body is the focus of the final stage of therapy.

### Educational Interventions

Nutritional and sociocultural education have been another component in the treatment of eating disorders (Garner, Rockert, Olmsted, Johnson, & Coscina, 1985; Hsu, Holben, & West, 1992). Dietary education is similar for patients with anorexia and bulimia and aims to teach them about good nutrition, establishing personal nutritional needs, and identifying the interrelationships between starvation, overeating, and metabolism and endocrine disturbances. The effects and dangers of self-induced vomiting and laxative abuse are also covered.

Some educational groups also discuss the sometimes opposing and difficult challenges to women in today's society. For example, often the role models of adolescents are successful athletes or performers in public view. Society has come to idealize the lean bodies of these successful individuals. But, a certain amount of body fat is necessary for women to function as sexually mature adults. For many adolescents, societal standards of slimness are often contradictory to biological makeup, and "slim body" goals may be unrealistic or unobtainable without posing severe threat of starvation.

One way to engage the family collaboratively in the treatment of anorexia or bulimia nervosa is to also provide educational materials. Books that describe the disorders in lay language and discuss treatment alternatives will emphasize the seriousness of the illness and the benefits of participation of the adolescent's family in her recovery. A list of some available literature is at the end of this chapter (Appendix A).

## Types of Treatment

### Inpatient versus Outpatient

The decision to treat an adolescent with an eating disorder as an inpatient or an outpatient is usually determined by the amount of assessed risk at any given time. The criteria for hospitalization versus outpatient treatment sometimes differ between professionals, yet most agree that certain conditions indicate an inpatient admission. Very low body weight (below 75 percent of average) or rapid weight reduction, physical complications (e.g., low serum potassium), severe depression or suicidal thoughts, lack of success or worsening condition in an outpatient setting, and an unsupportive family environment are indications for inpatient treatment for anorexia nervosa (Andersen, Morse, & Santmyer, 1985). Patients with bulimia nervosa may also require inpatient treatment if severe depression and suicidal thoughts occur, if there are severe physical complications, or if the patient is unable to break a chaotic binge-purge cycle in an outpatient treatment program.

Inpatient treatment is sometimes part of an emergency admission. At other times, it is elected by the patient. The type of admission should be clearly indicated to the patient. Emergency admissions result from severe metabolic instability, especially hypokalemia, weight loss below 70 percent of ideal body weight, or suicidal behaviors.

When a patient is admitted electively, preadmission assessments are completed by participating inpatient team members, such as the psychologist, physician, dietitian, social worker, and nursing staff. Discussion of the assessment from different disciplines is completed prior to admission, in order to establish treatment goals and options. Chronically ill patients with anorexia nervosa may have brief, time-limited admissions with modest goals.

Inpatient treatment, depending on the circumstances and availability, may occur on a special eating disorders unit, an adolescent psychiatric unit, or a general pediatric or medical ward. One view (Hsu, 1990) is that weight restoration is facilitated best on a unit that has a staff experienced in eating disorders and that has two or more eating-disordered patients at a time. It is important that a patient not feel isolated or different and that ward staff neither subvert treatment efforts nor make the patient feel uncomfortable or criticized.

Outpatient treatment for adolescents with anorexia nervosa usually consists mainly of psychotherapy, both individual and family, aimed at the underlying psychological factors that support the illness. This approach is offered for patients who are not in immediate medical danger. While weight restoration remains important, less emphasis is placed on this factor in outpatient treatment. Regular weigh-ins and monitoring of physical status to make sure the patient is not losing weight, as well as behavioral approaches—including contractual agreements to maintain or remain above a specified weight—are routinely employed in outpatient treatment to ensure patient safety. Patients previously seen as inpatient are referred for outpatient treatment to prevent relapse.

As mentioned previously, the person with bulimia nervosa is usually very distressed over her symptoms and therefore quite motivated for treatment. This is not to say that treatment of bulimia nervosa is easy. Frequently, because of shame or from a desire to please the therapist, the adolescent with bulimia nervosa will hide or minimize the extent of her bingeing or purging behaviors, particularly any relapses. Relapses are not so apparent in bulimia nervosa patients, due to the lack of visible physical signs such as emaciation. Thus, maintaining an open, nonjudgmental attitude on the part of the therapist is important in helping the adolescent cope with lowered self-esteem and embarrassment about her behaviors. With time and therapeutic skill, most patients can be treated successfully on an outpatient basis, and some argue that inpatient treatment is contraindicated (Freeman, 1991). Inpatient treatment is disruptive and costly to women who are attending school, working, or raising a family. Typically, outpatient treatment combines nutritional and educational components, in addition to psychotherapy. For both types of eating disorders—and whether treatment is inpatient or outpatient—a coordinated, interdisciplinary approach is necessary. Table 5 presents a summary of indications for outpatient and inpatient treatment. Most recognized centers for the treatment of eating disorders use a team approach, encompassing medical evaluation and monitoring, nutritional assessment and counseling, and psychotherapy.

**Table 5.**

**Indications for Outpatient versus Inpatient Treatment**

| Inpatient Treatment | Outpatient treatment |
| --- | --- |
| • Below 75% of average body weight<br>• Rapid weight reduction<br>• Physical complications (e.g., heart irregularities)<br>• Severe depression<br>• Suicidal thoughts<br>• Inability to disrupt chaotic binge-purge cycle as an outpatient | • No immediate medical danger<br>• Patient previously seen as an inpatient (relapse prevention)<br>• Lower cost than inpatient treatment<br>• Ability to maintain daily routines of school, work, or child care<br>• Recovery in realistic, less structured setting |

*Group versus Individual Therapy*

In general, the advantages of group therapy are that patients receive mutual support from others who have similar psychological and behavioral experiences. The power of the therapeutic intervention comes from the confrontation and pressure an individual receives from peers in the group. Additionally, a group setting provides the environment to test new ways of thinking or behaving, such as asserting oneself.

Group therapy for individuals with anorexia nervosa is considered to be quite difficult (Hall, 1985) because of the characteristic rigidity, withdrawal, high anxiety and dysphoria, outward compliance, hypersensitivity to criticism, competitiveness with one another, and total preoccupation with food. These characteristics make self-disclosure hard and identification with group goals difficult. Used as an adjunctive therapy, group work with anorexic patients may foster socialization and may be used for more structured educational purposes.

In contrast, group therapy for an adolescent with bulimia nervosa may have several advantages. It can provide an arena for sharing long-held secrets, instilling hope, and engaging in reality testing for irrational beliefs about food and weight. One primary goal of group therapy is to help an adolescent link specific emotions with eating behavior. This is accomplished through ongoing feedback from group members. Group therapy for persons with bulimia nervosa typically employs a combination of approaches, including psychodynamic, cognitive behavioral, and feminist approaches, and is usually offered in conjunction with individual therapy. While there seem to be several positive aspects of group therapy for the treatment of bulimia, systematic investigations of its effectiveness compared with that of other forms of treatment are still needed (Halvorson & Neuman, 1990). Within group therapy, important adjunctive treatment modalities (e.g., hypnosis and relaxation, social skills, and assertiveness training) can be effective.

Day hospital group treatment has been proposed for patients who commonly experience reduction of symptoms when externally controlled in a hospital setting but who have setbacks when external controls are lifted. Treatment occurs in groups and consists of nutritional and sociocultural interventions and of the identification of underlying disturbed psychological and family processes. Regression and dependency on hospital staff are minimized, since patients must maintain functioning outside the hospital and since the group treatment provides both mutual support and the impetus for change.

Support groups differ from group therapy in that the groups are usually led by a recovered patient or parent of a patient. These groups always recommend that professional treatment be sought simultaneously. A unique benefit of these groups is that they give information and peer support while encouraging reluctant patients to seek help.

One of the many group models proposed for the treatment of bulimia is Overeaters Anonymous (OA), which relies on the principles used by Alcoholics Anonymous (AA). OA assumes that obesity is a symptom of compulsive overeating that affects those of normal or subnormal weight. While OA offers practical advice, friendship, and support, Garner (1986) has pointed out that the program is predicated on a number of misdirected premises that may be harmful for the bulimia patient. For example, one OA premise is that bulimics are "sick people" who suffer from a progressive, incurable illness, with treatment aimed at arresting the sickness. Garner states that a person with bulimia can be treated successfully and that defining the problem as lifelong serves only to increase despair.

## Assessment of Eating Disorders

Except for obvious weight loss in anorexia nervosa, most of the symptoms of eating disorders occur privately, as in binge eating and purging, or are experienced subjectively, as in fear of becoming fat. Eventually family members may suspect a problem if noticeable changes occur, such as different or extreme patterns of eating, moodiness, increased need for sleep, exercise compulsions, changes in school performance, or seclusiveness. Physical symptoms of constipation, headache, abdominal pain, and fainting are often associated. While some parents notice that large amounts of food disappear from the home in which an adolescent has bulimia nervosa, this is not always the case. In some instances, adolescents may buy and eat their binge foods outside the home. One woman with bulimia nervosa, a twenty-nine-year-old mother of an infant, revealed that she had binged and vomited regularly since she was sixteen. Neither her parents nor her husband had ever been aware of her behaviors, which were carefully planned and hidden over the thirteen-year period. Adolescents with anorexia nervosa also find it easy to hide their food restriction in families in which two parents are working and there are a full social schedule and little time for family meals. Loose-fitting, colorful clothing and good facial makeup frequently mask the adolescent's emaciation until it is advanced.

When the symptoms come to the attention of those interacting with an adolescent, associated characteristics of eating disorders, such as overconcern with body weight and appearance and feelings of ineffectiveness, may not be obvious. Often an adolescent is reluctant to admit a problem exists or is unable to communicate areas of concern. For adolescents with anorexia nervosa, extreme denial is common, and their emotional reactions to parental probing may intimidate parents into ignoring the eating disorder. Adolescents with eating disorders frequently come to the attention of school personnel and their pediatricians through the physical symptoms associated with starvation, bingeing, or purging. Fainting, dizziness, abdominal pain, and headaches may also bring the adolescent with an eating disorder to the attention of professionals.

The preceding overview of etiologic theories, risk groups, and treatment interventions emphasizes that adolescents with specific subtypes of an eating disorder may vary in their presentation of symptoms. Early, accurate assessment of symptoms known to be related to the onset or maintenance of an eating disorder can mean the difference between successful, timely treatment and a serious, chronic condition affecting many domains of functioning and health.

### Initial Assessment

A comprehensive assessment, including medical, behavioral, psychological, family, and social aspects of eating disorders, is necessary, since eating disorders are multidetermined and symptoms may vary widely, depending on the individual. Reviews covering initial assessment of eating-disordered patients include those of Davis (1986), Johnson (1985), and McKenna (1989).

Typically, the first step in assessing a patient with an eating disorder is to take a weight history and assess eating behaviors physical symptoms, and experiences with prior treatment. A weight history should include present weight and height, and the highest and lowest weights since menarche, as well as ascertaining the adolescent's ideal weight and the number of times a day she weighs herself.

Although talking about specific eating behaviors can be particularly difficult for a patient, this information is essential to understand what her daily eating pattern is like. For example, how many calories are consumed, and what is the length of time between meals? If bingeing occurs, what amounts and types of foods constitute a binge? Which foods are forbidden, how often are the binges, and at what age did bingeing begin? Are there any specific circumstances that trigger a binge? Learning what follows a binge is also immediately important, since self-induced vomiting and laxative use have serious medical consequences. Time spent counting calories, planning meals, or obsessing about food is important as well as the extent to which eating and purging behaviors interfere with work or studies?

Since menstrual disturbances frequently accompany anorexia and bulimia nervosa, the age of menarche and the number of missed menstrual periods is important information. Current and past sexual interest and activity vary widely in patients with an eating disorder and can range from promiscuity to decreased interest in sex. Therefore, the adolescent's attitudes toward sex, current level of activity and method of birth control if sexually active should be determined. Another area of concern is alcohol or drug use, including duration and frequency. Problems, such as edema, hair loss, headaches, dental problems, and bloating should be evaluated to assess the extent of physical symptoms. Additionally, a complete physical should always accompany history taking.

An important step in evaluating a patient with an eating disorder is the psychological assessment, which will help to define psychological resources and barriers and to identify coexisting psychological disorders, if present. Assessment of character style, defense mechanisms, capacity for self-observation, and motivation for treatment can be accomplished through a combination of methods—for instance, an interview, observation, and standardized assessments. Screening for psychiatric disorders, including depression, other mood disorders, anxiety disorders, and personality disorders, is necessary, since rates of comorbidity are high and treatment implications are significant. It is important to assess for depression, mood swings, anxiety or phobias, memory or orientation difficulties, self-mutilation behavior, and especially suicidal thoughts or behavior. The risk of suicide should always be determined by asking specific questions in a clinical interview, even to those who do not report obvious symptoms of depression, such as feelings of sadness or worthlessness (see Chapter 6 on suicide risk).

Whether or not a family is directly involved in treatment, evaluation of family characteristics and functioning is important. Determine current family makeup and whether quarreling or a family breakup has recently occurred. Does the family permit open discussion over conflict, and are there opportunities for independence? How does the patient perceive her relationship with parents and siblings? Is there a family history of medical and psychiatric illness, substance abuse, or mood disorders? Screening for ongoing or prior physical or sexual abuse is also necessary. Family support and functioning may influence the determination of hospitalization versus outpatient treatment. Severely dysfunctional families whose members are unable to provide support for the adolescent may indicate the need for hospitalization.

Assessment spans several topics, many of which an adolescent may be reluctant to discuss. Often this information is gathered over more than one interview and sometimes by professionals from different disciplines, such as psychology, medicine, nursing and social work. Forming a supportive, honest alliance with the patient from the beginning of the interview is important.

McKenna (1989) suggests that a structured interview, conducted with a matter-of-fact, respectful attitude, is preferable to an open-ended interview, which may make the patient feel helpless and out of control.

Standardized, self-report questionnaires can be helpful in the evaluation and screening of symptoms associated with eating disorders. They may add supplemental information to a diagnostic interview by allowing the respondent to reply privately, avoiding direct responses that are often difficult to communicate. Additionally, normative values enable one to assess the severity of different symptoms compared with that of others with and without an eating disorder. The Eating Disorders Inventory 2 is one assessment tool that has been widely used by researchers and clinicians working with adolescents with eating disorders.

## Eating Disorders Inventory 2

The Eating Disorders Inventory 2 (EDI 2) is a self-report questionnaire developed to assess psychological traits and symptoms relevant to the treatment and understanding of eating disorders. It is intended to be part of a comprehensive assessment, including a diagnostic interview. It can also be used to screen individuals at risk for eating disorders and to assess change over the course of treatment (Garner, 1991). The EDI is based on the premise that eating disorders are multidetermined and can be the outcome of distinctly different developmental routes involving various biological, psychological, familial, and sociocultural factors.

The ninety-one-item questionnaire assesses eleven different psychological themes relevant to eating disorders. Eight subscales originally appeared in the first edition of the EDI. The original subscales were drive for thinness, bulimia, body dissatisfaction, ineffectiveness, perfectionism, interpersonal distrust, interoceptive awareness, and maturity fears. Three new, provisional subscales have recently been added: asceticism, impulse regulation, and social insecurity. While other psychological symptoms and behaviors, such as depression and substance abuse, have been related to eating disorders, the EDI 2 does not assess those areas. The following are brief descriptions of the eleven subscales and their relevance to anorexia and bulimia nervosa.

- *Drive for thinness.* Assesses concern over weight, intense fear of fatness, and excessive preoccupation with the pursuit of thinness. The drive for thinness is an important diagnostic indicator of anorexia nervosa and bulimia nervosa.
- *Bulimia.* Evaluates obsessiveness about food, episodes of uncontrollable overeating (bingeing), and anxiety about unwanted calories and impulses to purge. This theme is a central feature of bulimia nervosa and in cases of bulimic subtypes of anorexia nervosa.
- *Body dissatisfaction.* Assesses dissatisfaction with stomach, hips, thighs,

and buttock—those areas which often change during puberty. Body dissatisfaction is considered a feature of both anorexia and bulimia nervosa.

- *Ineffectiveness*. Assesses feelings of general inadequacy, insecurity, worthlessness, emptiness, and lack of control over one's circumstances. This subscale is related to poor self-esteem and negative evaluation but also includes feelings of loneliness or emptiness. Feelings of ineffectiveness have been implicated in the development of eating disorders.
- *Perfectionism*. Assesses the belief that only the highest standards of performance are acceptable to and expected by others, such as parents or teachers. This characteristic in an adolescent has been said to set the stage for the development of anorexia or bulimia nervosa.
- *Interpersonal distrust*. Appraises feelings of alienation and reluctance to form close relationships. This subscale also addresses the inability to express emotions or form attachments. The need to keep others at a distance psychologically has been related to eating disorders.
- *Interoceptive awareness*. Assesses the ability to recognize and respond accurately to different emotional states and sensations related to hunger and fullness. This characteristic has been suggested as a feature of both anorexia and bulimia nervosa.
- *Maturity fears*. Assesses the desire to retreat to the safety of childhood, where the challenges of adolescence and weight gain during puberty can be avoided. Fears about maturity can be a precipitating factor in the development of eating disorders.

### Provisional Subscales

- *Asceticism*. Assesses the tendency to seek virtue through pursuit of ideals, such as self-discipline, denial, restraint, sacrifice, and control over bodily urges. There are subgroups of patients with eating disorders whose behavior seems consistent with this theme.
- *Impulse regulation*. Assesses impulsive types of behavior, including substance abuse, hostility, recklessness, and destructiveness in interpersonal relationships. Difficulties with impulse regulation have been noted in persons with bulimia nervosa.
- *Social insecurity*. Gauges the belief that social relations are tense, disappointing, insecure, and of poor quality. The tendency to experience significant self-doubt and unhappiness in social situations has been described as a characteristic of patients with eating disorders.

The EDI 2 also has an independent symptom checklist, the EDI-SC, which is a structured self-report form. It provides detailed information about the frequency of specific symptoms, such as binge eating, self-induced vomiting, the use of laxatives, and exercise patterns, as well as about weight during different periods of life. It was designed to obtain current and historical information that can be used in making a diagnosis according to DSM III-R criteria. Those items denoted by an asterisk are among those required to make a DSM III-R diagnosis. The EDI-SC should always be used in conjunction with a clinical interview. It usually takes five to ten minutes to complete.

The EDI 2 has applications for use as a screening instrument for adolescents who are at risk for developing an eating disorder or who have subclinical forms of an eating disorder (i.e., those who do not meet the diagnostic criteria for an eating disorder, yet have significant symptoms). Criticism of the EDI 2 stems mainly from the fact that it is a self-report measure. As with any self-report measure, honest, thorough responses are necessary for an accurate assessment of symptoms. Results from this type of measure are susceptible to dishonesty and to minimization or denial of symptoms. A clinical interview and the establishment of a trusting therapeutic relationship are methods for clarification of symptoms if denial is suspected. Additionally, the tendency for an adolescent to minimize symptoms can be important information for treatment planning.

**Interpretation of EDI 2 scores.** Percentile scores and the mean standard error for each subscale are available in the EDI 2 manual. The lightly shaded plot on the profile form represents the average and standard error for each subscale for 889 eating-disordered (anorexia and bulimia nervosa) patients. The darkly shaded area represents the average and standard error scores of 205 female college freshmen. See Figures 1 and 2 for sample profiles of two cases, one of anorexia nervosa and the other of bulimia nervosa.

**Interpretation of Profiles.** The EDI 2 provides rich information regarding specific symptoms and psychological themes related to eating disorders. Figure 1 shows a sample profile of an initial assessment of a twelve-and-a-half-year-old female with anorexia nervosa. At the time of the assessment, she was severely emaciated, having lost over 25 percent of her body weight. She was described by her mother and adoptive father as having been cooperative, compliant, and eager to please before she began dieting. This profile reflects a substantial drive for thinness and considerable body dissatisfaction, even when compared with that of others with eating disorders. Maturity fears and, to a lesser extent, interpersonal distrust were relative concerns of this adolescent at the time of assessment. Bulimic tendencies, asceticism, impulse regulation, and perfectionism did not appear to be problems at this time, although a significant amount of social insecurity was evident.

Figure 2's sample profile shows the symptoms of a sixteen-year-old female with bulimia nervosa. At the time of assessment, she was slightly overweight and reported having been teased by her father for being "fat." She had been dieting to lose weight for about two years, although she had had little success. She usually binged five times a week, and she used self-induced vom-

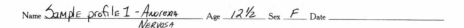

PROFILE FORM

Name Sample profile 1 - Anorexia   Age 12½  Sex F  Date _____
                     Nervosa

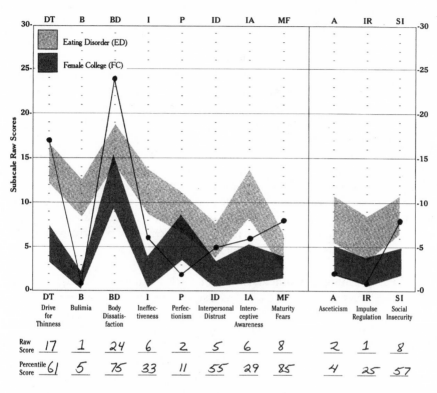

| | DT | B | BD | I | P | ID | IA | MF | A | IR | SI |
|---|---|---|---|---|---|---|---|---|---|---|---|
| Raw Score | 17 | 1 | 24 | 6 | 2 | 5 | 6 | 8 | 2 | 1 | 8 |
| Percentile Score | 61 | 5 | 75 | 33 | 11 | 55 | 29 | 85 | 4 | 25 | 57 |

Normative Group = Eating Disordered Patients   Normative Table = A1

**Figure 1. Sample Profile of a 12½-Year-Old Female with Anorexia Nervosa**

iting to control weight gain about ten times a week. Several subscales reflect the nature of her symptoms at the time the EDI 2 was completed. The drive for thinness, bulimia, and body dissatisfaction subscales were all elevated and consistent with the diagnosis of bulimia nervosa. Perfectionism, impulse regulation, social insecurity, and, to a lesser extent, interoceptive awareness were also areas of concern. Ineffectiveness, interpersonal distrust, maturity fears, and asceticism were not of particular concern at the time of the assessment.

**Implications for Treatment.** Elevations on particular subscales on the EDI 2 highlight relative areas of concern for an adolescent with an eating disorder. With this information, a counselor or therapist can tailor interventions toward these areas. For example, an adolescent with bulimia nervosa may initially be extremely dissatisfied with her body, in addition to feeling ineffective in her personal life and unable to assess thoughts or incidents that might precede a binge. Outpatient treatment might include a cognitive behavioral plan to stabilize eating patterns and learn to identify feelings or thoughts that may precede a binge. As treatment progresses and the EDI 2 is administered after eating patterns are stabilized, the interoceptive awareness score may be reduced; at the same time, another subscale might indicate new concern in a different area, such as maturity fears. Treatment would correspondingly change focus as assessed needs change.

**Use as a Screening Instrument.** Since the EDI 2 can easily and quickly be administered, it has been suggested as a screening device for suspected cases of eating disorders or for groups who have been identified as "body-focused" or at risk for some other reason. The second stage of the screening process would consist of a clinical interview with those adolescents who scored over a predetermined cutoff point. While the EDI 2 was not originally intended as a screening device, justification for this type of use comes from research on the Eating Attitude Test (EAT) (Garner, 1991). The EDI 2's drive for thinness subscale is reported to correlate highly with the Eating Attitude Test (EAT) (Garner, Olmsted, & Polivy, 1983).

Were the EDI 2 to be used as a screening device, identification of overconcern about body weight or shape might be addressed before a potential eating problem occurred. If an eating disorder had previously been suspected, information from the EDI 2 could be used as a means of addressing the problem with the adolescent and her family. With objective information at hand, suggestions for further assessment and treatment might be more readily accepted.

## Summary

Anorexia and bulimia nervosa are eating disorders of adolescence with significant negative medical and psychological consequences. Successful treat-

PROFILE FORM

Name _Sample profile 2 - Bulimia Nervosa_ Age __16__ Sex _F_ Date _____

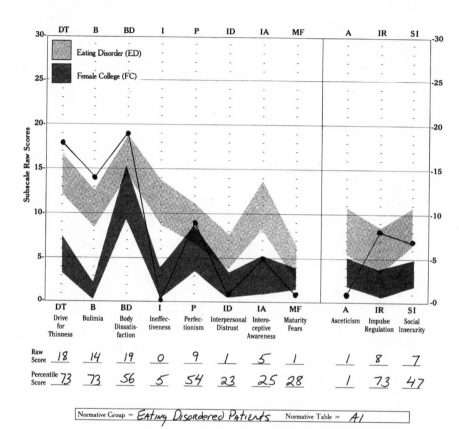

| | DT | B | BD | I | P | ID | IA | MF | A | IR | SI |
|---|---|---|---|---|---|---|---|---|---|---|---|
| | Drive for Thinness | Bulimia | Body Dissatis-faction | Ineffec-tiveness | Perfec-tionism | Interpersonal Distrust | Intero-ceptive Awareness | Maturity Fears | Asceticism | Impulse Regulation | Social Insecurity |
| Raw Score | 18 | 14 | 19 | 0 | 9 | 1 | 5 | 1 | 1 | 8 | 7 |
| Percentile Score | 73 | 73 | 56 | 5 | 54 | 23 | 25 | 28 | 1 | 73 | 47 |

Normative Group = _Eating Disordered Patients_    Normative Table = _A1_

### Figure 2.  Sample Profile of a 15-Year-Old with Bulimia Nervosa

ment requires attention to medical aspects, such as weight restoration and normalization of eating behaviors, as well as to psychological aspects, since abnormal beliefs, mood disturbances, social isolation, and family conflict may underlie the eating disorder. Prevention efforts, focusing on educating young adolescents and their families about the risks of dieting and the unrealistic role models thrust on women, may reverse the rise in the incidence of eating disorders. Early identification and referral for treatment of adolescents engaged in behaviors characteristic of eating disorders may prevent the development of chronic conditions and serious medical and psychological consequences.

## Suggested Reading

Brumberg, Jone, *Fasting Girls: The Emergence of Anorexia Nervosa as a Modern Disease*, Harvard University Press, 1988.

Cherinin, Kim, *The Obsession: Reflections on the Tyranny of Slenderness*, Harper and Row, 1981.

Garner, David, & Garfinkel, Paul, Editors, *Handbook of Psychotherapy for Anorexia Nervosa and Bulimia*, Guilford Press, 1985.

Hall, Lindsey, & Cohn, Leigh, *Bulimia: A Guide to Recovery*, Gurze Books, 1988.

Haskew, Paul, & Adams, Cynthia, *When Food Is a Four Letter Word*, Prentice Hall, 1985.

Hollis, Judi, *Fat Is a Family Affair: A Hope Filled Guide for Those Who Suffer from Eating Disorders and Those Who Love Them*, Harper and Row, 1985.

Levenkron, Steven, *The Best Little Girl in the World*, Warner, 1978.

Levenkron, Steven, *Treating and Overcoming Anorexia Nervosa*, Scribner's, 1982.

O'Neill, Cherry Boone, *Starving for Attention*, Continuum, 1982.

Orbach, Susie, *Fat Is a Feminist Issue*, Berkeley Book, 1978.

Pope, Harrison, & Hudson, James, *New Hope for Binge Eaters*, Basel, Karger Press, 1984.

Roth, Geneen, *Feeding the Hungry Heart*, Bobbs-Merrill, 1982.

Siegel, Michele, Brifman, Judith, & Weinshel, Margot, *Surviving an Eating Disorder: New Perspectives and Strategies for Family and Friends*, Harper and Row, 1988.

Weiss, Lillie, Katzman, Melanie, & Wolchik, Sharlene, *You Can't Have Your Cake and Eat It Too: A Program for Controlling Bulimia*, R & E Publishers, 1986.

## References

American Psychiatric Association. (1987). *Diagnostic and statistical manual of mental disorders*, (3rd ed. revised). Washington, DC: American Psychiatric Association.

Anderson, A. E., Morse, C. L., & Santmyer, K. S. (1985). Inpatient treatment for anorexia nervosa. In D. M. Garner & P. E. Garfinkel (Eds.), *Handbook of psychotherapy for anorexia nervosa and bulimia* (pp. 311–343). New York: Guilford Press.

Beary, M., Lacey, J., & Merry, J. (1986). Alcoholism and eating disorders in women of fertile age. *British Journal of Addictions, 81,* 685–689.

Biederman, J., Rivinus, T., Kemper, K., Hamilton, D., MacFadyen, T., & Harmatz, J. (1985). Depressive disorder in relatives of anorexia nervosa patients with and without a current episode of nonbipolar major depression. *American Journal of Psychiatry, 142,* 1495–1497.

Bruch, H. (1973). Eating disorders: Obesity, anorexia, and the person within. New York: Basic Books.

Brumberg, J. J. (1988). *Fasting girls: The emergence of anorexia nervosa as a modern disease.* Cambridge, MA: Harvard University Press.

Cavior, N., & Dokecki, P. (1973). Physical attractiveness, perceived attitude similarity, and academic achievement as contributors to interpersonal attraction among adolescents. *Developmental Psychology, 9,* 44–54.

Cavior, N., & Lombardi, D. A. (1973). Developmental aspects of judgment of physical attractiveness in children. *Developmental Psychology, 8,* 67–71.

Crawford, P. A., & Watts, D. (1992). Overview. In J. H. Gowther, O. L. Tennenbaum, S. E. Hobfoll, & M. A. Parris Stephens (Eds.), *The Etiology of Bulimia Nervosa: The Individual and Family Context* (pp. 29–33). Philadelphia, PA: Hemisphere Publishing Corporation.

Crisp, A. H., Hsu, L. K. G., Harding, B., & Hartshorn, J. (1980). Clinical features of anorexia nervosa. *Journal of Psychosomatic Research, 24,* 179–191.

Davis, R. (1986). Assessing the eating disorders. *The Clinical Psychologist, 39,* 33–36.

Dolan, B. (1991). Cross-cultural aspects of anorexia nervosa and bulimia: A review. *International Journal of Eating Disorders, 10,* 67–78.

Dornbusch, S. M., Carlsmith, J. M., Duncan, P. D., Gross, R. T., Martin, J. A., Ritter, P. L., & Siegel-Gorelick, B. (1984). Sexual maturation, social class, and the desire to be thin among adolescent females. *Developmental and Behavioral Pediatrics, 5,* 308–314.

Enns, M. P., Drewnowski, A., & Grinker, J. A. (1987). Body composition, body size estimation, and attitudes towards eating in male college athletes. *Psychosomatic Medicine, 49,* 56–64.

Fairburn, C. G. (1985). Cognitive-behavioral treatment for bulimia. In D. M. Garner & P. E. Garfinkel (Eds.), *Handbook on Psychotherapy for Anorexia Nervosa and Bulimia* (pp. 160–192). New York: Guilford Press.

Fairburn, C. G. (1988). The current status of the psychological treatments for bulimia nervosa. *Journal of Psychosomatic Research, 32,* 635–645.

Fairburn, C., & Cooper, P. J. (1982). Self-induced vomiting and bulimia: An undetected problem. *British Medical Journal, 284,* 1153–1155.

Fairburn, C. G., Jones, R., Peveler, R. K., Carr, S. J., Solomon, R. A., O'Connor, M. E., Burton, J., & Hope, R. A. (1991). Three psychological treatments for bulimia nervosa: A comparative trial. *Archives of General Psychiatry, 48,* 463–469.

Fallon, A. E., & Rosen, P. (1985). Sex differences in perceptions of desirable body shape. *Journal of Abnormal Psychology, 94,* 102–105.

Fava, M., Copeland, P., Schweiger, U., & Herzog, D. (19898). Neurochemical abnormalities of anorexia nervosa and bulimia nervosa. *American Journal of Psychiatry, 146,* 963–969.

Freeman, C. P. (1991). A practical guide to the treatment of bulimia nervosa. *Journal of Psychosomatic Research, 35,* 41–49.

Garfinkel, P., Garner, D., Kaplan, A., Rodin, G., & Kennedy, S. (1983). Differential diagnosis of emotional disorders that cause weight loss. *Canadian Medical Association Journal, 129,* 938'943.

Garner, D. M. (1986). Problems with the Overeaters Anonymous model in the treatment of bulimia. *National Anorexic Aid Society Newsletter, 13,* 1–2.

Garner, D. M. (1991). *Eating Disorder Inventory-2 Professional Manual.* Odessa, FL: Psychological Assessment Resources, Inc.

Garner, D. M., & Bemis, K. M. (1985). Cognitive therapy for anorexia nervosa. In D. M. Garner & P. E. Garfinkel (Eds.), *Handbook of psychotherapy for anorexia nervosa and bulimia* (pp. 107–146). New York: Guilford Press.

Garner, D. M., & Garfinkel, P. E. (1980). Social-cultural factors in the development of anorexia nervosa. *Psychological Medicine, 10,* 647–656.

Garner, D. M., Garfinkel, P. E. Rockert, W., & Olmsted, M. P. (1987). A prospective study of eating disturbance in the ballet. *Psychotherapy & Psychosomatic, 48,* 170–175.

Garner, D. M., Garfinkel, P. E., Schwartz, D., & Thomspon, M. (1980). Cultural expectations of thinness in women. *Psychological Reports, 47,* 483–491.

Garner, D. M., Olmsted, M. P., & Polivy, J. (1983). Development and validation of a multidimensional Eating Disorder Inventory for anorexia nervosa and bulimia. *International Journal of Eating Disorders, 2,* 15–34.

Garner, D. M., Rockert, W., Olmsted, M. R., Johnson, C., & Coscina, D. V. (1985). Psychoeducational principles in the treatment of bulimia and anorexia nervosa. In D. M. Garner & P. E. Garfinkel (Eds.), *Handbook of psychotherapy for anorexia nervosa and bulimia* (pp. 513–572). New York: Guilford Press.

Gayton, W. F., & Friedman, S. B. (1981). Psychosocial aspects of CF: A review of the literature. *American Journal of Diseases of Childhood, 56,* 538–543.

Giannini, A. J., Newman, M., & Gold, M. (1990). Anorexia and bulimia. *American Family Physician, 41,* 1169–1176.

Gilchrist, P. N., McFarlane, C. M., McFarlane, A. C., & Kalucy, R. S. (1986). Family therapy in the treatment of anorexia nervosa. *International Journal of Eating Disorders, 5,* 659–668.

Gowers, J., & McMahon, J. B. (1989). Social class and prognosis in anorexia nervosa. *International Journal of Eating Disorders, 8,* 105–109.

Hall, A. (1985). Group psychotherapy for anorexia nervosa. In D. M. Garner & P. E. Garfinkel (Eds.), *Handbook of psychotherapy for anorexia nervosa and bulimia* (pp. 213–53). New York: Guilford Press.

Halmi, K. A. (1974). Anorexia nervosa: Demographic and clinical features in 94 cases. *Psychosomatic Medicine, 36,* 18–26.

Halmi, K. A. (1985). Behavioral management for anorexia nervosa. In D. M. Garner & P. E. Garfinkel (Eds.), *Handbook of psychotherapy for anorexia nervosa and bulimia* (pp. 147–159). New York: Guilford Press.

Halmi, K. A., Casper, R., Eckert, E., Goldberg, S. C., & Davis, J. M. (1979). Unique features associated with age of onset of anorexia nervosa. *Psychiatry Research, 1,* 209–215.

Halmi, K. A., Falk, J. R., & Schwartz, E. (1981). Binge-eating and vomiting: A survey of a college population. *Psychological Medicine, 11,* 697–706.

Halvorson, P. A., & Neuman, P. A. (1990) A structured group therapy approach for clients with bulimia. In M. Seligman & L. E. Marshak (Eds.), *Group Psychotherapy Interventions with Special Populations* (pp. 243262). Boston MA: Allyn and Bacon.

Hamilton, L. H., Brook-Gunn, J., & Warren, M. P. (1985). Sociocultural influences on eating disorders in professional female ballet dancers. *International Journal of Eating Disorders, 4,* 465–477.

Heatherton, T. F., & Polivy, J. (1992). Chronic dieting and eating disorders: A spiral model. In J. H. Crowther, O. L. Tennenbaum, S. E. Hobfoll, & M. A. Parris Stephens (Eds.), *The Etiology of Bulimia Nervosa: The Individual and Family Context pp. 133155).* Philadelphia, PA: Hemisphere Publishing Corporation.

Herzog, D. B., Keller, M. B., & Lavori, P. W. (1988). Outcome in anorexia nervosa and bulimia nervosa: a review of the literature. *Journal of Nervous and Mental Disease, 176,* 131–143.

Hillard, J., & Hillard, P. (1984). Bulimia, anorexia nervosa, and diabetes: Deadly combinations. *Psychiatric Clinics of North America, 7,* 367–379.

Hsu, L. K. G. (1990). *Eating disorders.* New York: Guilford Press.

Hsu, L. K. G., Holben, B., & West, S. (1992). Nutritional counseling in bulimia nervosa. *International Journal of Eating Disorders, 11,* 55–62.

Hsu, L. K. G., & Holder, D. (1986). Bulimia nervosa: Treatment and short term outcome. *Psychological Medicine, 16,* 65–70.

Hudson, J., Pope, H., Jonas, J., & Yurgelun-Todd, D. (1983). Family history study of anorexia nervosa and bulimia. *British Journal of Psychiatry, 142,* 133–138.

Johnson, C. (1985). Initial consultation for patients with bulimia and anorexia nervosa. In D. M. Garner & P. E. Garfinkel (Eds.), *Handbook of Psychotherapy for Anorexia Nervosa and Bulimia* (pp. 83–104). New York: Guilford Press.

Johnson, C., & Flach, A. (1985). Family characteristics of 105 patients with bulimia. *American Journal of Psychiatry, 142,* 1321–1324.

Johnson, C., Tobin, D. L., & Lipkin, J. (1989). Epidemiologic changes in bulimic behavior among female adolescents over a five-year period. *International Journal of Eating Disorders, 8,* 647–655.

Jonas, J. M., Gold, M. S., Sweeney, D., & Pattash, A. L. C. (1987). Eating disorders and cocaine abuse: A survey of 259 cocaine abusers. *Journal of Clinical Psychiatry, 48,* 47–50.

Jones, D. J., Fox, M. M., Babigan, H. M., & Hutton, H. E. (1980). Epidemiology of anorexia nervosa in Monroe County, New York: 19601976. *Psychosomatic Medicine, 42,* 551–558.

Kalucy, R., Crisp, A. H., & Harding, B. (1977). A survey of 56 families with anorexia nervosa. *British Journal of Medical Psychology, 50,* 381–395.

Kaplan, A. S. (1990). Biomedical variables in the eating disorders. *Canadian Journal of Psychiatry, 35,* 745–753.

Kennedy, S. H., & Goldbloom, D. S. (1991). Current perspectives in drug therapies for anorexia nervosa and bulimia nervosa. *Drugs, 41,* 367–377.

Laessle, R. G., Kittl S., Fichter, M., Wittchen, H., & Pirke, K. M. (1987). Major affective disorder in anorexia nervosa and bulimia: A descriptive diagnostic study. *British Journal of Psychiatry, 151,* 785–789.

Laessle, R., Wittchen, H., Fichter, M., & Pirke, K. M. (1989) The significance of subgroups of bulimia and anorexia nervosa: Lifetime frequency of psychiatric disorders. *International Journal of Eating Disorders, 8,* 569–574.

Lambley, P., & Scott, D. (1988). An overview of bulimia nervosa. In D. Scott (Ed.), *Anorexia and Bulimia Nervosa* (pp. 24–36). London: Croom Helm.

Lipscomb, P. A. (1987). Bulimia: Diagnosis and management in the primary care setting. *Journal of Family Practice, 24,* 187–194.

Maloney, M. J., McGuire, J., Daniels, S. R., & Specker, B. (1989). Dieting behavior and eating attitudes in children. *Pediatrics, 84,* 482–487.

McKenna, M. S. (1989). Assessment of the eating disordered patient. *Psychiatric Annals, 19,* 467–472.

Minuchin, S. (1974). *Families and family therapy.* Cambridge, MA: Harvard University Press.

Mitchell, J. E., Hatsukami, D., Eckert, E. D., & Pyle, R. L. (1985). Characteristics of 275 patients with bulimia. *American Journal of Psychiatry, 142,* 482–485.

Mitchell, J. E., Pomeroy, C. & Colon, E. (1990). Medical complications in bulimia nervosa. In M. M. Fichter (Ed.), *Bulimia Nervosa: Basic Research Diagnosis and Therapy,* (pp. 71–83). New York: John Wiley & Sons.

Mitchell, J. E., Specker, S. M., & Zwaan, M. (1991). Co-morbidity and medical complications of bulimia nervosa. *Journal of Clinical Psychiatry, 52,* 13–20.

Nielsen, S., Borner, H., & Kabel, M. (1987). Anorexia nervosa/bulimia in diabetes mellitus. *Acta Psychiatrica Scandinavica, 75,* 474–473.

O'Leary, L. D., & Wilson, G. T. (1987). *Behavior therapy: Application and outcome.* Englewood Cliffs, NJ: Prentice Hall, Inc.

Orbach, S. (1985). Accepting the symptom: A feminist psychoanalytic treatment of anorexia nervosa. In D. M. Garner & P. E. Garfinkel (Eds.), *Handbook of Psychotherapy for Anorexia Nervosa and Bulimia* (pp. 83–104). New York: Guilford Press.

Palazzoli, M. S., Boscolo, L., Cecchin, G. C., & Prata, G. (1977). Family rituals: A powerful tool in family therapy. *Family Process, 16,* 445–453.

Palla, B., & Litt, I. F. (1988). Medical complications of eating disorders in adolescents. *Pediatrics, 81,* 613–623.

Patton, G. C. (1988). Mortality in eating disorders. *Psychological Medicine, 18,* 947–952.

Peveler, R., & Fairburn, C. (1990). Eating disorders in women who abuse alcohol. *British Journal of the Addictions, 85,* 1633–1638.

Pfeiffer, R. J., Lucas, A. R., & Ilstrup, D. M. (1986). Effect of anorexia nervosa on linear growth. *Clinical Pediatrics, 25,* 7–12.

Piran, N., Lerner, P., Garfinkel, P. E., Kennedy, S. H., & Brouillette, C. (1988). Personality disorders in restricting and bulimic forms of anorexia nervosa. *International Journal of Eating Disorders,* 589–599.

Pomeroy, C., & Mitchell, J.E. (1989). Medical complications and management of eating disorders. *Psychiatric Annals, 19,* 488–493.

Pumariega, A., Pursell, J., Spock, A., & Jounes, J. D. (1986). Eating disorders in adolescents with cystic fibrosis. *Journal of the American Academy of Child Psychiatry, 25,* 269–275.

Pyle, R. L., Mitchell, J. E., Eckert, E. D., Halvorson, P. A., Neuman, P. A., & Goff, G. M. (1983). The incidence of bulimia in freshman college students. *International Journal of Eating Disorders, 2,* 75–85.

Rigotti, N. A., Nussbaum, S. R., Herzog, D. B., & Neer, R. M. (1984). Osteoporosis in women with anorexia nervosa. *New England Journal of Medicine, 311,* 1601–1606.

Rivinus, T. M., Biederman, J., Herzog, D. B., Kemper, K., Harper, G. P., Harmatz, J. S., & Houseworth, S. (1984). Anorexia nervosa and affective disorders: A controlled family history. *American Journal of Psychiatry, 141,* 1414–1418.

Rosen, J. C., & Leitenberg, H. (1985). Exposure plus response prevention treatment of bulimia. In D. M. Garner & P. E. Garfinkel (Eds.), *Handbook of psychotherapy for anorexia nervosa and bulimia* (pp. 193–209). New York: Guilford Press.

Rosen, L. W., McKeag, D. B., Hough, D., & Curley, V. (1986). Pathogenic weight-control behavior in female athletes. *The Physician and Sports Medicine, 14,* 79–86.

Rosen, L. W., Shafer, C. L., Dummer, G. M., Cross, L. K., Deuman, G. W., & Malmberg, S. R. (1988). Relevance of pathogenic weight-control behaviors among Native American women and girls. *International Journal of Eating Disorders, 7,* 807–811.

Russell, G. F. (1979). Bulimia nervosa: An ominous variant of anorexia. *Psychological Medicine, 9,* 429–448.

Russell, G. F., Szmukler, G. I., Dare, C., & Eisler, I. (1987). An Evaluation of family therapy in anorexia nervosa and bulimia nervosa. *Archives of General Psychiatry, 44,* 1047–1056.

Schwartz, D. M., Thomspon, M. G., & Johnson, C. L. (1981). Anorexia nervosa and bulimia: The socio-cultural context. *International Journal of Eating Disorders, 1,* 20–36.

Singer, L. T., Yamashita, T., Benson-Szekely, L., & Jaffe, A. (1990, June). The diagnosis of eating disorders in a pediatric setting. Presented at *Treatment of Mental Disorders in a General Medical Setting,* HIMH research conference, Bethesda, MD.

Spitzer, R. L., Devlin, M., Walsh, B. T., Hasin, D., Wing, R., Marcus, M., Stunkard, A., Wadden, T., Yanovski, S., Agras, S., Mitchell, J., & Nonas, C. (1992). Binge eating disorder: A multisite field trial of the diagnostic criteria. *International Journal of Eating Disorders, 11,* 191–203.

Strober, M. (1991). Family-genetic studies of eating disorders. *Journal of Clinical Psychiatry, 52* (suppl.), 9–12.

Strober, M., Morrell, W., Burroughs, J., Salkin, B., & Jacobs, C. (1985). A controlled family study of anorexia nervosa. *Journal of Psychiatric Research, 19,* 239–246.

Swift, W. J., Ritholz, N. H., Kalin, F. S., & Kaslow, N. (1987). A follow-up study of thirty hospitalized bulimics. *Psychosomatic Medicine, 49,* 45–55.

Toner, B. B., Garfinkel, P. E., & Garner, D. M. (1986). Long term follow-up of anorexia nervosa. *Psychosomatic Medicine, 48,* 520–529.

Walsh, B. T. (1992). Diagnostic criteria for eating disorders in DSM IV: Work in progress. *International Journal of Eating Disorders, 11,* 301–304.

Walsh, B. T., Roose, S., Glassman, A., Gladis, M., & Sadik, C. (1985). Bulimia and depression. *Psychosomatic Medicine, 47,* 123–131.

Walsh, B. T., Roose, S. P., Lindy, D. C., Gladis, M., & Glassman, A. H. (1987). Hypothalamic-pituitary-adrenal axis in bulimia. In J. I. Hudson & H. G. Pope (Eds.), *The psychobiology of bulimia* (pp. 3–11). Washington, DC: American Psychiatric Press.

Wardle, J., & Beales, S. (1986). Restraint, body image and food attitudes in children from 1218 years. *Appetite, 7,* 209–217.

Willi, J., & Grossman, S. (1983). Epidemiology of anorexia nervosa in a defined region of Switzerland. *American Journal of Psychiatry, 140,* 564–567.

Yager, J. (1982). Family issues in the pathogenesis of anorexia nervosa. *Psychosomatic Medicine, 44,* 43–60.

Yates, A., Leehey, K., & Shisslak, C. M. (1983). Running—An analogue of anorexia? *The New England Journal of Medicine, 308,* 252–255.

# 4

# Sexual and Physical Abuse: The Adolescent Sexual Concern Questionnaire (ASC)

*David Hussey*
*Mark I. Singer*

The purpose of this chapter is to present an effective, structured interview format for interviewing adolescents regarding issues of sexual and physical abuse. The model of interviewing presented here can be used by a wide variety of clinicians and professionals working with adolescents. The requisite skills for using this format are a facility for interviewing adolescents and a general knowledge of abuse dynamics in individuals and families.

## Definition

Physical abuse is generally defined as inflicting injury—such as bruises, burns, head injuries, fractures, internal injuries, or lacerations—that has corporeal consequences lasting at least forty-eight hours (National Center on Child Abuse and Neglect, 1981). This category may also include excessive corporal punishment and close confinement, such as tying or binding the child and locking him or her in a closet.

While increasing emphasis is being placed on the circumstances and nature of the act, as opposed to merely the consequences, current definitions stress the presence of nonaccidental injury resulting from acts of commission (physical assault) or omission (failure to protect) by caretakers that requires medical attention or legal intervention (National Institute of Mental Health, 1977). Although the injury is not necessarily an accident, the parent or caretaker may not have intended to hurt the child. The injury may have resulted from overdiscipline or physical punishment that is inappropriate to the child's age. As a result of the Child Abuse Amendments of 1984 (PL 98-457), the definition of child abuse also includes as child abuse the withholding of medically indicated treatment for an infant's life-threatening conditions (U.S. Department of Health and Human Services, 1988).

There is no clear distinction in state statutes between acceptable forms of punishment on the one hand and child abuse on the other (National Institute of Mental Health, 1977). Legal definitions also fall short of practical requirements because, as a function of cultural values, history, and community standards, one person's "abuse" is another person's "discipline" (Wolfe, Kaufman, Aragona, & Sandler, 1981).

Defining child sexual abuse is also problematic due to societal and value-based difficulties. In understanding definitions of sexual abuse, it is important to realize that the major focus of concern is the inherent power imbalance between the perpetrator and the victim, not just the type of sexual act. A widely accepted definition emphasizes sexual experiences that occur between children and older persons (often defined as more than five years older; Finkelhor, 1979). Suzanne Sgroi has further clarified the definition to mean "a sexual act imposed on a child who lacks emotional, maturational, and cognitive development. The ability to lure a child into a sexual relationship is based upon the all-powerful and dominant position of the adult or older adolescent perpetrator, which is in sharp contrast to the child's age, dependency, and subordinate position. Authority and power enable the perpetrator, implicitly or directly, to coerce the child into sexual compliance" (Sgroi, 1982, p. 9). The Child Abuse Prevention and Treatment Act (Public Law 100-294) defines sexual abuse as the use, persuasion, or coercion of any child to engage in any sexually explicit conduct (or any simulation of such conduct) for the purpose of producing any visual depiction of such conduct, or rape, molestation, prostitution, or incest with children (U.S. Department of Health and Human Services, 1988). Sexual abuse includes fondling of the child's genitals, intercourse, incest, rape, sodomy, exhibitionism, and sexual exploitation. It is generally considered child abuse when such acts are committed by a person responsible for the care of a child (e.g., a parent, babysitter, or day-care provider). If a stranger commits these acts, they would more properly be considered sexual assault and handled solely by the police and criminal courts. In the past this distinction has often been characterized as the difference between "extrafamilial abuse" and "intrafamilial abuse," or "incest." Intrafamilial abuse refers to any type of exploitative sexual contact with a child or adolescent occurring between relatives, no matter how distant the relationship (Russell, 1983). This definition is not limited to a strictly genetic relationship but can include any individual who assumes a parental or familial role (e.g., stepparent, stepbrother, adoptive parent).

## Incidence

Incidence studies help to identify the overall probability and type of child maltreatment. The U.S. Department of Health and Human Services (1988) estimates from the reports received that approximately 1 to 1.5 million children were maltreated (physical abuse, sexual abuse, emotional abuse, and neglect) during 1986, the last year of its study. This range reflects the difference between (a) the original definitions used in 1980 and then again in 1986 and (b) expanded or revised definitions that were also added in the 1986 study. Even though the rate of reporting has increased each year within the past decade, the data provided by the U.S. Department of Health and Human Services are thought to be very conservative estimates of the numbers of abused and neglected children due to the high rate of underreporting.

The most frequent form of abuse by either set of definitional standards was physical abuse (53% of those abused, or 4.9 per 1,000), followed by emotional abuse (30%, or 2.8 per 1,000) and then sexual abuse (24%, or 2.2 per 1,000). Among abused children, there were significant increases in those physically and sexually abused. The rate of overall abuse in 1986 was 74 percent greater than it had been in 1980, involving 9.2 children per 1,000, or about 580,400 children. Physical abuse increased by 58 percent from 1980 levels, while sexual abuse tripled when comparing 1986 levels with 1980 levels. These increases are thought to be reflective of increases in the recognition of abuse by professionals and the public, rather than actual increases in the occurrence of abuse (U.S. Department of Health and Human Services, 1988).

Many children die as a result of abuse. In 1986, 1,100 children were known to have died as a result of abuse or neglect (U.S. Department of Health and Human Services, 1988). It has been estimated that between 1,000 and 5,000 children per year may suffer such a fate (American Medical Association, 1985). In the American Humane Association data, the average age of children who died as a result of abuse was 2.61 years, versus an overall average of 7.14 years for children maltreated (American Association for Protecting Children, 1985).

Compared with all U.S. families with children, maltreated children are twice as likely to live in a single-parent, female-headed household; are four times as likely to be supported by public assistance; and are affected by numerous family stress factors, such as health problems, alcohol abuse, and spouse abuse (Russel & Trainor, 1984). Family income was found to have profound effects on the incidence of abuse and neglect. Children from families whose income was less than $15,000 (in 1986) experienced more maltreatment and injury/impairment than those from families with incomes greater than $15,000 did. At every level of severity, lower-income children experienced more injury/impairment than upper-income children. They suffered three times the fatalities, nearly seven times the serious injuries, and more than five and a half times the moderate injuries compared with the experiences of the higher-income children. The rate of abuse was four times higher among lower-income children (16.6 per 1,000 children in this income category, or 275,500 children nationwide) than among the children in higher-income families (4.1 per 1,000, or 190,200 children nationwide).

Physical abuse was three and a half times more frequent and sexual abuse was five times more frequent among lower-income children (U.S. Department of Health and Human Services, 1988).

Reports of sexual and emotional maltreatment occur most frequently among adolescents. Surprisingly, physical abuse affects a sizable proportion of all age-groups; however, the highest rate of physical injury is found among the oldest children. Fatal and moderate injuries showed age relationships, but of reversed patterns: fatalities were more prevalent among younger children, whereas moderate injuries were more numerous among older children. Overall, it appears that while the youngest children were not as frequently maltreated as the older ones, when they did experience maltreatment it tended to be more injurious, perhaps due to their comparatively greater physical fragility (U.S. Department of Health and Human Services, 1988).

Sex of the victims has not shown a discriminatory pattern over the past years, with injuries to males and females being reported at approximately the same rate, with the exception of sexual abuse (Wolfe, 1988). A recent national study of child abuse and neglect found that 84 percent of sexual abuse victims were female (Jones & McCurdy, 1992). Although much sexual abuse occurs among younger children (even infants) and adolescents, the average victim age in sexual abuse appears to be about ten (Walker, Bonner, & Kaufman, 1988). Black families have been characterized by more neglect and less abuse, while white children, in contrast, are more often the victims of abuse or combined abuse and neglect (Wolfe, 1988). Overall, though, there are no significant relationships between the incidence of maltreatment and a child's race or ethnicity (U.S. Department of Health and Human Services, 1988).

The perpetrators of child maltreatment are, for the most part, the parents of the children (97%), with a large percentage being natural parents (American Humane Association, 1984). Incidence data have suggested that they had their children at a younger age than those in general did (Young, 1982). Parents may be more likely to maltreat their children if they are emotionally immature or needy; are socially isolated, with few supports; were emotionally deprived, abused, or neglected as children; are in poor health; or abuse drugs or alcohol (U.S. Department of Health and Human Services, 1988). Male perpetrators are associated with more major and minor physical injury, much more sexual abuse, and less neglect (Wolfe & Wolfe, 1988).

Walker et al. (1988), in reviewing the differences between physical and sexual abuse, notes that girls are predominately the victims of sexual abuse; however, in physical abuse there is more nearly equal distribution, with a slight tendency for boys to be more abused. Physical abuse is frequent at very young ages (two years and under). Sexual abuse is less frequent at very young ages but increases considerably from about age six (National Center on Child Abuse and Neglect, 1981). Physical abuse is almost always a result of actions by the parents, but in sexual abuse a substantial portion of abuse also occurs from relatives, acquaintances, and friends. In physical abuse, both mothers and fathers are frequently involved, with a slight tendency for mothers to be more involved. In sexual abuse, between 85 and 95 percent of the incidents are by males, frequently fathers or stepfathers. Females and mothers are rarely involved in sexual abuse, and if they are so involved, they are more likely to suffer from a primary psychiatric disorder. Statistically, physical abuse appears to be more prevalent, and obvious signs of injury or other trauma are generally present to substantiate the abuse. In sexual abuse, physical evidence or trauma is infrequently used to substantiate the abuse. Sexual abusers enjoy what they are doing; physical abusers seldom do.

In addressing gender differences among sex abuse victims specifically, Finkelhor (1984) reviews the available data and concludes (p. 166) that

- Two to three times as many girls are victimized as boys.
- Boys, like girls, are most commonly victimized by men.
- Boys are more likely than girls to be victimized by someone outside the family.
- Boys are more likely than girls to be victimized in conjunction with other children.
- Victimized boys are more likely than victimized girls to come from impoverished and single-parent families and to be victims of physical abuse as well.
- The abuse of boys is more likely to be reported to the police than to a hospital or child protective agency.

The main perpetrator in cases of sexual abuse clearly is a male, often middle-aged (average age: approximately thirty-five years), although in recent years more concern has been evidenced regarding the growing numbers of adolescent perpetrators. In a well-done study of college students in New England, Finkelhor (1979) reported in what he believed to be conservative estimates that 19.2 percent of women and 8.6 percent of men indicated they had been sexually abused as children. When combining these data with other findings, experts suspect that 20 to 25 percent of females and approximately 10 percent of males are sexually abused as children (Wolfe, 1988). Finkelhor's data further indicate that 43 percent of the girls were abused by family members, 33 percent by acquaintances, and 24 percent by strangers. For boys, the data are slightly different: only 17 percent were abused by family members, 53 percent by acquaintances, and 30 percent by strangers. His data also suggest that 60 percent of the cases of abuse were single occurrences. Therefore, the most common scenario is one in which the child is victimized only once, by an acquaintance (Walker et al., 1988).

The *Los Angeles Times* (Timnick, 1985) conducted a telephone survey of 2,628 adults chosen randomly from across the United States (in July 1985) to study their view of the problem of sexual abuse and their own childhood experiences. The sample included 1,145 men and 1,481 women. The survey revealed that 27 percent of women and 16 percent of men who participated said they had had a childhood sexual experience with an adult. The majority of these sexual molestations were isolated incidents, although 39 percent of the victims of intercourse reported repeated abuse. The vast majority of the abusers (93%) were male, and one-third of the victims had never told anyone about their sexual abuse until the survey. Only 3 percent had reported the incident to the police or another public agency. Of those who did disclose the abuse, most told a parent, another relative, or a friend. Surprisingly, 70 percent of those who had disclosed the experience said that no effective action was taken regarding their abuse.

Courtois (1979) estimates that sexual abuse typically begins when the victim is between ages four and twelve, with ages four and nine being especially high-risk years (Gelinas, 1983; Timnick, 1985). Suspected reasons that children of these ages are at higher risk of abuse include the four-year-old's naïveté and sexual curiosity and the nine-year-old's loyalty, desire to please, and trust of adults. Conversely, sexual abuse most often is terminated by age fourteen or fifteen, usually as a result of disclosure, threats of disclosure, or the child's running away (Curtois, 1980; Finkelhor, 1984).

## Etiology and Conceptual Models

Child abuse is not a single, unitary phenomenon caused by the same variables or mix of variables in every case. Yet it is possible to review the research and literature and organize the themes regarding the etiology of abusive behavior into several models.

Three general conceptual frameworks may be employed to understand child abuse. One, called the psychiatric model, assumes that the causes of abuse are to be found in the personality characteristics and/or psychopathology of the adults or children involved. This model has been used most dominantly to understand sexual abuse of children. A second model, the sociological model, has been more widely employed to explain neglect and physical abuse, and it proposes that the causes are to be found in societal conditions, such as poverty and unemployment. The third model, which might be termed an interactional model, assumes that variables in both of the first two models may be involved and that these variables interact within a social-situational context that results in abuse.

### Psychiatric Model

The use of the psychodynamic/individual approach to the problem of child abuse traces back to Freud's essay "A Child Is Being Beaten" (Zeigler, 1980), in which he used his theoretical formulations to describe the dynamics of a child abuser. Child abuse is conceptualized as a pathological phenomenon with roots in the character traits or psychodynamics of individual abusing parents, such as severe depression or extreme narcissism. A wide variety of less severe forms of psychopathology have also been described in connection with abusive parents, such as low self-esteem, immaturity, low frustration tolerance and impulsivity, difficulty controlling anger, extreme emotional affectivity, rigidity and inflexibility, low intelligence, and a lack of basic trust. In addition, other individual factors include having unrealistic or negative expectations of children, being deficient in child management skills, being under a high degree of stress, being involved in marital conflict, and having a history of abuse in one's own childhood.

Because the psychiatric or psychopathological model generally assumes that the causes of abuse lie in the personality of the parent or other abuser, many investigations have concentrated on that dimension. The general aim of a diagnostic definition is to identify a pathological condition in a way that enables therapeutic intervention. Thus, adult abusers are thought to be the source of the pathology and in need of cure on the individual case level. This somewhat limited approach is common in the health sciences because physicians require a diagnostic assessment tool and because each case is so different in terms of its symptoms, severity, and chronic or acute nature (Zigler, 1983). Some investigators, however, have noted that the characteristics of the child may also be an important factor, resulting in a situation in which the care of the child is more demanding and difficult than it would be were those factors not present. Children may be more likely to be at risk of maltreatment if they are unwanted, resemble someone the parent dislikes, or have physical or behavioral traits that make them different or especially difficult to care for (U.S. Department of Health and Human Services, 1988). Therefore, if there is a predisposition on the part of the parent to be abusive, such characteristics as child mental retardation, hyperactivity, and premature birth might elicit that abuse.

However tempting it has been to view child abuse as a general personality or impulse disorder, evidence has failed to support this illness-as-cause conclusion. Of course, a certain percentage of abusing parents are violent toward their children because of psychological impairments that can be defined in terms of psychiatric descriptions. But for the most part, interactions among parental characteristics, environmental factors, and child situations provide the best format for assessing abusive behavior from diverse sources and for avoiding an overreliance on purely psychiatric etiologies.

## Sociological Model

Turning to the sociological model to account for child abuse, David Gil (1970) argues that most societies, including American society, have not developed absolute cultural taboos and legal sanctions against the use of physical force against children by adults. Historically, children, being the biological offspring of their parents, tended to be considered the parents' property as well as their responsibility. This meant that parents had a wide range of rights and discretion in their treatment of their children and were also given the task of socializing them. This allocation of the socialization function to the family seems to be a further reason for condoning the use of physical force against children by parents, since the socialization situation is invariably structured in a manner that bestows dominant status, rights, and power on the adult, and subordinate status and minimal rights and power on the child. Significant differences exist between various segments of the American population concerning what extent of physical abuse of children is considered appropriate and what extent is actually practiced. Despite such differences, however, it cannot be denied that some measure of violence against children is patterned into the child-rearing philosophies and practices of nearly all Americans (Gil, 1970).

A number of general factors, as well as some specific situational factors, are thought to contribute to child abuse. For example, among the general factors are such factors as unemployment, low socioeconomic status, poverty, single-parent families, social isolation of the family, lack of an extended family or peer support network, and family mobility. Although many of these sociological factors are found in abusive families, they do not sufficiently explain the problem. Many families experience the same degree of environmental stress and do not abuse children.

Numerous scholars maintain that as long as corporal punishment remains an acceptable form of discipline, child abuse will continue to be a problem in this society (Gelles, 1973; Gil, 1970). The use of corporal punishment by teachers is commonplace in schools throughout the nation. Schools are probably the most important socializing agent, next to the family. The sociological model posits that the roots of violence and abuse run deep in society's structures, values, and practices and that socially sanctioned abuse in education is just one example.

The sociological explanation of child abuse allows for a broad definition that includes more minor forms of child neglect and "probable" hindrances to a child's development. The process of defining maltreatment is not done with clinical-scientific information; rather, it becomes a social judgmental task. That is, parental acts are considered abusive when they deviate from our culture's values of acceptable child rearing and adult role expectations. The judgment is made by social agents in order to protect social standards as well as to protect individual members of society (Zigler, 1983). Because child abuse is socially defined, social solutions are implied. Whereas the psychiatric definitions focus on the problem as caused by individuals and therefore requiring case-level solutions, the sociological definition sees its roots in political, economic, and human conditions over which individuals have little control. The latest study by the U.S. Department of Health and Human Services (1988) lends strong support for this model, due to the increased levels of physical, sexual, and emotional abuse found among children of lower-income families.

*Social-Interactional Model*

A combined social-interactional model of child abuse that incorporates the dynamic interplay among individual, family, and social factors has been suggested (Belsky, 1980, 1984; Burgess, 1979; Gil, 1970; Walker, 1988). This interactive systems model is aimed at understanding abusive behavior in relation to both past (e.g., exposure to parental violence during childhood) and present (e.g., a colicky child) contextual events that affect the parent-child relationship.

The social-interactional model maintains that there are factors in the parents, such as psychopathology or personality traits, that appear to predispose some individuals toward abusive behavior. Aside from these, there may also be a personal history of witnessing or experiencing abusive, exploitative, or oppressive behavior. As a result of these factors, parents may have a dysfunctional relationship with their child, a relationship that may take the form of a lack of nurturance or poor child management skills.

There is also evidence that factors within the child—such as unusual handicaps or behaviors that are difficult to manage—contribute to the abusive situation. To these can be added certain situational factors, such as recent social stress, family instability, and marital conflict. These factors can then interact with sociological variables, such as poverty and unemployment, to result in child abuse. This conceptual model currently is useful to the clinician in that it requires the clinician to look at a broad range of variables in a systematic way and to consider their interactions in terms of how abuse may be produced. The model remains, however, too broad and ill-defined to be empirically precise or predictive.

It is also not uncommon to find maltreated children who lack any signs of overt problems or internal distress. Rather than assuming that an apparent absence of problems is indicative of the benign effects of abuse, the clinician must carefully consider other alternatives. Certain children may temporarily disguise their distress; other, "resilient" children may possess specific coping abilities that help them to adapt in a positive manner or may have other positive life experiences (e.g., supportive adults) that serve as buffers against the development of traumatic behavioral sequelae. These observations indicate that ongoing assessment of abused children's development and behavior over an extended period may be necessary to understand the relationship of the behavior to past and present life experiences.

## General Perpetrator Characteristics: Sexual Abuse

*Pedophilia* is a term used to indicate that an adult finds children to be sexually appealing (Haden, 1986). Some authors (De Young, 1982) use the term *hebephilia* to further distinguish those who are attracted to adolescents from those who are attracted to younger-aged, prepubertal children. Lanning (1987), in material prepared for law enforcement officers, defines a pedophile as a "significantly older individual who prefers to have sex with individuals legally considered children. The pedophile is one whose sexual fantasies and erotic imagery focus on children" (p. 2). He goes on to note that not all pedophiles are child molesters, in that they may not act on their preferences for children. And he points out that not all child molesters—for example, those who act out of curiosity or due to simple availability—are by definition pedophiles.

Different schemata have been used to categorize and describe pedophiliac behavior. One of the better-known classifications originated with the work of Groth and Birnbaum (1978). In their schema they first divide sexual offenders against children into two major categories, molesters and rapists. Molesters are individuals who use enticement, negotiation, entrapment, and mild pressure to involve a child in sexual behavior. Rapists are individuals who use force and assault. Molesters may be further broken down, in this system, into those who are fixated and those who are regressed (Groth & Birnbaum, 1979). The authors' original findings and subsequent research indicate that these two groups are distinct in both their levels of sociosexual maturation and the nature of their offenses. Fixated abusers are individuals who have never matured sexually to the point where they relate effectively to adult, age-appropriate sexual partners. The regressed offender, within this classification system, is an individual who has a normal sexual orientation and relates in general to age-appropriate, adult partners; however, under certain circumstances (e.g., stress, conflict, rejection, use of mood-altering substances), the individual may impulsively choose a sexual partner of a younger age.

Lanning (1987) further elaborates on two broad categories of offenders termed situational and preferential. Situational offenders are characterized as typically regressed and inadequate social misfits. They are "morally indiscriminate," with an overall life pattern of using and abusing others, and "sexually indiscriminate," in that they are willing to try a wide variety of sexual behaviors with diverse partners. Preferential offenders have not only a clear sexual preference for children but also a need for frequent and repeated sex with them, leading to some predictability in the actions of this group. Preferential offenders are characterized by their skilled use of seduction, despite typically poor social skills and introversion, and their potential for sadism or brutality, although the actual incidence of sadistic child molestation is low.

To help investigators identify pedophiles in the latter group, Lanning offers some indicators, noting that these factors alone mean little; it is the accumulation of factors and the pattern they form that gives them significance. Knowledge of these factors can help assist in victim evaluation due to increased understanding of victim-perpetrator dynamics and interaction. Indicators (pp. 12–13) include

- Sexual abuse in their background
- Limited social contact as teenagers
- Being discharged prematurely from the military
- Frequent, unexpected moves to a new locale
- Multiple victims, with planned, repeated, high-risk attempts
- Limited dating relationships or a "special" marital relationship
- Associates and circle of friends who are young
- Activities with children that often exclude other adults
- An excessive interest in children

Groth and colleagues (1982) raise the connection between pedophilia and the offender's own history of abuse and neglect, and recommend exploration of what was going on for offenders when they were the age of the child they are offending. In a summary statement, Groth concludes:

> Generally speaking, the clinical impression that emerges in regard to a child molester is that of an immature individual whose pedophilic behavior serves to compensate for his relative helplessness in meeting adult bio-psychosocial life demands. It offers him a retreat from conflictual adult relationships. It provides a sense of power, control, and competence. It fulfills a longing for intimacy, affection and affiliation. It validates his worth. And it may provide some sexual gratification. However, all of this is basically illusionary and transient. The child will eventually mature and the offender must find another victim. (pp. 136–137)

Conte (1986) notes that the actual sexual behavior takes place only after "a considerable period of time during which the adult manipulates the child into an abusive relationship." In this "grooming process," the adult learns the child's likes and dislikes, concerns and fears, and uses this knowledge to entice him or her into the sexual contact. Such information may also be used to coerce or threaten the child as needed to continue the sexual relationship once it has begun. Burgess and Holmstrom (1980) found three main types of pressure used to sexually entice children: (a) the offer of material goods, (b) the misrepresentation of moral standards, and (c) the offer of warmth and social contact to youngsters or women who are isolated or impoverished emotionally or socially. Other methods of victim engagement include befriending the child; paying attention; having hobbies or interests appealing to children; having youth-oriented decorations in the house or room; showing sexually explicit material to the child; and using manipulation, through seduction, competition, peer pressure, motivational techniques, or child/group psychology to ultimately lower the inhibitions of the children (Lanning, 1987).

A thorough understanding of perpetrator dynamics, as well as victim grooming and enticement strategies, is an important prerequisite for skillful victim screening and evaluation.

## Victim Vulnerability Factors and Profile

A research review by Finkelhor and Baron (1986, pp. 79–80) helps isolate some of the factors associated with vulnerability to sexual abuse. While abuse appears to be democratic in its occurrence among all social classes and its proportionate distribution by race, these authors were able to conclude that girls are at higher risk than boys and that preadolescents are at greater risk than older or younger children. Strong associations were found across studies for both males and females concerning family characteristics, with risk associated with living without natural fathers; having mothers employed outside the home; being ill or disabled; having a poor relationship with one of their parents; living with stepfathers; and witnessing parental conflict. It must be recognized that some of these factors may in fact be proxies for other, more central risk factors, and that characteristics putting children at risk for abuse need to be differentiated from the effects of abuse itself.

Studies of abused children on standardized behavior and symptom scales are beginning to identify constellations of internalizing and externalizing symptoms found frequently in abused children (Fredrick, Urquiza, & Peilke, 1986; Gomes-Schwartz, Horowitz, & Sausier, 1985). Nevertheless, more than one pattern is emerging, and the patterns observed are not specific to abused children. It is also true that many children are not symptomatic subsequent to abuse. For instance, a situation of less severe abuse in an emotionally resilient child with a supportive family environment can produce a minimal acute-symptom response without long-term sequelae.

Given the above limitations, it is still useful to present in a concise format a schema for developing a victim profile checklist by enumerating some of the most common symptoms of both physical and sexual abuse. It is important to remember that many of these symptoms are applicable across a broad range of traumatic or stress-related events that influence childrens' behavior.

### Direct Communication or Evidence

1. Verbal disclosures from child
2. Reliable third-party reports or history
3. Physical evidence: bruises, welts, burns, fractures, lacerations or abrasions, abdominal injuries, central nervous system injuries, poisoning, severe developmental deficits, early pregnancy or abortion, STDs, physical evidence of sexual activity in children

*Cumulative Stress Symptoms/Undercontrolled and
Externalized Behaviors*

1. Aggressive, hostile, disruptive behavior
2. Animal torture/firesetting
3. Chronic running away
4. Alcohol and/or drug abuse
5. Compulsive lying
6. Age-inappropriate sexual acting-out
7. Prostitution/promiscuity
8. Over-seductive behavior or sexual preoccupation
9. Fear of touching or being touched/phobias
10. Ambiguous contextual statements referring to abuse

*Acute Trauma Symptoms/Overcontrolled and
Internalized Behaviors*

1. Dysphoria and crying for no apparent reason
2. Abuse-specific fears, probably associated with particular places or persons
3. Social withdrawal from peers
4. Self-regulation problems (e.g., sleep, appetite or weight, appearance)
5. Regressive behaviors (e.g., thumb sucking, enuresis, encopresis)
6. Severe nightmares/flashbacks/dissociative reactions
7. Suicide attempts/self-injurious or mutilating behavior

In evaluating adolescents, it is particularly important to remember that symptoms evolve and interact with human development in such a way that the further one moves in time from the abuse experience, the more transformed the initial reactions to it become. Because abuse is frequently disclosed long after the initial traumatic event, one may observe symptoms that began with the trauma of victimization but have evolved considerably in the meantime. Therefore, it is useful to understand how such events are transformed over time, especially from the perspective of memory storage and retrieval.

## Memory Phenomena

In order to understand a little more regarding evaluation methods for physical and sexual abuse, it is important to be able to develop "high-yield" interview strategies that will help identify victimized youngsters. To this end, we have familiarized ourselves with some of the more common dynamic characteristics and symptom formations emanating from abusive relationships. It is also helpful to be familiar with the memory processes suspected to underlie the storage and retrieval of information related to traumatic, confusing, or overwhelming events. One of the foundations of our interviewing protocol is to develop an awareness of information processing models and capitalize on techniques that will enhance the disclosure of sensitive information.

Bessel A. van der Kolk and Onno van der Hart (1989) have reviewed the work of Pierre Janet, who at the turn of the century explored memory storage and retrieval processes that transform traumatic experiences into psychopathology. Interest in Janet's work has reemerged, particularly in light of renewed inquiry into posttraumatic stress disorders.

It is thought that in the first few years of life, the quality of events, not the contexts, can be remembered (often as screen memories), creating context-free, fearful associations that are hard to locate in space and time. Memory, for Janet, is the enhanced capacity to categorize and generalize associatively, not the storage of features or objects as lists. Essentially, then, memory is an action of a constituting consciousness; it is the action of telling a story, which is why it often lends itself to metaphoric models of treatment and disclosure. For Janet, being able to reproduce negative memories verbally was essential to successful integration of such memories so that they would not have to be organized on a somatosensory or iconic level as behavioral reenactments, somatic responses, nightmares, or flashbacks. In treatment, we frequently attempt to move our clients from the behavioral or sensorimotor level of conflict expression to the talking or verbal level of working through conflict.

Cognitive psychologists (e.g., Piaget, Kihlstrom, Neisser) have long felt that memories often determine the interpretation of the present. The memory system maintains coherence of mental functioning and links the present with the past by continually organizing and categorizing new information in light of previously integrated memories. The harmonious operation of memory implies that we can cognitively store events in a comfortable, integrated manner. Unrelated memories can be distressing. Frightening experiences that do not fit into existing cognitive schemata can split off from voluntary consciousness and form separate, highly discrete states that are often referred to as dissociative states. In sustained trauma, a range of hysterical, narcissistic, multiple, or borderline personality disorders may present themselves (in a state-dependent learning paradigm). Dissociative reactions, then, are looked on as failed attempts to process and properly store overwhelming sensory or experiential phenomena.

In a ground-breaking study, Dodge, Bates, and Pettit (1990) investigated the idea that physically abused children may be deficient in interpreting environmental and interpersonal cues, due to their memories of abuse. That is, abused youth, due to their past memories of physical abuse, would have a propensity to incorrectly perceive the actions of others as hostile or threatening, and would therefore respond in kind. These authors found that (a) children who had been physically abused in early life (before age four) were more hostile and aggressive to their peers than children who were not so abused; (b) physically abused children developed different information processing styles than nonabused children, with abused children being more likely to attribute hostile intent to others and less likely to produce competent solutions to interpersonal problems; and (c) childrens' social information processing patterns at age five appeared to predict later aggressive behaviors. These findings are consistent with the idea that early experiences of physical abuse result in aberrant conceptualizations of social interactions, a result that in turn perpetuates violent behavior.

Clinical evidence suggests that as people mature, stressful life experiences are more likely either to be effectively processed and overcome or to be walled off and affect only isolated aspects of functioning. The age of the victim, predisposing personality factors, and the nature and duration of the trauma all seem to play a role in the way trauma is processed. What is of greater concern to evaluators is learning more about the way this potentially traumatic information is retrieved and reported in an interview setting. Janet used reframing techniques to help patients recall and work through traumatic events. He felt it was imperative to help patients forgive themselves for ineffectual behavior at the time of the trauma and thus decrease emotional attachment to the trauma. Unfortunately, trauma recall often isolates past, ineffectual behavior through the perspective of current empowerment patterns. It is not unusual to recall and process previous experiences from the vantage point of current perceptions.

Investigative techniques that offer clients more tenable explanations for their past ineffectual or compliant behavior can also elicit permission to share that traumatic past. The questioning process needs to "reframe" the client's previous, inadequate cognitive schemata and suggest a more acceptable explanation for his or her victimization experiences. The use of this type of reconstructive interviewing technique encourages the recoding of painful memories into more verbal disclosures.

Part of the reconstructive investigative technique requires that indirect measures be utilized to "soften" and "cue" victims in a way that supportively permits them not only to reveal to the interviewer what has happened to them but also to acknowledge to themselves that they have in fact been cleverly or painfully exploited. This requires a questioning process that not only suggests to the interviewer a profile of affects, cognitions, and behaviors congruent with victimization but also suggests and interprets this to the victim in an understandable and reassuring way. This type of interview process employs many didactic elements to help guide victims to discover their own buried secrets. Comparison among studies has shown that respondents disclose more experiences when they are given multiple opportunities for such disclosure and a variety of cues about the kinds of events researchers are interested in, as opposed to being asked single screening questions (Peters, Wyatt, & Finkelhor, 1986; Finkelhor et al., 1990).

As we explore the whole process of victim disclosure of physical and sexual abuse, one of the features we see is that most first-time disclosures are inaccurate. By "inaccurate" we do not mean that they are false; rather, we mean that they are greatly minimized and incomplete. This is due to a variety of reasons, which often include hesitancy, embarrassment, shame, guilt, repression, and fear of exposure and retaliation. This minimization is perhaps a defensive phenomenon that protects victims from the overwhelming realization of their own abusive experiences. Full and accurate disclosure of victimization experiences typically occurs progressively, in stages, over time. Our static models of victim disclosure emanate from criminal justice rules of evidence, which require that accurate initial victim statements be recorded and regard future deviations from the original statement as proof of incredulousness. Few of the law enforcement and protective service investigation models are equipped to deal with disclosure from this process-oriented perspective. Delays in time and changes of victim accounts can hamper and impede the judicial process. Our criminal justice models of victim reporting are often in conflict with information processing models in explaining the way in which traumatic events are retrieved from memory by victims and reported to interviewers. Therapy-based models of reporting are more likely to cultivate disclosures, due to the enhanced time frame and built-in sensitivity to retrieval and disclosure dynamics.

## Evaluation and Screening

Screening for physical and sexual abuse in high-risk clinical populations should be systematic, consistent, comprehensive, and documented. The quality-assurance aspects of conducting critical diagnostic evaluations are rarely prioritized in busy clinical settings. In addition, it is important that high-risk clinical populations be systematically screened for physical and sexual abuse in ways that maximize and initiate the process of disclosure. Such an approach is similar to obtaining key information about other issues adolescents are uncomfortable about discussing with adult authority figures. "Have you ever been physically or sexually abused?" is a good, direct question but is probably the equivalent of "Do you do drugs?" All too often, the question is perceived by the adolescent as too threatening and is simply met with a response of "No." In order to facilitate these types of disclosures, we need to use more sophisticated screening approaches that employ multiple measures of the variables thought to relate to physical and sexual abuse. Further, the method of collecting this information needs to be as supportive as possible and perceived by the adolescent as something that will help him or her feel better in the long run. The Adolescent Sexual Concern Questionnaire

(ASC) is an instrument we designed to help detect sexual and physical abuse (see Hussey & Singer, 1989). The usual way to find out if someone has been abused is to ask; however, one must ask in a way that gives teenagers permission to relate emotionally painful and confusing experiences. An understanding of disclosure dynamics, as well as the many ways in which adolescents react to past or present victimization, is an important screening prerequisite.

The ASC is designed to be used in the context of a structured interview by a professional familiar with the dynamics of sexual abuse and comfortable with discussing sexuality issues. The ASC is written at a sixth-grade level and is completed by twelve- to nineteen-year-old youngsters prior to their being interviewed. It has twenty-nine items, each presented in a Likert-type format to minimize simple true/false responses. The items screen for physical and sexual abuse and cover a wide range of issues, including physical appearance, birth control, concerns about sex, venereal disease, AIDS, homosexuality, homophobia, and sexual deviance. This clustering of issues reflects a logical, coherent questioning sequence. The ASC is structured so that it moves from less risky to more risky items, in order for the interviewer to establish rapport with the teenager and then choose points of emphasis for exploration. Use of a same-sex interviewer is thought to maximize discussion and disclosure of sensitive sexual material. The same types of critical questions are asked in different ways to serve as a validity check on responses and to help "cue" retrieval of memory associations by utilizing different semantic presentations of abusive experiences. The underlying premise is that disclosure is a process in which the victim is clinically prepared to accept a more accurate reality and redefine it in a healthier way. The instrument is meant to be used as a guide for the interviewer and to give him or her an opportunity to initiate the use of reframing techniques to provide educational information to the patient. Supportive generalizations that suggest, guide, and validate youngsters' responses to victimization are most often used. The ASC is simple, relatively short, and not too threatening. This is the delicate balance that needs to be achieved when creating instruments that are clinically useful and possess a research capability.

## Adolescent Sexual Concern Questionnaire (ASC)

Many teenagers have concerns or questions about health, relationships, and sexuality. The purpose of this form is to identify which areas you may have questions or concerns about so we can help you with them.

**I. The first is about your *health*. Please circle how often you have had concerns or questions about**

1. TROUBLE SLEEPING

    never          almost never          sometimes          often          very often

*Rationale for question:* Bedtime difficulties often correlate with abuse and psychiatric problems such as depression; sexual abuse often takes place at night and in the bedroom.

2. SLEEPING TOO MUCH

never          almost never          sometimes          often          very often

*Rationale for question:* Again, the question looks for signs of depression and withdrawal that may be associated with abuse.

3. WETTING THE BED

never          almost never          sometimes          often          very often

*Rationale for question:* A history of enuresis is associated with stress disorders. In addition, the interviewer needs to be sensitive to the triad of enuresis (or encopresis), firesetting, and animal torture that can indicate the youngster has a background of severe abuse. A simple way to remember this triad of important symptoms is by the phrase "to pee on a burning cat."

4. HAVING DREAMS OR NIGHTMARES

never          almost never          sometimes          often          very often

*Rationale for question:* Here we are attempting to explore access to unconscious or subconscious material and images. Asking about early dreams or memories may help to explore "screen memories" that serve as organizing residuals for early traumatic experiences. We are also concerned with possible dissociative experiences that may be evidence of serious trauma. Follow-up questions are

- Do you dream much?
- Does it ever feel like you're dreaming when you're awake?
- Can you tell me about a dream?
- Do you ever have any recurring dreams?
- What is the earliest event in your life you can remember?

5. HEADACHES OR STOMACHACHES

never          almost never          sometimes          often          very often

*Rationale for question:* Somatic complaints can also be related to trauma and stress. This frequently occurs with youngsters who are more likely to internalize than to act out their emotions and conflicts.

## II. The following is a list about *relationships* and *sex*. Please circle how often you have had questions or concerns about

1. BEING LIKED BY THE OPPOSITE SEX

never          almost never          sometimes          often          very often

*Rationale for question:* It is convenient and useful in the evaluation process to obtain a sexual history. One of the first steps is to talk about dating relationships. Most adolescents are concerned about how they are perceived by the opposite sex. A follow-up question is

- Do you have a boyfriend or girlfriend?

2. HOW FAR TO GO WITH SEX

never          almost never          sometimes          often          very often

*Rationale for question:* Many adolescents struggle with this issue in relationships and need to reach a satisfactory resolution to it. This question opens up discussion on how one chooses a sexual partner and what types of sexual expressions are comfortable for the individual. Issues around sexual victimization as well as sexual offending are suggested in this question.

3. SOMEONE IN YOUR FAMILY WANTING TO HAVE SEX WITH YOU

never        almost never        sometimes        often        very often

*Rationale for question:* This is a very direct question that explores the possibility of incestuous relationships. Perhaps a more useful approach in this line of questioning is to use a "projective questioning" technique—that is, one that parallels prototypal adolescent queries in which a teenager typically presents his or her own problems or concerns to a counselor couched in the rhetoric of "a friend of mine has this problem." The approach here is for the interviewer to use the same kind of technique to explore with adolescents what they would do in hypothetical situations involving abuse. This valuable technique can elicit critical information from an adolescent who is suspected of being abused but is afraid or embarrassed to tell. All too often, the teen will unknowingly list his or her own "hypothetical" barriers preventing disclosure of abuse, thereby providing the interviewer with useful clinical areas to address in further evaluation or therapy. Follow-up questions would include

- Do you know anyone who has ever been sexually abused?
- What did they do? Who did they tell?
- What would you do if that ever happened to you?
- Who would you tell?

4. USING BIRTH CONTROL

never        almost never        sometimes        often        very often

*Rationale for question:* This question relates to obtaining an accurate sexual history. It is important to use this opportunity in evaluating high-risk teenagers to educate them regarding pregnancy and birth control. It is also important to investigate for possible "sexual myths" or misunderstandings adolescents have regarding pregnancy and birth control.

Studies (see Strasburger, 1985) have shown that over 50 percent of teenage girls said they did not use birth control during intercourse because they thought they could not become pregnant. Teens do not think about a medical means of birth control until they've been sexually active for six months to a year, yet half of all teen pregnancies occur within the first six months after initiating intercourse (20% within the first month). Follow-up questions include

- Do you use any kind of protection during intercourse? What kind?
- Do you know you can get pregnant if you don't?
- Do you know you can get your partner pregnant if you don't use protection.

5. BEING RAPED OR SEXUALLY ABUSED

never        almost never        sometimes        often        very often

*Rationale for question:* This question is similar to question 3 in that it is a direct question, this time exploring sexual abuse by someone outside of the family. The same type of projective questioning techniques should be used as in #3 if the interviewer is suspicious of sexual abuse.

6. HOW YOU LOOK

never          almost never          sometimes          often          very often

*Rationale for question:* In adolescence, a teen's height increases by 25 percent, and his or her weight often doubles (Strasburger, 1985); only in early infancy is there also such a dramatic growth rate. Compared with nonabused youngsters, adolescents who have been sexually abused may be more conscious of bodily changes and alterations or feel more uncomfortable with their body and its appearance to others. Follow-up questions include

- How do you feel about your body and how you look?
- If you could change your appearance, what changes would you make?

7. CARING FOR PEOPLE OF YOUR SAME SEX

never          almost never          sometimes          often          very often

*Rationale for question:* People discover rather than choose their sexual identity, often during the period of adolescent development. Homosexual identity development is often hampered due to the fact that it typically takes place against the backdrop of social stigma.

Children and adolescents don't necessarily structure sexual experiences using sexual labels. It is clinically more useful to focus on the meaning of feelings. Clinicians can help teenagers by focusing on three levels of sexual identity formation. The first level is internal sexual orientation: "Do I feel and define myself as male or as female?" The second level is gender-role behavior referring to societal and cultural expectations: "Do I behave more male or more female?" The third level is sexual or erotic attraction: "Am I attracted to male or to female sexual partners?" Interviewers should treat sexual experiences as valid, but avoid premature labeling until further experience enables the adolescent to determine what sexual patterns most adequately express his or her own values, needs, and desires. If interviewers impose categories prematurely, it won't make the sexual feelings disappear; rather, it will only confuse and invalidate them, further amplifying the adolescent's distress.

Some research on homosexual identity development (Troiden, 1988) indicates that gay males first act on sexual feelings at a mean age of fifteen years; gay females, at a mean age of twenty years. Homosexual self-definition for gay males occurs on the average between nineteen and twenty-one years of age; for gay females, between twenty-one and twenty-three years of age. The final stage is a same-sex love relationship, which for gay males occurs on the average ages between twenty-one and twenty-four; for gay females, between ages twenty-two and twenty-three. A follow-up question is

- Do you have any concerns or questions about how you express positive feelings to people of your same sex?

8. GETTING VD OR AIDS

never          almost never          sometimes          often          very often

*Rationale for question:* AIDS education and prevention has become an important part of work with high-risk teens. This is an opportunity to provide educational counseling and to evaluate issues related to indiscriminate or promiscuous sexual relationships. A follow-up question is

- How can you protect yourself from getting sexually transmitted diseases?

9. BEING TALKED INTO DOING SEXUAL THINGS YOU DIDN'T WANT TO DO

never      almost never      sometimes      often      very often

*Rationale for question:* This question explores issues related to date rape and the whole phenomenon of sexual pressure in dating relationships. The key phrase is "being talked into," which opens up the discussion to experiences the adolescent isn't sure were abusive because they weren't physically coercive or because they occurred in an intimate relationship. A follow-up questions is

• Have you ever regretted having a sexual relationship with someone?

10. HAVING SEXUAL FEELINGS OTHERS THINK AREN'T RIGHT

never      almost never      sometimes      often      very often

*Rationale for question:* In this question we are beginning to look for sexual deviances, such as exhibitionism, voyeurism, cross-dressing, perpetrating, and deviant sexual fantasies. We are also exploring concerns regarding normal sexual behavior, such as masturbation, that more scrupulous teens might be struggling with.

11. GETTING AN ABORTION

never      almost never      sometimes      often      very often

*Rationale for question:* Teens have one-third of all abortions, although they represent only 16 percent of the childbearing population (Strasburger, 1985). Abortions can be significant life events that generate strong feelings and merit supportive discussion. Early pregnancy and abortion can represent incestuous family dynamics and sexual abuse.

12. SHOWING AFFECTION TO PEOPLE OF YOUR SAME SEX

never      almost never      sometimes      often      very often

*Rationale for question:* The rationale for this question is the same as that for question 7. An additional issue the interviewer is advised to watch for is extreme homophobia. Some young people who are severely homophobic may be more acutely disturbed than is immediately apparent and may even engage in highly aggressive behavior toward those whom they perceive to be gay.

**III. The following is a list about thoughts and feelings. Circle how often you have had questions or concerns about the following:**

1. BEING SCARED OF GETTING HURT OR KILLED

never      almost never      sometimes      often      very often

*Rationale for question:* This and the next question screen for physical abuse. This question is particularly concerned with harassment, intimidation, or physical abuse from someone outside the family, such as a peer. Some of the most emotionally and physically traumatic assaults on young people have been by their peers and, particularly for males, often are not labeled as such. For females, early discussion and screening for date-related violence can be preventive. Consequently, it is important to inquire directly about this. It is also useful to query the adolescent regarding his or her own use of physical aggression toward others. This question also seems to identify paranoid thinking patterns in some youngsters. Follow-up questions include

• Have you ever been in a fight? What happened?
• Have you ever been beaten up? Have you ever beaten anyone up?

2. GETTING HURT OR BEATEN UP BY SOMEONE IN YOUR FAMILY

   never          almost never          sometimes          often          very often

   *Rationale for question:* This critical question explores domestic violence. Research results support the overall conclusion that abusers are significantly less positive than nonabusers (primarily measured in terms of praise, physical contact, voice tone, and frequency of neutral and positive statements) and that abusers are proportionately more likely than nonabusers to rely on aversive control, such as threats and physical methods of punishment and control (Loeber et al., 1984; Reid et al., 1981).

   One form of domestic violence that is often unappreciated is sibling violence, particularly in very chaotic families. Normally, when children are abused by older siblings, parents intervene to stop the abuse and validate the issue for the victim. In highly chaotic families, however, this happens inconsistently or not at all. Consequently, the trauma of severe sibling abuse is legitimized by parental inaction. Follow-up questions are

   • How do your parents discipline you?
   • What's the worst punishment you ever received?
   • Were you ever hit by someone in your family in such a way that it left a mark or a bruise?
   • How do your parents behave when they are very angry?
   • How do your parents fight?

3. FEELING UPSET ABOUT SEXUAL THINGS YOU HAVE DONE

   never          almost never          sometimes          often          very often

   *Rationale for question:* In victims, this question looks for guilt or distress from perceived complicity in the abusive relationship. In perpetrators, the question attempts to explore conflict from sexually inappropriate behavior.

4. FEELING UPSET ABOUT SEXUAL THINGS THAT HAVE HAPPENED TO YOU

   never          almost never          sometimes          often          very often

   *Rationale for question:* This question explores conflicted feelings related to sexual behavior, including sexual abuse. A follow-up questions is

   • Has anything sexually confusing ever happened to you?

5. RUNNING AWAY

   never          almost never          sometimes          often          very often

   *Rationale for question:* Adolescents who run away from home have an unusually high rate of physical and sexual abuse. If adolescents have histories as runaways, the interviewer should evaluate what the adolescent is running away from in the home and family situation, or what the youth might be running to in terms of need for high levels of excitement or stimulation.

6. BEING AFRAID OF THE OPPOSITE SEX

   never          almost never          sometimes          often          very often

   *Rationale for question:* Female abuse victims sometimes develop phobic types of responses, particularly toward males. Both male and female abuse victims may have difficulties forming and maintaining intimate relationships. In addition, it is also useful to be sensitive to the "sexually shy" teenager, who may be sexually uninitiated or lack the social expertise for how to behave in opposite-sex relationships. This youngster can benefit from sensitive reassurance, and from social skill development.

7. HAVING A TERRIBLE SECRET

    never        almost never        sometimes        often        very often

    *Rationale for question:* Discovering the secret of abuse is the primary aim of this question. Oftentimes another secret—such as suicidal preoccupation or parental sexual misconduct in affairs—is revealed.

8. BEING DIFFERENT

    never        almost never        sometimes        often        very often

    *Rationale for question:* Victims of abuse often feel different from their peers by virtue of their traumatic experiences or their premature sexual initiation. The scourge of adolescence is to feel different from one's peers.

9. FEELING UNLOVED OR UNCARED ABOUT

    never        almost never        sometimes        often        very often

    *Rationale for question:* This question examines significant emotional attachments within the adolescent's life; it is used as a way to gauge emotional neglect or abuse. Interestingly, physically abused teens often report that the most painful part of abuse is the emotional rejection they experience from their families.

10. HAVING DIFFICULTY CONTROLLING SEXUAL FEELINGS

    never        almost never        sometimes        often        very often

    *Rationale for question:* This question is concerned with examining issues related to sexual promiscuity or sexual deviances, such as exhibitionism, obscene phone calling, and perpetrating. A follow-up question is

    • Have you ever had questions about how to control your sexual urges?

11. BEING TOUCHED IN A PRIVATE PART OF YOUR BODY AGAINST YOUR WISHES

    never        almost never        sometimes        often        very often

    *Rationale for question:* This question seeks to establish a history of sexual abuse by focusing in on inappropriate touch.

12. USING SEX TO GAIN AFFECTION

    never        almost never        sometimes        often        very often

    *Rationale for question:* This final question probes some of the emotional aspects underlying sexualized relationships. Victims may have been taught to seek affection through sexual expressions and behaviors. We are also concerned here with detecting possible evidence of prostitution.

---

In concluding the interview, it is important to remember the process-oriented perspective we've established. Oftentimes the interviewer may be suspicious that a youngster seems to have strong indications of being abused, even though the individual, in response to the interview and follow-up questions, has not disclosed a history of victimization. Here the use of generalizations and anticipatory guidance to help prepare the youngster for later disclosure become the focus. Sometimes saying such things as "I can't help but wonder if something very confusing or painful may have happened to you in the past that you've forgotten" allows the question of victimization to remain an open topic for further exploration. Supportive generalizations about some of the feelings and reactions of other victims of abuse and about issues of trust may speak directly to the current problems and struggles of the interviewee. This type of anticipatory guidance allows therapeutic intervention to begin without coercing a painful or premature disclosure.

If an adolescent has disclosed abuse for the first time, the interviewer should attempt to ascertain basic information about the abuse, such as who, what, when, where, and how. This will be important information to relay to the appropriate investigative agency. A note of caution is in order, however. The disclosure in itself may be a very traumatic or overwhelming event and in some instances can trigger suicidal or self-injurious feelings that need to be carefully assessed and monitored. A question such as "How do you feel about what you've just shared?" is a good way to begin the assessment.

Normally, the interview is ended by changing direction and asking about other issues, such as hobbies and career aspirations. This moves the discussion away from victimization issues and into lighter, less intensive subject matter. It is important to be able to use this technique at key points in an interview, particularly when interviewers sense that an adolescent is becoming disengaged from them. A great deal of valuable information can be gained through these types of questions.

## Research on ASC Responses

Francis Sink (1988), in his discussion of child sexual abuse evaluation, notes the need for improvements in the use of direct interview techniques with children who have been abused. Procedures with standards by which to refine and clarify questioning of children so that evaluators can be more certain of the meaning of what is heard have been enormously helpful to practitioners (MacFarlane & Waterman, 1986; White, 1986; White, Strom & Santilli, 1986). Opportunities to study styles of questioning about the specifics of abuse have enabled many clinicians to ask questions more directly and in a manner that children can understand (Sgroi, 1982). Research about the responses of children, abused and nonabused, to sexually anatomically correct dolls has helped lend credibility to the distinct quality of the abused child's responses (White et al., 1987). Investigators are now learning more specifics from children by using careful, direct questioning. When children are responsive to the direct-question format, the evaluator is much better equipped to assist them in telling about their abuse (Sink, 1988).

Initial data compiled on 260 consecutive admissions to an adolescent inpatient unit (Hussey & Singer, 1989) determined that 68 of these adolescents had been sexually abused (data on physical abuse are not yet available). The ASC was able to identify 21 patients with histories of sexual abuse that had never been disclosed. It also identified 30 patients with previously revealed histories of sexual abuse. An additional 17 patients had reported histories of sexual abuse during their inpatient stay but were not first identified through the ASC. Five of these patients had previously identified histories of abuse, and 12 were first-time disclosures. The positive prediction rate for those who for the first time disclosed being sexually abused was 64 percent (21 of 33); for youth who had previously revealed being sexually abused, the rate was 86 percent (30 of 35). These statistics cannot account for cases that remained undisclosed; however, an overall positive prediction rate of 75 percent (51 of 68) was achieved by the ASC for patients who were able to be classified as sexually abused.

More recent sexual abuse data using the ASC have been gathered from a separate sample of 410 consecutively admitted adolescent psychiatric inpatients. Table 1 displays the key sexual abuse screening responses for the ASC. These responses were obtained by comparing ASC answers from youth who were known to have been sexually abused (N = 113) with those of youth who had no known history of such abuse (N = 297), and then determining significant differences between the two groups through use of t-tests.

As can be seen in Table 1, significant differences in responses from sex-

**Table 1.**
**Key Screening Responses**

| Area of Question or Concern | Significance Level (P) |
|---|---|
| Having dreams or nightmares | .01 |
| Headaches or stomachaches | .01 |
| How far to go with sex | .01 |
| Someone in your family wanting to have sex with you | .00 |
| Using birth control | .00 |
| Being raped or sexually abused | .00 |
| How you look | .01 |
| Getting VD or AIDS | .01 |
| Being talked into doing sexual things you didn't want to do | .00 |
| Having sexual feelings others think aren't right | .01 |
| Getting hurt or beaten up by someone in your family | .00 |
| Feeling upset about sexual things you have done | .00 |
| Feeling upset about sexual things that have happened to you | .00 |
| Running away | .00 |
| Being afraid of the opposite sex | .00 |
| Having a terrible secret | .00 |
| Feeling unloved or uncared about | .01 |
| Having difficulty controlling sexual feelings | .00 |
| Being touched in a private part of your body against your wishes | .00 |
| Using sex to gain affection | .01 |

ually abused and non-sexually-abused adolescents emerged in twenty of the ASC questions. Further analyses of these differences using factor analysis and discriminant function analysis yielded six critical questions. When an adolescent endorsed *any* of these questions (i.e., indicated any category but "never"), there was a substantial likelihood of the adolescent having been sexually abused. By using these criteria, 78 percent of youth were able to be correctly classified into either the sexually abused or the non-sexually-abused group, with a false negative rate of 16.5 percent and a false positive rate of 32.9 percent. The six critical screening questions were

- Feeling upset about sexual things that have happened to you
- Being talked into doing sexual things you didn't want to do
- Someone in your family wanting to have sex with you
- Being afraid of the opposite sex
- Being raped or sexually abused
- Being touched in a private part of your body against your wishes

## Treatment

Due to the wide variety of abusive behaviors, there are many types of treatment interventions and modalities. In focusing on adolescents, we have found that developmental considerations suggest that the use of two kinds of therapeutic approaches might be particularly useful. The first approach involves the use of group therapy. Since adolescents are very peer-oriented, group therapy models are dynamically useful for addressing therapeutic issues and developing support systems. The second approach involves the use of creative media, such as art and music therapies. Adolescents are also very activity-oriented and often reluctant to initially process distressing emotions on a verbal level. The use of creative media techniques to encourage expression of affects and conflicts can be highly effective. It is important to remember as well that family-based treatments are often the most appropriate for family-based abuse. Determination of treatment options, of course, follows from careful assessment and evaluation of victimization issues. Treatment interventions may range from crisis intervention and brief counseling to long-term psychotherapy in an extended care setting.

In looking at treatment from an information processing model, the primary therapeutic goal is to correctly reinterpret and understand the meaning of the abuse experience in a way that can minimize its negative effects. For the victimized adolescent, these effects occur within the context of identity formation and fragmentation. The original defenses used to accommodate or adjust to the abuse have served as ego survival strategies. They now need to be transformed to integrate the meaning of the abuse with a healthier, non-fragmented identity. Residual effects of failing to do so can include low self-esteem, self-hatred, disturbed relationships, and poor impulse control.

The common features employed to accommodate to the abuse include denying the abuse, altering the affective responses to it, and changing the meaning of the abuse (Rieker & Carmen, 1986). In denying the abuse, one often finds minimizing and incomplete disclosure. For adolescents, such denial may be reflected in the development of distancing and dissociative strategies that frequently include heavy substance abuse patterns (Singer, Petchers, & Hussey, 1989). The altering of affective responses can result in sudden anger and impulsive or self-destructive behaviors.

In changing the meaning of the abuse, we frequently find that someone else besides the victim has defined the meaning of the abuse. All too often, it is actually the perpetrator who has determined that meaning; if not, then society, the media, the newspapers, or someone else may have inaccurately defined it. Adolescent victims need an accurate definition of the abuse experience and the right to own their feelings. The first treatment task, then, is to understand the victim's processing of the victimization experience. The ongoing therapeutic task will then be to allow the victim to own and accept the feelings associated with it and to reframe the meaning of the experience in a way that can allow for healthier identity development and future growth.

Family-based treatments for physical abuse attempt to intervene in ways that will reduce family dysfunction and enhance nurturance and skill development. Risk factors are identified, and interventions designed to remediate them are chosen. Risk factors include such things as marital discord, extreme affectivity, inappropriate child-rearing expectations, poor child management skills, and unhealthy familial coalitions and alliances. Interventions include use of treatment models employing strategic, structural, and cognitive-behavioral family therapy. In addition, if situational and environmental factors are thought to be significant factors, interventions designed to assist with such issues as financial management, unemployment, social isolation, and lack of adequate child-care options become important. In some cases, parents will be suffering from a primary psychiatric disorder or will have a primary contributing factor (e.g., alcoholism) requiring intensive treatment intervention. Parental self-help groups are another growing resource that combines supportive group treatments within the framework of a self-help model to assist physically and sexually abusive parents in learning new strategies for managing their own emotional reactions as well as the behavior of their children.

In terms of working with physically abused adolescents, problems often found relate to increased levels of anxiety, aggression, and behavioral difficulties. Practitioners may find that abused children exhibit a cluster of symptoms reflective of posttraumatic stress disorder (e.g., dysphoria, withdrawal, sleep disturbances). Treatment focuses can include the development of relaxation and communication skills, training in anger management and problem solving, and enhancement of self-esteem and social skills.

In regard to sexual abuse, incestuous families are often treated through a variety of combined individual, marital, family, group, and parent-child dyad therapy strategies. Level of perpetrator pathology, as well as the ability of the nonoffending parent to provide protection, is a primary concern. Treatment typically occurs over extended periods and may involve the use of a range of therapies focusing on issues related to communication, family boundaries, role and power distortions within relationships, cognitive distortions, and sexuality.

Work specifically with sexual offenders often relies heavily on group therapy models using cognitive-behavioral techniques to establish victim empathy and decrease power-distorted behaviors, increase impulse control, modify the offender's deviant sexual orientation and arousal patterns, and increase self-esteem and prosocial behavior. Aversive and satiation procedures, as well as biological interventions using medications and antiandrogenic preparations such as Depo-Provera, have been employed with some success (Berlin & Meinecke, 1981). Certain surgical procedures have also been tried.

In addition to the symptoms typically seen in female victims, such as shame, depression, guilt, and inappropriate sexual behavior, Rogers and Terry (1984) have described other issues encountered in the treatment of boy victims, including (a) confusion over sexual identity and fears of homosexuality, (b) a tendency to reenact the victimization by sexually abusing other children, (c) increased aggressive behavior, and (d) strong denial or minimization of the impact by the boy's parents. Because boys may typically attempt to reassert their masculinity through aggressive behavior, clinicians treating boy victims may want to implement a program that assists boys in channeling or redirecting those aggressive feelings in prosocial directions, such as asserting their masculinity by helping and protecting others. Thus, intervention with boy victims may be a productive long-term approach to preventing sexual crimes.

## Appendix
## Adolescent Sexual Concern Questionnaire (ASC)

Many teenagers have concerns or questions about health, relationships, and sexuality. The purpose of this form is to identify which areas you may have questions or concerns about so we can help you with them.

### I. The first is about your *health*. Please circle how often you have had concerns or questions about

1. TROUBLE SLEEPING

   never          almost never          sometimes          often          very often

2. SLEEPING TOO MUCH

   never          almost never          sometimes          often          very often

3. WETTING THE BED

never          almost never          sometimes          often          very often

4. HAVING DREAMS OR NIGHTMARES

never          almost never          sometimes          often          very often

5. HEADACHES OR STOMACHACHES

never          almost never          sometimes          often          very often

**II. The following is a list about *relationships* and *sex*. Please circle how often you have had questions or concerns about**

1. BEING LIKED BY THE OPPOSITE SEX

never          almost never          sometimes          often          very often

2. HOW FAR TO GO WITH SEX

never          almost never          sometimes          often          very often

3. SOMEONE IN YOUR FAMILY WANTING TO HAVE SEX WITH YOU

never          almost never          sometimes          often          very often

4. USING BIRTH CONTROL

never          almost never          sometimes          often          very often

5. BEING RAPED OR SEXUALLY ABUSED

never          almost never          sometimes          often          very often

6. HOW YOU LOOK

never          almost never          sometimes          often          very often

7. CARING FOR PEOPLE OF YOUR SAME SEX

never          almost never          sometimes          often          very often

8. GETTING VD OR AIDS

never          almost never          sometimes          often          very often

9. BEING TALKED INTO DOING SEXUAL THINGS YOU DIDN'T WANT TO DO

never          almost never          sometimes          often          very often

10. HAVING SEXUAL FEELINGS OTHERS THINK AREN'T RIGHT

never          almost never          sometimes          often          very often

11. GETTING AN ABORTION

never          almost never          sometimes          often          very often

12. SHOWING AFFECTION TO PEOPLE OF YOUR SAME SEX

never          almost never          sometimes          often          very often

**III. The following is a list about thoughts and feelings. Circle how often you have had questions or concerns about the following:**

1. BEING SCARED OF GETTING HURT OR KILLED

never          almost never          sometimes          often          very often

2. GETTING HURT OR BEATEN UP BY SOMEONE IN YOUR FAMILY

    never       almost never       sometimes       often       very often

3. FEELING UPSET ABOUT SEXUAL THINGS YOU HAVE DONE

    never       almost never       sometimes       often       very often

4. FEELING UPSET ABOUT SEXUAL THINGS THAT HAVE HAPPENED TO YOU

    never       almost never       sometimes       often       very often

5. RUNNING AWAY

    never       almost never       sometimes       often       very often

6. BEING AFRAID OF THE OPPOSITE SEX

    never       almost never       sometimes       often       very often

7. HAVING A TERRIBLE SECRET

    never       almost never       sometimes       often       very often

8. BEING DIFFERENT

    never       almost never       sometimes       often       very often

9. FEELING UNLOVED OR UNCARED ABOUT

    never       almost never       sometimes       often       very often

10. HAVING DIFFICULTY CONTROLLING SEXUAL FEELINGS

    never       almost never       sometimes       often       very often

11. BEING TOUCHED IN A PRIVATE PART OF YOUR BODY AGAINST YOUR WISHES

    never       almost never       sometimes       often       very often

12. USING SEX TO GAIN AFFECTION

    never       almost never       sometimes       often       very often

## References

American Association for Protecting Children, Inc. (1985). *Highlights of official child neglect and abuse reporting, 1983.* Denver, CO: The American Humane Association.

American Human Association. (1984). *Highlights of official child neglect and abuse reporting, 1982.* Denver, CO: Author.

American Medical Association, Council on Scientific Affairs. (1985). Diagnostic and treatment guidelines concerning child abuse and neglect. *Journal of the American Medical Association, 254,* 796–800.

Belsky, J. (1980). Child maltreatment: An ecological integration. *American Psychologist, 35,* 320–335.

Belsky, J. (1984). The determinants of parenting: A process model. *Child Development, 55,* 83–96.

Berlin, F. S., & Meinecke, D. F. (1981). Treatment of sex offenders with antiandrogenic medication: Conceptualization, review of treatment modalities, and preliminary findings. *American Journal of Psychiatry, 138,* 601–607.

Burgess, A. W., & Holmstrom, L. L. (1980). Sexual trauma of children and adolescents: Pressure, sex, secrecy. In L. G. Schultz (Ed.), *The sexual victimology of youth*. Springfield, IL: Charles C. Thomas.

Burgess, R. L. (1979). Child abuse: An interactional analysis. In B. B. Lahey & A. E. Kazdin (Eds.), *Advances in clinical child psychology* (Vol. 2, pp. 141–172). New York: Plenum Press.

Conte, J. R. (1986). *A look at child sexual abuse*. National Committee for the Prevention of Child Abuse.

Courtois, C. (1979). The incest experience and its aftermath. *Victimology: An International Journal, 4,* 337–347.

De Young, M. (1982). The sexual victimization of children. Jefferson, NC: McFarland.

Dodge, K. A., Bates, J. E., & Pettit, G. S. (1990). Mechanisms in the cycle of violence. *Science, 250,* 1678–1683.

Finkelhor, D. (1979). *Sexually victimized children*. New York: The Free Press.

Finkelhor, D. (1984). *Child sexual abuse: New theory and research*. New York: The Free Press.

Finkelhor, D. (1986). *A sourcebook on child sexual abuse*. Beverly Hills, CA: Sage Publications.

Finkelhor, D., & Baron, L. (1986). High risk children. In D. Finkelhor et al. (Eds.), *A sourcebook on child sexual abuse* (pp. 60–88). Beverly Hills, CA: Sage Publications.

Finkelhor, D., Hotaling, G., Lewis, I. A., & Smith, C. (1990). Sexual abuse in a national survey of adult men and women: Prevalence, characteristics, and risk factors. *Child Abuse and Neglect, 14,* 19–28.

Fredrick, W., Urquiza, A., & Peilke, R. (1986). Behavior problems in sexually abused young children. *Journal of Pediatric Psychology, 2,* 47–57.

Gelinas, D. J. (1983). The persisting negative effects of incest. *Psychiatry, 46,* 312–332.

Gelles, R. J. (1973). *Child abuse and neglect: biosocial dimensions*. New York: Aldine DeGruyter.

Gil, D. G. (1970). *Violence against children: Physical child abuse in the United States*. Cambridge, MA: Harvard University Press.

Gomes-Schwartz, B., Horowitz, J., & Sausier, M. (1985). Severity of emotional distress among sexually abused preschool, school-age, and adolescent children. *Hospital and Community Psychiatry, 36,* 503–508.

Groth, A. N., and Birnbaum, H. J. (1978). Adult sexual orientation and attraction to underage persons. *Archives of Sexual Behavior, 7*(3), 175–181.

Groth, A. N., & Birnbaum, H. H. (1979). *Men who rape: The psychology of the offender*. New York: Plenum Press.

Groth, A. N., Hobson, W. F., & Gary, T. S. (1982). The child molester: Clinical observations. In J. R. Conte & D. A. Shore (Eds.), *Social work and child sexual abuse* (pp. 129–144). New York: Haworth Press.

Haden, D. C. (Ed.). (1986). *Out of harm's way: Readings on child sexual abuse, its prevention and treatment*. Phoenix: Onyx.

Hussey, D. L., & Singer, M. (1989). Innovations in the assessment and treatment of sexually abused adolescents: An inpatient model. In S. Sgroi (Ed.), *Vulnerable populations,* (Vol. 2, 43–64). Lexington, MA: Lexington Books.

Jones, E.D., & McCurdy, K. (1992). The links between types of maltreatment and demographic characteristics of children. *Child Abuse and Neglect, 16*, 201–215.

Kaplan, H., & Sadock, B. (1988). *Synopsis of Psychiatry: Behavioral Sciences Clinical Psychiatry.* Baltimore, MD: Williams & Wilkins. 635–637.

Lanning, K. (1987). *Child molesters: A behavioral analysis.* Washington, DC: National Center for Missing and Exploited Children.

Loeber, R., Felton, D. K., & Reid, J. (1984). A social learning approach to the reduction of coercive processes in child abusive families: A molecular analysis. *Advances in Behavior Research and Therapy, 6*, 29–45.

McFarlane, K., & Waterman, J. (1986). *Sexual abuse of young children: Evaluation and treatment.* New York: Guilford Press.

National Center on Child Abuse and Neglect. (1981). *Study findings: National study of the incidence and severity of child abuse and neglect.* Washington, DC: U.S. Department of Health and Human Services (Publication #OHDS 81-30325).

National Institute of Mental Health. (1977). *Child abuse and neglect programs: Practice and theory.* Washington, DC: U.S. Government Printing Office.

Peters, S., Wyatt, G., & Finkelhor, D. (1986). Prevalence. In D. Finkelhor et al. (Ed.), *Sourcebook on child sexual abuse.* (pp. 15–59). Beverly Hills, CA: Sage.

Reid, J. R., Taplin, P., & Loeber, R. (1981). A social interactional approach to the treatment of abusive families. In R. B. Stuart (Ed.), *Violent behavior: Social learning approaches to prediction, management, and treatment* (pp. 83–101). New York: Brunner/Mazel.

Rieker, P., & Carmen, E. (1986). The victim-to-patient process: The disconfirmation and transformation of abuse. *American Journal of Orthopsychiatry, 56*, 360–370.

Rogers, C. M., & Terry, T. (1984). Clinical intervention with boy victims of sexual abuse. In J. R. Stuart & J. G. Greer (Eds.), *Victims of sexual aggression: Treatment of children, women, and men* (pp. 91–104). New York: Van Nostrand Reinhold Co.

Russell, D. E. H. (1983). The incidence and prevalence of intrafamilial and extrafamilial sexual abuse of female children. *Child Abuse and Neglect, 7*, 133–146.

Russell, A. B., & Trainor, C. M. (1984). *Trends in child abuse and neglect: A national perspective.* Denver, CO: American Humane Association.

Sgroi, S. M. (1982). *Handbook of clinical intervention in child sexual abuse.* Lexington, MA: Lexington Books.

Sink, F. (1988). A hierarchical model for evaluation of child sexual abuse. *American Journal of Orthopsychiatry, 58*(1), 129–135.

Singer, M. I., Petchers, M. K., & Hussey, D. L. (1989). The relationship between sexual abuse and substance among psychiatrically hospitalized adolescents. *Child Abuse and Neglect, 13*, 319–325.

Strasburger, V. C. (1985). Normal adolescent sexuality. *Seminars in Adolescent Medicine, 1*(2), 101–115.

Timnick, L. (1985, August 25). *Los Angeles Times.* 22% in survey were child abuse victims. The Times Mirror Company, p. 1.

Troiden, R. R., (1988). Homosexuality identity development. *Journal of Adolescent Health Care, 9*, 105–113.

U.S. Department of Health and Human Services. (1988). *Study findings: Study of* national incidence and prevalence of child abuse and neglect (Contract No. 105-85-1702). Washington, DC: Department of Health and Human Services.

van der Kolk, B. A., & van der Hart, O. (1989). Pierre Janet and the breakdown of adaptation in psychological trauma. *American Journal of Psychiatry, 146*(12), 1530–1540.

Walker, E. D., Bonner, B. L., & Kaufman, K. L. (1988). *The physically and sexually abused child—Evaluation and treatment.* New York: Pergamon Press.

White, S. (1986). Uses and abuses of the sexually anatomically correct dolls. *Newsletter of the Division of Child, Youth, and Family Services (APA), 9,* 3, 6.

White, S., Strom, G., & Santilli, G. (1986). Interviewing young sexual abuse victims with anatomically correct dolls. *Child Abuse and Neglect, 10,* 519–529.

Wolfe, D. A. (1988). Child abuse and neglect. In E. J. Mash & L. G. Terdal (Eds.), *Behavioral assessment of childhood disorders* (pp. 627–669). New York: Guilford Press.

Wolfe, D. A., Kaufman, K., Aragona, J., & Sandler, J. (1981). *The child management program for abusive parents: Procedures for developing a child abuse intervention program.* Winter Park, FL: Anna.

Wolfe, V. V., & Wolfe, D. A. (1988). The sexually abused child. In E. J. Mash & L. G. Terdal (Eds.), *Behavioral assessment of childhood disorders* (pp. 670–714). New York: Guilford Press.

Young, R. (1982). *Characteristics of families receiving services at Family and Children's Services of London/Middlesex: 1970–1980.* Unpublished manuscript.

Zeigler, E. (1980). Controlling child abuse: Do we have the knowledge and/or the will? In C. Gerbner, C. Ross, & E. Ziegler, (Eds.), *Child abuse: An agenda for action.* New York: Oxford University Press.

Zigler, E. F. (1983). Understanding child abuse: A dilemma for policy development. In E. F. Zigler, S. L. Kagan, & E. Klugman, (Eds.), *Children, families, and government* (pp. 331–352). Cambridge, England: Cambridge University Press.

# 5
# Depressive Disorders

*Harris Rabinowich*

All the psychiatric disorders of children and adolescents that have depressed mood as an integral part of their symptomatology will be discussed in this chapter. Each disorder will be discussed from the standpoint of symptoms, diagnosis, phenomenology, and treatment. The disorders to be discussed will include not only those disorders where depression is a primary symptom but also the disorders of unstable mood or cyclic disorders. In children and adolescents, the cyclic disorders have significant symptom overlap with depressive disorders. They are usually discovered when investigating complaints of depressed mood in a child or adolescent and therefore fit quite naturally into this chapter. Table 1 lists the disorders covered in this chapter.

The term *depression* can have a variety of meanings, and it is important to distinguish these meanings in order to avoid confusion. *Depression* is used to describe a normally occurring mood state, a symptom, a syndrome, and a psychiatric disorder. When we use the term *depression* to describe one of the normally occurring mood states that all of us experience, we are describing the dysphoric mood that occurs with normal fluctuations in mood state, separations from loved ones, losses of loved ones, or reversals of fortune. This dysphoric mood can also be brought about by physiological changes—typically, the hormonal changes of menstruation, pregnancy, and birthing, as well as seasonal variations. Some medications can produce dysphoric moods as well. Normally occurring dysphoric moods sometimes deepen in intensity, lengthen in duration, and become symptoms. How one distinguishes a normal dypshoria from dysphoric mood as a symptom can be troublesome. It is even more troublesome to discern in children and adolescents who have been depressed most or all of their lives and whose families or they themselves do not recognize that they are dysphoric.

Depression, as a symptom, can occur by itself as a reaction to some stressful event. It can also be accompanied by one of several sets of symptoms that regularly occur together, that is, syndromes. All of the syndromes that

**Table 1.**
**Psychiatric Disorders That Contain Depressed Mood as a Symptom**

| *Depressive Disorders* |
| --- |
| Major depressive disorder |
|   Melancholic subtype |
|   Psychotic subtype |
|   Seasonal pattern |
|   Atypical subtype |
| Dysthymic disorder |
| Adjustment disorder with depressed mood |
| Cyclothymic disorders |

have dysphoric mood as a cardinal symptom will be discussed in this chapter; however, they will be discussed not as syndromes but rather as mood disorders. When we discuss disorders rather than syndromes, the discussion goes beyond the symptoms that constitute the syndrome to include the natural history of the syndrome, the treatment implications, possible genetics, and biological correlates. Dysphoric mood, as a symptom, can be a cardinal feature of the following mood disorders: major depressive disorder, dysthymia, adjustment disorder with depressed mood, cyclothymia, and bipolar disorder. Dysphoric mood can also be a symptom that is seen in many of the other psychiatric disorders affecting children and adolescents.

## History of Depression Studies in Children and Adolescents

It has not always been accepted that children could experience depressive syndromes. The arguments for this were twofold. One set of objections was based on psychoanalytic theory, maintaining that children had not attained the level of psychological development necessary to experience many of the feelings seen in the clinical syndrome of depression as commonly observed in adolescents and adults. The second objection, based on developmental psychology, stated that many of the symptoms used to diagnose clinical depression in adults occur naturally, as transitory phenomena, in children and adolescents. While this may be true about individual symptoms, it is not the case when the cluster of symptoms that make up depressive disorders is observed as a set of symptoms.

The argument that the clinical syndrome of depression in children or adolescents is characterized by a unique set of symptoms that are specific to a developmental phase of childhood or adolescence has been rejected in favor of the idea that the same symptom criteria can be used to diagnose depressive syndromes in children, adolescents, and adults. This was first demonstrated by Puig-Antich (1978), who used the adult criteria and identified a group of children that met all the criteria for major depressive disorder. Proponents of the uniqueness of the depressive syndromes in childhood and adolescence were never able to come up with a coherent set of diagnostic criteria specific to developmental phases, and thus failed to convince the field of the correctness of their view. Rather, what has been accepted is that the core symptoms necessary for making a diagnosis of a depressive disorder in childhood, adolescence, and adulthood are the same. There may, however, be associated features that are specific for different ages and developmental levels. The best example of this is the separation anxiety that arises with the appearance of depressive disorders in some children and that is seen less frequently in adolescents and almost never in adults.

The current system used to diagnose depressive disorders in children, adolescents, and adults, the *Diagnostic and Statistical Manual of Mental Disorders,* Third Edition, Revised (DSM-III-R) (American Psychiatric Association, 1987), gives operationalized diagnostic criteria so that the clinician can make a diagnosis. This system of diagnostic classification is usually referred to as a categorical system based on categories or syndromes that have been clinically derived. The essential or required feature of depressive disorders is a dysphoric mood. The only exception is major depressive disorder, in which the pervasive loss of the ability to experience pleasure, anhedonia, or irritability can be the primary feature of the disorder. The operationalized diagnostic criteria for each depressive disorder give us required features of the disorder and a list of associated symptoms that must also be present in order for the diagnosis to be made. A result of the general acceptance and success of the DSM-III-R classification system has been substantial research on depressive disorders in children and adolescents. Now we can say much more about the associated features, course, predisposing factors, complications, differential diagnosis, and treatment of these disorders than we could in the past.

## Major Depressive Disorder

### Required Symptoms

The most serious depressive disorder in children and adolescents is major depressive disorder (MDD). It is serious because it is the most difficult to treat, and it confers a substantially increased risk for suicide in both male and female adolescents, particularly when accompanied by Conduct Disorder or substance abuse (Brent, Perper, Goldstein et al., 1988; Shaffer, 1988b). The required symptoms of MDD can be a dysphoric mood, pervasive anhedonia, or irritability. In children and adolescents, irritability may mask a dysphoric mood and is considered an equivalent essential symptom. The dysphoric mood should not be caused by another psychiatric disorder or have a physical cause. In fact, anytime a child or adolescent is evaluated for the existence of a mood disorder, his or her medications should be reviewed to determine if some medication is causing the mood symptoms. In young adolescent women, the most common medication causing dysphoric mood and associated symptoms of MDD is birth control pills. Frequently, when birth control pills are discontinued, the depressive symptoms vanish.

The presence of an essential symptom is a necessary condition in order to make a diagnosis of MDD. All DSM-III-R tells us about the persistence and severity of symptoms required for a diagnosis of MDD is that they must exist for at least two weeks and be "relatively persistent, that is they occur for most of the day, nearly every day" (American Psychiatric Association, 1987). The fact is that none of the symptoms of MDD, especially dysphoric mood, or the symptoms of any of the other depressive disorders are constant; they wax and wane. Thus, DSM-III-R leaves no place to draw the line for a threshold. One threshold that has been used in many research studies is the threshold for the presence of dysphoric mood contained in the Kiddie-Schedule for Affective Disorders and Schizophrenia (K-SADS). Puig-Antich and Ryan (1985) judged that three hours of dysphoric mood, at least three times a week, qualified as persistent depressed mood. This threshold has been used for biological studies, family studies, and treatment studies. In children and adolescents, it is frequently easier to elicit the symptom of boredom, rather than anhedonia and loss of interest. All three of these symptoms have been used interchangeably as an essential symptom in MDD but are not considered distinct essential symptoms.

*Associated Symptoms*

The associated symptoms of MDD include appetite changes, changes in sleep patterns, changes in psychomotor activity level, diminished energy or fatigue, feelings of worthlessness or guilt, diminished ability to think or concentrate, and morbid or suicidal thoughts or actions. The appetite changes can lead to either weight gain or weight loss, or, for adolescents, the failure to make expected weight gains. When substantial weight loss occurs in some depressed adolescents, it can be distinguished from the weight loss associated with anorexia nervosa, because there is no disturbance of body image or exaggerated fear of obesity in MDD. Many adolescents with bulimia nervosa have dysphoric moods and enough associated symptoms to qualify for the diagnosis of MDD. This association has had interesting implications in terms of the treatment of bulimia nervosa. The sleep disturbance is manifested by insomnia, hypersomnia, or significant shifts of sleep pattern over the diurnal cycle. Insomnia is initial insomnia (difficulty falling asleep), middle insomnia (waking up in the middle of the night), or terminal insomnia (waking up too early). Hypersomnia is sleep duration beyond the normal length of sleep for the child or adolescent. In adolescents, the sleep disturbance is sometimes manifest as a shift in the diurnal pattern of sleep and, in extreme cases, full phase reversal—that is, sleeping all day and being awake all night.

Symptomatic changes in psychomotor activity level are either agitation or retardation. Psychomotor agitation in children and adolescents is characterized by difficulty sitting still; pacing; hand wringing; pulling or rubbing hair, skin, or clothes; irritability; tantrums; yelling and shouting; and nonstop talking. Psychomotor retardation in children and adolescents is characterized by slower speech, increased speech latency (the time it takes to respond to another person), diminished amount of speech, lower speech tone, and slowed physical movement. The child or adolescent may even spend extended periods of time sitting or standing in one spot without moving or talking. This latter symptom is referred to as depressive stupor. While some children and adolescents display psychomotor agitation or retardation, others have alternating periods of retardation and agitation during the same episode of MDD.

Diminished energy is experienced as fatigue, tiredness, and the need to rest throughout the day. It is important to distinguish tiredness and lack of energy from the fact that most children and adolescents with MDD sleep poorly and complain of nonrestorative sleep. Children with MDD display exaggerated guilt by blaming themselves for events and incidents that are beyond their control or influence. In the psychotic subtype of MDD, the exaggerated guilt can take on delusional proportions. For example, adolescents display their feelings of worthlessness by their inability to correctly assess their abilities. In extreme cases, they may express self-hatred.

Diminished ability to think and concentrate in children and adolescents is typically expressed as increased difficulty with schoolwork for both children and adolescents. Declining school performance is the reason for referral for many children and adolescents with MDD. Many intelligent children and adolescents try to maintain their school grades by working harder in school. At times, the ability to think and concentrate is so impaired that the adolescent will have trouble following conversations or watching television or can appear to be confused.

Morbid thoughts are quite common, particularly, the thought that life is not worth living and that death is preferable. In a smaller number of teens with MDD, the morbid thoughts can evolve to thoughts of suicide, suicide plans, and suicide attempts. In the psychotic subtype, there can be a hallucinated voice telling the adolescent to commit suicide.

It is important to remember that associated symptoms like dysphoric mood wax and wane as well—psychomotor agitation may alternate with psychomotor retardation; diminished appetite may give way to increased appetite. This shifting of symptoms has sometimes fooled a clinician into thinking that a child or adolescent was recovering from an episode of MDD, when all that was occurring was some fluctuation in the character of the symptoms. Recovery from an episode of MDD is marked by sustained resolution of symptoms.

## Diagnostic Features

In order to make a diagnosis of MDD in an adolescent, the presence of five distinct essential or associated symptoms for a two-week period is required. At least one of the symptoms must be an essential symptom. The disturbance cannot have been caused by an organic factor, usually medications, or physical illness. Medications used by adolescents that have been known to produce the symptoms of MDD include birth control pills, anticonvulsants, systemic corticosteroids, neuroleptics, and cocaine. The medical condition most frequently masquerading as depression is hypothyroidism; every child and adolescent suspected of having MDD should be checked for hypothyroidism. Another factor excluding the diagnosis of MDD concerns disturbances caused by a reaction to the loss of a loved one, that is, normal bereavement; however, prolonged bereavement with morbid preoccupations, suicidal thoughts, and marked functional impairment does suggest MDD.

The key question is, How long is prolonged? Weller and colleagues found that 39 percent of bereaved children met criteria for MDD three months after the death of a parent (Weller, Weller, Fristad, et al., 1987). Those children who went on to have a depressive disorder could be predicted on the basis of preexisting psychiatric disorder or a family history of affective disorder. Therefore, it seems reasonable not to diagnose MDD for at least six months in an adolescent who has lost a parent or primary caretaker.

The final exclusion criterion is that schizophrenia or a schizophrenic spectrum disorder not be coexistent. The reason for this exclusion criterion is that the combination of schizophrenia and MDD is given its own diagnostic category, because it behaves differently from a pure mood disorder or pure schizophrenia.

## Nondiagnostic Features

A number of features are associated with MDD. While they do not have diagnostic significance, they can be troublesome to the child or adolescent and should be considered in treatment. The first feature is brooding, or worrying, the inability to get painful preoccupations or thoughts from one's mind. Brooding is distinct from the obsessions found in obsessive-compulsive disorder (OCD), because obsessions refer to stereotypical, repetitive words, ideas, phrases, or images that have meaningless content to the child or adolescent. Brooding, in contrast, refers to repetitious thinking about real or potentially unpleasant circumstances or events, such as an impending exam or a death.

Two other features are hopelessness and helplessness. The adolescent believes that he or she will never recover and can imagine nothing positive about the future. Plans to go to college or to prepare for a vocation are dropped. Relationships may be terminated and friends may be rejected, because everything is so hopeless. These characteristics are not unique to MDD, but it is rare to find an adolescent with MDD who does not express these feelings. Psychosomatic complaints include headaches, stomachaches, chest pains, and both generalized and specific aches and pains. With successful treatment of the MDD, these somatic complaints resolve.

Social withdrawal is more common in children with MDD who find it painful to spend time with peers. Some adolescents with MDD withdraw from peers, others from family, and find that a boyfriend or girlfriend may be the only person who can temporarily lift their mood. Nonsuicidal self-injury may also be seen.

Studies of the occurrence of MDD in prepubertal children have revealed a point prevalence, the percentage of the population that will have the disorder at any given time, from 1.8 to 2.5 percent. The point prevalence of MDD in adolescents is estimated to be three to four times the point prevalence in prepuberty (Fleming & Offord, 1990). It is not clear whether the difference in the occurrence in MDD in children and adolescents is a true age effect or is due to the difficulty in identifying MDD in children. MDD is equally common among prepubertal males and females but becomes more common for girls in adolescence. Studies of various kinds of diagnostic instruments show clearly that adolescent males underreport their symptoms, whereas girls are more forthcoming about their symptoms. This difference in acknowledgment of feelings is a possible explanation for the sex ratio difference between depressed prepubertal children and depressed adolescents (Ambrosini, Metz, Bianchi, Rabinovich, & Undie, 1991).

When symptom frequency and severity have been compared in groups of children and adolescents with MDD, there were no significant differences (Ryan, Puig-Antich, Rabinovich, et al., 1987). Children prior to the onset of puberty, had greater frequency of psychomotor agitation and hallucinations, as well as somatic complaints, separation anxiety, and phobias. Adolescents had greater degrees of anhedonia, hypersomnia, and weight change, together with the associated features of hopelessness and drug and/or alcohol abuse. Suicide attempts were more lethal in adolescents, but the severity of suicidal ideation was identical in children and adolescents. This confirms what many people had claimed for some time: depressed children are as suicidal as depressed adolescents. The explanation for the lower suicide rate among depressed children may be the lack of knowledge about how to kill themselves. One longitudinal study of untreated children with MDD gives us a picture of the natural course of this disorder (Kovacs, Feinberg, Crouse-Novak, et al., 1984a, 1984b). MDD lasts an average of 7.2 months, with 90 percent of the episodes lasting 8 months. Almost all children recovered from an episode of

MDD in 41 months. Seventy percent of these children will develop a second episode, with recurrence occurring within two years for 40 percent of them. Those children with dysthymia will develop their episode more quickly (Kovacs, Feinberg, Crouse-Novak, et al., 1984b). Children with MDD and an additional psychiatric diagnosis show a more prolonged course.

*Subtypes*

There are three subtypes of MDD recognized in DSM-III-R—melancholic, psychotic, and seasonal pattern—having important implications for assessment and treatment. A fourth subtype, atypical, has been identified in the literature.

**Melancholic Subtype.** The melancholic subtype is what most people consider to be the classic form of depression. Its associated features are quality of mood, lack of reactivity, diurnal variation, and pervasive anhedonia. Dysphoric mood is relatively constant; that is, there is no mood response to pleasurable stimuli, or there is a lack of mood reactivity. In addition, there is a daily pattern to the dysphoric mood, in that it is worse in the morning and improves as the day progresses. Dysphoric mood in the melancholic subtype is said to have "quality," meaning that the adolescent recognizes his or her mood as distinct from what he or she experiences with a separation or loss. As with mood in the melancholic subtype, anhedonia is constant and pervasive. In this subtype of MDD, the associated symptoms take particular forms. Typically, insomnia is terminal insomnia. Appetite suppression and weight loss can also occur, as can psychomotor agitation or retardation. The presence of at least one associated feature is a necessary condition, and a total of five associated symptoms and features are sufficient to make a diagnosis of melancholic subtype (American Psychiatric Association, 1987).

**Psychotic Subtype.** Of all the depressive disorders, MDD is the only one with a psychotic subtype. In general, psychotic mood disorders are the most severe form of the disorder, because of the additional difficulties psychosis adds to the treatment of mood disorders. The psychotic subtype of MDD is revealed by the presence of auditory hallucinations or delusions. Hallucinations or delusions must be thematically consistent with the depressive disorder and temporally congruent with the onset of the episode of MDD. For example, the content of the hallucinations and delusions must reflect or be connected to the depressive disorder, and the appearance of the hallucinations or delusions must coincide with the appearance of the depressive symptoms. Hallucinations are perceptions that occur in the absence of identifiable external stimulation. In order to be diagnostic, the hallucination should occur when the adolescent is fully awake, nonfebrile, and not under the influence of some medication or drug. The phenomena most frequently confused with the auditory hallucinations seen in the psychotic subtype of MDD are hypnogogic and hypnopompic hallucinations. Hypnogogic and hypnopompic hallucinations occur when individuals are falling asleep or waking up. Hallucinations should not be confused with illusions, in which an external stimulus is misperceived, or with a normal thought process that is exceptionally vivid. Elaborated fantasies are typical of play in younger children, and they should not be confused with hallucinations. Most children acknowledge that the fantasies are not real, but a few children cling to them. The most commonly experienced elaborated fantasies are imaginary companions.

The hallucinated voice in the psychotic subtype of MDD may make accusations about the child or adolescent having done something terrible or may make deprecating comments. The voice may even tell the child or adolescent to commit suicide. Delusions are convictions or beliefs that are not true and that are not shared with the individual's religious or cultural subgroup. Depressive delusions occur only in adolescents and usually involve wildly exaggerated guilt. Typically, the adolescent feels that he or she has done something so vile that he or she should be punished with death, or the individual may have a nihilistic delusion. The impending catastrophe in the nihilistic delusion is seen as a punishment for whatever the adolescent has done. Needless to say, MDD with psychosis in a child or adolescent is a psychiatric emergency and usually requires hospitalization.

**Seasonal Pattern Subtype.** The recognition that there is a seasonal pattern to the episodes of MDD and bipolar disorder in some adolescents and adults is recent; however, the evidence was apparent for some time. Suicide and psychiatric hospitalization rates show seasonal fluctuations in areas of the world with higher latitudes, where the seasonal fluctuations in light levels is the greatest. The effect of light on neuroendocrine control in humans is actively being studied. Even though the effects of light on the regulation of mood are not fully understood, some individuals with seasonal pattern mood disorders are using phototherapy or light therapy with success.

Diagnostic criteria for identifying a seasonal pattern include the following: a regular temporal relationship between the onset of episodes of MDD and a particular sixty-day period between the beginning of October and the end of November; the remission of episodes tending to occur during a sixty-day period from mid-February to mid-April; at least three episodes of mood disturbance in three separate years demonstrating the appropriate temporal, seasonal relationship, with at least two of the years being consecutive; and seasonal episodes of mood disturbance outnumbering any nonseasonal episodes by more than three to one (American Psychiatric Association, 1987). Seasonal pattern has been difficult to recognize in children, because of the necessity of observing episodes over at least three years. A further point of difficulty in diagnosing seasonal pattern is that many children and adolescents with depressive disorders become more symptomatic with the opening of school each year. The depressive symptoms seen typically in seasonal pattern of MDD include depressed mood, lethargy, difficulty concentrating, episodic bouts of overeating and weight gain, and hypersomnia. There is the associated feature of reverse diurnal variation of mood; that is, the depressed mood worsens as the day progresses. Preliminary evidence suggests that seasonal pattern of mood disorders may share pathophysiological mechanisms with carbohydrate-craving obesity and with premenstrual syndrome (Wurtman & Wurtman, 1989).

**Atypical Subtype.** The atypical subtype occurs not only in MDD but also in dysthymia. In many ways, its symptoms are the reverse of those found in the melancholic subtype. These include hypersomnia and increased appetite with weight gain. Associated features also have this reverse quality when compared with the melancholic subtype. For example, the associated features include mood reactivity (these individuals can be cheered up temporarily when presented with something they like doing), reverse diurnal variation, an absence of quality of mood, and strong sensitivity to rejection or criticism. Extreme fatigue and tiredness are characteristic but not unique to this subtype. Further, the atypical subtype of depression seems to respond to psychopharmacological treatment with only one type of antidepressant, the monoamine oxidase inhibitor family (MAOIs) (Liebowitz, Quitkin, Stewart, McGrath, et al., 1984; 1988). This pattern of response to medication is in contrast to that of the melancholic subtype, which does not respond preferentially to any one type of antidepressant. By symptoms, the atypical subtype appears to be related to seasonal pattern and to the depressive episodes seen in cyclic mood disorders.

*Etiology*

The most potent risk factor for developing a depressive disorder in childhood is having a parent who has suffered from a serious depression, particularly the child's mother. The risk of depression increases and the age of onset falls with greater family loading, early onset of depression in parents, and a family history of either recurrent depressive disorder or bipolar disorder (Ryan & Puig-Antich, 1986). Whether we examine the families of children with depressive disorders or examine the offspring of adults with depressive disorders, mood disorders are clustered in these families. Children with one parent with a mood disorder have double the risk of developing a mood disorder. Children whose parents have both had mood disorders are four times more likely to develop a mood disorder (Weissman, Gershon, Kidd, et al., 1984). While the evidence for the genetic transmission of MDD is accumulating, the method of genetic transmission is not clear. Studies of twins give strong but incomplete support to the idea that MDD is inherited. Monozygotic, or identical, twins are 76 percent concordant for depression when they are raised in the same environment and are 67 percent concordant for depression when raised apart; dizygotic, or fraternal, twins are 19 percent concordant for depression. These statistics suggest that genetic factors predominate in the etiology of MDD; however, they also suggest that nongenetic factors play a role (Tsuang, 1978).

The most potent psychosocial factor associated with MDD is life exits, such as the loss of loved ones through death, divorce, and other kinds of separation. Other psychosocial factors associated with depression are stressful life events, family discord, and physical or sexual abuse. Certain chronic physical illnesses, particularly epilepsy, chronic inflammatory bowel disease, and juvenile diabetes mellitus, predispose adolescents to MDD. It is interesting to note that, in adults, the absence or presence of a psychosocial precipitant has no effect on the symptom picture.

## Conditions Comorbid with Major Depressive Disorder

The psychiatric disorders that most frequently occur with MDD are anxiety disorders. One study reported that 33 percent of the children in the sample had comorbid anxiety disorders (Kovacs, Feinberg, Crouse-Novak, et al., 1984b). Other psychiatric disorders that have significant comorbidity with MDD include conduct disorder and attention-deficit hyperactivity disorder (ADHD). One study of adolescents with MDD describes conduct disorder symptoms (e.g., as stealing or destructive behavior) that start with the appearance of the MDD and resolve with the resolution of the MDD (Puig-Antich, 1982). The author is careful to point out that he believes MDD accounts for only a small portion of the cases of conduct disorder. He makes the point, however, that children and adolescents with conduct disorder should also be evaluated for MDD, because this is the only readily treatable cause of conduct disorder. The comorbidity of ADHD and MDD was found when a group of children and adolescents whose parents had depression were examined for psychiatric disturbance (Orvaschel, Ye, & Walsh-Allis, 1987).

## Biology of Major Depressive Disorder

Because the symptoms of MDD are under both biological and psychological influence, there has always been interest in the biological aspect of depressive disorders. The original hypothesis that depressive disorders represent a disturbance in catecholamines or neurotransmitters in the brain has opened the way so that we now understand that there are a number of biochemical and endocrine abnormalities in people suffering from depressive disorders. The initial evidence of biological MDD for adults has led to curiosity about it in depressed adolescents.

Two types of biological markers occur with physical disorders. The first is referred to as a marker of state. For example, when the individual is in the acute phase of the disorder, the marker is abnormal, and when the disorder resolves, the marker normalizes. Markers of state are of interest because they are helpful in diagnosis. Although to date, clinical interview by an experienced clinician is still the best way to make a diagnosis of a depressive disorder, there are special situations in which an individual cannot cooperate with a clinical interview, in which case a test for a state marker may be a useful aid in diagnosis.

The second type of marker is a marker of trait. This type of biological marker is abnormal independent of the activity of the disorder. Trait markers are of interest because they reveal information about the genetic transmission of disorders.

It has been difficult to learn much about the biological disturbance in MDD in adolescents by trying to study the neurotransmitters in the brain directly. These same neurotransmitters, however, also control the endocrine system, and studying endocrine function in individuals suffering from depressive disorders has been revealing. Abnormalities in the hypothalamic-pituitary-adrenal system, the growth hormone system, the luteinizing hormone system, and the hypothalamic-pituitary-thyroid stimulating hormone system are found in depressed adults. In depressed adults, the hypothalamic-pituitary-adrenal system has been shown to produce increased levels of cortisol, a hormone secreted by the adrenal cortex, and to exhibit a different diurnal pattern of cortisol secretion. This abnormality is the basis for the only marker of state that has been adapted as a diagnostic test, the Dexamethasone Suppression Test (DST) (Carroll, 1972).

**Dexamethasone Suppression Test (DST).** Dexamethasone is a synthetic adrenal hormone that, when administered orally to normal individuals, suppresses the function of the adrenal gland for twenty-four hours. When dexamethasone is given to depressed adults, however, it does not so readily suppress adrenal gland functioning in up to 70 percent of the cases. The degree of adrenal gland suppression is dependent on the severity of the depressive disorder. The DST involves giving dexamethasone and subsequently measuring the amount of cortisol in the blood during the period cortisol should be normally suppressed. In depressed adults, cortisol will be normal or increased; in nondepressed individuals, it will be decreased. When the DST has been used in depressed children, the results have been found to be similar to those of adults (Poznansky, Carroll, Banegas, et al., 1982). When depressed children were studied for cortisol hypersecretion, however, a much lower fraction of cortisol hypersecretors were found than were found in depressed adults. This suggests that some of the hypothalamic-pituitary-adrenal abnormalities seen in MDD may be age-dependent.

**Growth Hormone Abnormalities.** Disturbances in the growth hormone system are interesting because they have produced the only biological abnormality that may turn out to be a marker of trait. Such a marker would be abnormal in a depressed adolescent before, during, and after a depressive episode. The growth hormone system is evaluated by challenging it with various medications that stimulate the secretion of growth hormone. When the growth hormone system in depressed children was evaluated by challenging it with insulin, 50 percent of those children tested undersecreted growth hormone (Puig-Antich, Novachenko, Davies, et al., 1984a). When some of these children, particularly those with the melancholic subtype of MDD, recovered and were drug free, they were retested with insulin and were still found to hyposecrete growth hormone (Puig-Antich, Novachenko, Davies, et al., 1984b).

A second abnormality of growth hormone in some children with depression, both during the acute phase of the illness and on recovery, is overactive secretion during sleep (Puig-Antich, Goetz, Davies, et al., 1984a, 1984b). Again, the persistence of the abnormality on recovery suggests that growth hormone abnormalities could possibly provide a marker of trait. Growth hormone abnormalities have also been found in adolescents with MDD, particularly those who had a suicidal plan or had made a suicide attempt during the episode (Ryan, Puig-Antich, Rabinovich, et al., 1988).

**Sleep Abnormalities.** Sleep symptoms are not just subjective complaints among adolescents with MDD; they have also been documented in the sleep laboratory. The most commonly reported sleep abnormalities among adults with MDD are shortened period before the onset of REM or dream sleep, increased amount of dream sleep, decreased amount of the deeper stages of sleep, and decreased sleep efficiency (the amount of time spent in sleep versus the amount of time spent in bed) (Kupfer, 1976). One research group found that two-thirds of its group of children with MDD reported difficulty falling asleep or persistent middle-of-the-night awakenings. One-half of children with the melancholic subtype of MDD had early morning awakening. Only a minority of children with MDD had hypersomnia (Puig-Antich, Goetz, Davies, et al., 1984a, 1984b).

A second team of researchers found that the group of children with MDD had sleep disturbances, documented in the sleep laboratory, that resembled those of adults (Emslie, Rush, Weinberg et al., 1990). As this latter group were inpatients, they probably had a more severe form of MDD, thus accounting for the difference. Sleep studies of adolescents with MDD show them to have increased nighttime awakenings and decreased sleep efficiency (Goetz, Puig-Antich, Ryan, et al., 1987).

## Dysthymia

Dysthymia is a chronic disorder characterized by a depressed mood and associated symptoms. Dysthymia has a duration of at least a year in adolescents. For a diagnosis, the depressed mood should last much of the day and exist for more days than not. Associated symptoms are appetite disturbance, sleep disturbance, low energy or fatigue, low self-esteem, poor concentration, difficulty making decisions, and feelings of hopelessness (American Psychiatric Association, 1987). During the year of symptoms, no more than two months should be symptom free, and the diagnosis should not be made if an adolescent has MDD symptoms. In fact, some episodes of MDD resolve or end in euthymia; however, some resolve into dysthymia. Individuals whose mood state fluctuates between MDD and dysthymia have been said to suffer from "double depression" (Keller & Shapiro, 1982). Because this is a chronic condition, it may have significant negative effects on the adolescent's functioning at home and at school. Social interactions are frequently impaired.

Distinguishing between MDD and dysthymia can sometimes be difficult, since both disorders share many of the same symptoms. MDD occurs in discrete episodes, whereas dysthymia is a syndrome of chronic, mild depression of long duration. Dysthymia is especially difficult to diagnose in children or adolescents who have suffered from the disorder over the course of their whole lives. Either the symptoms are not recognized, or the symptoms are seen as the adolescent's normal functioning. When dysthymia was studied longitudinally in children, 50 percent of the children recovered after forty-five months. It took eighty-one months before all the children in the study recovered from an episode of dysthymia.

## Adjustment Disorder with Depressed Mood

A final disorder with depressed mood as an essential symptom is adjustment disorder with depressed mood (ADDM). An adjustment disorder is a maladaptive reaction to a readily identified psychosocial stressor. For example, a fifteen-year-old girl becomes sad and withdrawn from all school activities after the death of a close family friend from cancer. In ADDM, the maladaptive reaction is of recent origin, within three months after the appearance of the psychosocial stressor. The maladaptive nature of the reaction is manifest by disturbance in the child or adolescent's functioning at school, home, or both. It has been assumed that adjustment disorders remit after the stressor ceases, but this assumption has been called into question. There is such a wide variability in adolescents' reactions to stressors that it is difficult to generalize. Typical stressors for children and adolescents include family discord, physical abuse, sexual abuse, parental separation, moving, changing schools, birth of a sibling, and illness. No clear-cut relationship exists between the severity of the stressor and the intensity of the reaction.

The predominant symptoms of ADDM are depressed mood, tearfulness, and hopelessness. Children and adolescents with this disorder can be quite distraught and may even have suicidal thoughts and make suicide attempts on occasion. When ADDM was studied longitudinally in children, 50 percent recovered in six months, and all recovered within seventeen months. The probability of a child with ADDM subsequently developing MDD or dysthymia is quite low, in contrast to the number of children with MDD developing dysthymia and vice versa.

## Cyclothymic Disorders

This chapter could have been called "Mood Disorders of Children and Adolescents" as easily as "Depressive Disorders of Children and Adolescents," because whenever we look for, study, or treat depressive disorders, we always find some depressions that are accompanied by states of mania or hypomania.

### Mania and Hypomania

The history of a manic episode or a hypomanic episode changes the diagnosis of MDD to bipolar disorder. A history of a hypomanic episode changes the diagnosis of dysthymia to cyclothymia. The essential symptom of a manic episode is an elevated, irritable, or expansive mood. Associated symptoms are grandiosity, or inflated self-worth; decreased need for sleep; pressured speech; flight of ideas, or feeling that one's thoughts are going too fast, or racing; distractibility; being drawn to unimportant or irrelevant external stimuli; an increase in goal-directed activity, or psychomotor agitation; and excessive involvement in pleasurable activities that have a substantial potential for producing serious consequences. The presence of the essential symptom and three associated symptoms are necessary and sufficient conditions for a diagnosis of a manic episode (American Psychiatric Association, 1987).

Hypomanic episodes are distinguished from manic episodes by not causing serious impairment in functioning. The associated symptoms in hypomanic episodes are similar to the associated symptoms in a manic episode, except that they are less intense and are not accompanied by hallucinations or delusions. Any hallucinations and delusions in a manic episode should be temporally and thematically congruent with the manic episode. Typical delusions in a manic episode would reflect the grandiose, elevated, or expansive nature of the mood state. For example, one seventeen-year-old male in a residential treatment center became convinced that he was going to win an art prize, and he spent day and night constructing a new sculpture for entrance into a competition.

For many years it was believed that manic episodes did not occur before the onset of puberty. Manic episodes and hypomanic episodes are difficult to diagnose in children, because many of the associated symptoms of manic episodes and hypomanic episodes are difficult to distinguish from normal behavioral fluctuations. Fluctuations in activity level, self-concept, sleep requirements, energy level, and judgment occur all the time; however, these characteristics do not fluctuate together as a set in normal children, as they do in a manic episode or a hypomanic episode.

Again, all organic factors must be ruled out before a diagnosis of a manic episode or a hypomanic episode is made. The medications that most commonly induce mania or hypomania are antidepressants and corticosteroids. Manic episodes typically begin suddenly, with symptoms developing over a day or two. There is usually a dramatic shift in sleep pattern, from excess sleep or normal sleep to little or no sleep. The complications of a manic episode in adolescence can be serious and include sexual promiscuity, drug and alcohol abuse, and criminal activities. In children, manic episodes and hypomanic episodes have to be distinguished from attention-deficit hyperactivity disorder (ADHD) states, because all three disorders have excessive activity and restlessness as prominent symptoms; however, the mood in ADHD should be normal, or possibly depressed, and symptoms should be lifelong, in contrast to manic episodes or hypomanic episodes, in which symptoms have a relatively clear-cut onset and represent a departure from previously established mood states.

## Bipolar Disorder

The defining feature of a bipolar disorder is one or more manic episodes accompanied by one or more episodes of MDD. Bipolar disorder is classified as manic, depressed, or mixed, depending on the current mood state. A mixed state occurs when manic and depressive symptoms exist simultaneously or when the mood state is unstable and shifts rapidly from high to low, or vice versa. If there are more than two complete cycles, a cycle is a manic episode followed by an episode of MDD, or the reverse, within one year's time; then the condition is referred to as a bipolar disorder with rapid cycling.

Bipolar disorders with mixed mood states, or rapid cycling, are the most difficult mood disorders to treat, because it is frequently hard to maintain the individual in a stable mood state of any type—manic, depressive, or euthymic. Family studies have shown that bipolar disorder occurs much more frequently in the first-degree relatives of bipolar patients than in the general population. Hypomanic episodes followed by episodes of MDD are considered a variant of bipolar disorder, sometimes referred to as bipolar disorder type 2.

In the case of children and adolescents, cyclothymia occurs when hypomanic episodes are followed by depressive episodes that do not meet the criteria for MDD over a year's duration. The mood state must be either depressive or hypomanic for at least ten months of the year in question. There are some adolescents whose bipolar disorder begins with an episode of

MDD. Predictors of future bipolar disorder in adolescents with MDD include a family history of bipolar disorder, a hypomanic or manic response to antidepressant medication, and psychotic symptoms (Strober & Carlson, 1982).

## Assessment Methods

Assessment and diagnosis of mood disorders require careful examination of the relevant symptoms. Although adequate history taking should include a detailed inventory of symptoms, researchers in the field have developed a number of diagnostic interview instruments that have influenced clinical practice both directly and indirectly. Some clinicians use these diagnostic interview instruments in their practice, while others have used some of the conceptual thinking that went into these instruments' development to modify their clinical examination.

Briefly, there are two types of diagnostic interview instruments: semistructured and structured. In a structured diagnostic interview, questions about symptoms are asked in a fixed, consistent way. Structured diagnostic interview instruments are excellent for identifying symptoms. They are particularly useful in epidemiological studies. Examples include the Diagnostic Interview for Children and Adolescents (DICA) and the Diagnostic Interview Schedule for Children (DISC) (Welner & Reich, 1981; Costello, 1984).

Semistructured diagnostic interview instruments allow the interviewer some latitude in how questions about symptoms are asked. Using these instruments, the interviewer can adapt questions to the adolescent's developmental level.

Semistructured diagnostic interview schedules have more usefulness in clinical studies. Examples of these are the Interview Schedule for Children (ISC) and the Kiddie Schedule for Affective Disorders and Schizophrenia (K-SADS) (Kovacs, 1983; Puig-Antich & Ryan, 1985). Both types of interview schedules are used for youths ages six to eighteen. Although there are children younger than age six who suffer from depressive disorders, there are no standard methods of diagnosis. Only children younger than age six who display prominent, classic symptoms are identified. Unfortunately, others must wait until they are older before we can recognize these disorders.

Both structured and semistructured diagnostic interviews use the same strategy—that is, interviewing both the parent or caretaker and the adolescent. The reason for this approach is that some symptoms are better known to the adolescent, while others are more apparent to the parent. Symptoms better known to the adolescent reflect internal psychological processes and may or may not be shared with others. These include basic mood state, guilt, feelings of worthlessness, hopelessness, difficulties with concentration, hallucinations, delusions, and suicidal thoughts. Parents or caretakers are frequently surprised to find out that their children have suicidal thoughts or hallucinations, because these two symptoms are rarely shared with others, unless the adolescent is explicitly asked.

Symptoms that can be observed by others—external symptoms—can best be reported by parents or caretakers. These include appetite changes, changes in level of psychomotor activity, the ability to experience pleasure, and grandiosity or other symptoms of mania. In younger children, it is only by asking a parent or caretaker that a reliable sense of the time course of symptoms can be obtained. Most children are quite forthcoming about symptoms. Caregivers are helpful when assessing adolescents, however, because teenagers are more likely to conceal information about symptoms. Once the child or adolescent and the parent or caretaker has been interviewed, the two sets of symptom reports are combined to form a complete symptom picture. At times, significant discrepancies exist between the caretaker's report and the adolescent's report. When this situation occurs, the interviewer should meet with all parties to reconcile the differences.

Assessments are made not only for diagnostic purposes but also to track the course of the disorder and determine the efficacy of treatment. An assessment made at a single point in time reveals the current mood state in the case of mood disorders, but it does not reveal whether a disorder is progressing, resolving, or changing characteristics. Continuous monitoring of symptoms is necessary to reveal the complete nature of a mood disorder. The cycling of bipolar disorder or cyclothymia has been mistaken for recovery from a depressed state because the clinician lacked sufficient information about fluctuations in mood states over time.

## Treatment

The treatment of depressive disorders should be organized around the understanding of their etiology. Those disorders which have prominent, troublesome physical symptoms, generally the severe forms of MDD, should be treated simultaneously with psychological and somatic treatments. Those disorders whose manifestations are primarily psychological can successfully be treated with psychotherapy. Producing relief from the physical symptoms of a depressive disorder promotes the psychological treatment.

Treatment must include the adolescent and his or her family. Unless parents are informed about the nature of depressive disorders, they will be unable to understand their children's behavior or to separate symptoms from other behavior. Parents must also provide the environment in which the treatment can succeed. There may be times in the treatment of a severely depressed adolescent when the parent is required to monitor symptoms, as well as both therapeutic and side effects of medication. Finally, since the more severe depressive disorders are recurrent, chronic conditions, parents have to be taught to look for recurrences and prepare their children for living with a chronic psychiatric disorder, albeit one with a good possibility of being controlled.

The first treatment decision is the setting of the treatment. Does this child or adolescent require psychiatric hospitalization, or can he or she successfully be treated in an outpatient setting? Factors indicating the need for psychiatric hospitalization of a child or adolescent with a depressive disorder include suicidal intent, psychosis, rapidly changing mood states, the failure of prior outpatient treatment, and severe irritability with the possibility of violence. Hospitalization may be required only until the clinical situation is stabilized, and not necessarily for the full length of the treatment.

## Antidepressant Medication

The pharmacological treatment of depressive disorders in children and adolescents is confined to the treatment of MDD; table 2 lists antidepressants used to treat children and adolescents. Little or nothing is known about the use of medication to treat dysthymia and ADDM.

Antidepressant medications are grouped by similarity of action. Although three groups of antidepressants have been used to treat children and adolescents successfully, the rate of successful treatment is less than one would expect, based on experience in the treatment of adults. The most frequently used type of antidepressants are called tricyclic antidepressants (TCAs). These work by increasing the number of chemical messages that are sent to the mood regulation centers in the brain. Over time, the brain adjusts the balance between chemical messengers and receptor sites, a readjustment

**Table 2.**
**Antidepressants Used in the Treatment of Depressed Children and Adolescents**

*Tricyclic Antidepressants*

    Imipramine (Tofranil)

    Desipramine (Norpramin)

    Amitriptyline (Elavil)

    Nortriptyline (Pamelor, Aventyl)

*Monoamine Oxidase Inhibitor*

    Phenelzine (Nardil)

    Tranylcypromine (Parnate)

*Selective Serotonin Reuptake Inhibitors*

    Fluoxetine (Prozac)

    Sertraline (Zoloft)

Trade names are in parentheses.

process that takes several weeks to occur. Typically, TCAs take four to six weeks to work, and recent research suggests that some adolescents continue to improve up to ten weeks. A disappearance of symptoms is not the end of the use of antidepressant medication, because premature discontinuation of medication can result in relapse. Six months of treatment with TCAs is recommended.

In controlled studies of children with MDD, roughly 60 percent get symptomatic relief with TCAs. In adolescents, the response rate is somewhat smaller. The major difficulties with TCAs is their lethality, even in small multiples of therapeutic doses. The difference between a therapeutic dose and a lethal dose is not very large. As a result, whenever TCAs are used to treat a child or adolescent with a depressive disorder, the medication must be under the control of a parent or caretaker at all times.

Recently, a series of three deaths were caused by cardiac arrhythmia in children taking TCAs (Bartels, Varley, Mitchell, & Stamm, 1991). Guidelines for cardiac monitoring of TCAs are well established, but undetected cardiac disease remains a problem. A family history of sudden cardiac death should rule out their use. If treatment is not effective, it sometimes can be augmented by lithium. All children and adolescents with MDD, however, and especially those with a history of manic episodes or hypomanic episodes, should be observed carefully for the appearance of manic symptoms. If this should occur, lithium would be added as a mood stabilizer.

Other types of antidepressants are monoamine oxidase inhibitors (MAOIs) and serotonin agents. MAOIs are indicated for adolescents with the atypical subtype of MDD and for cases where TCAs are not effective. Their use is complicated, because certain foods cause hypertensive episodes when coupled with MAOIs. This side effect is managed by placing the adolescent on a diet that restricts those foods which interact with the MAOIs.

The best known of the serotonin agents is fluoxetine (Prozac). As Prozac is a relatively new agent, little is known about the use of Prozac for adolescents.

## Psychotherapy for Depression

Many types of therapies have been developed for treating depressive disorders (Clayton & Barrett, 1983). These different approaches include cognitive therapy, behavior therapy, social skills training, interpersonal psychotherapy, and problem-solving therapy. Outcome studies with adults with depressive disorders show that the various therapies alleviate the symptoms of depression (Beckham & Leber, 1985; Weissman, 1984). These treatments have all been superior to no treatment, but their relative efficacy is unclear.

Several studies have examined the effects of combining psychotherapy and medication. The combination of interpersonal psychotherapy and medication in adults with depressive disorders has been shown to be superior to either treatment alone (Klerman, 1982). In some studies, psychotherapy and medication alleviate different sets of symptoms: whereas psychotherapy influences problems with social functioning, medication improves vegetative signs. Controlled studies of the psychotherapeutic treatment of depressed adolescents are not available. Research with depressed children suggests that even when antidepressant medication works, there are significant residual difficulties in the day-to-day functioning of these children. In one study—the only study of its kind—antidepressant medication improved the way mothers and children interacted with each other when the children were depressed; however, that level of interaction was still below the level of mother-child interaction in normal children (Puig-Antich, et al, 1985).

Psychotherapeutic treatments have an important place in the treatment of depressive disorders in children and adolescents. Available evidence suggests that in the most severe forms of these disorders, medication is not helpful in repairing social functioning in mood-disordered adolescents. In the milder forms of these disorders, vegetative signs are not as prominent as in the severe forms, and the potential benefits of medication seem to be outweighed by its risks. In the milder forms of depressive disorder, psychotherapy would be the initial treatment of choice. Medication could always be added if there were treatment resistance or if significant vegetative symptoms developed.

## Clinical Vignette

The friends of a sixteen-year-old female became concerned because, after final exams, she does not seem very excited about the prospects of planning for the summer. Although she socializes with these friends by accompanying them to the movies and their favorite haunts at the mall, she does not enjoy herself. They also notice that she has trouble following conversations and is preoccupied about whether or not she is a good person. They express their concern to the girl's mother, who arranges for a psychiatric consultation.

During the evaluation, the girl reveals that she has been depressed for at least several months, since she broke up with a boyfriend. She is an honor student; however, her boyfriend performed only marginally academically and also had a drug abuse problem. Her current symptoms include depressed mood, anhedonia, anorexia, psychomotor retardation, impaired concentration, guilt, feelings of worthlessness, initial insomnia, and suicidal ideas.

This attractive, bright adolescent is unable to see herself accurately. She experiences her honor-roll status as accidental and feels that her "ugly" appearance will prevent her from having another boyfriend. Family history reveals that her mother is taking antidepressant medication and that an older sister has been hospitalized for MDD.

Since only suicidal ideas and not a suicide plan or attempt are present, the decision is made to treat the girl as an outpatient. The number of vegetative signs and their intensity suggest that antidepressant medication is indicated. Individual psychotherapy is also arranged, to deal with the girl's low self-esteem. The therapist is suspicious that the depression may be longerstanding than several months, or that this may not be the first episode of MDD, because of the severity of the self-esteem problem.

## Summary

In summary, this chapter attempts to describe the mood disorders of children and adolescents. The clinician's task does not end with treatment planning or referral but should continue with parent education, communication with school authorities, and education of peers, where appropriate. Friends and families of mood-disordered children and adolescents are quite understanding and accepting when they are informed that a child or adolescent suffers from a mood disorder. This explanation makes the social withdrawal of depression or the grandiosity of hypomania understandable and puts it in some context. Ideally, social stigma is minimized as well. When the child or adolescent tries to resume full functioning, recovery should be much easier. Again, many of the mood disorders that strike adolescents are chronic, recurrent disorders. These children will need well-informed parents, teachers, counselors, social workers, psychologists, and psychiatrists to help them make the transition to adulthood as smoothly as possible. Most children and adolescents get significantly better with treatment. Ongoing research in the treatment of mood disorders of children and adolescents promises even more success in the future.

## References

Ambrosini, P., Metz., C., Bianchi, M., Rabinovich, H., & Undie, A. (1991). Concurrent validity of the Beck Depression Inventory in outpatient adolescents. *J. Am. Acad. Child & Adol. Psychiatry, 30,* 51–57.

American Psychiatric Association. (1987). *Diagnostic and statistical manual of mental disorders.* Third Edition, Revised. Washington, DC: American Psychiatric Association.

Bartels, M., Varley, C., Mitchell, J., & Stamm, S. (1991). Pediatric cardiovascular effects of imipramine and desipramine. *Jl Am Acad Ch Adol Psychtr. 30,* 100–103.

Beckham, E. E., & Leber, W. R. (Eds.). (1985). *Handbook of depression: Treatment, assessment, and research.* Homewood, IL: Dorsey.

Brent, D. A., Perper, P. A., Goldstein, C. E., et al. (1988). Risk factors for adolescent suicide: A Comparison of adolescent suicide victims with suicidal inpatients. *Arch. Gen. Psychiat., 45,* 581–587.

Cable, P., Kupfer, D. J., Spiker, D. G., et al. (1980). EEG sleep and clinical characteristics in young primary depressives. *Sleep Res., 9,* 165.

Carroll, B. J. (1972). The hypothalamic-pituitary-adrenal axis in depression. In B. Davies, B. J. Carroll, & R. M. Mowbray (Eds.), *Depressive illness: Some research studies.* Springfield, IL: C. C. Thomas.

Clayton, P., & Barrett, J. E. (Eds.). (1983). *Treatment of depression.* New York: Raven Press.

Costello, A. (1984). *Diagnostic interview schedule for children.* Western Psychiatric Institute & Clinic, Pittsburgh, Pa.

Emslie, G. J., Rush, A. J., Weinberg, W. A., et al. (1990). Children with major depression show reduced rapid eye movement latencies. *J. Am. Acad. Child Adoles. Psychiatr., 47,* 119–124.

Fleming, J. E., & Offord, D. R. (1990). Epidemiology of childhood depressive disorders. *J. Am. Acad. Child & Adol. Psychiatry, 29,* 571–580.

Goetz, R., Puig-Antich, J., Ryan, N. D., et al. (1987). Electroencephalographic sleep of adolescents with major depression and normal controls. *Arch. Gen. Psychiat., 44,* 61–68.

Keller, M., & Shapiro, R. W. (1982). Double depression: Super-position of acute depression on chronic depressive disorders. *Am. J. Psychiatry, 139,* 438–442.

Klerman, G. L., & Schecter, G. (1982). Drugs and psychotherapy. In E. S. Paykel (Ed.), *Handbook of affective orders.* New York: Guilford Press, pp. 329–337.

Kovacs, M. (1983). *Interview schedule for children.* Western Psychiatric Institute and Clinic, Pittsburgh, Pa.

Kovacs, M., Feinberg, T. L., Crouse-Novak, M. A., et al. (1984a). Depressive disorders in childhood—I: A longitudinal prospective study of characteristics and recovery. *Arch. Gen. Psychiatry, 41,* 219–239.

Kovacs, M., Feinberg, T. L., Crouse-Novak, M. A., et al. (1984b). Depressive disorders in childhood—II: A longitudinal study of the risk for subsequent major depression. *Arch. Gen. Psychiatry, 41,* 643–649.

Kupfer, D. J. (1976). Rapid eye movement latency: A psychobiological marker for primary depressive disease. *Biol. Psychiatry, 11,* 159–174.

Liebowitz, M. R., Quitkin, F. M., Stewart, J. W., McGrath, P. J., et al. (1984). Phenelzine versus imipramine in atypical depression: A preliminary report. *Arch. Gen. Psychiatry, 41,* 669–677.

Liebowitz, M. R., Quitkin, F. M., Stewart, J. W., McGrath, P. J., et al. (1988). Antidepressant specificity in atypical depression. *Arch. Gen. Psychiatry, 45,* 129–137.

Orvaschel, J., Ye, W., & Walsh-Allis, G. (Oct. 1987). Comorbidity of ADD and depression in children at risk for affective disorder. Presented at the meeting of the American Academy of Child and Adolescent Psychiatry, Washington, DC.

Poznansky, E. O., Carroll, B. J., Banegas, M. C., et al. (1982). The dexamethasone test in prepubertal depressed children. *Am. J. Psychiatry, 139,* 321–324.

Puig-Antich, J. (1982). Major depression and conduct disorder in prepuberty. *J. Am. Acad. Child Psychiatry, 21,* 118–129.

Puig-Antich, J., Blau, S., Marx, S., et al. (1978). Prepubertal major depressive disorders: Pilot study. *J. Am. Acad. Child Psychiatry, 17,* 695–707.

Puig-Antich, J., Goetz, R., Davies M., et al. (1984a). Growth hormone secretion in prepubertal children with major depression—II: Sleep related plasma concentrations during a depressive episode. *Arch. Gen. Psychiat., 41*, 463–466.

Puig-Antich, J., Goetz, R., Davies M., et al. (1984b). Growth hormone secretion in prepubertal children with major depression—IV: Sleep related plasma concentrations in a drug free, fully recovered clinical state. *Arch. Gen. Psychiat., 41*, 479–483.

Puig-Antich, J., Lukens, E., Davies, M., Goetz, D., Brennan-Auattrock, J., & Todak, G. (1985a). Psychosocial functioning in prepubertal major depressive disorders—I: Interpersonal relationships during the depressive episode. *Arch. Gen. Psychiatr., 42*, 500–507.

Puig-Antich, J., Lukens, E., Davies, M., Goetz, D., Brennan-Auattrock, J., & Todak, G. (1985b). Psychosocial functioning in prepubertal major depressive disorders—II: Interpersonal relationships after sustained recovery from affective episode. *Arch. Gen. Psychiat., 42*, 511–517.

Puig-Antich, J., Novachenko, H., Davies, M., et al. (1984a). Growth hormone secretion in prepubertal children with major depression—I: Final report on response to insulin induced hypoglycemia during a depressive episode. *Arch. Gen. Psychiat., 41*, 453–460.

Puig-Antich, J., Novachenko, H., Davies, M., et al. (1984b). Growth hormone secretion in prepubertal children with major depression—III: Response to insulin induced hypoglycemia after recovery from a depressive episode, and in a drug free state. *Arch. Gen. Psychiat., 41*, 471–475.

Puig-Antich, J., & Ryan, N. D. (1985). Kiddie-Schedule for Affective Disorder and Schizophrenia. (3rd Ed), Western Psychiatric Institute and Clinic, Pittsburgh, Pa.

Ryan, N. H., & Puig-Antich, J. (1986). Affective illness in adolescents. In A. J. Frances & R. E. Hales (Eds.), *American Psychiatric Association Review*, Vol. 5. Washington, DC: American Psychiatric Press.

Ryan, N. D., Puig-Antich, J., Rabinovich, H., et al. (1987). The clinical picture of major depression in children and adolescents. *Arch. Gen. Psychiat., 44*, 854–861.

Ryan, N. D., Puig-Antich, J., Rabinovich, H., et al. (1988). Growth hormone response to desmethylimipramine in depressed and suicidal adolescents. *J. Affective Dis., 15*, 323–337.

Shaffer, D. (1988b). The epidemiology of teen suicide: An examination of risk factors. *J. Clin. Psychiatr., 49*(9), 36–41.

Strober, M., & Carlson, G. (1982). Bipolar illness in adolescents with major depression. *Arch. Gen. Psychiat., 39*, 549–555.

Tsuang, M. T. (1978). Genetic counseling for psychiatric patients and their families. *Am. J. Psychiatry, 135*, 1465–1475.

Weissman, M. M. (1984). The psychological treatment of depression: An update of clinical trials. In J. B. W. Williams & R. Spitzer (Eds.), *Psychotherapy research: Where are we, and where should we go?* New York: Guilford Press, pp. 89–103.

Weissman, M. M., Gershon, E. S., Kidd, K. K., et al. (1984). Psychiatric disorders in the relatives of probands with affective disorders: The Yale-NIMH collaborative family study. *Arch. Gen. Psychiatry, 41*, 13.

Weller, E. B., Weller, R. A., Fristad, M. A., et al. (October, 1987). Depressive symptoms in bereaved prepubertal children. Paper presented at the annual meeting of the American Academy of Child and Adolescent Psychiatry, Washington, DC.

Welner, Z., & Reich, W. (1981). *Diagnostic interview for children and adolescents.* Washington University School of Medicine, St. Louis, Missouri.

Wurtman, R. J., & Wurtman, J. J. (1989). Carbohydrates and depression. *Sci. Amer., 260,* 68–75.

# 6
# Suicide

*Howard S. Sudak*
*Norman B. Rushforth*

## Introduction

*Definitions*

At first glance, defining and classifying various forms of suicidal behavior might seem straightforward. This is hardly the case, however. For practical purposes, most suicidologists define suicidal behavior as conscious, deliberate acts that are self-harmful. Consequently, "completed suicide" indicates death brought about by such behavior and replaces the phrase "successful suicide," since the latter equates apparent failure with success. The term *success* may also connote a romanticization of suicide at the same time that it makes attempters feel unsuccessful. Suicide "attempts" are suicidal behaviors not resulting in death. How should we classify behaviors that do not so neatly fit these categories? What of the hallucinating schizophrenic patient whose voices tell him that if he shoots himself he will prove he is immortal? Is this suicidal behavior? Or what of the demented elderly patient who jumps out of her hospital window believing the building to be on fire? Neither is consciously self-destructive.

What of behavior generally acknowledged as self-harmful but not consciously self-destructive—smoking, substance abuse, high cholesterol diets, anabolic steroids, excessive exposure to ultraviolet rays? Most of these are viewed as representing psychological denial rather than suicide attempts per se, although the heavy smoker who persists, despite repeated heart attacks, certainly approximates the concept of suicide, for example. Such behaviors, along with other risk-taking behaviors like mountain climbing, motorcycle racing, and automobile racing, are sometimes classified as subintentional suicidal behavior. Kreitman (1976), a British psychiatrist, labels all nonfatal, deliberately self-harmful behaviors other than completions as parasuicidal.

Another problem arises when children and adults are compared, since many child psychiatrists and psychologists study suicidal thoughts and wishes in children, in addition to suicidal acts. Most adult psychiatrists focus

189

only on acts, presumably because thoughts and wishes are too ubiquitous to be useful in demarcating a suicidal subgroup.

Classificatory issues also arise when the decedent's intent is ambiguous—for example, a one-car auto accident, or death by hypnotics when the person may have taken additional pills while in a twilight state. Sometimes homicides represent suicides, as in the victim-precipitated homicides described by Wolfgang (1959), whereby a suicidal individual appears to have arranged for his or her own homicide (e.g., two men in a bar argue, and both escalate words to physical blows until one kills the other). Similar problems arise in classifying attempted suicides when individuals deny that their behavior was self-destructive in intent (e.g., "I was carrying a knife and accidentally fell on it"); in such instances, ascertaining the truth can be difficult if not impossible.

Wrist-cutting behavior and its variations pose yet another gray area. Although such acts are self-injurious, it appears that death is not sought. Wrist-cutters also tend to differ diagnostically and demographically from suicide attempters, in that they often experience a dramatic relief from anxiety immediately following cutting themselves. Many of these patients appear to suffer from borderline or other personality disorders, and a significant proportion ultimately make serious suicide attempts (Konicki, 1989).

Another common subclassification attempts to separate "gestures" from true attempts, presumably because the former are trying only to manipulate others to do their bidding via their pseudosuicidal behavior, while the latter either really wish to die or are at least more ambivalent about living. This is not a helpful distinction, however. Attempters range from those who were very intent on dying but miscalculated to those with little if any wish to die. Attempters, regrettably, are often treated cavalierly by health professionals, as though all of them were out only to manipulate their environments; thus, referring to a subgroup as "gestures" not only is pejorative but risks perpetuating a dangerous stereotype.

## Methods of Study

Suicidal behavior can be studied from many vantage points. One may study attempts (and extrapolate to completions) or completions. Since the dead tell fewer tales than the living, many experts feel that the dynamics of suicidal behavior can best be gleaned from studying individuals who have survived serious attempts. Others feel that the populations of those who attempt suicide are so different, diagnostically and demographically, from those who complete it that one can learn virtually nothing of true suicidal motivation from studying attempters.

Another dimension is provided along a macro/micro continuum. One can study attempted or completed suicide in normal groupings of individuals, comparing them with other "normal" groups (e.g., grouping by age, race, sex, religion, nationality, marital status, occupation, periods of birth), or study "pathological" groupings (e.g., diagnostic groups—such as major affective disorder patients versus normal subjects or versus other diagnostic groups). Such epidemiologically oriented studies are on a macro level. On a more micro level, one may try to understand what motivated a single individual to engage in suicidal behavior. Similar matrices can be created within or across other vantage points. The biopsychosocial model makes a wonderful holistic ideal, but it is difficult to investigate and disentangle all three spheres at once, let alone understand their interactions. Biological views can also be macro or micro, and views differ regarding what is most relevant biologically: neurotransmission, endocrine abnormalities, and so on. One may also approach psychological studies at varying depths—for example, looking at conscious, surface motives versus seeking deeper, unconscious ones. Obviously, the investigator's psychological bias or persuasion (psychoanalytic, cognitive-behavioral, interpersonal, etc.) will largely determine what levels appear relevant even within such a micro perspective. A more sociological view may also vary according to the investigator's persuasion, of course.

Data sources or bases also vary. That is, where and what is the source of information—suicide notes? interviews with decedents' families, friends, or therapists? hospital records? diaries or autobiographies (or biographies)? local, national, or international census data? registries of vital information? coroner's office records? obituaries? media accounts? large population surveys, such as the Environment Catchment Area (ECA) studies (Regier et al., 1984)? self-administered versus interviewer-administered questionnaires? open-ended versus closed-ended (multiple-choice type) interviews? Each has its usefulness, and each possesses its own potential for skewing and bias.

Time affords another dimension (and complexity). Retrospective studies are certainly problematic for completers, although psychological autopsies and interviews with families, friends, and therapists can provide important data. For attempters, however, retrospective studies are typical. The infrequency of suicide attempts, let alone completed suicide, makes prospective studies difficult. In order to generate a large enough sample of attempters or completers, one needs a large population to start with. One advantage of prospective studies is that one can make clear predictions and hypotheses and then measure the observed versus expected outcomes. In order to keep the base population studied as small as possible, most prospective studies begin with a study population at greater than average risk, comparing their suicide rates with those of a baseline reference group (e.g., rates in depressed individuals, alcoholics, or homosexuals versus those in "normals"). Since the best predictor we have of future suicide is a past history of suicide attempts, many prospective studies begin with attempters from one subgroup or another as the study population.

## Suicide Trends

Suicide occurs in virtually all cultures. It takes place across most phases of the life cycle but does so at widely different frequencies. In reviewing recent World Health Organization (WHO) statistics, it is noted that there is a broad range in reported suicide rates. Unfortunately, several countries do not provide suicide data. Of the 166 member-states of WHO, data on suicide rates are reported in 1987 for only 71 countries (Diekstra, 1990). From an inspection of the WHO data, it is seen that in general, Latin American and Arabic countries have the lowest suicide rates, in contrast to northern and middle European countries, which tend to have the highest rates. Southern European countries have below-average rates. Rates of countries with populations predominantly consisting of people of European ancestry (Australian, Canada, New Zealand, and the United States) have above-average suicide rates. Asian countries have rates throughout the range of reported values.

Globally, suicide rates have tended to increase over the past quarter-century, with relatively large increases in many northern and central European countries. For the vast majority of countries, suicide rates are higher in males than females for all age-groups; however, for some Latin American and Asian countries, the female suicide rate for the age-group fifteen to twenty-four years old is greater than the male rate for this age-group (Barraclough, 1988).

In 1980, approximately 27,000 deaths were classified as suicide in the United States, making it the tenth leading cause of death. For the age-group fifteen to thirty-four, suicide is the third leading cause of death, following death by unintentional injury and homicide (Baker, O'Neill, & Karpf, 1984). Thus, identification of and treatment for adolescents at risk for suicide are important aspects of mental health screening for teenagers. Suicide is quite rare prior to age fifteen; less than 1 percent of victims are younger than this age. Suicide rates are higher among whites and Native Americans (14 and 13 per 100,000) than in blacks and Asians (both 6 per 100,000); however, the age-specific rates of suicide are markedly different in the four racial groups (see Figure 1). In addition, the age- and sex-specific suicide rates exhibit very different patterns for the two prominent racial groups in the United States— blacks and whites (see Figure 2). The suicide rate is higher in large cities for both blacks and whites, and firearms are the predominant means of death for all race-sex-age groups. This contrasts with nonfatal self-inflicted injuries, for which drug ingestion is the most common means (Baker, O'Neill, & Karpf, 1984).

Since 1960, there has been a considerable increase in suicide rates among young people in the United States, Australia, and most European countries, peaking generally in the late 1970s or early 1980s, with subsequent slow declines, but not to original levels. Over this period, there have been significant declines in suicide rates for older white males in the United States and

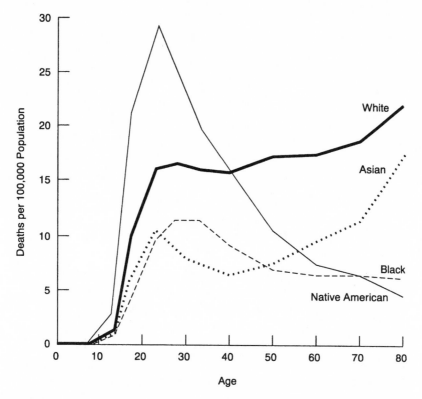

**Figure 1. Death Rates from Suicide by Age and Race, 1980–1986**

Reprinted from *The Injury Fact Book,* Second Edition by Baker, S. P., et al., Oxford University Press, 1992.

in some other Western countries, although these trends began reversing in the 1980s. Accompanying the increasing rates of suicide in the young in the 1960s and 1970s was a rise in attempted suicide, as determined in U.S. and European data from hospital admissions, suicide centers, and emergency rooms (Monk, 1988).

McCall (1991) examined the U.S. annual suicide rates for white male populations, ages fifteen to twenty-four and sixty-five and over, for the period 1946 to 1986, using a time series analysis that related these rates to a number of social variables. For adolescent and young adult white males, these variables were (a) percentage of white children ages eighteen and under in families living below the poverty level, (b) rates of children in families involved in divorces and annulments, (c) percentage of female-headed families with children present, (d) average monthly Aid to Families with Dependent Children payment per recipient in constant dollars, and (e) average annual salary for public school teachers. For the elderly males, the social

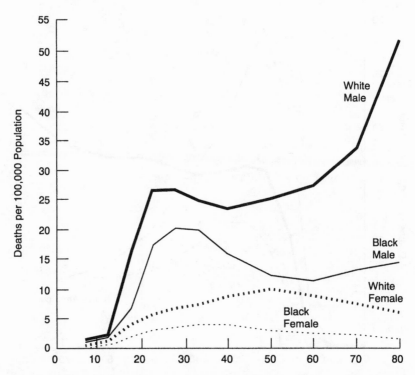

**Figure 2. Death Rates from Suicide by Age, Race, and Sex, 1980–1986**

Reprinted from *The Injury Fact Book,* second Edition by Baker, S. P., et al., Oxford University Press, 1992.

variables assessing their relative welfare were (a) percentage of white elderly living below the poverty level; (b) average Social Security payment for males, (c) percentage of elderly males enrolled in Medicare hospital insurance, and (d) the numbers of medical doctors per 1,000 population. On the basis of these analyses, McCall (1991) concluded that "family dissolution and white children living in poverty are associated with white male adolescent suicide trends, and that societal affluence is associated with white male elderly suicide trends."

Holinger and Offer (1982) found significant positive correlations between adolescent suicide rates and an increase in the proportion of adolescents in the United States, using data over the period 1933 to 1975. They predicted that with decreases in the proportion of adolescents in the U.S. population in the 1980s, there would be a decline in the suicide rates of this age-group—a result borne out by recent data. It has been suggested that increasing stress among the young is a result of their increasing percentage in the total population (Easterlin, 1980). Those born in a baby boom are less able to fulfill their aspirations as young adults, since they compete with larger numbers of adolescents in their birth cohort for a fixed number of educational, job, and housing opportunities. Easterlin (1980) predicted that in this situation, marital stress would be high, resulting in increased divorce rates. Higher levels of psychological stress also would result in more alienation, depression, crime, and suicide.

The importance of cohort effects to explain increases in suicide rates in the young was shown in studies in the early 1980s, using data from Alberta, Canada (Solomon & Hellon, 1980); the United States (Murphy & Wetzel, 1980); and Canada (Reed, Comus, & Last, 1985). A cohort effect was not found, however, for Australian (Goldney & Katsikitis, 1983) or British (Murphy, Lindesay, & Grundy, 1986) suicide rates. In addition, recent age-period-cohort analysis of Canadian (Trovato, 1988) and U.S. (Wasserman, 1987) data found no evidence of a significant cohort effect. In Trovato's analysis (1988), covariates measuring divorce, urbanization, and lack of religious affiliation were included. This analysis demonstrated that while suicide increased during the economic depression and declined during war years (period effects), age exerted the most pronounced effects on death due to suicide. He suggested that cohort effects are of limited value in explaining observed suicide rates, but additional factors such as divorce, gender, and urban living are important factors in understanding temporal variations in suicide rates.

The observed increases in suicide rates in the young are also accompanied by parallel increases in depression and affective disorder, as well as a rise in drug abuse in this age-group (Klerman, 1987). These are significant risk factors for suicide in the young.

## Risk Factors for Suicidal Behavior

### Socioenvironmental Factors

The socioenvironmental basis for suicide was first studied by Durkheim at the end of the 1800s. He emphasized factors leading to stronger societal cohesion, elements that tend to protect a society's members against suicide (Durkheim, 1952). Many subsequent studies have associated self-destructive behavior with social disorganization. Although for adolescents the data base is more limited, findings tend to relate suicide to family and environmental factors. Adolescents who attempt suicide have a greater number of negative life events and fewer personal resources and social supports than those who do not (Hirschfeld & Blumenthal, 1986).

**Family Instability.** Shaffer and Fisher (1981) propose that membership in a cohesive family protects children and adolescents against completed suicide.

In contrast, family dissolution, as with parental divorce or death, tends to increase an adolescent's risk for attempted (Garfinkel, Freese, & Hood, 1982) or completed suicide (Cain, 1972). Research has documented the relationship between divorce and suicide (Trovato, 1986), and the psychological trauma resulting from family disruption has been implicated as a factor contributing to adolescent suicide (Maris, 1985). McAnarney (1979) speculates that loosening or breaking of family ties is an important determinant of differing suicide rates in the young of various societies. On comparing suicide rates in differing geographic areas, she suggests that the prevalence of suicide is related to the degree of geographic mobility and family disruption found in the society—the lowest suicide rate, she noted, was in northern Sudan (1 per 100,000), characterized by closely knit Moslem family units, whereas the highest rate was on a Shoshonean Indian reservation (98 per 100,000) where there was little family stability. One-half of the suicides on the reservation were younger than twenty-five and, when compared with age-matched controls, had suffered more losses by parental desertion and divorce. A higher proportion of the young suicides had more than one caretaker in childhood.

**Marital Status.** Since the early study of Durkheim showing that marriage exerts a protective effect against suicide, investigations of adult populations find an overrepresentation of separated, divorced, and widowed individuals for both completed and attempted suicide (Adam, 1990). Widowers ages twenty to twenty-five have an exceptionally high rate of suicide. Suicide under the age of twenty-four, however, is more prevalent for married than single individuals (Petzel & Cline, 1978). In the United States, the suicide rate for fifteen- to nineteen-year-olds is at least 50 percent higher in married persons, compared with that for unmarried peers of both sexes. Young married women ages fifteen to nineteen have startlingly higher rates of parasuicide than single women of the same ages in Edinburgh, Scotland (Kreitman & Schreiber, 1980). Teenage wives are at greater risk for attempted suicide (Kreitman & Schreiber, 1979). This may be due to greater emotional immaturity and mismatch in teenage married couples (Maris, 1969) and to such marriages being an escape from unsupportive family backgrounds, likely to encounter a host of problems (Hawton, 1986).

**Teenage Pregnancy.** Reviews of the literature suggest a relationship between teenage pregnancy and attempted and completed suicide (Petzel & Cline, 1978). A history of previous pregnancy is found to be more common among girls who make suicide attempts than among girls in the general population (Bernstein, 1972); Holinger and Offer (1981), however, stress that the roles of intervening variables, such as the endocrinological state and psychological stress of the pregnancy, and the underlying psychopathology, which may covary with the risk of both teenage pregnancy and suicidal behavior, have not been assessed.

**Child Abuse and Neglect.** In retrospective studies, adolescents (Deykin, Alpert, & McNamarra, 1985) and children (Rosenthal & Rosenthal, 1984) who had attempted suicide were significantly more likely to have suffered abuse and neglect than nonsuicidal peer groups. Attempters have had more exposure to family violence than controls (Kosky, 1983; Kosky, Sullivan, & Zubrick, 1986) and have more frequently been victims of sexual or physical abuse (Hibbad et al., 1988). A parental history of emotional problems, absence, and abusiveness are found to be significant factors in completed suicides in children and adolescents (Shafii et al., 1985).

**Religious Affiliation.** The association between religious affiliation and suicide was first described in Durkheim's classic study (1952) in which he employed an ecological analysis to test certain causal hypotheses concerning suicide. Although this work has stimulated extensive subsequent research by others, it has been cited as an example of the ecological fallacy (Kleinbaum, Kupper, & Morgenstern, 1982). Durkheim found that, on the average, predominantly Protestant provinces in Western Europe had higher suicide rates than predominantly Catholic provinces, from which he concluded that Protestants are more likely to commit suicide than Catholics. While the conclusion may be correct, it is logically flawed, being an inference on the activities of individuals based on the observations of group behavior. In this case, it may have been primarily Catholics in the predominantly Protestant provinces who took their own lives. The risk of the ecological fallacy is present whenever the composition of each group in the analysis is not homogeneous with respect to the study factor (e.g., most of the provinces in this study had substantial members of Catholics and Protestants). Robinson (1950) has shown that the correlation between two ecological variables based on group data is frequently markedly different from individual correlations within the same populations. While ecological studies are useful for evaluating the impact of intervention programs on the health status of target populations, they have considerable limitations for testing etiological hypotheses. This should be kept in mind, particularly in evaluating the suicide literature, since studies of groups and geographic areas are not uncommon.

More recent ecological studies support Durkheim's initial findings. An inverse relationship has been reported between the suicide rate of U.S. states and the percentage of the state's Catholic population (Templer & Velaber, 1980). Suicide rates per 100,000 population in New York City (Cross & Hirschfeld, 1985) were found to be highest among Protestants and lowest among Catholics, with Jews having an intermediate rate. Catholic countries and Israel tend to have lower suicide rates than countries that are largely Protestant. Specific religious prohibitions against suicide and differing degrees of regulation by various religions of their members' behavior are considered important factors (Monk, 1988), but differential classification and reporting of deaths by suicide in the various societies may also play a role.

In a study of suicides in Sussex, England, church attendees were observed to be fewer in a control group (Sainsbury, 1986). In the United States, since 1960 there has been a major decline in membership in formal religious organizations (Monk, 1988), coupled with a breakdown of family patterns emphasizing religious beliefs and traditional moral values (Schall, 1981). It has been suggested that the decrease in such formal ties may be somewhat responsible for observed increases in the prevalence of suicide in the young (Monk, 1988).

## Socioeconomic Factors

The relationship between socioeconomic factors and suicidal behavior is not clear-cut. For adult populations in England and Wales over the period 1949–53, suicide rates were higher in the professional and high-status occupational class than in the unskilled class, but by 1970–72, rates for the unskilled were considerably higher (Monk, 1988). Occupational mortality rates for males in the United States were last determined for 1950, and at that time laborers and unskilled workers had the highest suicide rates (Guralnich, 1963). A more recent British study comparing the economic status of suicides and matched controls showed that a high risk of suicide characterized both the highest and the lowest socioeconomic classes (Shepherd & Barraclough, 1980).

There are conflicting findings on the socioeconomic status of adolescent suicide attempters. Two investigations found the social-class distributions of young attempters to be similar to those of the general population in the United Kingdom (White, 1974; Hawton et al., 1982). In a Swedish report, by contrast, adolescent suicide was found to be associated with lower social class (Bergstrand & Otto, 1962). In U.S. studies based on emergency room data, it has been suggested that suicidal behavior may be more prevalent among poor and minority youth (Garfinkel, Freese, & Hood, 1982; Kosky, 1983), but a community survey of children found no relationship between socioeconomic status and attempted suicide (Velez & Cohen, 1988). McIntire, Fine, and Fain (1984) point out that pediatricians can expect to encounter self-destructive children and adolescents from families of both high and low socioeconomic status—high-socioeconomic, overdemanding families (McIntire et al., 1977) and low-socioeconomic, socially isolated, disrupted families frequently living in inner-city areas (Rohn et al., 1977).

There is considerable evidence linking socioeconomic conditions and suicidal behavior from ecological analyses and studies of temporal trends in data from the United States and other countries. Causal inferences from such data must, however, be tempered by consideration of the ecological fallacy and possible effects of codependent variables.

Ecological studies of geographic units within cities have generally shown a relationship between adverse socioeconomic conditions and suicidal behavior. High levels of poverty and unemployment, social isolation, poor living conditions, transience, high crime rates, and other indices of social disorganization characterize areas with relatively more suicidal persons (Adam, 1990).

When trends in suicide rates are examined in relationship to socioeconomic events using WHO data for nations reporting mortality statistics, some fairly consistent patterns emerge. For nearly every country, suicide rates increased markedly during the 1930s economic depression and decreased during both world wars (Sainsbury, 1986). When suicide trends for European countries in the 1960s are assessed in relation to social variables, the findings are consistent with those generally found in ecological studies of areas within a country or city (Sainsbury, 1986)—suicide rates are related positively to measures of social disorganization. Successive increases in suicide rates for adolescents and young adults from the mid-1950s to 1980 have been observed in many populations. Such increases may be due to the declining social and economic well-being of these age-groups relative to other segments of the population over this period (Waldron & Eyer, 1975; Rushforth et al., 1984; McCall, 1991).

In reviews of studies comparing cases and controls, Platt (1984) notes that more suicides are found among the unemployed than would be expected, and that higher suicide rates are found in unemployed compared with employed groups. Unemployment, at the time of hospitalization for a suicide attempt, was found to be a risk factor for subsequent completed suicide in a five- to ten-year period (Beck & Steer, 1989). Little information is available on unemployment and suicidal behavior in older teenagers, and the findings are inconsistent. Suicidal ideation has been reported to be more common in unemployed than employed youth (Adam, 1986). The unemployment rate among sixteen- to eighteen-year-old attempters was observed to be in excess of that of other young people (Hawton et al., 1982). In contrast, unemployment has also been found to be associated with a decreased risk of completed suicide (Adam, 1986).

More recent thinking has moved away from considering social and occupational status as static variables in relation to suicidal behavior. Suicide is now considered to be associated more with a loss of social status and downward mobility, often resulting from unemployment, than with social status per se (Adam, 1990).

## Life Events

Adam (1990), in assessing the contemporary understanding of the role of social and environmental factors in suicidal behavior, emphasizes that suicidal behavior, like most psychiatric illnesses and behavioral disorders, "is best understood as being multi-determined and the result of an interaction between the more basic causal factors that render the individual susceptible, and those that interact with this susceptibility to produce symptoms, illness, or symptomatic behavior (p 40)." He stresses that "social and environmental factors may act in three main ways to produce suicidal behavior: 1) As predisposing factors producing a more or less specific vulnerability; 2) as precipitating factors to trigger suicidal activity in previously predisposed individuals whether or not this vulnerability is socially determined or otherwise; or 3) as contributing factors increasing the exposure of the individual in more general ways to other predisposing or precipitating conditions." While this view may provide a useful framework in which to consider risk factors relating to suicidal behavior, the various factors cannot be uniquely classified into one of these three categories. Some classifications may appear somewhat arbitrary, and other factors may operate in differing cases as predisposing, triggering, or contributing elements. Some life events, such as loss of a significant other, particularly when occurring in early childhood, are considered to act as predisposing factors to subsequent suicide. When such events occur later in the life cycle, they are frequently perceived as triggering stimuli.

**Family Characteristics.** In reviewing the literature, Adam (1986) found that since 1940, more than thirty studies have reported the prevalence of broken homes in the backgrounds of suicidal individuals, ranging from a low of 17 percent to a high of 76 percent, levels in general significantly greater than those of controls. He attributes the wide range in these percentages as due to differences in the methodologies of the studies, definitions of "a broken home" (parental deaths, divorce, separations of varying lengths, etc.), and the ages at which the child experiences such events. Ruther (1981) points out that the effects of a parental loss may depend not only on the age and developmental stage of the child but also on the context in which the loss occurs, the presence or absence of alternative parental care, and the long-term consequences to the family of a deterioration in their socioeconomic situation. Farberow (1980) found no significance in the prevalence of "loss" among psychiatric inpatients who had attempted suicide but did find more "family strife" in their backgrounds. Rohn and colleagues (1977) found that unemployment, high residential mobility, and marital disharmony were often found in the families of attempted suicides. In a study of adolescent suicide attempts, Haider (1968) found not only that many of these youths came from broken homes but that frequently the homes of those living with both parents were highly disorganized, characterized by frequent quarrels and problems in the families.

**Parental Psychopathology.** Parental alcoholism, parental mental and physical illness, and parental rejection appear in high frequencies in the families of children and adolescents exhibiting suicidal behavior (Adam, 1986). In a two-year follow-up study of 2,753 diagnoses who had been hospitalized for depression and/or a suicide state, Motto (1970) reported that approximately 5 percent of the group had committed suicide. A family history of alcoholism, depression, and other psychiatric illness was found to be correlated with the likelihood of suicide. There is considerable evidence that both fatal and nonfatal suicidal behavior tends to aggregate within families (Shaffer, 1988). Studies show that the prevalence of previous suicidal behavior is greater in the families of adolescent attempters than in the families of controls (Garfinkel, Freese, & Golombek, 1979). Data from family histories, family studies, and adoption studies indicate that a family history of suicide increases the risk of death by suicide (Klerman, 1987). Shafii and co-workers, in a psychological autopsy study (Shafii, Carrigan, & Whittinghill, 1985), found that variables discriminating between adolescents who committed suicide and matched-pair control subjects included having a sibling or friend who had attempted suicide, isolation (e.g., lack of close friends, loneliness, extreme sensitivity), physical or emotional abusiveness by parents, and having a parent or adult relation who had made suicidal threats, suicidal attempts, or an actual suicide. A family history of suicide was reported by Shaffer (1988) to be a risk factor in both male and female suicides in preliminary data from a larger psychological autopsy study on consecutive adolescent suicides in the New York metropolitan area.

**Previous Suicidal Behavior.** Many young people who kill themselves have previously engaged in suicidal behavior. Shaffer (1974), in an early study, found that 46 percent of suicides between the ages of twelve and fourteen had previously discussed, threatened, or attempted suicide. Forty percent had attempted suicide (Shaffer & Fisher, 1981), a figure similar to that reported in another study, by Cosand and co-workers (Cosand, Bourges, & Kraus, 1982). In a recent psychological autopsy study of 283 suicides of all ages in San Diego County, California, over the period 1981–83, Rich, Young, and Fowler (1986) found that 38 percent of the victims had made a previous suicide attempt. (The usefulness of these data are greatly restricted, however, by the lack of data on appropriate control groups.) A review of fifteen rating scales for the estimation of suicide risk led to the identification of previous suicidal behavior as a major predictor variable. Follow-up studies suggest that roughly 10 percent of young suicide attempters subsequently do kill themselves (Fawcett, 1988). In Shaffer's 1974 psychological autopsy study of risk factors for suicide of teenagers in New York, it was found that, compared with normal controls, male suicides have an 8.6-fold greater approximate odds ratio of prior attempts, while for female suicides this relative risk estimate is 49. In assessing risk factors for adolescents and young adult suicide attempts over recent decades and across various nations and societies, Klerman (1987) lists previous attempts as an important risk factor.

Females in these age-groups are more prone than males to make suicide attempts, such attempts frequently occurring in the context of a recent life event, following frustration in an interpersonal relationship. According to Klerman (1987), "Suicide attempts often occur as compulsive behavior and are seldom associated with a prolonged period of despair, hopelessness, or depression." Risk factors for suicide death in adolescents and youths also include previous suicide attempts. Completed suicide, in contrast to attempted suicide, is more prevalent in males, particularly those characterized by diagnosable psychiatric disorders. These include depression and affective disorders, as well as a family history of early-onset affective disorders (Klerman, 1987).

Fawcett (1988) points out that most data on completed suicide rely on the retrospective accumulation and analysis of information, with the attendant "possibility of memory distortion, inaccurate or incomplete information, and bias through selection attention and knowledge of the suicide (p. 7)." Prospective studies of deaths by suicide are much harder to execute, due to the relatively low frequency of the event and the difficulties in tracking subjects over long periods. In reporting the results of a study of 25 suicides in the initial four-year follow-up of 955 patients with major affective disorders, Fawcett (1988) distinguishes between various time-related risk factors for suicidal deaths. Previous suicide attempts were found to be a risk factor not for short-term suicide (less than one year after hospital discharge) but rather for longer-term suicide (one to five years to suicide).

**Precipitating Crises.** In addition to an array of predisposing factors, a review of the literature points to a variety of problems that may immediately precede suicide in young people. In a study of the characteristics of children and adolescents who committed suicide in England and Wales, Shaffer (1974) reported that interpersonal losses, disciplinary crises, and interpersonal conflicts were frequently precipitants for suicide. Interpersonal conflict and an increased number of stressful and humiliating events were found in other studies to precede adolescent suicide (Brent et al., 1988; Blumenthal & Kupfer, 1988). Compared with nonsuicidal children and adolescents, youthful suicide attempters appear to face more problems in their lives. Most common are problems with parents and siblings, schoolwork, and boyfriends or girlfriends (Hawton et al., 1982). In several studies, a preponderance of young suicide attempters with poor physical health has been reported (Walker, 1980). In addition, medical problems appear to be common in other family members of adolescent suicide attempters (Beck & Steer, 1989). Hawton (1986) suggests that parental physical illness may affect adolescents in two ways: "First, the adolescent may be concerned about the parent's ill-health, especially when the condition is life-threatening. Second, parents with chronic handicaps may not pay sufficient attention to the emotional needs of the children, being more concerned with their own plight, and in particular may be unable to provide support when the adolescent is under stress (p. 81)."

Sometimes the apparent precipitant of a suicide attempt is a cataclysmic event, such as the death of a family member; more frequently, however, the precipitating event appears to be of a relatively trivial nature—possibly the "final straw" superimposed on severe and long-standing problems, pushing the individual over the threshold into suicidal behavior (Hawton, 1986). Studies of adult attempters indicate that they experience many stressful life events during the six-month period before their attempt (Paykel, Prusoff, & Myers, 1975). Similar findings are seen for child and adolescent suicide attempters for a twelve-month period prior to an attempt leading to hospitalization. Attempters had experienced twice as much stress, compared with depressed nonsuicidal and nondepressed psychiatric controls (Cohen-Sandler, Berman, & King, 1982).

Several studies have shown the rate of suicide to be greater among individuals with selected medical illnesses than in the general population—for example, patients with chronic renal disease undergoing dialysis (Abram, Moore, & Westenell, 1976); with Huntington's disease (Schoenfeld et al., 1984); with cancer (Marshall, Burnett, & Brasure, 1983); with AIDS (Marzuk et al., 1988); and with epilepsy, musculoskeletal disorders, and peptic ulcer disease (Whitlock, 1986). As will be discussed later, some of the highest rates of suicide occur in patients who have mental illnesses. While the majority of the evidence for increased risk of suicidal behavior with medical illness is derived from studies on adult populations, there is some evidence that it holds for younger age-groups. Adolescent suicide attempters have rates of current illness 30 to 40 percent greater than age-matched controls (Hawton et al., 1982; Garfinkel, Freese, & Hood, 1982).

## Psychiatric Disorders

Recent research from psychological autopsy studies indicates that affective disorders, conduct disorders, and substance abuse are the most common psychiatric disorders associated with suicidal behavior in the young (Blumenthal & Kupfer, 1988).

Brent and colleagues (1988) found that 63 percent of suicide victims had an affective disorder, with more than one-fifth having a diagnosis of bipolar disorder. Shafii (1986) found that 76 percent of victims had a major affective disorder, or dysthymia, compared with only 28 percent in a control group. Substance abuse has been found either alone or together with affective disorder in more than one-third of young suicides (Brent et al., 1988; Rich et al., 1986; Shafii et al., 1985). In their psychological autopsy study, Shafii and his colleagues find a frequency of substance abuse as high as 70 percent and a similar prevalence of antisocial behavior in young suicides.

Data from an ongoing psychological autopsy study in New York (Shaffer, 1988), indicate that roughly half of the suicides had previous contact with a mental health professional. They had suffered from a range of psychiatric problems, including depression, drug and alcohol abuse, and antisocial behaviors; however, a subgroup with no evidence of antisocial behavior exhibited anxiety, perfectionism, and excessive distress when the routines of their lives were disrupted.

In follow-up studies of adolescent psychiatric patients and/or suicide attempters, the risk of completed suicide was high in patients with bipolar and schizophrenic disorders (Perris & D'Elia, 1986; Welner, Welner, & Fishman, 1979). Otto (1972) found that bipolar and schizophrenic disorder characterized children and adolescents who committed suicide following a previous suicide attempt. In a ten- to fifteen-year prospective study of hospitalized child psychiatry patients, the risk of completed suicide was greatest within the first two years after the attempt (Kuperman, Black, & Burns, 1988). In this study, schizophrenia was found to be a major risk factor for suicide.

Suicide attempts in the young are associated with depressive symptoms (Crumley, 1982). Taylor and Stronsfield (1984) found that depression was more prevalent among adolescent self-poisoners (26%) than among nonsuicidal psychiatric controls (2%). Depression and affective symptoms were common among adolescents and young adults referred to psychiatric units following suicide attempts (Clarkin et al., 1984). Although only a fraction of teenage attempters later commit suicide, follow-up studies show that their suicide rate is considerably higher than that for adolescents in the general population. According to Shaffer (1988, p. 38), "Observed rates range from approximately 9% of a group of male youths admitted to a psychiatric inpatient unit who had been depressed or had made a suicide attempt to less than 1% of youths who were presented at an emergency room after an overdose, but who were not admitted to a psychiatric hospital." Motto (1984) carried out a five- to fifteen-year prospective study of 335 adolescents ages ten to nineteen considered to be at high risk for suicide because of their admission to a hospital due to depression or suicidal behavior. The symptoms of severe depression (psychomotor retardation, difficulty in communicating, hypersomnia, hopelessness, fear of losing one's mind) were significantly associated with subsequent completed suicide. In reviewing other studies of attempted suicide in adolescents, Gammon, John, and Weissman (1986) document the following psychiatric disorders as significant risk factors: affective disorders (major depressive disorder and bipolar disorder), schizophrenia, and severe personality disorders (particularly borderline personality disorder), often with substance abuse. A recent study of over 18,000 adults drawn from five U.S. communities showed that panic disorder and attacks are associated with an increased risk of suicidal ideation and attempts. In the group with panic disorder, the risk of a suicide attempt was increased by the presence of drug abuse and an earlier age of onset of panic (Weissman et al., 1989).

While depressive disorder is a common thread in youthful attempted and completed suicide, the comorbidity of depressive symptoms with antisocial behavior—aggressivity and impulsivity, and/or substance abuse—appears to constitute a major risk factor for suicidal behavior (Blumenthal & Kupfer, 1988).

## Psychological Factors

Poldinger (1981) stresses the importance of the "psychological state" during the emergence of the "acute suicidal episode" leading to suicidal acts. This episode, superimposed on psychiatric illness, is frequently precipitated by psychosocial life events. While depressive symptoms are usually present, hopelessness, despair, pessimism, and helplessness appear to be more important factors in determining suicidal intent.

For some time, hopelessness has been considered one of the major cognitive factors in the suicidal behavior of adults (Beck, Kovacs, & Weissman, 1975). Reviews of more recent studies show it to be a key variable as well in child and adolescent suicide (Brent & Kolko, 1990). Such studies show that the hopelessness is greater in suicidal children and adolescents than in nonsuicidal psychiatric controls; associated with the severity of depression and suicidal ideation; more characteristic of those who construct suicidal plans or attempt suicide; and predictive of repeated suicide attempts. The central role given to hope as a protective factor against suicide is supported by successive studies showing that hopelessness is a stronger predictor than depression of suicidal intent (Adam, 1990).

Children and adolescents with a history of poor coping skills, rigidity of thought processes in response to problems, or impulsive problem-solving styles are at greater risk for suicidal behavior. They also have more interpersonal relationship problems with peers or family members than normal or nonsuicidal psychiatrically disturbed youth do (Brent & Kolko, 1990). Powerlessness and an external locus of control, associated with hopelessness and impulsive behavior, have been observed to be more prevalent among adolescent suicide attempters than in nonsuicidal control groups (Topol & Reznikoff, 1982). Neuringer (1974) has suggested that cognitively rigid individuals, when faced with naturally occurring stresses in life, cannot find alternative solutions. They tend to lapse into helplessness and hopelessness; become more isolated, with fewer social supports; and face increased risk for suicidal behavior.

## Biological Risk Factors

Until relatively recently, studies of suicide have centered on social and psychological factors involved with self-destructive behavior. Historically, biological factors were considered to play little role as causative agents. Asberg, Nordstrom, and Traskma-Bendy (1986) point out that only 5 of a total of 1,267 reports regarded as biological topics were contained in a bibliography of published suicide research covering the period 1958–67. More recent genetic and biochemical studies, however, indicate the importance of biological variables in predisposing a person to commit suicide.

Genetic Factors. As previously noted, a family history of suicide has been reported to be a risk factor for suicidal behavior. Such an association may result from several possible nongenetic mechanisms: early childhood loss of a significant other predisposing to later suicidal activities, increased stress placed on surviving members of the family, identification with and imitation of the family member who killed him- or herself (Blumenthal & Kupfer, 1988). Transmission of genetic factors for suicide, however, may also contribute to the observed familial association in suicidal behavior. This suggestion is supported by epidemiological research, including investigation of familial risk, studies of twins, and adoption studies.

Studies of suicides occurring during a hundred-year period in the Amish in southeastern Pennsylvania suggest possible genetic factors in both the transmission of affective disorders and suicide (Egeland & Sussex, 1985). Almost three-quarters of the twenty-six suicide victims were found to cluster in four family pedigrees, each of which contained a heavy genetic loading for both affective disorder and suicide. Other pedigrees, however, were found with heavy loading for affective disorder but not suicide.

Haberlandt (1967) reported an 18 percent concordance rate for suicide in fifty-one monozygotic twin pairs, in contrast to no dizygotic twins concordant for suicide. Zaw (1981) recorded nine sets of identical twin pairs in which both members died of suicide but no cases in which both fraternal twins did. Juel-Nielson and Videbeck (1970) reported significant numbers of monozygotic twins concordant for suicide, but with concordance rates lower than for depression or schizophrenia.

In an adoption study in Denmark comparing the incidence of suicide in the adoptive and biological relatives of adoptees who killed themselves, the biological relatives had a sixfold higher rate of suicide (Schulsinger et al., 1979). In another adoption study, one comparing suicide in individuals with depressive illness and matched controls, the incidence of suicide was again found to be greater in the biological relatives of adoptees who had killed themselves (Kety, 1986). The adoptee suicide victims with a diagnosis of "affective reaction" had significantly more biological relatives who had committed suicide. This diagnosis entails affective symptoms accompanying a situational crisis—frequently an impulsive suicide attempt. Kety (1986) suggests that a possible genetic factor in suicide may be an inability to control impulsive behavior and that such a genetic factor for impulsivity may be a result of inability to regulate serotonin systems.

Biochemical Factors. Recent biochemical studies indicate disturbances in metabolism of a brain neurotransmitter, serotonin, in suicide victims and violent suicide attempters (Stanley & Mann, 1988). Asberg, Traskman, and

Thoren (1976) were the first to show the association between suicidal behavior and low cerebrospinal fluid levels of the serotonin metabolite 5-hydroxyindoleacetic acid (CSF 5-HIAA). This association was confirmed in subsequent investigations in patients with several psychiatric conditions having an elevated risk for suicide (Mann, 1987). Several of these studies showed that low CSF 5-HIAA levels characterized individuals who had made violent or impulsive suicide attempts (e.g., hanging, shooting, drowning), compared with those whose self-destructive activities were more passive or less violent (e.g., drug overdoses). In addition, low CSF 5-HIAA has been shown to be associated with impulsive violent behavior manifesting as violence directed toward others (Brown, Linnoila, & Goodwin, 1990). Besides CSF 5-HIAA determinations, the measures of serotonin and imipramine binding in the brains of suicide victims and neuroendocrine challenge tests evaluating serotonergic function are generally consistent with a hypothesized relationship between decreased serotonergic functioning and suicidal behavior (Mann, 1987).

It is not clear whether serotonin measures are stable over time and therefore constitute a biochemical trait predictive of suicide. Serotonergic functioning may fluctuate, with lowered levels of CSF indicating an abnormal state, a relatively short-term correlate of a suicidal episode. Nevertheless, it appears to be a promising biological correlate, one that might significantly improve the clinician's ability to assess suicidal risk and ultimately result in improved pharmacological treatment.

## Imitation and Contagion Effects

A series of suicide clusters in teenagers and young adults in recent years increasingly points to the role of imitation and contagion as risk factors for suicidal behavior in the young (Gould, Wallenstein, & Kleinman, 1990). Such cluster suicides, occurring in excessive numbers in close temporal and geographic proximity, have been viewed in light of an infectious disease model. Terms such as "outbreak" of suicides in a community creating an "epidemic" through a "contagion process" among "susceptible hosts" have been used to describe the generation of suicidal clusters. Contagion pathways can occur through direct or indirect knowledge of the initial or index suicide. Direct transmission can occur through contact and friendship with a suicide victim. Indirect transmission may take place through the press or television media coverage of celebrities or even fictional characters. In both, however, a process of imitation and identification of susceptible individuals is the mechanism thought to underlie such contagion.

Suicide clusters are more characteristic of teenage and young adult populations than of individuals of other ages. Anecdotal reports of cluster suicides or suicide attempts include groups of high school and college students (Seiden, 1968; Robbins & Conroy, 1983), young marines (Hankoff, 1961), adolescent and young adult Native Americans (Ward & Fox, 1977), and Micronesian adolescents (Rubenstein, 1983). Such anecdotal reports of clusters are difficult to interpret without comparison groups and statistical analyses. More recent studies, however, have applied more appropriate methodologies. Davidson and co-workers (1989) used a case-control method to investigate two clusters of teenage suicides occurring in Texas between February 1983 and October 1984. In this study, case subjects were no more likely than control subjects to have had (a) direct acquaintance with a person who committed suicide or (b) greater indirect exposure to suicide through the media. They were, however, more likely to have attempted or threatened suicide previously, to have physically damaged themselves, to have been physically violent toward others, and to have known someone closely who died of unintentional injury or homicide. Case subjects were also more likely to have broken up with their girlfriends or boyfriends recently, moved more often, attended more schools, and lived with more parent figures than controls were.

Using statistical techniques adapted for studies to detect disease case interactions, U.S. mortality data for 1978–84 on suicides among adolescents ages fifteen to nineteen were examined. Gould and colleagues (1990) demonstrated significant time-space clustering in this age-group. There was some evidence that teenage clusters were more frequent in more recent time periods. Extending these analyses to other age-groups, they found that suicide clusters were two to four times more common in the fifteen- to nineteen- and the twenty- to twenty-four-year age-group than in all other age-groups (Gould et al., 1990). The magnitude of the clustering effect, however, even with teenagers and young adults, was quite small. The proportion of teenage suicides that occur in clusters was estimated as no greater than 5 percent.

A majority of studies of the impact of nonfictional suicide stories in the mass media on suicidal behavior supports a hypothesis of imitation. This is shown by increases in numbers of suicides and attempted suicides following the appearance of suicide stories in newspapers and television (Barraclough, Shepherd, & Jennings, 1977; Bollen & Phillips, 1982) and by decreases of suicides during periods when newspapers were not published (Motto, 1970). In a study of the effects of televised news or feature stories about suicide over the period 1973–79, Phillips and Carstensen (1986) found that teenage suicides increased more than adult suicides. Suicides increased as much after general information or feature stories about suicide as after news coverage of specific suicides. These investigators, after eliminating various possible explanations, including methodological artifacts, concluded that television stories about suicide trigger additional suicides through a mechanism of imitation. Nevertheless, in an attempted replication and extension of this study, using a longer time period (1973–84), Kessler and colleagues (1988) found no significant association between newscasts about suicide and subsequent teenage suicides.

Studies of the effects of fictional suicide stories on suicide have produced mixed results; some studies find no imitative effects, while others (Gould, 1990) find significant general effects or sex- and age-specific effects.

The studies to date examining the association of media coverage of suicides on suicide rates are limited in that only aggregate data are used. It is not known if the individuals reported as committing suicide actually were exposed to the media coverage. Inferences of imitative behavior by individuals based on population effects run the risk of the ecological fallacy. While clearly more research is needed to resolve some of the discrepancies found in the literature, the overall weight of evidence from media studies appears to support the concept of imitative suicides. Suicides, whether or not they occur in clusters or following media coverage of suicidal behavior, are determined by many risk factors. Nevertheless, suicide clusters among teenagers and young adults have received national attention, and public concern about the issue has increased. This has prompted the Centers for Disease Control (1988) to issue recommendations for community plans for the prevention and containment of suicide clusters.

## Availability and Accessibility of Firearms

Among adolescents and young adults in the United States, firearm suicide rates have increased systematically since 1950, while rates by other methods have shown only small increases, remained stable, or declined. The most substantial rise in firearm suicide rates has occurred primarily since 1970 among males ages fifteen to twenty-four. This corresponds to large increases in the numbers of civilian firearms produced in the United States over this period (Boyd & Moscicki, 1986). In 1982, among those ages fifteen to twenty-four, firearms were used in 64 percent of male and 57 percent of female suicides (Wintemute, et al., 1988). Deaths by firearms are a particularly common method of suicide when the victim is intoxicated (Brent, Perper, & Allman, 1987). The increasing availability of firearms and the use of alcohol among youth may have contributed to the observed increases in suicide rates among the young.

An analysis of regional U.S. suicide rates in the mid-1970s indicated that overall suicide rates and firearm suicide rates were significantly associated with the prevalence of firearms and the prevalence of pistols in households (Markush & Bartolucci, 1984). Lester and Murrell (1980) found an inverse correlation between the strictness of state gun control laws and state suicide rates in the United States, particularly for males. To investigate the possible association between firearm regulations and suicide, Sloan and colleagues (1990) compared the incidence of suicide from 1985 through 1987 in King County, Washington, with that of Vancouver, British Columbia, where firearm regulations are more restrictive. Although overall suicide rates were not found to be significantly different between the two metropolitan areas, the rate of suicide by firearms was higher in King County. The rate of suicide by handguns was almost sixfold greater. The Vancouver area, however, had a 1.5-fold higher rate of suicide by other means. Persons ages fifteen to twenty-four had a higher rate of suicide in King County, due primarily to an almost tenfold higher rate of handgun suicide. Sloan and colleagues (1990) concluded that while restricting access to handguns might reduce the suicide rate in those fifteen to twenty-four years old, it probably would not reduce the overall suicide rate. Older individuals, less compulsive, but with a sustained interest in self-destruction, would be sufficiently determined to switch to another lethal method if denied access to a firearm.

The phenomenon of "method substitution" has been seen in several situations. When domestic gas was detoxified in Basel, Switzerland, and in Australia, the decreased rates of suicide from domestic gas were offset by higher rates of suicide by other methods (Stengel, 1964; Burvill, 1980). Reductions in the numbers of young suicides in Australia by poisoning, attributed to the restriction of sales of sedatives, appear to have decreased suicide rates only for a short time, since total suicide rates soon began to rise again (Goldney & Katsikitis, 1983). The elimination of carbon monoxide from domestic gas in the United Kingdom led to a reduced rate of suicide from gas asphyxiation. The rate of suicide by other means increased among men ages fifteen to thirty-four, whereas for older men and for women the decline in suicide rates from domestic gas was accompanied by declines in total suicide rates (Kreitman, 1976). In the United States, where rates of suicide from domestic gas are much lower, detoxification led to a decrease in suicides by this means but to a rise in male suicide by car exhausts. Finally, in assessing possible effects of gun legislation on suicide rates in Toronto, Ontario, and San Diego, California, Rich and co-workers (1990) found that a decrease in the use of guns by suicidal men following gun control legislation was accompanied by an increase in suicide by leaping. Although these studies deal with aggregate data and thus are susceptible to the ecological fallacy, many of them support a hypothesis of substitution of suicide method. The results of such investigations suggest that reductions in suicide rates from restrictions on lethal methods may be limited and short-term.

The strongest evidence that firearm availability is a risk factor for completed suicide comes from a case-control study carried out by Brent and co-workers (1988). In this investigation, the characteristics of adolescent suicide victims were compared with those of a group at high risk for suicide: suicidal psychiatric inpatients who had either seriously considered suicide or actually attempted it. Firearms were found to be more frequently present in the homes of the completers than in the homes of the suicidal adolescent patients. Suicide by firearms was the manner of death in the majority of victims. The association between firearms and suicide was not confounded by suicidal intent, postsuicidal behavior, psychiatric diagnosis, or family history of psychiatric disorder. Between the households of cases and controls that contained firearms, no differences were found in the numbers of firearms or handguns and whether they were stored loaded or locked up. Brent and colleagues (1988) suggest that clinicians who work with suicidal adolescents should strongly advocate the removal of firearms from the home environment. They conclude that restricting the accessibility of a firearm in the home will not be as effective as its complete removal.

## Conceptual Models of Suicide

It is generally accepted that suicidal behavior is multidetermined. Biological and cultural factors, at least in contemporary Western society, appear to play secondary roles to social determinants in influencing its expression.

Adam (1986) emphasizes the role of a highly disorganized social environment and the psychological internalization of frustrating and disappointing family experiences as predisposing factors to self-destructive behavior. Parental loss through death, divorce, or permanent separation at an earlier age appears to set the stage for later disruptions in personal attachments, with catastrophic consequences. An acute suicidal event is frequently triggered by a crisis in a close interpersonal relationship and a threat of rejection. Self-destructive activities may be viewed in a model that emphasizes failed personal attachments (see Figure 3), wherein the suicidal behavior is "a desperate attempt to maintain relatedness to a vital attachment figure in the face of a threatening situation."

Blumenthal and Kupfer (1988) propose an overlap model of risk factor domains for suicidal behavior (see Figure 4). The domains consist of (a) psychiatric disorder (affective disorders, conduct disorders, and substance abuse); (b) personality traits (aggression, impulsivity, hopelessness, and personality disorders such as borderline personality disorder and antisocial personality disorder), (c) psychosocial factors (social supports, life events, and chronic medical illness), (d) family history and genetics, and (e) neurochemical and biochemical variables. This overlap model of risk factors stresses the interaction of predisposing variables increasing an individual's vulnerability for suicide. Blumenthal and Kupfer (1988) extend this model of multiple risk factor domains to one including protective and precipitating factors in relation to a threshold for suicidal behavior (see Figure 5). In this model, the predisposing risk factors (e.g., family history, biological and genetic vulnerability) interact with social factors (e.g., psychiatric illness, exposure to the suicidal behavior of others, the presence of a humiliating life event, easy access to a method of suicide) to lower the threshold for self-destruction. The presence of protective factors (e.g., strong social supports, treatment for psychiatric and personality disorders) raises the threshold and thus inhibits suicidal behavior. Such protective factors represent the opportunities for intervention and treatment.

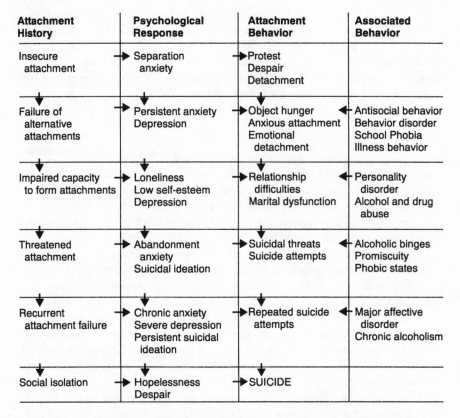

| Attachment History | Psychological Response | Attachment Behavior | Associated Behavior |
|---|---|---|---|
| Insecure attachment | → Separation anxiety | →Protest Despair Detachment | |
| Failure of alternative attachments | → Persistent anxiety Depression | →Object hunger Anxious attachment Emotional detachment | ← Antisocial behavior Behavior disorder School Phobia Illness behavior |
| Impaired capacity to form attachments | → Loneliness Low self-esteem Depression | →Relationship difficulties Marital dysfunction | ← Personality disorder Alcohol and drug abuse |
| Threatened attachment | → Abandonment anxiety Suicidal ideation | →Suicidal threats Suicide attempts | ← Alcoholic binges Promiscuity Phobic states |
| Recurrent attachment failure | → Chronic anxiety Severe depression Persistent suicidal ideation | →Repeated suicide attempts | ← Major affective disorder Chronic alcoholism |
| Social isolation | → Hopelessness Despair | →SUICIDE | |

**Figure 3. Model of Suicide Behavior in a Developmental Context**

From Adam, K. S., Early family influences on suicidal behavior, in psychobiology of suicide behavior, *Annals N.Y. Acad. Sci., 487*:63.

## Specific Screening Techniques

There is no entirely satisfactory method of screening adolescents or any other age population for suicidal tendencies. What methods there are can be divided into psychological tests and rating scales, biochemical correlates, and clinical assessment.

### Psychological Tests and Rating Scales

**General.** Paper-and-pencil tests such as the Minnesota Multiphasic Personality Inventory (MMPI) and other general tests may provide evidence of depression or impulsivity—either of which will correlate with attempted and completed suicide. Patterns indicative of psychotic thinking, borderline per-

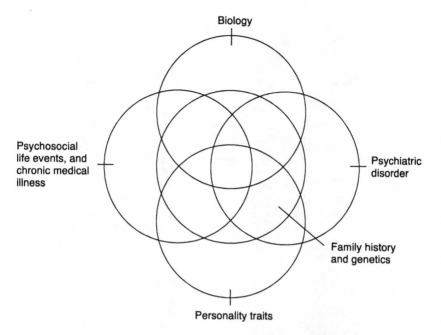

**Figure 4. Overlap Model (Five Domains)**

From Blumenthal, S. J., Kupfer, D. J., Generalizable treatment strategies for suicidal behavior, Annal N.Y. Acad Sci., 487:327–340, 1986.

sonality structure, and so forth, may also serve was warnings. A recent article by Eyman and Eyman (1991) reviews suicide prediction based on MMPIs.

**Projective Tests.** Thematic Apperception Test (TAT), Draw-a-Person Test, and Rorschach may all reveal patterns and themes suggestive of depression. Allusions to death or destruction or even direct references to suicide can sometimes be discerned. Here again evidence of fragmentation or disintegration may be indicative of a psychotic process and should alert one to higher risk. The skilled psychologist may learn a great deal regarding suicidal propensities from such tests. According to the Eymans (Eyman & Eyman, 1991), Rorschach data need to be combined with and corroborated by clinical data for maximum usefulness.

**Rating Scales.** A number of rating scales are suitable for adolescents and may be helpful in screening for suicidal risk. Among the most important are the following:

1. As mentioned earlier, perhaps of all the measures used to predict suicide, the Beck Hopelessness Scale (Steer & Beck, 1988) is the most im-

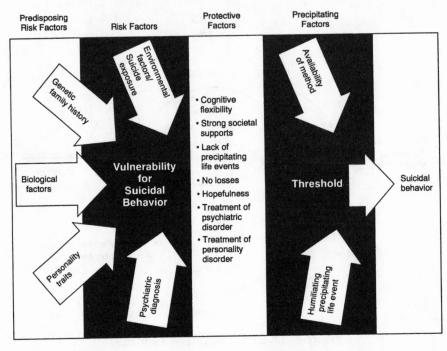

**Figure 5. Threshold Model for Suicidal Behavior**

From Blumenthal, S. J., Kupfer, D. J., Overview of early detection and treatment: strategies for suicidal behavior in young people, J. Youth & Adol., 17(1):1–23, 1988.

portant by virtue of its impressive predictive value—for example, of 165 inpatients, 11 suicided and 10 of these 11 (91%) had hopelessness scales of more than 9. Of 2,174 outpatients, 9 to 10 suicides had hopelessness scales of more than 9. The scale consists of twenty true/false statements to assess the degree of pessimism regarding the future. It has been validated for adolescents. Its shortcoming is that it will identify too many persons as being at high risk to be as useful as it would be were it more specific; that is, far more people will be predicted to be at high risk than will actually later kill themselves, or even make a very serious attempt. On the other hand, only very rarely will someone go on to suicide who has not been shown to have high hopelessness scores (i.e., high sensitivity).

2. The Beck Depression Inventory (Steer & Beck, 1988) is a useful test for measuring depression; however, not all people who are depressed are suicidal, so that this scale is even less specific than the Beck Hopelessness Scale. In this inventory, twenty-one symptoms of depression are rated from 0 to 3. This test has been validated for adolescents.

3. Hopelessness is not always the best predictor, however. In a study comparing 18 completers out of a follow-up of 161 alcohol-abusing attempt-

ers, both the Beck Depression Inventory and the Beck Hopelessness Scales statistically failed to predict significantly, although the Suicide Intent Scale (Beck, Steer, & Trexler, 1989) did. This negative prediction study was of 413 inpatient attempters from the period 1970–75, who were followed until 1982 and evaluated with the three instruments cited. The study showed that only a diagnosis of alcoholism and the "precautions against discovery" subscale of the Suicide Intent Scale significantly predicted suicide (Beck & Steer, 1989).

Other important rating scales are as follows:

1. The Schedule for Affective Disorders and Schizophrenia (SADS), developed by Spitzer and colleagues (Geller, Nelson, & Warham, 1988), was later modified by Puig-Antich and coworkers (1980) to accommodate children. Known as the "Kiddie-SADS" and designed for six- to sixteen-year-olds, the modified scale includes questions about school performance and other questions relevant to children and adolescents. It is administered first to parents and then to the child, and experienced administrators evaluate the responses and make an estimate of the most accurate combined child-parent response. It does inquire about suicidality and may be able to differentiate between those who are more seriously suicidal and those who are not.

2. The Hamilton Depression Scale (Hamilton, 1960), the Brief Psychiatric Rating Scale (BPRS) (Overall & Gorham, 1962), and other survey instruments can all be useful in assessing depression or other mental conditions that correlate with suicidal behavior. The Scale for suicidal ideation, also developed by Beck (Steer & Beck, 1988), is a clinician-administered, nineteen-item scale, scored 0 to 2, that apparently has not yet been validated for use with adolescents. Nonetheless, it adds a useful dimension following a suicide attempt to appraise how intent the attempter was on death from the attempt.

3. The Zung Self-Rating Depression Scale (Zung, 1965) is a self-rating depression scale that was estimated to be 82 percent effective in detecting major depressions in people fifty-three years of age or older in a Canadian report (Canadian Task Force, 1990). This same study rated the Beck Depression Inventory as 86 percent sensitive and 82 percent specific.

## Biochemical Screening

There have been numerous attempts to identify chemical tests (biological markers) that would help identify suicidal individuals. In 1968, Bunney and colleagues identified high adrenocortical steroid levels as indicating an increased risk for completed suicide. Work by Asberg, Traskman, and Thoren (1976), and later others, including Mann (1987) and Linnoila and colleagues (1983) (as mentioned earlier in this chapter in the "Risk Factors" section), have indicated that decreased levels of serotonin (5-HT) or its metabolite (5-hydroxyindoleacetic acid) in selected areas of the brain (in deceased patients) or of cerebrospinal fluid (CSF) (in living patients) correlates with completed or attempted suicide, respectively. This appears particularly true for violent means (jumping, stabbing, gunshot attempts, or completions) and may also hold true for other impulse dyscontrol disorders, as in the case of violent offenders or arsonists (Brown, Ebert, & Goyer, 1982; Virkunen, DeJong, Bartok, & Linnoila, 1989). The latter study revealed lower CSF 5-hydroxyindoleacetic acid levels and lower 3-methoxy, 4-hydroxy-phenylglycol (MHPG) levels in suicide attempters within a total population of fifty-three violent offenders and firesetters. A five-year follow-up of suicide attempts among depressed patients who had earlier cerebrospinal fluid studies (Roy, DeJong, & Linnoila, 1989) revealed that those who made repeated attempts had significantly lower CSF 5-hydroxyindoleacetic acid and homovanillic acid levels than those who did not make such attempts. This was particularly marked for patients who demonstrated melancholia. Interestingly, this marker (this genetic trait?) may be independent of the presence of depression.

## Clinical Screening

**Research on Assessment of Clinical Risk.** Just as epidemiological and biological studies are unreliable for ruling out suicidal risk (e.g., although black females have low completion rates in general, a given black female may be highly suicidal; a patient without abnormal CSF serotonin levels may nonetheless be suicidal), psychological tests and suicide rating scales are also limited when it comes to predicting suicide risk (i.e., none is totally reliable). Thus, the ultimate responsibility rests on the evaluator's own clinical assessment and judgment. A recent large and careful stepwise multiple logistic regression study (Goldstein, Black, Nasrallah, & Winoker, 1991) failed to identify any of the 46 out of 1,906 patients who went on to complete suicide, leading the authors to conclude that it is not possible to predict suicide based on present knowledge and that "the knowledge of health care professionals about their patients remains the best tool for the prediction of suicides." Great attention should be paid to searching for evidence of mental disorder because of the high correlation between psychiatric disorder and suicide attempts and completions. Blumenthal (1989) indicated that over 90 percent of individuals who kill themselves have a psychiatric disorder and that 60 to 80 percent of these 90 percent suffer from major affective illness. Fifteen percent of people suffering from affective disorders will, ultimately, kill themselves. Alcohol use is associated with 25 to 50 percent of suicides, and 5 to 27 percent of all alcoholics kill themselves. For adolescents, 70 percent of the victims suffer from alcohol or substance abuse (see also Shafii et al., 1985), and 95 percent of adolescent suicides had a psychiatric disorder. Seventy-six percent were depressed, compared with 28 percent of controls; 70 percent had antisocial personality disorder; and 50 percent had shown prior attempts. Blumenthal (1989) notes that conduct disorders and borderline personality disorders in adolescents were highly associated with suicidal behavior. Shafii and co-workers (1985) indicated in their study that 15 percent of people with schizophrenia commit suicide.

Brent and colleagues (1988) compared twenty-seven adolescent suicide victims with fifty-six suicidal inpatients, eighteen of whom had suicide thoughts and thirty-eight of whom had made attempts. They found similar rates of affective disorders and family histories of antisocial personality, affective disorder, and suicide. The victims, however, showed proportionally more diagnosis of bipolar illness, more affective disorder with comorbidity, more frequent absence of prior psychiatric treatment, and more guns in the home. These four variables provided an 81 percent correct classification. The authors noted that over 80 percent of the adolescent completers had expressed suicidal threats to others in the week prior to their death. One-half of these 80 percent revealed their intentions to a friend or sibling, however.

Another study (Garfinkel, Freese, & Hood, 1982) reviewed 505 child and adolescent attempters. They were 3 : 1 female to male, and the males were younger. They were more apt to be Protestant than Catholic or Jewish, and their living situation, propensity for substance abuse, current psychiatric illnesses, past treatment, and current medical illnesses differentiated them from matched controls. Their families had more psychiatric illnesses (primarily substance abuse) and a greater family history of suicide, paternal unemployment, and parental substance abuse than their controls.

A Swedish study (Allebeck, Algulander, & Fisher, 1988) followed 50,000 conscripts, of whom 247 killed themselves in the thirteen-year follow-up period. The diagnosis of antisocial personality was the most predictive. In this study none of the individuals with a diagnosis of schizophrenia or affective disorder killed themselves. There was a twofold increase in the risk rate if the conscript was diagnosed as neurotic; a threefold increase, if diagnosed as having a personality disorder. Subtle differences in diagnostic labels may account for some transnational discrepancies, however.

Increased risk rates or relative odds were also reported by Petronis, Samuels, Moscicki, and Anthony (1990). In this study, based on 13,673 Epidemiologic Catchment Area survey (ECA) participants and involving a one- to two-year follow-up period, the authors calculated increased risk rates of 41 for major depression, 19 for alcoholism, 11 for divorce or separation, and 62 for cocaine use.

Another study investigating risk factors within affective disorder subgroups (Fawcett, 1988) showed that in patients with major affective disorders (MADs), the presence of anhedonia, psychic anxiety (demonstrated clinically and also by elevated 17-hydroxycorticosteroids), panic attacks, depressive turmoil, and moderate alcohol abuse predicted suicide within one year of the diagnosis of MAD. This was a group of 1,955 patients with MAD, 25 of whom suicided within four years, 13 during the first year.

The combination of borderline personality disorder and dysthymic disorder appears particularly worrisome in adolescents (Friedman et al., 1984). Disorders of impulse control are also obviously of special concern.

Berman and Jobes (1991) separate risk factors from typological ones. Risk factors have been derived from research studies and include such items as family history of suicide, exposure to suicidal behavior in a friend or sibling, acting-out, substance abuse, and hopelessness. Typological factors are based on diagnostically derived clusters, such as the borderline or schizotypal adolescent with a history of rage, impulsivity, and interpersonal instability, or the rigid perfectionist who becomes depressed when he or she fails to excel.

**The Clinical Interview.** How does one ascertain suicide risk in the clinical interview? The first and most important principle is to ask. Every adolescent who is being evaluated and who shows the slightest hint of depression or is reported to be depressed or possibly depressed by friends, family, or teachers must be asked about suicidal wishes. Even one who shows no obvious signs of depression (e.g., no crying; no feelings of sadness, guilt, or worthlessness; no lack of pleasure in his or her usual interests [anhedonia]) yet does manifest some of the vegetative signs often accompanying depression (e.g., decreased or increased appetite or sleep) should also be asked.

Clinicians, particularly early in their careers, are often concerned that asking about suicide may be perceived as a suggestion or acceptance of the concept by the clinician. On the contrary, failure to ask may appear to the patient to be indifference (or stupidity) on the clinician's part. By the time of adolescence, everyone has thought of suicide—hopefully, only briefly and not very seriously—so that inquiring about it is hardly tantamount to suggesting it.

How does one inquire? Obviously, some tact is required, but it is not difficult to find a relatively graceful opening into the topic. For instance, if the youngster alludes to feelings of depression, one can ask, "Just how bad is it?" "How blue [or sad] do you get?" "Does it get so bad you wish you hadn't been born [or wish you were dead]?" "Have you thought about suicide?" "How would you do it?" "Do you have a gun [or pills, etc.]?" Each question is built on the preceding one and moves from the general to the specific. Are there suicidal thoughts? wishes? Does the adolescent have a plan and, if so, the means to carry out such a plan? It is often helpful to ask if the individual is frightened he or she might really act on the impulse. A negative answer hardly rules out suicide risk, since one may have resolved to do it and not feel frightened, but a positive answer should always alert the clinician that something needs to be done quickly to protect the youngster.

One of the difficulties in evaluating children and adolescents is that they may not manifest their depressions in ways typical of adults. Thus, the clinician dealing with them needs to maintain a high index of suspicion regarding depression and suicide. Indirect evidence of depression is all that one may see: "fatigue" or vague somatic complaints and disinterest in or withdrawal from school or social activities, impaired academic performance, change in developmental patterns or companions, increases or decreases in alcohol or drug use, the giving away of personal belongings, vague talk about death, or hopeless and helpless offhand remarks are all that may be seen. Although the surviving parents of adolescents who kill themselves not uncommonly remark just how normal their child seemed right up to the time of the suicide, close questioning of them often reveals clear evidence of depression or suicidal wishes that they either ignored or denied.

As part of the interview, the clinician should inquire about prior suicidal wishes and attempts (a past history of attempts being the best predictor of subsequent attempts), a past history of depression or mania, and a family history of suicide attempts or completions, depression, and mania. This should be rechecked with the adolescent's parents as well. In addition to questions about suicide, the adolescent should be asked specifically about recent losses (romantic, academic, or athletic losses, etc.) and about substance abuse. The clinician should not assume that romantic losses are necessarily heterosexual and should be aware that the risk of suicide is higher in those with AIDS (Marzuk et al., 1988), and that for some adolescents, fears regarding homosexual impulses may be so terrifying that they precipitate suicidal behavior. The clinician should also be attuned to anticipated losses, not just past ones. Particularly, impending separations from the family (e.g., camp or college) can be the stimulus for suicidal behavior. Emancipation from the family (object removal) is undoubtedly one of the key and most formidable tasks of adolescence. Reminiscences of past losses also serve as a frequent precipitant of depression and suicidal behavior; thus, anniversaries of prior losses (deaths, breakups, etc.) should be looked for. The adolescent may downplay the significance of such anniversaries, but this does not mean that they lack unconscious significance. Moreover, signal birthdays (e.g., turning sixteen or twenty-one) may have special significance for a given adolescent, representing failure, time to separate, and so forth.

## Current Treatment Options

### *Primary, Secondary, and Tertiary Prevention*

Primary prevention is the avoidance of the initiation of disease or injury, secondary prevention is aimed at preventing the extension of disease or injury, and tertiary prevention is intended to prevent death or disability. Thus, primary prevention efforts in suicide are aimed at preventing suicidal acts from occurring at all; examples are interfering with collective or individual conditions that predispose a person to commit suicide, facilitating programs aimed at preventing suicide, and decreasing the availability of agents used for suicide, such as guns and toxic pharmaceutical agents. Secondary prevention may be either treating the immediate attempt to prevent its extension or preventing a subsequent attempt. Tertiary prevention, in suicide, closely resembles secondary prevention in that both are aimed at avoiding recurrences, but tertiary prevention specifically focuses on avoiding death.

## Prevention, Intervention, and Postvention

A more typical continuum for suicidologists is represented by one addressing prevention, intervention, and postvention efforts, and many suicidologists equate these with primary, secondary, and tertiary prevention. The first, prevention, is obvious; the second, intervention, applies to working with an individual who either has already made an attempt or is perceived to be at high risk of doing so; and the third, postvention—ungainly term that it is—refers to efforts made to deal with the painful effects on the loved ones or friends of a suicide decedent. For adolescents in particular, programs in schools to help classmates (and teachers) work through their feelings and to avoid imitation ("copycat" or "contagion") effects are important. The dilemma for school prevention programs (i.e., those conducted prior to any completed suicide) is to avoid romanticizing suicide lest one increase its probability. Gould and Shaffer (1986) and Phillips and Carstenson (1988), in particular, have concluded that news stories and movies may generate suicidal behavior; however, it is unclear how to educate youth yet avoid such a paradoxical result. Klerman (1987) differentiates between local clusters, such as the ones in Westchester, New York, or Plano, Texas, as opposed to national ones seen after television stories. Phillips and Carstenson's (1988) contentions regarding contagion effects were refuted by a study whose authors were from the University of Michigan and the National Broadcasting Corporation (Kessler et al., 1988) but were then reinforced by a report of Gould, Wallenstein, and Davidson (1989) in which these investigators reviewed suicide clusters—here meaning both temporal and geographic clusters—and concluded that the phenomenon is real and primarily seen in youth.

## Pharmacological Approaches

To date, no direct antisuicide pharmacological approaches to suicide exist. There are, however, a number of approaches to the various psychiatric disorders predisposing one to suicide. Suicide is generally viewed as a symptom rather than an illness, and it is the primary illness that is targeted for treatment. Should suicide prove to be an independently inherited predisposition (e.g., related to impulse dyscontrol), we might in the future be able to provide primary treatment (genetic counseling or gene replacement therapy) or secondary treatment (that aimed at correcting or ameliorating the neurotransmitter imbalances caused by the abnormal gene). Perhaps we are already doing that when we treat depression (and its attendant suicidal risk) with serotonin-enhancing drugs.

Many effective chemical agents are available for the treatment of depression, including tricyclic antidepressants such as imipramine (Tofranil-R), amitriptyline (Elavil-R), the more potent but more difficult to use monoamine oxidase inhibitors such as phenelzine (Nardil-R), and newer agents such as fluoxytine (Prozac-R). For severely depressed patients—particularly elderly ones (as opposed to adolescents)—who are refractory to such treatments or whose cardiac status precludes the administration of such medications, electroconvulsive therapy (ECT) remains a rapid, safe, and highly effective therapy.

Effective treatments are also available for many other psychiatric disorders—for example, lithium for mania, major tranquilizers or neuroleptics for schizophrenia, and stimulants for hyperactivity and attention deficit disorder. There are no very satisfactory treatments for personality disorders, including borderline personality disorder, or disorders of impulse control; all of the above-mentioned pharmaceutical approaches have been tried with varying success. Another illness reported as having an intimate connection with suicide, especially in adults, is panic disorder (Weissman et al., 1989). In patients with panic disorder, suicidal ideation and attempts were reported as 2.62 times more likely than in patients with other psychiatric disorders, and panic attacks were 18 times more likely to occur in these patients than in normal controls. Fortunately, there are effective drugs to treat panic disorders, among them minor tranquilizers such as the benzodiazepines (e.g., Librium-R, Valium-R) and alprazolam (Xanax-R); tricyclic antidepressants have also been reported to be effective.

## Inpatient versus Ambulatory Treatment

An acutely suicidal youngster may require hospitalization to provide the secure environment required to help him or her from self-harm. Indeed, even if the adolescent refuses such treatment, if there appears to be sufficient risk of self-harm, hospitalization against his or her wishes may be necessary and justified. If the patient is younger than a given state's age of consent, the matter is facilitated, since parents may be able to sign the youngster into the hospital without court involvement. The adolescent who resists may feel relieved to be under surveillance despite protestations to the contrary. If an adolescent ward is available, it is preferable to a mixed-age unit, but any unit is better than none (when one is indicated). In the hospital one can examine precipitating factors, family dynamics, and the like, and perhaps begin the pharmacotherapy and/or psychotherapy that will continue postdischarge. Over the past few years, there have been instances where it appeared that adolescents were unnecessarily admitted to hospitals, using their allegedly high suicide risk as the pretext, when it may have been that the need to fill empty hospital beds with paying patients was a key motivation. Such machinations are obviously to be deplored, and hopefully more careful utilization review will decrease such abuses. It is equally obvious that an unnecessary hospitalization will be detrimental to an adolescent's self-image (but a necessary hospitalization may be essential to having any self-image at all).

## Individual, Group, and Family Approaches

Which approach indeed? and which persuasion—Freudian? Gestalt? neo-Freudian? T-groups? supportive? explorative? How can one know which to select—and are specific approaches more useful than others for a given patient or problem?

It would be wonderful to have answers to these questions, but we don't. We have strong evidence, employing meta-analyses, that psychotherapy is more effective than placebo (Smith & Glass, 1977; Steinbrueck et al., 1983) and good evidence that psychotherapy or cognitive/interpersonal therapy, when coupled with antidepressant pharmacotherapy, is more effective than pharmacotherapy alone (Weissman, 1973), but we know little more than that. The decisions usually are made according to the biases of the referring middle person or the referred-to therapist. Primary care physicians are often the front-line treaters, and when they feel the need for more specialized expertise, they refer directly either to therapists or to a therapist who will do his or her own triaging and then make a referral for therapy. Such referrals are more likely to be made on the basis of how one was trained (or received therapy oneself) and whom one knows and trusts, rather than according to some logical pattern or algorithm. Economic factors may also play a large role, since practical considerations may outweigh other factors.

Some general principles may, however, be useful. Psychotic adolescents should probably not be in deep-insight therapy. They are already having trouble keeping the lid on their impulses and feelings, and insight-oriented therapy can be further unsettling to them. Thus, medication and supportive therapy are likely to be more useful. It is often felt that young adolescent girls will do better with a female or an older male therapist, since they will have difficulty handling the feelings of excitement that might ensue with a young male therapist. This is probably true, but the competency of the therapist represents an even more overriding concern. Family problems would appear to be best treated in a family context, but this is true only if one has a family capable of such work. Sometimes a family (or parent) is so disordered that it is preferable to work with an adolescent individually to help him or her see how pathological the family is, in order to help the adolescent achieve emancipation. Heterogeneous insight-oriented groups are more interesting for therapists than homogeneous ones (mixed-diagnoses, mixed-sex, etc.) but can be too stimulating for the youngster. Depressed individuals may not do as well in groups as in individual therapy (though this is more anecdotally than scientifically verified); similarly, those with certain personality disorders may do better in groups than in individual therapy (a premise also based on anecdotal evidence). It appears important to allow the adolescent to ventilate feelings and to demonstrate that the therapist cares about what happens. It is necessary that the therapist be available by phone and that, if the adolescent is being treated on an outpatient basis, the therapist carefully evaluate the extent of family support and the family's capability of surveillance. Obviously, lethal objects should be made less accessible to the adolescent. The therapist needs to be aware of his or her countertransference feelings with such anxiety-producing patients and assess his or her own needs to be a rescuer. There are times when therapists have to rescue, but hopefully, at some opportune moment they can confront the issue with their patients. Alertness to missed appointments is necessary, and many therapists believe that a no-suicide "pact" or "contract" is an essential ingredient in working with such adolescents.

A comparable problem to the group versus individual and the "which kind of therapy" dilemmas is the "which discipline" one. Should the therapist be a psychiatrist, psychologist, social worker, nurse practitioner, pastoral counselor, and so on? Again, if the adolescent is psychotic or needs medication, the answer is relatively simple: a psychiatrist will need to be involved, even if he or she isn't the one performing the psychotherapy. Beyond that, it's not at all clear, and again, the biases of the referrer may be the primary determinants. Economic factors may also need to be considered, since therapists' fees appear to be in direct proportion with their years of training. A crude correlation between the depth of the therapy desired and the therapist's discipline may also be inferred, with psychiatrists and psychologists doing more intensive and deeper therapy and social workers or nurses doing less explorative and more supportive therapy. Although religious beliefs and affiliations are often quite helpful to many individuals, including depressed ones, having a minister as the primary therapist for an acutely suicidal adolescent may be inadvisable.

### Effectiveness of Crisis Hotlines and Suicide Prevention Centers

Clearly, crisis hotlines and suicide prevention centers (SPCs) can be effective ways to route troubled people into the mental health system (Hendin, 1982). What appears to be in question is whether their callers are truly suicidal or represent primarily those who are highly ambivalent about suicide and, in the absence of such a service, probably would not kill themselves or would make only mildly to moderately lethal attempts. Numerous studies have failed to show differences between comparable communities with and without SPCs (e.g., Shaffer et al., 1990). This is not to say that SPCs are not useful (since it is useful to assist disturbed individuals to receive help)—only that SPCs may not be effective in decreasing the suicide rate. Perhaps calling them "crisis centers" or "crisis services" might be more accurate. Shaffer and colleagues (1988) also feel that school programs are of little use in preventing suicide.

## Summary

Of all the psychosocial risks for adolescents that confront the mental health worker, it is clear that suicide (and homicide) is the most frightening. It is equally clear that there are no simple answers to such a complex phenomenon.

Suicidal behavior is multifactorial and multidetermined. No known single agent, by itself, has ever been revealed to be responsible in the absence of other factors. In other words, genetic loading does not result in 100 percent concordance in identical twins for suicide; incredibly terrible environmental circumstances may appear to lead to one individual's suicide but to no such action by others exposed to virtually identical events; severe depressive disorders may lead one person to suicide but not another; and so on. Predispositions, vulnerability, nurture effects, societal influences, and as-yet-unknown factors all converge to create a mosaic of influences that are never identical across individuals.

Consequently, the screening of individuals for suicidal behavior remains as problematic as should be inferred from the above paragraph. This becomes compounded by the fact that suicide is a relatively infrequent event and is therefore harder to predict and harder to study. Worse yet, much of the past research on suicide etiology and detection has been of poor quality—lacking adequate controls or appropriate statistical techniques. Many such studies are contradictory or confusing in other ways. Studying only one factor at a time, without adequately controlling for others, has led to much misinformation. Fortunately, more recent studies in this nascent computer age have employed more sophisticated methodology (e.g., logistic regression analyses, better control of variables) that will help us assign weights to factors such as those cited above and will help us understand how these factors interact.

We do not yet have biochemical markers that will predict suicide with sufficient precision to warrant employing them as screening devices; they lack both specificity and sensitivity. Some current psychological tests, however, do appear to have sufficient sensitivity, but regrettably, they lack the specificity to be satisfactory screening agents. Hopelessness scales provide the best example—high hopelessness scores will come very close to correctly predicting which pool of individuals will harm themselves—but the pool so identified as "at risk" is much larger than the number of individuals within it who do go on to harm themselves. Conversely, only rarely will individuals whose low hopelessness score has resulted in their being placed in a different pool go on to harm themselves.

Thus, we are left with the conclusion that the clinician must remain just that—a clinician, one who evaluates suicidal risk based on as much of the total clinical picture as he or she can discern. Knowing the risk factors dependent on the patient's age, race, sex, religion, ethnicity, social circumstances, economic factors, and so forth should increase the therapist's concern when they indicate greater risk, but these factors are less important than the patient's diagnosis, current mental state, and affect; his or her stated intent regarding suicide; the means available; family or other emotional support; history of losses; coexistent personality disorder; abuse of drugs or alcohol; past and family history of suicide and depression; impulsivity; sexual preference; and so on. Psychological tests are valuable adjuncts in assessing suicidal risks in many cases, yet the ultimate responsibility remains the clinician's, and his or her best estimate of risk must be through the total clinical assessment of the adolescent. Allowing ample interview time for the youngster to talk, employing open-ended questions, and interviewing parents or others should enable the therapist to decide whom to hospitalize and whom to initially treat on an ambulatory basis. Working with the adolescent, building trust, judiciously using psychoactive medications when they appear indicated, and keeping a high index of suspicion that the patient may, after all, require hospitalization should enable the clinician to safely and productively work with patients from this rewarding and frustrating age group.

## References

Abram, H. S., Moor, G. L., & Westenell, F. B. (1976). Suicidal behavior in chronic dialysis patients. *American Journal of Psychiatry, 127,* 119–124.

Adam, K. S. (1986). Early family influences on suicidal behavior. In J. J. Mann, & M. Stanley (Eds.), *Psychobiology of suicidal behavior,* Annals of the New York Academy of Sciences, *487,* 63–76.

Adam, K. S. (1990). Environmental, psychosocial, and psychoanalytic aspects of suicidal behavior. In S. J. Blumenthal & D. J. Kupfer (Eds.), *Suicide over the life cycle: Risk factors, assessment, and treatment* (pp. 39–96). Washington, DC: American Psychiatric Press, Inc.

Allebeck, P., Allgulander, C., & Fisher, L. (1988). Role of personality and deviant behavior. *British Medical Journal, 297,* 176–178.

Asberg, M., Nordstrom, P., and Traskma-Bendy, L. (1986). Biological factors in suicide. In A. Roy (Ed.), *Suicide.* Baltimore, MD: Williams & Williams.

Asberg, M., Traskman, L., & Thoren, P. (1976). Five-hydroxyindoleacetic acid in the cerebrospinal fluid: A biochemical suicide predictor? *Archives of General Psychiatry, 33,* 1193–1197.

Baker, S. P., O'Neill, B., & Karpf, R. S. (1984). *The injury fact book*. Lexington, MA: D. C. Heath and Co.

Barraclough, B. (1988). International variation in the suicide rate of 15–24 year olds. *Society of Psychiatric & Epidemiology, 23*, 75–84.

Barraclough, B., Shepherd, D., & Jennings, C. (1977). Do newspaper reports of coroner's inquests invite people to commit suicide? *British Journal of Psychiatry, 131*, 528–532.

Beck, A. T., Kovacs, M., & Weissman, A. (1975). Hopelessness and suicidal behavior: An overview. *Journal of the American Medical Association, 234*, 1146–1149.

Beck, A. T., & Steer, R. A. (1989). Clinical predictors of eventual suicide: A 5 to 10 year prospective study of suicide attempters. *Journal of Affective Disorders, 17*, 203–209.

Beck, A. T., Steer, R. A., & Trexler, L. D. (1989). Alcohol abuse and eventual suicide: A 5 to 10 year prospective study of alcohol-abusing suicide attempters. *Journal of Studies on Alcohol, 50*(3), 202–209.

Bergstrand, C. G., & Otto, V. (1962). Suicidal attempts in adolescence and childhood. *Acta Paediatrics, 51*, 17–26.

Berman, A. L., & Jobes, D. A. (1991). *Adolescent suicide: Assessment and intervention*. Washington, DC: American Psychological Association.

Bernstein, D. M. (1972). The distressed adolescent—pregnancy versus suicide. In Morris (Ed.), *Psychosomatic medicine in obstetrics and gynecology*. Basel, Switzerland: Karger.

Blumenthal, S. (1989). Suicide: A guide to risk factors, assessment, and treatment of suicide patients. *Medical Clinics of North America, 72*(4), 937–971.

Blumenthal, S. J., & Kupfer, D. J. (1988). Overview of early detection and treatment strategies for suicidal behavior in young people. *Journal of Youth and Adolescence, 17*, 1–23.

Bollen, K. A., & Phillips, D. P. (1982). Imitative suicides: A national study of the effects of television news stories. *American Social Review, 47*, 802–809.

Boyd, J. H., & Moscicki, E. K. (1986). Firearms and youth suicide. *American Journal of Public Health, 76*, 1240–1242.

Brent, D. A., & Kolko, D. J. (1990). The assessment and treatment of children and adolescents at risk for suicide. In S. J. Blumenthal & D. J. Kupfer (Eds.), *Suicide over the life cycle: Risk factors, assessment, and treatment of suicidal patients*. Washington, DC: American Psychiatric Press.

Brent, D. A., Perper, J. A., & Allman, C. J. (1987). Alcohol, firearms, and suicide among youth: Temporal trends in Allegheny County, Pennsylvania, 1960 to 1983. *Journal of the American Medical Association, 257*, 3369–3372.

Brent, D. A., Perper, J. A., Goldstein, C. E., Coco, D. J., Allen, M. J., Allman, C. J., & Zelenik, J. P. (1988). Risk factors for adolescent suicide: A comparison of adolescent suicide victims with suicidal inpatients. *Archives of General Psychiatry, 45*, 581–588.

Brown, G. L., Ebert, M. H., & Goyer, P. (1982). Aggression, suicide, and serotonin: Relationships to cerebrospinal fluid amine metabolites. *American Journal of Psychiatry, 139*, 741–764.

Brown, G. L., Linnoila, M., & Goodwin, F. K. (1990). Clinical assessment of human aggression and impulsivity in relationship to biochemical measures. In H. M.

Von Praag, R. Plutchik, & A. Apter (Eds.), *Violence & suicidality: Perspectives in clinical and psychobiological research.* New York: Brunner/Mazel.

Bunney, W. E., Fawcett, J. A., Davis, J. M., & Gifford, S. (1968). Further evaluation of urinary 17-hydroxycorticosteroids in suicidal patients. *Archives of General Psychiatry, 21,* 138–150.

Burvill, P. W. (1980). Changing patterns of suicide in Australia, 1910–1977. *Acta Psychiatrica Scandinavia, 62,* 258–268.

Cain, A. (Ed.). (1972). *Survivors of suicide.* Springfield, IL: Charles C. Thomas Co.

Canadian Task Force on Periodic Health Examinations, 1990 Update. (1990). 2. Early detection of depression and prevention of suicide. *Canadian Medical Association Journal, 142*(11), 1233–1238.

Centers for Disease Control, Division of Injury, Epidemiology, and Control. (1988). CDC recommendations for a community plan for the prevention and containment of suicide clusters. *Morbidity and Mortality Weekly Reports, 37,* 5–6; 1–12.

Clarkin, J. F., Friedman, R. C., Hurt, S. W., Com, R., & Aronoff, M. (1984). Affective and character pathology of suicidal adolescents and young adult inpatients. *Journal of Clinical Psychiatry, 45,* 19–22.

Cohen-Sandler, R., Berman, A. L., & King, R. A. (1982). Life stress and symptomology determinants of suicidal behavior in children. *Journal of the American Academy of Child Psychiatry, 21,* 178–186.

Cosand, B. J., Bourges, L. B., & Kraus, J. F. (1982). Suicide among adolescents in Sacramento County, California, 1950–1979. *Adolescence, 17,* 917–930.

Cross, C. K., & Hirschfeld, R. M. A. (1985). Epidemiology of disorders in adulthood: Suicide. In R. Michels, J. Covenar, & H. K. H. Brodie (Eds.), *Psychiatry* (Vol. 3) (pp. 1–15). Philadelphia, PA: J. B. Supply.

Crumley, F. E. (1982). The adolescent suicide attempt: A cardinal symptom of a serious psychiatric disorder. *American Journal of Psychotherapy, 36,* 158–165.

Davidson, L. E., Rosenberg, M. D., Mercy, J. A., Franklin, J., & Simmons, J. (1989). An epidemiological study of risk factors on two teenage suicide clusters. *Journal of the American Medical Association, 262,* 2687–2692.

Deykin, E. Y., Alpert, J. J., & McNamarra, J. J. (1985). A pilot study of the effect of exposure to child abuse or neglect on adolescent suicidal behavior. *American Journal of Psychiatry, 142,* 1299–1303.

Diekstra, R. F. W. (1990). An international perspective on the epidemiology and prevention of suicide. In S. J. Blumenthal & D. J. Kupfer (Eds.), *Suicide over the life cycle: Risk factors, assessment, and treatment of suicidal patients.* Washington, DC: American Psychiatric Press, Inc.

Durkheim, E. (1952). *Suicide: A study in sociology.* New York: Free Press. (Translated by J. A. Spaulding & G. Simpson from *Le suicide,* Paris, 1897).

Easterlin, R. (1980). *Birth and fortune: The Impact of numbers on personal welfare.* New York: Basic Books.

Egeland, J. A., & Sussex, J. N. (1985). Suicide and family loading for affective disorders. *Journal of the American Medical Association, 254,* 915–918.

Eyman, J. R., & Eyman, S. K. (1991). Personality assessment in suicide prediction. *Suicide and Life-Threatening Behavior, 21*(1), 37–55.

Farberow, N. (1980). Personality patterns of suicidal mental hospital patients. *Genetics & Psychological Monographs, 42,* 3–79.

Fawcett, J. (1988). Predictors of early suicide: Identification and appropriate interventions. *Journal of Clinical Psychiatry, 49*(10), 7–8.

Friedman, R. C., Corn, R., Aronoff, M. S., et al. (1984). The seriously suicidal adolescents: Affective and character pathology in hospitalized adolescents. In H. S. Sudak, A. B. Ford, & N. B. Rushforth (Eds.), *Suicide in the young.* Littleton, MA: Wright PSG.

Gammon, G. D., John, K., & Weissman, M. M. (1986). Adolescent suicide: Epidemiology, research, & prevention. *Advances in Adolescent Mental Health 1* (Part B), 91–117.

Garfinkel, B. D., Froese, A., & Golombek, A. (1979). Suicidal behavior in a pediatric population. In: *Proceedings of the 10th International Congress for Suicide Prevention & Crisis Intervention* (pp. 305–312).

Garfinkel, B., Froese, A., & Hood, J. (1982). Suicide attempts in children and adolescents. *American Journal of Psychiatry, 139*(10), 1257–1261.

Geller, A. B., Nelson, K., & Warham, J. (1988). Research assessment of depression and suicidal behavior using Kiddie-SADS. In: *Advances in Adolescent Mental Health 3* (pp. 209–218). London, England: Jai Press, Ltd.

Goldney, R. D., & Katsikites, M. (1983). Cohort analysis of suicide rates in Australia. *Archives of General Psychiatry, 40,* 71–76.

Goldstein, R. B., Black, W. W., Nasrallah, A., & Winoker, G. (1991). The prediction of suicide. *Archives of General Psychiatry, 48,* 418–422.

Gould, M., Wallenstein, S., & Davidson, L. (1989). Suicide clusters: A critical review. *Suicide and Life-Threatening Behavior, 19*(1, Chap. 2), 17–29.

Gould, M. S. (1990). Suicide clusters and media exposure. In S. J. Blumenthal & D. J. Kupfer (Eds.), *Suicide over the life cycle: Risk factors, assessment, and treatment of suicidal patients.* Washington, DC: American Psychiatric Press, Inc.

Gould, M. S., & Shaffer, D. (1986). The impact of suicide in television movies. *New England Journal of Medicine, 315,* 690–694.

Gould, M. S., Wallenstein, S., & Kleinman, M. H. (1990). Time-space clustering of teenage suicide. *American Journal of Epidemiology, 131,* 71–78.

Gould, M. S., Wallenstein, S., Kleinman, M. H., O'Carroll, P., & Mercy, J. (1990). Suicide clusters: An examination of age-specific effects. *American Journal of Public Health, 80,* 211–212.

Guralnich, L. (1963). *Mortality by occupation and cause of death among men 20 to 64 years of age: U.S. 1950.* Washington, DC: HEW Vital Statistics, Special Report No. 53.

Haberlandt, W. (1967). Aportacion a la genetica del suicidio. *Folio Clinics International, 17,* 319–322.

Haider, I. (1968). Suicidal attempts in children and adolescents. *British Journal of Psychiatry, 14,* 1133–1134.

Hamilton, M. (1960). A rating scale for depression. *Journal of Neurology, Neurosurgery, and Psychiatry, 23,* 56.

Hankoff, L. D. (1961). An epidemic of attempted suicide. *Comprehensive Psychiatry, 2,* 294–298.

Hawton, K. (1986). *Suicide and attempted suicide among children and adolescents.* Beverly Hills, CA: Sage Publications.

Hawton, K., O'Grady, J., Osborn, M., & Cole, D. (1982). Adolescents who take overdoses: Their characteristics, problems, and contacts with helping agencies. *British Journal of Psychiatry, 140,* 118–123.

Hendin, H. (1982). *Suicide in America,* New York, NY: W. W. Norton.

Hibbad, R. A., Brack, C. J., Rauchs, S., & Orr, D. P. (1988). Abuse, feelings, and health behaviors in a student population. *American Journal of Diseases of Children, 142,* 326–330.

Hirschfeld, R., & Blumenthal, S. (1986). Personality, life events, and other psychosocial factors in adolescent depression and suicide: A review. In G. Klerman (Ed.), *Suicide among adolescents and young adults.* Washington, DC: American Psychiatric Press.

Holinger, P. C., & Offer, D. (1981). Prediction on suicide and adolescence. In R. Simmons (Ed.). *Research in Community and Mental Health* (Vol. 2). (pp. 139–157). Greenwich, CT: JAI Press.

Holinger, P. C., & Offer, D. (1982). Prediction of adolescent suicide. *American Journal of Psychiatry, 136,* 1144–1147.

Juel-Nielson, N., & Videbeck, T. (1970). A twin study of suicide. *Acta Genetica Medical Gemellology, 19,* 307–310.

Kessler, R. C., Downey, G., Milavsky, J. R., & Stipp, H. (1988). Clustering of teenage suicides after television news stories about suicide: A reconstruction. *American Journal of Psychiatry, 145,* 1379–1383.

Kety, S. S. (1986). Genetic factors in suicide. In A. Roy (Ed.), *Suicide.* Baltimore, MD: Williams & Wilkins.

Kleinbaum, D. G., Kupper, L. L., & Morgenstern, T. (1982). *Epidemiologic Research.* Belmont, CA: Lifetime Learning Publications.

Klerman, G. L. (1987). Clinical epidemiology of suicide. *Journal of Clinical Psychiatry, 48* (Suppl. 12), 33–38.

Konicki, P. E. (1989). Rationale for clinical trials of opiate antagonists in treating patients with personality disorders and self-injurious behavior. *Psychopharmacology Bulletin, 25,* 556–563.

Kosky, R. (1983). Childhood suicidal behavior. *Journal of Child Psychology and Psychiatry, 24,* 457–468.

Kosky, R., Sullivan, S., & Zubrick, S. (1986). Symptomatic depression and suicidal ideation: A comparative study with 628 children. *Journal of Nervous Disorders, 174,* 523–528.

Kreitman, N. (1976a). The coal gas story: United Kingdom suicide rates, 1960–1971. *British Journal of Preventive Social Medicine, 30,* 86–93.

Kreitman, N. (1976b). Age and parasuicide ("attempted suicide"). *Psychological Medicine, 6,* 113–121.

Kreitman, N., & Schreiber, M. (1979). Parasuicide in young Edinburgh women, 1968–1975. *Psychological Medicine, 9,* 469–479.

Kreitman, N., & Schreiber, M. (1980). Parasuicide in young Edinburgh women: 1968–75. In R. Farmer & S. Hirsch (Eds.), *The suicide syndrome* (pp. 54–72). London: Crown Helm Ltd.

Kuperman, S., Black, C. W., & Burns, T. L. (1988). Excess suicide among formerly hospitalized child psychiatry patients. *Journal of Clinical Psychiatry, 49,* 88–93.

Lester, D., & Murrell, M. E. (1980). Influence of gun control laws on suicidal behavior. *American Journal of Psychiatry, 137,* 121–122.

Linnoila, M., Virkunnen, M., Scheinin, M., Nuutila, A., Rimon, R., & Goodwin,

F. K. (1983). How low cerebrospinal fluid 5-hydroxyindoleacetic acid concentration differentiates impulsive from non-impulsive violent behavior. *Life Sciences, 33,* 2609–2614.

Mann, J. J. (1987). Psychobiological predictors of suicide. *Journal of Clinical Psychiatry, 48* (Suppl. 12), 39–43.

Maris, R. (1969). *Social factors in urban suicide.* Homewood, IL: Dorsey Press.

Maris, R. (1985). The adolescent suicide problem. *Suicide and Life Threatening Behavior, 15,* 91–109.

Markush, R. E., & Bartolucci, A. A. (1984). Firearms and suicides in the United States. *American Journal of Public Health, 74,* 123–127.

Marshall, J. R., Burnett, W., & Brasure, J. (1983). On precipitating factors: Cancer as a cause of suicide. *Suicide & Life Threatening Behavior, 13,* 15–27.

Marzuk, P. M., Tierney, H., Tradiff, K., Gross, E. M., Morgan, E. B., Hsu, M., & Mann, J. J. (1988). Increased risk of suicide in persons with AIDS. *Journal of the American Medical Association, 259*(9), 1333–1337.

McAnarney, E. R. (1979). Adolescent and young adult suicide in the United States: A reflection of societal arrest? *Adolescence, 14,* 765–774.

McCall, P. L. (1991). Adolescent and elderly white male suicide trends: Evidence of changing well-being? *Journal of Gerontology* (Social Sciences), *46:* 343–51.

McIntire, M. S., Angle, C. R., Wikoff, R. L., & Schlicht, M. L. (1977). Recurrent adolescent suicidal behavior. *Pediatrics, 60,* 605–608.

McIntire, M. D., Fine, P., & Fain, P. R. (1984). Early indicators of self-destructive behaviors in children and adolescents: Primary detection by the pediatrician. In H. S. Sudak, A. B. Ford, & N. B. Rushforth (Eds.), *Suicide in the young* (pp. 259–270). Littleton, MA: John Wright PSG, Inc.

Monk, M. (1988). Suicide. In J. M. Last (Ed.), *Public health and preventive medicine,* 12th edition (pp. 1385–1397). Norwalk, CT: Appleton-Century-Crofts.

Motto, J. A. (1970). Newspaper influence on suicide. *Archives of General Psychiatry, 23,* 143–148.

Motto, J. A. (1984). Suicide in male adolescents. In H. S. Sudak, A. B. Ford, & N. B. Rushforth (Eds.), *Suicide in the young* (pp. 227–244). Littleton, MA: John Wright PSG, Inc.

Murphy, E., Lindesay, J., & Grundy, E. (1986). Sixty years of suicide in England and Wales: A cohort study. *Archives of General Psychiatry, 43,* 969–976.

Murphy, G. E., & Wetzel, R. D. (1980). Suicide risk by birth cohort in the United States, 1949 to 1974. *Archives of General Psychiatry, 37,* 517–523.

Neuringer, C. (1974). *Psychological assessment of suicidal risk.* Springfield, IL: Charles C. Thomas.

Otto, V. (1972). Suicidal acts by children and adolescents. *Acta Psychiatrica Scandinavia,* Suppl. 233, 7–120.

Overall, J. E., & Gorham, D. R. (1962). The Brief Psychiatric Rating Scale. *Psychological Reports, 10,* 99.

Paykel, E. S., Prusoff, B. A., & Myers, J. K. (1975). Suicide attempts and recent life events: A controlled comparison. *Archives of General Psychiatry, 32,* 327–333.

Perris, C., & D'Elia, G. (1986). A study of bipolar (manic-depressive) and unipolar recurrent depressive psychoses. X: Mortality, suicide, and life cycles. *Acta Psychiatrica Scandinavia, 42,* (Suppl), 172–183.

Petronis, K. R., Samuels, J. F., Moscicki, E., & Anthony, J. C. (1990). An epidemiologic investigation of potential risk factors for suicide attempts. *Society of Psychiatry & Psychiatric Epidemiology, 25,* 193–199.

Petzel, S. V., & Cline, D. W. (1978). Adolescent suicide: Epidemiological and biological aspects. *Adolescent Psychiatry, 6,* 239–266.

Phillips, D. P., & Carstensen, L. L. (1986). Clustering of teenage suicides after television news stories about suicide. *New England Journal of Medicine, 315,* 685–689.

Phillips, D. P., & Carstensen, L. L. (1988). The effect of suicide stories on various geographic groups, 1968–85. *Suicide and Life-Threatening Behavior, 18*(1, Chap. 10), 100–114.

Platt, S. (1984). Unemployment and suicidal behavior—A review of the literature. *Social Sciences and Medicine, 19,* 93–115.

Poldinger, W. J. (1981). Suicide and attempted suicide in the elderly. *Crisis: International Journal of Suicide and Crisis Studies, 2,* 117–121.

Puig-Antich, J., Orvaschel, J., Tabrize, M. A. (1980). The Schedule for Affective Disorders and Schizophrenia for School-Age Children—Epidemiologic Version (Kiddie-SADS-E), ed. 3. New York: New York Psychiatric Institute and Yale University School of Medicine.

Reed, J., Camus, J., & Last, J. M. (1985). Suicide in Canada: Birth-cohort analysis. *Canadian Journal of Public Health, 76,* 43–47.

Regier, D. A., Myers, J. K., Kramer, M., Robins, L. N., Blazer, D. G., Hough, R. L., Eaton, W. W., & Locke, B. Z. (1984). The NIMH environmental catchment area program: Historical context, major objectives, and study population characteristics. *Archives of General Psychiatry, 41,* 934–941.

Rich, C. L., Young, D., & Fowler, R. C. (1986). San Diego suicide study. I: Young versus old subjects. *Archives of General Psychiatry, 43,* 577–582.

Rich, C. L., Young, J. G., Fowler, R. C., Wagern, J., & Black, N.A. (1990). Guns and suicide: Possible effects of some specific legislation. *American Journal of Psychiatry, 167,* 362–366.

Robbins, D., & Conroy, R. C. (1983). A cluster of adolescent suicide attempts: Is suicide contagious? *Journal of Adolescent Health Care, 3,* 253–255.

Robinson, W. S. (1950). Ecological correlations and the behavior of individuals. *American Socialist Review, 15,* 351–357.

Rohn, R. D., Sarles, R. M., Kenney, T. J., et al. (1977). Adolescents who attempt suicide. *Pediatrics, 60,* 636–638.

Rosenthal, A., & Rosenthal, S. (1984). Suicidal behavior by preschool children. *American Journal of Psychiatry, 11,* 520–524.

Roy, A., DeJong, J., & Linnoila, M. (1989). Cerebrospinal fluid monoamine metabolites and suicidal behavior in depressed patients. *Archives of General Psychiatry, 46,* 609–612.

Rubenstein, D. H. (1983). Epidemic suicide among Micronesian adolescents. *Social Science and Medicine, 17,* 657–665.

Rushforth, N. B., Ford, A. B., Sudak, H. S., et al. (1984). Increasing suicide rates in adolescents and young adults in an urban community (1958–1982): Tests of hypotheses from national data. In H. S. Sudak, A. B. Ford, & N. B. Rushforth (Eds.), *Suicide in the young* (pp. 45–68). Littleton, MA: John Wright PSG, Inc.

Ruther, M. (1981). *Maternal deprivation reassessed.* (2nd ed.). Harmondsworth, England: Penguin Books.

Sainsbury, P. (1986). The epidemiology of suicide. In A. Roy (Ed.), *Suicide* (pp. 17–40). Baltimore, MD: Williams & Wilkins.

Schall, M. (1981). *Limits: A search for new values.* New York: C. N. Potter.

Schoenfeld, M., Myers, R. H., Cupples, L. H., Burkman, B., Sax, D. S., & Clark, E. (1984). Increased rate of suicide among patients with Huntington's disease. *Journal of Neurological Neurosurgery & Psychiatry, 47,* 1283–1287.

Schulsinger, R., Kety, S., Rosenthal, D., et al. (1979). A family study of suicide. In: *Origins, Prevention, and Treatment of Affective Disorders.* New York: Academic Press.

Seiden, R. H. (1968). Suicidal behavior contagion on a college campus: In: *Proceedings of the Fourth International Conference for Suicide Prevention.* Los Angeles, CA: Suicide Prevention Center.

Shaffer, D. (1974). Suicide in childhood & early adolescence. *Journal of Child Psychology & Psychiatry, 15,* 275–291.

Shaffer, D. (1988). The epidemiology of teen suicide: An examination of risk factors. *Journal of Clinical Psychiatry, 49* (9 Suppl.), 36–41.

Shaffer, D., & Fisher, P. (1981). The epidemiology of suicide in children and young adolescents. *Journal of the American Academy of Child Psychiatry, 20,* 545–565.

Shaffer, D., Garland, A., Gould, M., Fisher, P., & Trautman, P. (1988). Preventing teenage suicide: A critical review. *Journal of the American Academy of Children & Adolescent Psychiatry, 27*(6), 675–687.

Shaffer, D., Vieland, V., Garland, A., Rojas, M. M., Underwood, M., & Busner, C. (1990). Adolescent suicide attempters: Response to suicide prevention programs. *Journal of the American Medical Association, 264*(24), 3151–3155.

Shafii, M. (1986, October). Psychological autopsy study of suicide in adolescents. Paper presented at Child Depression Consortium, St. Louis, MO.

Shafii, M., Carrigan, S., & Whittinghill, J. R. (1985). Psychological autopsy of completed suicide in children and adolescents. *American Journal of Psychiatry, 142,* 1061–1064.

Shepherd, D. M., & Barraclough, B. M. (1980). Work and suicide—An empirical investigation. *British Journal of Psychiatry, 136,* 469.

Sloan, J. H., Rivara, F. P., Reay, D. T., Ferris, J., & Kellermann, A. L. (1990). Firearm regulations and rates of suicide: A comparison of two metropolitan areas. *New England Journal of Medicine, 322,* 369–373.

Smith, M. L., & Glass, G. V. (1977). Meta-analysis of psychotherapy outcome studies. *American Psychologist, 32,* 752–760.

Solomon, M. I., & Hellon, C. D. (1980). Suicide and age in Alberta, Canada, 1951 to 1977: A cohort analysis. *Archives of General Psychiatry, 37,* 511–513.

Stanley, M., & Mann, J. J. (1988). Biological factors associated with suicide. In A. J. Frances & R. E. Hales (Eds.), *American Psychiatric Association annual review* (Vol. 7). Washington, DC: American Psychiatric Press.

Steer, R. A., & Beck, A. T. (1988). Use of the Beck Depression Inventory, Hopelessness Scale, Scale for Suicidal Ideation, and Suicide Intent Scale with adolescents. In: *Advances in Adolescent Mental Health, 13* (pp. 219–231). London, England: Jai Press, Ltd.

Steinbrueck, S. M., et al. (1983). A meta-analysis of psychotherapy and drug therapy in the treatment of unipolar depression in adults. *Journal of Consulting & Clinical Psychology, 51,* 845–853.

Stengel, E. (1964). *Suicide and attempted suicide.* Baltimore, MD: Penguin.

Taylor, E. A., and Stronsfield, S. A. (1984). Children who poison themselves. I: A clinical comparison with psychiatric controls. *Br J Psychiatry, 145,* 127–132.

Templer, D. I., & Velaber, D. M. (1980). Suicide rate and religion within the United States. *Psychological Reports, 47,* 898.

Topol, P., & Reznikoff, M. (1982). Perceived peer and family relationships, hopelessness, and locus of control as factors in adolescent suicide attempts. *Suicide & Life Threatening Behavior, 12,* 141–150.

Trovato, F. (1986). The relationship between marital dissolution and suicide: The Canadian case. *Journal of Marriage & the Family, 48,* 341–348.

Trovato, F. (1988). Suicide in Canada: A further look at the effects of age, period, and cohort. *Canadian Journal of Public Health, 79,* 37–44.

Velez, C. N., & Cohen, P. (1988). Suicidal behavior and ideation in a community sample of children: Maternity and youth reports. *Journal of the American Academy of Child & Adolescent Psychiatry, 27,* 349–356.

Virkunen, M. D., DeJong, J., Bartok, J., & Linnoila, M. (1989). Psychobiological concomitants of history of suicide attempts among violent offenders and impulsive fire setters. *Archives of General Psychiatry, 46,* 604–606.

Waldron, I., & Eyer, J. (1975). Socioeconomic causes of the recent rise in death rates for 15–24 year olds. *Social Science Medicine, 9,* 383–396.

Walker, W. L. (1980). Intentional self-injury in school age children. *Journal of Adolescence, 3,* 217–228.

Ward, J. A., & Fox, J. A. (1977). A suicide epidemic on an Indian reserve. *Canadian Psychiatric Association, 22,* 423–426.

Wasserman, I. M. (1987). Cohort, age, and period effects in the analysis of U. S. suicide patterns: 1933–1978. *Suicide & Life Threatening Behavior, 17*(3), 179–193.

Weissman, M. M. (1973). The psychological treatment of depression: Evidence for the efficacy of therapy alone, in comparison with, and in combination with pharmacotherapy. *Archives of General Psychiatry, 29,* 407–413.

Weissman, M. M., Klerman, G. L., Markowitz, J. S., & Ovellette, R. (1989). Suicidal ideation and suicide attempts in panic disorder and attacks. *New England Journal of Medicine, 321,* 1209–1214.

Welner, A., Welner, Z., & Fishman, R. (1979). Psychiatric adolescent inpatients: Eight to ten-year follow-up. *Archives of General Psychiatry, 36,* 689–700.

White, H. C. (1974). Self-poisoning in adolescents. *British Journal of Psychiatry, 124,* 24–35.

Whitlock, F. A. (1986). *Suicide and physical illness in suicide.* In A. Roy (Ed.), *Suicide.* Baltimore, MD: Williams & Wilkins.

Wintemute, G. J., Teret, S. P., Kraus, J. F., et al. (1988). The choice of weapons in firearm suicides. *American Journal of Public Health, 78,* 824–826.

Wolfgang, M. (1959). Suicide by means of victim-precipitated homicide. *Journal of Clinical & Experimental Psychopathology and Quarterly Review of Psychiatry and Neurology, 20,* 335–349.

Zaw, K. (1981). A suicidal family. *British Journal of Psychiatry, 187,* 68–69.

Zung, W. W. K. (1965). A self-rating depression scale. *Archives of General Psychiatry, 12,* 63–70.

# 7
# Psychoses

*Debra Bendell Estroff*
*Miriam Friedland*

The purpose of this chapter is to present a format for interviewing adolescents in order to screen for the possibility of psychotic disorders. It cannot be assumed that differential diagnosis in adolescents is a straightforward task. Teenagers often devalue exploration of sensitive feelings and are deeply ambivalent about acknowledging distress or uncertainty (Strober, McCracken, & Hanna, 1989). Consequently, some will block, disguise, or explain away symptomatic behavior out of shame or embarrassment, whereas others will use anger, denial, or outright defiance to block disclosure. The knowledge necessary to recognize a possible psychotic disorder and refer the adolescent for further diagnosis and treatment will be summarized, as often a preliminary understanding of the adolescent's mental illness is necessary in order to design an effective referral strategy. An early and accurate referral leads to bettering the outcome for arresting the progression of the disorder and mitigating symptomatology for the adolescent and family.

## Incidence of Psychoses during Adolescence

Psychosis is a potentially disabling disorder of personality functioning that frequently runs a chronic or recurrent course. According to Weiner (1987), it is estimated that one to two out of one hundred people will suffer a psychotic episode during their lifetime, and the most likely age for the initial breakdown to occur is the adolescent or early adult years. Psychosis is diagnosed in 15 to 30 percent of adolescents admitted to psychiatric hospitals (Holzman & Grinker, 1987).

The DSM-III-R, which is the manual developed by the American Psychiatric Association (1986), stresses a characteristic symptom picture and a minimal duration to aid in diagnosis. The manual provides a detailed specification of symptoms, diagnostic criteria, and systematic descriptions of the disorder in a consistent fashion. A diagnosis of psychosis includes the presence of at least one of the following symptoms: delusions, hallucinations, incoherence or marked loosening of associations, catatonic behavior, and flat or inappropriate affect. A differentiation is made between prodromal symptoms, residual symptoms, and chronicity. The psychotic adolescent is often flooded with gross fantasies that can be impulsive, explosive, or destructive. There are a thought disorder, the substitution of fantasy for reality, labile emotionality, and shifting or confused identities, as well as an inconsistency in cognitive functioning. The adolescent responds as much to internal stimulation as to external real stimulation. There is often severe, regressive behavior under stress (Schwartz & Eagle, 1986).

Bleuler (1979) divided signs and symptoms of psychosis into two groupings of primary or secondary development, as a result of the deterioration in function that accompanies the illness. The primary, fundamental symptoms, often referred to as the "Four A's" (Flaherty and Sarles, 1981), include loosening of associated thoughts, inappropriate affect, ambivalence, and an absence of relationships that is labeled autism. Secondary symptoms include perceptual disturbances, impaired reality testing, speech and motor disturbances, and problems with sexuality.

A practical difficulty arises when evaluating psychotic manifestations that are superimposed on chronic personality difficulties and/or family turmoil. The diagnosis of psychoses is often difficult, and the adolescent may be assumed to be depressed, to have a conduct disorder, or to have poor interpersonal skills. Very often, parents' understanding of depressive symptomatology is deficient (Chambers, Puig-Antich, Hirsch, Paez, Ambrosini, Tabrizi, & Davis, 1985) and indicates a low correlation with how adolescents perceive themselves. An adolescent with a reactive psychosis has basically good ego strengths but, under the severe stress of a trauma or crisis, responds with explosive behavior, a thought disorder, fantasy overwhelming reality, and bizarre ideations. This adolescent is acutely uncomfortable and in great pain. There are no gross reversions to younger behavior in this disturbance, and the prognosis is more positive than when these regressive phenomena are present.

## Psychological Reorganizational Tasks of Adolescence

Erik Erikson's (1964) theory of psychosocial development is still relevant in understanding and conceptualizing the developmental changes that normally occur at adolescence. Erikson's schemata is especially helpful in understanding the normal cognitive changes occurring at adolescence.

As a child enters adolescence, thinking becomes less concrete and attains formal cognitive patterns that allow for abstractions and relativistic thinking. Evidence from both primate and human research demonstrates that the prefrontal cortex is a late part of the brain to develop. Thus, Hendren, Sholevar, Weinberger, and Wiener (1990) postulate that as one reaches adolescence, there are greater demands for autonomous cognitive functions that depend on prefrontal integrity. If the prefrontal cortex has been congenitally damaged or is dysfunctional, symptoms might not appear until adolescence. Normally, the adolescent begins questioning values, generating theories, and attempting to formulate a personal identity. A multitude of developmental tasks must be mastered in order to establish an adolescent identity. There is a need to define the self as separate and distinct; this comes with some rebelliousness and a judgmental stance toward the parents. Identification with the peer group is critically important for the adolescent, as this is inextricably tied to self-esteem. Because of growth and hormonal changes in the body, the body image and sexual identity must be formulated. Adolescents must also delineate occupational and educational goals and are faced with decisions for their lives. Erikson (1964) notes that adolescence is a time of turmoil, confusion, and ambivalence for the adolescent. Erikson's schemata, however, stresses that developmental tasks must be mastered at each stage so as to ensure optimal growth and mastery of later developmental tasks.

While the idea that psychic developmental turmoil is a universal feature of normal adolescence has had great historical attraction, research has shown that feelings of alienation and self-doubt, while highly characteristic of adolescence, are neither universal nor a cause or a precipitant of psychiatric disturbance (Rutter, Graham, Chadwick, & Yule, 1976; Offer & Offer, 1975). Rather, behavioral problems and adverse family experiences that begin in early childhood appear to become overt in adolescence. Perhaps a portion of this emergence can be traced to the greater ability of the adolescent to act out disturbance. With the tools of greater mobility (on foot or in an automobile), larger body size, and sexual maturation, there is an increased ability to impact negatively on the environment. Adolescents regularly and normally fear loss of control over themselves, their bodies, or their environments (Giuffra, 1985). It is important to realize that this fear of loss of control is exacerbated by hormonal changes and mood fluctuations.

The development of the capacity for intimacy is predicated on the ability to reveal the self. Thus, the formation of peer relationships intertwines with the capacity for intimacy. Patterns of peer relationships that are volatile and without depth protect the adolescent from intimacy.

The emission of behaviors that elicit positive reinforcement from others is a protective factor in the prevention of psychosis. Rutter, Tizard, and Whitmore (1970), in their Isle of Wight general population survey of two-year-old children, found that the description "not much liked by other children" was one of the best indicators of the presence of psychiatric disturbance. Rutter (1978) has reviewed the evidence and found that poor peer relationships are not only a good indicator of current problems but also a good indicator of later difficulties.

## Presentation of Symptoms

A psychosis involves a serious disorganization of thought processes, delusional thinking, or both of these factors, resulting in a deterioration from a previous level of functioning. The adolescent may fail to achieve the expected level of social development. Two different patterns of onset have been described, each having different prognostic implications (Arieti, 1974). The acute onset, or reactive, type is associated with a precipitating event. Physical and sexual abuse has specifically been linked with the development of psychosis (Chu & Dill, 1990; Emslie & Rosenfeld, 1983; Carmen, Rieker, & Mills, 1984).

The second pattern of onset, often called "process schizophrenia," is an insidious illness developing in a basically schizoid individual who has a long history of maladjustment (Flaherty & Sarles, 1981). There are often a progressive deterioration and a chronicity to the illness. This pattern of psychosis has a poorer prognosis than the acute onset psychosis. It is important to remember that not all psychoses are schizophrenic, even though, schizophrenia is a common cause.

The etiology of psychoses is unknown. There may be neurological, toxic, and metabolic causes (Cummings, 1986). Antecedents have been identified, such as parental death and neurodevelopmental problems (Hellgren, Gillberg, & Enerskog, 1987). That there is a high familial incidence of psychoses in adults and children with familial incidence of psychoses in adults and children demonstrates the contribution of genetic factors to the etiology of psychosis (Eggers, 1982). There is no evidence at this time for a specific brain abnormality causing psychoses (Maser & Keith, 1983).

## Primary Symptoms

Bleuler, in the early 1900s (Bleuler, 1908), classified primary symptoms of psychosis as a loosening of associative thought, inappropriate affect, ambivalence, and autism. Flaherty and Sarles (1981) have labeled these the "Four A's" (p. 302). This is still a helpful method of organizing observations of adolescents. That there is no one screening instrument used in the assessment of psychotic potential in adolescence is perhaps reflective of the personality disorganization and loss of contact with reality that make a tidy classification difficult; however, the presence of the symptoms described below indicate the need for further referral. The referral source will then be able to document the premorbid history and examine the underlying personality (Kestenbaum, 1985), steps that can lead to a differential diagnosis.

Incoherent thinking, which is often referred to as disassociation or the loosening of associative thought, involves a disruption in the sequence of thoughts so that one thought does not flow continuously from another. Very often the adolescent will express a series of loosely related ideas that do not seem to hang together and are difficult to follow (Weiner, 1987). Disassociation often occurs between a question asked and an answer given. A disassociated adolescent, when asked, "How are you doing today?" may reply, "An assignment is late for English" or "My brother is angry." Words are often used in a literal or concrete manner. Thus, an adolescent interprets the phrase "a stitch in time saves nine" by responding, "I don't know how to sew." There is often a sense of concreteness, vagueness, or abstractness, or a sense that two internal separate conversations are taking place at the same time (Flaherty & Sarles, 1981). Intense, bizarre convictions not shared by others of similar educational and cultural backgrounds are labeled delusions (Steinberg, 1985).

The psychotic adolescent presents with inappropriate affect (e.g., facial expressions), which probably reflects internal disorganization. This can range from blunted and flattened emotions to periods of intense anxiety, irritation, and agitation. This affect does not appear tied to external reality. Moods are often labile, ranging from intense sadness and crying bouts to being inappropriately humorous, often in the space of a few moments. Some adolescents may laugh while relating a violent, aggressive fantasy. Psychotic adolescents are frequently unable to prevent socially unacceptable and anxiety-provoking ideas from preoccupying their minds. The content of these ideas is often aggressive and sexual (Karon & Vandenbos, 1981) and at times may erupt into sudden outbursts of violence or assaultive sexual advances.

Simultaneous and opposite wishes, ideas, and feelings are another symptom of adolescent psychosis (Goldfarb, 1981). Concurrent and conflicting love-hate, like-dislike, or fascination-repulsion feelings are frequent. There is a confusion of thinking that is overwhelming to the adolescent.

A marked withdrawal from peers and adults that results in almost total isolation is labeled autism. This interpersonal isolation is accompanied by inadequate social skills. Social isolation, however, is related to unpopularity rather than shyness, as the adolescent's peers regard him or her as odd or eccentric. Very often, the adolescent behaves in an insensitive, argumentative, suspicious, or self-centered manner (Weiner, 1987), secondary to disordered thinking and inaccurate perceptions. This symptom is also reflective of judgmental distortions that indicate an unrealistic assessment of a situation.

## Secondary Symptoms

Secondary symptoms are defined by Bleuler (1908) as including perceptual disturbances, impaired reality testing, speech and motor disturbances, and problems with sexuality. The perceptual disturbances include hallucinations, which are most commonly auditory. The voices sometimes appear through

Ouija games or witchcraft rituals. These voices often comment critically on the adolescent's behavior or thoughts and order the adolescent to take specific behavioral actions. Sometimes two or more voices talk to each other. Some adolescents report their thoughts being broadcast so others can hear. Somatic hallucinations have been noted in the literature (Sholevar, 1986). Many times these hallucinations take the form of abnormal bodily sensations, such as the sensation of there being singing persons in the adolescent's head (Eggers, 1982). There are also passivity experiences, such as the sense that the adolescent's thoughts are being controlled by other people or social agencies (Steinberg, 1985). One adolescent reported the school principal's voice repeating and commenting on his thoughts. Evidence of a hallucination should always result in a referral for further evaluation, even without any additional evidence of a thought disorder.

Impaired reality testing is often tied to a lack of social understanding. Thus, an average pianist will audition for a scholarship for gifted musicians, or a slightly built, poorly coordinated freshman in high school will talk about going out for the basketball team. The behavior of psychotic adolescents involves multiple unrealistic assessments of themselves or the consequences of their actions.

Speech disturbances encompass unusual variations in stress, inflection, rate, or pitch. Speaking in a monotone or in a singsong tone may occur in psychotic adolescents. The most common speech disturbance, however, is the use of irrelevant or tangential speech. The adolescent often follows loosely connected aspects of a subject rather than the main topic. The speech of psychotic adolescents is often ungrammatical and does not serve interpersonal communication. Neologisms (i.e., invented words), often consisting of parts of two words merged together, and disturbances of the flow of speech are typical. Frequently the adolescent does not use the first person but speaks of him- or herself in the third person (Eggers, 1982). Motor disturbances of speed are often observed, ranging from extremely rapid movements to very slowed movements.

Problems with sexuality commonly focus on extreme sexual fantasies. These fantasies frequently evoke extreme anxiety and are surrounded by auras of shame and guilt. Inappropriate or assaultive sexual advances can occur around these fantasies. In a study of psychotic hospitalized adolescents, a majority of the adolescents had histories of assaultiveness before hospitalization (Inamdar, Lewis, Siomopoulos, Shanok, & Lamela, 1981).

## Secondary Psychosis

Neurological disorders occasionally cause psychotic states. Rivinus, Jamison, and Graham (1985) reported on twelve children, seen over the course of a year, in which neurological disease presented in the form of a psychiatric disorder. These diseases are rare, but the importance of proper diagnosis cannot be overemphasized.

Several studies (Akiskal, Walker, Puzantian, King, Rosenthal, & Dranon, 1983; Strober, 1985) have indicated that adolescents who present with a major depression and psychotic features often have a bipolar, or manic-depressive, outcome. Thus, these adolescents become manic-depressive.

A brief reactive psychosis occurs with sudden onset and a precipitating event in a personality that showed no prior illness. Precipitating events can range from rape to a dog bite to an auto accident (Munoz, Amado, & Hyatt, 1987). The prognosis for recovery from this type of psychosis is good. Varley (1984) has reported on mildly retarded adolescent girls who developed psychoses following sexual assault. In this sample, the assaults were not identified until the psychoses had cleared.

Drug intoxication can lead to a psychoticlike reaction (Kandel, 1982; Kestenbaum, 1985). Additionally, drugs can precipitate a psychotic disorder in a genetically vulnerable adolescent. A cross-sectional study (Kaplan, Landau, & Weinhold, 1984) found drug use to be associated with suicidal ideation and with helplessness. This association suggests that these characteristics might lead to the ingestion of unknown chemicals in great quantities. Aarkrog (1985) relates the case of a thirteen-year-old who took LSD and became psychotic. It was felt that the parents gave conflicting messages to this adolescent regarding life-style and the use of drugs. Flaherty and Sarles (1981) note that the drugs known to precipitate psychoses include amphetamines, marijuana, cocaine, and hallucinogenic drugs. Drug abusers can present with psychoses that sometimes continue for months after the drug has been discontinued.

## Case Studies

Psychosis is relatively rare in adolescence, whereas disruptive or externalizing disorders such as attention deficit disorders and conduct disorders are far more common. One method of beginning to separate these issues is through the careful examination of case study material.

### A Psychotic Adolescent

The first case presented is of a psychotic adolescent.

> The first contact regarding Ted was a telephone call from his father, who reported that he had taken his son Ted to a physician because Ted was excessively worried that several of his relatives might die. He talked to himself and cried a good deal. The physician advised his father to call the psychiatry department immediately.

The psychiatrist, on consultation, said Ted was obsessing and talked incessantly about people dying. He appeared agitated during the office visit. Additionally, the content of his speech was off the point. There was no history of drug abuse.

At the initial meeting, Ted was accompanied by his parents and three of his siblings. The history was obtained from Ted's mother and father, both of whom spoke English with strong accents that were difficult to understand. The parents had emigrated from China in the 1940s.

Ted is a sixteen-year-old Chinese American boy who lives with his biological parents and five siblings. He is the oldest child and has three sisters and two brothers. He is in the eighth grade in a public school. The mother's pregnancy and delivery were described as normal, and Ted reached developmental milestones at the expected times. The only childhood behavior that was different, according to his parents, was that Ted seemed less mature than others of his age and preferred to be with his younger siblings.

Ted had been anxious about the start of the school year, as was usual for him each year. One week prior to the referral, Ted had complained of feeling sick, as though he had a cold. Then he started talking continuously. It didn't matter whether anyone was listening or not; he just kept talking. He expressed concern about the possibility of grandparents, parents, and siblings dying. He cried frequently for long periods of time. Ted's parents were confused and overwhelmed by his behavior. They denied his accusations that his father beat him and his siblings with a stick. "I don't know why he says that; Father has not hit him in years, and then never with a stick," his mother commented.

Ted had always been a good student, getting mostly A's, except for a B in algebra; this B grade upset him a good deal. Ted's parents deny that they pressure him to get A's, and feel that he pressures himself excessively with regard to school performance. Apart from grades, Ted has always worried about his health, although the only health problems he has had is allergies causing hayfever; Ted has feared he would get pneumonia from this affliction. For years, he has had concerns regarding his parents' and relatives' health.

Ted has never played with other children of his age at school or in the neighborhood. His only playmates have been his siblings.

Ted's parents deny any knowledge of drug or alcohol use. They deny any particular stresses at home and report no history of mental illness in their families.

A clinical interview with Ted was difficult to follow, because he talked rapidly, switched subjects often, and repeated himself. He talked about his concern for his grandparents and for his aunt, who had a clot on her lung and was ill; later it was revealed that this aunt had died a year earlier. Ted talked of his father hitting him and his siblings with a stick. He also said his father was an alcoholic.

Previous history identified that a year earlier, after the start of the school year, Ted had become agitated and spoke to himself. This resolved after an aunt "spoke to him."

Diagnosis of psychosis was based on the following information: Ted, a sixteen-year-old Chinese American boy who is slightly overweight and casually dressed, was agitated, talked incessantly, and fluctuated between rapid, barely intelligible speech and calm, slower speech. He jumped from one subject to another without there being any connection. The subject matter didn't make sense at times (e.g., "My mother gave birth to me and is with me"). He repeated the same statements over and over. He was clingy, regressed, and scared and wanted either his mother or the therapist to sit next to him and hold his hand. He cried intermittently. When questioned about whether he heard voices, he said he heard a ghost telling him not to worry. He was oriented to time, place, and person. He did not respond to many questions, and kept on talking. This adolescent meets the criteria for psychosis because he has a thought disorder, as demonstrated by untrue accusations regarding his parents, aunt, and uncle. He talked about his uncle as if he were still alive, when he in fact was dead. He talked in a disorganized and pressured manner that was not logical.

## A Hyperactive Adolescent

The second case is of an attention deficit hyperactive adolescent.

This youth presented via a phone call from his mother, who reported that the school had called her for a conference regarding her son Tony. The school counselor had suggested to Tony's mother that Tony be seen by a therapist due to concerns regarding his classroom behavior and poor academic performance.

Tony was brought to the clinic by his mother, who stated that she was tired of getting "failing" notices and negative reports from Tony's school. At home, Tony was often noncompliant, defiant, and intimidating to his younger siblings. Tony lives with his mother, his stepfather, and his two brothers, who are nine and eleven years of age. He is in the eighth grade in public school, in a learning disability classroom. He rarely has contact with his biological father, visiting with him perhaps once every three months on an inconsistent basis.

Tony's teachers report that he fidgets in class, throws objects at other children, and frequently taps on the desk to a subvocalized rhythm or tune. He is distracting to other students and oppositional with the teacher. He will pace the classroom with a worried look on his face. At times, Tony will leave his seat and stand too close to a peer. He has been in physical fights with other children on a number of occasions during recess and frequently has been sent to the principal's office for discipline.

At the initial meeting with Tony and his parents, Tony presented as an attractive, fourteen-year-old who appeared nervous and embarrassed. He spoke in a pressured manner and appeared restless.

Tony's birth was normal. He was a difficult infant who did not self-console easily and was difficult for his mother to calm. His sleep patterns were irregular, and he was restless during his sleep, often throwing his blankets on the floor. He was moved to a second preschool at age four because the first school felt he was disruptive. In the second grade, he was diagnosed as having a learning disability that was visual-perceptual in nature. He has been in resource classrooms since then and is making slow progress academically.

Tony's speech was harried and jumped from topic to topic. He often switched to minor tangents in the conversation. Many of his sentences were run-on and somewhat fragmentary. He often blamed peers and teachers for what were obviously errors in his own behavior and judgment, insisting that his behavior was correct. He would become angry and frustrated at questions that deflected his attention. He made expressive sense, however, and showed through conversation that he was connected to reality. His behavior was immature but age-appropriate. He reported no hallucinations of any sort.

The second case displays elements of distractibility; intrusiveness; poor judgment; volatile and irritable behavior, especially when thwarted; impulsive risk taking; poor sleep habits; and denial of the prevalence of problems. There were, however, no symptoms of a thought disorder, hallucinations, or a loss of contact with reality. Table 1 summarizes symptoms for a differential diagnosis.

## Treatment Issues

It is important to refer an adolescent suspected of being psychotic to an appropriate therapist who has experience treating emotionally disturbed adolescents. Thus, treatment can be begun in order to prevent further psychological deterioration and dangerous behavior. The most helpful treatment for psychotic adolescents appears to be multifaceted. It includes (a) careful diagnosis, which may include referral to a substance abuse program; (b) antipsychotic medication, given under close supervision; (c) individual ther-

**Table 1.**
**Comparison of Symptoms between a Diagnosis of Psychosis and Attention Deficit Hyperactivity Disorder**

| Psychosis Symptoms | Attention Deficit Hyperactivity Symptoms |
|---|---|
| Disassociation | Distractibility |
| Inappropriate affect | Irritable behavior |
| Ambivalence | Impulsivity |
| Autism | Intrusiveness |
| Perceptual disturbances | Denial of problems |
| Impaired reality testing | Intrusiveness |
| Speech and motor disturbances | Poor sleep habits |
| Problems with sexuality | Problems with concentration |

apy, to aid in socialization and functioning; and (d) the adolescent living in a milieu where firm limits are set on behavior and where normal social behavior is consistently reinforced. Electroconvulsive therapy has not been seen as being of help with psychotic adolescents (Bertagnoli & Borchardt, 1990). Sedatives, stimulants, antianxiety tranquilizers, and antipsychotics have all been tried with psychotic adolescents. There is agreement that only the antipsychotic drugs are beneficial in diminishing or extinguishing psychomotor excitement, psychotic thinking, hallucinations, and disorganized behavior (McDaniel, 1986). Stelazine, Haldol, and Prolixin, among others, are effective antipsychotic drugs. Side effects consist of dry mouth, Parkinsonian tremors, sedation, and extrapyramidal effects. Extrapyramidal effects are muscle contractions, especially around the face and neck; these side effects can be frightening but are not dangerous for the patient. Of greater concern is the possibility of tardive dyskinesia, which often presents as repetitive movements around the mouth or tongue and can occur after a patient has been on medication for many years. Lithium is added in manic-depressive psychosis. The adolescent requires therapy to learn appropriate social skills and appropriate ways of controlling impulsive, disorganized thoughts and behaviors.

Parents must be involved in the successful treatment of severely disturbed adolescents. Family therapy is necessary to deal with clinical, legal, ethical, and financial issues (Peterson & Kelleher, 1987). Additionally, parents' groups with adolescents in a hospital setting have provided encouraging results (Pevsner, 1982; Rossman & Freedman, 1982; Peterson & Kelleher, 1987). One positive aspect of this group structure is the generation of a supportive network for parents.

Research reports indicate a bimodal distribution in outcome for the course of psychosis that begins in adolescence. A good outcome has been associated with relatively high intelligence, a normal EEG, and a late adolescent onset of psychosis (Steinberg, 1985). Having a large number of relatives with schizophrenia has been found to indicate a poor prognosis (McCabe, Fowler, Cadoret, & Winokur, 1971). One- to three-year outcomes of treated adolescent psychotics were assessed in Japan (Inoue, Nakajima, & Kato, 1986); this study found that being male, being of relatively younger age at the onset of the condition, and delaying obtaining psychiatric treatment were factors producing a less favorable outcome for the adolescent.

## Working with the Family

When a previously undiagnosed adolescent is exhibiting the signs of a severe mental disorder, diagnosis and referral to a mental health specialist for treatment need to occur without delay. Often further diagnostic evaluation and testing are necessary to help choose among several treatment options. When first presenting concerns to parents, it is wise to be informed regarding clinicians and facilities available for psychotic adolescents. It is usually helpful to stress the options that are available. Some acutely psychotic adolescents can be treated as outpatients, provided that they have a responsible parent to supervise them while the medication stabilizes them. In other cases, especially with the onset of psychosis, hospitalization will be needed. If the adolescent is underage (which qualifications may differ from state to state), there is no legal right for refusal of hospitalization, as the parent's signature suffices. If the adolescent is deemed imminently dangerous to him- or herself or to others, the parent can hospitalize the adolescent without his or her approval.

## Summary

This chapter has presented a format for the assessment of adolescents in order to screen for the possibility of a psychotic disorder. It is critical to identify and refer for treatment adolescents who are psychotic, because psychosis represents such a serious disorganization of the thought processes. Often a preliminary diagnosis is important so that an effective method of communicating concerns to the parents regarding the potential seriousness of the adolescent's psychiatric disturbance can occur and a referral strategy designed.

Diagnosis is difficult, because adolescents are often ambivalent about acknowledging their pain and distress. School personnel should be alert for sudden changes in personality or withdrawal from social contacts. Additionally, the adolescent will often attempt to disguise or explain away symptomatic behavior. Any evidence of hallucinations (whether related to drug abuse or not) should require a referral for evaluation.

# References

Aarkrog, T. (1985). Borderline and psychotic adolescents' relationship to their parents: A therapeutic point of view. *Adolescence, 20*(79), 681–687.

Akiskal, H., Walker, P., Puzantian, V., King, D., Rosenthal, T., & Dranon, M. (1983). Bipolar outcome in the course of depressive illness. *Journal of Affective Disorders, 5,* 115–128.

American Psychiatric Association. (1986). *Diagnostic and statistical manual of mental disorders* (rev. 3rd ed.). Washington, DC: American Psychiatric Association.

Arieti, S. (1974). *Interpretation of schizophrenia* (2nd ed.). New York: Basic Books.

Bertagnoli, M., & Borchardt, C. (1990). A review of ECT for children and adolescents. *Journal of American Academy of Child and Adolescent Psychiatry, 29*(2), 302–307.

Bleuler, M. (1908). Die prognoses der dementia praecox allgemeine zeitschrift fur Pssychiatric und Psychisch. *Gerichtliche Medezin, 65,* 436–464.

Bleuler, M. (1979). Schizophrenic psychoses. *American Journal of Psychiatry, 136,* 1403–1409.

Carmen, E., Rieker, P., & Mills, T. (1984). Victims of violence and psychiatric illness. *American Journal of Psychiatry, 141,* 378–383.

Chambers, W., Puig-Antich, J., Hirsch, M., Paez, P., Ambrosini, P., Tabrizi, M., & Davis, M. (1985). The assessment of affective disorders in children and adolescents by semistructured interview. *Archives of General Psychiatry, 42,* 696–702.

Chu, J., & Dill, D. (1990). Dissociative symptoms in relation to childhood physical and sexual abuse. *American Journal of Psychiatry, 147*(7), 887–891.

Cummings, J. (1986). Organic psychoses: delusional disorders and secondary mania. *Psychiatric Clinics of North America, 9,* 293–311.

Eggers, C. (1982). Psychoses in childhood and adolescence. *Acta Paeadopsychiatry, 48,* 81–98.

Emslie, G., & Rosenfeld, A. (1983). Incest reported by children and adolescents hospitalized for severe psychiatric problems. *American Journal of Psychiatry, 140,* 708–711.

Erikson, E. (1964). *Childhood, youth, and society.* New York: Norton.

Flaherty, L., & Sarles, R. (1981). Psychosis during adolescence: A review. *Journal of Adolescent Health Care, 1,* 301–307.

Giuffra, M. (1985). Demystifying adolescent behavior. *American Journal of Nursing, 75,* 1724–1727.

Goldfarb, W. (1981). *Childhood schizophrenia.* Cambridge, MA: Harvard University Press.

Hellgren, L., Gillberg, C., & Enerskog, I. (1987). Antecedents of adolescent psychoses: A population-based study of school health problems in children who develop psychosis in adolescence. *Journal of Child and Adolescent Psychiatry, 78,* 351–355.

Hendren, R. Sholevar, G., Weinberger, D., & Wiener, J. (1990). Schizophrenia in a fourteen-year-old boy. *Journal of the American Academy of Child and Adolescent Psychiatry, 29*(1), 141–148.

Holzman, P., & Grinker, R. (1987). Schizophrenia in adolescence. In S. Feinstein & P. Giovacchini (Eds.), *Adolescent psychiatry,* Vol. 5. (276–290). New York: Jason Aaronson.

Inamdar, S., Lewis, D., Siomopoulos, G., Shanok, S., & Lamela, M. (1981). Violent and suicidal behavior in psychotic adolescents. *American Journal of Psychiatry, 139*(7), 932–935.

Inoue, K., Nakajima, T., & Kato, N. (1986). A longitudinal study of schizophrenia in adolescence I: The one to three year outcome. *The Japanese Journal of Psychiatry and Neurology, 40*(2), 143–150.

Kandel, D. (1982). Epidemiological and psychosocial perspectives on adolescent drug use. *Journal of the American Academy of Child Psychiatry, 21*(4), 328–347.

Kaplan, S., Landau, B., & Weinhold, C. (1984). Adverse health behaviors and depressive symptomatology in adolescents. *Journal of the American Academy of Child Psychiatry, 233,* 595–601.

Karon, B., & Vandenbos, G. (1981). *Psychotherapy of schizophrenia.* New York: Jason Aronson.

Kestenbaum, C. (1985). Putting it all together: A multidimensional assessment of psychotic potential in adolescence. *Adolescent Psychiatry, 5,* 243–256.

Maser, J., & Keith, S. (1983). CT scans and schizophrenia: Report on a workshop. *Schizophrenia Bulletin, 9*(2), 265–283.

McCabe, M., Fowler, R., Cadoret, R., & Winokur, G. (1971). Familial differences in schizophrenia with good and poor prognosis. *Psychological Medicine, 1,* 326–322.

McDaniel, K. (1986). Pharmacological treatment of psychiatric and neurodevelopmental disorders in children and adolescents. *Clinical Pediatrics, 25*(3), 143–146.

Munoz, R., Amado, H., & Hyatt, S. (1987). Brief reactive psychosis. *Journal of Clinical Psychiatry, 48*(8), 324–327.

Offer, D., & Offer, J. (1975). *From teenager to young manhood.* New York: Basic Books.

Peterson, L., & Kelleher, C. (1987). Working with parents of disturbed adolescents: A multifaceted group approach. *Child Welfare, 66*(2), 139–148.

Pevsner, R. (1982). Group parent training versus individual family therapy: An outcome study. *Journal of Behavior Therapy and Experimental Psychiatry, 13,* 119–122.

Rivinus, T., Jamison, D., & Graham, P. (1985). Childhood organic neurological disease presenting as psychiatric disorder. *Archives of Diseases of Children, 50,* 115–119.

Rossman, P., & Freedman, J. (1982). Hospital treatment for disturbed adolescents: The role of parent counseling groups. *Adolescent Psychiatry, 10,* 391–406.

Rutter, M. (1978). Early sources of security and competence. In J. Bruner & A. Gaston (Eds.), *Human growth and development.* Oxford: Clarendon Press.

Rutter, M., Graham, P., Chadwick, O., & Yule, W. (1976). Adolescent turmoil: Fact or fiction? *Journal of Child Psychology and Psychiatry, 17,* 35–56.

Rutter, M., Tizard, J., & Whitmore, K. (1970). *Education, health, & behavior.* London: Longman.

Schwartz, L., & Eagle, C. (1986). *Psychological portraits of children: An integrated developmental approach to psychological test data.* Lexington, MA: Lexington Books.

Sholevar, G. (1986). Families of institutionalized children. In G. Sholevar (Ed.), *Emotional disorders in children and adolescents.* New York: Pergamon Press.

Steinberg, D. (1985). Psychotic and other severe disorders in adolescence. In M. Rutter & L. Hersov (Eds.), *Child and adolescent psychiatry.* Oxford: Blackwell Scientific Publications.

Strober, M. (1985). Depressive illness in adolescence. *Psychiatric Annals, 15,* 375–378.

Strober, M., McCracken, J., & Hanna, G. (1989). Affective disorders. In G. Hsu & M. Hersen (Eds.), *Recent developments in adolescent psychiatry* (pp. 202–232). New York: John Wiley & Sons.

Varley, C. (1984). Schizophreniform psychoses in mentally retarded adolescent girls following sexual assault. *American Journal of Psychiatry, 141*(1), 593–595.

Weiner, I. (1987). Identifying schizophrenia in adolescents. *Journal of Adolescent Health Care, 8,* 336–343.

# 8
# Sexuality and Reproductive Health Behavior

*Patricia K. Kokotailo*
*John N. Stephenson*

## Introduction

The culmination of adolescent sexuality is the establishment of intimacy with another human being. The teenage years are a critical time in the biopsychosocial process of human development during which this intimacy often occurs. Unfortunately, youth are prone to misconstrue their sexuality and to have misunderstandings concerning the consequences of sexual intercourse, contraception, pregnancy, abortion, parenting, and adoption. In addition, gay life-styles and sexual abuse have only recently become acceptable subjects for rational public discussion. Sexuality problems arise during adolescence as a result of insufficient and incorrect information, inexperience with sexuality, and unformed decision-making skills.

It is essential for professionals who work with youth and their parents to have a fundamental understanding of three concepts: (a) puberty, (b) maturational age and its asynchrony with respect to psychosocial and cognitive development, and (c) the normal unfolding of adolescent sexuality. The following section provides background information on these topics, in order to help the counselor address teenagers' sexual questions, feelings, and problems.

### Puberty

Virtually all bodily tissues are affected by the biological changes of puberty. The most dramatic of these changes are related to the maturation of the reproductive system and the appearance of secondary sexual characteristics. Sexual development in the female usually becomes apparent with the onset of breast development between ages 8 and 13. In the United States, the mean age of menarche (the first menstrual period) is 12.8 years, with a normal range of 10 to 16.5 years (Wyshak & Frish, 1982). Therefore, it is possible for pregnancy to occur in the preteen years. Sexual maturation in the male begins between 9.5 and 13.5 years of age (Neinstein & Kaufman, 1991), with testicular enlargement. Nearly 25 percent of final adult height is accounted for during pubertal growth, while weight gain during this time accounts for over 40 percent of the ultimate ideal adult weight in both sexes (Slap, 1986). These profound physical changes occur rapidly over a 3- to 5-year period.

## Psychosocial Development

Today a majority of youth are in school at least into young adulthood, and consequently remain at least partly dependent on their parents' financial support. Although this phenomenon may have become the norm in our society, the earlier onset of physiological maturity has encouraged adolescents to seek sexual and social independence. The result, according to Elkind (1990), represents a dramatic change from past eras. Elkind is concerned by this change because, in his view, sexual, social, and moral independence now seem to be granted on the basis of physical and physiological maturity, rather than intellectual and emotional maturity.

There is research evidence that adolescent intellectual, social, emotional, and cognitive development lags behind physical and physiological development (Elkind, 1990; Elkind & Bowen, 1978; Enright, Sapsley, and Shukla, 1979; Enright and Sutterfield, 1980). One consequence of this asynchrony is that teenagers are ready and able to engage in sexual activity before they are intellectually and socially prepared to cope with its ramifications. Coincidental with the dramatic increase in teenage sexual activity during the past twenty-five years have been the equally remarkable changes in the structure of the American family and the way in which society views adolescence.

Elkind (1990) argues that parents and society are beginning to view children and youth as ready and able to deal with life's vicissitudes, as a way of rationalizing the abrogation of many parental responsibilities. Adult guidance, supervision, and limit setting are often not followed through by tired, preoccupied, underinformed, and less determined parents. The asynchrony of adolescent biopsychosocial development is not being sufficiently appreciated. The marker events of growing up are being gradually downplayed for commercial and psychosocial reasons. Early adolescents were bestowed the rights and privileges of older youth without having first developed a sense of self and personal identity. When the adult sexual revolution occurred in the 1960s, changes in adolescent sexual attitudes and behavior quickly followed and were a mirror image of the U.S. population as a whole.

Society has discarded many of the roadmaps and signposts used by previous generations as guidelines for growing up. It has instead inadvertently cluttered the landscape with large, sexually biased billboards boldly proclaiming commercial products commonly used by adolescents (Strasburger,

1989), including diet cola, fragrances, jeans, beer, and tobacco. Once teenagers are in the privacy of their own homes, their sex education courses continue. Content analyses reveal that the average American teenager views over 14,000 sexual references, innuendos, and jokes per year on American television, yet less than 150 of the references deal with birth control, self-control, or abstinence (Harris & Associates, 1988). As noted by Strasburger (1989), sex is fine for selling prime-time programming, cars, shampoo, and beer, but contraception is a "dirty word." When viewing the teenage population as a whole, however, Offer and colleagues have argued that most teenagers are not adversely affected by early maturity or by society's demands for them to be grown up (Offer, Ostrov, & Howard, 1981, 1989). Some adolescents are more vulnerable and subject to risk taking than others. For example, an early-maturing girl in a sheltered, suburban community may be less stressed and therefore less vulnerable to external sexual pressures than an early-maturing girl in a working-class neighborhood (Elkind, 1990).

It is important for us to remember that it is normal for youth to be sexual. There would be something unhealthy about a fifteen-year-old who didn't have sexual thoughts, feelings, desires, and fantasies. The goal of adolescent sexuality is the establishment of intimacy with another person, although sexual intercourse is not essential for its attainment. Many youth, however, have equated sophistication and independence with early onset of sexual intercourse and its inherent risks.

## Exploration of Sexual Behavior

Because sexuality has such central importance for adolescent growth and development, it is frequently appropriate for professionals working with youth to assess a teenager's sexual knowledge, attitudes, and behavior. Ideally, such information gathering will appear relevant to the adolescent and be based on a relationship of trust, respect, and confidentiality. Whatever the circumstances, good rapport with the teenager is essential for obtaining accurate and helpful information. Although the evaluation may require the use of slang words to improve communication, correct terms and definitions should also be provided. Questions based on an interviewer's accurate estimate of a given adolescent's biopsychosocial and cognitive development are most likely to be viewed as unintrusive and helpful. How adolescents perceive their own behaviors is also critical in understanding how the counselor can help the adolescent minimize any risks to his or her health and well-being. There are three main categories of clinical circumstances in which a professional will need to assess an adolescent's sexual life: the new evaluation, the adolescent with an explicit sexual problem, and the evaluation of a suspected covert sexual difficulty.

## Table 1.
## Confidential Health Survey
## (to be filled in by teenager)

Date: _____

This questionnaire will help us get to know you better. Please answer the following questions, and feel free to ask a staff member about items that may be confusing to you.

1. What do you like to be called (nickname)? _____

2. Why are you coming to the clinic today? _____
_____

3. On a scale of 1 to 10, how would you rate your general health?

    1       2       3       4       5       6       7       8       9       10

awful                                                  great

4. Many teens and young adults have concerns about the following items. Please check any that may apply to you.

| | |
|---|---|
| _____ trouble sleeping | _____ parents/family |
| _____ being tired during the day | _____ grades/school |
| _____ headaches | _____ dreams or nightmares |
| _____ stomachaches | _____ fear of unplanned pregnancy |
| _____ dizzy/fainting spells | _____ fear of sexually transmitted diseases (STDs) |
| _____ height | |
| _____ weight | _____ controlling my temper |
| _____ muscle or joint pains | _____ nothing to do |
| _____ vision or hearing problems | _____ my future |
| _____ skin problems (acne, rashes) | _____ feeling down or depressed |
| _____ earaches | _____ a place to live |
| _____ sore throats | _____ getting enough to eat |
| _____ coughing | _____ family members drinking alcohol/ using drugs |
| _____ wheezing (asthma) | |
| _____ vomiting | _____ fighting |
| _____ diarrhea | _____ gangs |
| _____ pain with urination (passing water) | _____ racial problems |
| | _____ getting robbed or mugged |
| _____ allergies/hay fever | _____ getting killed |
| _____ privacy | _____ other (please describe) |
| _____ friends | |
| _____ no friends | _____ |
| _____ brothers/sisters | _____ |

## Table 1. (*continued*)

5. Would you like to know more about

| | |
|---|---|
| _____ menstruation | _____ physical abuse |
| _____ pregnancy | _____ my sexual development or feelings |
| _____ having children | _____ masturbation |
| _____ birth control | _____ drugs/alcohol |
| _____ dating | _____ gangs |
| _____ STDs | _____ cancer |
| _____ AIDS or HIV | _____ death and dying |
| _____ teenage body changes | _____ other (please describe) |
| _____ ways to deal with stress | _____ |
| _____ sexual assault or abuse | _____ |

6. Now think about these life-style patterns that may affect your health. Are there any you would like to change? If yes, please check them.

| | |
|---|---|
| _____ nutrition or diet | _____ making and keeping friends |
| _____ exercise | _____ drinking alcohol or using drugs |
| _____ smoking/chewing tobacco | _____ getting along with my family |
| _____ sleep | _____ sexuality |
| _____ my response to stress | _____ finding a job |
| _____ school performance | _____ communication with parents |
| _____ using a seat belt | _____ communication with friends |
| _____ wearing a motorcycle or bike helmet | _____ communication with adults |
| | _____ carrying a weapon |

## The New Evaluation

Most teenage medical clinics and social agencies serving youth have developed a confidential health and social questionnaire that the adolescent patient or client completes periodically. Table 1 provides an example of a personal survey. Such a questionnaire should include the following: general health concerns and a brief review of symptoms that might suggest a disease process; a psychosocial inventory that includes the chance to express concerns about home, school, and peers; and opportunities to ask questions about psychosexual feelings and behaviors and how various life-style patterns may affect the adolescent's health. Particular attention should be given to adolescents with a history of incarceration, psychiatric treatment, alcohol and drug abuse, previous pregnancy, sexual assault or incest, homelessness, and homosexual activity. Parenthood status should also be reviewed.

We view the health questionnaire as serving several purposes. It announces to the adolescent that we are willing to discuss these topics, either now or in the future. It also gives a message to any teenager answering the questionnaire that other young people have similar concerns. Although few adolescents ever check "yes" to an item on masturbation, we know that this topic represents the most frequently requested informational tape on our own program's free, anonymous call-in "Dial Access," a twenty-four-hour health information service for adolescents. We explain to adolescents that so many teenagers have asked questions regarding such topics as masturbation, sexual development and feelings, and prevention of STDs that we developed a questionnaire in order to give all individuals an opportunity to ask questions or share the concerns they might have. This approach is necessary because misinformation, misunderstanding, and social taboos continue to isolate adolescents whenever they believe they are engaged in sexual behaviors that are likely to be seen by others as perverted, and consequently subject to censorship. This issue is particularly true for homosexual youth, who will often need additional help and support in providing insight into conflicting or confusing identity struggles.

At present, teenage pregnancy and STDs are predominant morbidities of youth. Strongly positive correlations have been documented among substance use, dangerous vehicle use, and early sexual activity (Irwin, 1990). It stands to reason that a youth who is being screened or evaluated for one high-risk behavior should be questioned about other high-risk behaviors. For example, a detailed assessment for alcohol and other drug abuse should include screening-level questions about an adolescent's sexual behavior. Table 2 lists factors that may predispose adolescents to engage in sexual relationships.

One way of introducing sexuality as a legitimate subject is by saying, "I

**Table 2.**
**Identifying Teenagers Who Are at Risk for Sexual Relationships**

*Family factors*

Teenager's mother conceived her first child as an adolescent

History of teenaged parenthood among adolescent's siblings

Ambivalence about the value of education and school attendance

History of incest or sexual abuse

Chaotic or dysfunctional life-style

*Individual factors*

Engagement in other problem behaviors (e.g., substance use)

Poor school performance, ambivalence about the value of education, limited or vague aspirations about the future

Identifying with an older adolescent or young adult peer group

Becoming romantically involved with an older partner

History of sexual assault or incest

Learning disability, mild mental retardation, head injury, or certain psychiatric problems would like to ask you some questions about sex. It's an important part of your general health, and something I discuss with everyone when they reach your age." Questions should proceed from general, less sensitive topics to more specific and sensitive ones. Early adolescents may be asked whether they have any questions about their sexual development. They may say no while hoping that the counselor will anticipate their needs. We often ask what they have learned about this subject in school, at home, and from youth organizations to which they belong. Discussing developmental variations such as gynecomastia (transient breast development in males), asymmetrical breast development, menstrual regularity and cramps, nocturnal emissions (wet dreams), and masturbation suggests to the adolescent that the counselor is familiar and comfortable with these subjects, and may pave the way for a more frank discussion of sexual behaviors.

Assessing the need to evaluate an early adolescent's level of sexual activity is a matter of professional judgment (see Table 3). Malus and colleagues have shown that twelve years of age is not too young to begin discussion of such topics as contraception and sexually transmitted disease (Malus, LaChance, & Lamy, 1987). By age fifteen, three-quarters of adolescents in these authors' study were interested in discussing those issues. A noninvasive, open-ended approach should be used: "Do you have any friends with whom you have had a sexual relationship?" This approach avoids assigning a sexual preference before the teenager has had an opportunity to talk about it. Recent studies have reported that coital activity of adolescents younger than fifteen years ranges from 12 to 55 percent (Irwin, 1990). All youth who are involved in other risk-taking behaviors or are seen as vulnerable should be asked about their level of sexual activity, as well as the degree of sexual privacy they have within their own homes. All teenagers should be given the opportunity to talk about any unwanted or uncomfortable sexual experiences, including assault and incest. (See chapter 4 of this volume.)

## Table 3.
## Exploring Sexual Concerns and Behavior with Early Adolescents

1. Review the process and variations of puberty.

2. Discuss menstruation and ejaculation.

3. Discuss sexual outlets gently:
   - Masturbation
   - Sexual activity
   - Sexual preference

4. Discuss unwanted consequences of sexual activity:
   - Pregnancy
   - STDs

5. Assess the adolescent's risk for engaging in sexual activity.

6. Ascertain whether the teenager has had any uncomfortable sexual experiences at any time in his or her life.

For the middle and late adolescent, such topics as sexual preference, level of sexual intimacy, and pregnancy and STD/AIDS prevention measures are of increasing interest (see Table 4). If an adolescent is considering the possibility of having sexual intercourse, there is a strong likelihood that it will occur in the near future. Anticipatory guidance should be initiated to attempt to delay the onset of the behavior or to diminish the level of risk involved. For example, risk can be reduced through the use of condoms. Malus and colleagues have found that adolescents are willing to discuss a range of sexually related issues, provided that the professional gives them the opportunity (Malus, LaChance, and Lamy, 1987).

The following are examples of questions, both broad and specific, that we frequently ask middle and late adolescents in a medical setting.

- "Do you have a sexual relationship with someone now, or have you had one in the past?" Defining sexual preference and behavior in a frank but sensitive manner indicates to the teenager the counselor's comfort with and belief in the importance of this subject.
- "Do you have sex with members of your own sex, the other sex, or both?" Adolescents do not appear to be offended by this approach, and some have thanked us for our willingness to discuss homosexuality.
- "Do you find your current relationship satisfying? Have you had sex with one partner, or more than one? What are your methods for avoiding pregnancy or helping your partner avoid pregnancy?" Males have been traditionally omitted from a role in pregnancy prevention, yet are usually appreciative of their inclusion.

Such questions not only identify the adolescent with special needs but also help educate youth regarding their sexual feelings and behavior. Table 5 lists the specific elements of a comprehensive assessment of an adolescent's sexual behavior.

### The Adolescent with an Explicit Sexual Problem

When an adolescent presents with an explicit sexual problem, it usually means that he or she is concerned, angry, or afraid. Initially, such a visit calls

**Table 4.**
**Exploring Sexual Concerns and Behaviors with Middle and Late Adolescents**

1. Obtain a complete sexual history.
2. Help teenagers assess their knowledge about fertility and STDs, including HIV infection.
3. Ask about their comfort with sexuality and whether they find sex enjoyable or something they feel pressured into doing.
4. Discuss any previously uncomfortable sexual experiences.

for careful listening. It is important to establish what the problem is and not to accept too easily the label a teenager attaches to his or her difficulty. A recent example was a young man who thought he was impotent because he could not have intercourse five or six times a night, as, he believed, any "real man" should. More common concerns of teenagers include STDs and pregnancy scares. Even these complaints are not always what they first appear to be. An example concerns an adolescent female who requested a urine check for diabetes. After three negative tests, it became apparent that she thought she might be pregnant and that her diabetes test would demonstrate her pregnancy. She was familiar with an aunt who had been diagnosed as prediabetic during a recent pregnancy. The teenager logically thought that this test was a way of learning her own pregnancy status without having to discuss this concern directly with her health professional.

The adolescent's difficulty frequently stems from ignorance or misinformation. The counselor who is comfortable with the adolescent's problem should conduct a free and objective discussion, rather than merely recommending reading material. The counselor needs to convey that it is all right to discuss sexual behaviors and concerns openly.

### The Evaluation of a Suspected Covert Sexual Difficulty

Teenagers frequently complain of chronic fatigue or other vague symptoms. Occasionally, the cause is secondary to a concern the adolescent has about his or her sexual behavior. For example, sexual intercourse or a developing gay life-style may come into direct conflict with personal or religious values. A teenager who is involved in an incestuous relationship or has been raped may have been unable to disclose this problem in the past, and may present with symptoms suggestive of depression. An overemphasis on finding a medical cause for an adolescent's fatigue or vague symptoms may come at the expense of delayed counseling and continued risk-taking behavior. The health care provider needs to broach psychobehavioral etiologies, while simultaneously investigating possible medical etiologies for certain somatic symptoms.

## Counseling to Promote Sexual Abstinence

### Introduction/Definition of the Problem

With the extensive media coverage of the problem of premature sexual activity and the ensuing problems of sexually transmitted diseases, pregnancy, abortion, adoption, and adolescent parenthood, counselors and health professionals may feel that they have little influence on a teenager's decision to remain sexually abstinent. Although the United States has witnessed a trend

## Table 5.
## Assessment of an Adolescent's Sexuality and Sexual Behavior

Age (years, months)

Gender

Reason for visit

Overlying developmental, behavioral, psychiatric, or medical problems

Psychosocial profile

    Family: Family constellation (include ages)
           Relationships with family members

    School: Grade placement
           Attitude toward school
           Attendance
           Achievement
           Problems

    Employment:

    Future plans:

    Peers: Relationships and activities pursued together
           Ages and genders of friends
           Sexual behaviors
           Pregnancy and parenthood
           Involvement with police or court
           Involvement in gangs

    Substance use: Cigarettes
                Alcohol
                Marijuana
                Cocaine
                Other substances
                Routes of ingestion, including needles

    Institutional involvement (courts, group residence, social service agency):

    For females: Menarche
             Dates of last menstrual period and prior menstrual period
             Duration of flow
             Regularity of cycle
             Dysmenorrhea (menstrual pain)
             Concerns about menstrual periods

    For males: Erections
            Wet dreams
            Concerns about genitalia

    Sexual history: Romantic involvement
                Gender preference(s)
                Date (or age) of first sexual contact
                    Information about current and recent past partner(s) (age, school atten-
                    dance, employment, relationship with teenager's parents, duration of
                    relationship, degree of physical intimacy, emotional intensity, level of
                    communication, interest in preventing or promoting pregnancy, parent-
                    hood, substance use history, knowledge about other partners, history of
                    STD, involvement in gang activity, legal problems, violence or
                    intimidation)
                Number of partners (lifetime; within past year)
                History of sexually transmitted infection or pelvic infection
                Sexual practices
                Any symptoms suggestive of infection (discharge or drip, pain, dysuria)
                Parenthood

**Table 5. (*continued*)**

| |
|---|
| Sexual history: (*continued*) |
|         History of sexual assault, exploitation, incest |
|         Use of contraceptive methods |
|         Partner's use of contraceptive methods |
|         Sexual practices |
|         Enjoyment of sex |
|         Sexual dysfunction |
| Involvement of parents and other family members: |
|   Knowledge of visit |
|   Knowledge of sexual behavior |
|   Attitude toward adolescent's use of contraception |
|   Request by adolescent that parents be involved or not be involved |
| Formal assessment: |
|   Maturity |
|   Biopsychosocial functioning and sources of social support |
|   Risk for and motivation to prevent pregnancy, impregnation |
|   Risk for STD |
|   Risk for HIV infection |
|   History of sexual trauma |

of earlier and more frequent sexual activity by adolescents, many teenagers remain abstinent. The average age at first intercourse is approximately sixteen years for young men and young women (Deisher & Remafedi, 1989); the majority of early and middle adolescents are not sexually active. A thorough understanding of behavioral options may help a young person to make responsible decisions (Deisher & Remafedi, 1989). Abstinence should be seen as a viable option for young people. Delay of sexual activity allows an adolescent to mature cognitively, prior to assuming the responsibilities of expressing sexuality through intercourse.

There is growing evidence that education about sexuality encourages adolescents to postpone sexual activity until a later age. Howard and McCabe (1990) have found sexual educational programming involving peer counseling to be effective in postponing the onset of sexual activity for eighth- and ninth-graders. Educational programming, along with the provision of medical and contraceptive services, was also found to delay the onset of sexual activity in a group studied by Zabin, Hirsch, Smith, Streett, & Hardy (1986).

## Specific Counseling Strategies

Health care providers and counselors who deal with children and adolescents are often reluctant to offer education and counseling about abstinence and sexuality. They frequently feel uncomfortable in their own counseling skills, are concerned about time constraints, and regard counseling as value-laden. Time constraints can be handled by such methods as seeing adolescents earlier or later in the day, when interruptions are less likely to occur. Health care providers can also alternate counseling sessions with medical assessments for healthy adolescents. Moreover, the counselor can share values that are nonjudgmental. Deischer and Remafedi suggest that the following concepts of human sexuality are values that can be outlined with teenagers:

> (1) The goal of adolescent sexuality is the establishment of intimacy with another person (although physical intimacy is not essential for its attainment); (2) sexual behaviors are not intrinsically good or bad but derive their value and meaning from a social context; and (3) sexual intimacy is best reserved for people who can assume its responsibilities. (Deisher & Remafedi, 1989, p. 339).

A caring and interested counselor may also be seen by the teenager as an effective role model and can enhance the adolescent's own sense of worth and self-esteem (Hardy, 1988).

## Guided Decision Making

Further counseling strategies may be implemented in the form of guided decision making as described by Hofmann (1990). Health providers should begin discussion regarding sexuality early, as a natural part of a child's development, and encourage parents to do the same. Adolescents need facts about sexuality. For example, younger adolescents should learn that abstinence is the norm for their age-group and that most sexual fantasies are not unusual (Kenney, 1989). Exploration of an adolescent's emotions and behaviors may help define a problem behavior regarding early sexual activity. What may be responsible activity at an older age may be risky behavior at a younger age, based on the adolescent's developmental status. For example, a seventeen-year-old female may decide that she is ready to have sexual intercourse with her eighteen-year-old boyfriend of two years; he plans to wear a condom, she to take birth control pills. Even though the majority of adults may not want to encourage this adolescent couple's sexual behavior, they would no doubt acknowledge their thoughtful responsibility regarding the prevention of pregnancy and sexually transmitted infection. In contrast, a thirteen- or fourteen-year-old would probably be unable to understand the significance of sexual intercourse, discuss it with his or her partner, and plan ahead to prevent pregnancy and infection.

The next step in guided decision making is the definition of solutions or options. Kenney (1989) suggests that providers instruct adolescents about "safe-touch" areas and discuss alternatives to intercourse, such as masturbation, petting, and other forms of intimacy. Some adolescents may not realize that physical affection is possible without intercourse. Positive outcomes of abstinence, such as remaining worry free about infection and pregnancy, should be presented. The counselor should also offer strategies for handling sexual drives and peer pressure. The option of sexual intercourse should additionally be discussed with the adolescent, who should be asked to provide input regarding its personal risks and benefits. Asking the adolescent to make his or her own list of the risks and benefits of intercourse, or to dictate a list to the health provider or counselor, may be a concrete way of clarifying the consequences of intercourse. The health provider or counselor can dispel myths or misinformation about the options and their consequences, and help guide the adolescent to make an informed decision.

Once an option is chosen, the counselor can aid the adolescent to implement his or her decision. For example, if a teenager has decided to remain abstinent, the provider can help the adolescent to identify potentially high-pressure sexual situations that should be avoided, such as an empty house or the backseat of an automobile. Leaving the scene or double-dating may be an alternative.

Ideally, a couple can reach a mutual agreement to remain abstinent. Adolescents need to understand, however, that they have ownership of certain personal rights in social relationships. One is the right to say no to any activity or behavior that makes them uncomfortable. "No" may need to be emphatic and repetitive.

The counselor can also involve the youth in role-playing difficult situations and developing specific strategies to deal with peer or partner pressure. For example, a teenager might blame a parent for an early curfew, as a socially acceptable excuse for an uncomfortable situation. Teenagers can rehearse counters to common pressure tactics. For example, an effective response to "You would if you loved me" is "But if you really loved me, you wouldn't insist on my doing something I don't want to do." A counselor can also help adolescents decide in advance which sexual activities they will or will not agree to, and can assist them in learning how to communicate their decisions to their partners (Hatcher, Stewart, Trussell, Kowal, Gust, Stewart, & Cates, 1990–92).

If an adolescent decides to become sexually active, it is critical that the counselor provide referral or access to contraceptive counseling. Whatever option the adolescent chooses, continued support by the counselor needs to be given through regularly scheduled visits.

## Counseling to Prevent Pregnancy and to Promote Contraception

Teenagers in the United States are no more sexually active than youth who live in Western Europe, yet the incidence of pregnancy, live births, and abortion in this country exceeds the level of most other industrialized nations

(Jones, Forrest, & Goldman, 1985). These outcomes are partly due to limited sexuality education and poor contraceptive use among American youth. Case studies by the Alan Guttmacher Institute (1981) suggest that teenagers living in the United States are exposed to mixed messages about pregnancy prevention and that contraceptive services are not effectively delivered to the teenage population. Brooks-Gunn and Furstenberg (1989) have found that many American adults are poor contraceptive users as well. The most widely used method of contraception among married adults in their thirties is sterilization, presumably because they have many of the same apprehensions and problems with contraception that teenagers do.

## Failure to Use Contraception Effectively

The great majority of adolescent pregnancies are unintended (Alan Guttmacher Institute, 1981). The percentage of teenagers who use birth control only occasionally or not at all is substantial. The delay between the initiation of intercourse and the use of a prescription method of contraception averages one year. Such delays, as well as the inconsistent use of over-the-counter contraceptives (e.g., condoms), have serious consequences for youth. For example, nearly one-half of all first pregnancies occur in the first six months following the onset of intercourse, and one-fifth in the first month (Zabin, Kantner, & Zelnik, 1979).

Most teenagers engage in intercourse without fully understanding the immediate or long-term consequences of their actions. They do not consciously plan to become sexually active and frequently do not anticipate their first sexual experience. According to Chilman (1983), intercourse is often experienced not as a decision but rather as something that "happened." When teenagers first start having intercourse, they do so infrequently. One might view the teenager as more sexually "available" than sexually "active." It is not uncommon for an adolescent to have first intercourse at age fourteen or fifteen and then not to have sexual relations again for a year or two. Under these circumstances, adolescents are unlikely to view themselves as sexually active, capable of pregnancy, and in need of contraception.

## General Considerations for Contraceptive Counseling

To help adolescents avoid pregnancy, it is particularly important for the counselor to understand adolescent psychosocial and cognitive development. As Hofmann (1990) has noted, there can be no expectation that simply lecturing young people about the potential dangers of their sexual behavior and giving them factual information will result in substantial behavior change. Learning has to actively involve adolescents in the decision-making process through a joint analysis of the relevant issues and the young person's own decision about what action he or she wishes to take.

According to Davis (1990), successful contraceptive counseling rests on a foundation of trust, interactive communication, and continuity of care. A supportive, nonjudgmental environment is essential, as a teenager's compliance with contraception is more often a function of the effectiveness of counseling than of the inherent properties of a specific contraceptive device.

### Confidentiality

A statement from the counselor regarding confidentiality is a key factor in establishing trust. In our opinion, if one does not respect the confidentiality of the adolescent-counselor relationship, one will be seen as yet another surrogate parent, and the adolescent will provide little information concerning his or her level of sexual risk taking. Teenagers, as well as their parents, need to understand that confidentiality is one of the basic rules of counseling. The counselor or health care provider can make the following statement to an adolescent: "What you and I are discussing will not be shared with anyone unless you are in full agreement." The only obvious exception to this rule occurs when the adolescent has been a victim of incest or is threatening to hurt him- or herself or another individual. Such exceptions should also be explained to the teenager and, when appropriate, to his or her parents.

We encourage our patients to share information about their visit for contraception with their parents, and we volunteer to help them do this when and if they choose. Refusal by the adolescent may simply reflect testing the confidentiality statement. The counselor must not attempt to impose a solution to a given problem. Once the adolescent is comfortable with his or her decision, it will usually be shared with a parent. We view contraceptive use by sexually active adolescents as a responsible choice, and not something they need to hide in shame or embarrassment. Adolescents and parents need to hear this message clearly from adults they respect.

### Management

**Guided Decision Making.** Once it has been determined that a teenager is sexually active, the counselor should use a nonjudgmental, straightforward approach to estimate the degree of sexual risk taking (Hayes, 1987). The youth may be at risk not only for pregnancy or paternity but also for sexually transmitted disease and/or a significant clash with his or her own value system.

**Interventive Counseling.** The counselor, using an interventive approach, should offer the youth direction in his or her own decision making by (a) reviewing the issues and providing factual information, (b) exploring choices and decisions about the behavior, and (c) discussing and planning what to do, how to do it, and how to stick to the commitment (Hofmann, 1990). The process of guided decision making follows a logical sequence.

**Problem Definition.** Initially, the teenager and counselor need to decide what the problem is, what the risks are, and what behaviors may need modification. Once the counselor has obtained a psychosocial inventory, it should be an easy matter to ask about problems. Separate input from the adolescent and parent will be helpful, as each party has its own perspective. It is essential to give the adolescent sufficient time to talk about and define the problem as he or she sees it. For example, it may not be a problem for a boy or girl to be sexually active, but it may be a problem if pregnancy occurs. Another youth may wish to remain abstinent but recognize significant peer pressure to have sexual intercourse and a lack of parental support not to do so. Some female teenagers are put off by the need to have a pelvic examination when they want to use birth control pills. A common situation in our clinic is the teenager who has missed a menstrual period and fears she is pregnant. On learning that her pregnancy test is negative, she decides not to acquire contraception, because she no longer plans to be sexually active. There is a real possibility that pregnancy will eventually occur, however, unless true abstinence is practiced or effective contraception utilized.

Interactive counseling should allow sexually active adolescents who do not use contraception an opportunity to explore and appreciate the consequences of sexual activity on their own health, as well as on their personal and family value systems. The counselor may need to provide concrete situational examples to younger adolescents who lack life experience and the ability to see the future implications of their current behavior. Have they known anyone who has been pregnant or a teen parent? Have they talked with him or her about what that was like? How would their becoming pregnant affect their planned vacation at the beach this summer? Who would take care of their baby when they wanted to go to a basketball game with their friends? Have they discussed the need for contraception with a parent? In order to have personal meaning, the reality of eventual pregnancy needs to be explored within the framework of the adolescent's own life.

It is frequently helpful for the counselor to determine why an individual teenager is engaging in risk-taking behavior. Do significant predisposing and precipitating factors exist? An example of an adolescent who developed problematic sexual behavior but had sufficient insight to seek help for it concerns a sixteen-year-old male who claimed to have had over 200 female sexual partners but had never worn a condom. This information was offered nonchalantly during a routine interview. The initial health care provider thought the young man was bragging, and dismissed his statement. The physical examination, however, revealed that the young man was concerned about the relatively small size of his penis. As a younger adolescent, he had previously been too embarrassed to address this concern with a health care provider. Although no comment was made about the number of partners, the physician recommended that the young man wear a condom for each act of intercourse to help prevent pregnancy and the transmission of infection. The patient did not hesitate in accepting a supply of free condoms. During a subsequent visit with a second health care provider, the young man asked whether the size of a man's penis was related to homosexuality. Through gentle questioning, he disclosed that he was frightened about whether he was truly "male" and offered the insight that perhaps he needed to have sex with so many females to "prove [his] manhood." This youngster was very relieved to be able to discuss his basic concerns, and eagerly accepted referral to a mental health professional interested in helping teenagers with sexual identity problems. Although it was important for this young man to learn how to prevent an unplanned pregnancy, his basic problem and psychological dilemma had greatly enhanced his risk taking.

**Options and Possible Outcomes.** After identifying the problem(s) to be addressed, the adolescent's options should be reviewed (Hofmann, 1990). Both the counselor and the youth should contribute to this joint process. At the conclusion of this phase, the adolescent should fully understand all of the choices and the probable outcome for each one.

*Abstinence.* The benefits and problems associated with abstinence have already been discussed in this chapter. The majority of professionals working with youth see considerable benefits for youth in delaying sexual intercourse until they are older. Abstinence should be promoted as the most effective way for a teenager to avoid pregnancy, STDs, and a potential clash with his or her own value system. Many teenagers will acknowledge that abstinence may be advantageous, but still choose to become or remain sexually active (Sorenson, 1973). Coping with sexual drives and attempting to handle peer pressure do not make the practice of abstinence an easy one for an ambivalent teenager.

*To Be Sexually Active.* The risks of adolescent activity need to be acknowledged by the adolescent and the counselor. Reasons for using and not using contraception should be explored. Some teenagers may feel sufficiently insecure about themselves that they will risk pregnancy in order to achieve other goals. For example, a female adolescent with marginal self-esteem may feel that her refusal to have intercourse or to require her partner to use a condom will jeopardize their relationship. Denial and rationalization further complicate this social process. The adolescent should be encouraged to take personal control over his or her own life and choose contraception over no decision at all. The counseling approach should include gentle but firm reality testing as a strategy to enable the adolescent to choose an option and follow through with it. For example, the counselor can ask, "If you become infected with an STD, where will you and your partner go to get care?" or "If your girlfriend became pregnant, what plans would you make? Would she involve you in decisions about her pregnancy?"

**Option Choice/Commitment.** The adolescent now selects a solution and reviews in detail why it is what he or she wants to do. Hofmann warns that imposing a choice on the teenager at this time may invite rebellion (Henshaw & Van Vort, 1989). The adolescent may test the counselor's position by making an unwise initial choice. When the youth is satisfied that the counselor will not intervene, he or she will feel free to make another choice.

**Option Implementation.** Once the adolescent has selected an option, the counselor will often need to be a source of practical information, as well as an active listener (Hofmann, 1990).

*Abstinence.* The reader is referred to the earlier discussion of abstinence.

*Sexual Activity with Contraception.* The teenager will require information not only about contraceptive methods but also about which ones offer protection against sexually transmitted diseases, including HIV infection. Table 6 lists the reliability of contemporary contraceptive methods and comments on each method's protection against STDs. When two methods are used together, the pregnancy risk can be dramatically decreased. If one of these methods is a condom, protection against sexually transmitted disease is significantly increased. Although a majority of teenagers are aware of the concept of safer sex, the 1989 National Adolescent Student Health Survey found that more than 50 percent of the 11,000 eighth- and tenth-graders questioned did not know that taking birth control pills will not protect against STDs ("National Adolescent Student Health Survey," 1989).

Contraceptive use should be not only discussed but also demonstrated. Having the adolescent open a sealed condom pack and correctly position the condom over a banana is a humorous but effective way to teach correct technique. Pill packs for birth control pills can be confusing. Having various sample packs available for hands-on experience will help prepare the female adolescent for her visit to a clinic offering family planning services. Although birth control pills are extremely safe and effective, many teenagers remain ambivalent about their use. They have heard that the pill may cause cancer and heart disease. They may have heard the myth that birth control pills decrease a woman's fertility. Frustration concerning weight gain, breast tenderness, and spotting has caused teenagers to discontinue this contraceptive method without consulting their health care providers. A host of questions may arise in the course of a frank discussion of family planning: "Will I need to have a pelvic exam? What is it like?" "Can I have a female examiner?" "How will I remember to take the pill each day?"

Table 6.
Contraception and STD Protection*

| | Contraceptive Reliability (%) | STD Protection, Including HIV |
|---|---|---|
| Abstinence | 100 | Most protective |
| Condom—latex | 88 | Protective |
| Condom—natural membrane | 88 | Not protective for HIV, Hepatitis B |
| Natural family planning | 80 | Not protective |
| Withdrawal | 82 | Not protective |
| Spermicide | 79 | Protective against gonorrhea and several other STDs |
| Contraceptive sponge | 82 | Probably protective |
| Diaphragm with spermicide | 82 | Protects against STDs that infect the cervix |
| Cervical cap with spermicide | 82 | Similar to diaphragm |
| IUD | 97 | Increases risks |
| Oral contraceptive pill | 97 | Increased risk of chlamydial cervicitis; may protect against pelvic infection |
| Norplant® | 99.5 | Unknown—probably resembles oral contraception |

* Adapted from Hatcher, R. A., Stewart, L., Trussell, J., Kowal, D., Guest, F., Stewart, G. K., Cates, W. (1990–1992). *Contraceptive Technology.* New York: Irvington Publishers, Inc.


Many gynecologists and family planning agencies are gaining experience with Norplant®, a long-term but reversible contraceptive system. This new method involves the insertion of six small capsules containing a progestin hormone just beneath the skin of a woman's upper arm. Although it is too early to determine how acceptable this method will be to teenagers, it is believed that it will be successful for individuals who have difficulty complying with daily oral contraceptive pills.

Counselors should be able to discuss myths and practicalities of birth control. For example, telling a young woman to keep her pill pack with her toothbrush or in her fresh panty drawer may be a helpful answer to the question of how to remember to take a pill daily. Female teenagers may have a difficult time discussing consistent condom use with their partners. The counselor should find out what the teenager thinks her partner will say when he objects to using condoms and help her practice her reply so that she can insist on condom use. The partner may say he doesn't have a condom and doesn't want to get one right now, even though he wants to have sex. She might reply, "Well, I just happen to have some condoms with me. What color do you like most?" (Hatcher, Stewart, Trussell, et al., 1990–92). Humor and firmness help a lot. Sources of free condoms should also be discussed. Males are more likely to use condoms if they have done so previously and do not perceive condom use as interfering with sexual enjoyment. Moreover, males are also influenced by their girlfriends' attitudes toward condoms (Pendergrast, Durant, & Gaillard, 1991).

Cost and geographic access to a family planning program are major hurdles for many adolescents. Is the clinic open at a time convenient for the adolescent's school, work, and family schedules? A visit to procure contraception may represent the first time a teenager sees a health professional without a parent's presence. If the teenager chooses to attend a public family planning program, it is helpful for the counselor to be familiar with it and to have a personal contact whom the adolescent can call. The youth needs to know where he or she is going, whom he or she will be seeing, what will happen, and how much it will cost. The availability of a sliding scale or no fee at all will reassure the adolescent with limited funds. Before the youth leaves the counselor's office, a specific appointment for contraception should be scheduled.

**Reinforcement.** Continued support from the counselor during the transition to using a contraceptive method is essential. Asking a female adolescent to call about the success of her (and her partner's) visit for contraception or how their decision to be abstinent is working out may help to sustain their option choice. Here the counselor might say, "If I don't hear from you by the end of next week, I will be calling to see how things are going. What would be a good time to reach you so we could talk?"

The adolescent should be encouraged to share his or her concerns with a parent throughout the counseling process. Parents can be a prime source of emotional as well as financial support. For an early adolescent, parental involvement may be the only way of achieving any level of contraceptive compliance. Various strategies of telling parents can be reviewed. The counselor should offer his or her own involvement in the discussion process. This message is important for the adolescent to hear, while at the same time assuring the youth of his or her right to privacy. Here the counselor might ask:

- What do you think your mother or dad would say or do if you told them you were sexually active and needed contraception?
- What if you had to tell them you or your sexual partner was pregnant? Would it help if you wrote them a note or called them on the phone? How have they handled unexpected news in the past?

Adolescents who cope well but come from highly dysfunctional environments usually have at least one significant positive adult model. At times, the counselor may find him- or herself playing that role until the teenager is well into young adult life.

Contraceptive use averts 680,000 teenage pregnancies each year, but consistent use of any method could prevent another 313,000 cases per year (State of Wisconsin, Department of Health and Social Services, 1988). Combinations such as mechanical and chemical barriers add to contraceptive effectiveness and offer protection against STDs. The counselor may not only accelerate the social process whereby adolescents decide to use contraception but also help them choose a method with which they are comfortable.

## Pregnancy Counseling

### Introduction

Close to a million teenagers in the United States become pregnant each year. About 31,000 pregnant adolescents are younger than fifteen (National Academy of Sciences, 1987). It is estimated that 47 percent of adolescent pregnancies culminate in delivery, that 40 percent are aborted, and that 13 percent miscarry. Teenage women account for 13 percent of the nation's births and 26 percent of all abortions (Henshaw & Van Vort, 1989). In 1986, the pregnancy rate for nonwhite teenagers ages fifteen to nineteen was twice that of white teenagers. For adolescents younger than fifteen, the differential was fivefold greater in nonwhite youth. In 1985, 92 percent of these births were to unmarried adolescents, and less than 7 percent of teenage parents placed their infants for adoption (Advance Report of Final Natality Statistics, 1985," 1987). Approximately 87 percent of births to teenagers are described as unintended (Moore, Snyder, & Daly, 1992).

There is no unique psychological profile common to pregnant teenagers. Many, however, suffer from poverty, a dysfunctional family environment, low self-esteem, and poor academic achievement. For some, a familial/cultural acceptance of adolescent childbearing is present. As discussed elsewhere in this chapter, teenagers in the United States do not use contraception effectively.

Adolescents who become parents are seriously risking their futures (Hayes, 1987). Withdrawal from school, low occupational attainment, and poverty await many of these young people. Studies of the effects of teenage paternity have now documented the educational and financial disadvantages of being a teenage father as well (Enright & Sutterfield, 1980). For those teenage parents who choose to marry, the strains of early marriage in combination with parenting responsibilities are often insurmountable. It is estimated that 75 percent of such marriages end in divorce (American Academy of Pediatrics, Committee on Adolescence, 1989b).

Improvements in perinatal care have markedly decreased medical complications among babies born to teenage mothers, but pregnant adolescents ages fourteen and younger continue to experience unacceptably high rates of adverse outcomes (McAnarney, 1987). Infants of young mothers have increased rates of hospitalization and increased risks of accidents, poisonings, burns, and superficial injuries (Taylor, Wadsworth, & Butler, 1983). These statistics are sobering. Anyone engaged in pregnancy counseling must consider them carefully.

## Identifying a Counselor

A female adolescent who thinks she may be pregnant is usually initially reluctant to share this concern with her family. Her decision regarding the person to whom she initially turns for help will be influenced by her prior experience. Who was willing to listen and respond to her in a respectful and nonjudgmental manner in the past? If she turns to a professional, she will consider accessibility. For example, how long does it take to get an appointment? Is a monetary cost involved? Such teenagers frequently seek out school nurses, social workers, and counselors for help because these persons' judgment is trusted and they have a reputation for helping other students in crisis. Other young women may call their physicians, have pregnancy tests at local public family planning clinics, or perform their own home pregnancy tests.

## Counseling Bias

Professionals who become involved in pregnancy counseling need to examine their own attitudes about premarital sex, pregnancy, and abortion, as these personal beliefs can be deeply rooted. Pregnancy counselors must refrain from allowing their own sexual and moral standards to interfere with adolescents' decision making. Professionals who are not able to provide unbiased options counseling for adolescents should recognize their biases and make a conscious decision not to offer counseling services in this area. They do, however, have the responsibility of referring pregnant adolescents to other professionals and facilities experienced with and sensitive to the needs of adolescents (American Academy of Pediatrics, Committee on Adolescence, 1989a).

## The Process of Pregnancy Counseling

Pregnancy assessment and counseling should be initiated even before the pregnancy test result is available, in order to take advantage of the reality of the event as an actual life experience. The following information should be routinely gathered:

- Why the adolescent thinks she may be pregnant (missed or abnormal menstrual period)

- General health, including possible symptoms of pregnancy (breast tenderness or enlargement, weight changes, thickening of waist, nausea and vomiting, urinary frequency), nutritional status, and tobacco, alcohol, or other drug use
- Gynecological and pregnancy history
- Sexual history
- Contraceptive history
- Family and partner involvement
- Financial aid and social service support

The counselor may ask such open-ended questions as "If the test comes back positive for pregnancy, how would you feel? What do you think you would do?" Although current pregnancy testing methods available through hospital, clinic, and commercial laboratories are highly accurate, they should nevertheless be interpreted in conjunction with clinical and other laboratory data available to a knowledgeable health care professional.

Pregnancy counseling frequently needs to address the needs of a teenager in crisis. A variety of emotions, including panic, disbelief, fear, anger, and guilt, may surface and will need to be acknowledged. The counselor will also need to explore the pregnancy itself, including pregnancy options, community resources, and the adolescent's relationships with her partner(s), parent(s), and other significant individuals. If the patient is not pregnant (i.e., she has experienced a pregnancy "scare"), the counselor needs to discuss pregnancy prevention and refer the teenager for contraceptive care.

*Confidentiality*

In most states, adolescents of minority age have legal rights protecting their privacy regarding the diagnosis and treatment of pregnancy. Information should not be offered to anyone, including the youth's parents and sexual partner, without the adolescent's knowledge and permission. It is hoped that at some point during the process of pregnancy counseling, the young woman will be able to include her parents or adult surrogates, as well as her sexual partner, in a full discussion of the issue.

To determine what the adolescent truly needs and desires, the following open-ended questions are helpful: "Could you tell me how you are feeling about your pregnancy?" and "How can I help you at this time?" Looking for nonverbal cues of depression or anxiety will allow the counselor to address these feelings more effectively. During counseling, the provider should keep the teenager focused on the issue of her pregnancy, for there is often a tendency to attempt to handle too wide a range of problems during a single session. If digression occurs, the counselor will need to practice active listening ("It sounds like you are feeling overwhelmed by a number of difficult problems . . .") and then refocus the adolescent on the immediate concern

("... but you need to take things one step at a time. Let's look at what you need to do about your pregnancy, and then perhaps address these other concerns in another session"). Examples of common issues contributing to an adolescent's perception of crisis include previous sexual trauma, school problems, family dysfunction, substance use, and financial difficulty. The counselor and adolescent need to prioritize these issues so that they can be addressed in the near future.

In interacting with the pregnant adolescent, the counselor needs to pay careful attention to vocabulary. For example, the word *partner* is preferred to *father*. The counselor should try not to refer to the adolescent as *mother* or call the fetus *baby*. The adolescent should be allowed to choose her own vocabulary, as her choice of words will help convey how she feels. The teenager should also be encouraged to identify any barriers she perceives as deterring her from gaining the support of her parent(s), partner(s), and friends. If the adolescent remains isolated, or indiscriminately seeks support and sanction for her pregnancy, she clearly needs a greater intensity of help.

Most teenagers are uninformed regarding state laws that address abortion, adoption, child support, paternal rights, and marriage. A brief overview of laws and recent court decisions is often helpful. Information about minors' rights can be obtained from one or more of the following sources: city and state bar associations, county and state medical societies, state and city departments of health and social service, state attorney general offices, Planned Parenthood and other family planning programs, the Children's Rights Project of the American Civil Liberties Union, attorneys specializing in health care law, and attorneys representing hospitals and malpractice carriers (Hofmann & Greydanus, 1989). Referral to knowledgeable legal counsel should be made when indicated.

## Management

Three basic options are available to a pregnant adolescent (Stephenson, 1989). The first option is to continue the pregnancy and raise the child. She may raise the child together with the father, as a family unit; raise the child with the help of other family members; or raise the child alone, as a single parent. Her second option is to continue the pregnancy but relinquish the infant for adoption. Third, she may choose to have an abortion. Although we need to understand the expedient nature of her decision, the pregnant teenager should be encouraged to consider these options and return for as many visits as may be needed to reach a decision.

**The Decision to Remain Pregnant.** If the teenager decides to continue her pregnancy, the counselor should suggest immediate referral to a special adolescent maternity program or obstetrician known to have acceptable standards for managing both the medical and the emotional aspects of adolescent pregnancy. The decision-making process may require several visits. Staff at local family planning programs are a good source of information, as they are aware of teen-oriented obstetric services, as well as how teenagers can enroll in the following supportive programs: Women Infants Children (WIC), Medical Assistance (MA), Aid to Families with Dependent Children (AFDC), and food stamps. Optimally, an appointment should be arranged with a specific individual in the referral facility. If parents are still not involved, the counselor may offer to attend the first obstetric visit with the adolescent. In reality, pregnant teenagers who will continue to live at home need to involve their families at an early point during the pregnancy. The counselor may need to take an active role in helping an adolescent communicate with her family.

**The Choice of Adoption.** Although the vast majority of infants born to teenagers remain with their mothers, any counselor working with pregnant youth should not assume this to be the case. The important option of adoption should be discussed initially, as well as at appropriate intervals during the course of the pregnancy. The importance of regular prenatal care with respect to healthy maternal-infant outcome should be stressed prior to actual referral. Continued support by the counselor is essential even after the adolescent has been referred for obstetric management. Initially, the counselor needs to ensure that the adolescent did indeed follow through with her scheduled appointment, perhaps by saying, "Please call me next week to let me know how your first appointment turned out. If I don't hear from you by next Thursday, I'll try to reach you. What would be a good time for me to phone?"

**Additional Issues for the Adolescent Who Remains Pregnant.** The adolescent should be encouraged to include her family and sexual partner in counseling sessions. If she is reluctant to reveal the identity of the father, the possibility of sexual abuse or incest should be considered. For some adolescents, individual and family psychotherapy may be necessary and early referral should be initiated. It is of great importance that the teenager's formal education continue during her pregnancy and following delivery. Many school districts maintain flexible school-aged mother programs, and other community resources may be available.

**Adolescents Who Choose Abortion.** Deciding to have an abortion is a highly ambivalent process for many adolescents. These feelings may be masked by an attitude of indifference or flippancy, both of which belie the individual's true feelings. Biro and colleagues have recently reviewed the acute and long-term psychosocial and medical consequences for adolescents who choose abortion (Biro, Wildey, & Hillary, 1986). The experience of the procedure itself is considered by many to be stressful and associated with feelings of guilt and depression and a sense of isolation. These feelings appear to be of relatively short duration, however, and the majority of adolescents who have undergone an abortion believe that it helped them to mature and accept responsibility.

**Parental Notification.** It has been our experience that adolescents who choose not to tell a parent of their pregnancy or planned abortion often show an impressive degree of sensitivity and maturity in making that decision. Rosen (1980) found that although few adolescents consulted their parents when they first thought they might be pregnant, more than half ultimately involved their mothers in pregnancy-resolution decision making. The U.S. Supreme Court has allowed states to establish requirements for parental notification concerning therapeutic abortion. The Court has determined, however, that parental notification may be waived for a pregnancy in a minor deemed by the state court or administrative agency to be mature enough to give informed consent. Many health care professionals believe that the judicial-bypass process interferes with their ability to prepare the minor psychologically and medically for the abortion procedure. In addition, there is no guarantee that the judge or referee making a decision about the level of an adolescent's maturity will use logic or respect health care professionals' judgments. Finally, the judicial-bypass procedure can be time-consuming for youngsters who, because they delayed seeking help for a suspected pregnancy, have little time to spare for an abortion procedure to be performed. These factors need to be taken into account by the adolescent's primary counselor in helping the pregnant teenager prepare for her abortion, as well as the process leading to it.

When an adolescent elects to have an abortion, she needs to learn in more detail what an early or midtrimester abortion is, how it is done, and what complications can occur. This information is equivalent to that given to any patient prior to an operative procedure. The teenager also needs to be given a description of the clinic and where it is located. She needs to know the cost of the procedure, in order to find the money for it. Specific names of the abortion clinic's staff, as well as the facility's phone number, should be given to the adolescent. Members of our teenage clinic staff have occasionally, at adolescents' requests, accompanied them when they have had their abortion procedures performed.

**Abortion Methods.** A wide variety of surgical and medical procedures are available to the gynecologist performing an abortion on an adolescent who is requesting termination of her pregnancy. The counselor should be aware of these procedures and be able to reassure the adolescent as to their efficacy and safety. The goal of an abortion procedure is to remove the products of conception, which include the placenta or chorionic villi and fetal parts.

A first-trimester abortion is performed within the first thirteen weeks of pregnancy. Gestational age is determined from the first day of the last menstrual period. Vacuum curettage is the procedure of choice for first-trimester pregnancies. Following local anesthesia, the woman's cervix is dilated. After inserting a vacuum curette and introducing a negative pressure from an electrical pump or other means, the gynecologist evacuates the products of conception. This procedure can be safely performed in an office or outpatient hospital setting until the sixteenth week of pregnancy, provided that the office is equipped to handle medical complications. Many health care providers are reluctant to use this procedure beyond thirteen to fourteen weeks, due to higher complication rates. Although RU 486 and prostaglandin agents have been used as early abortificants in Europe, they are not ready for marketing in the United States (Couzinet, Le Strat, & Ulmann, 1986).

A second-trimester abortion involves terminating pregnancy from fourteen to twenty-four weeks of gestation. Four agents can be used to induce a second-trimester abortion: prostaglandin F2, prostaglandin E, hypertonic saline, and hypertonic urea. One of these agents is instilled in the uterine cavity, and the cervix is dilated, frequently by placement of laminaria. These procedures are more complex than vacuum curettage, and have higher complication rates. Hospitalization is usually required for these procedures.

Both short- and long-term complications can occur with any of the abortion methods currently in use. Complications are less likely to occur when the patient is healthy, is in early pregnancy, is free of STDs such as gonorrhea and chlamydia, and is psychologically prepared to terminate her pregnancy. The overall risk of a woman's dying from a legal abortion is 1 per 100,000; however, procedures such as intrauterine instillations carry five times the risk that instrumental evacuation does (*Abortion Surveillance Report, 1981, 1985*). By comparison, pregnancy has a higher mortality rate than abortion performed by appropriately trained personnel. Tietze and colleagues noted a mortality rate of 11.1 per 100,000 in fifteen- to nineteen-year-old pregnant adolescents who deliver (Tietze, Bongaarts, & Schearer, 1976). Short-term postabortion complications include the following: infection, retained products of conception and blood clots, continuing pregnancy, cervical or uterine trauma, and bleeding. Long-term complications associated with legal abortion do not reveal major risks for the most commonly utilized methods, but this issue remains under study (Hatcher, Stewart, Trussell, et al., 1990–92).

**Abortion Follow-Up.** The adolescent should be encouraged to keep a postabortion follow-up appointment with the counselor within the following week and to call sooner if she would like. Family planning methods are usually discussed at the abortion facility, but their initiation may require additional visits and review. This transition period is a vulnerable time for repeat pregnancy to occur.

**Facts about Adoption.** An important option for the counselor to discuss with the pregnant adolescent is the possibility of adoption. In order to facilitate appropriate referral, the counselor should be familiar with the medical, legal, and specialized counseling resources available in the adolescent's community. The adolescent's basic options, which are subject to the laws of each state, include the traditional agency-based adoption, an open agency-based adoption, and an independent adoption.

The traditional agency-based adoption provides the birth mother with the following: crisis and options of counseling, careful review and home study of prospective adoptive families, coordination of the termination of parental rights, access to temporary foster care, and social service referral.

The open agency-based adoption provides the same services as the traditional agency but in addition allows the birth mother to participate in the selection of the adoptive family. The degree to which the adoptive parents remain anonymous depends on the parties involved.

Independent adoption allows the birth mother total control over the selection of the adoptive family. Rather than relinquishing custody to the adoption agency, she locates an adoptive family and places the child directly with that family. She must also consult a reputable attorney to protect her legal rights. Attorneys for the birth and the adoptive parents petition the court for placement of the child and termination of parental rights. The court then holds a hearing and orders a home study to be done by a voluntary adoption agency, the county department of social services, or the state department of social services. If the court then approves, the child is placed in the home of the adoptive parents, and guardianship is transferred to the agency conducting the home study. After six months of home supervision by the guardianship agency, a report of the placement is made to the court, which makes the final decision.

Since the Reagan presidency years, adoption has been advocated politically as an option to abortion. Nevertheless, ambivalence among pregnant teenagers remains strong. Many adolescents recognize that the best interests of the child may very well rest with adoption. At the same time, however, they face peers and possibly family members who may view their adoption plans as selfish, unloving, and even incomprehensible (Rosen, 1980).

## Counseling to Prevent Sexually Transmitted Diseases

### Extent of the Problem

Although public health programs have historically monitored five STDs, it is currently recognized that at least thirty-two organisms and twenty-six syndromes are sexually transmitted (Wisconsin Department of Health and Social Services, 1990). The true incidence of many of these diseases is probably underestimated, because of lack of required reporting, absence of diagnostic validation, and underreporting.

The increased rates of adolescent sexual activity in the United States have brought a concomitant increase in STDs. When rates are corrected to control for sexual experience, the age-specific rates for many STDs are highest in the adolescent age-group. The two most common sexually transmitted organisms, *Neisseria gonorrhoeae* and *Chlamydia trachomatis,* have the highest prevalence rates among adolescents and young adults (Adger, 1990).

In 1989, approximately 175,000 cases of gonorrhea in teenagers were reported to the Centers for Disease Control (CDC), the section of the U.S. Public Health Service that is responsible for disease-monitoring efforts. During the 1980s, the incidence of gonorrhea in fifteen- to nineteen-year-old males rose, although it declined for all other age-groups. At present, females ages fifteen to nineteen continue to have the highest age-specific rates of gonorrhea.

Cervical and urethral chlamydial infections in adolescent females and males are estimated to be at least two times more common than gonorrheal infections. Visits to private clinicians for consultations for genital herpes in fifteen- to nineteen-year-old females rose from 15,000 yearly visits in 1966 to over 125,000 visits in 1988. For genital warts caused by human papilloma virus (HPV), yearly visits rose from approximately 50,000 in 1966 to over 300,000 in 1988 for fifteen- to nineteen-year-old females. Reported visits for these two viral STDs probably greatly underestimated the incidence of these diseases in males and females (Cates, 1990).

Although reasons for the increased risk for STD acquisition among adolescents have not been entirely delineated, several adolescent health habits and behaviors increase risks. With the early onset of sexual activity, the adolescent may be exposed to multiple partners. Although most adolescents have only one partner at a time, partnerships may be short-lived, leading to many partners over time. Adolescent females frequently have significant cervical ectopy, or columnar-type epithelial cells, present on the ectocervix, or outer surface of the cervix. Gonorrhea and chlamydia have a predilection for columnar epithelium. In contrast, this type of epithelium is usually not exposed among adult women. It is also postulated that adolescents have less immune experience with STDs and are therefore more susceptible to infection (Neinstein, 1991). Bacterial diseases such as gonorrhea and syphilis, as well as chlamydia, are easily treated with antibiotics; however, adolescents may be less compliant than adults with using antibiotics for the treatment of STDs. As a result, any remaining untreated infection may serve as a source of continued transmission to other individuals. Viral infections, such as HIV and HPV, cannot be effectively treated with antimicrobial medication. Mechanical and chemical barrier methods of contraception (e.g., condoms, vaginal spermicides), the best methods for reducing viral and bacterial STD transmission, are often utilized inconsistently by adolescents. An adolescent's feeling of invulnerability to disease may also lead to risk-taking behavior. Education about STDs and how to access services for STDs is often not available for teenagers (Cates, 1990).

Morbidity due to STDs includes not only the monetary costs of treatment but medical complications. Female adolescents are particularly vulnerable to serious medical sequelae, which include pelvic inflammatory disease, chronic pain, ectopic pregnancy, impaired fertility, and genital cancer. Pregnant teenagers may transmit the infection to the fetus during the course of the pregnancy, or to the newborn infant during the birth process.

Table 7 outlines general counseling strategies for the prevention of sexually transmitted diseases, and Table 8 provides specific points that should be reviewed with an adolescent who has a sexually transmitted infection.

### Current Issues and Research regarding Human Immunodeficiency Virus

Although much of the current research in STD acquisition among adolescents has focused on prevention and transmission of HIV, many of the issues are applicable to the prevention and transmission of other STDs as well.

**Table 7.**
**General Counseling Strategies to Prevent Sexually Transmitted Disease***

| General preventive measures | Specific Recommendations |
|---|---|
| Maintain healthy sexual behavior | Postpone initiation of sexual intercourse until at least 2–3 years following menarche. |
| | Limit number of sex partners. |
| | Avoid "casual" sex and sex with high-risk partners. |
| | Question potential sex partners about STD and inspect their genitals for lesions or discharge. |
| | Avoid sex with infected persons |
| | Abstain from sex if STD symptoms appear. |
| Use barrier methods | Use condoms, diaphragms, and/or vaginal spermicides for protection against STD, even if contraception is not needed. |
| | Use condoms consistently and correctly throughout all sexual acts and with every partner. |
| Adopt healthy medical-care-seeking behavior | Seek medical evaluation promptly after having unprotected sex (intercourse without a condom) with someone who is suspected of having an STD. |
| | Seek medical care immediately when genital lesions or discharge appears. |
| | Seek routine checkups for STD if in nonmutually monogamous relationship(s), even if symptoms are not present. |
| Comply with management instructions | Take all medications as directed, regardless of symptoms. |
| | Return for follow-up evaluation as instructed. |
| | Abstain from sex until symptoms disappear and appropriate treatment is completed. |
| Ensure examination of sex partners | When diagnosed as having an STD, notify all sex partners in need of medical assessment. |
| | If preferred, assist health providers in identifying sex partners. |

* Adapted from Table 2. "Recommendations for Individuals to Prevent STD/PID", Centers for Disease Control. Pelvic inflammatory disease: Guidelines for Prevention and Management. MMWR 1991; 40 (no. RR-5): 9.

**Table 8.**
**General Counseling Strategies for Use When a Diagnosis of an STD Has Been Made**

1. Explain in concrete terms (understandable to the patient) how the infection was acquired (nearly all disease is spread by sexual activity, *not* toilet seats, towels, etc.).
2. Investigate the possibility of sexual abuse.
3. Emphasize the need for antimicrobial treatment for *patient and partner(s)*, with abstinence, until both have completed the treatment course.
4. Test the teenager after completion of the treatment course to ensure that reinfection has not occurred.
5. Review safer sex techniques. Emphasize in particular that a latex condom should be worn for every act of sexual intercourse, regardless of the use of other contraceptive methods.
6. Use barrier contraceptives after diagnosis of a viral disease (e.g., human papilloma virus, herpes), with abstinence recommended with active herpes lesions. Explain that condoms or other barrier method use may not prevent the spread of infection by viral lesions not covered by the barrier, but barriers will help prevent the spread of other STDs.
7. For heterosexual relationships, explore the motivation to prevent pregnancy. Discuss contraception and help the adolescent to acquire a contraceptive method.

As of July 1989, the CDC estimated that the prevalence of HIV, the causative agent of AIDS, is approximately 1,000,000 cases in the United States. The annual incidence of new HIV infections in adults and adolescents is estimated at greater than or equal to 40,000 infections per year (Centers for Disease Control, 1990a). Less than 1 percent of AIDS cases reported to the CDC through December 31, 1988, were in adolescents thirteen to nineteen years old (Centers for Disease Control, 1989), but approximately 20 percent of all AIDS cases are diagnosed in persons between twenty and twenty-nine years of age (Centers for Disease Control, 1990b). Since HIV infection has such a long latency period (eight to ten years), many of these cases probably resulted from infection acquired during adolescence.

Are adolescents increasing their knowledge about HIV infection and AIDS, and changing their high-risk behaviors? Educational efforts have increased adolescents' knowledge about AIDS in some research samples (Steiner, Sorakin, Schiedermayer, & Van Susteren, 1990), but other studies have shown only a variable knowledge about AIDS or HIV transmission by adolescents (Centers for Disease Control, 1990c; DiClemente, Boyer, & Morales, 1988). Surveys have also shown that significant numbers of adolescents report intravenous drug use, multiple sexual partners, and low use of condoms (Centers for Disease Control, 1990c; Kegeles, Adler, & Irwin, 1988; Strunin & Hingson, 1987). The assumption is that knowledge of risks may not always affect behavior. The continued high rates of other STDs in adolescents also indicate inconsistent use of barrier methods and other safer sexual practices. Moreover, use of alcohol or other drugs before or during sexual activity may additionally make it difficult for one to practice safer sex.

## Counseling Strategies

Given adolescents' high risks of acquiring STDs, it is clearly important to provide access to education and counseling for this age-group. Many people have looked to the school system to provide such education and counseling, but community counseling resources are also necessary, as many young people at risk for contracting an STD do not attend school. Guidelines for school health programs regarding AIDS education are well outlined by the CDC (Centers for Disease Control, 1988). These guidelines state that education about AIDS may be most appropriate and effective when carried out in the context of a more comprehensive health program. Education about AIDS should be linked with information about other sexually transmitted diseases, drug abuse, and community health. AIDS education may have greater impact when students are also able to develop skills in communication, decision making, and resistance to persuasion. The guidelines include suggestions for the preparation of education personnel and for the content of programs for early elementary school, late elementary/middle school, junior high, and senior high school age-groups. The CDC has also included guidelines for curriculum time and resources, as well as program assessment.

Community resources are vital in spreading educational messages about preventing AIDS and other STDs. Youth groups, teen clinics, STD treatment and mental health facilities, detention centers, and youth shelters can all address high-risk behaviors and STD prevention. In larger cities, youth outreach workers may aid homeless and other vulnerable youth (Remafedi, 1988).

### Specific Counseling Strategies

In counseling an adolescent regarding STD prevention, it is essential to remain nonjudgmental and to protect confidentiality. Counseling regarding AIDS and other STDs should be provided in the context of other sexuality counseling. Developmental considerations should guide timing regarding the provision of specific information, but such considerations should generally parallel information about pregnancy prevention and risky behaviors such as alcohol and drug use.

Because there are many myths and misconceptions regarding STDs and AIDS, a counselor should provide facts regarding STD transmission and behavioral risk factors for acquiring STDs. Although all adolescents should be encouraged to practice sexual abstinence and to avoid intravenous drug use, a special focus should be placed on targeting younger adolescents with these primary prevention strategies. Similarly, those adolescents who choose not to abstain need to be informed of ways to reduce their risks and enhance their prevention skills. Table 9 lists key AIDS prevention strategies that should be discussed.

## Table 9.
## Components of Pre- and Posttest Counseling for HIV Infection

*Pretest Counseling Components*

At the pretest counseling session(s), the counselor should

1. Introduce him- or herself and explain his or her professional role.
2. Reassure confidentiality and/or anonymity.
3. Take a psychosocial history.
4. Assess risk for HIV infection.
5. Explain the meaning of the HIV antibody test and interpret the test results. Being HIV positive does not equal AIDS.
6. State the voluntary nature of the test.
7. Explain risk-reduction guidelines, whether the test result is positive or negative.
8. Explain the benefits of early intervention (monitoring and therapy) if the test result is HIV positive.
9. Ask with whom the patient will share the test results. Help the patient identify an adult support person, and explain that the support person should be available at the time of the posttest visit.
10. Explain issues of confidentiality regarding medical records, employment, and health insurance.
11. Follow individual state policy regarding informed consent for testing.
12. Emphasize the importance of follow-up and explain that test results will be given only in person, not over the telephone.
13. Reassure the teenager that it is normal to feel anxious during the waiting period for the results, and provide suggestions for coping.

*Posttest Counseling Components*

At the posttest counseling session(s), the counselor should

1. Inform the patient of the test results.
2. Interpret the results.
3. Give risk-reduction recommendations.
4. Assess the needs for further medical and mental health follow-up care and social support services. Make referrals or arrange for needed care.
5. Provide guidance for patients who are HIV positive regarding partner notification, support groups, and referrals for ongoing monitoring and therapy.
6. If the test result is negative, help the teenager to understand that he or she may still be at risk of acquiring HIV infection, and that it is still vitally important to practice risk-reduction behaviors.

A counselor needs to be specific in delineating which sexual activities to avoid in order to prevent HIV infection as well as other STD transmission. The riskiest behaviors are receptive ("passive") and insertive ("active") anal intercourse without a condom, between a man and a man or between a man and a woman, as well as unprotected vaginal intercourse. Although controversy exists (Darrow, Echenberg, Jaffe, O'Malley, Byers, Getchel, & Curran, 1984; Fischl, Dickinson, Scott, Klimas, Fletcher, & Parks, 1987), many studies (Moss, Osmond, Bacchetti, Chermann, Barre-Sinoussi, & Carlson, 1987; Padian, Marquis, Francis, Anderson, Rutherford, O'Malley, & Winkelstein, 1987; Winkelstein, Lyman, Padian, Grant, Samuel, Wiley, Anderson, Lang, Riggs, & Levy, 1987) have shown that oral sex and swallowing semen cause considerably lower risk for acquisition of the HIV infection than unprotected vaginal or anal intercourse, but because of potential risk, they should be avoided or partners protected by use of condoms. Oral-anal contact ("rimming"), hand-anal contact ("fisting"), and urinating on or around the genitalia ("water sports") have not been well studied; however, these activities are considered risky because they cause contact of semen/vaginal secretions or blood with mucous membrane surfaces such as the lining of the mouth or vagina.

Adolescents also need to learn how they *won't* get HIV infection. Transmission does not occur through casual contact, mosquito bites, or toilet seats. Sharing utensils, hugging or kissing, and eating food prepared or served by someone who has HIV infection do not transmit the virus. Giving blood is totally safe, and the risk of receiving HIV through a blood transfusion has been virtually eliminated due to improved screening techniques.

It is also important for the counselor to provide specific, practical instruction in the application and use of condoms. Good illustrations or models are very helpful. An adolescent should be instructed to roll the condom on the erect penis before any intimate activity, leaving a reservoir space free of air at the tip of the condom, and to use only water-based lubricants. Instructions should also be given to withdraw the penis from the vagina or anus carefully while it is still erect and never to reuse a condom. The use of other chemical and mechanical barrier methods of contraception, including spermicides (especially Nonoxynyl-9, which has been shown to kill HIV and other viruses) and diaphragms, should also be encouraged, although condoms should continue to be used. The counselor can also help adolescents increase communication with their partners about the use of barrier contraceptive methods; practicing typical scenarios with youth will enhance such communication. Again, adolescents need follow-up reinforcement about decisions to remain sexually abstinent or to practice safer sex techniques.

(Again, Table 8 summarizes counseling strategies that can be used when an adolescent has been diagnosed with an STD.)

### Specific Issues related to HIV

Many issues related to HIV prevention counseling have been discussed within the context of preventing other STDs. Several issues, such as risk assessment for HIV acquisition and HIV pre- and posttest counseling, are specific for prevention of this infection. Detailed assessment, counseling, and testing protocols (Planned Parenthood of Wisconsin, Inc., 1987; Rosenfeld, 1991; State of Wisconsin, Department of Health and Social Services, 1988) have been developed, some of which focus on adolescents. Counseling and testing components based on these protocols will be discussed briefly below, with an emphasis on adolescent-oriented considerations.

**Assessing for HIV Risk Factors.** Adolescents can become very worried about HIV infection and AIDS. Their fears may be founded on misconceptions, or may accurately reflect a truly high-risk status. Adolescents who present with such concerns or with apparent risk factors require full assessment. A counselor may begin to differentiate fear from concern based on knowledge about risk factors by asking such questions as "Is there a special reason why you are concerned about AIDS?" "What makes you believe you may have been exposed to the virus?" and "Did a friend or sex partner suggest you come in for a test?" (Planned Parenthood of Wisconsin, Inc., 1987). These questions allow the counselor a good entry into a discussion of risk factors for HIV infection, which include a history of IV drug use or sexual relations with an IV-drug-using partner; a history of unprotected anal intercourse; multiple sexual partners; especially if their drug or sexual histories are not known; a history of hemophilia or sexual relations with a hemophiliac; and sex with someone from a Caribbean or African country where HIV is prevalent. After discussing these and other possible risk factors with the adolescent, the counselor can better explain the adolescent's risk level and help him or her decide whether HIV antibody testing is appropriate.

**Special Considerations regarding HIV Antibody Testing for Youth.** Confidentiality regarding HIV-related counseling and testing must be ensured. Adolescents have the same legal rights to confidentiality and anonymous testing as do adults. Two testing options are available—anonymous and name-associated testing—and their implications should be explained to the adolescent. Teenagers whose names will be linked with the test results should be informed of local reporting and medical records requirements and of the possible risks of discrimination in health insurance and employment if the test is positive, especially if a health insurer requests access to the medical records.

Legal ability for an adolescent to give informed consent for HIV antibody testing may vary by state. In general, however, a minor may be legally able to give informed consent under statutes defining mature minors, statutes providing minors with access to sexually transmitted disease evaluation and treatment, or statutes addressing exposure to dangerous diseases.

Adolescents must receive pre- and posttest counseling. Counseling and testing are ideally done at a site where ongoing medical and mental health care is available, where the environment is trusting, and where continuity of health care is practiced. Counselors need to have knowledge of HIV- and AIDS-related issues, and have an understanding of adolescent growth and cognitive and psychosocial development. A younger adolescent, for example, may need far more concrete information regarding risky behaviors or advice regarding whom to tell about the testing than a college student requires. Counseling may require more than one set of pre- and posttest sessions.

Whether the test result is positive or negative, follow-up must be provided to reevaluate the need for further testing, to reinforce risk-reduction behaviors, and to ensure that the adolescent has completed any referrals for medical, mental health, and social support services. Table 9 lists the components of both pre- and posttest counseling for HIV infection.

## Issues for Gay and Lesbian Youth

### Homosexuality in the Adolescent Population

Human sexual development is a process that extends across the entire life cycle, and adolescence is but one critical period in the process. Although adolescence is the time when it appears that many gender issues emerge, determinations of gender and related concepts are actually processes that develop over long periods. Deisher and Remafedi (1989) state that during the early years of childhood, environmental influences such as nurturing combine with genetic and hormonal influences to establish a child's *core morphological gender identity,* or the child's sense of being male or female. *Sexual orientation* is defined as an individual's affinity toward persons of the same or opposite gender and appears to be in place by middle childhood. In this conceptualization, sexual orientation also includes sexual fantasies and behaviors, self-identification, and community affiliation. *Gender role,* or the adoption of stereotypically male or female social roles and mannerisms, appears to be more flexible than gender identity or sexual orientation. Gender role, however, also appears to be well established before adolescence.

Homosexuality is generally defined as sexual orientation directed predominantly toward persons of the same gender. Adolescent homosexuality is a controversial and often emotionally charged issue. Neinstein and Cohen (1991) point out several considerations in sexual development applicable to adolescent homosexuality. It is important to realize that heterosexuality and homosexuality are not dichotomous but rather part of a continuum of sexual orientation; between the domains of people who are exclusively heterosexual and those who are exclusively homosexual there probably lie many people with varying degrees of homosexual and heterosexual fantasy and behavior. An example illustrating this concept is the normal sexual play of adolescents with same-sex friends. Many children and adolescents experiment with such play, and it appears to be part of the process of heterosexual development. Such experimentation can lead to confusion or unease in some adolescents. In what is probably a small subset of adolescents, the young person has the feeling that his or her experimentation has a deeper significance. These youngsters sense that from an early age, their feelings regarding sexuality have been different from that of their peers.

In what is probably an even smaller subset, adolescents may clearly identify themselves as homosexual, although expression of same-sex sexual orientation can be suppressed until early adulthood, or it can be delayed indefinitely. Sexual behavior during early adolescence may or may not parallel eventual adult sexual behavior. Sexual experimentation during adolescence, however, can be seen as helping to confirm a teenager's sexual orientation. Neinstein and Cohen (1991) state that some heterosexually oriented adolescents may become involved in homosexual behaviors when the environment creates an opportunity for these behaviors. Such situations include attendance at same-sex boarding schools and camps, or incarceration. These settings may also involve exploitation or coercion. When the environment changes, most individuals will revert to heterosexual behavior.

Prevalence of homosexuality among adolescents, especially in females, is not well documented. Deisher and Remafedi (1989) state that approximately 17 percent of boys and 11 percent of girls report at least one homosexual experience by age nineteen, and that approximately half as many teenagers are or ultimately will become self-identified as homosexual.

The etiology of homosexual identity is not clear. Genetic, hormonal, psychoanalytic, social process, and combination theories have been proposed regarding the etiology and acquisition of homosexual orientation. It is likely that each theory may act to some extent in determining sexual orientation.

## Youth Counseling Issues and Strategies

Counseling issues for gay and lesbian youth include the medical risks of their sexual activity, especially regarding STD and AIDS risks, and the psychosocial stresses and problems that may arise because of their sexual orientation. In order to deal with these issues, it is necessary for the provider to obtain a sexual history from the adolescent. Sharing this information may be especially difficult for younger adolescents, adolescents just becoming aware of their sexual orientation, or any teenager who lacks a trusting relationship with the counselor or medical provider.

Key approaches to obtaining a sexual history from a gay or lesbian youth should be similar to those used with any youth. First, confidentiality must be ensured. This requirement is particularly important for any youth who has witnessed societal homophobia and its sometimes violent repercussions. A counselor or health care provider should explain that honest answers will help provide the best care. It is essential for a provider to ask questions nonjudgmentally. Assuming heterosexuality when asking about partners may lead to an instant dead end with homosexual youth. Examples of nonjudgmental interviewing approaches include, "Is there one person to whom you're especially attracted? What is that person's name?" or "Do you have sex with men or with women or with both?" or "Do you have sexual feelings for men or women or both?" Again, the developmental stage of the youth must be considered when phrasing these questions, and a trusting relationship, possibly developed over several visits, needs to be established before more sensitive or specific questions can be asked.

Once basic information about sexuality has been obtained, inquiries should be made regarding specific sexual practices. Neinstein and Cohen (1991) suggest that sexual questions be directed to fellatio, anal intercourse, anilingus, multiple sexual partners, frequency of sexual contact, use of condoms, prior history of STDs, HIV status (if known), and whether acts are active or receptive. It may also become necessary to ask about use of sex toys, digital or fist manipulation, or violence relating to sexual activity.

Neinstein and Cohen (1991) also outline key counseling points to cover with gay and lesbian youth, as well as with adolescents who are concerned about their sexual orientation. Again, the provider must establish a nonjudgmental and accepting atmosphere in order to gain the adolescent's trust. The teenager should be told in understandable terms that homosexuality is not a disease or a mental illness but a variation on the continuum of sexual orientation that was established long before adolescence and is therefore not easily changed. Neinstein and Cohen (1991) suggest that since sexual orientation is rarely if ever a choice for a person, the word *preference* should be avoided when referring to sexual orientation. It is important not to minimize an adolescent's concerns about his or her sexual orientation. It is also essential to help adolescents realize that they do not need to confirm their sexual orientation quickly.

Whether an adolescent is comfortable with or is concerned about his or her sexual orientation, it is critical that the counselor deliver accurate and specific information regarding safer sexual practices and AIDS risk-reduction techniques. Teens may think that having sex with someone their own age is safe if they perceive AIDS as an "adult" problem. Or a teen may state, "I was with a married man and I figured he would be safe." Lesbians are believed to be at much less medical risk from their sexual practices than gay men are. On the other hand, some heterosexual couples practice anal intercourse in the hope of preventing pregnancy but are unaware of the heightened risk for HIV infection. All adolescents need information and supportive STD prevention and treatment services, regardless of sexual orientation.

The American Academy of Pediatrics noted in a 1983 policy statement that "the social consequences of homosexual orientation in an adolescent include potential difficulties in peer group acceptance, family rejection, school and institutional harassment, limited employment opportunities, legal difficulties and social isolation. Although homosexual orientation does not appear to predispose to mental illness, the social consequences of this life-style in a teenager may create serious secondary emotional problems" (American Academy of Pediatrics, Committee on Adolescence, 1983). Counselors and health care personnel have the responsibility of providing guidance for young people who are struggling with problems of sexual orientation and expression. Guidance can also include referral to community support groups and referral for mental health counseling regarding adjustment difficulties.

The counselor can help to promote the individual adolescent's self-esteem through an accepting, nonjudgmental, matter-of-fact attitude, and an acknowledgment that the adolescent is not alone. There are many gay, lesbian, and bisexual youth and adults who, despite society's homophobia, lead productive and well-adjusted lives. At the same time, the counselor should present a realistic picture of the challenges and struggles that may be faced, and offer supportive services as needed.

### Parental Counseling

Counseling needs may also include supporting concerned parents. Parents of a gay or lesbian adolescent may feel many negative emotions regarding their child's sexuality, among them grief, anger, guilt, shame, and fear. It is important for parents to appreciate that sexual orientation appears to be determined early and that its origins are unclear. Alleviating guilt that the parents have "done something" to cause homosexuality in their child is essential. Parents also need correct information about homosexuality, as outlined earlier in this section, including facts about HIV risk and transmission. Parents may also need appropriate reading material, referral to parent support groups in the community, or further counseling by mental health professionals with suitable experience and interests. Finally, parents need to understand that not every emotional or adjustment problem an adolescent presents is a direct result of his or her homosexuality.

### Option Reinforcement

Gonsiorek (1988) states that the majority of gay and lesbian youth, given the opportunity to mature in a supportive environment, present no more serious mental health problems than the general adolescent population does. It is especially important for health providers and counselors to maintain regular contact with homosexual youth to ensure that their medical and psychological needs are being met. Safer sex practices and other ways to reduce risk-taking behavior can be reinforced during these visits.

## Summary

Establishing intimacy with another human being, the goal of adolescent sexuality, is not without potentially harmful repercussions, as demonstrated by the consequences of unintended pregnancy or the acquisition of HIV and other STDs. Both heterosexual and homosexual youth may meet considerable biopsychosocial challenges during their adolescence. As counselors, we can guide youth through this period of development by helping them define problems, as well as choose and implement options in order to diminish their risk-taking behaviors. Providing a safe and confidential environment for adolescents—and for their parents, when appropriate—to seek information and discuss problems will greatly help a counselor to implement the assessment and counseling strategies suggested in this chapter.

## References

*Abortion surveillance report, 1981.* (1985). Washington, DC: U.S. Department of Health and Human Services, Center for Disease Control for Health Promotion and Education, Division of Reproductive Health, Pregnancy Epidemiology Branch.

Adger, H. (1990). Sexually transmitted disease. In F. A. Oski, C. DeAngelis, R. B. Feigin, & J. B. Warshaw (Eds.), *Principles and practices of pediatrics* (pp. 730–737). Philadelphia, PA: Lippincott.

Advance report of final natality statistics, 1985. (1987). *Monthly Vital Statistics Report, 36*(Suppl. 4), 1–43.

Alan Guttmacher Institute. (1981). *Teenage pregnancy: The problem that hasn't gone away.* New York: Alan Guttmacher Institute.

American Academy of Pediatrics, Committee on Adolescence (1989a). Counseling the adolescent about pregnancy options. *Pediatrics, 83*(1), 135–137.

American Academy of Pediatrics, Committee on Adolescence (1989b). Care of adolescent parents and their children. *Pediatrics, 83,* 138–140.

American Academy of Pediatrics, Committee on Adolescence (1983). Homosexuality and adolescence. *Pediatrics, 72*(2), 249–250.

Biro, F. M., Wildey, L. S., & Hillary, P. G. (1986). Acute and long-term consequences of adolescents who choose abortions. *Pediatric Annals, 15,* 667–673.

Brooks-Gunn, J., & Furstenberg, F. F. (1989). Adolescent sexual behavior. *American Psychiatrist, 249–257.*

Cates, W. (1990). The epidemiology and control of sexually transmitted diseases in adolescents. *Adolescent Medicine: State of the Art Reviews, 1,* 409–427.

Centers for Disease Control. (1990a). HIV prevalence estimates and AIDS care projections for the United States: Report based upon a workshop. *Morbidity and Mortality Weekly Report, 39*(RR-16), 6–7.

Centers for Disease Control. (1990b). Update: Acquired immunodeficiency syndrome–United States, 1989. *Morbidity and Mortality Weekly Report, 39*(5), 82.

Centers for Disease Control. (1990c). HIV-related knowledge and behaviors among high school students—selected U.S. sites, 1989. *Morbidity and Mortality Weekly Report, 39*(23), 385–397.

Centers for Disease Control. (1989). AIDS and human immunodeficiency virus infection in the United States: 1988 update. *Morbidity and Mortality Weekly Report, 38*(suppl. S-4), 2.

Centers for Disease Control. (1988). Guidelines for effective school health education to prevent the spread of AIDS. *Morbidity and Mortality Weekly Report, 37*(Suppl. no-2), 1–14.

Chilman, C. S. (1983). *Adolescent sexuality in a changing American society: Social and psychological perspectives for the human services professions* (2nd ed.). New York: Wiley.

Couzinet, B., Le Strat, N., & Ulmann, A. (1986). Termination of early pregnancy by the progesterone antagonist RU486 (Mifepristone). *New England Journal of Medicine, 315,* 1665–1670.

Darrow, W. W., Echenberg, M. D., Jaffe, H. W., O'Malley, P. M., Byers, R. H., Getchel, J. P., & Curran, J. W. (1984). Risk factors for human immunodeficiency virus (HIV) infections in homosexual men. *American Journal of Public Health, 77*(4), 479–483.

Davis, A. J. (1990). Teenagers' sexuality and contraception. *Dialogues in Contraception* (University of Southern California School of Medicine), *3*(2), 1.

Deisher, R., & Remafedi, G. (1989). Adolescent sexuality. In A. D. Hofmann & D. E. Greydanus (Eds.), *Adolescent medicine,* (pp. 337–346). Norwalk, CT: Appleton & Lange.

DiClemente, R. J., Boyer, C. B., & Morales, E. S. (1988). Minorities and AIDS: Knowledge, attitudes, and misconceptions among black and Latino adolescents. *American Journal of Public Health, 78*(1), 55–57.

Elkind, D. (1990). Are today's adolescents growing up too fast? *Adolescent Medicine: State of the Art Reviews, 1,* 71–79.

Elkind, D., & Bowen, R. (1978). Imaginary audience behavior in children and adolescents. *Developmental Psychology, 15,* 38–44.

Enright, R., Sapsley, D., & Shukla, D. (1979). Adolescent egocentrism in early and late adolescence. *Adolescence, 14,* 687–695.

Enright, R., & Sutterfield, S. (1980). An ecological evaluation of social cognitive development. *Child Development, 51,* 156–161.

Fischl, M. A., Dickinson, G. M., Scott, G. B., Klimas, N., Fletcher, M. A., & Parks, W. (1987). Evaluation of heterosexual partners, children, and household contacts of adults with AIDS. *Journal of the American Medical Association, 257*(5), 640–644.

Gonsiorek, J. C. (1988). Mental health issues of gay and lesbian adolescents. *Journal of Adolescent Health Care, 9*(2), 114–122.

Hardy, J. B. (1988). Premature sexual activity, pregnancy, and sexually transmitted diseases: The pediatrician's role as a counselor. *Pediatrics in Review, 10*(3), 69–76.

Harris, L., & Associates. (1988). *Sexual material on American network television during the 1987–88 season.* New York, NY: Planned Parenthood Federation of America.

Hatcher, R. A., Stewart, L., Trussell, J., Kowal, D., Guest, F., Stewart, G. K., & Cates, W. (1990–92). *Contraceptive technology* (pp. 155–158). New York: Irvington Publishers, Inc.

Hatcher, R. A., Stewart, L., Trussell, J., Kowal, D., Guest, F., Stewart, G. K., & Cates, W. (1990–92). *Contraceptive technology* (pp. 447–460). New York: Irvington Publishers, Inc.

Hatcher, R. A., Stewart, L., Trussell, J., Kowal, D., Guest, F., Stewart, G. K., & Cates,

W. (1990–92). *Contraceptive technology* (p. 166). New York: Irvington Publishers, Inc.

Hayes, C. D. (Ed.). (1987). *Risking the future: Adolescent sexuality, pregnancy, and childbearing,* Washington, DC: National Academy Press.

Henshaw, S. K., & Van Vort, J. (1989). Teenage abortion, birth, and pregnancy statistics: An update. *Family Planning Perspectives, 21, 85.*

Hofmann, A. E. (1990). Clinical management of health risk behaviors in adolescents. *Adolescent Medicine: State of the Art Reviews, 1*(1), 33–44.

Hofmann, A. E., & Greydanus, D. E. (1989). *Adolescent medicine* (pp. 519–520). Norwalk, Conn.: Appleton & Lange.

Howard, M., & McCabe, J. B. (1990). Helping teenagers postpone sexual involvement. *Family Planing Perspectives, 22*(1), 21–26.

Irwin, C. E. (1990). The theoretical concept of at-risk adolescents. *Adolescent Medicine: State of the Art Reviews, 1,* 1–14.

Jones, E. F., Forrest, J. D., & Goldman, N. (1985). Teenage pregnancy in developed countries: Determinants and policy implications. *Family Planning Perspectives, 17,* 53–63.

Kegeles, S. M., Adler, N. E., & Irwin, C. E. (1988). Sexually active adolescents and condoms: Changes over one year in knowledge, attitudes, and use. *American Journal of Public Health, 78*(4), 460–461.

Kenney, R. D. (1989). A guide to sexual abstinence counseling. *Contemporary Pediatrics, 6*(12), 83–95.

Malus, M., LaChance, P. A., & Lamy, L. (1987). Priorities in adolescent health care: The teenager's viewpoint. *Journal of Family Practice, 25,* 159–162.

McAnarney, E. R. (1987). Young maternal age and adverse neonatal outcome. *American Journal Diseases of Children, 141,* 1053–1059.

Moore, K. A., Snyder, N. O., & Daly, M. (1992). *Facts At a Glance,* January. Washington, D.C.: Child Trends, Inc.

Moss, A. R., Osmond, D., Bacchetti, P., Chermann, J., Barre-Sinoussi, F., & Carlson, J. (1987). Risk factors for AIDS and HIV seropositivity in homosexual men. *American Journal of Epidemiology, 125*(6), 1035–1047.

National Academy of Sciences. (1987). Risking the future: A symposium on the National Academy of Sciences report on teenage pregnancy. *Family Planning Perspectives, 19,* 119–125.

National adolescent student health survey. (1989). *Morbidity and Mortality Weekly Report, 38,* 147.

Neinstein, L. S. (1991). Overview of sexually transmitted disease. In L. S. Neinstein, *Adolescent health care: A practical guide* (pp. 725–726). Baltimore, MD: Urban and Schwarzenberg.

Neinstein, L. S., & Cohen, E. (1991). Homosexuality. In L. S. Neinstein, *Adolescent health care: A practical guide* (pp. 547–560). Baltimore, MD: Urban and Schwarzenberg.

Neinstein, L. S., & Kaufman, F. R. (1991). Normal physical growth and development. In L. S. Neinstein, *Adolescent health care: A practical guide* (p. 21). Baltimore, MD: Urban and Schwarzenberg.

Offer, D., Ostrov, E., & Howard, K. (1989). Adolescence: What is normal? *American Journal of Diseases of Children, 143,* 731–736.

Offer, D., Ostrov, E., & Howard, K. (1981). *The adolescent.* New York: Basic Books.

Padian, M., Marquis, L., Francis, D. P., Anderson, R. E., Rutherford, G. W., O'Malley, P. M., & Winkelstein, W. (1987). Male-to-female transmission of human immunodeficiency virus. *Journal of the American Medical Association, 258*(6), 788–790.

Pendergrast, R. A., Durant, R. H., & Gaillard, G. L. (1991). Sexual behavior and condom use in adolescent males. *Journal of Adolescent Health Care, 12*(2), 168.

Planned Parenthood of Wisconsin, Inc. (1987). *Protocol for AIDS/HIV antibody screening and counseling.*

Remafedi, G. J. (1988). Preventing the sexual transmission of AIDS during adolescence. *Journal of Adolescent Health Care, 9*(2), 139–143.

Rosen, R. H. (1980). Adolescent pregnancy decision making: Are parents important? *Adolescence, 15,* 43–54.

Rosenfeld, S. (1990). *Recommended guidelines: Adolescent HIV antibody counseling and testing.* Boston: Massachusetts Department of Public Health.

Slap, G. B. (1986). Normal physiological and psychosocial growth in the adolescent. *Journal of Adolescent Health Care, 7,* 145–155.

Sorenson, R. C. (1973). *Adolescent sexuality in contemporary America.* New York: World Publishing.

State of Wisconsin, Department of Health and Social Services. (1988). *Pre-test counseling and information about the HIV antibody test; post-test counseling of persons with seropositive HIV antibody test results; post-test counseling of persons with seronegative HIV antibody test results; and recommendations for counseling individuals with positive HIV antibody test results.* Madison, WI.

Steiner, J. D., Sorakin, G., Schiedermayer, D. L., & Van Susteren, T. J. (1990). Are adolescents getting smarter about acquired immunodeficiency syndrome? *American Journal of Diseases of Children, 144,* 302–306.

Stephenson, J. N. (1989). Pregnancy testing and counseling. *Pediatric Clinics of North America, 36,* 747–773.

Strasburger, V. C. (1989). Adolescent sexuality and the media. *Pediatric Clinics of North America, 36,* 752.

Strunin, L., & Hingson, R. (1987). Acquired immunodeficiency syndrome and adolescents: Knowledge, beliefs, attitudes, and behaviors. *Pediatrics, 79*(5), 825–828.

Taylor, B., Wadsworth, J., & Butler, N. R. (1983). Teenage mothering, admission to hospital, and accidents during the first five years. *Archives Diseases of Children, 58,* 6–11.

Tietze, C., Bongaarts, J., & Schearer, B. (1976). Mortality associated with the control of fertility. *Family Planning Perspectives, 8,* 14–15.

Winkelstein, W., Lyman, D. M., Padian, N., Grant, R., Samuel, M., Wiley, J. A., Anderson, R. E., Lang, W., Riggs, J., & Levy, J. A. (1987). Sexual practices and risk of infection by the human immunodeficiency virus. *Journal of the American Medical Association, 257*(3), 321–325.

Wisconsin Department of Health and Social Services. (1990). *Healthier people in Wisconsin: A public health agenda for the year 2000, 15.* Madison, WI (Self-published).

Wyshak, G., & Frisch, R. E. (1982). Evidence for a secular trend in age of menarche. *New England Journal of Medicine, 306,* 1033–1035.

Zabin, L. S., Hirsch, M. B., Smith, E. A., Streett, R., & Hardy, J. B. (1986). Evaluation of a pregnancy prevention program for urban teenagers. *Family Planning Perspectives, 18*(3), 119–126.

Zabin, L. S., Kantner, J. F., & Zelnik, M. (1979). The risk of adolescent pregnancy in the first months of intercourse. *Family Planning Perspectives, 11*(4), 215–222.

## Resources

1. AIDS National Hotline 1-800-342-2437.
2. American Academy of Pediatrics. (1990–91). *Sex education: A bibliography of educational materials for children, adolescents, and their families.* Elk Grove Village, IL. (Self-published).
3. Bell, R. (1987). *Changing bodies, changing lives.* New York: Vintage Books.
4. Boston Women's Health Book Collective. (1984). *The new our bodies, ourselves.* New York: Simon and Schuster.
5. Hearing Impaired AIDS National Hotline 1-800-AIDS-TTY
6. National AIDS Information Clearinghouse 1-800-458-5231
7. Sexually Transmitted Diseases National Hotline 1-800-227-8922
8. Spanish AIDS National Hotline 1-800-344-7432

# 9
# Traumatic Brain Injury

*Grant J. Butterbaugh*

## Introduction

Traumatic brain injury (TBI) should be considered in the context of the larger public health epidemic of injury. Injuries have a variety of causes; motor vehicle accidents (MVAs), falls, assaults, attempted suicide, fire, and drowning are common examples. The scope of the injury epidemic as a major public health problem is often underestimated, as has been noted by three important publications, *Injury in America* (National Research Council, 1985), *Injury Prevention: Meeting the Challenge* (National Committee on Injury Prevention and Control [NCICP], 1989), and the *Surgeon General's Workshop on Violence and Public Health Report* (1986). Unfortunately, this underestimation contributes to delays in providing treatment services for injured adolescents and their families, as well as to difficulties in the initiation and funding of injury prevention programs.

This chapter provides a selective review of research and clinical findings regarding (a) the epidemiology and risk of injury, including TBI; (b) the diagnosis and classification of TBI; (c) the risks and types of neuropsychological and psychosocial sequelae following TBI; and (d) trauma care models and services. The chapter's main theme is the risk of neuropsychological sequelae after severe blunt TBI, although the risk for injury is also briefly addressed. The medical, rehabilitation, and educational management of TBI is beyond the scope of this chapter.

### Epidemiology of Injury

Injury is the leading cause of death for individuals ages one to forty-four in the United States, and the fourth leading cause of death—behind heart, neoplastic, and cerebrovascular disease—for all ages. Because young people die from injuries at a rate much greater than that of older members of society, injury is the leading cause of life-years lost (National Research Council, 1985). Nearly 80 percent of all injuries occur in those less than forty-five years old (Rice, MacKenzie, & Associates, 1989).

Motor vehicle accidents, including vehicle-vehicle and vehicle-pedestrian accidents, are the leading cause of injury-related deaths across most ages, with fifteen- to twenty-four-year old adolescents and young adults being at greatest risk (Rice, MacKenzie, & Associates, 1989). For all ages, the rates for MVA-related injuries and hospitalization are ranked only second, behind injuries and hospitalization due to falls. In a recent community epidemiological study of pediatric accidental deaths and injuries, Gallagher and colleagues (1982) reported that 58 percent of all deaths in one- to nineteen-year-olds were due to injury, including 58 percent of these injury deaths caused by MVA-related incidents. In thirteen- to nineteen-year-olds, 77 percent of all deaths were caused by MVAs. The gender ratio for MVA-related deaths was three males for every female. In this study, emergency room treatment was 773 times greater, and hospitalization for injuries was 44 times greater, than the rate of injury-related mortality, indicating the relative frequency of nonfatal injuries for this community.

The second and third leading causes of death among adolescents are homicide and suicide, with homicide being the leading cause of death among African-American adolescents and young adults (Baker, O'Neill, & Karpf, 1984; Blum, 1987). Acknowledging that underreporting of intentional injuries and deaths is widely expected, Guyer, Lescohier, Gallagher, Housman, and Azzara (1989) estimated from a large community survey of newborns to nineteen-year-olds that 83 percent of patients with self-inflicted wounds were in the fifteen- to nineteen-year-old range. They found that girls were twice as likely as boys to self-inflict wounds. Assaults occurred 8 times more often than self-inflicted injuries, with boys being 2.3 times more likely than girls to be assaulted. In contrast, girls had higher rates than boys for being victims of rape and child abuse. These intentional injuries accounted for 3.4 percent of injuries, 9.8 percent of hospitalizations, and 15.7 percent of injury-related deaths in this survey. The large increase in death due to intentional causes is a tragic reminder of the personal and community threats faced by many adolescents.

Based on the 1987 National Hospital Discharge Survey, McManus, McCarthy, Kozak, and Newacheck (1991) reported hospital discharge rates for injuries per 10,000 population in adolescents and young adults. They found that younger adolescents, ages ten to fourteen, had a lower rate (71 per 10,000) than older adolescents, ages fifteen to eighteen (136 per 10,000), and young adults, ages nineteen to twenty-four, (135 per 10,000) did. The respective discharge rates for each of these three age-groups for all other categories, including mental disorders, were 26, 78, and 78 per 10,000 population, indicating the comparative hospitalization rates for these major public health problems of adolescents. Both injured and mentally ill adolescents face unique postdischarge challenges, although the risk of adverse outcomes for injured adolescents has been less well recognized.

Because of definitional and methodological difficulties, it is uncertain just how many injuries involve TBI. For example, is TBI to be defined by functional or physiological alterations? Is TBI defined by temporary or persistent neurobehavioral disturbances? In addition, the practice of grouping adolescents with adults in TBI epidemiology and outcome research limits our understanding of the risks of injury for adolescents and the developmental impact of adverse neuropsychological and psychosocial sequelae.

Using a coma scale (described below) to define the severity of TBI in a different large-community epidemiological study, Kraus, Rock, and Hemyari (1990) have reported the incidence of brain injuries in newborns to nineteen-year-olds based on 1981 hospitalization rates in San Diego. In this pediatric sample, about 5 percent of children and adolescents died, 6 percent had severe TBI, 8 percent had moderate TBI, and 82 percent had mild TBI, although the "mild" TBI group included patients with what many researchers would consider to be moderate TBI. Across this general age-group, 37 percent of TBIs were caused by MVAs, 24 percent by falls, 21 percent by sports or recreation activities, 10 percent by assaults, and 8 percent by miscellaneous causes. The rates of various causes of TBI differed across specific age subgroups. As age increased, both the proportion of more severe TBIs and the number of MVA-related TBIs increased. In addition, gender-specific age differences were observed. This study found that the rate of TBI increased in males older than five years and peaked for adolescents ages fifteen to nineteen. In contrast, the rate of TBI for females was found to decline after three years of age, with a slight elevation around twelve years of age (Kraus et al., 1990). Unfortunately, the risks of adverse neurobehavioral sequelae can persist even for mild or moderate TBI cases (as described by Rimel, Giordani, Barth, Boll, & Jane, 1982, and by Rimel, Giordani, Barth, & Jane, 1982).

*Epidemiological Model of Injury Control*

This section briefly reviews injury control research and describes analyses of various risk factors, as well as injury prevention research findings. Haddon (1972, 1980) proposed an epidemiological model for examining injuries as an interactional function of hosts (e.g., humans), inanimate (vehicles) or animate (vectors) agents, and physical and social environments, as well as preinjury, injury onset, and postinjury temporal events. Haddon (1980) believed that injuries could be understood as nonrandom phenomena similar to infectious diseases, with seasonal variation and socioeconomic and geographic characteristics. This model has shifted injury control analysis away from the traditional focus on human factors to include the mechanisms of injury (e.g., physical energy involved in a motor vehicle injury) and physical or socioenvironmental factors (e.g., poor road or walkway design and inadequate funding for urban street repair). The preinjury, injury, and postinjury phases are each associated with human, vehicle, and environmental injury-related factors. See Table 1 for examples.

**Table 1.**
**Injury Phase-Factor Matrix**

|  | Injury Factors | | |
| --- | --- | --- | --- |
|  | Host | Agent | Environment |
| *Temporal Phase* | | | |
| Preinjury | | | |
|  | Driver intoxication | Unsafe cars | Poor road design |
|  | Conflict resolution skills | Gun availability | Social modeling of violence and risk taking |
| Injury | | | |
|  | No seat belt usage | No air bags | No guard rails |
|  | Intoxication | Automatic weapons | No emergency phones |
| Postinjury | | | |
|  | Poor health | Unsafe fuel system | Slow medical services |
|  | Uninsured | Fragmenting bullets | No rehabilitation services |

Source: Modified from Haddon (1972, 1980).

Tonkin (1987) reviewed adolescent risk taking using Haddon's (1972) injury control matrix. He emphasized human factors and concluded that technological advances may be creating "risk-filled situations" for adolescents.

Jessor (1984) suggested a multifactorial social theory of "problem behaviors," including health risk behaviors, and argued that adolescence may well include the developmental task of becoming responsible for health behaviors. The importance of this assertion is underscored through Jessor's (1984) observations that the highest numbers of deaths and injuries in adolescents have a behavioral basis, such as MVAs, homicides, and suicide: however, based on empirical findings of continuity of health risk behaviors across adolescent and young adult development stages, Jessor (1984) also suggested that no clear developmental demarcation distinguishes adolescents and adults. Therefore, problem behaviors in both developmental stages may be the result of a common underlying interaction among personality, perceived environmental factors, and behavioral factors. The covarying nature of risk behaviors suggests a syndrome of problem behaviors that may result from these three health risk factors. This model primarily addresses the perspective of human or socioenvironmental factors in approaching such public health problems as injury control and substance use. The paradigm of a health risk syndrome implies that strategies for prevention also need to address multiple health risk behaviors (Jessor, 1984). The role of biological maturation was not considered a major factor in Jessor's model.

Irwin and Millstein (1986) have elaborated a biopsychosocial model of risk-taking behavior that is based on biological maturation. For example, this model postulates that the gender-specific timing of puberty directly influences cognitive, self-perception, and perceived socioenvironmental and personal values. Risk perception and peer-related influences are specified as mediating factors that can contribute to risk-taking behaviors. For example, MVA-related events are analyzed as a function of endogenous biopsychosocial factors (i.e., human factors, including inexperience and gender), exogenous environmental factors (e.g., driving regulations, lack of public transportation), critical precipitating endogenous factors (e.g., substance use), and exogenous factors (e.g., peer pressure). This model emphasizes the important role of biodevelopmental factors in understanding risk-taking behaviors.

Jeffrey (1989) provided a review of health risk behaviors and listed several decision-making biases that may contribute to such behaviors. These biases include individuals' tendencies to prefer immediate rather than future gratification, to display optimistic biases about their own risks, to act more readily to avoid losses than to obtain gains, and to prefer certainty over uncertainty. These human biases are observed to significant extent in children, adolescents, and adults across various conceptual developmental stages and may contribute to risk perception and health risk behavior.

The developmental and social factors responsible for the elevated risk of injury for both adolescents and young adults are speculative. Traditional psychodevelopmental stage theories may, however, need to be revised in order to account for the significance of gender-specific and sociocultural injury risk factors. As an example, the well-known differences among individual countries' rates of homicide (Wolfgang, 1986) suggest the importance of weapon availability and sociocultural factors in addition to age-related developmental factors. Current risk-taking models focus primarily on the role of human risk taking, while epidemiological injury models consider a broader array of factors in regard to injury control analyses and prevention strategies. We need risk models that include biodevelopmental, social, other environmental, and individual difference factors. Using Haddon's (1980) terminology, several injury risk factors specific to hosts (people) and environments, including gender, race, socioeconomic status, age, and substance use, are discussed below.

## Injury Risk Factors

**Gender.** It is well known that males have a disproportionately greater risk of death or injury than females do, across categories of unintentional and intentional injuries. For example, firearm-related deaths are 5 times greater and MVA-related deaths are 2.8 times greater in males than in females. The differences in community and international injury studies suggest that socioeconomic, cultural, transportation system, and health care system factors must be considered in developing risk models and prevention strategies (Baker et al., 1984; Rice, MacKenzie, & Associates, 1989).

**Socioeconomic and Ethnoracial Status.** Among African-American fifteen- to nineteen-year-old males and females, homicide is the leading cause of death, while MVAs are the leading cause of death for their Native American and Caucasian peers (Baker et al., 1984). Although the relationships between racial and socioeconomic (SES) class factors are complex, homicide appears to be more closely associated with SES factors than with racial ones (Baker et al., 1984; Centerwall, 1984). Caucasian adolescents commit suicide at a higher rate than their non-Caucasian peers do (Hollinger, 1990).

**Developmental Status.** Interestingly, experience factors do not appear to account for the age-related differences rates of MVAs. For example, Robertson (1983) reported that eighteen-year-olds with three years of driving experience had the same rate of crashes as did newly licensed nineteen-year-olds. As noted above, developmental risk models need to be refined, especially given the enduring risk of unintentional and intentional injury long past the time that more mature adult reasoning and knowledge are thought to be established.

**Intoxicants.** Alcohol and other intoxicants are well-known factors in intentional and unintentional violence and MVA-related deaths and injuries. Recent data suggest that alcohol is involved in 50 percent of all fatal MVAs and in 20 percent of MVAs that produce serious injury (Haddon & Blumenthal, 1984). Pipkin, Walker, and Thomason (1989) reported that 50 percent of all sixteen- to twenty-year-olds who were tested at admission following an MVA-related injury had a measurable blood alcohol concentration (BAC). Although a BAC level of 0.10 percent is used widely as a definition of intoxication, recent recommendations have urged that 0.05 percent BAC be adopted as the legal limit because driving skills can be impaired below 0.10 percent (Council on Scientific Affairs, 1986). It is obviously necessary to screen systematically for alcohol and other drugs in injury events in order to clarify the true extent of their contributions.

Although the role of alcohol in MVAs is well known, a comparable public health education and research campaign is needed to address the roles of drugs and alcohol in community and domestic violence. The role of alcohol and substance use in violence-related injury has been demonstrated repeatedly, with one classic study finding that 66 percent of homicide cases involve alcohol use by the victim, the perpetrator, or both (Wolfgang, 1958). Violence can arise in drug deals and is often related to territorial and financial disputes (NCICP, 1989). The number of drug-related assaults is difficult to establish; however, about 33 percent of all homicides are attributed to drug-related factors in a recent study of inner-city injury deaths (Tardiff & Gross, 1986).

Thus, risk of injury involves agent-related and environmental factors that exceed the personal decision-making capabilities of many adolescents. Personal health risk models may lead to more effective, active strategies to prevent intentional and unintentional injuries. The adoption of the epidemiological analysis of Haddon (1972, 1980) into empirical models may lead to a greater range of prevention strategies (Wilson & Baker, 1987).

## Risk Assessment of Individuals

It is difficult to conduct research about the clinical health risk assessment of individuals, because of the rarity of adverse health events. For example, whereas the likelihood of any specific individual dying in an MVA is very low, it would be extremely expensive to conduct prospective individual risk assessment research. Although at-risk individuals might be identified through formal risk assessment, a restriction of the personal liberties of these innocent, but "at-risk" citizens could result from the application of individual risk control strategies. For example, were the driving privileges of some high-risk groups of drivers to be restricted on the basis of prior driving history, an unacceptably high number of unjustified decisions might occur, without a major reduction in the rate of MVAs (see Robertson, 1983; Waller, 1985).

Despite the uncertainties of risk of injury for any particular adolescent, education and health care professionals can use clinical risk assessment models to provide guidance both to help prevent health risk behaviors and to design interventions to reduce already established health risk behaviors (Hofmann, 1990). Given the wide scope of risk-taking behavior and the expression of imperfect decision making by both adolescents and adults, it is unrealistic to expect the elimination of risk taking. Instead, the goal of clinical risk assessment and intervention should be to delay the onset of or reduce the health risk behaviors of adolescents with regard to injuries and other health-threatening conditions (Hofmann, 1990).

## Injury Prevention Strategies

Haddon (1980) proposed ten injury control strategies derived from his matrix of injury-related factors and temporal phases of injury events. He also advanced the distinction between active and passive injury control strategies (see also Wilson & Baker, 1987). Active strategies rely on actions individuals can take (e.g., using seat belts, not drinking and driving, not using firearms to settle conflicts). Passive strategies require no action by the individual (e.g., cars equipped with air bags). Although he considered injuries to be subject to epidemiological and preventive methods, Haddon did not reject the value of active injury control strategies. He argued that

> with injuries, as with various other pathological conditions long since brought under control, this preference for emphasizing the individual typi-

cally results in blame being placed on the victim. As a result, it is argued that measures directed elsewhere and the idea that a responsibility exists to employ them deserve no consideration. (Haddon, 1980, p. 416)

Haddon (1980, p. 416) provided the following injury control strategies, which are supplemented here by Robertson's (1983) creative prevention proposals and examples:

1. Prevent the creation of hazard in the first place (eliminate dangerous vehicles and firearms).
2. Reduce the amount of hazard brought into being (reduce the availability of dangerous vehicles and firearms).
3. Prevent release of hazard that already exists (improve road construction and drivers' skills; reduce drug trade).
4. Modify the rate or spatial distribution of release of the hazard from its source (use vehicle safety belts and air bags; eliminate automatic weapons).
5. Separate, in time and space, the hazard and that which is to be protected (increase distances between sidewalks/bicycle paths and streets, and between traffic lanes flowing in opposite directions; restrict hunting ranges to unpopulated areas).
6. Separate the hazard and that which is to be protected by interposition of a material barrier (require mandatory motorcycle helmet laws and air bags; use energy-absorbing, rigid off-road structures).
7. Modify relevant basic qualities of the hazard (use energy-absorbing materials and designs in cars; adopt plastic and nonfragmenting bullets).
8. Make what is to be protected more resistant to damage from the hazard (protect fuel systems from crashes; use bulletproof glass).
9. Counter the damage already done by the environmental hazard (use rapid emergency medical services to transport victims to acute trauma care).
10. Stabilize, repair, and rehabilitate the object of damage (provide affordable and available long-term individual and family trauma care services).

Hofmann (1990) presented a five-step sequence of guided decision making that educators, counselors, and health care professionals can employ in working with adolescents (see Table 2). This strategy assumes that adolescents lack information about the consequences of and alternatives to their individual health risk behaviors.

The first step of the model is to define the problem. It involves establishing an agreement with the adolescent regarding what behaviors may be a risk to health, such as driving while intoxicated or carrying weapons for self-protection. The second step is to explore behavioral options that could replace the targeted health risk. The objective is for the adolescent to consider

**Table 2.**
**Guided Health Risk Counseling**

1. Agreement about health risks
2. Exploration of risk-reduction behavioral options
3. Choice of behavioral option
4. Implementation of behavioral option
5. Ongoing health risk counseling

Source: Modified from Hofmann (1990).

safer alternatives (e.g., drinking, but planning to walk home). During the third step, choice of options, adolescents actively choose to avoid or to adopt risky behaviors. The fourth step involves implementation of the chosen behavioral option. The professional should not assume that adolescents have the skills to implement their conscious choices. For example, the counselor may need to help an adolescent develop assertiveness skills regarding the choice to walk home rather than accept a ride from an intoxicated peer. The fifth step is continued follow-up and support, which help maintain adolescents' appropriate preventive actions and enable the professional to address other risk-taking behaviors that may emerge.

## Diagnosis and Classification of TBI

TBI includes penetrating, perforating, and blunt brain injuries. In a penetrating TBI, an object is lodged in the brain; in a perforating injury, it has entered and exited the brain. For the third type of TBI, this chapter uses the phrase "blunt TBI," because the phrase "closed head injury" fails to differentiate between injuries to the head and injuries to the brain, both of which can be mutually exclusive. Because blunt TBIs are nonpenetrating, they can be more difficult to diagnose using standard medical procedures. These techniques, which include general physical and neurological examinations and brain imaging studies, may not accurately detect brain impairment. For example, relying on neuroradiological techniques to detect traumatic brain lesions will underdiagnose blunt TBI in patients who exhibit only disturbances in consciousness. On the other hand, the use of physical examination findings such as extracranial lacerations and bruises alone to diagnose blunt TBI will overdiagnose it in cases where none has occurred. Some TBIs can also occur without loss of consciousness, thereby further complicating diagnosis. Obviously, these diagnostic difficulties hamper the establishment of the true incidence, prevalence, and clinical course of TBI.

Neuropathological findings in TBI have been reviewed by Levin, Benton, and Grossman (1982). TBI can involve immediate primary macroscopic lesions (e.g., cerebral hemorrhages and lacerations) and microscopic lesions (e.g., nerve fiber stretching and tearing), as well as secondary posttraumatic causes of injury (including brain swelling, increased intracranial pressure, and brain mass shifts). Delayed posttraumatic effects of TBI can involve hydrocephalus and white matter degeneration, which appear in the post-acute period as brain abnormalities on imaging studies. Although the functional neuropsychological and psychosocial course of mild or moderate TBI in pediatric and adult TBI is not fully understood, increasing experimental and clinical neuropathological evidence indicates that centripetal diffuse axonal injury (DAI) underlies various severities of blunt TBI. This hypothesis is supported by the increased vulnerability to TBI of cortical and frontal brain regions, compared with that to lower brain stem regions. In addition, clinical recovery patterns include the sequential recovery of consciousness, sensorimotor, and finally memory and other higher cortical functions (Ommaya & Gennarelli, 1974; Stalhammar, 1990).

Emergency medical services and many hospitals utilize clinical observational measures such as the Glasgow Coma Scale (GCS) (Teasdale & Jennett, 1974) to assess patients' level of consciousness. The GCS has been used in numerous research studies as an index of the severity of TBI. Scores are obtained for three categories of patients' responses—eye-opening response, best motor response to commands, and verbal response. The scale has a minimum of 3 and a maximum of 15 possible points. Patients can have a GCS score of 15, yet have suffered a TBI. The limitations of this scale in predicting individual outcomes and in estimating severity of injury while patients are receiving various acute medical interventions are well known.

Although definitions and measures vary across studies of TBI, patients with GCS scores of 8 or below are considered to be severe TBI cases. Coma is traditionally defined as no eye-opening, no utterances of recognizable words, and inability to follow simple commands, or a GCS score of 8 or below, even though 10 percent of individuals with these low scores will not be technically comatose (Jennett & Frankowski, 1990). Patients with momentary or brief loss of consciousness but without neuroradiological evidence of skull fractures, brain swelling, and intracranial mass lesions and with GCS scores of 13 to 15 are considered to be mild TBI cases. Moderate TBI cases include (a) patients with a GCS score of 9 to 12 and (b) those with GCS scores of 13 to 15 and positive neuroradiological evidence of skull fractures, brain swelling, and intracranial mass lesions (Levin et al., 1982). Recent evidence that magnetic resonance imaging (MRI) may be a more sensitive neuroradiological technique than computerized tomography (CT) for mild and moderate TBI (Levin et al., 1987) suggests the need for revision in how the severity of TBI is determined. Other TBI studies have used clinical estimates of the duration of posttraumatic memory impairment to estimate the severity of TBI (e.g., Rutter, Chadwick, Shaffer, & Brown, 1980), although to date validation of reliable methods of evaluating posttraumatic memory impairment on pediatric patients has been limited.

A selective review of pediatric and adult outcome studies of blunt TBI will serve to discuss the diverse effects of TBI on the development of children, adolescents and their families. The inclusion of some preadolescent and adult research data may be helpful to the reader, as chronic neuropsychological and psychosocial deficits from TBI in children may continue through adolescence and into adulthood. Although this qualification will be made only once, the reader should bear in mind that only a few TBI outcome studies have systematically followed patients for more than two years, and as a consequence, there are many unanswered clinical and theoretical questions.

## Neuropsychological Outcomes of Pediatric TBI

Neuropsychology is the interdisciplinary study of brain-behavior relationships. Clinical neuropsychological approaches to the study of a variety of medical, psychiatric, and developmental disorders have recently become more prominent in basic and applied diagnostic and treatment research. Different patterns of memory, language, visual-perceptual, problem solving, and psychosocial functioning characterize the developmental ability profiles and courses of any acquired and congenital disorders that have either neurological bases or neurological consequences (Spreen, Tupper, Risser, Tuokko, & Edgell, 1984). Clinical neuropsychological assessment is based on the application of specialized professional knowledge to the results of standardized tests that have been validated with patients with brain-related disorders.

As clinical child neuropsychology is a recent specialization, several issues require clarification. Various neuropsychological tests, test batteries, and clinical test interpretation approaches are acknowledged and accepted by neuropsychologists. The professional knowledge, training, and experience of the neuropsychologist may be as important as the specific choice of which neuropsychological tests will be used for assessment.

Despite the preeminent role of mental status examinations and intelligence tests in health care and educational settings, the study of patients with brain-related disorders has revealed that more refined measures are essential to assess the diverse patterns of dysfunction (Lezak, 1988a). Though brief mental status examinations are often used to screen patients, it is clearly recognized that these can underdiagnose brain impairment in a significant number of cases (Strub & Black, 1988). In addition, such examinations have no real value in adequately assessing the nature and severity of a patient's impairment for educational or rehabilitation treatment planning. Many educational tests have not been well validated on different samples of brain-impaired adolescents, so that their value for neuropsychological diagnostic purposes is limited. In addition to test-related factors, developmental considerations are important in neuropsychological assessment. It has been traditionally assumed that fewer functional deficits are observed in younger as compared with older persons following brain insult, but contradictory findings have appeared in both experimental animal studies and clinical human studies (Kolb, 1989). Some neurobehavioral functions are affected more severely following brain insults in early childhood as compared with similar insults in later years. No simple generalizations can be made regarding the neurobehavioral effects of traumatic lesions acquired early versus later in life. Only limited research has been reported comparing adolescents with younger and older patients regarding selective vulnerabilities or sparing of abilities after TBI. It is clear, however, that brain insults in children can produce both a loss of already established neuropsychological abilities and an impairment to their developing abilities to acquire new skills and information (Hebb, 1942; Rourke, Bakker, Fisk, & Strang, 1983).

## Consciousness and Memory Abilities

Disturbances of consciousness, orientation, and/or memory are consistent acute symptoms of TBI and are associated with risk of neuropsychological sequelae (Levin et al., 1982). Measurement of these abilities is not well standardized. Disturbances in patients' pre- and postinjury memories may compromise their reports about the circumstances of their injury and their level of consciousness. For example, a patient may be observed to be talking at the scene of the accident and yet later fail to recall these events due to his or her impaired memory status. Premorbid memory and general cognitive abilities should also be considered in evaluating whether any memory-related effects of TBI are present.

TBI produces both retrograde amnesia (impairment in memory for events occurring immediately—and sometimes more remotely—before the TBI) and anterograde memory disturbance (varying durations of memory impairment for events occurring post TBI). Posttraumatic amnesia (PTA) is a common, typically transient condition following any degree of TBI that represents disturbances in orientation and anterograde memory. PTA generally lasts three to four times longer than the loss of consciousness does (Jennett & Frankowski, 1990). Clinical evidence of PTA in patients may include disorientation and anterograde amnesia with rapid forgetting of daily events. Even in severe TBI patients with significant anterograde memory deficits, "islands" of brief memories may survive after the resolution of the PTA. For example, a patient may remember the sounds of a helicopter, or a brief moment with a family member in the hospital. Orientation can be adequate, despite anterograde memory impairment, for learning, retaining, and/or recalling new information. Remote memories of pre-TBI personal events or general knowledge may be recalled despite the presence of anterograde memory problems. These dissociations among different memory phenomena limit the usefulness of referring to patients' "memory" ability as a unitary global ability.

Recent neuroscience research also indicates that qualitatively different memory systems exist and may be subserved by different brain areas (Squire, 1987). Long-term memory systems include episodic, semantic, and procedural memory systems. Episodic memory consists of personally experienced events, and semantic memory consists of general factual knowledge; both episodic and semantic memory are thought to be components of the declarative (or explicit) memory system, impairments of which can result in difficulties in learning new episodic or factual information. Although a less-researched long-term memory system, procedural (or implicit) memory includes habit and perceptual learning. Whereas declarative memory involves patients' conscious recollection of new verbal information, procedural memory involves patients' nonconscious recollection of new verbal or nonverbal information or skills; however, the commonly made distinctions between the domains of material-specific memory, such as memory for verbal information and for nonverbal visual information, do not adequately describe impairments of different memory systems.

Because children and adolescents experience multiple daily demands on memory, the sensitivity of memory abilities to TBI is especially important. Disproportionate deficits in verbal memory compared with intelligence have been observed in adolescent and adult TBI patients. For example, declarative verbal memory can be disturbed following TBI in the presence of normal intelligence (Levin, Eisenberg, Wigg, & Kobayashi, 1982; Levin, Goldstein, High, & Eisenberg, 1988). These data also provide evidence of the relatively low sensitivity of intelligence tests in measuring the effects of TBI in some patients with declarative verbal memory deficits.

One study used the GCS to define severity of blunt TBI. Levin, High, Ewing-Cobbs, and colleagues (1988) compared groups of children ages six to eight and nine to twelve and groups of adolescents ages twelve to fifteen with either severe TBI (GCS score ≤ 8) or mild/moderate TBI (GCS score > 8) on declarative memory tests. The measures included a word-list learning and memory test as well as a visual memory test. The results of this study suggested that severe TBI produced immediate and persisting declarative memory deficits. Adolescents with severe TBI demonstrated grater verbal memory impairment than younger children did. Visual memory problems were related to severity of injury and showed less selective deficits, perhaps because this function develops during early childhood (Levin et al., 1988). The educational implications of these memory data suggest that children and adolescents with TBI may fail to acquire new declarative memory information in the classroom and in other settings. Adolescents may exhibit a selective developmental vulnerability because their learning and memorization strategies are developing more rapidly than those of younger children are (Levin, High, Ewing-Cobbs, et al., 1988).

Procedural memory is the long-term memory system that involves the acquisition of new perceptual-motor and cognitive skills or information.

Some patients with TBI fail, however, to recollect their learning such new skills or information (Squire, 1987). As mentioned, TBI patients are amnesic for new episodic and semantic memories to varying degrees during the period of PTA. Rapid forgetting of new information and events may leave these patients confused at this stage of their recovery (Levin, High, & Eisenberg, 1988). In a recent study, procedural memory abilities following severe TBI (GCS ≤ 8) were evaluated in patients ages fifteen to fifty who had PTA at the time of testing; the control group were of similar educational and ages status (Ewert, Levin, Watson, & Kalisky, 1989). Half of the sixteen members of the severe TBI group were twenty-one years old or younger. Procedural memory tasks were administered each day for three days. Patients' abilities to acquire new procedural skills were assessed using tests of timed mirror reading of words, negotiation of visual mazes, and visual motor tracking. Declarative memory was assessed using a recognition memory test based on the words in the mirror reading test. Significant improvements in skill acquisition on the procedural memory tests were observed for the severe TBI group, despite their impairment on the verbal declarative memory test. Further increases in skill acquisition on these tests were observed for patients following the resolution of PTA, indicating that both declarative and procedural memories were impaired during PTA. For the control group, the procedural memory tests were generally too easy, thereby precluding control subjects from showing greater learning effects.

These data provide encouraging evidence that patients in PTA can acquire new skills during the PTA phase. This finding provides some promise for utilizing the adaptive potential of patients' procedural memory abilities when their declarative memory abilities are compromised. Although postinjury memory impairments are typically less severe, they do indicate that adolescents with TBI are at risk for significant educational and social problems.

*Case Study*

A fifteen-year-old, previously healthy ninth-grade male student who held a part-time job was admitted to the hospital on a weekend night following an MVA in which he was an unbelted passenger. An Emergency Medical Service worker reported that the teen was unconscious at the scene of the accident. On admission to the hospital, the teen was combative. CT exams revealed bilateral fronto-temporal lobe contusions, right parietal skull fracture, and various orthopedic injuries to the right shoulder area. His early hospital course involved periods of disorientation, confusion, restlessness, and agitation. He had no recall of the events leading up to or following the accident. A brief neuropsychological screening examination was administered eleven days following admission. He was alert, friendly, cooperative, able to listen and to talk, and oriented for person, place, and date. No spontaneous cognitive, emotional, or physical complaints were volunteered by the patient, except for his complaint of "a little pain" in his right shoulder. No gross aphasia or visual perceptual deficits were found on standardized tests, although his drawing, writing, and reading comprehension speed was mildly deficient. Despite his intact orientation and only mildly deficient immediately recall and thirty-minute recall for several visual designs, his immediate recall of verbal stories was poor. He could not recall any story details after a thirty-minute delay and could not recognize the correct story details from the multiple choices presented to him. After this screening examination, he was asked whether he had any difficulties and he complained again only of "a little pain" in his right shoulder.

These selective screening examination results provide a clinical example of a patient with severe TBI. He exhibited some retrograde amnesia and anterograde memory impairment for new verbal information and slowed mental processing, despite his adequate orientation and lack of aphasia or visual perceptual deficits. This case exemplifies the limits of patients' insights into their own mental status and the inadequacies of bedside conversations and orientation testing in determining a patient's mental status.

### Intellectual Abilities

Despite the limitations of intelligence tests for assessing brain-related disorders, patients with TBI are at risk for intellectual deficits. Chadwick, Rutter, Brown, Shaffer, and Traub (1981) conducted a two-and-a-quarter-year follow-up study of twenty-five orthopedically injured control (OC) patients, twenty-nine "mild" blunt TBI (duration of PTA > 1 hour and < 7 days) patients, and twenty-five "severe" blunt TBI (duration of PTA ≥ 7 days) patients, all of whom were between ages five and fourteen. This study also provided data on other neuropsychological measures, which will be discussed later. The mild TBI group demonstrated no significant mean increase, and hence no evidence of recovery, in either the verbal (VIQ) or the performance (PIQ) intelligence scores of the Wechsler Intelligence Scale for Children (WISC) at one year and at two and a quarter years following the injury. In contrast, the severe TBI group showed a significant mean improvement, and hence recovery, in VIQ and PIQ scores when compared with the OC group. No further improvement in PIQ was observed for either the severe TBI group or the OC group between the one-year and the two-and-a-quarter-year intervals. Unfortunately, mean VIQ change scores were not reported for the two-and-a-quarter-year follow-up assessment. Therefore, this study was unable to evaluate whether "late" recovery in verbal intellectual abilities was possible. The study's authors argued that WISC PIQ scores were more sensitive to the effects of TBI than the VIQ scores were.

Gulbrandsen (1984) studied fifty-six children and early adolescents ages nine to thirteen who had sustained mild TBI with less than fifteen minutes of unconsciousness four to eight months following their injuries. These TBI patients were compared with gender- and grade-matched classmates with similar levels of academic abilities based on the preinjury performance of the TBI patients. No significant WISC VIQ and PIQ score differences were observed between the TBI group and the matched group, and only minor mean differences were observed on two subtests. These results are consistent with the findings of Chadwick, Rutter, Brown, and colleagues (1981), in which no WISC VIQ or PIQ score differences were observed in the mild TBI group as compared with a control group. Gulbrandsen's (1984) study, however, also included neuropsychological testing. These findings will be discussed in a later section.

It is not clear whether intelligence test performances return to preinjury levels. Little work has been conducted in this area. Using school records, Richardson (1963) reported that two adolescents with severe TBI obtained IQ scores at two to three years following injury that were 20 to 35 points below their objectively measured preinjury IQ scores. Levin and Eisenberg (1979), evaluating children and adolescents with TBI about six months postinjury, found patients' postinjury PIQ-related scores to be significantly lower than the preinjury academic scores taken from their school records, even though some patients obtained average postinjury PIQ scores.

The above studies of intellectual outcomes following TBI provide some evidence that more severe TBI is associated with greater risks of cognitive deficits, particularly on PIQ scores. The finding that greater increases occur in postinjury PIQ scores as compared with VIQ scores has been interpreted to suggest that timed visual-perceptual and motor-related tasks may be more sensitive to the effects of TBI than verbal intellectual performances. In addition, average intelligence test scores may not rule out a history of TBI or the presence of other post-TBI cognitive deficits.

## Problem Solving

Neuropsychological studies of problem solving, including concept formation and reasoning abilities, have typically been based on available pediatric neuropsychological measures, rather than on developmental theories of thinking (see Dennis, in press). Nonetheless, problem-solving deficits have been reported in pediatric patients who have sustained a TBI.

Gulbrandsen's (1984) study of children and young adolescents with TBI at four to eight months postinjury revealed no group differences on IQ scores compared with those of their classmates. The TBI group, however, performed significantly lower than the noninjured group on both an untimed concept-formation/nonverbal reasoning test and a timed tactile-kinesthetic problem-solving test.

In a preliminary report, Levin and colleagues (1991) compared nonverbal planning and problem-solving tests in children ages six to nine with moderate to severe TBI with frontal and extrafrontal lobe lesions as defined by imaging studies. The frontal lobe lesion group solved significantly fewer of these novel problems than the extrafrontal lobe lesion group did, a finding consistent with both theoretical notions about frontal lobe functioning and empirical results in adult patients (see Stuss, 1987). No follow-up data were available on the duration of such problem-solving deficits, however. In addition, it is not known whether selective deficits are noted at different ages.

These preliminary studies demonstrate that problem-solving abilities may be impaired despite normal intelligence test results (Gulbrandsen, 1984), and that hypothesized frontal lobe functions may be operational in preadolescents and are vulnerable to localized effects of TBI. Gulbrandsen's (1984) findings are disturbing for two reasons: (a) his sample consisted of young patients with relatively mild TBI, and (b) the problem-solving deficits endured to at least four to eight months postinjury. The relationship between neuropsychological impairment and problem solving as described by tradition psychodevelopmental theorists remains poorly understood.

## Visuomotor Abilities

Visual-perceptual abilities include tests of visual discrimination of faces or designs and visual-spatial relations, as well as tests of recognition of the type and familiarity of objects. Constructional tests include puzzle and design construction or copying tasks. It is clear that the clinical assessment of visual-perceptual abilities is frequently complicated by the dependence of such tests on motor-related functions. For example, design copying and puzzle construction tests fail to separate patients' perception of the design from their graphic copying or manual construction of puzzles. Levin and Eisenberg (1979) found an association between severity of injury and impairment on a composite "visual-spatial" score based on copying, puzzle construction, motor-free facial discrimination tests. The patterns of impairment on motor-dependent performance and "motor free" visual-perceptual tests were not reported.

In a study described earlier, Chadwick, Rutter, Shaffer, and Shrout (1981) compared groups of children and adolescents ages five to fourteen who had severe TBI with a control group of children with orthopedic injuries (OC). The groups were asked to perform on a variety of measured tasks, including timed design copying tests. The severe TBI group was more impaired than the OC group on a timed copying test at two and a quarter years postinjury. Design copying deficits have also been reported in a longitudinal study in which children with a GCS of below 12 showed relatively less recovery, compared with a group of similarly severely injured adolescents during the first postinjury year (Thompson et al., 1990), indicating a possible selective developmental vulnerability for younger children.

Bawden, Knights, and Winogron (1985) compared "mild" (less than twenty minutes of loss of consciousness [LOC] or minor skull injuries; n = 17), "moderate" (greater than twenty minutes of LOC; n = 17), and "severe" (GCS ≤ 7; n = 17) TBI groups of children and adolescents ages five to seventeen at approximately one year postinjury. Each group received purely motor as well as visual-motor tests with varying motor speed demands. Results revealed greater deficits on timed tests in the severe TBI group, compared with the mild and moderate TBI groups, whose performances did not differ. In contrast to Chadwick, Rutter, Shaffer, and Shrout (1981), who reported deficits in severe TBI subjects' timed copying performance, Bawden and colleagues (1985) observed no deficits on untimed design copying tests in their study.

These findings suggest that the speeded visual-perceptual-motor abilities of some patients are susceptible to the effects of severe TBI. That visual-motor tasks involving graphic or construction tasks are performed less efficiently may challenge patients' performances in the classroom or on the job.

### Language Abilities

The clinical assessment of basic language abilities typically includes tests of auditory verbal comprehension, verbal repetition, verbal expression, and auditory perception. Only recently has research focused on the pragmatic application of these basic language abilities for social communication. Research on the language and communication abilities of adolescents with TBI contributes to our understanding of their risks for educational and social difficulties.

Initial studies of basic language abilities in pediatric TBI patients found that deficits in verbal naming and fluency were linked to severity of TBI (Chadwick, Rutter, Shaffer, & Shrout, 1981). Levin and Eisenberg (1979) also found that 31 percent of a sample of children and adolescents with different severities of TBI and at varying stages of recovery had impairment in some basic language abilities.

A more recent study of children and adolescents with either mild or moderate/severe TBI, conducted at one month following injury, revealed that 18 percent of the sample was impaired on tests of verbal expression, sentence repetition, and auditory comprehension (Ewing-Cobbs, Levin, Eisenberg & Fletcher, 1987). A significant association existed between severity of TBI and the presence of verbal expressive, comprehension, and repetition deficits. Youngsters in the moderate/severe TBI group were more impaired than those in the mild TBI group were on graphic, expressive, and naming tests, but not on comprehension tests. An age-related vulnerability in writing to dictation was observed in children relative to adolescents with TBI. Analyses of these writing-to-dictation performances revealed primarily errors in spelling, capitalization, and word omission. Although this report described a variety of deficits in basic language abilities in children and adolescents with TBI, it concluded that classic aphasia syndromes were rarely observed in this age-group (Ewing-Cobbs, Levin, Eisenberg, & Fletcher, 1987). These observations suggest a possible sparing of language abilities in pediatric patients with TBI, as compared with adult TBI patients, in whom classic aphasia syndromes may sometimes be observed (Sarno, Buonagurno, & Levita, 1986).

Study of social communication abilities following TBI has shown that daily social communication is disturbed. Basic expressive and receptive linguistic and social perceptual abilities, as well as immediate memory and stored social and semantic knowledge, contribute to competent social communication (Dennis & Barnes, in press). Preliminary evidence in a sample of TBI patients ages six to twenty-two who were at least three years postinjury indicated that nearly 80 percent of patients exhibited deficits on standardized tests of pragmatic communication. Basic language abilities did not consistently predict their performance on tests related to social communication. This group of TBI patients showed diverse patterns of deficits in inferential reasoning about story scripts, expressing appropriate descriptions of social activities, and understanding figurative or metaphoric statements.

These findings indicate that the evaluation of social communication contributes unique information about the verbal abilities of children and adolescents with TBI, and should be performed in addition to assessment of basic language abilities. Such results may prove useful in explicating the nature of communication problems in TBI patients who are not aphasic. It is important to note that these social communication deficits may be neither reliably nor easily detected by clinical interviews. Additional standardized measures need to be developed to ascertain the domains of deficit more accurately, so that more effective treatments can be developed.

### Academic Skills

Academic achievement tests have been used to evaluate the risk of academic skill deficits following TBI. The educational consequences for pediatric TBI were noted in a five-year prospective study (Klonoff & Paris, 1974) of patients ages two to sixteen years with relatively mild TBI. Although the results of the study may be qualified by the attrition of some subjects, school performance at follow-up in younger TBI patients (age at injury < nine years) revealed that 74 percent had attained "normal" progress, 15 percent had failed a grade but were in regular classes, and 10 percent were in remedial classes. Similarly, older TBI patients (age at injury > nine years) showed a 67 percent rate of "normal" progress, an 18 percent rate of grade failure but placement in regular classes, a 3 percent rate of remedial placement, and a 13 percent rate of either successive grade failures or quitting school. No objective academic test results were reported.

Chadwick, Rutter, Shaffer, and Shrout (1981) observed initial reading deficits at about one month following injury in a group of children and adolescents with severe TBI, compared with a control group, as described earlier. This deficit had, however, resolved by the time of the one-year postinjury assessment. Because no TBI-related reading deficits were observed initially in the mild/moderate TBI group, it is not surprising that this group did not demonstrate a "recovery" effect in subsequent one-year and two-and-a-quarter-year assessments. Interviews with teachers of the group with severe TBI revealed that nearly all of these children and adolescents were experiencing academic difficulties.

Levin and Benton (1986) assessed children and adolescents at six months following TBI and reported a decline in performance on arithmetic but not on oral reading or spelling tests. Examination of subjects' preinjury academic records revealed their mathematics scores to be similar to their reading scores, indicating that their arithmetic abilities had been impaired selectively.

Preliminary results from a recent prospective, although uncontrolled, study (Ewing-Cobbs et al., 1991) of children and adolescents ages five to fifteen with mild, moderate, and severe TBI revealed no apparent academic deficits in oral reading, spelling, arithmetic, and reading comprehension in the youngsters with mild or moderate TBI. In contrast, patients with severe TBI experienced significant deficits in reading comprehension, spelling, and arithmetic during the two-year follow-up period. Unexpectedly, adolescents with severe TBI exhibited greater deficits than children with comparably severe TBI in reading comprehension, reading recognition, spelling, and arithmetic, even when IQ was controlled.

These studies demonstrate persistent and selective academic deficits and comprehension, depending on the age of the patient, the length of follow-up intervals, and the severity of TBI. When educational outcome studies are reviewed in the context of known neuropsychological deficits, including intellectual and memory impairments, there can be little doubt that TBI has a significant adverse educational impact on children and adolescents. Many adolescents with TBI clearly need educational interventions. Table 3 lists the possible neuropsychological sequelae of TBI.

### Case Study

While riding his bicycle, an eleven-year-old boy was struck by a car traveling at fifty miles per hour. He sustained a severe TBI, associated with a coma of three weeks' duration, and a left parietal-occipital skull fracture with epidural and subdural hematomas. Prior to the trauma, he had had a history of estimated average in-

**Table 3.**
**Possible Neuropsychological Sequelae of TBI**

Intellectual skills
Language/academic skills
Visuoperceptual-motor skills
Learning, declarative, and procedural memory skills
Problem-solving skills
Sensorimotor skills

telligence, and had attended regular education classes, although he needed remedial reading instruction. The first neuropsychological examination at two months postinjury revealed a WISC-R VIQ score of less than 45 and a PIQ score of 47, which falls in the moderate range of mental retardation. His daily abilities, however, indicated adequate social independence and competence. Assessment of language revealed a global aphasia with severely impaired verbal expression, repetition, and comprehension. As he had difficulty in talking, he gestured to communicate and even used gestures to make jokes. His ability to comprehend the examiner's gestural and facial communication behavior appeared adequate, as did his visual-perceptual-motor abilities. On a test measuring concept formation/nonverbal reasoning, he fell near the average range for nine-year-olds and enjoyed the cognitive challenge.

The second neuropsychological examination was conducted about one year later, after he had received daily outpatient rehabilitation. His WISC-R VIQ score was 50, and his PIQ score was 75, which continued to fall in the mild-borderline range of mental retardation. Assessment of language revealed a nonfluent aphasia, with modest improvement in his verbal comprehension and much less improvement in his verbal repetition and expression. Adequate visual-perceptual-motor abilities were noted. On a difficult concept formation/nonverbal reasoning test, he obtained an average score and again enjoyed the cognitive challenge involved in nonverbal problem solving.

This patient represents a case of acquired traumatic aphasia in which the VIQ and PIQ scores were similarly impaired at the initial assessment. The case demonstrates that verbal intellectual abilities can be seriously impaired by TBI. The follow-up assessment provides further indication of this patient's apparently greater left (than right) hemisphere impairment, consistent with the nature of his injury. This extroverted and socially competent youngster displayed social communication abilities well beyond his language abilities. An important finding was that his intelligence test results underestimated his cognitive abilities, given his adequate concept formation/nonverbal reasoning abilities and social communication. Identifying patients' neuropsychological strengths as well as their weaknesses is crucial to understanding their academic and psychosocial needs. His parents also reported improvement in their relationships, because of the reciprocal support of family members, a psychosocial outcome that is desirable but all too infrequent.

### Psychosocial Outcomes

Few longitudinal studies have been conducted on the nature and risk of psychosocial sequelae for pediatric and adolescent TBI patients and their families. This circumstance is unfortunate, given the clinically known risk for long-term psychosocial sequelae following TBI, the increased incidence of more severe TBIs in adolescents (Kraus et al., 1990), the enhanced risk for psychosocial sequelae with more severe TBIs (Brown et al., 1981), and the relatively greater family burden posed by psychosocial versus physical and cognitive sequelae (Blazyk, 1983; Lezak, 1988b; Thomsen, 1974, 1984). Patients' psychosocial adjustment after TBI is related to a combination of preinjury developmental and psychological status, injury-related factors, and social and health care resources. Adolescents with TBI, like adolescents with other medical and psychosocial handicaps, share the same developmental challenges in attaining successful independence, intimacy, and adequate self-concept and self-esteem (McAnarney, 1985; Slater & Rubenstein, 1987). Patients' neurological and functional psychosocial courses following blunt TBI will be discussed below.

### Recovery Models

Several descriptive neurobehavioral models of patients' recovery from severe TBI have been proposed, including the Rancho Los Amigos Hospital Levels of Cognitive Functioning Scale (Hagan, Malkmus, & Durham, 1979) and Alexander's (1982) stage model of recovery. Although the psychometric properties of recovery scales have not been well studied (Gouvier, Blanton, LaPorte, & Nupomuceno, 1987), the scales provide a descriptive sequence of stages of neurological and behavioral recovery that are clinically useful for families and professional staff. Alexander's (1982) descriptive model will be reviewed to familiarize readers with the recovery stages of TBI patients. The model proposes seven stages of functional neurological recovery, each of varying duration, that are primarily applicable to cases of severe TBI.

*Coma* is usually defined as the inability to follow commands. It represents the antithesis of full consciousness and is the lowest functional neurological stage associated with severe TBI. Comatose patients are thought not to be aware of themselves or their environment. Families may see that their comatose adolescent is unable to respond, looks badly damaged, and is connected to multiple pieces of medical equipment. Families and health care professionals alike are concerned whether the injured adolescent will live. Alexander (1982) noted that the primary medical intervention during the stages of coma and unresponsive vigilance centers on neurosurgical efforts to eliminate factors that impede recovery and maintenance of wakefulness.

The return of wakefulness without significant cognition and responsiveness represents the stage of *unresponsive vigilance,* which arouses the family's hope that further recovery will soon occur. Family members may focus their attention on looking for additional signs of recovery, and frequently experience an understandable degree of heightened anticipation. The parents' attribution of cause regarding their adolescent's injury and their associated feelings about it may continue to be appropriately or inappropriately directed toward themselves or others (Lehr, 1990). Crisis interventions can be very helpful for family members.

*Mute responsiveness* is the third stage of functional recovery. It may be gradually observed as patients make simple efforts to cooperate with staff in a variety of simple in-bed activities, such as repositioning or orienting toward others' activities. As Lehr (1990) noted, patients in this stage may respond more reliably to family members than to health care staff, a situation that can produce conflicting perceptions of patients' recovery by the staff and the families. Patients are not yet, however, vocalizing or writing verbal responses. The major medical challenges include continued monitoring of neurological complications. The return of communication by patients marks the end of this recovery stage.

*Confusional states* are represented by significant attentional, amnesic, social-emotional, and cognitive organizational disturbances. The term *delirium* and the phrase "clouding of consciousness" similarly characterize the confused states arising from various medical disorders, including TBI (Plum & Posner, 1980). Patients continue to be in posttraumatic amnesia (PTA), may deny having obvious cognitive or physical problems, may not recall visits by family members, and may become anxious and confused. The sometimes bizarre or confused behavior of patients in this stage can be frightening to family members, whose bewilderment may be reduced by reassurance and information about the cause of these behavioral, emotional, and cognitive symptoms. Both families and staff continue the unsettling task of evaluating the patient's current cognitive and behavioral status in relation to preinjury functioning. As the patient's adequate arousal and capacity for mobility increase, behavior and safety become more important ward management issues (Alexander, 1982). Patients' self-awareness can be profoundly impaired, resulting in their inability to understand why they cannot go home and why others are so concerned about them. Families require education about patients' denial of their problems and anterograde memory loss. Denial or minimization of illness can represent a neurological symptom in many TBI cases, although psychological reactions may co-occur (Lezak, 1988b). Medical and inpatient management of confused patients involves an individualized combination of redirection, reassurance, limit setting, and, if necessary, pharmacotherapy (Alexander, 1982).

The resolution of coma, confusion, and PTA brings the return of *greater independent self-care* by patients, who at this stage may be discharged home or to rehabilitation facilities. Much to the dismay of staff, parents may believe that they are ready to handle all possible problems. Their naive confidence can lead to misunderstandings between family and staff (Lehr, 1990). Such readiness can be based on a lack of experience and/or minimization of their adolescent's deficits. Others, including peers, frequently expect survivors to perform up to their preinjury levels of social and cognitive functioning. These expectations are based on the often normal physical appearance of patients recovering from TBI. Thus, patients' behavioral changes may be viewed as inappropriate and willful, and frequently result in the patient's being rejected by peers and others (Richardson, 1963). Such social isolation from peers can be confusing and frustrating for survivors. Parents may feel understandably distressed and helpless to alter the social isolation of their son or daughter.

At this stage of recovery, management issues include the completion of relevant interdisciplinary assessments to determine placement and treatment needs. These assessment results can be helpful in altering any overestimates of the survivor's abilities and in reducing others' excessive cognitive, educational, and social demands. Following even mild TBI, patients may complain of postconcussive symptoms, which include headache, insomnia, hypersensitivity to light or noise, dizziness, fatigue, and problems with concentration, memory, and irritability (Levin et al., 1982). Patients' continued fatigue and irritability are especially common. Their impaired self-awareness can lead to overestimation of their own cognitive and social abilities. Professionals and families may struggle between the perils of inadequate supervision of the adolescent and the strife of adolescent-adult conflict generated by overprotectiveness.

The recovery stage of attaining *greater intellectual independence* continues to include late and residual problems of TBI, such as fatigue, "forgetfulness," judgment, and psychosocial difficulties. The psychological changes of survivors may become more burdensome to parents as emotional liability, irritability, silliness, apathy, self-centeredness, and organizational and motivational problems become more apparent (Blazyk, 1983; Lezak, 1988b). The latter can be especially troubling for families whose adolescent's postinjury empathy and understanding of others' perspectives is deficit (Blazyk, 1983; Thomsen, 1974, 1984). The reestablishment of goal-directed behavior in school, home, and community settings is the primary challenge and treatment objective at this stage of recovery, which, if negotiated successfully, leads to the last stage of *complete social recovery* (Alexander, 1982).

The frequently dynamic rapid behavioral changes in and diverse individual differences among patients cannot be easily characterized. Nevertheless, several psychiatric disorders relevant to TBI have been proposed as part of the *Diagnostic and Statistical Manual III-R* (DSM III-R) (American Psychiatric Association, 1987; Grant & Alves, 1987). The relevant so-called organic diagnoses for TBI-related psychiatric disorders have not, however, been well studied. DSM III-R includes so-called organic and other, nonorganic major psychiatric disorders, such as delirium, dementia, and amnesic and organic mood, or delusional, personality, and hallucinosis disorders (Axis I); personality or specific developmental disorders (Axis II); medical disorders, such as TBI or other medical diagnoses (Axis III); various circumstantial stressors (Axis IV); and global social-adaptive functioning (Axis V). Preexisting behavioral problems in adolescent patients and their families should also be evaluated; these include well-known risk factors, such as learning disability or substance abuse, that must be considered as part of clinical assessments in addition to patients' postinjury psychosocial problems (Gerring, 1986). Nevertheless, the many patterns of psychosocial sequelae of patients with the same severity of TBI should give anyone pause before making simple generalizations about the "traumatic brain injured" adolescent. Further, the relevance of DSM III-R is also uncertain, given the limited research on the psychosocial measurement and course of TBI in children and adolescents. For example, the number of clinically observed, apparently TBI-related psychosocial disturbances exceeds the number of available DSM III-R diagnoses.

Long-term psychosocial changes in some patients with severe TBI may persist for years and be a greater burden for families than the physical and cognitive changes that occur (Brooks, 1991; Thomsen, 1974, 1984). The pediatric studies of psychosocial sequelae reviewed below are based entirely on the post-PTA stages of recovery.

## Psychosocial Outcome Research

Research into psychosocial outcomes in pediatric TBI patients has had three important methodological limitations: the failures to (a) consider differing levels of severity of TBI, (b) control for preinjury psychosocial problems, and (c) include control groups for comparison purposes. Indeed, there is controversy about whether the population of pediatric and adolescent TBI cases is representative of the pediatric population as a whole. That a variety of individual and environmental risk factors have been linked empirically to these patients and their families further complicates the attribution of adverse psychosocial outcomes to TBI (Rutter et al., 1983). Determination of which TBI patients are at greatest risk for psychosocial problems is a critical research and clinical issue.

Brown and colleagues (1981) reported results from a controlled, psychosocial outcome study of TBI in the same five- to fourteen-year-old males and females that participated in Chadwick and colleagues (1981) study. Control patients with orthopedic injuries (OC) were compared with same-age peers with either severe TBI (STBI; duration of PTA ≥ one week) or mild TBI (MTBI; duration of PTA < one week) for about two years postinjury. The frequency of developing new psychosocial problems across the two-year postinjury follow-up period did not differ significantly in the MTBI (15 to 20 percent) and OC (5 to 14 percent) groups. The STBI group, however, expressed a 48 to 62 percent rate of developing new psychosocial problems. The MTBI group's preinjury behavioral scores (as measured by parent report) were higher than the scores of the OC group, but there was no evidence of a significant increase in the nature or mean severity of the behavioral problems of the MTBI group following individuals' TBI. The pattern of behavioral disturbances observed in the STBI group included socially inappropriate acts—for example, being outspoken or loud, asking others embarrassing questions, being careless in dress and hygiene, and exhibiting inappropriate "sexual" behavior, such as undressing in public or demonstrating excessive physical expression of affection. "Hyperactivity" did not develop in members of the TBI group. The presence of neurological abnormalities, intellectual deficits, and familial psychosocial adversity was associated with post-TBI psychosocial problems, but some patients with STBI develop new psychiatric problems without the presence of coexisting neurological, intellectual, and familial problems (Brown et al., 1981). This study helps demonstrate that STBI, but not MTBI, is frequently associated with the development of new psychosocial problems.

Fletcher, Ewing-Cobbs, Miner, Levin, and Eisenberg (1990) followed male and female patients ages three to fifteen with mild, moderate, and severe TBI (as defined in Levin, Goldstein, et al., 1988). Because the measures in this study used good age-specific norms for comparative purposes, no control group was necessary. Parents completed the Child Behavior Checklist (CBCL) (Achenbach & Edelbrock, 1983) and were interviewed using the Vineland Adaptive Behavior Scales (VABS) (Sparrow, Balla, & Cicchetti, 1984) immediately following the injury and during clinical assessments occurring at six- and twelve-month intervals following the injury. The severe TBI group's overall adaptive behavior levels were lower than its estimated preinjury levels at both the six-month and the twelve-month follow-up assessments, when compared with both the mild and the moderate TBI groups. The latter two groups did not differ from each other or their own respective preinjury scores as estimated at baseline. VABS domain-specific scale scores in functional communication, daily living skills, and social behavior also declined from preinjury baseline levels to the levels observed at the times of the six-month and/or twelve-month follow-up assessments for the severe but not the mild or moderate TBI groups.

On the CBCL, the global "internalized" (e.g., somatic or mood symptoms) and "externalized" (e.g., disruptive behavior symptoms) psychopathology scale scores did not significantly differ among the three groups, indicating that no parent-reported differences existed among these groups, and that no apparent behavioral postinjury changes occurred, compared with estimates of patients' preinjury behavior. Fletcher and colleagues' (1990) failure to find behavioral sequelae among severe TBI patients is inconsistent with Brown and colleagues' (1981) findings of new psychosocial problems in their severe TBI group. Fletcher and colleagues (1990) suggested that the CBCL format and/or items may not have been as sensitive to the existence of brain-related behavioral sequelae as the interview format of the VABS or other measures of psychosocial status. This interpretation also holds true in clinical assessments of patients' psychosocial adjustment.

Thomsen (1974, 1984) reported on patient and family outcomes at two to five years and at ten to fifteen years post-TBI for a sample of fifty adolescent and adult patients with severe TBI, twenty-three of whom were fifteen to twenty-one years old at the time of their injury. At first follow-up, relatives' complaints were greatest for personality changes, followed by neuropsychological and motor deficits. Although the neurological examination revealed motor deficits that were severe (e.g., inability to walk) or mild (motor problems, but independently functioning) in all but fifteen patients, no relatives complained of patients' physical disabilities. All but eight relatives, however, complained of changes in the patients' character, including childishness, irritability, lack of spontaneity, stubbornness, and emotional lability. Eighty percent of the sample was interviewed again at ten to fifteen years following injury (6 percent of the sample had died in the interim). Although some gradual improvement in patients' behavior had occurred in subsequent years postinjury, 65 percent of patients continued to demonstrate emotional or personality changes, generally consisting of lack of initiative, apathy, irritability, and emotional lability. "Childish" behavior was an early symptom that resolved for some patients. Posttraumatic psychosis was observed in eight patients (16 percent), seven of whom were twenty-two years old or younger at the time of injury. Thomsen (1984) also reported that the only symptoms that appeared more often among patients below age twenty-one than among those above age twenty-one at the time of TBI were greater irritability, restlessness, and disturbed behavior that included aggression or sexual disinhibition. The long-term developmental challenges faced by these patients were clearly evident by the social effects of their emotional, neuropsychological, and physical deficits. At ten to fifteen years postinjury, 66 percent of the sample had no social contacts outside the close family, 93 percent were receiving disability payments, few were employed on a regular basis, and half continued to be dependent on others for activities of daily living. Patients who had been single at the time of injury were unlikely to wed, and married patients sustained a high divorce rate. Importantly, patients' greatest subjective burden was their social isolation, while their relatives' greatest burden was a patient's personality and emotional changes. Patients with bifronto-temporal and brain stem lesions had the worst outcomes (Thomsen, 1984). This study is not usually discussed in the pediatric neuropsychology literature, but it deserves greater attention, given both the large number of adolescent subjects and the long follow-up clinical assessment of patients' psychosocial outcomes.

All these studies provide valuable information about adolescents' postinjury risk of developing adaptive, neuropsychological, and psychosocial problems. The outcomes for patients with mild or moderate TBI appear to be more favorable, with less risk of adverse psychosocial sequelae. Table 4 lists general domains of psychosocial sequelae of TBI. The search continues for pre- and postinjury factors that account for the heterogeneous patterns of psychosocial disturbances among patients. Methodological considerations are important, and include the severity of TBI and how individual and family psychosocial outcomes are measured. The effects of TBI on psychosocial competence is a critical topic in the evaluation of adolescents' outcomes.

## Trauma Care Models and Services

The significant advances in delivery of emergency trauma services have increased both the number of survivors and their need for postacute and long-term care. Emergency medical systems save lives and improve outcomes when coordinated trauma communication, transport, acute care, intermediate care, rehabilitation, and community services are available (Haller & Beaver, 1990). Still, not all communities may have readily available or affordable postacute medical, rehabilitation, psychosocial, and educational services for adolescents with TBI and their families. Continuity of trauma care provides for the psychosocial needs of adolescents and their families during acute, intermediate, and long-term phases of recovery and adjustment. Unfortu-

**Table 4.**
**Domains of Psychosocial Sequelae of TBI**

*Psychological*

    Self-concept and self-esteem

    Behavioral initiation and disinhibition

    Mood disturbances

    Social skills

*Adaptive*

    Family and peer relations

    Recreational, vocational, and community skills

    Daily living skills

nately, the development of efficacious long-term services may not have kept pace with the advances in acute trauma care. Further, the long-term needs of adolescents with TBI may not currently be recognized, partly because of the limited training of medical, psychosocial, and educational professionals (Tyler, Mira, & Hollowell, 1989; Savage, 1991), a factor that in turn may impede the development of long-term services.

A second, disturbing trend is the reduction in the number of trauma centers, some of which have closed because of their financial costs, even though their long-term savings to society have been demonstrated (Garza, 1990). A variety of long-term trauma care services may be essential for op-timal functional outcomes for some trauma survivors, and include medical, family, rehabilitation, and educational services. Some of these services are discussed below.

### Adolescent and Family Services

Psychosocial services are essential components of rehabilitation in order to reduce immediate and chronic personal and social distress in adolescents and the families. In addition to Alexander's (1982) neurologically based recovery factors, patients' psychosocial adjustment after TBI involves a combination of preinjury developmental and psychological factors and available social and health care resources. Adolescents with TBI, like adolescents with other medical and psychosocial handicaps, share the same developmental chal-lenges in attaining successful independence, intimacy, and adequate self-concept and self-esteem (McAnarney, 1985; Slater & Rubenstein, 1987).

Patients' psychosocial changes can be the result of both direct neurolog-ical disturbances and indirect or personal psychological reactions of patients to their altered cognitive social, and physical status. As Boll (1983) has re-ported, the failure to detect and address these TBI-related deficits can pro-duce "a negative cycle of failure, anxiety, and assumptions of incompetence which may long out-live the actual behavioral sequelae of the head injury itself" (p. 79).

The need to include families in the delivery of trauma services to adoles-cent patients is obvious. Families often serve as the primary or only consis-tent caretakers, supporters, and advocates for patients. Turnbull and Turnbull (1991) have argued that "the basic unit of considerate in policy and services is the individual and family, rather than solely the individual with the disability" (p. 37).

Clinical observations about family responses to TBI (and other medical and nonmedical stresses and strains) have utilized several traditional models of psychosocial adjustment. Hill's (1958) ABCX crisis model has served to highlight that a crisis (X) is a function of the event (A), the family's available resources (B), and the family's perception of the event (C). As applied to a family's process of coping with recovering adolescents, this model emphasizes the family's unique perceptions and resources in adjusting to postinjury events. For example, parents' reactions to their adolescent's injury understandably vary according to their attribution of responsibility for the injury event; their financial, social, and psychological resources; and their interpretation of the significance of the injury in relation to such concerns as their son's or daughter's aspirations and their own personal aspirations.

Models of grieving (Kubler-Ross, 1969) and chronic sorrow (Olshansky, 1962) have been important in normalizing the emotional experience of loss for many people, including those of TBI survivors and their family members (Lezak, 1988b). The episodic nature of sorrow is thought to be a normal reaction to loss that can be precipitated by various events, such as an adolescent's failure to attain developmental milestones on schedule (Copley & Bodensteiner, 1987; Williams, 1991). Education about typical neuropsychological and psychosocial sequelae of TBI may help patients and families to seek earlier therapeutic interventions and to understand better their psychosocial adjustment, including accepting their current, and perhaps chronic, sorrow as normal.

Family systems models have been adapted to address the treatment needs of adolescents with disabilities and their families. In addition to the injured adolescent's treatment needs, critical family factors, including cultural, communication, and life cycle issues, may need to be assessed and integrated with the successful provision of long-term medical, rehabilitation, and supportive service plans (Muir, Rosenthal, & Diehl, 1990; Slater & Rubenstein, 1987; Turnbull & Turnbull, 1991). TBI research has been conducted too infrequently on families' outcomes following their adolescent's TBI, although recent clinical reviews of families' adjustment needs indicate their many understandable concerns and persistent daily struggles in their caretaking demands (Muir et al., 1990; Williams & Kay, 1991).

## Rehabilitation Services

Rehabilitation has been defined by Diller and Gordon (1981) as services "provided to the disabled person in order to reduce impairment, to facilitate optimum acquisition of skills, and to overcome the disability" (p. 703). Impairment represents an adverse change in function, whereas disability represents difficulty meeting the functional expectations of others (Diller & Gordon, 1981).

Interdisciplinary rehabilitation assessment of TBI patients may require services from various medical specialists. In addition, physical, occupational, speech/language, audiological, educational, psychological, and neuropsychological specialists are frequently necessary to evaluate adequately many TBI patients' functional capacities. The assessment of severely injured patients should occur both in the acute phase of recovery to determine discharge and follow-up interdisciplinary management plans and in later stages of recovery to determine patients' continuing need for treatment services. Trauma care and rehabilitation systems routinely utilize an interdisciplinary assessment and intervention model because of some patients' multiple medical, psychosocial, educational, and vocational sequelae. Although determination of rehabilitation needs should be considered for each patient, many less severely injured patients may not require comprehensive interdisciplinary assessments and treatment services. Detailed discipline-specific assessment and intervention issues are addressed elsewhere (Rosenthal et al., 1990; Ylvisaker, 1985).

Rourke and colleagues (1983) proposed a neuropsychological assessment model that integrates patient- and disorder-specific findings within developmental, social, educational, and vocational contexts for intervention planning. In order to develop a realistic immediate and long-term treatment plan, the adolescent's neuropsychological and psychosocial impairments and capabilities are considered in regard to the type, acuity, extent, and location of the brain impairment. For example, some brain-related impairments associated with TBI may resolve rapidly during the acute recovery period, limiting the long-term significance of "early" neuropsychological and other discipline-specific results for long-term treatment planning. Findings are valuable, however, for developing immediate discharge plans. Short- and long-term social, educational, and vocational demands on adolescents are integrated with neuropsychological and other interdisciplinary assessment findings to estimate the patients' short- and long-term outcomes. Estimates about patients' short- and long-term outcomes are then considered in relation to the available remedial resources to develop realistic short- and long-term remedial plans. These assessment findings serve to inform families of an adolescent survivor's limitations and strengths, to set appropriate expectations, and to implement interventions.

A critical component of patient rehabilitation concerns the personal and social adjustment to one's disabilities. The psychosocial sequelae that sometimes follow TBI can impede rehabilitation, educational, and eventual vocational adjustment due to the functional communicational, emotional, and behavioral challenges for patients, families, and professionals. As evident in Table 5, psychosocial sequelae of injury present both subjective and social changes that can profoundly influence adolescents' ability to participate fully in rehabilitation and educational settings. Indeed, the adjustment by adolescents and their families can be quite difficult at times, with increasing stresses as some adolescents fail to fulfill expected developmental, social, educational, and vocational roles. Wright (1983) has asserted that there is often too great an emphasis on what the person cannot do versus what he or she can do. This approach can lead to viewing survivors as passive victims to be pitied, rather than active participants who help shape their futures and achieve their maximum potential.

The efficacy of rehabilitation treatment for TBI and other neurological disorders is a controversial issue that has received surprisingly limited empirical study (Prigatano, Fordyce, Zeiner, Roueche, Pepping, & Wood, 1984). Nonetheless, a central concern of many researchers and clinicians is not whether traditional interdisciplinary rehabilitation is worthwhile for TBI patients but whether any proof exists for the additional benefits of so-called cognitive rehabilitation techniques. For example, while several promising studies support the potential efficacy of a few cognitive rehabilitation strategies, there has been no controlled empirical evaluation of many cognitive rehabilitation techniques. As Hachinski (1990) noted about the many diverse techniques that have been called cognitive rehabilitation, "Something is better than nothing in the rehabilitation of brain-injured patients. . . . Without therapeutic enthusiasm there would be no innovation and without skepticism, there would be no proof. Cognitive rehabilitation deserves further evaluation" (p. 224). Because the controversy and existing studies of cognitive rehabilitation cannot be covered adequately here, interested readers are referred to (a) several critical reviews of research on diverse traditional and cognitive rehabilitation approaches (Benedict, 1989; Diller & Gordon, 1981; Grimm & Bleiberg, 1986; McGlynn, 1990) and (b) interdisciplinary rehabilitation textbooks on TBI (Rosenthal, Griffith, Bond, & Miller, 1990; Ylvisaker, 1985).

Despite the controversy about the efficacy of cognitive rehabilitation, the special educational needs of some adolescents with TBI are becoming more widely appreciated, although, as with cognitive rehabilitation techniques, special education instruction strategies for TBI adolescents have not received sufficient study. Given the persisting psychological and adaptive sequelae with which adolescents, families, and professionals are challenged, the need to address psychosocial issues in inpatient and outpatient rehabilitation settings is critical.

## Educational Services

Educational reentry, from either an acute care or a rehabilitation setting, may be challenging for injured students, as well as for their teachers and families. Some TBI studies suggest that brain impairment may produce selective neuropsychological deficits in patients at various developmental stages. Thus, although brain impairment may produce a loss of established cognitive, psychosocial, and physical abilities, the acquisition of new abilities and information is also adversely affected (Hebb, 1942). For some survivors, previous academic, social, and physical expectations may no longer be appropriate. Interdisciplinary assessments, not medical diagnoses alone, are necessary to document whether educationally significant handicaps are present. It should be stressed, however, that the structured and supportive nature of one-to-one neuropsychological and educational assessments may mask underlying cognitive, psychosocial, and adaptive deficits that could emerge later in the classroom (Baxter, Cohen, & Ylvisaker, 1985). More complex cognitive and social abilities may not be required from survivors until reentry into the classroom occurs. On the other hand, adolescents with only mild to moderate injuries but educationally significant neuropsychological deficits may escape notice in large busy classrooms. Therefore, health care professionals may need to educate teachers and parents to become advocates for brain-injured adolescents in obtaining additional special education services (Martin, 1988). Such advocacy is particularly necessary, given the limited professional preparation of many educators about the special needs of students with TBI (Carney & Gerring, 1990; Savage, 1991).

Except in cases of severe postinjury disability, adolescents with mild to moderate TBI-related deficits have not often been recognized as requiring special education services. Determination of the degree of cognitive, psychosocial, and physical difficulties necessary for an adolescent with TBI to be eligible for such services or other accommodations is not well established. Such determination is made jointly with the parents, school officials, and health care professionals, including trauma care specialists. The certification criteria for special education services for those with mild/moderate TBI are even less clear (Savage, 1991). Generally, a medical diagnosis (e.g., TBI) in a student is not a sufficient basis for establishing that a student has an educational handicap. Rather, a student's certification for special education is based on whether a cognitive, psychological, or sensorimotor deficits condition adversely affects his or her educational progress (Carney & Gerring, 1990; Martin, 1988).

Ylvisaker, Hartwick, and Stevens (1991) have developed a helpful sequence of school reentry steps for students with TBI that includes hospital-school communication and planning, staff and peer education, utilization of individual instructional strategies, and ongoing follow-up and family treatment services. Recent reviews concerning the education of students with TBI can be found in special issues of the *Journal of Head Trauma Rehabilitation* (1991) and the *Journal of Learning Disabilities* (1987, 1988). The National Head Injury Foundation may be contacted through its state representatives for various informational, referral, and support services. This organization has published a manual with background information on TBI and instructional ideas for teachers (National Head Injury Foundation, 1988). A resource guide about colleges and other helpful organizations for students with TBI and their families is also available (Heath Resource Center, 1988).

New educational programs and instructional technologies for students with TBI are expected to develop as research advances demonstrably efficacious rehabilitation techniques that can be adapted for classroom use. The development of regional special education programs has been proposed or implemented in several school systems as a possible solution for the inability of many local districts to provide appropriate instruction and psychological support for students with TBI (Carney & Gerring, 1990).

## Summary

TBI represents one aspect of the leading adolescent public health problems of "unintentional" injuries caused primarily by MVAs and "intentional" injuries caused by assaults and self-inflicted trauma. Epidemiological and health risk models of factors contributing to injuries are necessary to reduce injury-related deaths and disabilities by active and passive prevention strategies that target host, agent, environmental, and temporal injury-related phase factors (Waller, 1985; NCICP, 1989).

Until more effective injury control strategies are developed and adopted that can reduce the number of cases of TBI in adolescents, the management of postinjury neuropsychological and psychosocial sequelae will depend on the development of long-term services provided by adolescents and their families by health care, rehabilitation, and education professionals, as well as community support groups. There is an obvious need for improved education and research in the health care, psychosocial, and educational fields in order to prevent injury and to understand and reduce the adverse sequelae of TBI and other injuries.

## References

Achenbach, T., & Edelbrock, C. (1983). *Manual for the Child Behavior Checklist and Revised Behavior Profile*. Burlington, VT: University of Vermont.

Alexander, M. (1982). Traumatic brain injury. In D. Benson & D. Blumer (Eds.), *Psychiatric aspects of neurologic disease* Vol. II (pp. 219–250). New York: Grune & Stratton.

American Psychiatric Association. (1987). *Diagnostic and statistical manual* (3rd ed., revised). Washington, DC: Author.

Baker, S., O'Neill, B., & Karpf, R. (1984). *The injury fact book*. Lexington, MA: Heath.

Bawden, H., Knights, R., & Winogron, W. (1985). Speeded performance following head injury in children. *Journal of Clinical and Experimental Neuropsychology, 7*, 39–54.

Baxter, R., Cohen, S., & Ylvisaker, M. (1985). Comprehensive cognitive assessment. In M. Ylvisaker (Ed.), *Head injury rehabilitation: Children and adolescents* (pp. 219–246). San Diego, CA: College Hill.

Benedict, R. (1989). The effectiveness of cognitive remediation strategies for victims of traumatic head-injury: A review of the literature. *Clinical Psychology Review, 9*, 605–626.

Blazyk, S. (1983). Developmental crisis in adolescents following severe head injury. *Social Work in Health Care, 8*, 55–67.

Blum, R. (1987). Contemporary threats to adolescent health in the United States. *Journal of the American Medical Association, 257*, 3390–3395.

Boll, T. (1983). Minor head injury in children—Out of sight but not out of mind. *Journal of Clinical Child Psychology, 12*, 74–80.

Brooks, D. (1991). The head-injured family. *Journal of Clinical and Experimental Neuropsychology, 13,* 155–188.

Brown, G., Chadwick, O., Shaffer, D., Rutter, M., & Traub, M. (1981). A prospective study of children with head injuries: III. Psychiatric sequelae. *Psychological Medicine, 11,* 63–78.

Carney, J., & Gerring, J. (1990). Return to school following severe closed head injury: A critical phase in pediatric rehabilitation. *Pediatrician, 17,* 222–229.

Centerwall, B. (1984). Race, socioeconomic status, and domestic homicide, Atlanta, 1971–72. *American Journal of Public Health, 74,* 813–815.

Chadwick, O., Rutter, M., Brown, G., Shaffer, D., & Traub, M. (1981). A prospective study of children with head injuries: II. Cognitive sequelae. *Psychological Medicine, 11,* 49–61.

Chadwick, O., Rutter, M., Shaffer, D., & Shrout, P. (1981). A prospective study of children with head injuries: IV. Specific cognitive deficits. *Journal of Clinical Neuropsychology, 3,* 101–120.

Copley, M., & Bodensteiner, J. (1987). Chronic sorrow in families of disabled children. *Journal of Child Neurology, 2,* 67–70.

Council on Scientific Affairs. (1986). Alcohol and the driver. *Journal of the American Medical Association, 255,* 522–527.

Dennis, M. (in press). Frontal lobe function in childhood and adolescence: A heuristic for assessing attention regulation, executive control, and the intentional states important for social discourse. *Developmental Neurology, 6.*

Dennis, M., & Barnes M. (in press). Knowing the meaning, getting the point, bridging the gap, and carrying the message: Aspects of discourse following closed head injury in childhood and adolescence. *Brain and Language.*

Diller, L., & Gordon, W. (1981). Rehabilitation and clinical neuropsychology. In S. Filskov & T. Boll (Eds.), *Handbook of clinical neuropsychology* (Vol. 1), (pp. 702–733). New York: Wiley.

Ewert, J., Levin, H., Watson, M., & Kalisky, Z. (1989). Procedural memory during posttraumatic amnesia in survivors of severe closed head injury. *Archives of Neurology, 46,* 911–916.

Ewing-Cobbs, L., Iovino, I., Fletcher, J., Miner M., & Levin, H. (1991). Academic achievement following traumatic brain injury in children and adolescents. *Journal of Clinical and Experimental Neuropsychology, 13,* 93.

Ewing-Cobbs, L., Levin, H., Eisenberg, H., & Fletcher, J. (1987). Language functions following closed head injury in children and adolescents. *Journal of Clinical and Experimental Neuropsychology, 9,* 572–592.

Fletcher, J., Ewing-Cobbs, L., Miner, M., Levin, H., & Eisenberg, H. (1990). Behavioral changes after closed head injury in children. *Journal of Consulting and Clinical Psychology, 58,* 93–98.

Gallagher, S., Guyer, B., Kotelchuck, M., Bass, J., Lovejoy, F., McLoughlin, E., & Mehta, K. (1982). A strategy for the reduction of childhood injuries in Massachusetts: SCIPP. *New England Journal of Medicine, 307,* 1015–1019.

Garza, M. (1990). Who cares about trauma? *Journal of Emergency Medical Services, 15,* 32–39.

Gerring, J. (1986). Psychiatric sequelae of severe closed head injury. *Pediatrics in Review, 8,* 115–121.

Gouvier, W., Blanton, P., LaPorte, K., & Nupomuceno, C. (1987). Reliability and validity of the Disability Rating Scale and the Levels of Cognitive Functioning Scale in monitoring recovery from severe head injury. *Archives of Physical Medicine and Rehabilitation, 68,* 94–97.

Grant, I., & Alves, W. (1987). Psychiatric and psychosocial disturbances in head injury. In H. Levin, J. Grafman, & H. Eisenberg (Eds.), *Neurobehavioral recovery from head injury* (pp. 232–261). New York: Oxford.

Grimm, B. & Bleiberg, J. (1986). Psychological rehabilitation in traumatic brain injury. In S. Filskov & T. Toll (Eds.), *Handbook of clinical neuropsychology* (Vol. 2), (pp. 495–560). New York: Wiley.

Gulbrandsen, G. (1984). Neuropsychological sequelae of light head injuries in older children 6 months after trauma. *Journal of Clinical Neuropsychology, 6,* 257–268.

Guyer, B., Lescohier, I., Gallagher, S., Hausman, A., & Azzara, C. (1989). Intentional injuries among children and adolescents in Massachusetts. *New England Journal of Medicine, 321,* 1584–1589.

Hachinski, V. (1990). Cognitive rehabilitation. *Archives of Neurology, 47,* 224.

Haddon, W. (1972). A logical framework for categorizing highway safety phenomena and activity. *The Journal of Trauma, 12,* 193–207.

Haddon, W. (1980). Advances in the epidemiology of injuries as a basis for public policy. *Public Health Reports, 95,* 411–421.

Haddon, W., & Blumenthal, M. (1984). Foreword. In H. Ross (Ed.), *Deterring the drinking driver: Legal policy and social control.* Lexington, MA: Heath.

Hagan, C., Malkmus, D., & Durham, P. 1979). Levels of cognitive functioning. *Rehabilitation of the head injured adult: Comprehensive physical management.* Downey, CA: Professional Staff Association of Ranchos Los Amigos Hospital, Inc.

Haller, J., & Beaver, B. (1990). Overview of pediatric trauma. In R. Touloukian (Ed.), *Pediatric trauma* (pp. 3–13). Baltimore, MD: Mosby Year Book.

Heath Resource Center. (1988). *The head injury survivor on campus: Issues and resources.* Washington, DC: American Council on Education.

Hebb, D. (1942). The effect of early and late brain injury upon tests scores, and the nature of normal adult intelligence. *Proceedings of the American Philosophical Society, 85,* 275–292.

Hill, R. (1958). Social stresses on the family. *Social Casework, 38,* 139–158.

Hofmann, A. (1990). Clinical assessment and management of health risk behaviors in adolescents. *Adolescent Medicine: State of the Art Reviews, 1,* 33–44.

Hollinger, P. (1990). The causes, impact, and preventability of childhood injuries in the United States. *American Journal of Diseases of Children, 144,* 670–676.

Irwin, C., & Millstein, S. (1986). Biopsychosocial correlates of risk-taking behaviors during adolescence. *Journal of Adolescent Health Care, 7,* 82s–96s.

Jeffrey, R. (1989). Risk behaviors and health. *American Psychologist, 44,* 1194–1202.

Jennett, B., & Frankowski, R. (1990). The epidemiology of head injury. In R. Braakman (Ed.), *Handbook of clinical neurology* (pp. 1–16). New York: Elsevier.

Jessor, R. (1984). Adolescent development and behavioral health. In J. Matarazzo, S. Weiss, & J. Herd (Eds.), *Behavioral health: An overview* (pp. 69–100). New York: Wiley.

Klonoff, H., & Paris, R. (1974). Immediate, short-term, and residual effects of acute head injuries in children: Neuropsychological and neurological correlates. In R. Reitan & L. Davison (Eds.), *Clinical neuropsychology: Current status and applications* (pp. 179–210). New York: Wiley.

Kolb, B. (1989). Brain development, plasticity, and behavior. *American Psychologist, 44,* 1203–1212.

Kraus, J., Rock, A., & Hemayari, P. (1990). Brain injuries among infants, children, adolescents, and young adults. *American Journal of Diseases of Children, 144,* 684–691.

Kubler-Ross, E. (1969). *On death and dying.* New York: Macmillan.

Lehr, E. (1990). *Psychological management of traumatic brain injuries in children and adolescents.* Rockville, MD: Aspen.

Levin, H., Anparo, E., Eisenberg, H., Williams, D., High, W., McArdle, C., & Weiner, R. (1987). Magnetic resonance imaging and computerized tomography in relation to the neurobehavioral sequelae of mild and moderate head injuries. *Journal of Neurosurgery, 66,* 706–713.

Levin, H., & Benton, A. (1986). Developmental and acquired dyscalculia in children. In I. Fleming (Ed.), *Second European symposium on developmental neurology.* Stuttgart: Gustav Fisher Verlag.

Levin, H., Benton, A., & Grossman, R. (1982). *Neurobehavioral consequences of closed head injury.* New York: Oxford.

Levin, H., Culhane, K., Mendelsohn, D., Chapman, S., Harward, H., Hartmann, J., Bruce, D., Fletcher, J., & Ewing-Cobbs, L. (1991). Effects of frontal vs. extrafrontal lesions on planning ability on head-injured children. *Journal of Clinical and Experimental Neuropsychology, 13,* 63.

Levin, H., & Eisenberg, H. (1979). Neuropsychological outcome of closed head injury in children and adolescents. *Child's Brain, 5,* 281–292.

Levin, H., Eisenberg, H., Wigg, N., & Kobayashi, K. (1982). Memory and intellectual ability after head injury in children and adolescence. *Neurosurgery, 11,* 668–672.

Levin, H., Goldstein, F., High, W., & Eisenberg, H. (1988). Disproportionately severe memory deficit in relation to normal intellectual functioning after closed head injury. *Journal of Neurology, Neurosurgery, and Psychiatry, 51,* 1294–1301.

Levin, H., High, W., & Eisenberg, H. (1988). Learning and forgetting during posttramatic amnesia in head injured patients. *Journal of Neurology, Neurosurgery, and Psychiatry, 51,* 14–20.

Levin, H., High, W., Ewing-Cobbs, L., Fletcher J., Eisenberg, H., Miner, M., & Goldstein, F. (1988). Memory functioning during the first year after closed head injury in children and adolescents. *Neurology, 22,* 1043–1051.

Lezak, M. (1988a). IQ: R.I.P. *Journal of Clinical and Experimental Neuropsychology, 10,* 351–361.

Lezak, M. (1988b). Brain damage is a family affair. *Journal of Clinical and Experimental Neuropsychology, 10,* 111–123.

Martin, R. (1988). Legal challenges in educating traumatic brain injured students. *Journal of Learning Disabilities, 21,* 471–485.

McAnarney, E. (1985). Social maturation: A challenge for handicapped and chronically ill adolescents. *Journal of Adolescent Health Care, 6,* 90–101.

McGlynn, S. (1990). Behavioral approaches to neuropsychological rehabilitation. *Psychological Bulletin, 108,* 420–441.

McManus, M., McCarthy, E., Kozak, L., & Newacheck, P. (1991). Hospital use by adolescents and young adults. *Journal of Adolescent Health, 12,* 107–115.

Morbidity and Mortality Weekly Report. (1989). Results from the National Adolescent Student Health Survey. *Journal of the American Medical Association, 261,* 2025, 2031.

Muir, C., Rosenthal, M., & Diehl, L. (1990). Methods of family intervention. In M. Rosenthal, E. Griffith, M. Bond, & J. Miller (Eds.), *Rehabilitation of the adult and child with traumatic brain injury* (pp. 433–448). Philadelphia, PA: F. A. Davis.

National Committee on Injury Prevention and Control. (1989). *Injury prevention: Meeting the challenge.* New York: Oxford.

National Head Injury Foundation. (1988). *An educator's manual: What educators need to know about students with traumatic brain injury.* Southborough, MA: Author.

National Research Council (1985). *Injury in America.* Washington, DC: National Academy Press.

Olshansky, S. (1962). Chronic sorrow: A response to having a mentally defective child. *Social Casework, 43,* 190–193.

Ommaya, A., & Gennarelli, T. (1974). Cerebral concussion and traumatic unconsciousness: Correlation of experimental and clinical observations on blunt head injuries. *Brain, 97,* 633–654.

Pipken, N., Walker, L., & Thomason, M. (1989). Alcohol and vehicular injuries in adolescents. *Journal of Adolescent Health Care, 10,* 119–121.

Plum, F., & Posner, J. (1980). *The diagnosis of stupor and coma.* Philadelphia, PA: Davis.

Prigatano, G., Fordyce, D., Zeiner, H., Roueche, J., Pepping, M., & Wood, B. (1984). Neuropsychological rehabilitation after closed head injury in young adults. *Journal of Neurology, Neurosurgery, and Psychiatry, 47,* 505–513.

Prothrow-Smith, D. (1986). Interdisciplinary interventions applicable to prevention of interpersonal violence and homicide in black youth. In *Surgeon General's workshop on violence and public health report* (pp. 35–43). Rockville, MD: U.S. Dept. of Health & Human Services.

Rice, D., MacKenzie, E., & Associates. (1989). *Cost of injury in the United States: A report to Congress.* Institute for Health and Aging, University of California and Injury Prevention Center, Johns Hopkins University.

Richardson, F. (1963). Some effects of severe head injury: A follow-up study of children and adolescents after protracted coma. *Developmental Medicine and Child Neurology, 5,* 471–482.

Rimel, R., Giordani, B., Barth, J., Boll, T., & Jane, J. (1982). Disability caused by minor head injury. *Neurosurgery, 9,* 221–228.

Rimel, R., Giordani, B., Barth, J., & Jane, J. (1982). Moderate head injury: Completing the clinical spectrum of brain trauma. *Neurosurgery, 11,* 344–351.

Robertson, L. (1980). Crash involvement of teenaged drivers when driver education is eliminated from high schools. *American Journal of Public Health, 70,* 599–603.

Robertson, L. (1983). *Injuries.* Lexington, MA: Heath.

Rosenthal, M., Griffith, E., Bond, M., & Miller, J. (1990). *Rehabilitation of the adult and child with traumatic brain injury* (2nd ed.). Philadelphia: Davis.

Rourke, B., Bakker, D., Fisk, J., & Strang, J. (1983). *Child neuropsychology.* New York: Guilford.

Rutter, M., Chadwick, O., & Shaffer, D. (1983). Head injury. In M. Rutter (Ed.), *Developmental neuropsychiatry* (pp. 83–111). New York: Guilford.

Rutter, M., Chadwick, O., Shaffer, D., & Brown, G. (1980). A prospective study of children with head injuries: I. Design and methods. *Psychological Medicine, 10,* 633–645.

Sarno, M., Buonagurno, A., & Levita, E. (1986). Characteristics of verbal impairment in closed head injured patients. *Archives of Physical Medicine and Rehabilitation, 67,* 400–405.

Savage, R. (1991). Identification, classification, and placement issues for students with traumatic brain injuries. *Journal of Head Trauma Rehabilitation, 6,* 1–9.

Slater, E., & Rubenstein, E. (1987). Family coping with trauma in adolescents. *Psychiatric Annals, 12,* 786–790, 794.

Sparrow, S., Balla, D., & Cicchetti, D. (1984). *The Vineland Adaptive Behavior Scales.* Circle Pines, MN: American Guidance Services.

Spreen, O., Tupper, D., Risser, A., Tuokko, H., & Edgell, D. (1984). *Human developmental neuropsychology.* New York: Oxford.

Squire, L. (1987). *Memory and brain.* New York: Oxford.

Stalhammar, D. (1990). The mechanism of brain injuries. In R. Braakman (Ed.), *Handbook of clinical neurology* (pp. 17–41). New York: Elsevier.

Strub, R., & Black, F. (1988). The bedside mental status examination. In F. Boller & J. Grafman (Eds.), *Handbook of neuropsychology* Vol. 1 (pp. 29–46). New York: Elsevier.

Stuss, D. (1987). Contribution of frontal lobe injury to cognitive impairment after closed head injury: Methods of assessment and recent findings. In H. Levin, J. Grafman, & H. Eisenberg (Eds.), *Neurobehavioral recovery from head injury* (pp. 166–177). New York: Oxford.

*Surgeon General's workshop on violence and public health report.* (1986). Rockville, MD: U.S. Dept. of Health & Human Services.

Tardiff, K., & Gross, E. (1986). Homicide in New York City. *Bulletin of the New York Academy of Medicine, 62,* 413–426.

Teasdale, G., & Jennett, B. (1974). Assessment of coma and impaired consciousness: A practical scale. *Lancet, 2,* 81–84.

Thomsen, I. (1974). The patient with severe head injury and his family. *Scandanavian Journal of Rehabilitation Medicine, 6,* 180–183.

Thomsen, I. (1984). Late outcome of very severe blunt head trauma: A 10–15 year second follow-up. *Journal of Neurology, Neurosurgery, and Psychiatry, 47,* 260–268.

Thompson, N., Francis, D., Fletcher, J., Ewing-Cobbs, L., Levin, H., & Miner, M. (1990). Recovery of spatial, motor, and perceptual skills following closed head injury in children. *Journal of Clinical and Experimental Neuropsychology, 12,* 104.

Tonkin, R. (1987). Adolescent risk-taking behavior. *Journal of Adolescent Health Care, 8,* 213–330.

Turnbull, A., & Turnbull, H. (1991). Understanding families from a systems perspective. In J. Williams & T. Kay (Eds.), *Head injury: A family matter* (pp. 37–64). Baltimore, MD: Brookes.

Tyler, J., Mira, M., & Hollowell, J. (1989). Head injury training for pediatric residents. *American Journal of Diseases of Children, 143,* 930–932.

Waller, J. (1985). *Injury control: A guide to the causes and prevention of trauma.* Lexington, MA: Heath.

Williams, J. (1991). Family reaction to head injury. In J. Williams & T. Kay (Eds.), *Head injury: A family matter* (pp. 81–100). Baltimore, MD: Brookes.

Williams, J., & Kay, T. (1991). *Head injury: A family matter.* Baltimore, MD: Brookes.

Wilson, M. (1990). Epidemiology of injury in childhood and adolescence. In F. Oskie (Ed.), *Principles and practices of pediatrics* (pp. 569–585). Philadelphia, PA: Lippincott.

Wilson, M., & Baker, S. (1987). Structural approach to injury control. *Journal of Social Issues, 43,* 73–86.

Wolfgang, M. (1958). *Patterns in criminal homicide.* Philadelphia, PA: University of Pennsylvania Press.

Wolfgang, M. (1986). Homicide in other industrialized countries. *Bulletin of the New York Academy of Medicine, 62,* 400–412.

Wright, B. (1983). *Physical disability—A psychosocial approach.* New York: Harper & Row.

Ylvisaker, M. (1985). *Head injury rehabilitation: Children and adolescents.* San Diego, CA: College Hill Press.

Ylvisaker, M., Hartwick, P., & Stevens, M. (1991). School reentry following head injury: Managing the transition from hospital to school. *Journal of Head Trauma Rehabilitation, 6,* 10–22.

# 10
# Attention Deficit Hyperactivity Disorder

*Deborah Rich*
*H. Gerry Taylor*

## Introduction

According to the *Diagnostic and Statistical Manual of Mental Disorders, Third Edition-Revised* (DSM III-R) (American Psychiatric Association, 1987), the hallmarks of attention deficit hyperactivity disorder (ADHD) are "developmentally inappropriate degrees of inattention, impulsiveness, and hyperactivity" (p. 50). The DSM III-R lists fourteen symptoms of ADHD. To meet DSM III-R criteria for ADHD, children or adolescents must manifest a majority of these behavioral symptoms. Individual symptoms represent one or more variants of the following presenting complaints: (a) motoric restlessness, or activity levels that are exaggerated for age; (b) poor impulse control; (c) a tendency to be readily distracted, or to shift activities often; (d) difficulty completing assigned tasks, or following rules or routines; (e) difficulty attending to directions given by others, or in organizing oneself; and (f) social disruptiveness. Symptoms must be of at least six month's duration and evident prior to age seven. A further stipulation is that the child or adolescent not have a pervasive developmental disorder.

Recent formulations by Barkley (1990) and Douglas (1988) are similar to that espoused in DSM III-R. In Barkley's (1990) view,

> ADHD consists of developmental deficiencies in the regulation and maintenance of behavior by rules and consequences. These deficiencies give rise to problems with inhibiting, initiating, or sustaining responses to tasks or stimuli, and adhering to rules or instructions, particularly in situations where consequences for such behavior are delayed, weak, or nonexistent. (p. 71)

Douglas (1988) also stresses core self-regulatory deficiencies. According to her conceptualization, these deficiencies are manifest in any or all of three

333

ways: (a) impaired organization of information processing (planning, executive functions, use of appropriate mental strategies); (b) difficulties in "mobilization" of attention (deploying appropriate effort, staying focused, maintaining attention to task demands); and (c) inhibiting inappropriate responding (withholding inappropriate responses, or responses to inappropriate reinforcers). The appeal of Douglas's conceptualization is that it accounts for the perplexing variability of attentional problems in terms of such factors as information processing load, amount of external structuring or regulation available, and task salience.

A condition once believed to be "outgrown" by adolescence (Laufer, Denhoff, & Solomons, 1957), ADHD is now known to persist throughout the teenage years and into adulthood, at least in a majority of cases (Barkley, Fischer, Edelbrock, & Smallish, 1990; Hoy, Weiss, Minde, & Cohen, 1978; Weiss, Hechtman, Milroy, & Perlman, 1985). The primary symptoms may decrease in severity over time or change in form, for example, from "overactivity" to "rebelliousness" (Mendelson, Johnson, & Stewart, 1971; Minde, Weiss, & Mendelson, 1972). Nevertheless, significant academic, behavioral, and social difficulties are more the rule than the exception as children with ADHD enter adolescence.

The primary aims of this chapter are to review this disorder and to describe methods of psychological assessment appropriate for its diagnosis and treatment. We begin by summarizing major historical antecedents, along with current thinking regarding etiology. We then review problems characteristic of adolescents with ADHD, assessment procedures, and treatment approaches. Within the assessment section, we address several issues critical in evaluating adolescents for ADHD, including the principles that guide our approach, the essential elements of the assessment process, and clinical and pragmatic considerations involved in assessment and screening. Throughout the chapter, we place special emphasis on problems and methods particular to the adolescent with ADHD.

## Historical Background

Some of the first descriptions of ADHD-like behaviors were made by Still in 1902. Still observed that neurological disorders of childhood were frequently manifest by what he referred to as deficiencies in the "volitional inhibition" of behavior. He portrayed such children as aggressive, defiant, resistant to discipline, highly emotional, and lacking in self control—all of which he believed stemmed from "defects in moral control." Still also noted excessive activity and difficulty in sustained attention. He stressed that these behaviors could occur in the absence of any concurrent neurological abnormality, and that males were more frequently affected than females.

Another historical precedent for the belief that hyperactivity was the result of neurological impairment was the observation of unusual behavioral sequelae following a World War I epidemic of encephalitis lethargica (Kessler, 1980). What came to be characterized as "postencephalitic behavior disorder" included sleep disturbance, emotional instability, irritability, obstinacy, lying, thieving, impaired attention and memory, poor motor control, and hyperactivity (Stryker, 1925). Descriptions of the behavioral sequelae of head injury and of birth trauma further reinforced the perception that neurological dysfunction had distinct effects on children's behavior (Blau, 1936; Schilder, 1931; Shirley, 1939; Strecker & Ebaugh, 1924). The notion that hyperactivity was a consequence of neurological impairment was so widely accepted that many researchers in the late 1940s interpreted this clinical disorder as prima facie evidence for brain damage (Strauss & Lehtinen, 1947).

Not everyone, however, was comfortable with the idea that all hyperactive children were brain-damaged, or with the concept of the "brain-damaged child" (Birch, 1964; Herbert, 1964). Birch (1964) noted that the latter concept was used erroneously to describe a pattern of behavior disorders that frequently failed to apply to children with verified brain damage. Other problems with the term *brain-damaged* included the reluctance of many neurologists to diagnose brain damage on the basis of behavioral or learning problems alone and the shock of parents presented with this diagnosis (Kessler, 1980). To acknowledge that the term was not synonymous with documented brain damage, the phrases "minimal brain damage" and then "minimal brain dysfunction" came into subsequent use, and the range of possible causes of the disorder was broadened to include such factors as genetic variations and biochemical irregularities (Clements, 1966; Taylor, 1983). The link between hyperactivity and neurological damage was eventually dropped altogether. By 1968 the official diagnosis of the American Psychiatric Association (APA) was "hyperkinetic disorder of childhood."

New perspectives on hyperactivity emerged in the 1970s and 1980s (Barkley, 1990). Hyperactivity was no longer considered the single primary manifestation of this disorder. Researchers instead viewed deficiencies in sustained attention, impulse control, and executive functioning or self-regulation of behavior as the major hallmarks of this condition (Barkley, 1981; Douglas, 1972, 1983; Routh, 1978). Accordingly, the syndrome was relabeled by the APA in 1980 as "attention deficit disorder with or without hyperactivity."

In the more recent DSM III-R, the distinction "with or without hyperactivity" has been eliminated and the condition renamed "attention deficit hyperactivity disorder." The authors of DSM III-R recognized that some children have attention deficits without hyperactivity (referred to in DSM III-R as "undifferentiated attention deficit disorder"), but apparently were hesitant to take theoretical distinctions for granted and sought instead to place emphasis on behavioral characteristics. Nevertheless, there is a good deal of empirical support for a distinction between attentional problems and hyperactivity (Barkley, DuPaul, & McMurray, 1991; Brown, 1986; Lahey & Carlson, 1991; McGee, Williams, & Silva, 1985). There is also considerable support for distinguishing symptoms of inattention/overactivity and aggressive behavior (Loney, 1987; Loney & Milich, 1982; McGee, Williams, & Silva, 1985; Pelham, Milich, Murphy, & Murphy, 1989; Shaywitz & Shaywitz, 1991b). Identification of meaningful variations, or subtypes, within the broader category of ADHD is in fact a major focus of current research on ADHD (Shaywitz & Shaywitz, 1991a).

## Etiology

### Genetic Factors

Evidence that ADHD has a genetic basis is provided by familial aggregation and twin studies. Numerous investigations have revealed a greater degree of concordance for high activity levels in monozygotic pairs than in dizygotic pairs (Lopez, 1965; Matheny, Dolan, & Wilson, 1976; Rutter, Korn, & Burch, 1963). The incidence of hyperactivity also appears to be higher in nontwin siblings and parents of hyperactive children than in families of children who are not hyperactive (Safer, 1973; Welner, Wilner, Stewart, Palkes, & Wish, 1977). Morrison and Stewart (1971), for example, reported a significantly higher prevalence of hyperactivity in parents, particularly fathers and second-degree relatives of hyperactive children as compared with the relatives of control children. Similar findings were obtained by Cantwell (1972).

Studies of the parents and other family members of children with hyperactivity also document higher than expected rates of alcoholism, antisocial personality, and hysteria (Cantwell, 1972; Morrison & Stewart, 1971). The raised incidence of these disorders appears specific to blood relatives, as it is not found among adoptive parents (Morrison & Stewart, 1973a). Although symptoms of ADHD would appear to be heritable and not just a function of the family social environment, the exact mode of genetic transmission is not well established (Pennington, 1991). Some researchers have proposed a polygenetic model of transmission, suggesting that hyperactivity can be inherited from both maternal and paternal relatives (Morrison & Stewart, 1973b; Wender, 1971).

### Brain Damage

Although we now know that most children and adolescents with ADHD do not have histories suggestive of unequivocal brain disease (Rutter, 1982; Barkley, 1990), attentional problems and behavioral disinhibition frequently accompany documented brain disease (Brown, Chadwick, Shaffer, Rutter, & Traub, 1981; Levin, Eisenberg, Wigg, & Kobayashi, 1982; Rutter, 1982; Taylor, Schatschneider, & Rich, 1991). Attentional problems are especially prominent in children who have sustained serious traumatic brain injury (Levin et al., 1982). Lead poisoning has also been linked to hyperactivity, short attention span, and impulsivity (Byers & Lord, 1943; David, 1974). Even mild elevations in lead burden (well below 40 micrograms per deciliter) may contribute to symptoms of hyperactivity (David, Clark, & Voeller, 1972). Further evidence for a specific link between lead poisoning and and hyperactivity comes from a study conducted by David, Hoffman, Sverd, Clark, and Voeller (1976), wherein behavioral improvement following chelation therapy (chemically removing lead from the body) was found to occur more for hyperactive children with high lead levels than for hyperactive children whose problems may have related to other etiologies.

Although a variety of other etiologies have also been proposed, ranging from food allergies to toxic effects of food additives, excessive intake of sugar, and even reactions to fluorescent lights, research findings have failed to offer unequivocal support for any single dietary or environmental account for ADHD (Barkley, 1981, 1990; Taylor & Fletcher, 1983). Empirical work does, however, implicate endogenous factors. There is mounting evidence, for example, for pathophysiological abnormalities in individuals with ADHD, including aberrant patterns of cerebral blood flow (Low, Henriksen, Bruhn, Borner, & Neilsen, 1989) and depletion of the neurotransmitters dopamine and norepinephrine (Pennington, 1991; Raskin, Shaywitz, Shaywitz, Anderson, & Cohen, 1984; Zametkin & Rapoport, 1987). Certain pre- and perinatal conditions, such as low birthweight, respiratory distress, and maternal substance abuse, also pose clear risks for attentional problems (Denson, Nanson, & MacWatters, 1975; Hack, Breslau, Weissman, Aram, Klein, & Borowski, 1991; Nichols & Chen, 1981; Shaywitz, Cohen, & Shaywitz, 1980; Streissguth, Martin, Barr, Sandman, Kirchner, & Darby, 1984).

## Manifestations of ADHD in Adolescence

Table 1 summarizes ADHD behaviors and related problems in adolescents with ADHD. The persistence of ADHD from childhood into adolescence is well documented. Barkley et al. (1990) found that 71.5 percent of 123 adolescents who were diagnosed as hyperactive eight years previous to follow-up continued to meet DSM III criteria for this disorder. The mean number of symptoms of ADHD in the latter subgroup of adolescents was 9, compared with a mean of 1.5 symptoms for adolescents without past or present symptoms of ADHD. Similar longitudinal findings are reported by Gittelman, Manuzza, Shenker, and Banagura (1985). Hyperactive adolescents themselves admit to being restless, impulsive, and easily upset, as well

**Table 1.**
**Manifestations of ADHD in Adolescents**

| Area | Associated Problems |
| --- | --- |
| Behavior | Hyperactivity |
| | Distractibility |
| | Restlessness |
| | Excitability |
| | Impulsiveness |
| | Immaturity |
| | Rebelliousness |
| | Excessive talking |
| | Failure to finish task |
| Conduct disorder/antisocial behavior | Delinquent acts (e.g., thefts, assaults) |
| | Contact with police |
| | Drug/alcohol use |
| | Institutionalization (juvenile delinquent/psychiatric facilities) |
| School performance | Poor academic achievement |
| | Academic failure |
| | Grade retention |
| | Special educational placement |
| | Suspensions |
| | Expulsions |
| Peer relations/self-esteem | Low self-esteem |
| | Poor peer relationships |
| | Few close friends within age-group |
| | Low expectations for success |

as to having difficulties concentrating and finishing tasks (Stewart, Mendelson, & Johnson, 1973).

In a seminal study in this area, Weiss, Minde, Werry, Douglas, and Nemeth (1971) found significant decreases across adolescence in the target symptoms of hyperactivity, distractibility, aggressiveness, and excitability. Each of these symptoms, however, was more frequent in the adolescents with histories of ADHD than in peers without histories of ADHD. According to the investigators, complaints of restlessness were less prominent during adolescence but continued to be reported to some degree in 30 percent of the cases. Classroom behavioral observations revealed that hyperactive children exhibited more behavior "unrelated to classroom activity" (e.g., playing with pencils) than normal controls did. The investigators concluded that hyperactive children, rather than outgrowing their restlessness, merely expressed it in less disturbing ways.

Others researchers stress that core childhood symptoms carry over into adolescence, despite developmental changes in the nature of the presenting problems. In a study by Mendelson, Johnson, and Stewart (1971), a rebellious attitude was the most frequent complaint of mothers of hyperactive adolescents. The combination of overactivity and overtalkativeness, although the most common complaint made two to six years earlier, was only the third most frequent complaint at follow-up. In a study by Ackerman, Dykman, and Peters (1977), complaints of management problems at home distinguished a sample of teenagers who met criteria for both hyperactivity and learning disabilities from a group of adolescents who had learning disabilities only, as well as from individuals without either of these disorders. Other presenting problems included fidgetiness, excessive talking, impulsivity, inability to delay gratification, and immaturity. Consistent with observations of Weiss and colleagues (1971), the single most common parental complaint was emotional immaturity.

## Academic/School Problems

Existing research indicates that teachers of children and adolescents with ADHD describe them as loud, inattentive, uncooperative, lazy, sneaky, immature, annoying, inconsiderate, easily discouraged, distractable, and attention-seeking (Heusey & Cohen, 1976). Teachers rate adolescents with ADHD as more restless and inattentive than their peers, less able to concentrate, and more antisocial (Weiss et al., 1971).

Adolescents with ADHD also perform more poorly than their peers on tests of academic achievement and have elevated rates of academic failure, grade retentions, suspensions, expulsions, and school dropout (Ackerman et al., 1977; Fischer, Barkley, Edelbrock, & Smallish, 1990; Huessy, Metoyer, & Townsend, 1974; Weiss et al., 1971). As hyperactive children approach adolescence, they are also more likely to have spent time in a special educational setting when compared with their nonhyperactive classmates (Mendelson, Johnson, & Stewart, 1971; Weiss et al., 1971). In a study summarized by Barkley (1990), 19 to 26 percent of a sample of children with ADHD met conservative criteria for learning disabilities. An even higher incidence of learning disabilities among this population has been reported in several other studies (Cantwell & Baker, 1991; Dykman & Ackerman, 1991; McGee & Share, 1988). Weiss and colleagues (1971) found academic difficulty to be the most consistent feature of the disorder, characterizing 80 percent of adolescents in these researchers' longitudinal study. Seventy percent of the hyperactive subjects studied by Weiss and colleagues (1971), 57 percent of those evaluated by Ackerman, Dykman, and Peters (1977), and 33 percent of those in the Huesey and Cohen (1976) study had repeated at least one grade by the time they reached adolescence.

More recently, Barkley and colleagues (1990) found that grade repetition or school suspensions or expulsions were three times more common in students with ADHD than in students without ADHD. Hyperactivity alone increased the risk of suspension and school dropout, but the additional diagnosis of conduct disorder added appreciably to these risks. Associated conduct disorder accounted almost entirely for the greater prevalence of expulsions in the ADHD group.

*Conduct Disorders/Antisocial Behavior*

In addition to experiencing greater difficulties at school, adolescents with ADHD are more likely than their non-ADHD peers to have contact with the police (Hoy et al., 1978; Mendelson, Johnson, & Stewart, 1971), to be arrested (Satterfield, Hoppe, & Schell, 1982; Wallander, 1988), and to spend time in either a facility for juvenile delinquents or a psychiatric institution (Mendelson, Johnson, & Stewart, 1971; Satterfield, Hoppe, & Schell, 1982). Compared with same-age youths without hyperactivity, adolescents with ADHD also commit significantly more thefts and assaults (Barkley, Fischer, Edelbrock, & Smallish, 1990; Satterfield, Hoppe, & Schell, 1982; Stewart, Mendelson, & Johnson, 1973), use weapons more frequently (Barkley et al., 1990; Satterfield, Hoppe, & Schell, 1982), and have a higher incidence of drug and alcohol use (Ackerman, Dykman, & Peters, 1977; Barkley et al., 1990; Gittelman, Manuzza, Shenker, & Banagura, 1985). The absolute incidence of these problems is also high, with as many as 65 percent of adolescents meeting criteria for oppositional-defiant disorder and as many as 50 percent meeting criteria for conduct disorder (Barkley et al., 1990; Gittelman et al., 1985). Differentiation of ADHD from conduct disorder can be made through examination of DSM III-R criteria. For a diagnosis of ADHD, criteria include the presence of such behaviors as excessive fidgeting; difficulty with sustaining attention, awaiting turns, playing quietly, following directions, or staying seated; excessive talking and interrupting; easy distractibility; and engaging in physically dangerous activities because of poor judgment. A diagnosis of conduct disorder requires the presence of such antisocial activities as stealing, running away, lying, firesetting, truancy, destruction of property, breaking and entering, forced sexual activity, physical fighting, and cruelty to animals and people.

Research indicates that factors in addition to hyperactivity may contribute to the higher rate of antisocial behavior among these youths. Barkley and colleagues (1990), for example, found that hyperactive adolescents with conduct disorders reported higher levels of cigarette and marijuana use than either hyperactive adolescents without conduct disorder or controls without hyperactivity did. Research findings further suggest that the relationship between childhood attention problems and later antisocial behavior may be moderated by family factors, including paternal alcohol consumption (Wallander, 1988). Other family variables, such as poor mother-child relationships, poor parental mental health, and punitive child-rearing practices, also seem to distinguish groups of hyperactive youths with and without delinquent behaviors. Given that hyperactive adolescents from lower socioeconomic strata are more likely to have multiple arrests for serious crimes than middle- or upper-class hyperactive teenagers are, sociodemographic factors may additionally contribute to antisocial acts.

## *Peer Relationships/Self-Esteem*

Although poor peer relationships and low self-esteem are problems for many children with ADHD, these symptoms are especially marked during adolescence. In the words of Ross and Ross (1982), "The best single descriptor for the social adjustment of the hyperactive adolescent is *lonely*." Research confirms the impression that hyperactive adolescents tend to have few close friends within their age-group. According to maternal reports, 30 percent of the children with ADHD followed by Weiss, Minde, Werry, Douglas, and Nemeth (1971) had no steady friends. Mendelson, Johnson, and Stewart (1971), who also documented mothers' concerns over poor peer relationships, found an even higher percentage of friendless adolescents in their sample (46%). In comparison with other adolescents, hyperactive youths themselves report spending significantly more of their spare time alone or with younger children, and feeling less well liked by their peers (Hoy et al., 1978; Mendelson, Johnson & Stewart, 1971). Given the high incidence of unsatisfactory social relationships, it is not surprising that these adolescents frequently suffer from low self-esteem (Ackerman, Dykman, & Peters, 1977; Hoy et al, 1978; Mendelson, Johnson, & Stewart, 1971; Weiss et al., 1971), are less pleased with themselves in comparison with nonhyperactive peers (Hoy et al., 1978), and have low expectations for success (Weiss et al., 1971).

# Assessment

## *Overview and Guiding Principles*

Proper assessment of ADHD in adolescents requires knowledge of the diverse manifestations and correlates of this disorder as described in the previous section. Assessment is also founded on three fundamental principles. The first is that certain inherent, or brain-related, core deficits are responsible for the diverse behavioral manifestations of the disorder, and that the assessment methods described below ("Evaluation Procedures") are capable of discerning these deficits. A second assumption is that the behavioral expression of underlying brain-based deficiencies will vary substantially as a function of other factors, including such variables as cognitive capabilities, personality traits and copying styles, and family and school stressors and supports. The third assumption is that the ultimate aim of assessment is to understand reasons for presenting problems rather than to assign a given diagnosis. Whereas a diagnosis of ADHD and any comorbid disorders has clear implications for the understanding and treatment of the adolescent's problems, the diagnosis itself is usually insufficient for either purpose.

A clinically relevant assessment is one that considers all potential contributing factors in the adolescent and his or her environment. The method we advocate for assessment of ADHD is the "biobehavioral systems model" described by Taylor and Fletcher (1990) and by Taylor (1988, 1989). According to this neuropsychologically based approach, evaluation of ADHD requires analysis of (a) the manifest or presenting problems; (b) the adolescent's cognitive, academic, and psychosocial characteristics; (c) potential environmental influences on the problems or the adolescent's ability to cope with them; and (d) biological-genetic factors. The manifest disability, in this instance, refers to functional problems reported by the adolescent and his or her parents or teachers. Cognitive, academic, and psychosocial traits refer to strengths and weaknesses on specific tasks or in social interaction. Environmental influences include parent attitudes and management practices, assistance and accommodations available to the individual in coping with weaknesses, and family resources and stressors. Biological-genetic factors include history of neurological diseases or insults, family history of ADHD or associated disorders, chronic illnesses or other comorbid medical conditions that might have a bearing on diagnosis or treatment, and medications taken.

The biobehavioral systems model as it applies to the assessment of ADHD is depicted schematically in Figure 1. The "hub" of the model comprises criteria for ADHD itself, for example, as formally defined by DSM III-R and ADHD behavioral rating scales. The model assumes, however, that the clinical phenomenon of ADHD is embedded in a more complex system of variables. Consideration of this system of variables is needed to more firmly establish the diagnosis, to rule out other bases of presenting symptoms, and to understand the full implications of ADHD.

### Evaluation Procedures

The multimodal nature of assessment necessitates collection of data from several sources, using a variety of assessment methods. Procedures undertaken as part of a comprehensive evaluation of ADHD include (a) parent,

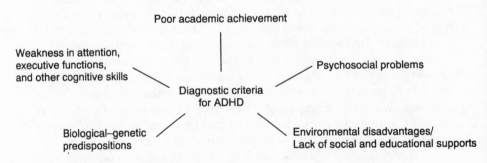

**Figure 1. A Biobehavioral Schema for Assessment of ADHD**

teacher, and adolescent interviews and questionnaires; (b) parent and teacher ratings of behavior; (c) adolescent self-report measures; (d) neuropsychological evaluation of attention and other cognitive abilities; (e) direct observation of ADHD behaviors; and (f) assessment of family functioning. Each of these procedures is taken up in greater detail below.

**Parent Interview and Parent Questionnaire.** The parent interview serves several purposes. Primary aims are to build rapport with the family, obtain information on the nature and history of the presenting complaints, observe interactions among family members, and narrow in on diagnostic possibilities and relevant and feasible treatment strategies (Barkley, 1990; Taylor, 1988).

Barkley's (1990) ADHD Clinic Parent Interview is recommended as a resource for anyone intending to develop a comprehensive interview format. Our practice in evaluating ADHD and other developmental disorders, like Barkley's, has been to focus initially on parent concerns and behavioral complaints (Taylor, 1988). Parents of an adolescent with ADHD typically state that their son or daughter does not finish assigned work or chores, does not listen to instructions, has poor work habits, needs close supervision, and is disorganized, distractable, and restless. Impulsivity, low frustration tolerance, and excessive talking are also frequently reported, along with oppositional behavior, argumentativeness, rebelliousness, defiance, and even aggressiveness. For example, a parent at our clinic stated that his daughter was receiving D's in several of her classes because of incomplete assignments. He also reported that her teachers' main complaints were that she talked too much and was easily distracted. There were frequent arguments between the patient and her father, mostly centering on her poor study habits and failure to do her chores.

When addressing specific complaints, the examiner may find it informative to inquire about the circumstances in which behavioral problems occur, that is, antecedents and consequences, frequency, age of onset, chronicity of behavior, and situational and temporal variations. A substantial history of attention problems is particularly critical to the diagnosis of ADHD. Determining why parents chose to have the problem addressed at the time of referral is also informative with regard to the family's primary concerns, motivation for treatment, and recent family events.

The examiner can then explore current problems in other developmental domains, including motor, language, intellectual, academic, emotional, self-help, social functioning, and physical health domains. The ADHD adolescent is likely to have problems in at least some of these areas. Moreover, information in this regard is important in making a differential diagnosis (e.g., in ruling out autistic spectrum disorder, depression, or anxiety disorder as the primary basis for presenting symptoms) and in deciding whether further evaluations might be appropriate. Questions as to presence of motor tics are also indicated. If present, tics suggestive of Tourette's disorder may contraindicate potential treatment with stimulant medications.

After obtaining a thorough description of the behavioral problems of concern to the family, queries can be made regarding the adolescent's current medical history of illnesses, injuries, and hospitalizations; pregnancy and birth complications; and maternal history of smoking, drinking, and drug abuse during pregnancy. In addition to the fact that conditions such as head injury or pre- and perinatal complications may predispose the child to attentional problems, there is some tendency for individuals with ADHD to have elevated rates of colds, upper respiratory infections, otitis media, and allergies (Barkley, 1990; Taylor & Fletcher, 1983). Medication effects are of additional concern, especially in cases of chronic illness (Taylor, 1988).

Questioning next centers on the adolescent's developmental history. Problems in fine motor skills are often apparent in younger children with ADHD. Parents may report that their child had difficulties as a youngster in learning to tie shoes, use scissors, or button or zip clothes. If language delays are reported, the examiner will want to make inquiries regarding the nature of the delay and any past speech/language evaluations or interventions. Answers to questions about early temperament and activity level can be especially telling. Parents of adolescents with ADHD will often report that their child was constantly "on the go" as toddler, ran rather than walked, and could not stay focused on any one activity for long. Early problems in social interactions are frequently characterized by aggressiveness toward peers, a tendency to boss other children around, and difficulty playing "by the rules." The importance of taking a careful developmental history is illustrated by the following example:

> When the parents of a fifteen-year-old male were questioned regarding early development, they reported that his language skills had seemed delayed and that he had received occupational therapy as a preschooler because of poor fine motor control. In addition, he had related well with other children so long as they played games "his way." His preschool and kindergarten teacher had frequently expressed concerns regarding his aggressive behavior, such as hitting and pushing others.

Taking a careful educational history is another essential part of the interview. Parents are asked to chronicle any behavior or learning difficulties in school, beginning with the individual's entry to school, including preschool. Problems with inattentiveness, overactivity, and impulsivity are often first noticed by preschool or kindergarten teachers, as are delays in fine and gross motor coordination and in language skills. Grade repetitions and special education placement are common later in school. When ADHD is compounded with conduct disorder, the adolescent is also more likely to be suspended or expelled from school. Even if the adolescent has not been identified as having a behavior problem and has not been deemed eligible for assistance in a special education program, neurocognitive deficiencies in attention and other skill areas may compromise the individual's academic productivity and ability to profit from instruction. Handwriting, for example, may be difficult due to visual-motor weaknesses, or writing and text comprehension may be impaired as a consequence of specific language disabilities.

A further topic to explore in the parent interview is the adolescent's interactions with family members and peers. Compliance with rules and parental directives, follow-through on daily chores, and social interactions are especially relevant. Additional concerns include ways in which the family has attempted to cope with the problems to date, previous interventions, and family stressors and resources. More likely than not, the family of an adolescent with ADHD will report a great deal of tension and stress within the home, most of it attributed to the adolescent's behavior. For example, a mother of a thirteen-year-old adolescent with ADHD reported that she frequently dreaded going home after work because of the tension she felt as the result of her son's behavior. Information on previous interventions and family stressors helps in evaluating current needs. This information is also useful in uncovering the parents' beliefs regarding reasons behind the presenting complaints, and in gauging the family's abilities to comply with alternative treatment recommendations.

Obtaining a family history of school, attentional, and behavioral problems is another important component of the interview. It is not unusual for at least one parent to have residual attention deficit disorder (see Barkley, 1990, and Denckla, 1991, for assessment considerations) or to report having had difficulty attending or sitting still as a child. Attentional problems may be similarly noted in siblings. Given the raised incidence of other mental health problems in parents of children and adolescents with ADHD, questions pertaining to personal or family history of depression, alcoholism, and personality or conduct problems are likewise appropriate (Biederman, Munir, Knee, et al., 1987). Information of this nature assists the clinician in sorting out factors that may be contributing to the adolescent's problems. Such information is also useful for treatment planning, as a parent with ADHD may have difficulty providing the kind of structure and consistency that would be optimal for some types of behavioral interventions.

Inquiry as to the adolescent's strengths can be used to close out the interview on a positive note. Parents' responses to this question reveal more about their feelings toward their child and may suggest ways to build self-esteem and establish more constructive parent-child interactions.

Much of the above information can be obtained through administration of questionnaires. Questionnaires either can be completed by parents prior to the interview or can be used as the basis of the interview. The former arrangement allows the examiner to focus on issues of primary interest without

## Table 2.
## Outline of Parent Questionnaire

I. Identifying information and persons living with child or adolescent

II. Current problems

    A. Please describe what you consider your child's main difficulties now, or the problems that you would most like help with.

    B. When and how did you first become aware of these problems?

    B. Why do you think your child has these problems?

    D. If your child has already been evaluated by the school or other professions, what were the results?

    E. What has been done to help your child, and how has this worked?

    F. What specific questions about your child would you like us to try to answer in our evaluation?

III. Behavior, interests, and accomplishments

    A. If your child is difficult to manage at home, please describe the situation.

    B. If there are other problems or anything unusual with regard to your child's behavior at home, at school, or in the neighborhood, please describe the situation.

    C. If your child has any difficulty getting along with others his or her age, please describe this difficulty.

    D. If there are any problems completing homework, please describe those problems.

    E. What are you child's main strengths, positive personality traits, special interests, or areas of accomplishment?

IV. School history

    A. Please list the school your child attended each school year, beginning with the first year of school, preschool, or day care outside the home.

    B. Please check areas of special difficulty for your child and indicate his or her age when the difficulties were first noticed and if the area is still a problem: reading, spelling, math, handwriting, composition, speech or language, fine motor coordination, gross motor coordination, behavior, other.

    C. Please check if your child has ever been in any of the following special classes: learning disabilities, transitional classroom, behavioral handicapped, mentally handicapped, developmentally handicapped, visually handicapped, hearing handicapped, multihandicapped, other.

V. Social history and family background

    A. Names, occupations, and educational status of parents or guardians.

    B. Relationship of biological parents and guardians to each other and to the child.

    C. Please check if any family members have ever had any of the following difficulties, and indicate the relationship to the child of the family member: trouble learning to read or spell, trouble with math, speech and language problems, repeated a grade, hyperactive or attention problems, mentally handicapped, mental health problems, alcoholism or drug abuse, problems with law, other.

VI. Pregnancy, birth, and early development

    A. If the child's mother had any illnesses or complications during her pregnancy with this child, please describe them.

    B. If the child's mother did any of the following during her pregnancy with this child, please check and describe the circumstances: smoked, drank alcohol, took medications, took drugs, other.

    C. If the child was premature, how many weeks? What was the birthweight?

    D. If there were any problems during delivery, please describe them.

**Table 2.** (*continued*)

|  |  |
|---|---|
| | E. If there was any special care given to the infant after delivery, please describe that care (e.g., neonatal intensive care, placement on respirator). |
| | F. If your child had any medical problems in the first few weeks of life, please describe them. |
| | G. Please indicate the approximate age of your child at the time he or she first walked without support, spoke in single words, and combined words. |
| | H. If you feel that your child's early development (ages 1–5) was delayed in any way, please describe the situation (e.g., speech and language, motor skills, social behavior). |
| VII. | Past medical events |
| | A. If your child has had or still has any of the following medical problems, please check the problem, indicate the child's age at the time, and describe the problem: poor growth, hospitalizations or operations, poisonings, head injury, loss of consciousness, seizures/convulsions, other neurological disorder, other physical injury, physical abuse/neglect or sexual abuse, drug use, other medical problems. |
| | B. If your child has had or still has problems in any of the following areas, please check the areas and describe the problems: seeing; moving eyes; hearing; understanding; swallowing; walking; talking; coordination/clumsiness; funny feelings on the body, such as numbness, tingling, or buzzing; decreased strength or stiffness of one part of the body; tics or twitching of the face or other body parts or unusual movements or sounds; staring spells or trances; wetting or other problems in urination; soiling or other problems moving bowels; noticeable loss of or change in abilities; unusual physical complaints. |
| VIII. | Current health |
| | A. Current physician following child. |
| | B. Please describe any medical problems or concerns about your child. |
| | C. If your child sees any other professional, please describe that person (e.g., physician, psychologist, social worker, counselor, speech therapist, special tutor, other specialist). |
| | D. If your child takes any medication, please describe it. |
| | E. Parent's consent for release of information to child's physician. |
| IX. | Additional comments/information |

sacrifice of background data, and hence results in a saving of time and expense; its disadvantages are that much of the information covered in the questionnaire has to be taken up again in the interview and that a time investment is required of parents, with attendant delays in scheduling of the parent interviews. The questionnaire we use in our clinic in evaluating referrals for ADHD and other developmental disorders is outlined in Table 2.

**Teacher Questionnaire.** The different demands placed on adolescents at home and at school make it imperative to obtain teacher impressions regarding learning and behavior. Given that most adolescents have multiple teachers, and given the practical difficulties involved in arranging for personal meetings with teachers, we prefer to ask teachers who are well acquainted with the adolescent to write down their answers to a few basic questions about the individual. Questions pertain to the individual's classroom functioning (strengths and weaknesses), factors the teacher has identified as contributing to the problems, strategies that have been used in dealing with the student, and the success or failure of those strategies. Information regarding the length of time each teacher has known the student and the nature of the relationship (e.g., homeroom teacher, resource room teacher, gym instructor) is useful in interpreting the teacher reports. Requests for commentaries of this sort take the form of the teacher questionnaire outlined in Table 3. Our practice is to submit the teacher questionnaire, along with the more formal rating scales described below (see "Teacher Ratings"), either prior to or immediately after the parent interview.

**Interview of the Adolescent.** The last step in evaluation is a one-to-one interview with the adolescent (i.e., without parents or other family members present). Areas of inquiry include the adolescent's understanding of the reasons for the assessment and descriptions of personal problems, family functioning, school performance, and peer relationships. It is also useful to explore attitudes towards self and attributions of problems. Low self-esteem is common in adolescents with ADHD (Stewart, Mendelson, & Johnson, 1973). Although adolescents are likely to report behaviors associated with hyperactivity, they tend to underestimate or deny the severity of their problems. Answers to questions about social relationships are particularly suspect, and denial of any problems by the adolescent cannot be taken as an indication that problems do not exist. For example, a fourteen-year-old girl reported that she had many friends and a busy social life; her parents and teachers, however, indicated that she was unpopular with peers and often teased by her classmates. Traditional psychological assessment techniques, such as sentence completion or other projective tests, are often worthwhile. We have also found a formal but brief interview, such as the Structured

**Table 3.**
**Outline of Teacher Questionnaire**

I. Background information: child's name, school, type of class, teacher completing the form, date

II. Problem identification

A. Please describe the major problems or issues you would like us to evaluate or help you with.

B. Why do you think the child is having these problems?

C. What has been done, past or present, to deal with the problems (special modifications, programs, strategies)?

D. How effective have these interventions been?

E. What are the child's strengths?

III. Requests for previous test results, samples of schoolwork, and completion of treatment ratings

Pediatric Psychosocial Interview (Webb & Van Devre, 1985), to be clinically revealing.

**Standardized Ratings Scales.** Behavioral rating scales are integral to assessment. The major virtue of standardized ratings is that they quantify the extent to which the adolescent's behavior is deviant in relation to normative standards for sex and age. Rating scales are easily administered and require relatively little time to complete or score. An additional advantage is that they can be given to multiple observers as a means to determining consensus of opinion regarding the adolescent's behavior and learning. Their only major drawback is that age norms for adolescents are not yet available for a number of instruments discussed in this section. In these instances, the clinician has the option of using norms for older children as rough guidelines or, better still, of collecting local adolescent norms.

*Parent Ratings.* Two of the most commonly used parent questionnaires are the Child Behavior Checklist (CBCL) (Achenbach & Edelbrock, 1983) and the Conners Parent Rating Scale—Revised (CPRS-R) (Goyette, Conners, & Ulrich, 1978). Other relevant parent questionnaires include the ADHD Rating Scale (Barkley, 1990), the Home Situations Questionnaire (HSQ) (Barkley & Edelbrock, 1987), the Home Situations Questionnaire—Revised (HSQ-R) (Barkley, 1990), and the Attention Deficit Disorders Evaluation Scale—Home Version (McCarney, 1989a) (see Barkley, 1990, for comprehensive review of these and other questionnaires).

The CBCL consists of a Social Competence Scale and a Behavioral Problems Scale. Behavioral profiles are standardized for age and sex. Test-retest reliability and interparent agreement are high (Achenbach & Edelbrock, 1983; Barkley, 1987). Validity has been documented by studies showing that CBCL ratings discriminate children with ADHD from same-age normal peers and from children with other psychiatric conditions (Mash & Johnston, 1983). In a review of parent ratings for use in evaluating ADHD, Blondis, Accardo, and Snow (1989) found the CBCL to be the best rating available for reliable assessment of attentional and related behavioral dysfunctions.

The ADHD Rating Scale (Barkley, 1990) represents the fourteen DSM III-R criteria for ADHD, translated into parent ratings. Parents are asked to rate each criterion on a 4-point scale, from "not at all" to "very much," as it applies to their child. Cutoffs for ADHD can be based either on the number of items given excessive ratings ("pretty much" or "very much") or on the parent norms provided by Barkley (1990) for the total numerical score.

The CPRS-R is a forty-eight-item questionnaire comprised of scales labeled Conduct Problems, Learning Problems, Psychosomatic, Impulsive-Hyperactive, and Anxiety (Goyette, Conners, & Ulrich, 1987). The Hyperactivity Index score from the CPSR-R is based on ten of the items and is probably the most commonly applied parent rating of ADHD in the literature. The Hyperactivity Index has been shown to discriminate groups of children with ADHD from non-ADHD groups and is sensitive to the effects of stimulant medication and parent training intervention (Barkley, 1987).

The HSQ (Barkley, 1990) supplements the CBCL and CPSR-R by targeting circumstances in which behavior problems are most likely to arise. To complete this scale, parents indicate the circumstances under which behavior problems are apparent at home. A total of sixteen circumstances are listed (e.g., during meals, while parent is on the phone). A severity rating (1 to 9) is then assigned for each circumstance in which behavior problems are noted. Normative data are available, and reliability is acceptable (Barkley & Edelbrock, 1987). Validity studies confirm that the HSQ ratings discriminate children with ADHD from other children, and that these ratings are sensitive to the effects of treatment with stimulants and to parent training interventions (Barkley, Karlsson, Polland, & Murphy, 1985). The HSQ-R (Barkley, 1990) has a similar format but instead asks the parent to rate situations in which their child manifests difficulties in paying attention or concentrating, as opposed to behavior problems more generally.

Because aggressiveness, noncompliance, and other behavior problems not necessarily related to ADHD per se can contribute to elevated problem scores on the CPRS-R and HSQ, we commonly administer additional scales to sort out symptoms of inattention, hyperactivity, and oppositional behavior. Parent measures useful for this purpose are the Attentional Problem Disorder, Aggressive Behavior Disorder, and Hyperactive Impulse Disorder scales described by Loney (1987); the Attention Deficit Disorders Evaluation Scale (ADDES) (McCarney, 1989a); and the DSM III-R checklists provided in Barkley's ADHD Clinic Parent Interview (Barkley, 1990).

*Teacher Ratings.* Teacher impressions of ADHD behaviors can be obtained by administering any of several available rating scales. Examples include the Child Behavior Rating Scale—Teacher's Report Form (CBCL-TRF) (Achenbach & Edelbrock, 1986), the Conners Teacher Rating Scales (CTRS) (Goyette, Conners, & Ulrich, 1978), the School Situations Questionnaire (SSQ) (Barkley, 1990), the School Situations Questionnaire—Revised (SSQ-R) (Barkley, 1990), the ADHD Rating Scale (see teacher norms given in Barkley, 1990), the Child Attentional Problems Scale (CAP) (Edelbrock, 1986), the Attention Deficit Disorders Evaluation Scale—Teacher Version (McCarney, 1989b) and the ADD-H Comprehensive Teacher Rating Scale (ACTeRS) (Ullman, Sleator, & Sprague, 1988).

The CBCL-TRF consists of two scales, Adaptive Functioning and Behavior Problems. It is normed by age (six to eleven years and twelve to sixteen years) and sex, and has adequate test-retest reliability. Like the CBCL, the CBCL-TRF discriminates children with ADHD from children with other behavior disorders. Ratings also distinguish children with ADHD from those with attention deficit without hyperactivity (Edelbrock, Costello, & Kessler, 1984).

There are two versions of the CTRS. The original, thirty-nine-item scale (Conners, 1969) is the most widely used. Test-retest and interrater reliability are satisfactory, and the scale is sensitive to effects of stimulant medication and to parent training interventions. The Conners Teaching Rating Scale—Revised (CTRS-R) is a shorter, twenty-eight-item questionnaire, comprised of subscales labeled Conduct Problems, Hyperactivity, and Inattentive-Passive (Goyette, Connors, & Ulrich, 1978). A ten-item Hyperactivity Index provides a criterial measure of ADHD. Like the CPRS-R, the CTRS-R is also well normed, test-retest reliability is adequate, and ratings are valid in discriminating children with ADHD from controls and in measuring responsiveness to treatment with stimulants (Barkley, 1987).

The SSQ is the teacher analogue for the HSQ. Teachers are asked to indicate those circumstances, from a total of twelve listed, in which children problems are apparent at school (e.g., in the hallways, during small-group work). As in the case of the HSQ, scores include both the number of circumstances in which problems are observed and the severity of each problem area (scale of 1 to 9). Barkley and Edelbrock (1987) provide data on normative standards and test-retest reliability. These authors also describe findings documenting the validity of the SSQ in discriminating children and adolescents with ADHD from unaffected peers, and in determining response to stimulants. The SSQ-R is similar to the SSQ in design but instead focuses on the pervasiveness of problems in attention and concentration at school.

Supplementary ratings useful in distinguishing attentional problems with and without hyperactivity and in isolating attentional problems from oppositional-defiant disorder, conduct disorder, or other behavioral disturbances include the ADD-H Comprehensive Teacher Rating Scale (ACTeRS) (Ullmann, Sleator, & Sprague, 1984) and the Iowa Conners Teacher Rating Scale (Loney & Milich, 1982).

*Self-Ratings.* The Child Behavior Checklist—Youth Self-Report (CBCL-YSR) (Achenbach & Edelbrock, 1987) was designed to provide a self-report of problems in adjustment and behavior, including ADHD symptomatology. This scale parallels the CBCL and CBCL-TRF conceptually and is normed for the eleven- to eighteen-year-old age-group. Test-retest reliabilities are satisfactory, and validity is documented in comparisons between adolescents with ADHD and non-ADHD peers (Barkley et al., 1990). Additional self-report scales useful in assessing problems often associated with ADHD in adolescence include the Children's Depression Inventory (CDI) (Kovacs, 1981) for children and adolescents ages eight to fourteen, the Reynolds Adolescent Depression Scale (Reynolds, 1987), and the Beck Depression Inventory (BDI) (Beck, Ward, Mendelson, Mack, & Erbaugh, 1961) for older persons.

**Neuropsychological Testing.** Neuropsychological assessment consists of evaluation of intelligence, language, memory, sensorimotor skills, visual-spatial and constructional abilities, nonverbal problem solving/abstract reasoning, and attention and organizational functions (Taylor & Fletcher, 1990). In our experience, ADHD is most consistently accompanied by weaknesses on measures of sustained attention and response inhibition (impulsivity), language processing and mental set shifting, psychomotor efficiency, visual/spatial constructional skills, fine motor dexterity, and memory. Relatively depressed performance on the Freedom from Distractibility factor on the Wechsler Intelligence Scale for Children—Revised (WISC-R) (Wechsler, 1974) is another common correlate of this disorder, although not necessarily diagnostic (Barkley, 1990). Assessments of overall intelligence, although useful in determining if attentional problems are greater than expected given the individual's mental age and processing capacity, are also of limited value in examining attentional status. Although most studies of ADHD reveal IQ scores well within the average range (Douglas, 1980), relative weaknesses in attention and impulse control can occur across the full range of mental abilities. Evaluation is therefore indicated regardless of IQ (Handen, Breaux, Gosling, Ploof, & Feldman, 1990).

Assessment of attention is an especially critical element of neuropsychological evaluation (Pennington, 1991; Voeller, 1991). The types of tests most essential in evaluating adolescents for ADHD are those which measure sustained attention, selective attention-impulsivity, and executive functions (i.e., mental planning and organizational skills). Testing of these and related abilities is also dictated both by theories regarding attentional processes and by current thinking regarding the "core" deficits responsible for ADHD (Cooley & Morris, 1990; Douglas, 1988; Mirsky, 1987).

The Continuous Performance Test (CPT) (Rosvold, Mirsky, Sarason, Bransome, & Beck, 1956) is the most common method for assessing two fundamental aspects of attention: the ability to sustain attention and the ability to resist impulsive responding. Although procedures vary, testing typically involves presentation on a computer screen of a series of numbers, letters, or shapes. The stimuli are presented at either a fixed or a variable rate, and the child is required to press a button whenever a predesignated target or series of targets appears. Performance is assessed in terms of the numbers of correct responses (hits), missed targets (misses), and incorrect responses (false alarms). The first two scores measure sustained attention; the last score assesses impulsivity. In the case of procedures involving varying presentation rates (i.e., rates that increase or decrease in relation to the accuracy of the subject's performance), the average presentation rate (interstimulus interval) provides an alternative measure of efficiency of target detection. Examples of CPT tasks include the Gordon Diagnostic System (Gordon, 1983; Gordon & Mettleman, 1988); the Computerized Test of Attention (Barkley, 1988), developed by Dr. Greg Wright; the Pediatric Assessment of Cognitive Efficiency

(Lindgren & Lyons, 1984); and the Continuous Performance Task (Shapiro & Garfinkel, 1985). Several of these measures, like parent and teacher ratings of attention, have proved useful both in diagnosis and in gauging response to treatment (Douglas, 1983; Barkley, 1990).

The task that has probably been used more often than any other to assess selective attention and impulsivity is the Matching Familiar Figures Test (MFFT, Kagan, 1966). In this test, a series of recognizable line drawings are presented to the examinee one at a time. After each presentation, the target drawing is taken away, and the examinee is shown an array of six drawings from which he or she must identify the original drawing. Two scores are derived from the MFFT: the mean time taken to first response (latency) and the total number of errors. Although past research on the MFFT supported its utility in clinical diagnosis and in determining response to medications (Campbell, Douglas, & Morgenstern, 1971; Weithorn, Kagen, & Marcus, 1984), more recent findings summarized by Barkley (1990) raise some doubts in this regard. Lack of norms for adolescents further detracts from its appeal in the identification or management of ADHD in this age-group.

Our choice for measuring selective attention in a format similar to the MFFT is the Underlining Test (Rourke & Orr, 1977). This task, for which norms are available across most of the adolescent years, requires the examinee to match a series of relatively simple forms (e.g., line drawings, letter groupings), each of which places different demands on processing. A different target stimulus appears at the top of each page of the test, and the examinee is asked to search through rows of similar stimuli on that page and to underline all stimuli identical with the one at the top. The virtue of this test is that it assesses the individual's ability to work quickly and to sustain attention and inhibit impulsive responding under self-paced conditions.

A number of other tests are also useful in assessing ADHD. To assess response inhibition, the examiner may wish to administer either the Delay task from the Gordon Diagnostic System (Gordon, 1983) or the Delayed Responding task from the Pediatric Assessment of Cognitive Efficiency (Lindgren & Lyons, 1984), both of which make correct responses contingent on the examinee's ability to withhold responding for a few seconds. Procedures we have found useful in evaluating executive functions are those which require the examinee to keep several bits of information in mind at once (i.e., working memory), to shift mental sets, and to engage in linguistic or perceptual processing. Tests that satisfy this need include the Token Test (DeSimoni, 1978), portions of the Clinical Evaluation of Language Fundamental—Revised (CELF-R) (Semel, Wiig, Secord, & Sabers, 1987), the Verbal Selective Reminding Test (Wilkinson, 1981), the Contingency Naming Test (Taylor, Albo, Phebus, Sachs, & Bierl, 1987), and the Developmental Test of Visual-Motor Integration (Beery, 1989).

It should be emphasized, however, that few attempts have been made to validate the sensitivity and specificity of most psychometric procedures in identifying ADHD. There is little doubt that *groups* of children and adolescents score relatively poorly on tests described in this section, or on ones similar to them (Barkley, Dupaul, & McMurray, 1991; Douglas, 1988; Gordon, 1983). The issue is the utility of these measures in identifying individuals with ADHD. Laboratory measures of attention have little utility when considered in isolation. Failure on the CPT, for instance, does not necessarily imply that an individual has ADHD (false positive); nor does a passing score rule out the disorder (false negatives) (Trommer, Hoeppner, Lorber, & Armstrong, 1988). This is particularly the case for relatively simple procedures that involve following a straightforward rule or sustained vigilance. Further doubts regarding test utility are raised by the fact that psychometric performance is not closely related to behavioral ratings and that attention deficits are dependent on contextual demands not present in formal testing (Barkley, 1990; Douglas, 1988).

In our own experience and in Pennington's (1991), attentional problems are usually apparent in comprehensive neuropsychological assessment of ADHD, and test findings help the examiner gauge the extent and nature of attentional weaknesses. We do not believe, however, that performance on any one test or group of tests bears a consistent enough association with ADHD to merit its use in diagnosis. The role of neuropsychological testing is to help validate the diagnosis and to explore its cognitive implications. Whether or not neuropsychological testing is considered an essential part of the evaluation process will therefore depend on the aims of the assessment (see "Clinical Considerations for Assessment and Screening").

**Direct Observation.** Despite the sensitivity of neuropsychological testing to underlying weaknesses in attention, test results frequently fail to capture the inattention, impulsivity, and executive dysfunctions evident in behavioral observation during testing. The most straightforward way to quantify behavior characteristics during testing is to have the examiner rate the examinee's behavior after completion of testing. We have found the Behavioral Attitude Checklist (Sattler, 1988) useful for this purpose. Lack of normative standards and questions regarding examiner reliability prevent us from depending too heavily on ratings of this nature. But such ratings do permit experienced examiners to convey general impressions of a given adolescent as compared with other adolescents with and without ADHD. A more rigorous method of making in-clinic behavior observations is to formally rate the adolescent's behavior during independent engagement in testing or in assigned "homework" tasks. Examples of these methods include the Structured Observation of Academic and Play Settings (SOAPS) (Roberts, Milich, & Loney, 1984) and Barkley's (1990) Restricted Academic Situation.

Similar coding systems could be applied in making in-class observations of behavior, with unidentified adolescents from the same classroom used as a standard of comparison (Barkley, 1990). Parent-adolescent interactions can also be subjected to formal observation, using either modifications of procedures developed for in-home observations of children or procedures specifically developed for adolescents (e.g., Parent-Adolescent Interaction Coding System; Robin & Foster, 1989). Whereas parent and teacher ratings are usually sufficient for diagnosis, direct observations of behavior at home, in interaction with parents, or at school are occasionally helpful in (a) verifying the diagnosis, (b) making a differential diagnosis (e.g., ADHD versus learning disabilities), (c) monitoring response to treatment, and (d) identifying contextual factors that may be contributing to difficulties the adolescent is having in coping with attentional weaknesses. Some of the reasons in situ observation procedures are not routinely used include the facts that they are time-consuming, that they require extensive observer training, and that they afford the examiner little control over situational demands. Additional disadvantages include the shuffling between classes that most adolescents do throughout the day and the stigma associated with observer presence (Barkley, 1990).

**Measures of Family Functioning.** A final set of considerations in the assessment process entails parental psychological status, the marital relationship, and the quality of communication between family members and of family functioning more generally. As a rule, families of children and adolescents with ADHD exhibit higher than normal rates of parental psychopathology, marital discord, conflict among family members, and parenting stress (Barkley, 1990; Breen & Barkley, 1988; Offord, Boyle, & Racine, 1989). Scales useful in evaluating these dimensions of family functioning include the Brief Symptom Inventory (BSI) (Derogatis & Melilsaratos, 1983), the Beck Depression Inventory (BDI) (Beck, Ward, Mendelson, Mack, & Erbaugh, 1961), the Dyadic Adjustment Scale (Spanier, 1976), and the Parenting Stress Index (PSI) (Abidin, 1990). The Conflict Behavior Questionnaire and the Issues Checklist (Robin & Foster, 1989), which assess conflicts and communication problems between adolescents and their parents, are particularly relevant for adolescents with ADHD. Other measures of the family environment and of family resources and stressors include the Family Environment Scale (FES) (Moos & Moos, 1986), the Family Environment Questionnaire (Sines, Clark, & Lauer, 1984), the Family Assessment Device (FAD) (Miller, Bishop, Epstein, & Keitner, 1985), and the Life Stressors and Resources Inventory (Moos & Moos, 1988).

## Clinical Considerations in Assessment and Screening

Considerations of expense and efficiency make it unnecessary to administer all of the procedures described above to all adolescents seen for possible ADHD. Factors that influence the number of procedures and time required include the extent to which critical information is already available, the complexity of issues involved, and the intent of the evaluation (comprehensive assessment or screening).

Our assessment philosophy mandates evaluation of the broader "network" of variables depicted in Figure 1 for comprehensive evaluation and treatment planning. Frequently, however, psychoeduational testing or other assessments, along with medical examinations, have already been performed. Communication with other specialists who have seen the child, or review of relevant written findings, may limit the amount of testing needed or "review of systems" necessary to ensure that all bases are covered. In cases where the adolescent has not been followed by a physician, we recommend that the family arrange for a physical examination to evaluate general health and to explore past or present conditions that might be relevant to school problems (Barkley, 1990). Collaboration with the adolescent's physician is also critical in orchestrating follow-up care and in potential medication treatment. If the individual has not yet received a school psychological assessment, and if such an assessment is justified, we recommend that this be conducted prior to our evaluation. Since the parent interview is generally revealing with regard to contributing environmental and neurobehavioral factors, decisions regarding appropriate evaluation procedures are also based on this information.

Our own practice is to obtain information regarding the presenting complaints and existing medical, educational, and psychological findings from the parents by phone in a brief intake interview. At this point, referrals are made to other specialists or for further preliminary assessments, as deemed appropriate. Once the request for evaluation at our clinic has been accepted, an interview appointment with our clinical staff is scheduled and parents are sent a standard package of forms. Our current procedure is to send parents a parent questionnaire (Table 2), the CBCL, the HSQ, and the Abbreviated Symptom Questionnaire (Hyperactivity Index) from the CPRS-R. We also send parents the teacher questionnaire (Table 3), the CBCL-TRF, the Abbreviated Symptom Questionnaire (Hyperactivity Index) from the CTRS-R, and the ACTeRS, asking that the parents have the teacher who best knows their child (or, if possible, several teachers) complete these forms. Parents are occasionally asked to send the completed forms back to us by mail, for scoring prior to the interview; in most instances, however, we merely request that the parents bring the completed parent and teacher forms with them to the interview. In the materials for teachers, we include a self-addressed envelope and give the teachers the choice of returning their questionnaires directly to us by mail or via the parents.

Following our interview of the parents and adolescent, the parents' completion of the ADHD Rating Scale, the CAP, and the HSQ-R, and the adolescent's completion of the CBCL-YSR, we ask the adolescent and his or her parents to complete any additional self-ratings we feel would be useful in exploring family or parental functioning, or in refining our understanding of the nature of attentional or other behavioral problems in the adolescent. Appointments for testing typically are scheduled immediately after the interview. The time set aside for testing (usually one or two two- to three-hour session) varies with the amount of previous testing conducted and the purposes of assessment. For example, evidence of solid academic achievement from the parents' report and previous school testing would contraindicate further testing of this nature. Relatively recent administration of intelligence testing might also allow us to omit or shorten our assessment of general cognitive abilities. In almost all cases, however, we find it useful to administer neuropsychological tests of attention and executive functions (see "Neuropsychological Testing").

Impressions and treatment recommendations are communicated to the family at a subsequent feedback session. Depending on the complexity of the case, the adolescent might then be referred for additional evaluations (e.g., for further assessment of emotional problems or for a pediatric neurological exam). Occasionally, formal test results and in-clinic observations may be inconclusive, or the clinician may wish to isolate specific problem areas for treatment. In these instances, final decisions regarding diagnosis and treatment may best await additional observations of the adolescent at school or in interaction with parents, or further follow-up to determine the individual's response to a given treatment strategy (e.g., placement in an alternative educational setting, psychotherapy with the adolescent or the family).

The major virtue of the individualized approach advocated here is that it permits adolescents who have relatively straightforward problems or for whom test data and other findings are already available to be assessed in a relatively efficient manner, while preserving more in-depth evaluations for those with more complex or multifaceted problems. A primary disadvantage is that most assessments carried out at tertiary referral centers such as ours are relatively expensive, both for the family and in terms of the heavy demands placed on the examiner to collect and score test data. Assessment of this type is clearly more than would be necessary for screening, or for determining if the individual qualifies for the diagnosis of ADHD per se.

In our view, differences between screening, diagnosis, and more comprehensive assessment fall along a continuum of assessment priorities, as shown in Table 4. The most critical components of the assessment process are: (1) systematic and probing examination of the presenting problems and ADHD-related symptoms, based on interview and standardized parent and teacher questionnaires; (2) a careful history of the problems, based on interview of the parents and adolescent; and (3) efforts to rule out other possible explanations for problems, or to make a differential diagnosis, again by means of interview and standardized questionnaires. Of lesser priority from the perspective of diagnosis per se, but just as critical for a more complete picture of the adolescent's problems and needs, are: (4) neuropsychological testing of attention and executive functions, and (5) examination of other adolescent characteristics (broader sampling of cognitive strengths and weaknesses, psychosocial adjustment, and academic achievement). Elements of the assessment having lowest priority, or as mentioned earlier, portions best left to a second stage of assessment, include: (6) direct observations of the adolescent at school or interacting with family members; and (7) follow-up to determine the adolescent's response to a given intervention.

Administration of questionnaires and a brief interview targeted at the history of ADHD symptomatology constitute a reasonable *screening* for ADHD. For such screening to be clinically acceptable, however, it is imperative that the examiner (a) recognize the risks of underidentification associated with gathering information from limited sources (e.g., ratings by parents only, compared with the combination of ratings by multiple informants and test findings) and (b) recognize that clinical impressions of attentional problems based on brief encounters with adolescents are notoriously inaccurate (Klein & Gittelman-Klein, 1975; Sleator & Ullmann, 1981). Given the possibility of underidentification, as well as difficulties in assessing residual forms of ADHD, it is unwise to rule out ADHD on the basis of screening alone, at least in individuals in whom behavior or learning problems have been substantiated. As is the case for behavioral screening more generally, decisions for further assessment should be fairly liberal, and the aims of screening should be to decide if further assessment might be warranted, rather than to establish a diagnosis (Simonian, Tarnowski, Stancin, Friman, & Atkins, 1991).

Assessments that entail components 1 to 3 above, or what we would

**Table 4.**
**Components of Assessment for ADHD by Priority Level**

| Priority Level | Component of Assessment | Evaluation Procedures |
|---|---|---|
| 1 | Examination of presenting problem | Parent and teacher behavior ratings; self-ratings; interview |
| 2 | History of problems and symptoms | Parent questionnaire; interview; review of previous findings |
| 3 | Differential diagnosis | Behavior ratings; interview; additional evaluations or referrals as appropriate |
| 4 | Neuropsychological evaluation of attention and executive functions | Testing |
| 5 | Evaluation of other cognitive skills, psychosocial adjustment, and academic achievement | Testing; review of previous findings; additional interviews, ratings, or referrals |
| 6 | Direct observation | Observations of behavior at school or in interaction with family members |
| 7 | Response across follow-up to suggested interventions | Interview; reports from teachers |

refer to as a *diagnostic evaluation,* are required for even a provisional diagnosis of ADHD. Assessing presenting complaints and determining if the adolescent's medical, educational, and developmental history is consistent with ADHD require knowledge of the manifestations of attentional problems at various ages but are otherwise relatively straightforward. Barkley's (1990) handbook is an excellent resource in this regard, and highly recommended for anyone undertaking assessments of ADHD. A recent article by Voeller (1991) is also helpful. Barkley (1990) recommends that actual diagnosis be reserved for those individuals (a) who meet DSM III-R criteria, as judged from interview and the ADHD Rating Scale; (b) who have manifested symptoms for at least twelve months; (c) whose ratings on a standardized ADHD behavior checklist completed by parents *or* teachers fall more than 1.5 standard deviations above the mean for sex and age; and (d) who present with relatively pervasive attentional problems at home *or* at school, as judged, for example, by ratings on the HSQ-R or SSQ-R that fall more than 1.5 standard deviations above norms. Since DSM III-R criteria specify that symptoms be manifest prior to age seven, the duration requirement as applied to adolescents would imply a continuance of symptoms from an early age, taking for granted some developmental and situational variations across time.

Establishing a differential diagnosis (component 3) is the most challenging element of this level of assessment. Symptoms of ADHD can present either as a primary disorder associated with other comorbidities or as a secondary consequence of other conditions. Examples include learning disabilities, conduct or oppositional-defiant disorders, depression, anxiety disorders, Tourette's disorder, pervasive developmental disorders, fragile X syndrome, birth complications/prematurity, prenatal exposure to drugs, elevated lead burden, and brain injury. The evaluator must also consider potential environmental influences, such as a chaotic home environment or family stress. Proper management necessitates recognition of coexisting conditions and determination of whether attentional problems are primary or secondary. Making this determination requires that diagnosticians be familiar with a wide range of clinical conditions, and that they be able and willing either to evaluate these problems themselves or to recognize circumstances under which further assessment elsewhere is in order.

One of the benefits of a *comprehensive assessment for ADHD,* involving components 1 to 8, or at least 1 to 5, is that it provides confirmatory evidence for ADHD. Confirmation is especially useful in cases in which coexisting problems are in fact present, or where symptoms are obscured by situational variations or cognitive or social strengths. These complexities are common occurrences in the general population of persons with ADHD but are especially prominent in the adolescent age group. The other major advantage of comprehensive assessment, as previously noted, is that it enhances understanding of the cognitive, academic, and behavioral correlates of ADHD and is therefore vital to treatment planning. While we would not argue that comprehensive assessments are indicated in every case, we do believe that they are an essential option in centers specializing in ADHD and other specific developmental disorders.

## Treatment

### *Empirically Validated Approaches*

According to the existing literature, the three most promising interventions for ADHD are pharmacotherapy, cognitive therapy and other unimodal approaches, and multimodal approaches. Whereas direct comparisons of these approaches with one another or with other treatments are uncommon and few studies have focused on adolescents, findings suggest that each approach has some merit in managing the problems associated with ADHD.

**Pharmacotherapy.** In one of the few studies that has focused on the adolescent age group, Varley (1988) assessed the effects of Ritalin (methylphenidate), the most widely prescribed stimulant medication. Using a placebo double-blind cross-over design, Varley found that administration of Ritalin was associated with less deviant parent and teacher behavior ratings. In another study of the effects of Ritalin on adolescents with ADHD, Coons, Klorman, and Borgstedt (1987) administered a vigilance test both on and off the medication. Behavior ratings were also collected under the two conditions. Findings showed that the study participants not only were rated as less behaviorally deviant when taking Ritalin but also performed better in testing. On the basis of these and similar findings (Lerer & Lerer, 1977; Safer & Allen, 1975), Varley (1985) concludes that adolescents respond in much the same fashion as children to stimulants. Stimulants other than Ritalin (Cylert and Dexedrine) also enjoy a broad base of experimental support, and tricyclic antidepressants and neuroleptics have proved useful when stimulants are ineffective or when other conditions, such as anxiety or depression, accompany ADHD (Barkley& Murphy, 1991).

**Cognitive Therapy and Other Unimodal Approaches.** Although cognitive-behavior modification has been only partly successful with younger age-groups (Brown & Borden, 1986), the dependence of this method on higher-level thinking and reasoning skills makes it particularly suitable to adolescents. In their work with institutionalized adolescents with conduct disorder, Synder and White (1979) found that a cognitive self-instruction approach was superior to both an operant approach and an assessment-only control condition in improving behavior and reducing impulsivity. Further examples of effective cognitive self-control training programs are those described by Barkley, Copeland, and Sivage (1980), Douglas (1980), Deshler, Warner, Schumaker, and Alley (1983), and Kendall and Braswell (1985).

Additional unimodal treatments to be considered include individual psychotherapy, family systems therapy, biofeedback, parent training, and behavior management. This last approach has received the most empirical support (Barkley & Murphy, 1991). Efforts to clarify expectations, establish behavioral contracts, and institute appropriate schedules of rewards and response costs are nearly always worthwhile. Psychoeducational techniques (Brown, 1986) and vocational training (Conners, 1984) are two other approaches that may prove effective in working with adolescents.

**Multimodal Approaches.** Most researchers advocate an approach that combines more than one of the specific approaches listed above (Brown, Borden, & Clingerman, 1986; Cantwell, 1986). Examples of such multimodal approaches to treatment include the programs described by Brown, Borden, and Clingerman (1986), Cantwell (1986), and Robin (1990). The major advantage of more global interventions is that they address the multitude of problems characteristic of many adolescents with ADHD. Cantwell (1986) recommends that the elements of the multimodal treatment program include family work, environmental manipulation, possible use of medication, skills remediation, behavior modification, social skills training, and psychotherapy.

Despite the appeal of a multimodal approach, Robin (1990) is one of the few researchers who has tailored such a program for adolescents with ADHD and their families. His program is based on a biobehavioral–family systems model and incorporates family ADHD education, stimulant medication, behavioral contracting, strategic-structural family therapy techniques, individual therapy for the adolescent, work on study skills and cognitive strategies, and training in problem solving and communication. To date, the only component of the treatment package that had been formally investigated is training in problem solving and communication (Barkley, 1990). Although such combined treatment programs are promising, more research is needed to determine their benefits (Barkley, 1990; Robin, 1990).

## Treatment Planning and Recommendations

Planning treatment for the individual adolescent is based on impressions as to the severity of the problems, environmental and historical influences on coping, and psychological, cognitive, and academic comorbidities. The most effective approach is one that considers all aspects of ADHD (Barkley & Murphy, 1991; Keogh & Barkett, 1980). Whether or not there are coexisting academic weaknesses, the intervention approaches detailed by Taylor (1989) for children with learning disabilities are equally appropriate for the adolescent with ADHD. Effective instructional principles—that is, direct teaching and individual attention, seeing that the student spends as much time as possible engaged in academic tasks, mastery learning, and establishing attainable objectives and incentives—are an important goal for everyone with ADHD. Other environmental interventions include (a) remediation of any basic language or academic weaknesses; (b) establishment of realistic expectations and promotion of independence; (c) motivation-enhancing techniques, such as student involvement in program planning, cooperative learning groups, and opportunities to develop strengths and participate in extracurricular activities; (d) behavior contracting, social skills training, and individual and family therapy; and (e) cognitive-behavior modification. A listing of several of the recommendations we routinely include in reports to parents and teachers is given in Table 5.

Our personal experience, clearly supported by the empirical literature, is that stimulant medications can also play an important role in treatment. Like other clinicians, however, we believe that drug treatment should be undertaken only if certain minimal conditions are met (Barkley, 1990). First, medications should be used only in conjunction with other interventions. Second, a careful trial placement of medications should be undertaken prior to longer-term use, with efforts to systematically validate drug effectiveness (parent and teacher ratings before and after, or a double-blind placebo-drug trial), evaluate potential side effects, and determine optimal dosage level. Finally,

**Table 5.**
**Behavioral Interventions Helpful in Managing ADHD**

---

1. Provide as much individual attention as possible, involving directed teaching: highly structured, step-by-step methods, with ample opportunities for practice, targeting of goals, and regular monitoring of performance.

2. Modify work demands to increase success rate, break tasks into manageable segments, set task priorities, establish fixed work periods, intersperse breaks of high-interest activities to maintain motivation, and promote consistent study habits and the sense of responsibility for completing tasks.

3. Present directions in parts, use demonstrations and models of what is to be done, monitor understanding by asking for evidence of understanding (samples of work, verbal repetition), and ensure mastery of initial elements before proceeding.

4. Incorporate as much routine as possible in home and school environments, and establish clear guidelines and limits for behavior, understood and consistently maintained consequences, rewards for achieving goals, and positive expectations for success.

5. Plan ahead or restructure situations that tend to lead to failure or noncompliance.

6. Allow and even encourage participation in high-interest activities and appropriate social interactions, setting aside time irrespective of ability to keep up with schoolwork.

7. Have a special staff member at school serve as "case manager" to help troubleshoot, provide counseling and support, check work, serve as a liaison between teachers and between school and home, and assist in the implementation and overseeing of any behavioral interventions.

8. Encourage the use of organizational aids, such as assignment logs or memory and study strategies.

9. Encourage parents' participation in support groups and the involvement of the adolescent and family in therapy as indicated.

---

strong consideration should be given to adolescents' and parents' attitudes toward medication, as well as to the likelihood that the medications will be used as prescribed. Appropriate drug treatment demands that adolescents be fully aware of the purposes of medications, view the medications as a facilitator rather than as something they are dependent on, and be willing collaborators in treatment. Lack of a similar understanding and willingness on the part of the adolescent's parents is also likely to sabotage this intervention.

Some parents and professionals may be reluctant to use pharmacotherapy with adolescents for fear that this procedure might promote drug abuse. While acceptance of medications as a means for dealing with behavior problems may well convey an unintended and undesirable message to adolescents (Whalen & Henker, 1980), neither the use of stimulant medication nor the duration of treatment has been specifically tied to subsequent drug abuse during adolescence (Kramer & Loney, 1981). Loney, Kramer, and Milich (1981) in fact found that a positive response to Ritalin was associated with a lesser rather than a greater risk for drug abuse. It remains imperative, nonetheless, to consider potential noncompliance or other misuse of medication, along with side effects, social stigma, and effects on self-perceptions (Barkley, 1990; Sleator, Ullman, & von Neumann, 1982; Whalen & Henker, 1980).

Taking steps to assist adolescents with ADHD also requires that the clinician attempt to engender a common understanding of the disorder, common goals, and open lines of communication (i.e., involving parents, teachers, and the adolescents themselves); make it clear that treatment will involve efforts for change on behalf of *both* adolescents and those persons who live or work with them; set treatment priorities; and determine the feasibility of different treatment options. Although it is wise to deal with problems on as many fronts as possible, it is sometimes necessary to deal exclusively with behavioral or adjustment issues prior to tackling other contributing factors. Given the frequent lack of opportunity for intensive academic remediation at the junior or senior high school level, as well as developmental considerations, work on strategies for compensating for attentional and executive dysfunctions may often take priority. Financial resources may also set constraints on options such as outside tutoring or extended individual psychotherapy. Interventions that are likely to have the highest yield are those which address multiple needs over an extended period and encourage the development of interests and talents, as well as work on areas of weakness (Taylor, 1989).

## Summary

A review of a number of recent longitudinal studies of ADHD substantiates the continuation of this disorder into adolescence, at least for the majority of affected individuals (Barkley et al., 1990; Brown & Borden, 1986; Gittelman, Manuzza, Shenker, & Banagura, 1985; Thorley, 1984). Adolescents with ADHD manifest a high incidence of behavior disorders, antisocial acts and other interpersonal problems, school and learning problems, positive family histories of parental mental health problems, and family dysfunction/ instability. As Barkley and colleagues (1990) conclude, "Childhood hyperactivity represents a chronic and often socially disabling condition, placing the children at high risk for later negative outcomes across many domains of adjustment" (p. 556). While there are undoubtedly many children with ADHD for whom symptoms either dissipate or are well compensated by adolescence, findings in general run counter to previous notions that ADHD is "outgrown," or that the condition is merely a modified and less severe expression of earlier childhood symptoms (Cantwell, 1986).

One factor that may contribute to the persistence of the theory that ADHD is outgrown, and that may also result in underidentification of this condition, is the prominence of coexisting problems in the adolescent with ADHD. Difficulties in adjustment, motivation, and academic achievement are more apparent to the observer than subtle attentional problems are. Further, the adolescent with ADHD is typically caught up in a self-defeating cycle in which attentional and organizational problems make learning and interaction with others frustrating. Such frustration may in turn lead to diminished incentive to persist on school tasks, apathy, avoidance, cumulative weaknesses in academic skills, and poor study habits. By adolescence, poor motivation and behavior problems may therefore no longer be merely a secondary consequence of ADHD but may instead have become entrenched in a more pervasive pattern of maladaptation. It is easy to see how one might overlook a primary attentional problem, especially given that this problem may be variably expressed and difficult to detect or to document historically.

Identification and proper management of ADHD in adolescence require familiarity with the developmental manifestations of the disorder, behavioral and learning comorbidities, the manner in which symptoms vary with situational demands, environmental factors, and the adolescent's cognitive abilities and coping style. A sensitivity to core deficits in sustained attention, executive function, and impulse control is also essential, as is appreciation of subtypes of ADHD.

Although there is good reason to conceive of the disorder as inherent, biologically based, and incurable (Barkley, 1990; Taylor & Fletcher, 1983), recognition can lead to any of several effective treatments. Nonmedical interventions that are likely to improve behavior and school performance include helping the adolescent to better cope with attentional weaknesses and encouraging parents and teachers to make reasonable accommodations and to apply appropriate management techniques. Treatment with attention-enhancing medications is also warranted, at least in cases where medications are useful adjuncts to other interventions and where the adolescent and family are in agreement with this option. Efforts to identify and treat this disorder prior to adolescence and to encourage more systematic follow-up may be one way to improve the longer-term outlook.

The overall theme of this chapter is that assessment and treatment are both multimodal in nature. Screening is possible but should be undertaken with full knowledge of the complexities of ADHD and as a stepping-stone to further and more comprehensive assessment. Diagnosis of ADHD is also relatively straightforward and need not involve more than the collection of information from interviews and behavioral rating scales. Our position, however, is that diagnosis is often not possible without more comprehensive neuropsychological evaluation and that it is not feasible to base treatment decisions on the diagnosis alone. Working toward constructive changes on behalf of the adolescent with ADHD demands a further understanding of environmental influences and medical history, coexisting behavior and learning disorders, and associated cognitive, psychosocial, and academic competencies. Despite sobering statistics on the intransigence of ADHD and on behavioral outcomes, much can be done to promote a healthy adjustment and a successful school career.

## Acknowledgments

Preparation of this chapter was undertaken during the first author's postdoctoral fellowship at the Rainbow Learning Center, Department of Pediatrics, Rainbow Babies and Children's Hospital. Appreciation is extended to the board of trustees of Rainbow Babies and Children's Hospital for its support of Dr. Rich's fellowship. We are also indebted to Learning Center staff members Ruth Johnson-Straub, Ann Foreman, and Christine Barry, not only for their suggestions on the manuscript but for their contributions to the development and implementation of the assessment model advocated herein.

## References

Abidin, R. R. (1990). *Parenting Stress Index manual* (3rd ed.). Charlottesville, VA: Pediatric Psychology.

Achenbach, T. M., & Edelbrock, C. (1983). *Manual for the Child Behavior Checklist and Revised Child Behavior Profile.* Burlington, VT: Department of Psychiatry, University of Vermont.

Achenbach, T. M., & Edelbrock, C. (1986). *Manual for the Teacher Report Form and the Child Behavior Profile.* Burlington, VT: Department of Psychiatry, University of Vermont.

Achenbach, T. M., & Edelbrock, C. (1987). *Manual for the Child Behavior Checklist Youth Self-Report.* Burlington, VT: Department of Psychiatry, University of Vermont.

Ackerman, P. T., Dykman, R. A., & Peters, J. E. (1977). Teenage status of hyperactive and nonhyperactive learning disabled boys. *American Journal of Orthopsychiatry, 47,* 577–596.

American Psychiatric Association (1987). *Diagnostic and statistical manual of mental disorders* (Third Edition-Revised). Washington, DC: American Psychiatric Association.

Barkley, R. A. (1981). Hyperactive children: A handbook for diagnosis and treatment. New York: Guilford.

Barkley, R. A. (1987). A review of child behavior rating scales and checklists for research in child psychopathology. In M. Rutter, A. H. Tuma, & I. Lann (Eds.), *Assessment and diagnosis in child psychopathology.* New York: Guilford.

Barkley, R. A., (1988). Attention deficit hyperactivity disorders: A handbook for diagnosis and treatment. New York: Guilford.

Barkley, R. A., Copeland, A. P., & Sivage, C. (1980). A self-control classroom for children. *Autism and Developmental Disorders, 10,* 75–89.

Barkley, R. A., DuPaul, G. J., & McMurray, M. B. (1991). Attention deficit disorder with and without hyperactivity: Clinical response to three dose levels of methylphenidate. *Pediatrics, 87,* 519–531.

Barkley, R. A., & Edelbrock, C. S. (1987). Assessing attentional variation in children's behavior problems: The Home and School Situation Questionnaires. In R. Prinz (Ed.), *Advances in behavioral assessment of children and families* (Vol. 3, pp. 157–176). Greenwich, CT: JAI.

Barkley, R. A., Fischer, M., Edelbrock, C. S., & Smallish, L.H. (1990). The adolescent outcome of hyperactive children diagnosed by research criteria: I. An eight-year prospective follow-up study. *Journal of the American Academy of Child and Adolescent Psychiatry, 29,* 546–557.

Barkley, R. A., Fischer, M., Newby, R., & Breen, M. (1988). Development of a multi-method clinical protocol for assessing stimulant drug responses in ADHD children. *Journal of Clinical Child Psychology, 17,* 14–24.

Barkley, R. A., Karlsson, J., Polland, S., & Murphy, J. (1985). Developmental changes in the mother-child interactions of hyperactive children. *Journal of Abnormal Child Psychology, 13,* 631–638.

Barkley, R. A., and Murphy, J. V. (1991). Treating attention-deficit hyperactivity disorder: Medication and behavior management training. *Pediatric Annals, 20*(5), 256–266.

Beck, A. T., Ward, C. H., Mendelson, M., Mack, J., & Erbaugh, J. (1961). An inventory for measuring depression. *Archives of General Psychiatry, 4,* 561–571.

Beery, K. E. (1989). *Revised administration, scoring, and teaching manual for the Developmental Test of Visual-Motor Integration.* Cleveland, OH: Modern Curriculum.

Biederman, J., Munir, K., Knee, D., Armentano, M., Autor, S., Waternaux, C., & Tsuang, M. (1987). High rate of affective disorders in probands with attention deficit disorders and in their relatives: A controlled family study. *American Journal of Psychiatry, 144,* 330–333.

Birch, H. G. (1964). *Brain damage in children: The biological and social aspects.* Baltimore, MD: Williams & Wilkens.

Blau, A. (1936). Mental changes following head trauma in children. *Archives of Neurological Psychiatry, 35,* 722–769.

Blondis, T. A., Accardo, P. J., & Snow, J. H. (1989). Measures of attention: Part I. Questionnaires. *Clinical Pediatrics, 28*(5), 222–228.

Breen, M. H., & Barkley R. A. (1988). Child psychopathology and parenting stress in girls and boys having attention deficit disorder with hyperactivity. *Journal of Psychology, 13,* 265–280.

Brown, G., Chadwick, O., Shaffer, D., Rutter, M., & Traub, M. (1981). A prospective study of children with head injuries: III. Psychiatric sequelae. *Psychological Medicine, 11,* 63–78.

Brown, R. T. (1986). Teacher ratings and the assessment of attention deficit disordered children. *Journal of Learning Disabilities, 19*(2), 95–100.

Brown, R. T., & Borden, K. A. (1986). Hyperactivity at adolescence: Some misconceptions and new directions. *Journal of Clinical Child Psychology, 15,* 194–209.

Brown, R. T., Borden, A., & Clingerman, S. R. (1986). Pharmacotherapy in ADD adolescents with special attention to multimodality treatments. *Psychopharmacology Bulletin, 21,* 192–211.

Byers, R. K., & Lord, E. E. (1943). Late effects of lead poisoning on mental development. *American Journal of Diseases of Children, 66,* 471–490.

Campbell, S. B., Douglas, V. I., & Morganstern, G. (1971). Cognitive styles in hyperactive children and the effect of methylphenidate. *Journal of Child Psychology and Psychiatry, 12,* 55–67.

Cantwell, D. P. (1972). Psychiatric illness in the families of hyperactive children. *Archives of General Psychiatry, 27,* 414–417.

Cantwell, D. P. (1986). Attention deficit disorder in adolescents. *Clinical Psychology Review, 6,* 237–247.

Cantwell, D. P., & Baker, L. (1991). Association between attention deficit-hyperactivity disorder and learning disorders. *Journal of Learning Disabilities, 24*(2), 88–95.

Clements, S. D. (1966). *Minimal brain dysfunction in children: Terminology and identification.* NINDB Monograph No. 3. Washington, DC: U.S. Public Health Service.

Conners, C. K. (1969). A teacher rating scale for use in drug studies with children. *American Journal of Psychiatry, 126,* 884.

Conners, C. K. (1984, September). *Selection of dependent and independent variables.* Paper presented at Pharmacotherapy for ADD/H Adolescents, a workshop sponsored by the Special Populations Section, Pharmacologic and Somatic Treatments Research Branch, National Institute of Mental Health. Washington, DC.

Cooley, E. L., & Morris, R. D. (1990). Attention in children: A neuropsychologically based model for assessment. *Developmental Neuropsychology, 6*(3), 239–274.

Coons, H. W., Klorman, R., & Borgstedt, A.D. (1987). Effects of methylphenidate on adolescents with a childhood history of ADD: II. Information processing. *Journal of the American Academy of Child and Adolescent Psychiatry, 26,* 368–374.

David, O. J. (1974). Association between lower level lead concentrations and hyperactivity. *Environmental Health perspective, 7,* 17–25.

David, O. J., Clark, J., & Voeller, K. (1972). Lead and hyperactivity. *Lancet, 2,* 900–903.

David, O. J., Hoffman, S. P., Sverd, J., Clark, J., & Voeller, K. (1976). Lead and hyperactivity: Behavioral response to chelation. A pilot study. *American Journal of Psychiatry, 133,* 1155–1158.

Denckla, M. B. (1991). Attention deficit hyperactivity disorder—Residual type. *Journal of Child Neurology, 6*(Suppl.), 542–548.

Denson, R., Nanson, J. L., & MacWatters, M. A. (1975). Hyperkinesis and maternal smoking. *Canadian Psychiatric Association Journal, 20,* 183–187.

Derogatis, L. R., & Melilsaratos, N. (1983). The Brief Symptom Inventory: An introductory report. *Psychological Medicine, 13,* 595–605.

Deshler, D. D., Warner, M. M., Schumaker, J. B., & Alley, G. R. (1983). Learning strategies intervention models: Key components and current status. In J. D. McKinney & L. Ferguson (Eds.), *Current topics in learning disabilities* (Vol. 1, pp. 245–283). Norwood, NJ: Ablex.

DeSimoni, F. G. (1978). *The Token Test for Children.* Boston, MA: Teaching Resources.

Douglas, V. I. (1972). Stop, look, and listen: The problem of sustained attention and impulse control in hyperactive and normal children. *Canadian Journal of Behavioral Science, 4,* 259–282.

Douglas, V. I. (1980). Higher mental processes in hyperactive children: Implications for training. In R. M. Knights & D. J. Bakker (Eds.), *Treatment of hyperactive and learning disordered children: Current research* (pp. 65–91). Baltimore, MD: University Park.

Douglas, V. I. (1983). Attention and cognitive problems. In M. Rutter (Ed.), *Developmental neuropsychiatry* (pp. 280–329). New York: Guilford.

Douglas, V. I. (1988). Cognitive deficits in children with attention deficit disorder with hyperactivity. In L. M. Bloomindale & J. Sergeant (Eds.), *Attention deficit disorder: Criteria, cognition, and intervention* (pp. 65–81). A book supplement of the *Journal of Child Psychology and Psychiatry* (No. 5). New York: Pergamon.

Dykman, R. A., & Ackerman, P. T. (1991). Attention deficit disorder and specific reading disability: Separate, but often overlapping disorders. *Journal of Learning Disabilities, 24*(2), 96.

Edelbrock, C. (1986). *Child Assessment Profile.* Worcester, MA: Department of Psychiatry, University of Massachusetts Medical School.

Edelbrock, C., Costello, A., & Kessler, M. D. (1984). Emperical corroboration of attention deficit disorder. *Journal of the American Academy of Child Psychiatry, 23,* 285–290.

Fischer, M., Barkley, R. A., Edelbrook, C. S., & Smallish, L. (1990). The adolescent outcome of hyperactive children diagnosed by research criteria: II. Academic, attentional, and neuropsychological status. *Journal of Consulting and Clinical Psychology, 38,* 580–588.

Gittelman, R., Manuzza, S., Shenker, R., & Banagura, N. (1985). Hyperactive boys almost grown up. *Archives of General Psychiatry, 42,* 937–947.

Gordon, M. (1983). *The Gordon Diagnostic System.* Boulder, CO: Clinical Diagnostic Systems.

Gordon, M., & Mettleman, B. B. (1988). The assessment of attention: I. Standardization and reliability of a behavior based measure. *Journal of Clinical Psychology, 44,* 682–690.

Goyette, C. H., Conners, C. K., & Ulrich, R. F. (1978). Normative data for Revised

Conners Parent and Teacher Rating Scales. *Journal of Abnormal Child Psychology, 6,* 221–236.

Hack, M., Breslau, N., Weissman, B., Aram, D., Klein, N., & Borowski, E. (1991). Effects of very low birthweight and subnormal head size on cognitive abilities at school age. *New England Journal of Medicine, 325,* 231–237.

Handen, B. L., Breaux, A. M., Gosling, A., Ploof, D.L., & Feldman, H. (1990). Efficacy of methylphenidate among mentally retarded children with attention deficit disorder. *Pediatrics. 86,* 922–930.

Herbert, M. (1964). The concept and testing of brain damage in children: A review. *Journal of Child Psychology and Psychiatry, 5*(3, 24), 197–217.

Hoy, E., Weiss, G., Minde, K., & Cohen, H. (1978). The hyperactive child at adolescence: Cognitive, emotional, and social functioning. *Journal of Abnormal Child Psychology, 6,* 311–324.

Huessy, H. R., & Cohen, A. H. (1978). Hyperkinetic behaviors and learning disabilities followed over several years. *Pediatrics, 57,* 4–10.

Huessy, H. R., Metoyer, M., & Townsend, M. (1974). Eight to ten-year follow-up of 84 children treated in rural Vermont for behavioral disorder. *Acta Paedopsychiatrica, 40,* 230–235.

Kagan, J. (1966). Reflection-impulsivity: The generality and dynamics of conceptual tempo. *Journal of Abnormal Psychology, 71,* 17–24.

Kendall, P. C., & Braswell, L. (1985). *Cognitive-behavioral therapy for impulsive children.* New York: Guilford.

Keogh, B. K., & Barkett, C. J. (1980). An educational analysis of hyperactive children's achievement problems. In C. K. Whalen & B. Henker (Eds), *Hyperactive children: The social ecology of identification and treatment* (pp. 259–282). New York: Academic.

Kessler, J. W. (1980). History of minimal brain dysfunctions. In H. E. Rie & E. D. Rie (Eds.), *Handbook of minimal brain dysfunctions: A critical review.* New York: Wiley.

Klein, D. R., & Gittleman-Klein, R. (1975). Problems in diagnosis of minimal brain dysfunction and the hyperkinetic syndrome. *International Journal of Mental Health, 4,* 45–60.

Kovacs, M. (1981). Rating scales to assess depression in school-aged children. *Acta Paedopsychiatry, 46,* 305–315.

Kramer, J., & Loney, J. (1981). Childhood hyperactivity and substance abuse: A review of the literature. In K. Gadow & I. Bialer (Eds.), *Advances in learning and behavior disabilities* (Vol. 1, pp. 225–229). Greenwich, CT: JAI.

Lahey, B. B., & Carlson, C. L. (1991). Validity of the diagnostic category of attention deficit disorder without hyperactivity: A review of the literature. *Journal of Learning Disabilities, 24*(2), 110.

Laufer, M., Denoff, E., & Solomons, G. (1957). Hyperkinetic impulse disorder in children's behavior problems. *Psychosomatic Medicine, 19,* 38–49.

Lerer, R. J., & Lerer, M. P. (1977). Responses of adolescents with minimal brain dysfunction to methylphenidate. *Journal of Learning Disabilities, 10,* 223–228.

Levin, H. S., Eisenberg, H. M., Wigg, N. R., & Kobayashi, K. (1982). Memory and intellectual ability after head injury in children and adolescents. *Neurosurgery, 11,* 668–673.

Lindgren, S. D., & Lyons, D. A. (1984). *Pediatric Assessment of Cognitive Efficiency (PACE)*. Iowa City: University of Iowa, Department of Pediatrics.

Loney, J. (1987). Hyperactivity and aggression in the diagnosis of attention deficit disorder. In B. B. Lahey & A. E. Kazdin (Eds), *Advances in clinical child psychology* (Vol. 10, pp. 1–54). New York: Pergamon.

Loney, J., Kramer, J., & Milich, R. S. (1981). The hyperactive child grows up: Predictors of symptoms, delinquency, and achievement at follow-up. In K. Gadow & J. Loney (Eds.), *Psychosocial aspects of drug treatment of hyperactivity* (pp. 381–415). Boulder, CO: Westview.

Loney, J., & Milich, R. (1982). Hyperactivity, inattention, and aggression in clinic practice. In M. Wolraich & D. K. Routh (Eds.), *Advances in behavioral pediatrics* (Vol 2, pp. 113–147). Greenwich, CT: JAI.

Lopez, R. E. (1965). Hyperactivity in twins. *Canadian Psychiatric Association Journal, 10,* 421–426.

Low, H. C., Henriksen, L., Bruhn, P., Borner, H., & Neilsen, J. B. (1989). Striatal dysfunction in attention deficit and hyperkinetic disorder. *Archives of Neurology, 46,* 48–52.

Mash, E. J., & Johnston, C. (1983). Parental perceptions of child behavior problems, parenting self-esteem, and mothers' reported stress in younger and older hyperactive and normal children. *Journal of Consulting and Clinical Psychology, 51,* 68–99.

Matheny, A. P., Dolan, A. B., & Wilson, R. S. (1976). Twins with academic learning problems: Antecedent characteristics. American Journal of Orthopsychiatry, 46, 464–469.

McCarney, S. B. (1989a). *Attention Deficit Disorders Evaluation Scale—Home Version*. Columbia, MO: Hawthorne Educational Services.

McCarney, S. B., (1989b). *Attention Deficit Disorders Evaluation Scale—School Version*. Columbia, MO: Hawthorne Educational Services.

McGee, R., & Share, D. L. (1988). Attention deficit-hyperactivity disorder and academic failure: Which comes first, and what should be treated? *Journal of the American Academy of Child and Adolescent Psychiatry, 27,* 318–325.

Mendelson, W. B., Johnson, N. E., & Stewart, M. A. (1971). Hyperactive children as adolescents: A follow up study. *Journal of Nervous and Mental Diseases, 153,* 273–279.

Miller, I. W., Bishop, D. S., Epstein, N. B., & Keitner, G. I. (1985). The McMaster Family Assessment Device: Reliability and validity. *Journal of Marital and Family Therapy, 11*(4), 345–356.

Minde, K., Weiss, G., & Mendelson, B. A. (1972). A 5-year follow up of 91 hyperactive school children. *Journal of the American Academy of Child Psychiatry, 11,* 595–610.

Mirsky, A. F. (1987). Behavioral and psychophysiological markers of disordered attention. *Environmental Health Perspective, 74,* 191–199.

Moos, R. H., & Moos, B. S. (1986). *Family Environment Scale*. Palo Alto, CA: Consulting Psychologists.

Moos, R. H., & Moos, B. S. (1988). *Life Stressors and Social Resources Inventory: Preliminary manual*. Palo Alto, CA: Stanford University and VA Medical Centers.

Morrison, J. R., & Stewart, M. A. (1971). A family study of the hyperactive child syndrome. *Biological Psychiatry, 3,* 189–195.

Morrison, J., & Stewart, M. (1973a). The psychiatric status of legal families of adopted hyperactive children. *Archives of General Psychiatry, 28,* 888–891.

Morrison, J., & Stewart, M. (1973b). Evidence for a polygenetic inheritance in the hyperactive child syndrome. *American Journal of Psychiatry, 130,* 791–792.

Nichols, P. L., & Chen, T. C. (1981). *Minimal brain dysfunction: A prospective study.* Hillsdale, NJ: Erlbaum.

Offord, D. R., Boyle, M. H., & Racine, Y. (1989). Ontario child health study: Correlates of disorder. *Journal of the American Academy of Child and Adolescent Psychiatry, 28,* 856–860.

Pelham, W. E., Jr., Milich, R., Murphy, D. A., & Murphy, H. A. (1989). Normative data on the IOWA Conners Teacher Rating Scale. *Journal of Clinical Child Psychology, 18*(3), 259–262.

Pennington, B. F. (1991). *Diagnosing learning disorders: A neuropsychological framework.* New York: Guilford.

Raskin, L. A., Shaywitz, S. E., Shaywitz, B. A., Anderson, G. M., & Cohen, D. J. (1984). Neurochemical correlates of attention deficit disorder. *Pediatric Clinics of North America, 31,* 387–396.

Reynolds, W. M. (1987). *Reynolds Adolescent Depression Scale.* Odessa, FL: Psychological Assessment Resources.

Roberts, M. A., Milich, R., & Loney, J. (1984). *Structured observations of academic and play settings.* Iowa City, IA: University Hospital School, University of Iowa.

Robin, A. L. (1990). Training families with ADHD adolescent. In R.A. Barkley (Ed.), *Attention deficit hyperactivity disorder: A handbook for diagnosis and treatment* (pp. 462–497). New York: Guilford.

Robin, A. L., & Foster, S. L. (1989). *Negotiating parent-adolescent conflict: A behavioral family systems approach.* New York: Guilford.

Ross, D. M., & Ross, S. A. (1982). *Hyperactivity: Current issues, research, and theory* (2nd ed.). New York: Wiley.

Rosvold, H. E., Mirsky, A. F., Sarason, E. D., Bransome, E. D., & Beck, L. H. (1956). A continuous performance test of brain damage. *Journal of Consulting Psychology, 20,* 343–350.

Rourke, B. P. (1991). If it's worth doing . . . *Contemporary Psychology, 36*(5), 425–426.

Rourke, B. P., & Orr, R. R. (1977). Prediction of the reading and spelling performances of normal and retarded readers: A four-year follow up. *Journal of Abnormal Child Psychology, 5,* 9–20.

Routh, D. K. (1978). Hyperactivity. In P. Magrab (Ed.), *Psychological management of pediatric problems.* Baltimore, MD: University Park.

Rutter, M. (1982). Syndromes attributed to "minimal brain dysfunction" in childhood. *American Journal of Psychiatry, 139,* 21–33.

Rutter, M., Korn, S., & Birch, H.G. (1963). Genetic and environmental factors in the development of "primary reaction patterns." *British Journal of Social and Clinical Psychology, 2,* 161–173.

Safer, D. J. (1973). A familial factor in minimal brain dysfunction. *Behavior Genetics, 3,* 175–186.

Safer, D., & Allen, R. (1975). Stimulant drug treatment of hyperactive adolescents. *Diseases of the Nervous System, 368,* 454–457.

Satterfield, J. H., Hoppe, C. M., & Schell, A. M. (1982). A prospective study of delinquency in 110 adolescent boys with attention deficit disorder, and 88 normal adolescent boys. *American Journal of Psychiatry, 139,* 795–798.

Sattler, J. M. (1988). *Assessment of children* (3rd ed.). San Diego, CA: Jerome M. Sattler.

Schilder, S. (1931). Organic problems in child guidance. *Mental Hygiene, 15,* 480–486.

Semel, E., Wiig, E. H., Secord, W., & Sabers, D. (1987). *CELF-R: Clinical Evaluation of Language Fundamentals—Revised* (Technical Manual). New York: Psychological Corporation.

Shapiro, S. K., & Garfinkel, B. D. (1985). The Continuous Performance Task (Version 3.1): An operating manual. Minneapolis, MN: Division of Child and Adolescent Psychiatry, University of Minnesota.

Shaywitz, B. A., 7 Shaywitz, S. E. (1991a). Comorbidity: A critical issue in attention deficit disorder. *Journal of Child Neurology, 6*(Supple.), 513–520.

Shaywitz, S. E., Cohen, D. J., 7 Shaywitz, B. E. (1980). Behavior and learning difficulty in children of normal intelligence born to alcoholic mothers. *Journal of Pediatrics, 96,* 978–982.

Shaywitz, S. E., & Shaywitz, B. A. (1991b). Introduction to the special series on attention deficit disorder. *Journal of Learning Disabilities, 24*(2), 68–72.

Shirley, M. (1939). A behavior syndrome characterizing prematurely born children. *Child Development, 10*(2), 115–128.

Simonian, S. J., Tarnowski, K. J., Stancin, T., Friman, P. C., & Atkins, M. S. (1991). Disadvantaged children and families in pediatric primary care settings: II. Screening for behavior disturbance. *Journal of Clinical Child Psychology, 20*(4), 360–371.

Sines, J. O., Clark, W. M., & Lauer, R. M. (1984). Home Environment Questionnaire. *Journal of Abnormal Child Psychology, 12,* 519–529.

Sleator, E. K., & Ullman, R. K. (1981). Can the physician diagnose hyperactivity in the office? *Pediatrics, 67*(1), 13–17.

Sleator, E. K., Ullman, R. K., & von Neumann, A. (1982). How do hyperactive children feel about taking stimulants and will they tell the doctor? *Clinical Pediatrics, 21,* 474–479.

Snyder J. J., & White, M. J. (1979). The use of cognitive self-instructions in the treatment of behaviorally disturbed adolescents. *Behavior Therapy, 10,* 227–235.

Spanier, G. B. (1976). Measuring dyadic adjustment: New scales for assessing the quality of marriage and similar dyads. *Journal of Marriage and Family, 38,* 15–28.

Stewart, M. A., Mendelson, W. B., & Johnson, N. F. (1973). Hyperactive children as adolescents: How they describe themselves. *Child Psychiatry and Human Development, 4,* 3–11.

Still, G. F. (1902). Some abnormal psychical conditions in children. *Lancet, i,* 1008–1012, 1077–1082, 1163–1168.

Strauss, A. A., & Lehtinen, L. E. (1947). *Psychopathology and education of the brain injured child* (Vol. 2). New York: Grune & Stratton.

Strecker, E., & Ebaugh, F. (1924). Neuropsychiatric sequelae of cerebral trauma in children. *Archives of Neurology and Psychiatry, 12,* 443–453.

Streissguth, A. P., Martin, D. C., Barr, H. M., Sandman, B. M., Kirchner, G. L., & Darby, B. L. (1984). Intrauterin alcohol and nicotine exposure: Attention and reaction time in four-year-old children. *Development Psychology, 20,* 533–541.

Stryker, S. (1925). Encephalitis lethargica: The behavior residuals. *Training School Bulletin, 22,* 152–157.

Taylor, H. G. (1983). MBD: Meanings and misconceptions. *Journal of Clinical Neuropsychology, 5*(3), 271–287.

Taylor, H. G. (1988). Learning disabilities. In E. J. Mash & L. G. Terdal (Eds.), *Behavioral assessment of childhood disorders* (2nd ed., pp 402–450). New York: Guilford.

Taylor, H. G. (1989). Learning disabilities. In E. J. Mash & R. Barkley (Eds.), *Behavioral treatment of childhood disorders* (pp. 347–380). New York: Guilford.

Taylor, H. G., Albo, V., Phebus, C., Sachs, B., & Bierl, P. (1987). Postirradiation treatment outcomes for children with acute lymphocytic leukemia: Clarification of risks. *Journal of Pediatric Psychology, 12,* 395–411.

Taylor, H. G., & Fletcher, J. M. (1983). Biological foundations of specific developmental disorders: Methods, findings, and future directions. *Journal of Clinical Child Psychology, 12*(1), 46–65.

Taylor, H. G., & Fletcher, J. M. (1990). Neuropsychological assessment of children. In M. Hersen & G. Goldstein (Eds.), *Handbook of psychological assessment* (pp. 228–255). New York: Plenum.

Taylor, H. G., Schatschneider, C., & Rich, D. (1992). Sequelae of *Haemophilus influenzae* meningitis: Implications for the study of brain disease and development. In M. Tramontana & S. Hooper (Eds.), *Advances in child neuropsychology* (Vol. 1). New York: Springer-Verlqag.

Thorley, G. (1984). Review of follow-up and follow-back studies of childhood hyperactivity. *Psychological Bulletin, 96,* 116–132.

Trommer, B. L., Hoeppner, J. B., Lorber, R., & Armstrong, K. (1988). Pitfalls in the use of a continuous performance test as a diagnostic tool in attention deficit disorder. *Developmental and Behavioral Pediatrics, 9*(5), 339–345.

Ullman, R. K., Sleator, E. K., & Sprague, R. (1984). A new rating scale for diagnosis and monitoring of ADD children. *Psychopharmacology Bulletin, 20,* 160–164.

Ullman, R. K., Sleator, E. K., & Sprague, R. (1988). *ADD-H Comprehensive Teacher Rating Scale.* Champaign, IL: Meritech Inc.

Varley, C. K. (1985). A review of studies of drug treatment efficacy for attention deficit disorder with hyperactivity in adolescents. *Psychopharmacology Bulletin, 21,* 216–221.

Varley, C. K. (1988). Effects of methylphenidate in adolescents with attention deficit disorder. *Journal of the American Academy of Child Psychiatry, 22,* 351–354.

Voeller, K. K. S. (1991). Clinical management of attention deficit hyperactivity disorder. *Journal of Child Neurology, 6*(Suppl.), 551–567.

Wallander, J. L. (1988). The relationship between attention problems in childhood and antisocial behavior eight-year later. *Journal of Child Psychology and Psychiatry, 29,* 53–61.

Webb, T. E., & Van Devre, C. A. (1985). SPPI manual for the Structured Pediatric Psychosocial Interview. Akron, OH: Fourier.

Wechsler, D. (1974). *Wechsler Intelligence Scale for Children—Revised*. New York: The Psychological Corporation.

Weinberg, W. A., & Emslie, G. J. (1991). Attention deficit hyperactivity disorder: The differential diagnosis. *Journal of Child Neurology, 6*(Suppl.), 523–536.

Weiss, G., Hechtman, L., Milroy, T., & Perlman, T. (1985). Psychiatric status of hyperactive as adults: A controlled prospective 15-year follow up of 63 hyperactive children. *Journal of the American Academy of Child Psychiatry, 24*, 211–220.

Weiss, G., Minde, K., Werry, J. S., Douglas, J. I., & Nemeth, E. (1971). Studies on the hyperactive child VIII: Five-year follow up. *Archives of General Psychiatry, 24*, 409–414.

Weithorn, C. J., Kagen, E., & Marcus, M. (1984). The relationship of activity level ratings and cognitive impulsivity to task performance and academic achievement. *Journal of Child Psychology and Psychiatry, 25*, 587–606.

Welner, Z., Welner A., Stewart, M. A., Palkes, A., & Wish, E. (1977). A controlled study of siblings of hyperactive children. *Journal of Nervous and Mental Disease, 165*, 110–117.

Wender, P. H. (1971). *Minimal brain dysfunction in children*. New York: Wiley.

Whalen, C. K., & Henker, B. (Eds.). (1980). *Hyperactive children: The social ecology of identification and treatment*. New York: Academic.

Wilkinson, A. L. (1981). Growth functions in rapid remembering. *Journal of Experimental Child Psychology, 32*, 354–371.

Zametkin, A. J., & Rapaport, J. L. (1987). Neurobiology of attention deficit disorder with hyperactivity: Where have we come in 50 years? *Journal of the American Academy of Child and Adolescent Psychiatry, 26*, 676–686.

# 11
# Antisocial Behavior: Using a Multiple Gating Strategy

*Thomas J. Dishion*
*Gerald R. Patterson*

## Introduction

*Overview*

The term *antisocial* refers to disruptive behavior, aggressiveness, lawbreaking, stealing, lying, and noncompliance. These behaviors tend to come in a "package," whereby children who lie are likely to be disruptive at school as well as aggressive. Although it is possible to define subgroups of Pure Stealers or Fighters, these children represent a small percentage, and the children most at risk are quite versatile in their antisocial repertoire (Loeber & Schmaling, 1985). Children who display antisocial behavior early in their development are likely to become the versatile delinquents in early adolescence, with accumulative arrest records that testify to energetic delinquent offending (Patterson, Crosby, & Vuichinich, 1991). Some studies of delinquency have estimated that these early starting youngsters place disproportionate demands on police, with 5 to 10 percent of such youth composing as much as 50 percent of the arrests (Wolfgang, Figlio & Sellin, 1972). In the beginning stages of the early starting progression, these children might be called oppositional- or behavior-disordered. When they become older, the label changes to conduct-disordered or delinquent. We use the term *antisocial* in a way that loosely maps onto these more specific labels, referring to troubled and troublesome youth who are at high risk for several adjustment problems.

Some forms of adolescent psychopathology (e.g., depression, eating disorders) emerge around adolescence and are relatively difficult to predict from children's adjustment in middle childhood. This is not true for adolescent antisocial behavior. Many adolescents who are seriously engaged in antisocial or delinquent conduct showed similar patterns in the middle childhood years (Olweus, 1979). In fact, early antisocial behavior is quite predictive of adolescent delinquency, at least for males (Loeber & Dishion, 1983; Patterson, Dishion, & Yoeger, 1991).

375

Most clinicians would agree that the multiple problems and lack of parental control in adolescence underlie the lament that "we are getting them too late." Even with the most effective treatment strategies for seriously delinquent youth (e.g., Chamberlain & Reid, 1987), there is a sense that reducing the level of problem behavior will only partly meet the needs of troubled adolescents, and that the correlated difficulties, such as academic and social skill deficits, will continue to compromise the adolescent's adjustment well into adulthood. It is these early starters (Patterson, Reid, & Dishion, in press) who experience tremendous difficulty in normative social contexts, such as in the classroom with peers and, later, in work settings and in marital and parental responsibilities (Caspi & Elder, 1988; Dishion, Loeber, Stouthamer-Loeber, & Patterson, 1984; Patterson, 1982; Robins, 1978). This chapter develops and discusses a cost-effective screening procedure to identify fourth-grade children whose antisocial behavior patterns will persist into adolescence. It is assumed that early screening is the initial step toward intervention with high-risk families, most likely within a public school context.

Early identification is more than prediction technology. Studies over the past twenty years have shown that we can predict, at a group level, with relative accuracy those children who are likely to become delinquent (Loeber & Dishion, 1983, 1987). What has lagged behind is our understanding of the developmental processes explaining why some children start early and persist into adolescence. Assuming that the usefulness of theoretical models of antisocial behavior is reflected in the effectiveness to change the developmental course, then the record is dismal. Most interventions for children with conduct problems are simply ineffective (Kazdin, 1987). Effective primary and secondary preventive interventions are especially dependent on good theory, as theory will provide a guiding light to the optimal target of the interventions.

Both longitudinal studies of children's social development and clinical outcome literature help focus attention on the family as a key social context in the etiology of children antisocial behavior. Interventions that systematically enhance parents' family management practices are the most efficacious in reducing child behavior problems (Kazdin, 1987; Patterson, Chamberlain, & Reid, 1982; Webster-Stratton, 1988). Similarly, reviews of longitudinal studies involving the prediction of adolescent delinquency reveal that chaotic, harsh, lax, and generally poorly managed families best predict later delinquency (Loeber & Dishion, 1983). Thus, two very different research literatures converge on the importance of maladaptive family management practices to children's development of antisocial patterns, patterns that are potentially consistent across settings (the home and school) and stable through time into adulthood.

Research by Patterson (1982, 1986) and colleagues (Patterson, Dishion, & Bank, 1984; Patterson & Bank, 1987; Patterson, Reid, & Dishion, in press) has concentrated on detailing the importance of coercive family processes in children's development of antisocial behavior. We are also working on better understanding the interrelation between maladaptive family socialization practices and other socialization experiences not directly involving the parent (e.g., experiences in school [Walker, Shinn, O'Neill, & Ramsey, 1987] and relations with close friends [Dishion, Andrews, & Patterson, 1990]).

The working model shown in Figure 1 represents a consensus among a group of investigators at the Oregon Social Learning Center (OSLC) who have studied parenting processes related to child antisocial behavior (Chamberlain & Patterson, 1984; Dishion, Patterson, Stoolmiller, & Skinner, 1991; Fagot & Kavanagh, 1988; Patterson & Forgatch, 1987; Patterson & Bank, 1987; Patterson & Reid, 1984; Patterson et al., in press; Reid, 1986). We use the term *working* to describe the model, because the key hypotheses are subject to revision depending on new information. In our earlier research on adolescent delinquency (Patterson & Dishion, 1985), we incorporated the concept of the deviant peer group into our family management model based on the research findings reported by sociological investigators such as Delbert Elliott (Elliott, Huizinga, & Ageton, 1985). This led us to examine the interrelation between family and peer processes that may lead to an adolescent's being exposed and vulnerable to the influence of deviant peers.

Figure 1 reveals that the model is family-based and places parenting practices as central in the process of children's becoming persistently troublesome. Family management practices (discipline, monitoring, positive reinforcement, parent involvement, problem solving, and parent modeling) have been identified primarily on the basis of twenty years of clinical experience using the parent training model with conduct-problem children (Patterson, 1982; Patterson et al., in press). The relation between parenting practices and future problem behavior is well established. In a review of longitudinal research reporting the prediction of male delinquency, it was found that disorganized, chaotic, and lax supervision were found to be among the best predictors, even when compared with earlier behavior problems (Loeber & Dishion, 1983).

Our recent work with the Oregon Youth Study (OYS) also shows a direct and strong association between family management practices and antisocial child behavior (Loeber & Dishion, 1984; Patterson, 1986; Patterson & Bank, 1987; Patterson & Forgatch, 1987; Patterson & Stouthamer-Loeber, 1984; Patterson et al., in press), adolescent delinquency (Patterson, Capaldi, & Bank, 1989; Patterson & Dishion, 1985), and drug use (Dishion, Reid, & Patterson 1988; Dishion & Loeber, 1985). In developing a model for child antisocial behavior, we relied on intensive measurement of parenting processes, including home observations, daily telephone interviews, and detailed structured interviews with both the child and the parent. The cost of such measurement, however, is often prohibitive in applied settings, and es-

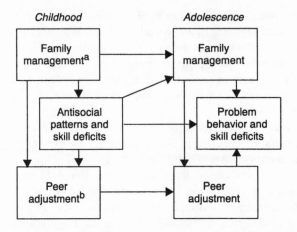

a Family management summarizes several key parenting practices including discipline, monitoring, positive reinforcement, involvement with the child, and problem solving.

b Peer adjustment includes rejection by the conventional peer group and association with antisocial peers.

**Figure 1. Overview of Coercion Model Applied to Screening for Risk of Adolescent Antisocial Behavior**

pecially in developing screening procedures for large populations of school-children.

The coercion model shows promise in explaining several features of chronic antisocial behavior. First, the process is unintentional and largely takes place outside the awareness of the child and parent. Moment-by-moment interchanges between the child and parent are gradually shaped over time based on immediate consequences. The development of maladaptive parenting can sometimes be insidious, whereby disruptions in family structure or context (e.g., divorce, unemployment) can initiate or exacerbate maladaptive interaction patterns.

Second, when children are provided with multiple opportunities to escape demands to cooperate with adults in the family, they are likely to be particularly troublesome to adults in other settings (in particular, schools). This is especially true for children whose parents have been violent and abusive. In adapting to the abusive parenting, these children may resort to violent social tactics when professionals make demands that resemble the abusive interchanges within the family. These tactics can be especially difficult to manage for most middle-class professionals operating in institutions such as schools, where contingencies are loose and violence relatively rare.

Third, the antisocial child is an unhappy and unskilled child. He or she experiences failure in most conventional settings, and these failures lead to depressed mood and low self-esteem (Patterson & Stoolmiller, 1991).

Fourth, the child who displays problem behaviors both at home and in school is a sure sign of more severe family disruption, arrested skill development (Loeber & Dishion, 1984), delinquent behavior, and early substance use (Robins & Przybeck, 1985). Figure 1 suggests that the child's early manifestation of antisocial patterns is both directly and indirectly related to later problem behavior. Early antisocial behavior is indirectly related to later delinquency by disrupting the parents' child-rearing practices and by peer rejection, as well as involvement in a deviant peer group. In this respect, the early antisocial behavior of the child is causally surely not the most important, but, rather, the clearest signal of past and future disrupted socialization. Measuring antisocial behavior in childhood is therefore a critical feature of any screening procedure.

## Screening Terminology

Screening procedures are one component of an overall prevention strategy. We must identify measures that are theoretically guided, inexpensive, available, normatively based, and predictively effective.

The critical issue is determining prediction effectiveness. The prediction literature is full of spectacular statements, such as that 80 percent of those identified went on to commit serious offenses, without giving due consideration to accompanying prediction errors (e.g., those youngsters who were not identified as being at risk but who committed serious offenses [i.e., false negatives]). The point is that, when evaluating screening effectiveness, the full range of resulting prediction outcomes needs consideration. A standard terminology is required that describes screening predictions and their outcomes. We follow the language described by Wiggins (1973), based on the personality assessment and personnel selection tradition within clinical psychology: "valid positives" refer to correctly identifying children at risk, "false positives" refer to incorrectly identifying children at risk, "false negatives" describe children who are considered not at risk but who later develop a problem, and "valid negatives" are those who were accurately predicted not to be at risk.

In previous research, an index was developed (Goldberg, cited in Loeber & Dishion, 1983) called Relative Improvement over Chance (RIOC). The RIOC provides an overall summary of the predictive efficiency of an early identification strategy. The RIOC index is expressed as a percentage, ranging from 0 percent (no improvement over chance) to 100 percent (perfect possible prediction). The advantage of the RIOC index is that it allows research consumers to compare the predictive efficiency of different screening strategies that use disparate selection ratios (proportion of population defined as being at risk) and base rates (proportion of individuals with adjustment problems). The RIOC provides a standard rule to compare results of various screening strategies. For more details on the computation of RIOC and the issues underlying the evaluation of predictive efficiency in screening, see Appendix A in this chapter.

In previous research on the development of cost-effective screening procedures for adolescent delinquency, we described what was called a "multiple gating" screening procedure (Loeber & Dishion, 1987; Loeber, Dishion, & Patterson, 1984). The concept is based on personnel selection procedures referred to as multistage assessments (Cronbach & Glaser, 1965). The idea is to identify a set of screening measures with established predictive validity, with each measure adding uniquely to predict children at risk. The measures are then administered sequentially. The least expensive measure is first given to an entire population, for example, a fourth-grade class in a public school setting. Only those individuals defined as at risk are then given the second most expensive measure, to further identify children at risk. In our earlier work on multiple gating (Loeber & Dishion, 1987; Loeber, Dishion, & Patterson, 1984), we used teacher ratings as the first gate, parent telephone report as the second gate, and an assessment of family management as the third gate, Note that only a minority of the original sample was administered the more expensive and intensive assessment of family management. Therefore, a relatively thorough screening battery can be used in a cost-effective fashion to identify a high-risk sample. The inclusion of expensive screening measures is justified only if it adds to the overall accuracy of prediction (i.e., the RIOC gets higher); otherwise we might simply use a relatively inexpensive measure to define a risk sample.

Our earlier research on the multiple gating procedure was based on a planning sample for the Oregon Youth Study (OYS) and combined concurrent arrests with those acquired up to two years after the assessment as outcome criteria. Further, children included in those studies were as old as twelve years at the time of assessment and therefore could not be considered as being identified early.

## Summary

In this chapter, we test our earlier ideas on the multiple gating approach to screening high-risk boys. We used data from 206 boys and their families, constituting the OYS sample (Capaldi & Patterson, 1987; Patterson, 1986; Patterson, Reid, & Dishion, in press). As of this writing, these boys have been followed to age sixteen; data were collected on the boys' contacts with the police and their involvement in adolescent problem behavior. We present data on the boys' tobacco use in an effort to establish the relevance of these early identification procedures for multiple adjustment outcomes. The chapter will end with a data-based recommendation for screening boys at risk for adolescent delinquency. These findings apply only to boys; the research procedure would need to be repeated using a female sample to identify girls at risk for delinquency and antisocial behavior in adolescence.

## The Oregon Youth Study

### The Sample and Procedures

The Oregon Youth Study (OYS) is a longitudinal study of boys in high-risk neighborhoods. The study focuses on the role of family management practices, family contextual variables, and peer influences in the development of antisocial behavior, chronic delinquency, drug (ab)use, and depression (Patterson et al., in press). The OYS sample comprises two cohorts of 102 and 104 boys and their families, recruited, respectively, in 1983–84 and 1984–85. The study was conducted in a Northwest community with a population of 150,000. Three school districts in the area participated in the research project.

Boys and their families were recruited from the schools. Ten elementary schools with the highest density of neighborhood delinquency (i.e., arrest records within school districts) were selected from the forty-three public elementary schools within the study community. The sampling order was randomly selected among ten schools for each cohort. Families were considered ineligible for the study if they had plans to move from the area during the initial assessment period or if a foreign language was the primary language. Thirteen percent and seven percent of cohorts 1 and 2, respectively, were considered ineligible for one of these two reasons.

Of all families eligible to participate in the OYS, 74.4 percent agreed to participate (Capaldi & Patterson, 1987). Capaldi and Patterson (1987) compared the participant boys with the refusers and found that there were no reliable differences between the boys on the primary clinical scales of the teacher version of the Child Behavior Checklist (Achenbach & Edelbrock, 1986). When compared with national norms (Patterson et al., in press), families in both cohorts were found to be of lower socioeconomic status and to have a somewhat higher percentage of unemployed parents than would be expected. Both Cohorts were predominantly white (99%).

### Measurement Strategy

Every other year, the boys and their families in the OYS were assessed on a full range of independent and dependent variables. To accomplish this, families were observed in the home (Dishion, Garner, Patterson, Reid, & Thibodeaux, 1983) and were interviewed, school data were collected (school records, teacher ratings), telephone interviews were conducted, and a family problem-solving task (Forgatch, Fetrow, & Lathrop, 1985) was videotaped.

The entire battery took approximately twenty hours for two-parent families to complete.

Consistent with the ideas of Campbell and Fiske (1959) and Cronbach and Meehl (1955), each construct in the model was operationally defined by multiple measures, as well as multiple reporting agents. An intensive discussion of the measurement model and basic findings for the first wave of the OYS are described in detail in *Antisocial Boys* (Patterson et al., in press).

Because this handbook is intended as an applied discussion of early identification, an effort was made to develop a screening battery based on published measures with established scoring procedures and normative data. The Child Behavior Checklist (CBCL) was administered to the parent (Achenbach & Edelbrock, 1983) and to the teacher (Achenbach & Edelbrock, 1986). Two scale scorers were used for predicting later delinquent behavior. For the parent, the Delinquency Scale (six- to eleven-year-old boys) was used; the items for this measure are listed in Table 1. Also listed in Table 1 are the items from the teacher CBCL, formulating the Aggression Scale. The scoring for these scales is available in published reports.

In addition to the reports of the parent and teacher, family management

**Table 1.**
**Items for the Teacher and Parent CBCL Scales Used for Screening.**

| *Teacher CBCL (Aggression Scale)* | |
|---|---|
| Argues | Talks out of turn |
| Defiant | Attacks people |
| Bragging | Disrupts class |
| Fidgets | Screams |
| Cruelty | Acts irresponsibly |
| Demands attention | Shows off |
| Destroys own things | Explosive |
| Destroys others' things | Easily frustrated |
| Disobedient at school | Steals |
| Disturbs others | Stubborn |
| Poor peer relations | Moody |
| Lacks guilt | Sulks |
| Jealous | Suspicious |
| Feels persecuted | Swearing |
| Fights | Talks too much |
| Bad friends | Teases |
| Impulsive | Temper tantrums |
| Lying, cheating | Threatens |
| Not liked | Loud |

| *Parent CBCL (Delinquency Scale)* | |
|---|---|
| Destroys own things | Sets fires |
| Destroys others' things | Steals at home |
| Disobeys at school | Steals outside home |
| Bad friends | Swearing |
| Lies, cheats | Truant |
| Runs away | Vandalism |

practices were considered for their predictive efficiency. Following earlier research on the multiple gating procedure (Loeber & Schmaling, 1985), we included three measures of family functioning: family structure, parent discipline, and parent monitoring. These were considered candidates for the third gate of the multiple gating procedures, since they were by far the most expensive measures to collect, and therefore should be applied to the smallest-risk population. The brief interview assessment of family structure, as well as the constructs of parent discipline and parent monitoring, is described below; Capaldi and Patterson (1987) provide more details on the scoring of the parent discipline and parent monitoring measures for the interested reader. Also described below are measures of antisocial behavior and police contacts obtained during adolescence.

## Family Structure at Ages Nine to Ten

The least expensive measure available on family adjustment was a brief interview with questions about the number of transitions the family had experienced since the study boy's birth. These were coded 0 if the boy was currently residing with both biological or adoptive parents, and 1 if there had been at least one divorce or other marital transition (e.g., never married to married), and for single-parent, never-married parents. A score of 0 reflects a low-risk family context; a score of 1, a higher-risk family context.

## Parent Discipline at Ages Nine to Ten

All families in the study were observed in the home on three occasions, using a structured home observation format developed for clinical evaluation of parent training (Reid, 1987). The measure of parent discipline was based on scores describing a parent's behavior toward the child during these sessions. Four scores were combined to describe harsh, erratic, and noncontingent discipline practices. These were called "parent nattering," the "abuse cluster," "observer impressions" on the parent's discipline skill, and the parent's report of "harsh discipline practices," in a structured interview. The reader may note that this construct score would be difficult, at best, to use in an applied setting to screen at-risk youngsters. It is thought, however, that consideration of this variable would provide a basis for evaluating the potential of observations of parent-child interaction for predictive screening.

## Parent Monitoring at Ages Nine to Ten

This score assessed the parents' supervision of the child in relation to establishing clear guidelines of conduct and monitoring his daily activities. The construct score was based on the following:

1. The parent and child interview's global ratings on the extent to which the child was well supervised by parents. One item was included on each Interviewer Impression Inventory: "How well is this child monitored?"
2. The child's report of house rules in the structured interview at the research center. The six items in this scale reflect the child's perception of his parents' rules concerning telling parents when he would be home, leaving a note about where he was going, checking in after school, whether there was someone home after school, knowing how to reach parents when they were out, and talking to parents about daily plans.
3. In the parent telephone interview, the primary caretaker—usually the mother—was asked about the number of hours she had spent with her son in the previous twenty-four hours. Her response to this question was aggregated over six telephone calls.

### Child Antisocial Behaviors at Ages Thirteen to Fourteen

A construct score was formulated to represent the boy's antisocial behavior across settings in early adolescence. This score followed the guidelines of the Antisocial construct score reported by Capaldi and Patterson (1987), a measure that combined the reports of teachers, the parents, and the child across questionnaires and in telephone interviews.

### Police Contact at Ages Fifteen to Sixteen

Six years after the original recruitment and assessment, data were collected on the extent of the boy's police contact for criminal offenses, in addition to the typical assessment of interviews, videotaped interactional tasks, and school data. To date, we have follow-up data on all of the original cohort for police contact, and 98 percent of the boys were followed up to obtain their reports of substance use at ages fifteen to sixteen and of delinquent behavior.

## Battery Development and Results

The initial step in finding the best set of measures for high-risk screening was to look at how well the measures, collected when the boys were ages nine to ten, predicted antisocial behavior when the boys were ages fourteen to sixteen. Those measures which did not correlate with antisocial behavior were immediately rejected. Those which did correlate were compared with one another to determine which predictors were the most powerful, controlling statistically for the power of all other viable screening measures. In this way, we selected the optimal screening battery based on empirical data. Incidentally, empirically developed screening procedures such as the one reported in this chapter have been repeatedly shown to be superior to astute predictions of the best-trained clinicians (Meehl, 1954).

Table 2 shows the correlations between (a) the measures of the boys' adaptation at home and at school, together with family management practices, at ages nine to ten and (b) measures of their antisocial behavior at fourteen. We also computed correlations between screening scores and the boys' arrest status at ages fifteen to sixteen. Inspection of Table 2 reveals that teacher and parents CBCL reports were highly correlated with later antisocial behavior and police contact at a level that was statistically significant and extremely high for a sample of 206. Poor parent discipline practices with the boys at ages nine to ten correlated reliably with their adolescent antisocial behavior, in terms of both the composite score and official records of arrests. Parent discipline is an expensive measure, consisting of three home observations. In this respect, it is interesting that the one question on the families' marital history (i.e., family structure) correlated with adolescent antisocial behavior at a level equal to the expensive parent discipline measure. Capaldi and Patterson (1989) have reported that the number of marital/structural changes the OYS families experienced was associated with lower family management skills and poor child adjustment.

Based on the correlations shown in Table 2, it is difficult to judge which measures to select for a multistage screening procedure. In developing a multiple gating strategy, it is critical that the subset of screening measures selected account for a maximum amount of variance in later antisocial behavior. Multivariate data analyses were necessary to address this question. In Appendix B of this chapter, the results of the multiple regressions (antisocial behavior composite as dependent variable) and logistic regressions (arrests as dependent variable) are provided, showing the predictive power of each viable screening measure in the context of all other possible screening measures. Based on the correlational results, the following measures were

**Table 2.**
**Correlations between Screening Measures Assessed at Ages 9 to 10 and Antisocial Behavior at Ages 13 to 14 and Delinquency at Ages 15 to 16.**

| Measures Assessed at Ages 9 to 10 | Antisocial Behavior at ages 13 to 14 | At Least Two Police Contacts at Ages 15 to 16 |
|---|---|---|
| Teacher CBCL Aggression Scale | .55** | .39** |
| Parent CBCL Delinquency Scale | .59** | .30** |
| Parent discipline | −.39** | −.24** |
| Parent monitoring | −.19** | −.12 |
| Family structure | .23** | .22** |

*p < .05
**P < .01

used to predict adolescent antisocial behavior and police contact: parent discipline, family structure, Parent CBCL Delinquency Scale, and Teacher CBCL Aggression Scale. In summary (see Appendix B for specific findings), we found that the more expensive measure of parent discipline did not add predictive power to the teacher or parent ratings of problem behavior when considering the boys' general antisocial behavior score or their record of arrests. The inexpensive family structure score, however, did reliably contribute to the statistical prediction of adolescent antisocial behavior.

Based on these multivariate analyses, we tested a three-gate screening strategy for predictive efficiency, examining the incremental efficiency achieved by adding each gate sequentially, beginning with teacher ratings in the school, followed by parent ratings, and then a brief interview on family structure. We used the dichotomous outcome of police contact as the dependent variable (1 = at least two police contacts: 0 = one or no contacts. The results of these analyses are provided in Table 3. Teacher ratings on the CBCL Aggression Scale served as an excellent first-stage screening measure. Selecting those boys who had a t-score over 65 on the teacher Aggression Scale predicted those boys with police contact by ages fifteen to sixteen, producing a RIOC score of 41 percent, comparing well with other longitudinal studies predicting male adolescent delinquency from elementary school teacher ratings. This finding is consistent with the idea that schools are an important social field within which a boy's adaptation is critical for long-term adjustment (Kellam, 1990). The addition of the parent CBCL to the teacher CBCL ratings improved prediction of those boys most likely to be arrested at least twice in adolescence, yielding a RIOC of 43 percent. Adding the family structure variable as a third screening gate did not improve predictions of those adolescents to be picked up by the police at least twice (RIOC = 35%).

By following this procedure for the OYS boys, the prediction results shown in Figure 2 were obtained. Out of the 64 boys defined as being at risk, 29 were picked up by the police at least twice by ages fifteen to sixteen (45.3%). This is a high density of accurate predictions in the risk cell, espe-

Table 3.
Predictive Efficiency of One-, Two-, and
Three-Stage Screening Strategies (N = 206).

|  |  | RIOC |
|---|---|---|
| Stage 1 | Teacher CBCL Aggression Scale | 34.8% |
| Stage 2 | 1. Teacher CBCL Aggression Scale<br>2. Parent CBCL Delinquency Sale | 42.6% |
| Stage 3 | 1. Teacher CBCL Aggression Scale<br>2. Parent CBCL Delinquency Scale<br>3. Family structure | 35.3% |

cially considering that all predicted cases were early starters—a group of boys whose long-term prognosis for both continuity and rate of offending is extremely dim (Loeber & LeBlanc, in press). Of the 48 boys who acquired police contact, 29 were correctly predicted and 17 missed (i.e., false negative errors). Therefore, 60.4 percent of the future antisocial adolescents were accurately acquired into a risk sample by using parent and teacher ratings alone. In general, the predictive efficiency of the two-gate procedure compared favorably with that of the three-gate procedure described by Loeber and Schmaling (1985), despite the short prediction interval of the latter study. It is also worth noting that 8 of the 17 youths who eventually became violent, repeat offenders were entered in the risk sample, which represented 47 percent of this serious population, a considerable improvement over the base rate (8%) of violent offenders in the sample.

### Self-Reported Problem Behavior

Within the framework of problem behavior theory (Jessor & Jessor, 1977), one might expect that the "early starters" predicted by the two-stage screening procedure were engaging in more serious levels of substance use by ages fifteen to sixteen (see Figure 2). As with antisocial behavior, early onset substance use is a risk factor for later substance abuse (Robins & Pryzabeck, 1985), especially when initiated prior to age fifteen (Anthony & Petronis, in press). Consistent with problem behavior theory (Jessor & Jessor, 1977), screening for adolescent antisocial behavior captured 50 percent of the boys who became daily smokers, 48.5 percent of the boys who became heavy drinkers, and 51.4 percent of the boys who became marijuana smokers, compared with the base rate figure of 19, 16, and 17 percent, respectively.

Looking at the boys' self-reported involvement in major index offenses at ages fifteen to sixteen, the identified risk group reported an average of 1.67 offenses per year, whereas the nonrisk group reported an average of .66. A difference in reported serious criminal activity was statistically reliable ($F$ [1,200] = 6.10, $p < .01$).

## Conclusions and Future Directions

### Summary

The analyses of the OYS boys supported the validity of a two-stage screening procedure for identifying boys at risk for adolescent antisocial behavior. Consistent with earlier work on multiple gating procedures (Loeber & Dishion, 1987; Loeber, Dishion, & Patterson, 1984), the combination of parent and teacher ratings seems to be one screening strategy that is both cost-effective and predictively efficient, predicting adjustment at ages nine to ten

| Age 9–10 | 2 or more police contacts | 1 or fewer police contacts | Number and percent of group substance abuse by age 15–16 | | |
|---|---|---|---|---|---|
| | | | Daily smokers | Heavy drinkers | Marijuana use |
| At-risk | 29 | 35 | 20 (50%) | 16 (48.5%) | 18 (51.4%) |
| Not-at-risk | 19 | 123 | 20 (50%) | 17 (51.5%) | 17 (48.6%) |
| | 48 | 158 | 206 | | |

Parent CBCL–Delinquency Scale (T>, 60) and Teacher CBCL–Aggression Scale (T255).
Improvement Over Chance = 12.1%; RIOC = 42.6%
V = Number of violent, repeat offenders

**Figure 2. Two-Stage Screening Procedure for Early Adolescent Antisocial Behavior**

to antisocial behavior at ages thirteen to fourteen, a five-year prediction interval. Although family management constructs correlated highly with concurrent (Patterson & Bank, 1986) and later child antisocial behavior, these construct scores did not have predictive power over the less costly teacher and parent ratings. It is clear that prediction and explanation are two distinct research aims, and the measures that provide the best predictive validity do not necessarily help explain the development of the antisocial pattern. In this sense, these findings are consistent with a family-based model that sees the development of antisocial behavior patterns as originating within the family and, under the same conditions, persisting over time. These data do support the importance of evaluating the cross-setting (e.g., home and school) characteristics of child antisocial behavior.

The combination of the parent and teacher ratings of boys' early antisocial behavior appears to be the least expensive and most predictively efficient screening strategy for identifying boys who initiate offending by early adolescence. It is clear, however, that the use of teacher ratings alone is nearly equal to combining teachers' and parents' reports. In a two-state screening procedure, boys were identified initially by teachers as one-half standard deviation above the national mean on aggressive behavior (t > 55%). This subsample of boys was then administered the parent CBCL, and those boys 1 standard deviation above the mean (t = 60 or above) on the Delinquency subscale were retained as high-risk boys. The parent and teacher cutting scores could vary according to the resources available and the school population being served. Higher cutting scores would yield a clinically more difficult but smaller risk group; lower cutting scores would provide a larger intervention sample, with some mild cases.

## Early Screening and Intervention

In this section, we will discuss the practical application of these findings. We assume the real world of a public school with limited resources but an interest in preventing more serious delinquent behavior in adolescence. Schools typically screen young children in kindergarten and first grade for learning or language difficulties that might interfere with their potential to profit from the mainstream classroom environment. With the passage of Public Law 91-942, it became necessary for schools to supply the additional resources for any child defined as handicapped. For reading, learning, or language disabilities, this process is formalized, and assessment strategies developed with norms that provide some guidance for the decision-making process. "Child antisocial behavior," or "behavior disorders," are typically defined in the context of the school, based on the professional judgment of staff psychologists, usually by a professional team. The data analyzed in this chapter suggest that the decision-making process can be very systematic and data-based. By combining teachers' and parents' ratings of children's current behavior, a risk group that will probably escalate their antisocial behavior and eventually come to the attention of the community police can be defined.

We suggest, at this point, that it is feasible for schools and parents to take a more active, voluntary approach to reducing the level of antisocial conduct in the schools. Figure 3 outlines the sequential procedures that might be followed in screening and early intervention. The dental model of health care may be the most appropriate (Dishion, Reid & Patterson, 1988). In this framework, the community views the development of antisocial behavior as a virtual risk process, as is the development of tooth decay. Periodic, behaviorally descriptive assessments of children's antisocial behavior might serve as the signpost for intervention. Once risk status is identified, parents and teachers can collaborate to form an intervention team to reduce these youngsters' antisocial behavior and promote their education.

To ensure maximizing the likelihood of parent engagement, a range of options can be provided, including (a) videotapes of parents of child management (Webster-Stratton, Kolpacoff, & Hollinsworth, 1988), (b) parenting groups (Webster-Stratton, 1984), (c) home/school notes (Blechman, Taylor, & Schrader, 1981), and (d) individualized parent training (Patterson, Chamberlain, & Reid, 1984). Special consultation services to teachers

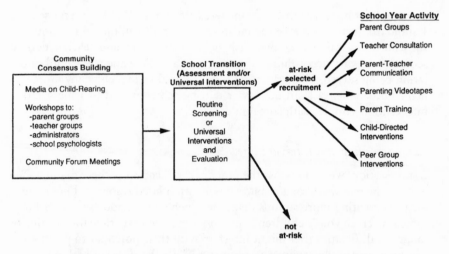

Figure 3. Early Screening and Intervention Scenario

regarding child management or parent-teacher communication skills might be offered as well.

Such a scenario assumes cooperation from parents. Many school professionals feel this cooperation is difficult to achieve at best. We have recently had a different experience, however, at the Oregon Social Learning Center (OSLC). In the past year, we have worked in middle schools identifying young teenagers at risk for problem behavior and substance abuse. At the end of the sixth grade, teachers were asked to simply check off the names of those students they deemed to be at risk on a number of factors (e.g., antisocial behavior, academic skills, and emotional adjustment). Prior to the risk assessment, parents were given the opportunity to refuse participation with a negative consent procedure. At this juncture, only 10 percent of all parents of the sixth-grade youngsters preferred that their child not be assessed by teachers. In the fall of the seventh grade, parents of youngsters identified as being at risk were contacted by OSLC staff to participate in a twelve-week intervention—called the Adolescent Transitions Program—involving joint parent and teen groups. Parents had to be willing to make this time commitment; for two-parent families, both parents had to agree to their involvement. Sixty percent of the parents of children at-risk agreed. As one might expect, at least some of the parents refusing participation were seen by school personnel as having children who were highly at risk. It might be noted that the OSLC staff responsible for the recruitment of families thought a major barrier to recruitment was the parents' lack of name recognition of the Adolescent Transitions Program. Had the schools built the program up in communication with parents, the likelihood of recruitment might well have increased.

For this reason, we suggest broad-based community interventions to precede the screening and early intervention program, maximizing cooperation and involvement of school personnel, parents, and the community. Viewing early intervention as a community intervention opens the possibilities of addressing some contextual issues perpetuating poor child-rearing practices (Biglan, Glasgow, & Singer, in press). Community interventions can be systematic, while incorporating the various resources of any given school community, such as media, natural resources, and participant ownership of the early intervention program (Kelly, 1989).

Screening interventions could also be a routine component of a primary prevention program. Individuals not responding to primary prevention and deemed being at risk could be identified for a selected intervention, analogous to secondary prevention. In this sense, screenings and interventions would be practically and theoretically linked. Primary prevention interventions (e.g., the "Good Behavior Game," Kellam, 1990) in school settings could rely on measures of school antisocial behavior as outcome variables. Children unresponsive to such interventions could be targeted for a second-stage intervention and assessment, this one targeting the child's adaptation in the home and relying on home-based measures (e.g., parent report) as outcome/screening measures.

At some future point, research might identify other social contexts that maintain, exacerbate, or cause antisocial behavior problems in children and therefore require innovative thinking to develop interventions that enhance the socialization of at-risk children. Recent studies by peer relations researchers (Asher & Coie, 1990; Dishion, 1990; Hartup, 1983; Parker & Asher, 1987) indicate that the peer context of antisocial behavior may be an important component for any model of antisocial behavior in adolescence and possibly a context in which to target intervention research. Using the OYS boys, we looked at the combined effectiveness of teacher ratings on the Aggression Scale and peer nominations of "social preference" and "deviant peers" ("kids who hang around with tough peers") at ages nine to ten. Combining the teacher report and the peer nomination into a two-gate screening measure provided very good predictive efficiency, producing a RIOC of 47 percent, very near to that provided by the combination of parent and teacher ratings of antisocial behavior. Studies focusing on which key aspects of children's experience with peers especially undermine children's adjustment and predict later adjustment problems will guide us in incorporating peer experiences within a multiple gating strategy.

## Limits of Prediction

It is tempting to wish for screening measures that predict with perfect accuracy who, five to ten years later, will fit a particular diagnostic category. We suspect, however, that social development does not allow for such accurate predictions, since the very socialization contexts (e.g., family, school, neighborhoods) themselves are in a state of perpetual flux. Perhaps the best we can hope for is the identification of an extreme subgroup of children who may share the misfortune of extremely pathogenic environments. There are significant numbers of children who may develop maladaptive trajectories at several stages of development from childhood to adolescence. The duration of maladaptive behavior may be shorter for these children but nonetheless associated with negative consequences to the child. To meet the needs of these youngsters, as well as those of youngsters with chronic behaviors, we could begin thinking about more circumscribed predictions that center on both major (elementary to middle school to high school) and minor academic transitions—for example, predicting from kindergarten data who will experience adjustment problems in first grade. The more specifically we target our models, screening, and intervention procedures, the clearer our successes and the reasons for our failures will be.

Behavioral science must move further away from a disease model for some adjustment problems; an alternative model might be the dental model (Dishion, Reid, & Patterson, 1988). In such a model, the probability of children and adolescents being at risk is fluid, potentially changing from year to year. Within this framework assessments of risk might be incorporated into cultural practices defining socialization. Professionals and parents might establish as routine the collection of objective measures of children's behavioral adaptation at school. Assessments of the child's behavior by parents might also be considered standard diagnostic information that assists in formulating an educational plan and an environment that best meets the needs of the child and the family. Certainly, if measures of academic performance are standard cultural practices, then at some point professionals might collaborate with parents to prioritize other types of information to be shared by adults concerned with the welfare of children.

## Appendix A: Computation of RIOC

Figure 4 is provided as a hypothetical example of a screening procedure for adolescent delinquency and antisocial behavior.

Two types of correct predictions (See Figure 4) can result from a screening prediction: valid positives and valid negatives. The former refers to those youngsters who are defined as being at risk and who in fact develop problems; the latter refers to those youngsters who are defined as not being at risk and who in fact do not develop problems. The two types of prediction errors are false positives and false negatives; the former describes those youngsters who are predicted to have future problems but who do not, and the latter describes incorrect predictions about the nonrisk group. The percentage of each prediction outcome is computed by dividing the number of persons in each outcome by the total $N$ in the prediction sample. In the hypothetical

Based on early
screening
cutoff score

Actual outcome
in adolescence

| Based on early screening cutoff score | Delinquent | Nondelinquent | |
|---|---|---|---|
| At-risk | Valid positives<br><br>30<br>(30%) | False positives<br><br>0 | 30 |
| Not-at-risk | False negatives<br><br>0 | Valid negatives<br><br>70<br>(70%) | 70 |
| | 30 | 70 | N=100 |

Percent correct = 70%
Percent chance correct=58%
Percent improvement over chance=12%

**Figure 4. Hypothetical Early Screening Procedure, Outcome, and Terminology**

example considered in Figure 5, there was a 15 percent rate of valid positives, false positives, and false negatives, and a 55 percent rate of valid negatives. One can easily compute the total percentage correct by summing the percentage of valid positives and negatives, which in the hypothetical example is 70 percent (15% + 55%). This can be compared with the percentage correct one could expect by simple chance, assuming no relation between the screening measure and the outcome, and knowing the selection ratio and base rate, which is 58 percent in the hypothetical example. Percentage improvement over chance (Wiggins, 1973), then, is derived by subtracting percentage chance correct from the total percentage correct, yielding 12 percent in the example shown in Figure 4. Thus, we can be sure that our screening procedure was at least better than chance in predicting those who would be delinquent in adolescence. The question remains, however, as to just how well this screening procedure, compared with other possible strategies, works.

The number of children defined as being at risk (i.e., selection ratio ) is commonly smaller than the nonrisk sample, primarily because the implicit goal of screening is to define a subgroup of individuals who might especially benefit from secondary prevention. Often the selection ratio is matched with the projected base rate of the problem to be prevented, in this case, contact with police for a delinquent offense.

**Actual outcome in Adolescence**

| Based on early screening cutoff score | Delinquent | Nondelinquent | |
|---|---|---|---|
| At-risk (positives) | Valid positives 15 (15%) | False positives 15 (15%) | 30 |
| Not-at-risk (negatives) | False negatives 15 (15%) | Valid negatives 55 (55%) | 70 |
| | 30 | 70 | N=100 |

(MC) Maximum percent correct = 100%
(RC) Percent chance correct = 58%
(MC–RC) Maximum percent improvement over chance = 42%
RIOC = 29%

**Figure 5. Maximum Possible Correct of a Hypothetical Screening Procedure**

Interpretation of the prediction outcomes are somewhat more complicated, although nonetheless important. The match or mismatch between the selection ratios and base rates has an impact on the prediction outcome. If one were to select very few children as being at risk (i.e., small selection ratio), then there would naturally be fewer false positive errors, at the expense of more false negatives. Moreover, it is nearly impossible to evaluate two different prediction strategies in two different studies, because of disparate selection ratio/base rate matches. For this reason, the Relative Improvement over Chance (RIOC) index was developed by L. Goldberg (cited in Loeber & Dishion, 1983). The RIOC provides a standard index for evaluating screening predictions across studies using different measures, predictors, study samples, developmental time spans, dependent variables, and selection ratio/base rate matches.

The RIOC index compares the improvement over chance index with yet one more consideration, the maximum possible correct, given the selection ratio/base rate match. In the example shown in Figure 5, the selection ratio and base rate are identical, and therefore the best possible prediction is 100 percent, 42 percent better than the chance prediction. The maximum percentage correct assumes a perfect correlation between the screening procedure and the predicted outcome, an unlikely state of affairs. As shown in the bottom of Figure 5, the RIOC can be computed by all the information available when it represents where in the interval between the chance correct and the maximum correct the empirical truth lies for this hypothetical example, which is 29 percent (see Figure 5). Compared with other studies where RIOC was computed, this is a moderately low level of predictive accuracy (Loeber & Dishion, 1983; Loeber, Green, & Stouthamer-Loeber, 1989). Criminologists interested in the statistical characteristics of RIOC have looked extensively at the relation between RIOC and other categorical measures of association (Farrington & Loeber, 1988), and its distributional qualities (Copas & Loeber, 1988).

## Appendix B: Multivariate Analyses of Possible Screening Measures on Antisocial Behavior and Police Contact

| Age 9 to 10 | Multiple Regression Model (Antisocial Construct Ages 13 to 14) | Logit Model (Police Contact at Least Two Arrests Ages 15 to 16) |
|---|---|---|
| | Beta Coefficients | Logit Coefficients/ Stardard Error |
| Parent discipline | -.09 | -1.35 |
| Family structure | .11* | 2.46 |
| Parent CBCL Delinquency Scale | .41* | 2.00 |
| Teacher CBCL Aggression Scale | .33* | 3.27 |
| | $F (4,196 = 45.9^{***} R^2 = .48$ | $X^2 (201) = 199, p = .53$ |

## Author Notes

This chapter is based on data collected in Oregon Youth Study, funded by a grant from the National Institute of Mental Health to Gerald R. Patterson (MH 37940). The writing of this chapter was supported by the above grant, as well as by a grant from the National Institute on Drug Abuse to Thomas J. Dishion (DA07031). Carol Kimball is gratefully acknowledged for her efforts in preparing this report, as is Mary Perry for her editorial assistance.

## References

Achenbach, T. M., & Edelbrock, C. (1983). *Manual for the Child Behavior Checklist and revised Child Behavior Profile*. Burlington, VT: University of Vermont Press.

Achenbach, T. M., & Edelbrock, C. (1986). *Manual for the teacher's report form and teacher version of the Child Behavior Profile*. Burlington, VT: University of Vermont Press.

Anthony, J. C., & Petronis, K. R. (in press). Early-onset drug use and later drug problems. *American Journal of Public Health*.

Asher, S. R., & Coie, J. D. (Eds.). (1990). Peer rejection in childhood. Cambridge, MA: Cambridge University Press.

Barkley, R. A. (1987). *Defiant children: Parent-teacher assignments.* New York: Guilford Press.

Bierman, K. L., & O'Brian, S. F. (1989, April). *Enchancing the prediction of future peer rejection with behavior problem ratings and sociometric nominations.* Abstracts (Vol. 6) of the Society of Research in Child Development Biennial Meeting, Kansas City, MO.

Biglan, A., Glasgow, R. E., & Singer, G. (in press). The need for a science of large social units: A contextual approach. *Behavior Therapy.*

Blechman, E. A. Taylor, C. J., & Schrader, S. M. (1981). Family problem solving versus home notes as early intervention with high-risk children. *Journal of Consulting and Clinical Psychology, 49*(6), 919–926.

Blumstein, A., Farrington, D. P., & Moitra, S. (1985). *Delinquency careers: Innocents, desisters, and persisters.* Chicago, IL: University of Chicago Press.

Bronfenbrenner, U. (1986). Ecology of the family as a context for human development. *Developmental Psychology, 22,* 723–742.

Campbell, D. T., & Fiske, D. W. (1959). Conversant and discriminant validation of the multitrait and multimethod matrix. *Psychological Bulletin, 56,* 81–105.

Capaldi, D., & Patterson, G. R. (1987). An approach to the problem of recruitment and retention rates for longitudinal research. *Behavioral Assessment, 9,* 169–177.

Capaldi, D., & Patterson, G. R. (1989). *Psychometric properties of fourteen latent constructs from the Oregon Youth Study.* New York: Springer-Verlag.

Caspi, A., & Elder, G. H., Jr. (1988). Emergent family patterns: The intergenerational construction of problem behavior and relationships. In R. A. Hinde & J. Stevenson-Hinde (Eds.), *Relationships within families: Mutual influences* (pp. 218–240). Oxford: Clarendon.

Caspi, A., Elder, G. H., & Bern, T. J. (1987). Moving against the world: Life-course patterns of explosive children. *Developmental Psychology, 23,* 308–313.

Chamberlain, P., & Patterson, G. R. (1984). Aggressive behavior in middle childhood. In D. Schaffer, A. A. Ehrhardt, & L. L. Greenhill (Eds.), *The clinical guide to child psychiatry.* New York: Free Press.

Chamberlain, P., & Reid, J. B. (1987). Parent observation and report of child symptoms. *Behavioral Assessment, 9,* 97–109.

Chamberlain, P., & Weinrott, M. (1990). Specialized foster care: Treating seriously emotionally disturbed children. *Children Today, January–February,* 24–27.

Copas, J. B., & Loeber, R. (1988). *Relative Improvement over Chance (RIOC) for 2 × 2 tables.* Unpublished manuscript. Available from Western Psychiatric Institute and Clinic, 3811 O'Hara Street, Pittsburgh, PA 15213.

Cronbach, L. J., & Glaser, G. C. (1965) *Psychological tests and personal decisions.* Urban, IL: University of Illinois Press.

Cronbach, L. J., & Meehl, P. E. (1955). Construct validity in psychological tests. *Psychological Bulletin, 52,* 281–302.

Dishion, T. J. (1990). The peer context of child and adolescent troublesome behavior. In P. Leone (Ed.), *Understanding troublesome and troubled youth* (pp. 128–153). Newberry Park, CA: Sage Publications.

Dishion, T. J., Andrews, D. A., & Patterson, G. R. (1990). *Adolescent boys and their friends: Dyadic interactions related to antisocial behavior.* Manuscript submitted for publication.

Dishion, T. J., Garner, K., Patterson, G. R., Reid, J. B. & Thibodeaux, S. (1983). *The family process code: A multidimensional system for observing family interactions.* Technical manual, (Available from Oregon Social Learning Center, 207 East Fifth Avenue, Suite 202, Eugene, OR 97401).

Dishion, T. J., & Loeber, R. (1985). Adolescent marijuana and alcohol use: The role of parents and peers revisited. *American Journal of Drug and Alcohol Abuse, 11,* 11–25.

Dishion, T. J., Loeber, R., Stouthamer-Loeber, M., & Patterson, G. R. (1984). Skill deficits and male adolescent delinquency. *Journal of Abnormal Psychology, 12,* 37–54.

Dishion, T. J., Patterson, G. R., Stoolmiller, M., & Skinner, M. (1991). Family, school, and behavioral antecedents to early adolescent involvement with antisocial peers. *Development Psychology, 27,* 172–180.

Dishion, T. J., Reid, J. B., & Patterson, G. R. (1988). Empirical guidelines for a family intervention for adolescent drug use. *Journal of Chemical Dependency Treatment, 1,* 189–214.

Elliott, D., Huizinga, D., & Ageton, S. (1985). *Explaining delinquency and drug use.* Beverly Hills, CA: Sage Publications.

Fagot, B., & Kavanagh, K. (1988). *Context of attachment.* Unpublished manuscript. (Available from Oregon Social Learning Center, 207 East Fifth Avenue, Suite 202, Eugene, OR 97401).

Farrington, D. P., & Loeber, R. (1988). *RIOC and Phi as measures of predictive efficiency and strength of association in 2 × 2 tables.* Unpublished manuscript. (Available from Western Psychiatric Institute and Clinic, 3811 O'Hara Street, Pittsburgh, PA 15213).

Forgatch, M. S., Fetrow, B., & Lathrop, M. (1985). *Solving problems in family interaction.* Unpublished training manual. (Available from Oregon Social Learning Center, 207 East Fifth Avenue, Suite 202, Eugene, OR 97401).

Hartup, W. W. (1983). The peer system. In E. M. Hetherington (Ed.), *Handbook of child psychology: Volume 4, Socialization, personality, and social development* (pp. 103–196). New York: John Wiley and Sons.

Jessor, R., & Jessor, S. L. (1977). *Problem behavior and psychosocial development: A longitudinal study of youth.* New York: Academic Press.

Kandel, D. B. (1973). Adolescent marijuana use: Role of parents and peers. *Science, 181,* 1067–1081.

Kandel, D., Simcha-Fagan, O., & Davies, M. (1986). Risk factors for delinquency and illicit drug use from adolescence to young adulthood. *Journal of Drug Issues, 16,* 67–90.

Kazdin, A. (1987). Treatment of antisocial behavior in children: Current status and future directions. *Psychological Bulletin, 102,* 187–203.

Kellam, S. (1990). Developmental epidemiological framework for family research on depression and aggression. In G. R. Patterson (Ed.), *Depression and aggression in family interaction* (pp. 11–48). Hillsdale, NJ: Lawrence Erlbaum Associates.

Kelly, J. (1989). *A guide to conducting prevention research in the community: First steps.* New York: The Haworth Press.

Loeber, R., & Dishion, T. J. (1983). Early predictors of male delinquency: A review. *Psychological Bulletin, 94,* 68–98.

Loeber, R., & Dishion, T. J. (1984). Boys who fight at home and school: Family conditions influencing cross setting consistency. *Journal of Consulting and Clinical Psychology, 52,* 759–768.

Loeber, R., & Dishion, T. J. (1987). Antisocial and delinquent youths: Methods for their early identification. In J. D. Burchard & S. N. Burchard (Eds.), *Prevention of delinquent behavior* (Vol. 10, pp. 75–89). Newberry Park, CA: Sage Publications.

Loeber, R., Dishion, T. J., & Patterson, G. R. (1984). Multiple gating: A multistage assessment procedure for identifying youths at risk for delinquency. *Journal of Research in Crime and Delinquency, 21,* 7–32.

Loeber, R., Green, S. M., & Stouthamer-Loeber, M. (1989). Optimal informants on childhood disruptive behaviors. *Development and Psychopathology, 1,* 317–337.

Loeber, R., & LeBlanc, M. (in press). Toward a developmental criminology. In N. Morris & M. Tonry (Eds.), *Crime and Justice* (Vol. 12), pp. 375–473). Chicago, IL: University of Chicago Press.

Loeber, R., & Schmaling, K. B. (1985). Empirical evidence for overt and covert patterns of antisocial conduct problems: A meta-analysis. *Journal of Abnormal Child Psychology, 13,* 337–352.

Meehl, P. (1954). *Clinical versus statistical prediction: A theoretical analysis and a review of the evidence.* Minneapolis, MN: University of Minnesota Press.

Olweus, D. (1979). Stability of aggressive reaction patterns in males: A review. *Psychological Bulletin, 86,* 852–875.

Parker, J. G., & Asher, S. R. (1987). Peer relations and later personal adjustment: Are low-accepted children at risk? *Psychological Bulletin, 102,* 357–389.

Patterson, G. R. (1982). *Coercive family process.* Eugene, OR: Castalia Publishing Company.

Patterson, G. P. (1986). Performance models for antisocial boys. *American Psychologist, 41,* 432–444.

Patterson, G. R., & Bank, L. (1986). Bootstrapping your way in the nomological thicket. *Behavioral Assessment, 8,* 49–73.

Patterson, G. R., & Bank L. (1987). When is a nomological network a construct? In D. R. Peterson & D. B. Fishman (Eds.), *Assessment for decision: Psychology in action* (pp. 249–279). New Brunswick, NJ: Rutgers University Press.

Patterson, G. R., Capaldi, D., & Bank, L. (1989). An early starter model for predicting delinquency. In D. Pepler & K. H. Rubin (Eds.), *The development and treatment of childhood aggression.* Hillsdale, NJ: Lawrence Erlbaum Associates.

Patterson, G. R., Chamberlain, P., & Reid, J. R. (1982). A comparative evaluation of parent training procedures. *Behavior Therapy, 3,* 638–650.

Patterson, G. R., Crosby, L., & Vuichinich, S. (1991). An empirical test of the early starter model. *Journal of Quantitative Criminology.* Manuscript submitted for publication.

Patterson, G. R., & Dishion, T. J. (1985). Contributions of families and peers to delinquency. *Criminology, 23,* 63–79.

Patterson, G. R., Dishion, T. L., & Bank, L. (1984). Family interaction: A process model of deviancy training. *Aggressive Behavior, 10,* 253–267.

Patterson, G. R., Dishion, T. J., & Yoeger, K. (1991). *Using latent constructs to predict early-starting delinquents.* Unpublished manuscript.

Patterson, G. R., & Forgatch, M. S. (1987). *Parents and adolescents: 1. Living together.* Eugene, OR: Castalia Publishing Company.

Patterson, G. R., & Reid, J. B. (1984). Social interactional processes within the family: The study of moment-by-moment family transactions in which human development is embedded. *Journal of Applied Developmental Psychology, 5,* 237–262.

Patterson, G. R., Reid, J. B., & Dishion, T. J. (in press). *Antisocial boys.* Eugene, OR: Castalia.

Patterson, G. R., & Stouthamer-Loeber, M. (1984). The correlation of family management practices and delinquency. *Child Development, 55,* 1299–1307.

Patterson, G. R., & Stoolmiller, M. (1991). Replications of a dual failure model for boys' depressed mood. *Journal of Consulting and Clinical Psychology, 59*(4), 491–498.

Reid, J. B. (Ed.) (1978). *A social learning approach to family intervention: II. Observation in home settings.* Eugene, OR: Castalia Publishing Company.

Reid, J. B. (1986). Social-interactional patterns in families of abused and nonabused children. In C. Zahn Waxler, E. M. Cummings, & R. Iannotti (Eds.), *Altruism and aggression: Biological and social origins* (pp. 238–255). New York: Cambridge University Press.

Reid, J. B., Patterson, G. R., Baldwin, D. V., & Dishion, T. J. (1988). Observations in the assessment of childhood disorders. In M. Rutter, A. H. Tuma, & I. S. Lann (Eds.), *Assessment and diagnosis in child psychopathology* (pp. 156–195). New York: Guilford Press.

Robins, L. H. (1978). Study of childhood predictors of adult antisocial behavior: Replication from longitudinal studies. *Psychological Medicine, 8,* 611–622.

Robins, L. N., & Przybeck, T. R. (1985). Age of onset of drug use as a factor in drug and other disorders. In C. L. Jones & R. J. Battjes (Eds.), *Etiology of drug abuse: Implications for prevention* (National Institute of Drug Abuse (NIDA) Research Monograph 56). Washington, D.C.: NIDA.

Walker, H. M., Shinn, M. R., O'Neill, R. E., & Ramsey, E. (1987). A longitudinal assessment of the development of antisocial behavior in boys: Rationale, methodology, and first year results. *Remedial and Special Education, 8,* 7–16.

Webster-Stratton, C. (1984). Randomized trail of two parent-training programs for families with conduct-disordered children. *Journal of Consulting and Clinical Psychology, 52,* 666–678.

Webster-Stratton, C. (1988). Mothers' and fathers' perceptions of child deviance: Roles of parent and child behaviors and parent adjustment. *Journal of Consulting and Clinical Psychology, 56,* 909–915.

Webster-Stratton, C., Kolpacoff, M., & Hollinsworth, T. (1988). Self-administered videotape therapy for families with conduct problem children: Comparison with two cost-effective treatments and a control group. *Journal of Consulting and Clinical Psychology, 56,* 558–566.

Wiggins, J. S. (1973). *Personality and prediction: Principles of personality assessment.* Menlo Park, CA: Addison Wesley Publishing Company.

Wolfgang, M. E., Figlio, R. M., & Sellin, T. (1972). *Delinquency in a birth cohort.* Chicago, IL: University of Chicago Press.

# 12
# Youth Gangs

*Michael L. Walker*
*Linda M. Schmidt*
*Lisa Lunghofer*

## Introduction

Youth gangs have recently drawn increasing public and media attention throughout the United States. Although gangs are not a new phenomenon, the violence in which young members currently engage has proved exceptionally deadly. The growth of youth gangs, which has been associated with low socioeconomic status, life in inner cities, and the proliferation of drug use and sales (National Committee for Injury Prevention and Control, 1989), has increased the risk that young people will be the victims and/or the perpetrators of violence.

A study of gang membership in forty-five cities found 1,439 gangs, with 120,636 members (Spergel, Curry, Change et. al., 1990). Of these gang members, 54.6 percent were African-American and 32.6 percent were Hispanic. Spergel and colleagues also found that gang members were involved in violent crimes three times more often than juvenile delinquents who were not gang members. Those crimes have become more deadly as shotguns and automatic weapons are increasingly the weapons of choice among warring gangs (National School Safety Center, 1988).

The growth of gangs and gang violence has made familiarity with the gang subculture a necessity among professionals working with adolescents. Understanding possible precursors to violent behavior and knowing how to identify signs of gang involvement may provide insight into an adolescent's problems, as well as facilitate selection of intervention strategies.

## Gangs

A gang is any group of three or more individuals that has an identifiable leadership, structure, and symbols and is engaged in antisocial or criminal

400

behavior. There are many types of gangs—for example, African-American gangs, Asian gangs, hate groups, Hispanic gangs, Jamaican posses, motor-cycle gangs, stoner gangs, organized crime families, rural gangs, and prison gangs.

## Why Do Young People Join Gangs?

Young people join gangs for a variety of reasons, many of which are similar to the reasons children join other, more prosocial groups, such as the Boy Scouts or the Girl Scouts. Many join in search of love, structure, discipline, recognition, and a sense of belonging. Gang membership allows a young person to establish an identity in an atmosphere where brotherhood and respect are essential virtues. One young female gang member explained the depth of that commitment to brotherhood. One of her "boys" was shot and his fellow gang members could not take him to the hospital because there were warrants outstanding for all of them. They took him to a friend's base-ment and called her. She went to the house, picked him up and took him to the hospital. She was subsequently questioned by police and involved in a homicide investigation. Brotherhood and commitment can have legal rami-fications.

In addition to searching for commitment and a sense of belonging, some youth join gangs in search of protection. These young people join out of necessity: the need for physical safety is a powerful motivator for joining a gang. There are neighborhoods where young people must join a gang in order to survive in the community. Children regularly explain that they would not feel safe walking to and from school unless they knew their posse would provide protection.

Some young people join gangs in search of power. There is a great deal of power in the fear engendered by young men and women wearing colors. This fear can facilitate control of an environment that may often seem equally uncontrollable to children, their parents, and law enforcement officials. The ability to intimidate can be a game and an addiction, as well as a means of bolstering self-esteem. By designating turf and intimidating anyone who chal-lenges this territorial claim, gang members reinforce their sense of power and control.

Gang activity in shopping malls on Friday night and Saturday afternoons reflects the search for power and control. Unprovoked attacks at malls are a common gang activity. Gang members go to malls looking for unsuspecting shoppers to scare, youths from rival gangs, or young people who are "false-flagging" (wearing a gang's colors but not belonging to it). False-flagging, which is usually an accident, is one of the most common causes of unpro-voked attacks. The desire to dress fashionably (e.g., wearing Los Angeles Raiders sportswear) can be dangerous, particularly if a young person unsus-pectingly wanders into a rival gang's turf. Unknowingly using gang hand signs in the wrong area of a mall or a neighborhood can be equally deadly.

Finally, growing up in a family in which gang membership has become a tradition can be a motivator for joining a gang. Cases are not uncommon in which the father was a gang member ("gangbanger") in the 1960s and is currently in prison, his son is a member of a local gang, and the boy is about to become the father of a thirteen-year-old girl's baby. The gang can become a child's family, his or her religion, and the only way of life he or she knows.

### Levels of Organization

Most gang members range in age from eight to thirty years. The youngest members begin their gang involvement as scavengers. Scavengers do not wear colors or have a leader. They congregate in neighborhoods or local malls and are involved primarily in minor mischief.

Territorial gangs, the largest of the organizational levels, constitute the next stratum. Scavengers who look up to these gang members often become part of territorial gangs. These gangs have leaders, wear colors, have structure and rank, and are involved in antisocial and criminal activity.

As territorial gang members become more sophisticated in their criminal activity, they climb the organizational ladder to the corporate level. The primary purpose of corporate gangs, like that of any big business, is profitmaking. Their crimes are generally premeditated and committed in pursuit of their business objectives. The Bloods and the Crips are well-known examples of corporate gangs. These gangs are increasingly sending some of their members to college in an attempt to develop their own cadre of lawyers and accountants. One of the gang rules is to "keep it in the family."

### Levels of Involvement

There are three levels of gang involvement: committed, marginal, and wannabe. Committed members, the most involved of the three levels, will be tattooed. They will attend gang meetings once each week. The "rag" (bandanna) representing their gang's colors will be their ticket into the meeting. Committed members will fight when ordered to by their "OG" (original gangster/leader). They are dangerous and unlikely to think independently. Their behaviors are often determined by the needs of the gang.

Marginal members, who compose the largest contingent of gang members, will not be tattooed. They attend a sufficient number of meetings to show affiliation but avoid involvement in major criminal activity. Marginal members, unlike their committed counterparts, retain the ability to think for themselves. Their decisions to fight are generally consciously debated on the basis of risk and potential reward. These members can be dangerous, but the danger is primarily to themselves. They are often found guilty by association with young people involved in serious criminal activity. A marginal member is most likely to find himself saying, "But I thought we were just going to the show. I didn't know Jo-Jo had a gun. I didn't know they were planning to do a driveby. I'm innocent!" or "The six of us were going to the mall to play video games. I didn't know Jo-Jo had crack on him. I didn't know Jo-Jo was a trafficker. I'm innocent!" Under circumstances such as these, all parties present get a police record. The youth may be telling the truth, but he has jeopardized his future, and possibly his life, by knowingly associating with committed gang members.

A wannabe is a youth who decides to start a gang. This young person may begin a no-name gang or claim that the fledgling group is an organized set of a corporate gang such as the Crips. This group is not sophisticated or knowledgeable about gang philosophies or activities; however, its members take the little knowledge they have and channel it into criminal activity. If they are successful in this activity, they eventually "flip" (join) a larger, established gang.

Level of involvement and associated responsibilities are denoted within the gang by a hierarchy of ranks. Each gang nation has its own list of ranks. These may include generals, princes, 1st C, 2nd C, right-hand man, left-hand man, enforcers, footsoldiers, and peewees. Each member of a gang has a rank. The higher the rank, the more involved the youth is in criminal activity and the harder it is to help him or her leave the gang.

The problems of an eighteen-year-old enforcer for a gang reflect the difficulties of relinquishing rank. The rank of enforcer carries with it responsibility for making gang hits and disciplining members. After a short time as an enforcer, this young man found the responsibilities of his rank overwhelming. He moved to another city in order to get away from the gang and his position. After relocating, however, he felt compelled to join another gang. He explained that he missed the excitement of gang life but wanted to remain at the low level of footsoldier, where he would not have the pressure and responsibility of his former rank. This, however, did not keep him out of trouble. He was arrested for assaulting his mother after she attempted to take his "lit book" (gang handbook) away from him.

## Rites of Passage: The Initiation

Initiation is the rite of passage during which potential gang members demonstrate their fearlessness, willingness to fight, and ability to carry out orders. Rituals vary depending on the set a member is joining and the neighborhood in which he or she is joining it. For boys, initiation can involve a variety of activities: fighting in a "360" (a circle of gang members) for a designated period, fighting in a "180" (a half-circle of gang members standing in front of the initiate), "walking the line" (walking past a line of gang members who beat the new gang member), getting through a neighborhood within twenty-four hours while being attacked by a designated number of gang members during that period, doing a driveby shooting, shooting an innocent person, stealing something, doing a home invasion, or snatching a car. After the youth has passed these tests of initiation, he is "blessed in" and hugged by each gang member as a symbol of their unity and brotherhood. Thus, he becomes part of a group demanding his unwavering dedication and loyalty.

Initiations always involve violence and humiliation. For example, one OG commanded that a youth be beaten until he bled enough to fill a cup with his blood. Each gang member in the 360 then drank from the cup of the young man's blood. Their brotherhood was cemented.

For girls, initiation can also involve performance of a range of rituals: standing naked in the middle of a busy street for a certain number of minutes; beating up a senior citizen, robbing him or her, and then being graded on the performance; stealing; and being gang-raped. Gang rape is the most popular form of initiation for females who join the four major gang nations—the Bloods, the Crips, the Folks, and the People. The initiate is raped by approximately five gang members while the rest of the gang watches. She is then told that speaking of this initiation is a violation of gang rules. She has become a member of the set, and the only way out is death. Gang norms and expectations can seductively pervade every aspect of a young person's life. This makes both leaving the gang and remaining a member potentially deadly.

Although most gang members join willingly, some are "jumped in" (initiated against their will). Regardless of the circumstances of initiation, however, membership can become addictive; that is, youth can become psychologically fused to gang relationships, excitement, and violence. One thirteen-year-old girl thought that her sixteen-year-old boyfriend was taking her to a party. He was actually taking her to a gang meeting to be initiated into his set. After the gang rape through which she was initiated, she wandered the streets aimlessly. The police picked her up. Although she refused to explain why, she begged not to have to face her mother. After many professionals tried unsuccessfully to work with her at home, she was sent to live with relatives in another state. It was hoped that she could receive counseling to help her deal with the rape and with her gang involvement. Unfortunately, her family could not afford to pay for therapy. Four months later, she returned to the gang. She is now pregnant.

A fifteen-year-old female attempted suicide after her OG refused to allow her to leave the gang. She was a high-ranking member whose responsibilities included carrying out gang hits, disciplining members, and finding young females to be initiated. She explained to her OG that she could no longer watch eight- and nine-year-olds gang-raped into the set. The OG responded that death was the only way out of the set. Although her suicide attempt was unsuccessful, she remains in a psychiatric hospital.

Another female gang member refuses to leave the gang, although she has had three abortions, has had numerous bouts with STDs, and, at age sixteen, is now sterile. Two of her boyfriends, neither of whom made it to the age of twenty, are dead. She is intelligent, articulate, and, given the opportunity, hardworking. All attempts, however, to keep her away from the gang have failed. She explains that she likes the fast money and the excitement brought by living on the edge.

## Being a Member: Gang Tradition and Ritual

**The Lit Book.** A lit (short for *literature*) book includes everything there is to know about a gang member's set. It is usually handwritten, often photocopied, and passed to new members. The lit book and the rag are a gang member's two most important representations of his or her gang. Lit books generally contain a history of the gang, rules and/or code numbers, an organizational chart (sometimes, but not always), ranks, gang prayers, hand signs and handshakes, symbols/graffiti, disrespect symbols/graffiti for rival gangs, gang poetry, and, occasionally, a list of members' names. Familiarity with every part of the book is essential. If a higher-ranking gang member tells a lower-ranking gang member to "spit lit" (recite the literature) and the person is unable to do so, he or she is in violation of gang rules and is disciplined.

Figure 1 provides an example of a Folks lit book.

**Gang Prayers.** Each gang nation has a prayer that members are required to say every night before going to bed. Examples of some of the major gang prayers are depicted in Figure 2 (terms to note: *slob* is a term of disrespect for the Blood nation, and *crab* is a term of disrespect for the Crip nation).

**Hand Signs and Handshakes.** Each gang uses hand signs and special handshakes. The Folks use their pitchfork symbol as a hand sign. The Rice and Beans use the American Sign Language sign of "I love you" as their hand sign. The Vice Lords sign the V-L combination.

Gangs also use hand signs to "disrespect" (insult) rival gangs. As a sign of disrespect, a gang member will give the hand sign of a rival gang, then raise his or her arm and lower it quickly, thus "throwing down" the rival gang's hand sign. This behavior often provokes gang fights, particularly at high school basketball games. It is interesting to note that a basketball court is an insufficient barrier between rival gangs intent on showing disrespect to one another.

**Gang Terms.** All gangs use street language. The following is a list of the most commonly used gang terms.

*CK*—Crip killer

*Claim*—announce your gang affiliation

*Cluckhead*—crack addict

*Crab*—insulting term for Crips

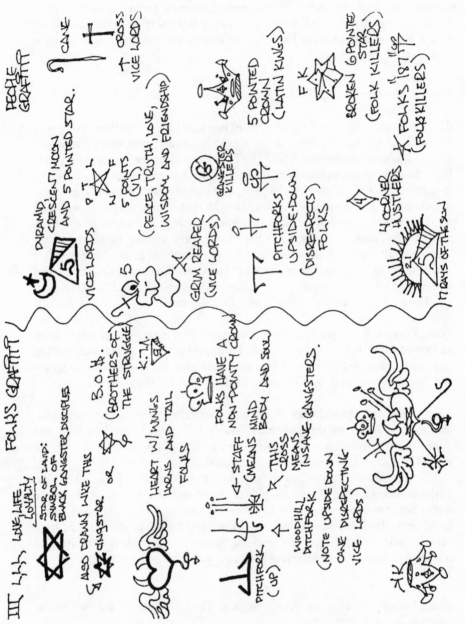

Figure 1. Excerpt from Folks Lit Book

GANG PRAYERS

**CRIP NATION**

LORD, I LAY ME DOWN TO SLEEP
ON MY SIDE MY RAGS TO KEEP
IF I DIE BEFORE I WAKE
LET ME WASTE A SLOB WITH MY 38.

**BLOOD NATION**

I LAY MY RED RAG DOWN TO SLEEP
PRAY THE LORD MY SOUL TO KEEP
IF I SHALL DIE BEFORE I WAKE
I SHALL KILL A CRAB WITH A 38.

**FOLKS NATION**

IF I DIE SHOW NO PITY
BURY ME DEEP IN MANIAC CITY
LAY TWO PITCH FORKS ACROSS MY CHEST
AND TELL MY FOLKS I DONE MY BEST.

**PEOPLE NATION SETS**

**BLACKSTONE RANGERS**

BLACKSTONES ARE MY BROTHERS FOR THAT
I KILL, WALK THROUGH A VALLEY OF
FOLKS DEVILS AND SHOW THEM HOW I
FEEL FOR WHEN I BATTLE I SHALL TAKE
NO DEFEAT AND IF I SHALL DIE BURY A
FIVE POINT STAR AT MY FEET.

**VICE LORDS**

WHEN I DIE, BURY ME DEEP, PLACE TWO
CANES AT MY FEET, A FIVE POINT STAR
ACROSS MY CHEST AND TELL MY BROTHERS
I DID MY BEST.

**Figure 2. Gang Prayers**

*Dis*—disrespect

*Down*—loyal to the set, ready to fight

*Essay*—Hispanic gang member

*Flaggin'*—throwing signs

*G'd up*—wearing gang attire

*G ster*—gangster

*Jack*—holdup

*Loc*—generic gang term:

  Loc—Crips

  Lok—Bloods

*Off-Brands*—local gangs, not with the real G sters

*Outs*—out of prison or detention

*Pocket*—with a gun

*Saggin'*—wearing your pants hanging low

*Slangin'*—hanging out, selling dope

*Slob, Snoop*—insulting terms for Bloods

*Vicci Lou*—Insulting term for Vice-Lords

It is important to note the disrespect terms for rival gangs. Awareness of these terms may provide clues to potentially volatile situations. For example, in one school discipline incident, a principal told a youth to sit next to another student. The student shouted vehemently, "You can't make me sit next to that Slob!" Had the principal known that *Slob* is a disrespect term for a Blood nation gang member, he might have been able to prevent the violence that resulted from having two rival gang members in his office.

**Gang Alphabet and Symbols.** Each gang nation has its own alphabet and symbols (see Figure 3). There are some similarities between Crip and Folks alphabets, as well as between Blood and People alphabets. Each letter has a meaning based on respect for the gang's symbols or disrespect of rivals. Familiarity with the respect symbols for each nation will help professionals to identify the gang nation to which an alphabet belongs. Disrespect of rival gangs often involves altering their symbols by, for example, drawing them upside down. It is therefore important to note whether symbols have been transformed in any way.

*Gang Nations*

As noted earlier, there are four national gang nations: the Bloods, the Crips, the Folks, and the People. Each has unique sets, colors, means of representing, symbols, rivals, lit books, prayers and alphabets. Familiarity with their traditions and rituals will facilitate identification of members of each nation.

**The Bloods.** The Bloods, the most sophisticated of the gang nations, began in Los Angeles during the early 1970s. The nation was created in reaction to formation of the Crip nation. Bloods are predominantly African-American, but there are some white, Hispanic, and interracial sets. Piru is the largest of the 150 sets belonging to the nation. The Bloods are aligned with the People, such as the Vice Lords, the Blackstone Rangers, the Kings, and Rice and Beans, and their major rivals are the Crips and the Folks.

Bloods rarely "flash colors" (wear identifiable gang colors). When they do, it is a sign that something significant is about to happen. When flashing colors, they wear red pants, red tennis shoes or Converse Allstars (because of the five-point star on the shoe), and a red rag. Because Bloods "represent" (give evidence of the specific gang to which they belong) on the left side of the body, the tattoo showing respect for their gang will be on a member's left side

( ) = disrespect terms    [ ] = colors gang wears

| Gang Nations | | Symbols | Alphabets |
|---|---|---|---|
| Bloods | [red] | | |
| Piru | (Slobs) | | |
| Rollin 60s | | | |
| Crips | [blue] | | |
| Rollin' 20s | (Crabs) | | |
| Nuttywood Blocc | | | |
| Hoover W. 59 St. | | | |
| Folks | [black & white] | | Gangster Alphabet--BGD |
| Black Gangster Disciples | | | |
| Insane Gangster Disciples | | | |
| Maniac Gangster Disciples | | | |
| People | [red & black] | | Vice Lord Alphabet--VL |
| Vice Lords | (Vicci-Lou's) | | |
| Blackstone Rangers | | | |
| Rice & Beans | | | |
| Hate Groups | | | Look for local patterns. |
| Supreme White People | | | |
| Skinheads | | | |
| Aryan Brotherhood | | | |
| Neo-Nazis | | | |
| Cults | [black] | | Runic Alphabet |
| Stoners | | | |
| Satanic | | | |
| Off-Brands | | | Look for local patterns. |
| West Side Posse (suburb) | | | |
| Loped Out Posse (suburb) | | | |
| Cute Ass Pimps (female) | | | |
| E. 61 St. Posse (female) | | | |

Figure 3. Youth Gangs

and a tattoo showing disrespect for their rivals will be on the right side. Members will "sag" their pants (wear them very low on the hips) to the left, as well as position belt buckles, beepers, and hats on the left side of their bodies.

The Bloods, like other gangs, have a lit book containing all information relevant to the gang, including the alphabet, prayers, and symbols. The Blood alphabet is the most complicated of the four nations. Their prayer is very similar to that of their rival, the Crips. The number 5 and the five-point star are the Bloods' most significant symbols; other symbols include the top hat, glove, pyramid, champagne glass, cane, and staff.

**The Crips.** The Crips, the most violent of the gang nations, began in Los Angeles during the early 1970s. The Crips have approximately 150 sets. Their major sets are the Rollin' 20s, the Nuttywood Blocc, the Hoover West 59th Street Gangster Crips, the Blue Devils, and the Rollin' 60s. The Crips are rivals of the Blood and People nations; currently, they are also fighting with some Folks sets over drug turf.

Crips wear "heavy colors" (blatant gang identifiers). Los Angeles Raiders sportswear, including hats (boonies or baseball), T-shirts, jackets, and long coats, is a major Crip identifier. Crips also carry a blue rag. Because they represent on the right side of the body, Crips hang their rag out of their right pocket; keep their hats, belt buckles, and beepers tilted to the right; and wear their pants sagging to the right. A member's respect tattoo will be on the right side of the body, and his or her disrespect tattoo will be on the left. Members may also have three slashes through the right eyebrow or on the right side of the head and wear the tongue of their right shoe pulled down under the laces; females sometimes pull up their right pant leg as an identifier.

Crips have a strong sense of ritual and tradition that is reflected in their symbols, lit books, alphabet, prayers, and rules. Crips use the number 6, the roman numeral III, and the Star of David as symbols. The Folks also use the number 6 and the Star of David as symbols. The two nations are aligned, however, only if members of both nations are carrying blue rags.

Some Crip lit books include an explanation of the meaning behind each of the letters of their alphabet. The *A* is upside down because it is taking half a pyramid down. The *B* is crossed out for disrespect to Bloods. The *S* is an upside-down 5 for disrespect to all who run under the five-point star, and the *V* is upside down for disrespect to the Vice Lords.

One lit book included Crip poems:

Chitty Chitty Bang Bang Nothin' but a Crip Thang
Thought I was Piru nothing but a True Blue.
Whether it rains, pours or drips I'll socc a Slob
In his lip. And if he asks me what's my trip, I'll tell
Him Rollin' 60s Loco Gangster Crip!!!

To be a Crip you're put to the test to put a sorry
Ass Slob to rest. If I die in Gangster City tell my
C-Dogg to show no pity. Lay two-C-rags across my
Chest and all Crips know I Did my very best.

United we stand. Divided we fall. Combined as one,
Crips stand tall. Crips to the sky. Slobs must die.

Taking out Slobs is my job. Gang banging is my thing.
Killing Pirus with a bang.
Crippin' ain't easy but it won't stop 'til my coffin drops.

Like other gang nations, Crips have an extensive list of rules. Some of these include the following:

1. Never tell anyone your lit.
2. Anything spelled with a CK must be changed to a CC because CK stands for Crip killer.
3. Always attend meetings with your rag.
4. Do nothing on the fifth day [Friday is considered the fifth day] except kill Slobs and gangbang.
5. Always wear your colors to funerals of gang members.
6. Say your Crip prayer every night.

**The Folks.** The Folks gang nation began in Chicago in the 1950s. Originally they were organized to protect their mothers and sisters from dangers in the streets of Chicago. Their good intentions were short-lived, however, and their protective behaviors were quickly replaced by criminal activity and gang violence. They have numerous sets, including the Black Gangster Disciples, the Gangster Disciples, the Insane Gangster Disciples, and the Maniac Latin Disciples. They also have junior members, called Junior Folks. The Folks are rivals of the Bloods, the People, and some Crip sets.

Folks bear a number of similarities to Crips. Like Crips, Folks wear Los Angeles Raiders sportswear. They also wear Chicago White Sox and, occasionally, Los Angeles Kings sportswear (depending on their neighborhood). They carry a blue rag if they are aligned with the Crips and a black rag if they are not so aligned. Their alphabet is similar to that of the Crips.

Like Crips, Folks use the number 6 and the Star of David as symbols. In addition, Folks use the pitchfork as a primary symbol. For Folks, the six points of the Star of David represent love, life, loyalty, wisdom, understanding, and knowledge. The Folks also use the three-point crown, symbolizing the Third World; the heart and wings, signifying spreading love over the nation; an upside-down champagne glass, representing the celebration of victory and disrespect for the Vice Lords; a cane with the handle pointing down, representing a disciple; an upside-down top hat, symbolizing shelter; and horns, signifying the voice of the gang.

**The People.** Like the Folks, the People nation began in Chicago during the 1950s. The People nation has numerous large sets, including the Latin Kings, the Vice Lords, the Blackstone Rangers, Rice and Beans, and the Kings. The People are rivals of the Folks and the Crips.

People colors are red and black. Members often wear Chicago Bulls starter sets, jackets, hats, and pants. Converse Allstars, red tennis shoes with black laces, and black tennis shoes with red laces are also identifiers of this nation.

The number 5 and the five-point star are the People nation's primary symbols. The five points of the star stand for love, truth, peace, freedom, and justice. People members also use the king symbol, which is the Folks symbol inverted. Other People symbols include the champagne glass in the upright position, representing the defeat of the gangsters; a crescent moon, symbolizing unity of the five-point star; the top hat in the upright position, signifying shelter; the pyramid, representing shelter and strength; a five-point crown, symbolizing the supreme almighty nation; a cane with the handle up, signifying strength or power; and a Playboy bunny, representing a profile of all brothers of the almighty nation.

### Suburban Gangs, Cults, and Skinheads

**Suburban Gangs.** Like their urban counterparts, suburban youth are interested in the gang culture. They are not, however, as sophisticated as the gang nations. Although suburban juvenile assaults, drug use, sex offenses, vandalism, and weapons violations are increasing, the prevalence of these problems has not yet reached the levels found among inner-city youth gangs. Suburban gangs have also not yet established the solidarity and focus of the gang nations: some dabble in Satanism, while others experiment with the Skinhead movement. Their lack of consensus on colors reflects their lack of strong organization. Only the Stoner set appears to be well established. Stoners are unified by their dress, wearing black clothing and Satanic jewelry, and by their experimentation with Satanism.

In addition to being aware of emerging suburban gangs, it is also important to remember that gang members belonging to the four major gang nations reside in the suburbs as well as in inner cities. The suburbs are not immune to the destruction of gang warfare and criminal activity. Gang members are found among all races and all socioeconomic backgrounds.

**Cults.** Young people join cults for many of the same reasons that motivate children to join gangs. They join in search of a sense of belonging, recognition, structure, adventure, security, and attention. Cults are similar to gangs in that they both attempt to shape and control members' behaviors and attitudes by emphasizing "group thought" rather than independent thinking. Like gangs, Satanic cults have their own alphabets, graffiti, symbols, and handbook. The "book of shadows," like the gang lit book, contains essential information concerning the cult. The most sacred symbols of Satanism include the triple 6 (the sign of the beast), the upside-down cross (the denial of Christianity), and the six-point star in a circle (the Seal of Solomon). Members wear colors and special jewelry to signify their commitment to the cult.

The similarities between cults and gangs increase the likelihood that, if a young person is attracted to one of these groups, he or she may also be attracted to the other. Thus, it is important to be aware of the possibility of a youth's membership in both a gang and a cult. One young man, incarcerated in one of Ohio's juvenile detention facilities, was involved in Satanism at the time of his arrest. During his incarceration, he was jumped into the Hoover West 59th Street Gangster Crips. His drawing (Figure 4) reflects this dual membership: a mirror drawing of himself as Satan with Crip graffiti throughout, including tattoos and symbols of disrespect for Bloods.

**Skinheads.** Like suburban gangs and Satanic cults, racist movements, such as the Skinhead movement, are gaining increasing strength. There are approximately 3,000 Skinheads in the United States today. They should not be confused with the wannabe Skinheads who experiment with Satanism and drugs. The devoted Skinheads can be recognized by their military bearing, steel-toed workboots, tight jeans with rolled cuffs, workshirts or tennis shirts, military jackets, and, occasionally, shaved heads. Many are tatooed with swastikas, lightning bolts, and chains of strength around the wrist. Skinheads are known to use their boots as deadly weapons. Their language is similar in some respects to that used by gang members; for example, they use the phrase "jump in" to signify initiation into the group. They also paint graffiti, often on elementary schools. As is the case for each of these groups, recruiting young members is an integral part of sustaining and perpetuating the organization.

## Adolescents' Exposure to Violence

### The Incidence of Violence in the Lives of Adolescents

No discussion of gangs can be complete without mentioning the important role that violence plays in the day-to-day lives of adolescents. Violence has become a way of life not only for gang members but for adolescents outside of gang membership as well. Indeed, protection from violence and "safety in numbers" have been considered among the chief contributory factors to gang

**Figure 4. Mirror Drawing of Satanic Cult and Crip Dual Membership**

membership. As violence among young people intensifies, gang membership becomes increasingly attractive.

Homicide poses a significant threat to all young people, particularly those living in inner cities. Among fifteen- to nineteen-year-olds, the murder rate increased by 103 percent between 1985 and 1990, whereas the murder rate for the entire population rose by only nineteen percent (Stokes, 1991). Homicide is the leading cause of death among African-American males and females between ages fifteen and twenty-four (Children's Defense Fund, 1990). For young black males, the risk of death by homicide ranges from five to twenty-two times higher than the national norm (Centers for Disease Control, 1990), a risk associated with the poverty and illicit drug markets of the urban areas in which many live (Spivak et al., 1988).

Although most adolescents will not be the victims of homicide, they are not immune to other types of violence. *The National Adolescent Student Health Survey* asked a nationally representative sample of 11,449 eighth-

and tenth-graders about their exposure to violence. Survey results showed that these adolescents had both engaged in and been the victims of violence. Thirty-nine percent of students had been in at least one physical fight within the past year, and students reported significant exposure to violence in their neighborhoods: 33 percent had been threatened with bodily harm, fifteen percent had been robbed, and sixteen percent had been attacked (American School Health Association, 1989).

Studies limited to inner-city populations paint an even more dismal picture of adolescent exposure to violence. A 1988 Urban Institute study involving interviews with 387 randomly selected, ninth- and tenth-grade males from inner city Washington, D.C. schools found high rates of victimization: 27 percent had been attacked, threatened, or robbed by a person with a weapon, and 12 percent had been badly beaten by a nonhousehold member (Brounstein, Hatry, Altschuler, & Blair, 1989). These young men also engaged in violence: 22 percent had been part of a group that attacked or threatened someone, 9 percent had robbed, and 4 percent had shot, stabbed, or killed someone.

Gustavsson and Balgopal (1990) contend that adolescents face danger at school, as well as on the street. They report that 250,000 students are attacked at school in an average month (U.S. Senate Subcommittee on Juvenile Justice, 1981). A survey by a Boston commission to study high school safety found that 37 percent of boys and seventeen percent of girls had carried a weapon to school at least once (Boston Commission Survey, 1983). *The National Adolescent Student Health Survey* (American School Health Association 1989) found that, while at school, 34 percent of students said someone threatened to hurt them, fourteen percent had been robbed, and thirteen percent had been attacked.

## Repercussions of Adolescents' Exposure to Violence

The escalation of violence in the lives of young people has been accompanied by growing feelings among children on the street that social control mechanisms cannot or will not protect them. Conversations with these children reveal that they feel increasingly compelled to take the search for retribution and justice into their own hands. The story of Zone (a street name) and his "boys" illustrates this point. After Zone was "hit" (murdered) by a rival gang in October 1990, his boys "posse'd up" on the corner in their "hood" (neighborhood). They painted graffiti insulting to the rival gang (disrespect graffiti) on the corner store. The owner of the store immediately painted over it. The police monitored the neighborhood and broke up a crowd of gang members on the corner, but all to no avail. A rival gang member was shot, and one of Zone's boys went to prison. They handled it themselves.

A number of studies have examined the relationship between exposure to violence and delinquent behavior among adolescents. Some (e.g., Lewis,

Shanok, Pincus, & Glaser, 1979; Lewis, Shanok, & Balla, 1979; Gray, 1984) suggest that violent delinquents are more likely than nonviolent delinquents to have experienced physical abuse. Thus, early exposure to abuse may be an important precursor to involvement with violent youth gangs.

Kratcoski (1982) examined case files of 863 incarcerated male juvenile delinquents and found that twenty-six percent had been physically abused. Of the abused, 86 percent had experienced violence more than once. An Arkansas survey of 60 delinquent girls referred to a diagnostic center found that 53 percent reported sexual abuse and 51 percent injury from physical punishment (Mouzakitis, 1981). In a study of a Connecticut correctional school, 75 percent of 78 violent juveniles had been abused, while only 33 percent of 19 nonviolent juveniles had been abused (Lewis, Shanok, Pincus, & Glaser, 1979). Rivera and Widom (1990) compared the criminal histories of (a) 908 confirmed victims of physical and sexual abuse documented between 1967 and 1971 and (b) 667 matched control subjects who had not been abused. They found that childhood abuse increased the risk for offenses involving violence, particularly among males and blacks.

## Violence and Popular Culture

Violence in the lives of adolescents is compounded by exposure to violence in the form of entertainment, particularly in music and movies. From informal conversations with young people, there emerges a picture of the extent to which popular culture bombards them with messages of violence and death. Many children talk of regularly listening to rap by groups such as NWA (Niggers with an Attitude). A July 1991 *Time Magazine* article questioned why NWA's "grotesque new rap album soars to No. 1 . . . and . . . why ghetto rage and the brutal abuse of women appeal to mainstream listeners." (p. 56) Young people are particularly susceptible to the messages popular music conveys. One fourteen-year-old, in a detention facility for selling drugs, explained that he did not use drugs because the rappers told him he would be a fool to use his own. They did not, however, tell him not to sell drugs. They also failed to tell him about what life in the detention center would be like.

Research on the effects of viewing media violence has confirmed many of the fears arising from casual conversations with young adults about their preferences in movies and music. Robinson and Bachman (1972) reported a relationship between the number of hours of television an adolescent watched and his or her self-reports of aggressive and antisocial behavior. A number of researchers have conducted studies, in both laboratories and natural settings, of the relationship between watching violence and acting it out. Bandura, Ross and Ross (1961) Bobo doll experiment is perhaps one of the best known of these studies. In this study, young children watched a film of violent treatment of a doll, and their aggressiveness in a playroom was subsequently measured. Those observing aggression in the film were more aggressive in the playroom than their control group counterparts who had not seen that film.

Criticism that such studies were conducted in artificial environments led to the replication of the experiment in natural settings. Stein and Friedrich (1975) conducted one such study. They assigned ninety-seven preschool children to one of the following television "diets" for four weeks: antisocial, prosocial, or neutral. The researchers observed children's behavior before, during, and after viewing these television diets. They found that those who were aggressive before the experiment began became significantly more aggressive after watching antisocial programs. Those watching prosocial programs were less aggressive and more cooperative than children watching both neutral and antisocial programs. Lefkowitz (1972) reported that for boys these effects persisted over time. He found that there was a significant relationship between eight-year-olds' preferences for violent programs and eighteen-year-olds' aggressive behavior.

Illustrative of this relationship is a Teenage Mutant Ninja Turtle drawn by a member of the Folks gang (see Figure 5). Obviously influenced by the violent theme these children's toys portray, the gang member drew the turtle named Rafael holding the Folks symbol as his raised weapon.

Television teaches rules, norms, and standards of behavior. As Liebert and Sprafkin (1988) argue, repeated exposure to violence in the media can normalize antisocial and aggressive attitudes and actions. The extent to which these messages are acted out depends on both the individual child and

**Figure 5. Gang Member's Drawing of Teenage Mutant Ninja Turtle**

his or her environment. The marketing of violence in popular culture cannot, however, be dismissed as a potential factor in the perpetuation of violence against and by young people in our society.

## Screening for Gang Involvement

Professionals working with young people should be aware of a number of sources of gang information, as well as being alert to signs of gang involvement. These signs and pieces of information can be significant for children of all ages. Eight- and nine-year-olds are increasingly becoming involved in gangs. It is therefore important not to dismiss signs of gang involvement in children of any age.

Children's nicknames, writing, and graffiti can provide information concerning their gang involvement. Knowledge of a young person's name on the street can be very informative, allowing assessment of his or her rank, level of involvement, and type of criminal activity. As noted earlier, each gang member has a rank, and each gang nation has it own hierarchy of ranks. Those with the highest ranks, such as generals and princes, are typically also the most involved in criminal activity. A young person's street name is likely to reflect his or her position and level of involvement in the gang. Similarly, the enforcer, or member who enforces gang discipline and carries out gang hits, can sometimes be recognized by the handgun jewelry he wears to distinguish himself from members of lower rank.

All gang members have nicknames that often reveal additional information about the young person. For example, those with the rank of enforcer may be called Assassin. There will typically be a reason and a related story when a child calls himself Crazy or Psycho. "Lil" is often a preface to a Crip nickname, such as Lil Crazy.

A child's writing can also provide clues as to his or her gang involvement. Gang rules require that members always write in their gang alphabet—even statements to police must be given using the alphabet. Reading a young person's writing may therefore provide clues concerning drug trafficking and the nation and set to which he or she belongs.

Graffiti provide additional information about gangs, their members, and their activities. Graffiti can indicate how much of a community a gang has claimed as its turf, members' names, the presence of drug trafficking activity, and death threats on gang members. Crossing out graffiti bearing a member's name is a sign that a death threat has been made against that gang member.

"Lil Frank $" is another example of informative graffiti. As noted, "Lil" indicates that Frank is a Crip. The dollar sign, made out of an upside-down 5, indicates that Frank is selling drugs in the area, and the upside-down 5 shows disrespect for the Blood and People gang nations.

Graffiti are found not only on abandoned neighborhood buildings but also in school artwork and notebooks. Such depictions are often dismissed as attractive drawings, yet insufficient attention to the meaning behind the drawings can have serious consequences. A drawing of Bart Simpson, for which a youth in a detention facility received an A+, illustrates this point. The young man was rewarded for his effort by having the picture displayed on a dorm wall. Fighting subsequently began in the dorm. Closer inspection of the drawing revealed the reason for the violence: the youth was a Folks member who had very subtly disrespected the Blood and People nations by using an upside-down 5 throughout the picture. Sensitivity among teachers and therapists to these subtleties may alert them to gang involvement and potential gang-related problems.

In addition to these sources of information, it is also important to check for other gang identifiers. These include the following:

1. *Self-admission.* If a youth belongs to one of the four major gang nations, he is required by his rules to "claim his set" (admit belonging to his gang), regardless of the circumstances.
2. *Tattoos.* A committed gang member will be tattooed with his gang's symbols on the side of the body on which the gang represents and an optional disrespect tattoo on the opposite side.
3. *Special clothing.* A gang member can be identified by the clothes he wears, the color of his rag, and the way he represents.
4. *Gestures.* Hand signs and handshakes identify a member's gang set and nation.
5. *Personal relationships.* Friends can be an important clue to gang membership.
6. *Home address.* Neighborhood can provide information about a youth's gang membership or level of involvement.
7. *Photos.* Most gangs like to keep pictures of themselves in their colors, holding their weapons, or flashing their hand signs.
8. *Letters.* Gang members will write to their friends using their gang alphabets.
9. *Schoolbooks.* Gang members will often write their alphabet and draw their graffiti in schoolbooks.

In screening for gang involvement, it is essential to remember that simply because a young person is wearing a Los Angeles Raiders hat or one such "identifier," he or she is not necessarily a gang member. It is important to look for three or more identifiers. Professionals should be careful not to misidentify a youth who is trying to dress fashionably. Young people want to dress alike and to fit in; some, unfortunately, do not realize the dangers involved.

## Working with Gang Members

Currently, gang members are viewed as criminals, rather than as victims of brainwashing and indoctrination. Approaches to dealing with gang members, such as arrest and incarceration without treatment, are consistent with this view. The continued escalation of gang violence suggests that this solution is inadequate. Interventions involving treatment strategies must be explored. Youth gang members require treatment for their addictions to power, violence, and/or drugs. Those attempting to leave gangs also need a safe, positive environment that provides the structure, discipline, and support once offered by the gang. Interventions with young children trying to avoid gang involvement might include arrangements for someone to meet them at the bus stop after school, provision of a structured and supervised after-school program, and enforcement of a curfew. Older youths might benefit from sports programs, after-school jobs, or volunteer work. Enlisting parental support is important in helping young people of all ages.

Implementing these interventions will not be an easy task. Working with a gang member, particularly one who has had significant long-term involvement with gang life and has adopted the pervasive mindset of the gang, is a challenge. It is not impossible. It is important, however, that the young person be committed to making changes in his or her life.

If the young person is willing to discuss personal issues, there are a number of interview tips to keep in mind:

1. Listen. Watch for body language. Have a pad of paper and colored pencils for children to use while you are talking to them. It will relax them and may also provide you with insight into their gang involvement. If the youth is a gang member, he or she may draw gang symbols. Although you should not ask for it, the hope is that the children will leave their work behind. It is appropriate to show interest and to ask what they are drawing, as well as to ask them to explain the meaning of their pictures.
2. Never tell a young person what another youth told you. Repeating what you have heard from another child is a signal to the young person that "If you talk about them, you'll talk about me."
3. Do not show shock or surprise. Be prepared for anything.
4. Do not be judgmental.
5. Be flexible. Allow the young person to initiate discussion of important topics.
6. Be understanding. Try to determine whether the youth feels he or she has a problem that requires a solution. If a solution is needed, be sensitive to the context and complexity of the problem.

Establishing trust and mutual respect is essential. Adults need to develop meaningful communication with young people. It must be sincere communication. If children use expressions we do not understand, we must ask them to explain. Young people respect sincere interest and honesty. In working with gang members, it is also important to be firm, fair, and consistent. Firmness in discipline, fairness under all circumstances, and consistency in treatment will help establish a safe environment in which the young person can develop trust without fear of the unexpected.

There are, of course, some young people who are not ready, willing, or able to respond to efforts to help them leave a gang. We must be willing to accept that and move on to the next young person who is ready to receive help in regaining control of his or her life. The ultimate goal is to help youth become adults who can think independently, tolerate frustration, deal effectively with the inevitable problems of life, develop a sense of humor, and build lasting relationships based on mutual respect.

Gangs are a symptom of problems we, as a society, have failed to solve and, in some cases, have failed to recognize. They are a problem, however, that we can no longer continue to ignore. Gangs affect all of us. We must acknowledge that. The future of all our children depends on our awareness and our action.

# References

American School Health Association. (1989). *The national adolescent student health survey: A report on the health of America's youth.* Oakland, CA: Third Party Publishing Company.

Bandura, A., Ross, D., & Ross, S. (1961). Transmission of aggression through imitation of aggressive models. *Journal of Abnormal and Social Psychology, 63,* 575–582.

Boston Commission on Safe Public Schools. (1983, November). Boston Commission Survey of weapons-carrying: making our schools safe for learning, pp. 12–16.

Brounstein, P. S., Hatry H. P., Altschuler, D. M., & Blair, L. H. (1989). *Patterns of substance abuse and delinquency among inner city adolescents.* Report to the National Institute of Justice. Washington, DC: The Urban Institute.

Centers for Disease Control. (1990). Homicide among black males—United States, 1978–1987. Morbidity & Mortality Weekly Report *MMWR, 39,* 629–633.

Gray, E. (1984). *Child abuse: Prelude to delinquency?* Washington, DC: Office of Juvenile Justice and Delinquency Prevention.

Gustavsson N., & Balgopal, P. (1990). Violence and minority youth: An ecological perspective. In A. Stiffman & L. Davis (Eds.), *Ethnic issues in adolescent mental health* (pp. 115–130). Newbury Park, CA: Sage Publications, Inc.

Huff, C. R. (1990). *Gangs in America.* Newbury Park, CA: Sage Publications, Inc.

Kratcoski, P. (1982). Child abuse and violence against the family. *Child Welfare, 7*(61), 435–444.

Lefkowitz, M., Eron L., Walder, L., & Huesmann, L. R. (1972). Television violence and child aggression: A followup study. In G. A. Comstock & E. A. Rubinstein (Eds.), *Television and social behavior. Vol. 3: Television and adolescent aggres-*

*siveness*. (pp. 35–135). Washington, DC: United States Government Printing Office.

Lewis, D., Shanok, S., & Balla, D. (1979). Perinatal difficulties, head and face trauma, and child abuse in the medical histories of seriously delinquent children. *American Journal of Psychiatry, 136:4A,*(13), 419–423.

Lewis, D., Shanok, S., Pincus, J., & Glaser G. (1979). Violent juvenile delinquents: Psychiatric, neurological, psychological, and abuse factors. *Journal of the American Academy of Child Psychiatry, 4*(18), 307–319.

Liebert, R. M., & Sprafkin, J. (1988). *The Early window: Effects of television on children and youth.* New York: Pergamon Press.

Mouzakitis, C. (1981). An inquiry into the problem of child abuse and juvenile delinquency. In R. J. Hunner & Y. E. Walker (Eds.), *Exploring the relationship between child abuse and delinquency.* Montclair, N.J.: Allanheld, Osmun.

Murry, J. (1988). On TV violence. *Division of Child, Youth, and Family Services Newsletter, 11*(3), 12–13.

National Committee for Injury Prevention and Control. (1989) *Injury prevention: Meeting the challenge.* New York: Oxford University Press.

National School Safety Center. (1988). *Gangs in schools: Breaking up is hard to do.* Washington, DC: Office of Juvenile Justice and Delinquency Prevention.

Rivera, B., & Widom, C. (1990). Childhood victimization and violent offending. *Violence and Victims, 5*(1), 19–35.

Robinson, J. P., & Bachman, J. G. (1972). Television viewing habits and aggression. In G. A. Comstock & E. A. Rubinstein (Eds.), *Television and social behavior. Vol. 3: Television and adolescent aggressiveness.* (pp. 372–382) Washington, DC: United States Government Printing Office.

Spergel, I. A., Curry, D., Change, R., Kane, C., Ross, R., Alexander, A., Simmons, E., & Oh, S. (1990). *Youth gangs: Problem and response. National youth gang suppression and intervention research and development program.* (Executive summary). Chicago, IL: University of Chicago, School of Social Service Administration.

Spivak, H., Prothrow-Smith, D. & Hauseman, A. (1988). Dying is no accident: Adolescents, violence, and unintentional injury. *Pediatric Clinics of North America, 35*(6), 1339–1347.

Stein, A. H., & Friedrich, L. K. (1975). Impact of television on children and youth. In E. M. Hetherington (Ed.), *Review of child development research* (Vol. 5). (pp. 202–252) Chicago, IL: University of Chicago Press.

Stokes L. (1991, December). Paper presented at the Youth Violence Prevention Conference, Cleveland, OH. *Youth Violence Prevention.*

Staff. (1991, July). A nasty jolt for the pop stars. *Time,* p. 56.

U.S. Department of Health and Human Services. (1986). *Health, United States, 1986.* Washington, DC: National Center for Health Statistics.

U.S. Senate Subcommittee on Juvenile Justice. (1981). *The problem of juvenile crime* (Serial No. J–97–48). Washington, DC: United States Government Printing Office.

# Index

# About the Contributors

**Grant J. Butterbaugh, Ph.D.,** is an assistant professor of pediatrics in the Division of Adolescent Medicine at the University of Maryland School of Medicine. He has clinical and research interests in pediatric neuropsychology. He is neuropsychology coordinator at Children's Hospital in New Orleans.

**Kathleen Cole-Kelly, M.S.W.,** is assistant professor in the Department of Family Medicine at Case Western Reserve University. She is the director of behavioral sciences in the Family Medicine Department at Metro Health Medical Center. Kathy also has a private practice in marital and family therapy.

**Thomas J. Dishion, Ph.D.,** is a research scientist and clinical psychologist at the Oregon Social Learning Center. Over the past ten years, Dr. Dishion has been involved in research on the influence of peers and parents on adolescent delinquency. The focus of his research is on understanding the unique contribution of peers to social development, formulating a model of substance abuse in adolescents, and advancing research methodology.

**Debra Bendell Estroff, Ph.D.,** is a child psychologist at Kaiser Permanente Medical Center, Department of Psychiatry and is an associate clinical professor of pediatrics at the University of California-San Francisco. She has authored chapters and articles in the area of pediatric psychology and adolescents. She is active in the American Psychological Association.

**Miriam Friedland, M.D.,** is chief of child psychiatry at Kaiser Permanente Medical Center in Fremont, California. She works extensively with adolescents, including the psychopharmacology needs of this population. She is a member of the American Academy of Child and Adolescent Psychiatry.

**David L. Hussey, Ph.D.,** is the clinical director of Beech Brook, a large, multiservice, children's mental health agency in Cleveland, Ohio. Dr. Hussey also maintains a private practice and is an adjunct instructor at Case Western Reserve University in Cleveland. He has over fifteen years of clinical experience in working with children and their families, and specializes in the areas of child mental health, victimization, and substance abuse.

**David Kaye, M.D.,** is clinical assistant professor of psychiatry and director of training in child psychiatry at the School of Medicine at the State University of New York, Buffalo.

**Patricia K. Kokotailo, M.D., M.P.H.,** is an assistant professor of pediatrics and director of pediatric medical education at the University of Wisconsin-Madison. Dr. Kokotailo has research and clinical interests in adolescent risk-taking behavior, including adolescent sexuality and alcohol and other drug use. Other interests include health-risk behavior of minority youth, and pediatric faculty development in alcohol and other drug issues in which she has taught at a national level.

**Lisa Lunghofer** is a doctoral candidate in social welfare policy at Case Western Reserve University. She directs a tutoring program for at-risk inner city adolescents. Her research interests include domestic violence, incarcerated women, and gender differences. Currently, she is studying the relationship between exposure to violence and mental health among adolescent girls.

**Sonia Minnes** is a masters level psychologist currently working at Rainbow Babies and Childrens Hospital in Cleveland Ohio. Her B.S. and M.A. in psychology are from Pennsylvania State and Cleveland State Universities. Special areas of interest are childhood and adolescent behavioral disorders complicated by medical factors.

**Gerald R. Patterson, Ph.D.,** is a research scientist and clinical psychologist at the Oregon Social Learning Center. During the course of his research, Dr. Patterson has addressed a wide range of related topics in the areas of intervention, assessment, evaluation of treatment outcome, and research methodology. More recently, he has been working on the social interactional theory of delinquency and antisocial behavior outlined in this volume.

**Harris Rabinovich, M.D.,** is an associate professor of psychiatry at Medical College of Pennsylvania, Eastern Pennsylvania Psychiatric Institute. He is the director of training in the Division of Child and Adolescent Psychiatry, as well as the director of the Children's Inpatient Psychiatric Unit. Areas of special interest include: psychiatric assessment of children and adolescents, psychiatric diagnosis, and mood disorders in children and adolescents. He writes "Help" column for a children's newspaper.

**Deborah Rich, Ph.D.,** is an assistant professor of pediatric psychology in the Department of Pediatrics and Human Development at Michigan State University. Her Ph.D. is in clinical psychology from Bowling Green State University. Dr. Rich's postdoctoral training in pediatric neuropsychology was completed at Case Western Reserve University School of Medicine.

**Norman B. Rushforth, Ph.D.,** is professor and chair of the Department of Biology and associate professor of epidemiology and biostatistics at Case Western Reserve University. His current research interests include epidemiological studies of violent death in urban communities. He is undertaking analyses of long-term trends in homicide, suicide, and fatal injuries in the Cleveland region and, with Drs. Howard S. Sudak and Amasa B. Ford, has edited a book on suicide in the young.

**Linda M. Schmidt** is the project director of the Youth Gang Diversion project of The Task Force on Violent Crime. She is a respected authority in the area of youth violence and youth gangs. She is a member of the Midwest Gang Investigators Association and the Center for Adolescent Health's Task Force on Adolescent Violence. She has authored *Youth Gangs: A Parents Guide for the '90s,* and co-authored *Criminal Street Gangs in Greater Cleveland.*

**Pamela Senders, Ph.D.,** has a doctorate in clinical psychology from Case Western Reserve University. She has completed an assistantship in adolescent psychology at University Hospitals of Cleveland, and is currently a psychology fellow in private practice.

**John N. Stephenson, M.D.,** is a professor of pediatrics and director of the Teenage and Young Adult Clinic at the University of Wisconsin-Madison. Dr. Stephenson has worked in the field of adolescent medicine for 25 years. His areas of research and teaching have included eating disorders, adolescent alcohol and other drug abuse, contraceptive use by adolescents, and school-based health programs. In addition to his University of Wisconsin Medical School activities he is medical consultant to the Madison Metropolitan School District.

**Howard S. Sudak, M.D.,** is the chairman of the Department of Psychiatry at The Pennsylvania Hospital and psychiatrist-in-chief at the Institute of Pennsylvania Hospital, Philadelphia, Pennsylvania. Prior to that, he was a vice dean of the School of Medicine, an associate vice president for Medical Affairs, and a professor of psychiatry at Case Western Reserve University, Cleveland, Ohio. He has authored many articles on suicide and, along with

Dr. Norman Rushforth and Amasa Ford, edited *Suicide in the Young*. He also has edited a general textbook, *Clinical Psychiatry*.

**H. Gerry Taylor, Ph.D.,** is an associate professor of pediatrics at Case Western Reserve University School of Medicine, and is director of pediatric psychology at Rainbow Babies and Childrens Hospital. He received his Ph.D. from the University of Iowa in child behavior and development. His research interests include the neuropsychological consequences of childhood brain injuries and cognitive and social antecedents in children's learning problems.

**Michael L. Walker** is the executive director of The Task Force on Violent Crime. He received his B.A. degree in political science/communications from The Ohio State University. He is a member of the Midwest Gang Investigators Association and the Center for Adolescent Health's Task Force on Adolescent Violence. He was appointed to the Governor's Council on Alcohol and Drug Addiction Services in December 1991. Mr. Walker is also a special advisor to the American Bar Association's special committee on the drug crisis. He has spoken throughout the country on issues related to the reduction of youth violence and the drug crisis. He has appeared on the Today Show and 48 Hours.

# About the Editors

**Mark I Singer, Ph.D.,** is an associate professor of social work at the Mandel School of Applied Social Sciences and an assistant professor of pediatrics at the School of Medicine, Case Western Reserve University. He specializes in mental health and drug abuse treatment with adolescents and young adults. Dr. Singer has an extensive clinical and administrative background in youth services, including directing two adolescent inpatient psychiatric units. He is currently investigating the mental health consequences of adolescents' exposure to violence.

**Lynn T. Singer, Ph.D.,** is an associate professor of psychology in pediatrics and psychiatry at Case Western Reserve University School of Medicine. She is also a pediatric psychologist at Rainbow Babies and Children's Hospital, Cleveland, Ohio, with extensive experience treating adolescents with eating disorders. She currently is principal investigator of longitudinal studies of feeding and growth disorders in preterm infants.

**Trina M. Anglin, M.D., Ph.D.,** is an associate professor of pediatrics at the University of Colorado School of Medicine, and an associate chief of the Section of Adolescent Medicine at The Children's Hospital in Denver. In addition to her work as a physician, Dr. Anglin holds a doctorate in sociology. Her professional interests include the identification of psychosocial and behavioral problems in adolescents, school-based health care, and physician education. She is nationally recognized for her work aimed at helping health care professionals to recognize the problems of substance abuse in their adolescent patients.